Learning Theories

An Educational Perspective

Eighth Edition

Dale H. Schunk
The University of North Carolina at Greensboro

Pearson

Director and Publisher: Kevin M. Davis
Content Producer: Janelle Rogers
Media Producer: Lauren Carlson
Portfolio Management Assistant: Casey Coriell
Executive Field Marketing Manager: Krista Clark
Executive Product Marketing Manager: Christopher Barry
Procurement Specialist: Carol Melville
Full-Service Project Management: Thistle Hill Publishing Services, LLC
Cover Designer: Carie Keller, Pearson CSC
Cover Image: Tom Gril / JGI / Blend Images / Getty Images
Composition: Pearson CSC
Printer/Binder: LSC Communications, Inc. / Crawfordsville
Cover Printer: Phoenix Color/Hagerstown
Text Font: 10/12 ITC Garamond Std

Credits and acknowledgments borrowed from other sources and reproduced, with permission, in this textbook appear on the appropriate page within the text.

Every effort has been made to provide accurate and current Internet information in this book. However, the Internet and information posted on it are constantly changing, so it is inevitable that some of the Internet addresses listed in this textbook will change.

Library of Congress Cataloging-in-Publication Data

Names: Schunk, Dale H., author.
  Title: Learning theories : an educational perspective / Dale H. Schunk, The
    University of North Carolina at Greensboro.
  Description: Eighth Edition. | New York, NY : Pearson, [2018] | Includes
    bibliographical references and index.
  Identifiers: LCCN 2018034999| ISBN 9780134893754 (paperback) | ISBN
    0134893751 (paperback)
  Subjects: LCSH: Learning. | Cognition. | Learning, Psychology of.
  Classification: LCC LB1060 .S37 2018 | DDC 370.15/23—dc23
  LC record available at https://lccn.loc.gov/2018034999

8 2020

ISBN 13:   978-0-13-489375-4
ISBN 10:   0-13-489375-1

Dedication

*To Albert Bandura, for helping me develop self-efficacy
for leading a fulfilling life*

Preface

Learning is a lifelong activity and fundamental to education. And the study of learning is crucial for everyone who wants to live a fulfilling life and help others do so. The better we understand learning, the better we can determine how to improve it.

Over the past several years, the study of learning by researchers has continued at a strong pace. This situation is desirable because it has resulted in theoretical refinements, improved research methodologies, and implications for instruction based on sound theory and research.

Although the study of learning has changed a lot since the first edition of this book was published in 1991, the primary objectives of this eighth edition remain much the same as those of the first edition: (a) to help students become knowledgeable of learning theoretical principles, concepts, and research findings, especially as they relate to education, and (b) to provide applications of principles and concepts in settings where teaching and learning occur. As in previous editions, the focus of the current edition is on cognition. Cognitive constructivist perspectives emphasize that learners are not passive recipients of information but rather actively seek, construct, and adapt their knowledge, skills, strategies, and beliefs.

STRUCTURE OF THIS TEXT

The text's 12 chapters are organized as follows. The introductory chapter covers learning theory, research methods, and learning issues, as well as historical foundations of the study of learning. Chapter 2 discusses the neuroscience of learning. A basic understanding of neuroscience assists readers in understanding the links between brain functions and cognitive and constructivist learning principles. Chapter 3 covers behaviorism, a dominant learning theory for many years. Current cognitive and constructivist theories and principles are the subject of Chapters 4–8: social cognitive theory; information processing theory—encoding and storage; information processing theory—retrieval and forgetting; cognitive learning processes; and constructivism. Chapters 9–11 cover topics relevant to and integrated with learning: motivation, self-regulated learning, and contextual influences. The final chapter asks learners to develop their own perspective on learning.

NEW TO THIS EDITION

Readers familiar with prior editions will notice content and organizational changes in this edition, which reflect new theoretical and research emphases. Several topics have been added including sections on educational data mining, positive behavior supports, metacognition and epistemic thinking, Neo-Piagetian theories, self-regulation and technology, and future developments in the study of learning. The text has been revised to incorporate newer theoretical principles and research findings. These revisions are most evident in the chapters on constructivism and contextual influences. Sections on technology throughout the text have been revised to keep up with the latest educational uses of technology. Added to the ends of each of the first eleven chapters are two new sections: a chapter critique and a set of reflection questions that students can think about as they review the chapter and can be discussed in classes. To keep the text current and timely, new terms have been incorporated into the glossary. More than 200 new references have been added, and several dated references have been dropped.

Applications of learning principles have been a hallmark of this text since its inception and these continue to be present in this new edition. Each chapter except the introductory and concluding chapters contains a section on instructional applications. All chapters begin with vignettes that illustrate some principles discussed in the chapters. Throughout the chapters, there are many informal examples and detailed applications. Most of the applications involve K–12 settings, but applications also address other learning contexts including college students.

The text is designed for graduate students in education or related disciplines, as well as upper-level undergraduates interested in education. It is assumed that most students have taken a course in education or psychology and currently work in an educational capacity or anticipate pursuing an educational career. The text is appropriate for courses on learning and cognition, as well as any course that covers learning in some depth such as courses on motivation, educational psychology, human development, and instructional design.

ACKNOWLEDGEMENTS

Many people deserve thanks for their contributions to this edition. Over many years, there have been numerous professional colleagues who have assisted me to develop my thinking about learning processes and applications. I have acknowledged the contributions of these individuals in previous editions. For this edition, I want to gratefully thank Héfer Bembenutty, Herb Clark, Maria DiBenedetto, Jeff Greene, Judith Meece, Ellen Usher, Bernard Weiner, Allan Wigfield, Phil Winne, and Barry Zimmerman. My association with members of professional organizations has been most beneficial, especially the Motivation in Education and the Studying and Self-Regulated Learning Special Interest Groups of the American Educational Research Association, and Division 15 (Educational Psychology) of the American Psychological Association. It has been an honor for me to work with many excellent students, teachers, counselors, administrators, and superintendents. I also am indebted to several graduate and undergraduate student collaborators who assisted me on research projects.

I am most fortunate that again for this edition my editor at Pearson Education is Kevin Davis. Kevin unquestionably is one of the finest editors anyone could work with. He is highly encouraging and supportive, and his continued guidance has resulted in a better product. I also express appreciation to Casey Coriell and Janelle Rogers at Pearson

Education for their editorial assistance. I owe sincere thanks to the following reviewers of the eighth edition: Oris Griffin, James Madison University; James R. May, Oklahoma State University; Kerry Rice, Boise State University; Melissa Stormont, University of Missouri; and Ellie L. Young, Brigham Young University.

It is hard to believe that it has been almost 30 years since the first edition of this book was published. At that time, I proudly gave a copy to my parents, the late Mil and Al Schunk, for their love, encouragement and support. Since then, several friends have served as inspirations to me to continue to produce new editions. For this edition, I graciously thank Bill Gattis. And I am most grateful for my wife Maria and my daughter Laura, who was born shortly before the first edition was released. Laura is a remarkable young woman from whom I have learned so much and in whose life learning has made a profound difference.

Brief Contents

Contents

1 Introduction to the Study of Learning

Russ Nyland teaches a graduate education course on learning and cognition. Toward the end of the semester, three students approach him: Jeri Kendall, Matt Bowers, and Trisha Pascella.

Jeri: Dr. Nyland, can we talk with you? It's late in the course, and we're still confused.

Russ: About what?

Jeri: Well, we've been studying all these theorists. It seems like they're saying different things, but maybe not. Skinner, Bandura, Vygotsky, and the others. They make different points, but then some of what they say seems to overlap what others say.

Matt: I'm confused too. I read these theorists and agree with what they're saying. But am I supposed to have only one theory, to believe one way and not others? There's a lot of overlap between theories.

Russ: You're right, Jeri and Matt; there is overlap. Most of what we've studied in this course involves cognition. Cognitive theories are alike because they say that learning involves changes in cognitions—knowledge, skills, beliefs. Most theorists also say that learners construct their knowledge and beliefs; they don't automatically adopt what somebody tells them.

Trisha: So then what should we do? Am I supposed to be something like an information processing theorist, a social cognitive theorist, a constructivist? That's what I'm confused about.

Russ: No, you don't have to be only one. There may be one theory that you like better than the others, but maybe that theory doesn't address everything you want it to. So then you can borrow from other theories. For example, when I was in grad school, I did research with a professor whose specialty was cognitive learning. There was another professor who did developmental research. I really liked her research, probably because I had been a teacher and was interested in development, especially the changes in students from elementary to middle school. So I was a learning theorist who borrowed from the developmental literature. I still do. It's okay to do that!

Jeri: Well, that makes me feel better. But it's late in the course, and I want to know what I should be doing next.

Russ: Tell you what—next class I'll spend some time on this. A good place to start is not to decide which type of theorist you are but rather determine what you believe about learning and what types of learning you're interested in. Then you can see which theory matches up well to your beliefs and assumptions and maybe do as I did—borrow from others.

Matt: Isn't that being eclectic?

Russ: Perhaps, but you may still have one preferred theory that you adapt as needed. It's okay to do that. In fact, that's how theories are improved—by revising and incorporating ideas that weren't in them originally.

Trisha: Thanks Dr. Nyland. This is really helpful.

Learning involves acquiring and modifying knowledge, skills, strategies, beliefs, attitudes, and behaviors. People learn cognitive, behavioral, linguistic, motor, and social skills, and these can take many forms. At a simple level, children learn to solve $2 + 2 = ?$, to recognize *y* in the word *daddy*, to tie their shoes, and to play with other children. At a more complex level, students learn to solve long-division problems, write term papers, ride a bicycle, and work cooperatively on group projects.

This book focuses on how human learning occurs, which factors influence it, and how learning principles apply in educational contexts. Animal learning is de-emphasized, which is not intended to downgrade its importance because we have gained much knowledge about learning from animal research. But human learning is fundamentally different from animal learning because human learning typically involves language and is more complex, elaborate, and rapid.

This chapter provides an overview of the study of learning. Initially, learning is defined and examined in settings where it occurs. An overview is given of some important philosophical and psychological precursors of contemporary theories that helped to establish the groundwork for the application of learning theories to education. The roles of learning theory

and research are discussed, and methods commonly used to assess learning are described. The links between learning theories and instruction are explained, after which some critical issues in the study of learning are presented.

The opening scenario describes a situation that many students find themselves in when they take a course in learning, instruction, or motivation and are exposed to different theories. Students often think that they are supposed to believe in one theory and adopt the views of those theorists. They may be confused by the perceived overlap between theories.

As Russ Nyland says, that is normal. Although theories differ in many ways, including their general assumptions and guiding principles, many rest on a common foundation of cognition. This text focuses on these cognitive theories of learning, which contend that learning involves changes in learners' constructions: their thoughts, beliefs, knowledge, strategies, and skills. These theories differ in how they predict that learning occurs, which learning processes are important, and which aspects of learning they stress. Some theories are oriented more toward basic learning and others toward applied learning (and, within that, in different content areas); some stress the role of development, others are strongly linked with instruction; and some emphasize motivation (Bruner, 1985).

Russ advises students to examine their beliefs and assumptions about learning rather than decide which type of theorist they are. This is good advice. Theories are perspectives on learning. They are neither right nor wrong. Rather, they help us understand learning and act accordingly. Once we are clear about where we stand on learning in general, then the theoretical perspective or perspectives that are most relevant will emerge. As you study this text, it will help if you reflect on your beliefs and assumptions about learning and decide how these align with the theories.

This introductory chapter is important because it should prepare you for an in-depth study of learning by providing a framework for understanding learning and some background material against which to view contemporary theories. It also covers types of research to investigate learning and ways to assess it. These are topics that everyone interested in learning should be familiar with.

When you finish studying this chapter, you should be able to do the following:

- Define learning and identify instances of learned and unlearned phenomena.

- Distinguish between rationalism and empiricism, explain the major tenets of each, and discuss how rationalism and empiricism are reflected in contemporary learning theories and research.

- Discuss how the work of Wundt, Ebbinghaus, the Structuralists, and the Functionalists helped to establish psychology as a science.

- Describe the major features of different research paradigms.

- Discuss the central features of different methods of assessing learning, including educational data mining and criteria for assessment methods.

- Explain what value-added assessment of learning is and how it can be used to determine progress in student learning.

- Explicate the ways that learning theory and educational practice complement and refine one another.

- Explain differences between behavior and cognitive theories with respect to various issues in the study of learning.

LEARNING DEFINED

Although people agree that learning is important, they hold different views on the causes, processes, and consequences of learning (Alexander, Schallert, & Reynolds, 2009; Geary, 2009). There is no one definition of learning that is universally accepted by theorists, researchers, and practitioners. Despite disagreement about the precise nature of learning, the following is a general definition of learning that is consistent with this book's cognitive focus and that captures the criteria most educational professionals consider central to learning.

Learning is an enduring change in behavior, or in the capacity to behave in a given fashion, which results from practice or other forms of experience.

Let us examine this definition in depth to identify three criteria of learning (Table 1.1). One criterion is that *learning involves change*—in behavior or in the capacity for behavior. Change is a central ingredient of learning (Alexander et al., 2009). When people learn, they become capable of doing something differently. A key point is that we do not

Table 1.1
Criteria of learning.

- Learning involves change
- Learning endures over time
- Learning occurs through experience

observe learning directly but rather its products or outcomes. In other words, *learning is inferential*—it is demonstrated based on what people say, write, and do. The definition also says that learning involves a changed capacity to behave in a given fashion because people can learn skills, knowledge, beliefs, and behaviors without demonstrating them at the time they learn them (Chapter 4).

A second criterion is that *learning endures over time*. This criterion excludes temporary behavioral changes (e.g., slurred speech) brought about by such factors as drugs, alcohol, and fatigue. Such changes are temporary because when the cause is removed, the behavior returns to its original state. Although learning is enduring, it may not last forever because forgetting occurs. Researchers debate how long changes must last to be classified as learned, but most people agree that changes of brief duration (e.g., a few seconds) do not qualify as learning.

A third criterion is that *learning occurs through experience* (e.g., practice, thinking, observation of others). This criterion excludes behavioral changes that are primarily determined by heredity, such as maturational changes in children (e.g., crawling, standing). Nonetheless, the distinction between maturation and learning often is not clear-cut. People may be genetically predisposed to act in given ways, but the actual development of the particular behaviors depends on the environment. Language offers a good example. As the human vocal apparatus matures, it becomes able to produce language such that children acquire language in much the same type of trajectory (Goldin-Meadow et al., 2014). The actual words produced, however, are learned from interactions with others. Although genetics are critical for children's language acquisition, teaching and social interactions with parents, teachers, and peers exert a strong influence on children's language achievements (Mashburn, Justice, Downer, & Pianta, 2009). In similar fashion, with normal development, children crawl and stand, but the environment must be responsive and allow these behaviors to occur. Children whose language and movements cannot be expressed freely in an environment may not develop normally.

PRECURSORS OF MODERN LEARNING THEORIES

The roots of contemporary theories of learning extend far into the past. Many issues addressed and questions asked by researchers today are not new but rather reflect the continuing desire for people to understand themselves, others, and the world about them.

It is important to understand the origins of contemporary learning theories, which this section traces beginning with philosophical positions on the origin of knowledge and its relation to the environment and concluding with some early psychological views on learning. This review is selective and includes historical material relevant to learning in educational settings. Readers interested in a more comprehensive discussion should consult historical sources (Bower & Hilgard, 1981; Heidbreder, 1933; Hunt, 1993).

Learning Theory and Philosophy

From a philosophical perspective, learning can be discussed under the heading of *epistemology*, which refers to the study of the origin, nature, limits, and methods of knowledge. How do we know? How do we learn something new? What is the source of knowledge? The complexity of how humans learn is illustrated in Plato's *Meno* (427?–347? B.C.):

> I know, Meno, what you mean . . . You argue that a man cannot enquire (*sic*) either about that which he knows, or about that which he does not know; for if he knows, he has no need to enquire (*sic*); and if not, he cannot; for he does not know the very subject about which he is to enquire (*sic*). (Plato, 1965, p. 16)

Two positions on the origin of knowledge and its relationship to the environment are rationalism and empiricism. These philosophies are recognizable in current learning theories.

Rationalism. *Rationalism* reflects the idea that knowledge derives from reason without recourse to the senses. The distinction between mind and matter, which figures prominently in rationalist views of human knowledge, can be traced to Plato, who distinguished knowledge acquired via the senses from that gained by reason. Plato believed that things (e.g., houses, trees) are revealed to people via the senses, whereas individuals acquire knowledge of ideas by reasoning or thinking about what they know. People have ideas about the world, and they learn (discover) these ideas by reflecting upon them. Reason is the highest mental faculty because through reason, people discover abstract ideas. The true nature of houses and trees can be known only by reflecting upon the ideas of houses and trees.

Plato escaped the dilemma expressed in *Meno* by assuming that true knowledge, or the knowledge of ideas, is innate and is brought into awareness through reflection. Learning is recalling what exists in the mind. Information acquired via the senses by seeing, hearing, tasting, smelling, or touching constitutes raw materials rather than ideas. The mind is innately structured to reason and provide meaning to incoming sensory information.

The rationalist doctrine also is evident in the writings of René Descartes (1596–1650), a French philosopher and mathematician. Descartes employed doubt as a method of inquiry. By doubting, he arrived at conclusions that were absolute truths and not subject to doubt. The fact that he could doubt led him to believe that the mind (thought) exists, as reflected in his dictum, "I think, therefore I am." Through deductive reasoning from general premises to specific instances, he showed that God existed and concluded that ideas arrived at through reason must be true.

Like Plato, Descartes established a mind–matter dualism; however, for Descartes, the external world was mechanical, as were the actions of animals. People are distinguished by their ability to reason. The human soul, or the capacity for thought, influences the body's mechanical actions, but the body acts on the mind by bringing in sensory experiences. Although Descartes postulated dualism, he also hypothesized mind–matter interaction.

The rationalist perspective was extended by the German philosopher Immanuel Kant (1724–1804). In his *Critique of Pure Reason* (1781), Kant addressed mind–matter dualism and noted that the external world is disordered but is perceived as orderly because order is imposed by the mind. The mind takes in the external world through the senses and alters it according to subjective, innate laws. The world never can be known as it exists but only as it is perceived. People's perceptions give the world its order. Kant reaffirmed the role of reason as a source of knowledge but contended that reason operates within the realm of experience. Absolute knowledge untouched by the external world does not exist. Rather, knowledge is empirical in the sense that information is taken in from the world and interpreted by the mind.

In summary, rationalism is the doctrine that knowledge arises through the mind. Although there is an external world from which people acquire sensory information, ideas originate from the workings of the mind. Descartes and Kant believed that reason acts upon information acquired from the world; Plato thought that knowledge can be absolute and acquired by pure reason.

Empiricism. In contrast to rationalism, *empiricism* reflects the idea that experience is the only source of knowledge. This position derives from Aristotle (384–322 B.C.), who was Plato's student and successor. Aristotle drew no sharp distinction between mind and matter. The external world is the basis for human sense impressions, which, in turn, are interpreted as lawful (consistent, unchanging) by the mind. The laws of nature cannot be discovered through sensory impressions but rather through reason as the mind takes in data from the environment. Unlike Plato, Aristotle believed that ideas do not exist independently of the external world, which is the source of all knowledge.

Aristotle's contribution to psychology was his principles of association as applied to memory. The recall of an object or idea triggers recall of other objects or ideas similar to, different from, or experienced close in time or space, to the original object or idea. The more that two objects or ideas are associated, the more likely that recall of one will trigger recall of the other. Such associative learning is reflected in many learning theories (Shanks, 2010).

Another influential figure was British philosopher John Locke (1632–1704), who developed an empirical school of thought that stopped short of being truly experimental. In his *Essay Concerning Human Understanding* (1690), Locke noted that there are no innate ideas; all knowledge derives from two types of experience: sensory impressions of the external world and personal awareness. At birth, the mind is a *tabula rasa* (blank tablet). Ideas are acquired from sensory impressions and personal reflections on these impressions. What is in the mind originated in the senses. The mind is composed of ideas that have been combined in different ways. The mind can be understood only by breaking down ideas into simple units. This atomistic view of thought is associationist; complex ideas are collections of simple ones.

The issues Locke raised were debated by such profound thinkers as George Berkeley (1685–1753), David Hume (1711–1776), and John Stuart Mill (1806–1873). Berkeley believed that mind is the only reality. He was an empiricist because he believed that ideas derive from experiences. Hume agreed that people never can be certain about external reality, but he also believed that people cannot be certain about their own ideas. Individuals experience external reality through their ideas, which constitute the only reality. At the same time, Hume accepted the empiricist doctrine that ideas derive from experience and become associated with one another. Mill was an empiricist and associationist, but he rejected the idea that simple ideas combine in orderly ways to form complex ones.

Mill argued that simple ideas generate complex ideas, although the latter need not be composed of the former. Simple ideas can produce a complex thought that might bear little relation to the ideas of which it is composed. Mill's beliefs reflect the notion that the whole is greater than the sum of its parts, which is an integral assumption of Gestalt psychology (Chapter 5).

In summary, empiricism holds that experience is the only form of knowledge. Beginning with Aristotle, empiricists have contended that the external world serves as the basis for people's impressions. Most accept the notion that objects or ideas associate to form complex stimuli or mental patterns. Locke, Berkeley, Hume, and Mill are among the better-known philosophers who espoused empiricist views.

Knowing about philosophical positions that underlie learning theories helps us better understand the latter. Philosophical positions suggest the types of research conducted by researchers adopting different theoretical positions. Thus, theories that reflect a rationalist perspective are apt to be concerned with learners' perceptions of learning environments and ways that learners construct knowledge. These research methods might try to tap qualitative measures such as learners' reflections at various points during learning. In contrast, theories that reflect empiricism may place greater emphasis on environmental variables and the effects these might have on the associations made by learners. These theories may also examine how complex types of learning are built up from more basic ones. The research methods are likely to include measures and variables that can be quantified.

It should be emphasized that philosophical positions and learning theories do not neatly map onto one another; however, behavior theories (Chapter 3) typically are empiricist in their orientation whereas cognitive theories (Chapters 4–8) are more rationalistic. But overlap and exceptions occur. For example, most theories posit that some learning occurs through association. Cognitive theories stress association between cognitions and emotions; behavior theories emphasize the association of stimuli with responses and consequences. And more recent behavior theories have begun to include cognition (Chapter 3). Information processing (Chapters 5 and 6) seems highly empiricist at times, but it does emphasize the construction of knowledge. So we are left with complexity such that it is best not to overgeneralize how a particular philosophical position may manifest itself in a given learning theory.

Beginnings of the Psychological Study of Learning

Although the study of learning is probably "as old as the sun," the formal beginning of the psychological study of learning is more recent but difficult to pinpoint. Systematic psychological research began to appear in the latter part of the 19th century. Two persons who had a significant impact on learning theory are Wundt and Ebbinghaus.

Wundt's Psychological Laboratory. The first psychological laboratory was opened by Wilhelm Wundt (1832–1920) in Leipzig, Germany, in 1879, although William James had started a teaching laboratory at Harvard University four years earlier (Dewsbury, 2000). Wundt wanted to establish psychology as a new science. His laboratory acquired an international reputation with an impressive group of visitors, and he founded a journal to report psychological research. The first research laboratory in the United States was opened in 1883 by G. Stanley Hall (Dewsbury, 2000).

Establishing a psychological laboratory was particularly significant because it marked the transition from philosophical theorizing to an emphasis on experimentation and instrumentation (Evans, 2000). The laboratory included scholars who conducted research aimed at scientifically explaining phenomena (Benjamin, 2000). In his 1873 book *Principles of Physiological Psychology*, Wundt contended that psychology is the study of the mind. The psychological method should be patterned after the physiological method; that is, the process being studied should be experimentally investigated in terms of controlled stimuli and measured responses.

Wundt's researchers investigated such phenomena as sensation, perception, reaction times, verbal associations, attention, feelings, and emotions. Wundt also was a mentor for many psychologists who subsequently opened laboratories in the United States (Benjamin, Durkin, Link, Vestal, & Acord, 1992). Although Wundt's laboratory produced no great psychological discoveries or critical experiments, it established psychology as a discipline and experimentation as the method of acquiring and refining knowledge.

Ebbinghaus's Verbal Learning. Hermann Ebbinghaus (1850–1909) was a German psychologist who helped to validate the experimental method and establish psychology as a science. Ebbinghaus investigated higher mental processes by conducting research on memory (Erdelyi, 2010). He accepted the principles of association and believed that learning and the recall of learned information depend on the frequency of exposure to the material. Properly testing this hypothesis required using material with which participants were unfamiliar. Ebbinghaus invented *nonsense syllables*, which are three-letter consonant-vowel-consonant combinations (e.g., cew, tij).

Ebbinghaus often used himself as the subject of study (Erdelyi, 2010). In a typical experiment, he would devise a list of nonsense syllables, look at each syllable briefly, pause, and then look at the next syllable. He determined how many times through the list (trials) it took to him learn the entire list. He made fewer errors with repeated study of the list, needed more trials to learn more syllables, forgot rapidly at first but then more gradually, and required fewer trials to relearn syllables than to learn them the first time. He also studied a list of syllables some time after original learning and calculated a *savings score*, defined as the time or trials necessary for relearning as a percentage of the time or trials required for original learning. He found that meaningfulness of material made learning easier. The results of his research are compiled in the 1885/1964 book *Memory*.

Although important historically, there are concerns about this research. Ebbinghaus typically employed only one participant (himself), and it is unlikely he was unbiased or a typical learner. We also might question how well results for learning nonsense syllables generalize to meaningful learning (e.g., text passages). Nonetheless, Ebbinghaus was a careful researcher, and many of his findings later were validated experimentally. He was a pioneer in bringing higher mental processes into the experimental laboratory.

Structuralism and Functionalism

The work by Wundt and Ebbinghaus was systematic but confined to particular locations and of limited influence on psychological theory. The turn of the century marked the beginning of more widespread schools of psychological thought. Two perspectives that emerged were structuralism and functionalism. Although neither exists as a unified doctrine today, their early proponents were influential in the history of psychology as it relates to learning.

Structuralism. Edward B. Titchener (1867–1927) was Wundt's student in Leipzig. Titchener became the director of the psychology laboratory at Cornell University in 1892 and imported Wundt's experimental methods into U.S. psychology.

Titchener's psychology, which eventually became known as *structuralism*, reflected empiricism because it represented a combination of associationism with the experimental method. Structuralists believed that human consciousness is a legitimate area of scientific investigation, and they studied the structure or makeup of mental processes. They postulated that the mind is composed of associations of ideas that to be studied must be broken down into single ideas (Titchener, 1909).

The experimental method used often by Wundt, Titchener, and other structuralists was *introspection*, a type of self-analysis. Participants in introspection studies verbally reported their immediate experiences following exposure to objects or events. For example, if shown a table, they might report their perceptions of shape, size, color, and texture. They were told not to label or report their knowledge about the object or the meanings of their perceptions. Thus, if they verbalized "table" while viewing a table, they were attending to the stimulus rather than to their conscious processes.

Introspection was a uniquely psychological process and helped to demarcate psychology from the other sciences. It was a professional method that required training in its use so that an introspectionist could determine when individuals were examining their own conscious processes rather than their interpretations of phenomena.

Unfortunately, introspection often was problematic and unreliable. It is difficult and unrealistic to expect people to ignore meanings and labels. When shown a table, it is natural that people say "table," think of uses, and draw on related knowledge. The mind is not structured to compartmentalize information so neatly, so by ignoring meanings introspectionists disregarded a central aspect of the mind. Watson (Chapter 3) decried the use of introspection, and its problems helped to rally support for an objective psychology that studied only observable behavior (Heidbreder, 1933). Edward L. Thorndike, a prominent psychologist (Chapter 3), contended that education should be based on scientific facts, not opinions (Popkewitz, 1998). The ensuing emphasis on behavioral psychology dominated U.S. psychology for the first half of the 20th century.

Another problem was that structuralists studied associations of ideas, but they had little to say about how these associations are acquired. Further, it was not clear that introspection was the appropriate method to study such higher mental processes as reasoning and problem solving, which are more complex than immediate sensation and perception.

Functionalism. While Titchener was at Cornell, other developments challenged the validity of structuralism. Among these was *functionalism*, the view that mental processes and behaviors of living organisms help them adapt to their environments (Heidbreder, 1933). This school of thought flourished at the University of Chicago with John Dewey (1867–1949) and James Angell (1869–1949). Another prominent functionalist was William James (1842–1910). Functionalism was the dominant American psychological perspective from the 1890s until World War I (Green, 2009).

James's principal work was the two-volume series, *The Principles of Psychology* (1890), which is considered one of the greatest psychology texts (Hall, 2003). An abridged version was published for classroom use (James, 1892). James was an empiricist who believed that experience is the starting point for examining thought, but he was not an associationist. He thought that simple ideas are not passive copies of environmental inputs but rather are the product of abstract thought and study (Pajares, 2003).

James (1890) postulated that consciousness is a continuous process rather than a collection of discrete bits of information. One's "stream of thought" changes as experiences change. James described the purpose of consciousness as helping individuals adapt to their environments.

Functionalists incorporated James's ideas into their doctrine. Dewey (1896) believed that psychological processes could not be broken into discrete parts and that consciousness must be viewed holistically. "Stimulus" and "response" describe the roles played by objects or events, but these roles could not be separated from the overall reality (Bredo, 2003). Dewey cited an example from James (1890) about a baby who sees a candle burning, reaches out to grasp it, and experiences burned fingers. From a stimulus–response perspective, the sight of the candle is a stimulus, and reaching is a response; getting burned (pain) is a stimulus for the response of withdrawing the hand. Dewey argued that this sequence is better viewed as one large coordinated act in which seeing and reaching influence each other.

Functionalists were influenced by Darwin's writings on evolution and studied how mental processes helped organisms adapt to their environments and survive (Bredo, 2003; Green, 2009). Functionalists were interested in how mental processes (e.g., thinking, feeling, judging) operate, what they accomplish, and how they vary with environmental conditions. They also saw the mind and body as interacting rather than existing separately.

Functionalists opposed the introspection method, not because it studied consciousness but rather because of how it studied consciousness. Introspection attempted to reduce consciousness to discrete elements, which functionalists believed was not possible. Studying a phenomenon in isolation does not reveal how it contributes to an organism's survival.

Dewey (1900) argued that the results of psychological experiments should be applicable to education and daily life. Although this goal was laudable, it also was problematic because the research agenda of functionalism was too broad to offer a clear focus. Structuralists and functionalists believed in the value of research, but they approached it differently. Structuralism reflected the tenets of empiricism, whereas functionalism was better aligned with rationalism. But both perspectives had weaknesses involving research. These weaknesses paved the way for the rise of behaviorism as the dominant force in U.S. psychology (Chapter 3). Behaviorism reflected empiricism because it emphasized experimentation and observable phenomena, which helped to secure psychology's standing as a science (Asher, 2003; Tweney & Budzynski, 2000).

LEARNING THEORY AND RESEARCH

Theory and research are integral to the study of learning. This section discusses some general functions of theory, along with key aspects of the research process. Readers who are knowledgeable about these topics may wish to omit this section.

Functions of Theory

A *theory* is a scientifically acceptable set of principles offered to explain a phenomenon. Theories are perspectives on learning that provide frameworks for interpreting environmental observations. They also help to bridge the gap between research and education. Research findings can be organized and systematically linked to theories. Theories provide a scientific basis for education regarding how people think, feel, and act (Sternberg, 2008). Without theories, people might view research findings as disorganized collections of data, because researchers and practitioners would have no overarching frameworks to which the data could be linked. Even when researchers obtain findings that do not seem to be directly linked to theories, they still must attempt to make sense of data and determine whether the data support theoretical predictions.

Theories reflect environmental phenomena and generate new research through *hypotheses*, or assumptions that can be empirically tested. Hypotheses can be cast as statements of relation, such as, "X should relate positively to Y," or as if–then statements (e.g., "If I do X, then Y should occur)," where X and Y might be such events as "give students feedback on their progress in learning" and "promote their learning," respectively. Thus, we might test the hypothesis, "If we give students feedback on their progress in learning, then they should display better learning." A theory is strengthened when hypotheses are supported by data. Theories may require revision if data do not support hypotheses.

When researchers explore areas where there is little theory to guide them, they formulate research objectives or questions to be answered (e.g., "How will students' learning be affected when they receive feedback on their learning progress?"). Regardless of whether researchers are testing hypotheses or exploring questions, they need to specify the research conditions as precisely as possible.

Because research forms the basis for theory development and has important implications for teaching, the next section examines types of research and the process of conducting research. Readers familiar with this material may wish to omit this section.

Conducting Research

To specify the research conditions, researchers need to answer such questions as: Who will participate? Where will the research study be conducted? What procedures will be employed? What are the variables and outcomes to be assessed?

Researchers must define precisely the phenomena they are studying by providing conceptual and operational definitions. An *operational definition* defines a phenomenon in terms of the measures and procedures used to assess it. For example, a researcher might define *self-efficacy* (covered in Chapter 4) conceptually as one's perceived capabilities for learning or performing a task and operationally by specifying the measures and procedure used to assess self-efficacy in the research study (e.g., one's score on a 30-item questionnaire administered privately before students received instruction). Ideally, conditions are specified so precisely that, after reading the description, another researcher could replicate the study.

Research studies that explore learning employ various types of *paradigms* (or *models*; Table 1.2). The following paragraphs describe the correlational, experimental, and qualitative paradigms, followed by a discussion of laboratory and field studies.

Correlational Research. *Correlational research* deals with exploring relations that exist between variables. A researcher might hypothesize that self-efficacy is positively correlated with (related to) achievement such that the higher the students' self-efficacy, the higher they achieve. To test this relation, the researcher might measure students' self-efficacy for solving mathematical problems and then assess how well they solve the problems. The researcher could statistically correlate the self-efficacy and achievement scores to determine the direction of the relation (positive, negative) and its strength (high, medium, low).

Correlational research helps to clarify relations among variables. Correlational findings often suggest directions for further research. If the researcher were to obtain a high positive correlation between self-efficacy and achievement, the next study might be an experiment that attempts to raise students' self-efficacy for learning and determine whether such an increase produces higher achievement.

A limitation of correlational research is that it cannot identify cause and effect. A positive correlation between self-efficacy and achievement could mean that (a) self-efficacy influences achievement, (b) achievement influences self-efficacy, (c) self-efficacy and achievement influence each other, or (d) both self-efficacy and achievement are influenced by other, nonmeasured variables (e.g., parents, teachers). To determine cause and effect, experimental studies are necessary.

Experimental Research. In *experimental research*, the researcher changes one or more (independent) variables and determines the effects on other (dependent) variables. A researcher could form two groups of students, systematically raise self-efficacy beliefs among students in one group and not among students in the other group, and assess achievement in the two groups. If the first group performs better, the researcher might

Table 1.2
Learning research paradigms.

Type	Qualities
Correlational	Examines relations between variables
Experimental	One or more variables are altered and effects on other variables are assessed
Qualitative	Concerned with description of events and interpretation of meanings
Laboratory	Project conducted in a controlled setting
Field	Project conducted in a natural setting (e.g., school, home, work)

conclude that self-efficacy influences achievement. While the researcher alters variables and assesses their effects on outcomes, she or he must hold constant other variables that potentially can affect outcomes (e.g., learning conditions).

Experimental research, which often is conducted by researchers in the empiricism tradition, can clarify cause–effect relations, which helps us understand the nature of learning. At the same time, experimental research often is narrow in scope. Such research typically involved quantitative data, which includes closed-ended information on beliefs and performance instruments (Creswell & Plano-Clark, 2007). Researchers typically study only a few variables and try to minimize effects of others, which is difficult to do and often unrealistic. Classrooms and other learning settings are complex places where many variables operate at once. To say that one or two variables cause outcomes may overemphasize their importance. It is necessary to replicate experiments and examine other variables to better understand effects.

Qualitative Research. The *qualitative research* paradigm is characterized by intensive study, descriptions of events, and interpretation of meanings. The theories and methods used are referred to with various labels including qualitative, ethnographic, participant observation, phenomenological, constructivist, and interpretative (Erickson, 1986). It is often conducted by researchers in the rationalist tradition.

Qualitative research is especially useful when researchers are interested in the structure of events rather than their overall distributions, when the meanings and perspectives of individuals are important, when actual experiments are impractical or unethical, and when there is a desire to search for new potential causal linkages that have not been discovered by experimental methods (Erickson, 1986). Qualitative research is varied and can range from analyses of verbal and nonverbal interactions within single lessons to in-depth observations and interviews over longer periods. Methods may include observations, use of existing records, interviews, and think-aloud protocols (i.e., participants talk aloud while performing tasks). It is not the choice of method that characterizes this approach—all of the aforementioned methods could be used in correlational or experimental studies—but rather the depth and quality of data analysis and interpretation.

A qualitative researcher might be curious about how self-efficacy contributes to the development of skills over time. She or he might work with a small group of students for several weeks. Through observations, interviews, and other forms of data collection, the researcher might examine how students' self-efficacy for learning changes in relation to their learning in reading, writing, and mathematics.

Quantitative and qualitative methods can be used together in a research study, which is known as *mixed-methods research* (Creswell & Plano-Clark, 2007). Qualitative research yields rich sources of open-ended data, which are more intensive and thorough than those typically obtained with quantitative methods. This model also can raise new questions and fresh perspectives on old questions that often are missed by traditional methods. A potential limitation is that qualitative studies typically include only a few participants, who may not be representative of a larger population of students or teachers. This limits generalization of findings beyond the research context. Another limitation is that data collection, analysis, and interpretation can be time-consuming and therefore impractical for students wanting to graduate and professors wanting to build their publication records! But as a research model, this paradigm offers a useful approach for obtaining data typically not collected with other methods.

Laboratory and Field Research. *Laboratory research* is conducted in controlled settings, whereas *field research* is conducted where participants live, work, or attend school. During the first half of the 20th century, most learning research was conducted on animals in laboratories. Today most learning research is conducted with people, and much is done in field settings. Any of the preceding research models (experimental, correlational, qualitative) can be applied in the laboratory or the field.

Laboratories offer a high degree of control over extraneous factors that can affect results, such as equipment noises (e.g., ringing phones), people talking, windows to look out of, and other persons in the room who are not part of the study. Light, sound, and temperature can be regulated. Laboratories also allow researchers to leave their equipment set up over lengthy periods and have all materials at their immediate disposal.

Such control is not possible in the field. Schools are noisy, and often it is difficult to find space to work. There are numerous distractions: Students and teachers walk by, bells ring, public announcements are made, and fire drills are held. Rooms may be too bright or dark, cold or warm, and they may be used for other purposes so researchers have to set up equipment each time they work. Interpreting results in light of these distractions can be a problem.

An advantage of field research is that results are highly generalizable to other similar settings because studies are conducted where people typically learn. In contrast, generalization of laboratory findings to the field is done with less confidence. Laboratory research has yielded many important insights on learning, and researchers often attempt to replicate laboratory findings in the field.

Whether the laboratory or the field is employed depends on such factors as the purpose of the research, availability of participants, costs, and how the results will be used. The laboratory adds control but loses some generalizability, and vice versa with the field. In the field, researchers try to minimize extraneous influences so that they can be more confident that their results are due to the variables they are studying.

ASSESSMENT OF LEARNING

Because learning is inferential, we do not directly observe it but rather its products—what learners say and do. Researchers and practitioners who work with students may believe that students have learned, but to be more certain, they must assess learning's outcomes. *Assessment* involves "a formal attempt to determine students' status with respect to educational variables of interest" (Popham, 2014, p. 8). In school, the educational variable of interest most often is student achievement in different areas (e.g., reading, writing, mathematics, science).

Student achievement always has been critical, but its importance has been underscored in recent years by legislation and standards. For example, the federal government's No Child Left Behind (NCLB) Act of 2001 (Shaul & Ganson, 2005) has many provisions. Among the most significant are the requirements for annual testing of students in grades 3 through 8 and again in high school in reading and mathematics and for school systems to show increases in students making adequate yearly progress in these subjects. *The Common Core State Standards for English Language Arts and Mathematics* (National Governors Association Center for Best Practices and Council of Chief State School Officers, 2010; White & DiBenedetto, 2015), which are designed to promote college and career readiness, were adopted by many states. The Every Student Succeeds Act of 2015 made several changes to NCLB's provisions including giving states freedom to select their goals for test proficiency, English language proficiency, and graduation rates. However, states remain accountable to the federal government, and their accountability systems must include at least four indicators: proficiency on state tests, English language proficiency, a third academic indicator, and one other indicator such as student engagement and postsecondary readiness. Collectively, these standards and legislation ensure that accountability for student learning will continue to receive attention.

Two points are noteworthy with respect to this text. Although accountability often leads to testing being the means of assessment, the latter includes many measurement procedures besides testing (described below). Researchers and practitioners want to know whether learning has occurred, and there may be procedures other than testing that provide evidence of student learning (Popham, 2014). Second, students' skills in content areas often are the learning outcomes assessed, but researchers and practitioners may also be interested in other forms of learning. For example, they may want to know whether students have learned new attitudes or self-regulation skills or whether students' interests, values, self-efficacy, and motivation have increased as a result of content learning.

This section covers ways to assess outcomes of learning. These methods include direct observations, written responses, oral responses, ratings by others, and self-reports (Table 1.3).

Table 1.3
Methods of assessing learning.

Category	Definition
Direct observations	Instances of behavior that demonstrate learning
Written responses	Written performances on tests, quizzes, homework, papers, and projects
Oral responses	Verbalized questions, comments, and responses during learning
Ratings by others	Observers' judgments of learners on attributes indicative of learning
Self-reports	People's judgments of themselves
■ Questionnaires	Written ratings of items or answers to questions
■ Interviews	Oral responses to questions
■ Stimulated recalls	Recall of thoughts accompanying one's performances at given times
■ Think-alouds	Verbalizing aloud one's thoughts, actions, and feelings while performing a task
■ Dialogues	Conversations between two or more persons

Direct Observations

Direct observations are instances of student behavior that we observe to assess whether learning has occurred. Direct observations are contrasted with reported observations, where others inform us that they observed instances of student behavior. Teachers employ direct observations frequently. A chemistry teacher wants students to learn laboratory procedures. The teacher observes students in the laboratory to determine whether they are implementing procedures properly. A physical education instructor observes students dribble a basketball to assess how well they have learned the skill. An elementary teacher gauges how well students have learned classroom rules based on their behavior.

Direct observations are valid indexes of learning if they are straightforward and involve little inference by observers. Direct observations work best when the desired behaviors can be specified and then the students are observed to ascertain whether their behaviors match the standards.

A problem with direct observations is that they focus only on what can be observed and therefore bypass the cognitive and affective processes that underlie actions. For example, the chemistry teacher knows that students have learned laboratory procedures but not what the students are thinking about while they are performing the procedures or how confident they feel about performing them.

A second problem is that, although observing a behavior indicates that learning has occurred, the absence of appropriate behavior does not mean that learning has not occurred. Learning is not the same as performance. Many factors other than learning can affect performance. Students may not perform learned actions because they are not motivated, are ill, or are busy doing other things. We have to rule out these other factors to conclude from the absence of performance that learning has not occurred. That requires making the assumption—which at times may be unwarranted—that since students usually try to do their best, if they do not perform, they have not learned.

Written Responses

Learning often is assessed based on students' *written responses* on tests, quizzes, homework, term papers, and reports. Based on the level of mastery indicated in the responses, teachers decide whether adequate learning has taken place or whether additional instruction is needed because students do not fully comprehend the material. For example, assume that a teacher is planning a unit on the geography of Hawaii. Initially the teacher assumes that students know little about this topic. A pretest given prior to the start of instruction will support the teacher's belief if the students score poorly. The teacher retests students following the instructional unit. Gains in test scores lead the teacher to conclude that learners have acquired some knowledge.

Their relative ease of use and capacity for covering a wide variety of material makes written responses desirable indicators of learning. With technology (e.g., computers, clickers), many written responses can be recorded electronically for assignments, blogs, and other products. We assume that written responses reflect learning, but many factors can affect performance of behavior even when students have learned. Written responses require us to believe that students are trying their best and that no extraneous factors (e.g., fatigue, illness, cheating) are operating such that their written work does not represent what they have learned. We must try to identify extraneous factors that can affect performance and cloud learning assessments.

Oral Responses

Oral responses are an integral part of the school culture. Teachers call on students to answer questions and assess learning based on what they say. Students also ask questions during lessons. If their questions indicate a lack of understanding, this is a signal that proper learning has not occurred.

Like written responses, we assume that oral responses are valid reflections of what students know, which may not always be true. Further, verbalization is a task, and some students may have problems translating what they know into oral expressions due to unfamiliar terminology, anxiety about speaking, or language difficulties. Teachers may rephrase what students say, but such rephrasing may not accurately reflect the nature of students' thoughts.

Ratings by Others

Another way to assess learning is for individuals (e.g., teachers, parents, administrators, researchers, peers) to rate students on the quantity or quality of their learning. These *ratings by others* (e.g., "How well can Tim solve problems of the type $52 \times 36 = ?$" "How much progress has Olivia made in her printing skills in the past 6 months?") provide useful data and can help to identify students with exceptional needs (e.g., "How often does Matt need extra time to learn?" "How quickly does Jenny finish her work?").

An advantage of ratings by others is that observers may be more objective about students than students are about themselves (self-reports, discussed next). Ratings also can be made for learning processes that underlie actions (e.g., comprehension, motivation, attitudes) and thereby provide data not attainable through direct observations; for example, "How well does Seth comprehend the causes of World War II?" But ratings by others require more inference than do direct observations. It may be problematic to accurately rate students' ease of learning, depth of understanding, or attitudes. Further, ratings require observers to remember what students do and will be distorted when raters selectively remember only positive or negative behaviors.

Self-Reports

Self-reports are people's assessments of and statements about themselves. Self-reports take various forms: questionnaires, interviews, stimulated recalls, think-alouds, and dialogues.

Questionnaires present respondents with items or questions asking about their thoughts and actions. Respondents may record the types of activities they engage in, rate their perceived levels of competence, and judge how often or how long they engage in them (e.g., "How long have you been studying Spanish?" "How difficult is it for you to learn geometric theorems?"). Many self-report instruments ask respondents to record ratings on numerical scales (e.g., "On a 10-point scale, where $1 =$ low and $10 =$ high, rate how good you are at reducing fractions.").

Interviews are a type of questionnaire in which an interviewer presents the questions or discussion points and the respondent answers orally. Interviews typically are conducted individually, although groups can be interviewed. A researcher might describe a learning context and ask students how they typically learn in that setting (e.g., "When the French teacher begins a lesson, what are your thoughts? How well do you think you will do?"). Interviewers may need to prompt respondents if replies are too brief or not forthcoming.

In the *stimulated recall* procedure, people work on a task and afterward recall their thoughts at various points during the task. Interviewers query them (e.g., "What were you thinking about when you got stuck here?"). If the performance was video recorded, respondents subsequently watch the recording and recollect, especially when interviewers stop the recording and ask questions. It is desirable that the recall procedure be accomplished soon after the performance so that participants do not forget their thoughts.

Think-alouds are procedures in which students verbalize their thoughts, actions, and feelings while working on a task (Greene, Deekens, Copeland, & Yu, 2018). Verbalizations may be recorded by observers and subsequently scored for level of understanding. Think-alouds require that respondents verbalize; many students are not used to talking aloud while working in school. Talking aloud may seem awkward to some, and they may feel self-conscious or otherwise have difficulty expressing their thoughts. Investigators can prompt students if they do not verbalize.

Dialogues are conversations between two or more persons while engaged in a learning task. Like think-alouds, dialogues can be recorded and analyzed for statements indicating learning and factors that seem to affect learning in the setting. Although dialogues use actual interactions while students are working on a task, their analyses require interpretations that may go beyond the actual elements in the situations.

The choice of self-report measure should match the purpose of the assessment. Questionnaires can cover a lot of material; interviews are better for exploring a few issues in depth. Stimulated recalls ask respondents to recall their thoughts at the time actions took place; think-alouds examine present (real-time) thoughts. Dialogues allow for investigation of social interaction patterns.

Self-report instruments typically are easy to develop and administer; questionnaires usually are easy to complete and score. A problem can arise when inferences have to be drawn about students' responses. It is essential to have a reliable scoring system. Other concerns about self-reports are whether students are giving socially acceptable answers that do not match their beliefs, whether self-reported information corresponds to actual behavior, and whether young children are capable of self-reporting accurately. By guaranteeing that data are confidential, researchers can help promote truthful answering. There is evidence that, beginning around the third grade, self-reports are valid and reliable indicators of the beliefs and actions they are designed to assess (Assor & Connell, 1992), but researchers need to use self-reports cautiously to minimize potential problems. A good way to validate self-reports is to use multiple forms of assessment (e.g., self-reports, direct observations, oral and written responses).

Educational Data Mining

In recent years, a trend has emerged—largely the result of advances in technology—of delving into large data sets in fine-grained fashion to explore learners' processes while they are engaged in learning. *Educational data mining* refers to the tools and techniques used to find meanings in large data repositories generated during learners' activities. Developments in technology have created new opportunities for researchers. Particularly with the growth of computer-supported learning environments (CSLEs) and learning management systems (LMSs), researchers can determine the activities students engage in as they work with the system. For example, it is possible to track how many minutes learners spend on particular content, which links they explore, how long they spend working on a problem, whether their solutions are correct, what their grades are on assignments, and, in some cases, what their eye movements are to determine to which aspects on a screen they are attending.

Information obtained from educational data mining can be useful in discerning students' learning patterns and relating these to learning outcomes. For example, by studying data from a LMS, researchers can determine students' grades on tests, assignments, and courses, and look for patterns in the activities they engaged in during the course. This might reveal that students who utilized more of the LMS's resources performed better in the course, as well as whether the timing of resource use related differentially to outcomes. Such results provide insight into the processes students use during learning and offer suggestions for ways to design learning environments to promote student success.

Various uses of educational data mining have been identified (Biswas, Baker, & Paquette, 2018). An important use is predicting students' future behaviors while engaged in learning. Models can be developed for particular learners by entering data on their characteristics such as their entry level of knowledge and the steps they accomplish as they are engaged in learning. By relating these steps to their learning outcomes, models can show which steps lead to better outcomes for which learners. This type of model development is helpful as it suggests how instructional environments might be designed to be maximally effective for each student.

A second important use is to map the course of learning in a particular content domain. By mining particular learner responses while they are engaged in learning specific content (e.g., algebra, marine science), the procedure can show what successful learners do and how their actions are distinguished from those of less successful students. This knowledge has key implications for instructional design because it suggests how to structure learning experiences that are likely to lead to success with specific content learning.

Data mining also can evaluate the effectiveness of instructional conditions and learner supports. Students' responses can be tracked before and after supports are in effect to determine how their responses change and what effects these changes might have on achievement and other outcomes. The results of this type of data mining can result in positive changes in learning conditions.

A closely aligned field is *learning analytics*, which involves the use of learner-generated data and analysis models to discover how students learn and connect with one another for the purpose of predicting future learning. The methods and tools of learning analytics are substantially similar to those of educational data mining. The difference in terms might arise in part from where the field began. Learning analytics reflects more of a background in LMSs, whereas educational data mining has been explored by researchers from intelligent tutoring systems. Regardless of perspective, these ways to explore data offer new insights on the processes students engage in while learning and can lead to positive changes in students' learning.

Assessment Issues

Given the current educational emphasis on accountability, there are issues that should be addressed in assessment. This section discusses issues involving assessment criteria and value-added assessment.

Assessment Criteria. Regardless of the method of assessment of learning, there are three criteria that are important: reliability, validity, and absence of bias (Popham, 2014).

Reliability involves consistency of assessment (Popham, 2014). This means that the assessment will produce comparable results if given on different occasions with no intervening events that could influence learning. For example, a reliable algebra test is one that will produce similar results for each student if given in the morning and again in the afternoon of the same day, where students have had no exposure to algebra in between test occasions. Reliability is important because unreliable assessments affect research results and lead researchers to draw erroneous conclusions.

Validity refers to the extent that evidence supports the accuracy of interpretations about students (Popham, 2014). Validity pertains not to assessments themselves but rather to their interpretations. When students are assessed in some content area (e.g., reading) or on a psychological variable (e.g., interest), researchers draw conclusions about students based on their scores. Thus, if a student scores low on an interest assessment, researchers want to be confident in concluding that this student's interest is low. Validity is important for research because if a test purports to measure one variable (e.g., learning) but actually measures something different (e.g., intelligence), then researchers will make incorrect interpretations of the results.

A third criterion is *absence of bias,* defined as an assessment being free of qualities that offend or penalize students because of their group characteristics (e.g., gender, ethnicity, religion) (Popham, 2014). Absence of bias is important because when bias exists, it can skew (raise or lower) results due to students' personal characteristics. Thus, questions on a mathematics test that involve a soccer game might favor students who are familiar with the game even though that has nothing to do with the mathematical knowledge presumably being assessed.

Value-Added Assessment Models. Value-added assessment models have gained popularity in education. A *value-added assessment model* is one that attempts to determine the causes of students' learning progress (Popham, 2014). Students' prior achievement and background variables (e.g., socioeconomic status, gender) are statistically controlled to isolate the role of instructional variables (e.g., school, teacher) on learning progress. The "value added" aspect then is the gain attributed to school or teacher, which presumably provides a measure of effectiveness. This measure can be used by school systems as a basis for evaluations and funding.

One presumed advantage of value-added assessments is that since they track students' progress from their baseline levels, this allows for schools to be compared even if they have different baselines. This has been a persistent problem in education because it is not legitimate to compare students from schools with different demographics and baseline levels.

Although value-added assessments are popular, they contain some problems (Darling-Hammond, Amrein-Beardsley, Haertel, & Rothstein, 2012). Learning is affected by many variables, only some of which are under the school and teacher's control. It is difficult to attempt to statistically control all potentially relevant ones. Another issue is that it is risky to ascribe student progress to schools or teachers because those assessments only provide estimates of their contribution. Gains in student achievement can be affected by multiple variables such as peer culture, prior teachers, home and community influences, and individual student needs (Darling-Hammond et al., 2012). These assessments also take a limited view of learning by equating it with achievement, but as explained earlier, achievement is a performance measure and may not fully reflect learning.

If value-added assessment models are used, it is better to employ them to track students' progress over a longer time rather than at only one point in time (Anderman, Anderman, Yough, & Gimbert, 2010). Monitoring individual students' growth and progress could help teachers better differentiate instruction according to needs, which also can yield motivational benefits for students (Anderman et al., 2010). Further, diversified assessments that contain many indicators of student learning (e.g., tests, papers, class participation) should provide a more accurate picture of learning (Darling-Hammond et al., 2012). Tests should be designed and their results reported so as to accurately capture each student's mastery of each curricular learning objective (Wiliam, 2010), which requires that tests reflect the criteria of reliability, validity, and absence of bias.

The American Educational Research Association (2015) developed standards for the use of value-added assessment models for evaluation of educators. These standards include such points as using assessments that meet professional standards of reliability and validity, basing assessments on multiple years of assessments, calculating value-added scores from tests that are comparable over time, and not using value-added scores alone or in isolation in evaluation systems. Properly adhered to, these standards should minimize or prevent misinterpretations of value-added assessments to inform teacher evaluations.

RELATION OF LEARNING AND INSTRUCTION

Theories and research findings help to advance the field of learning, but their ultimate contribution must be to improve teaching. Although it may seem odd, historically there was little overlap between the fields of learning and instruction (Sternberg, 2008; Sztajn, Confrey, Wilson, & Edgington, 2012). One reason may have been that these fields traditionally were dominated by persons with different interests. Most learning theorists and researchers have been psychologists. Much early learning research used nonhuman species. Animal research has benefits, but animals do not allow for proper exploration of instructional processes. In contrast, instruction was the domain of educators, who were primarily concerned with directly applying teaching methods to classrooms and other learning environments. This applied focus has not always lent itself well to exploring how learning is affected by instructional variables.

A second reason derives from the idea that teaching is an art and not a science like psychology. As Highet (1950) wrote: "[This book] is called *The Art of Teaching* because I believe that teaching is an art, not a science. It seems to me very dangerous to apply the aims and methods of science to human beings as individuals" (p. vii). Highet stated, however, that teaching is inseparable from learning. Gage (1978) noted that the use of "art" in reference to teaching is a metaphor. In fact, teaching as an art can undergo the same type of scrutiny and scientific investigation as any other type of art, including drawing, painting, and musical composition.

A third possible reason stems from the idea that different theoretical principles may govern the two domains. Sternberg (1986) contended that cognition (or learning) and instruction require separate theories. This may be true for learning and instruction by themselves, but as Shuell (1988) noted: "Learning from instruction differs from traditional conceptions of learning and teaching considered separately" (p. 282). Researchers today view learning from instruction as involving an interaction between learners and contexts (e.g., teachers, peers, materials, settings). Sequencing of material, for example, affects learners' cognitive organizations and development of memory structures. In turn, how these structures develop affects what teachers do. Teachers who realize that instruction is not being comprehended will alter their approach. As the opening scenario makes clear, learning theories should be adapted to fit specific instructional contexts.

Fourth, traditional research methods may be inadequate to study instruction and learning simultaneously. Much learning research has used experimental methods in which some conditions are varied and changes in outcomes are determined. Teaching methods often are held constant across changes in variables, which negates the dynamic nature of teaching. In education, *process–product research* conducted in the 1970s and 1980s related changes in teaching processes (such as number and type of questions asked, amount of warmth and enthusiasm displayed) to student products or outcomes (e.g., achievement, attitudes; Pianta & Hamre, 2009). Although this research paradigm produced many useful results, it neglected the important roles of teacher and student thoughts. Thus, we might know which type of questions produce higher student achievement but not why they do so (i.e., how questions affect students' thinking). Process–product research also focused primarily on student achievement at the expense of other outcomes relevant to learning (e.g., expectations, values). In short, a process–product model is not well designed to examine how students learn.

Fortunately, the situation has changed. Researchers increasingly are viewing teaching as the creation of learning environments that assist students in executing the cognitive activities necessary to develop skills (Floden, 2001). Researchers are examining student learning by observing teaching during instruction, (Pellegrino, Baxter, & Glaser, 1999; Pianta & Hamre, 2009). Researchers are more concerned with analyzing teaching patterns rather than discrete teaching behaviors (Seidel & Shavelson, 2007). Children's learning has received increased attention (Siegler, 2005), and more research is being devoted to how what is learned in school is related to what skills are important outside of school (Anderson, Reder, & Simon, 1996).

A promising development is to determine students' learning trajectories, or the paths they might take from their starting points to the intended learning goal (Sztajn et al., 2012). Teachers then can combine their knowledge of these trajectories with contextual factors to make instructional decisions. Instructional research can have a profound impact on learning theories and their applications to promote student learning (Pianta & Hamre, 2009).

A goal of this book is to help you understand how learning theory and educational practice complement one another. Learning theory is no substitute for experience. Theory without experience can be misguided because it may underestimate the effects of situational factors. When properly used, theory provides a framework to use in making educational decisions.

Conversely, experience without theory can be wasteful and potentially damaging. Experience without a guiding framework means that each situation is treated as unique, so decision making is based on trial and error until something works. Learning how to teach involves learning what to do in specific situations. Although learning research results at times conflict with common instructional practices (Rohrer & Pashler, 2010), research on learning will continue to have an effect on educational practices.

Educational professionals should strive to integrate theory, research, and practice. We should ask how learning principles and research findings might apply in and out of school. In turn, we should seek to advance our theoretical knowledge through results of informed teaching practice.

CRITICAL ISSUES FOR LEARNING THEORIES

Although most professionals accept in principle the definition of learning given at the outset of this chapter, there is less agreement on many learning issues. Some key issues are discussed in this section (Table 1.4). These issues are addressed in subsequent chapters as different learning theories are discussed. First, however, a short explanation of behavior and cognitive theories is given to provide a background against which to frame learning theories.

Table 1.4
Critical issues in the study of learning.

- How does learning occur?
- How does memory function?
- What is the role of motivation?
- How does transfer occur?
- How does self-regulated learning operate?
- What are the implications for instruction?

Behavior theories view learning as a change in the rate, frequency, or form of behavior or response, which occurs primarily as a function of environmental factors (Chapter 3). Behavior theories contend that learning involves the formation of associations between stimuli and responses. In Skinner's (1953) view, a response to a stimulus is more likely to occur in the future as a function of the consequences of prior responding: Reinforcing consequences make the response more likely to occur, whereas punishing consequences make it less likely.

Behaviorism was a powerful force in psychology in the first half of the 20th century. These theories explain learning in terms of observable phenomena. Behavior theorists contend that explanations for learning need not include internal events (e.g., thoughts, beliefs, feelings), not because these processes do not exist (because they do—even behavior theorists have to think about their theories!) but, rather, because the causes of learning are observable environmental events.

In contrast, *cognitive theories* stress the construction of knowledge and skills, the development of mental structures and memory networks, and the cognitive processing of information and beliefs. Learning is an internal mental phenomenon inferred from what people say and do. A central theme is the mental processing of information: its construction, acquisition, organization, coding, rehearsal, storage in and retrieval from memory, and adaptation. The theories covered in Chapters 4–8 are cognitive, as are the principles discussed in later chapters.

These two conceptualizations of learning have important implications for educational practice. Behavior theories imply that teachers should arrange the environment so that students can respond properly to stimuli. Cognitive theories emphasize making learning meaningful and taking into account learners' perceptions of themselves, others, and learning environments. Teachers need to consider how instruction affects students' thinking during learning.

How Does Learning Occur?

Behavior and cognitive theories agree that differences among learners and in the environment can affect learning, but they diverge in the relative emphasis they give to these two factors. Behavior theories stress the role of the environment—specifically, how stimuli are arranged and presented and how responses are reinforced. Behavior theories assign less importance to learner differences than do cognitive theories. Two learner variables that behavior theories consider are *reinforcement history* (the extent to which the individual was reinforced in the past for performing the same or similar behavior) and *developmental status* (what the individual is capable of doing given his or her present level of development). Thus, cognitive handicaps will hinder learning of complex skills, and physical disabilities may preclude acquisition of motor behaviors.

Cognitive theories stress the role of contexts and environmental conditions as influences on learning. Instructional explanations and demonstrations serve as environmental inputs for students who, with practice and feedback, construct knowledge and learn. Cognitive theories contend that instructional factors alone do not fully account for students' learning. What students do with knowledge—how they attend to, rehearse, transform, code, store, and retrieve it—is critically important. The ways that learners process knowledge determine what, when, and how they learn, as well as what use they will make of the learning.

Cognitive theories emphasize the role of learners' thoughts, beliefs, attitudes, and values. Learners who doubt their capabilities to learn may not properly attend to the task or may work halfheartedly on it. Such learner thoughts as "Why is this important?" or "How well am I doing?" can affect learning and need to be considered in instructional planning.

How Does Memory Function?

Learning theories differ in the role they assign to memory. Some behavior theories conceive of memory in terms of neurological connections established as a function of behaviors being associated with external stimuli. More commonly, theorists discuss the formation of habitual ways of responding with little attention to how these behavior patterns are retained in memory and activated by external events. Most behavior theories view forgetting as caused by lack of responding over time.

Cognitive theories assign a prominent role to memory. Information processing theories equate learning with *encoding*, or constructing and storing knowledge in memory in an organized, meaningful fashion. Knowledge is retrieved from memory in response to relevant cues that activate the appropriate memory structures. Forgetting is the inability to retrieve knowledge from memory caused by interference, memory loss, or inadequate cues to access information. Memory is critical for learning, and how information is learned determines how it is stored in and retrieved from memory.

One's perspective on the role of memory has important implications for teaching. Behavior theories posit that periodic, spaced reviews maintain the strength of responses in learners' repertoires. Cognitive theories place greater emphasis on presenting material to be learned in such a way that learners can organize it, relate it to what they know, and remember it in a meaningful fashion.

What Is the Role of Motivation?

Motivation can affect all phases of learning and performance (Chapter 9). Behavior theories define motivation as an increased rate or probability of occurrence of behavior, which results from repeating behaviors in response to stimuli or as a consequence of reinforcement. Skinner's (1968) operant conditioning theory contains no new principles to account for motivation: Motivated behavior is increased or continued behavior produced by reinforcement. Students display motivated behavior because they previously were reinforced for it and because effective reinforcers are present.

In contrast, cognitive theories view motivation and learning as related but not identical. One can be motivated but not learn and one can learn without being motivated. Cognitive theories emphasize that motivation can help to direct attention and influence how knowledge is constructed. Although reinforcement can motivate students, its effects on behavior are not automatic but instead depend on how students interpret it. When reinforcement history (what one has been reinforced for doing in the past) conflicts with present beliefs, people are more likely to act based on their beliefs (Bandura, 1986; Brewer, 1974). Research has identified many cognitive processes that motivate students; for example, goals, social comparisons, self-efficacy, values, and interests. Teachers need to consider the motivational effects of instructional practices and environmental features to ensure that students remain motivated to learn.

How Does Transfer Occur?

Transfer refers to knowledge and skills being applied in new ways, with new content, or in situations different from where they were acquired (Chapter 6). Transfer also explains the effect of prior learning on new learning—whether the former facilitates, hinders, or has no effect on the latter. Transfer is critical, for without it, all learning would be situationally specific. Transfer lies at the heart of our system of education.

Behavior theories stress that transfer depends on identical elements or similar features (stimuli) between situations. Behaviors transfer (or *generalize*) when the old and new situations share common elements. Thus, a student who learns that $6 \times 3 = 18$ should be able to perform this multiplication in different settings (school, home) and when the same numbers appear in a similar problem format (e.g., $36 \times 23 = ?$).

Cognitive theories postulate that transfer occurs when learners understand how to apply knowledge in different settings. How information is stored in memory is important. The uses of knowledge are stored along with the knowledge itself or can be easily accessed from another memory storage location. Situations need not share common elements.

Instructional implications of these views diverge. From a behavioral view, teachers should enhance the similarity between situations and point out common elements. Cognitive theories supplement these factors by emphasizing that students' perceptions of the value of learning are critical. Teachers can address these perceptions by including in lessons information on how knowledge can be used in different settings, by teaching students rules and procedures to apply in situations to determine what knowledge will be needed, and by providing students with feedback on how skills and strategies can benefit them in different ways.

How Does Self-Regulated Learning Operate?

Self-regulated learning refers to the process whereby learners systematically direct their thoughts, feelings, and actions toward the attainment of their learning goals (Zimmerman & Schunk, 2011; Chapter 10). Researchers of different theoretical traditions postulate that self-regulated learning involves having a purpose or goal, employing goal-directed actions, and monitoring strategies and actions and adjusting them to ensure success. Theories differ in the mechanisms postulated to underlie students' use of cognitive, metacognitive, motivational, and behavioral processes to regulate their activities.

From a behavior theory perspective, self-regulated learning involves setting up one's own contingencies of reinforcement; that is, the stimuli to which one responds and the consequences of one's responses. No new processes are needed to account for self-regulated behavior, which includes learners' self-monitoring, self-instructing, and self-reinforcing.

Cognitive researchers emphasize mental activities such as attention, planning, rehearsal, goal setting, use of learning strategies, and comprehension monitoring. These theorists also stress motivational beliefs about self-efficacy, outcomes, and perceived value of learning. A key element is *choice:* For self-regulated learning to occur, learners must have some choice in their motives or methods for learning, time spent learning, criterion level of learning, the setting where learning occurs, and the social conditions in effect. When learners have few choices, their behaviors are largely externally regulated rather than self-regulated.

What Are the Implications for Instruction?

Theories attempt to explain various types of learning but differ in their ability to do so (Bruner, 1985). Behavior theories emphasize the forming of associations between stimuli and responses through selective reinforcement of correct responding. Behavior theories seem best suited to explain simpler forms of learning that involve associations, such as multiplication facts, foreign language word meanings, and state capitals.

Cognitive theories explain learning with such factors as knowledge construction, information processing, memory networks, and student perceptions and interpretations of classroom factors (teachers, peers, materials, organization). Cognitive theories are more appropriate for explaining complex forms of learning, such as solving mathematical word problems, drawing inferences from text, and writing essays.

But commonalities often exist among different forms of learning (Bruner, 1985). Learning to read is fundamentally different from learning to play the violin, but both benefit from attention, effort, and persistence. Learning to write term papers and learning to throw the javelin may not appear to be similar, but both are promoted by goal setting, self-monitoring of progress, feedback from teachers and coaches, and motivation to achieve.

Effective teaching requires that we determine the best theoretical perspectives for the types of learning we deal with and their implications for teaching. When reinforced practice is important for learning, then teachers should schedule it. When learning problem-solving strategies is important, then we should study the implications of information processing theory. A continuing challenge for researchers is to specify similarities and differences among types of learning and identify effective instructional approaches for each.

SUMMARY AND CRITIQUE

Chapter Summary

The study of human learning focuses on how individuals acquire and modify their knowledge, skills, strategies, beliefs, and behaviors. Learning represents an enduring change in behavior or in the capacity to behave in a given fashion, which results from practice or other experiences. This definition excludes temporary changes in behavior due to illness, fatigue, or drugs, as well as behaviors reflecting genetic and maturational factors, although many of the latter require responsive environments to manifest themselves.

The scientific study of learning had its beginnings in writings of such early philosophers as Plato and Aristotle. Two prominent positions on how knowledge is acquired are rationalism and empiricism. The psychological study of learning began late in the 19th century. Structuralism and functionalism were active schools of thought at the beginning of the 20th century with such proponents as Titchener, Dewey, and James, but these positions suffered from problems that limited widespread applicability to psychology.

Theories are perspectives or frameworks that help us make sense of environmental events. Theories serve as bridges between research and educational practices and as tools to organize and translate research findings into recommendations for educational practice. Types of research include correlational, experimental, and qualitative. Research may be conducted in laboratories or in field settings. Common ways to assess learning include direct observations, written and oral responses, ratings by others, and self-reports. Aided with advances in technology, newer methods such as educational data mining and learning analytics explore large data sets to determine learners' cognitive and behavioral activities during task engagement and how these predict achievement outcomes. Assessments should satisfy the criteria of reliability, validity, and absence of bias. Value-added assessment models track students' learning progress and can be used as a basis for differentiating instruction according to student needs.

Learning theory and educational practice often are viewed as distinct, but, in fact, they complement and help refine one another. Neither is sufficient to ensure good teaching and learning. Theory alone may not fully capture the importance of situational factors. Practical experience without theory is situationally specific and lacks an overarching framework to organize knowledge of teaching and learning.

Behavior theories explain learning in terms of observable events, whereas cognitive theories also consider the cognitions, beliefs, values, and affects of learners. Theories of learning differ in how they address critical issues. Some of the more important issues concern how learning occurs, how memory functions, the role of motivation, how transfer occurs, how self-regulated learning operates, and the implications for instruction.

Chapter Critique

Learning is a well-researched topic, but research on learning continues at a strong pace today. The more that researchers investigate learning, the more complex the field becomes. The days of simple explanations for learning seem to be over.

Even once-mundane topics have seen new life. For many years, assessment of learning was relatively straightforward: Measure it before and after instruction or an intervention. Researchers today take a more nuanced view of learning and often explore as it occurs. Learning is a dynamic process; exploring it while it is happening shows in more fine-grained fashion how it changes over time and in response to experiences.

The field has benefited from recent advances in educational data mining and learning analytics. It seems clear that data techniques will receive increased emphasis in the future.

Learning is an exciting topic to investigate. It is the bedrock of educational systems. Regarding any instructional procedure, the bottom-line question is whether it helps students learn. As long as that question stays at the forefront of education, we can expect continued high emphasis on the study of learning.

REFLECTION QUESTIONS

- We do not measure learning directly, but rather we infer it from performances. Accurate assessment of learning requires that students' performances closely correspond to what they have learned. Yet performances may be incomplete (i.e., not fully reflect what students have learned) or may be influenced by factors other than learning (e.g., illness, motivation). What are some ways that educators can help ensure that students' performances closely correspond to their actual learning?

- Learning theories and teaching practices ideally should affect one another. Think of some specific examples of how learning theories might affect teaching practices and how teaching practices might influence learning theories.

- For any given type of learning, the answer to the question "How does learning occur?" is critical. Pick a type of learning (e.g., dividing fractions, comprehending main ideas in text) and explain how the answer to that question might affect lesson design, instructional practices, and student activities.

FURTHER READING

Alexander, P. A., Schallert, D. L., & Reynolds, R. E. (2009). What is learning anyway? A topographical perspective considered. *Educational Psychologist, 44*, 176–192.

Anderman, E. M., Anderman, L. H., Yough, M. S., & Gimbert, B. G. (2010). Value-added models of assessment: Implications for motivation and accountability. *Educational Psychologist, 45*, 123–137.

Bruner, J. (1985). Models of the learner. *Educational Researcher, 14*(6), 5–8.

Popham, W. J. (2014). *Classroom assessment: What teachers need to know* (7th ed.). Boston: Allyn & Bacon.

Sztajn, P., Confrey, J., Wilson, P. H., & Edgington, C. (2012). Learning trajectory based instruction: Toward a theory of teaching. *Educational Researcher, 41*, 147–156.

Tweney, R. D., & Budzynski, C. A. (2000). The scientific status of American psychology in 1900. *American Psychologist, 55*, 1014–1017.

2 Neuroscience of Learning

The Tarrytown Unified School District was holding an all-day workshop for teachers and administrators on the topic of "Using Brain Research to Design Effective Instruction." During the afternoon break, a group of four participants—Joe Michela, assistant principal at North Tarrytown Middle School; Claudia Orondez, principal of Templeton Elementary School; Emma Thomas, teacher at Tarrytown Central High School; and Bryan Young, teacher at South Tarrytown Middle School—were discussing the day's session.

Joe: So, what do you think of this so far?

Bryan: It's really confusing. I followed pretty well the part about the functions of different areas of the brain, but I'm having a hard time connecting that with what I do as a teacher.

Emma: Me, too. The presenters are saying things that contradict what I thought. I had heard that each student has a dominant side of the brain so we should design instruction to match those preferences, but these presenters say that isn't true.

Joe: Well they're not exactly saying it isn't true. What I understood was that different parts of the brain have different primary functions but that there's a lot of crossover and that many parts of the brain have to work at once for learning to occur.

Claudia: That's what I heard too. But I agree with Bryan—it's confusing to know what a teacher is to do. We're supposed to appeal to all parts of the brain, and isn't that what teachers try to do now? For years, we've been telling teachers to design instruction to accommodate different student learning styles—visual, auditory, hands-on. Seems like brain research says the same thing.

Joe: Especially seeing. They said how important the visual sense is. I tell teachers not to lecture so much since that's not an effective way to learn.

Bryan: True, Joe. Another thing they said that threw me was how much teens' brains are developing. I thought their unusual behaviors were due to hormones. I see now that I need to be helping them more to make good decisions.

Emma: I think this really is fascinating. This session has made me aware of how the brain receives and uses information. But it's so complex! For me, the challenge is to match brain functioning with how I organize and present information and the activities I design for students.

Claudia: I've got lots of questions to ask. I know there's much that researchers don't know, but I'm ready to start working with elementary teachers to use brain research to benefit our children.

Many different learning theories and processes are discussed in subsequent chapters in this text. Behavior theories (Chapter 3) focus on external behaviors and consequences, whereas cognitive and constructivist theories—the focus of this text—posit that learning occurs internally. Cognitive processes include thoughts, beliefs, and emotions, all of which have neural representations.

This chapter addresses the *neuroscience of learning*, or the science of the relation of the nervous system to learning and behavior (Ludvik, 2016). Although neuroscience is not a learning theory, being familiar with neuroscience will give you a better foundation to understand the learning chapters that follow. And you will see that many findings from neuroscience research are highly compatible with principles of cognitive information processing (Chapters 5–7).

The focus of this chapter is on the *central nervous system (CNS)*, which comprises the brain and spinal cord. Most of the chapter covers brain rather than spinal cord functions. The *autonomic nervous system (ANS)*, which regulates involuntary actions (e.g., respiration, secretions), is mentioned where relevant.

The role of the brain in learning and behavior is not a new topic, but its significance among educators has increased in recent years. Although educators always have been concerned about the brain because the business of educators is learning and the brain is where learning occurs, much brain research has investigated brain dysfunctions. To some extent, this research is relevant to education because

educators have students in their classes with handicaps. But because most students do not have brain dysfunctions, findings from brain research have not been viewed as highly applicable to typical learners.

The advances in technology have made possible new methods that show how the brain functions while people perform mental operations involving learning and memory. The data yielded by these new methods are highly relevant to classroom teaching and learning and suggest implications for student motivation and learning and teacher professional development (Dubinsky, Roehrig, & Varma, 2013). Although to date there has been little direct influence of neuroscience research on instruction (Bowers, 2016), educators are interested in findings from neuroscience research as they seek ways to improve teaching and learning for all students (Byrnes, 2012; Scalise & Felde, 2017). This interest is evident in the opening vignette.

This chapter begins by reviewing the brain's neural organization and major structures involved in learning, motivation, and development. The topics of localization and interconnections of brain structures are discussed, along with methods used to conduct brain research. The neurophysiology of learning is covered, which includes the neural organization of information processing, executive function, memory networks, brain plasticity, and language learning. The important topic of brain development is discussed to include the influential factors on development, phases of development, critical periods of development, language development, and the role of technology. How motivation and emotions are represented in the brain is explained, and the chapter concludes with a discussion of the major implications of brain research for teaching and learning.

Discussions of the CNS are necessarily complex, as Emma notes in the opening scenario. Many structures are involved, there is much technical terminology, and CNS operation is complicated. The material in this chapter is presented as clearly as possible, but a certain degree of technicality is needed to preserve the accuracy of information. Readers who seek more technical descriptions of CNS structures and functions as they relate to learning, motivation, self-regulation, and development are referred to other sources (Byrnes, 2012; Centre for Educational Research and Innovation, 2007; Heatherton, 2011; Jensen, 2005; National Research Council, 2000; Wang & Morris, 2010; Wolfe, 2010).

When you finish studying this chapter, you should be able to do the following:

■ Describe the neural organization and functions of axons, dendrites, and glial cells.

■ Discuss the primary functions of the major areas of the brain.

■ Identify some brain functions that are highly localized in the right and left hemispheres.

■ Discuss the uses of different brain research technologies.

■ Explain how learning occurs from a neuroscience perspective to include executive function, consolidation, and memory networks.

■ Discuss how neural connections are formed and interact during language acquisition and use.

■ Discuss the key changes and critical periods in brain development as a function of maturation and experience.

■ Explain the role of the brain in the regulation of motivation and emotions.

■ Discuss some instructional implications of brain research for teaching and learning.

ORGANIZATION AND STRUCTURES

The central nervous system (CNS) is composed of the brain and spinal cord and is the body's central mechanism for control of voluntary behavior (e.g., thinking, acting). The autonomic nervous system (ANS) regulates involuntary activities, such as those involved in digestion, respiration, and blood circulation. These systems are not independent. People can, for example, exert some control over their heart rates, which means that they are voluntarily controlling an involuntary activity.

The spinal cord is about 18 inches long and the width of an index finger. It runs from the base of the brain down the middle of the back. It is essentially an extension of the brain. Its primary function is to carry signals to and from the brain, making it the central messenger between the brain and the rest of the body. Its ascending pathway carries signals from body locations to the brain, and its descending pathway carries messages from the brain to the appropriate body structure (e.g., to cause movement). The spinal cord also is involved in some reactions independently of the brain (e.g., knee-jerk reflex). Damage to the spinal cord, such as from an accident, can result in symptoms ranging from numbness to total paralysis (Jensen, 2005; Wolfe, 2010).

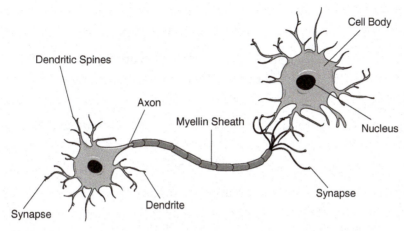

Figure 2.1
Structure of neurons.

Neural Organization

The CNS is composed of billions of cells in the brain and spinal cord. There are two major types of cells: neurons and glial cells. A depiction of neural organization is shown in Figure 2.1.

Neurons. The brain and spinal cord contain 90–100 billion neurons that send and receive information across muscles and organs (Evrard, Annese, & Ludvik, 2016; Wolfe, 2010). Most of the body's neurons are found in the CNS. Neurons are different from other body cells (e.g., skin, blood) in two important ways. For one, most body cells regularly regenerate. This continual renewal is desirable; for example, when we cut ourselves, new cells regenerate to replace those that were damaged. But neurons do not regenerate in the same fashion. Brain and spinal cord cells destroyed by a stroke, disease, or accident may be permanently lost. On a positive note, however, there is evidence that neurons can show some regeneration (Kempermann & Gage, 1999), although the extent to which this occurs and the process by which it occurs are not well understood.

Neurons are also different from other body cells because they communicate with one another through electrical signals and chemical reactions. They thus are organized differently than other body cells. This organization is discussed later in this section.

Glial Cells. The second type of cell in the CNS is the *glial cell*. Glial cells are far more numerous than neurons. They may be thought of as supporting cells since they support the work of the neurons. They do not transmit signals like neurons, but they assist in the process.

Glial cells perform many functions. A key one is to ensure that neurons operate in a good environment. Glial cells help to remove chemicals that may interfere with neuron operation. Glial cells also remove dead brain cells. Another important function is that glial cells put down myelin, a sheathlike wrapping around axons that helps transmit brain signals (discussed in the next section). Glial cells also appear to play key functions in the development of the fetal brain (Wolfe, 2010). In short, glial cells work in concert with neurons to ensure effective CNS functioning.

Synapses. Figure 2.1 shows neural organization with cell bodies, axons, and dendrites. Each neuron is composed of a cell body, thousands of short dendrites, and one axon. A *dendrite* is an elongated tissue that receives information from other cells. An *axon* is a long thread of tissue that sends messages to other cells. *Myelin sheath* surrounds the axon and facilitates the travel of signals.

Each axon ends in a branching structure. The ends of these branching structures connect with the ends of dendrites. Each of these connections is a *synapse*. We have 90–100 billion neurons and 10 times that number of synapses (Evrard et al., 2016). The interconnected structure is the key to how neurons communicate, because messages are passed among neurons at the synapses.

The process by which neurons communicate is complex. At the end of each axon are chemical *neurotransmitters*. They do not quite touch dendrites of another cell. The gap is called the *synaptic gap*. When electrical and chemical signals reach a high enough level, neurotransmitters are released into the gap. The neurotransmitters will either activate or inhibit a reaction in the contacted dendrite. Thus, the process begins as an electrical reaction in the neuron and axon, changes to a chemical reaction in the gap, and then reconverts to an electrical response in the dendrite. This process continues from neuron to neuron in lightning speed. As discussed later in this chapter, the role of the neurotransmitters in the synaptic gap is critical for learning. From a neuroscience perspective, *learning* is a change in the receptivity of cells brought about by neural connections formed, strengthened, and connected with others through use (Jensen, 2005; Wolfe, 2010).

Brain Structures

The human adult brain (*cerebrum*) weighs approximately three pounds and is about the size of a cantaloupe or large grapefruit (Tolson, 2006; Wolfe, 2010). Its outward texture has a series of folds and is wrinkly in appearance, resembling a cauliflower. Its composition is mostly water (78%), with the rest fat and protein. Its texture is generally soft. The major brain structures involved in learning are shown in Figure 2.2 (Jensen, 2005; Scalise & Felde, 2017; Wolfe, 2010) and described in the following paragraphs.

Cerebral Cortex. Covering the brain is the *cerebral cortex*, which is a thin layer about the thickness of an orange peel (less than one quarter of an inch). The cerebral cortex is the wrinkled "gray matter" of the brain. The wrinkles allow the cerebral cortex to have more surface area, which allows for more neurons and neural connections. The cerebral cortex has two hemispheres (right and left), each of which has four lobes (occipital, parietal, temporal, and frontal). The cortex is the central area involved in learning, memory, and processing of sensory information.

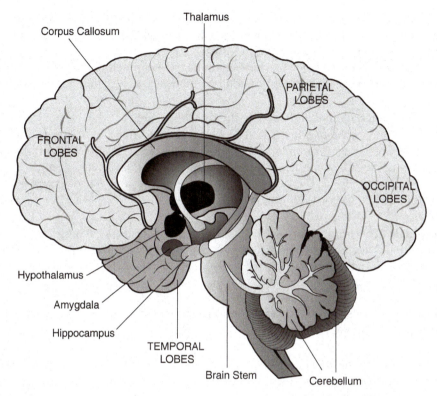

Figure 2.2
Major brain structures.

Brain Stem and Reticular Formation. At the base of the brain is the *brain stem*. The brain stem handles ANS (involuntary) functions through its *reticular formation*, which is a network of neurons and fibers that regulates control of basic bodily functions, such as breathing, heart rate, blood pressure, eyeball movement, salivation, and taste. The reticular formation also is involved in awareness levels (e.g., sleep, wakefulness). For example, when you go into a quiet, dark room, the reticular formation decreases brain activation and allows you to sleep. The reticular formation also helps to control sensory inputs. Although we constantly are bombarded by multiple stimuli, the reticular formation allows us to focus on relevant stimuli. This is critical for attention and perception (Chapter 5), which are key components of the human information processing system. The reticular formation also produces many of the chemical messengers for the brain.

Cerebellum. The *cerebellum* at the back of the brain regulates body balance, muscular control, movement, and body posture. Although these activities are largely under conscious control (and therefore the domain of the cortex), the cortex does not have all the equipment it needs to regulate them. It works in concert with the cerebellum to coordinate movements. The cerebellum is the key to motor skill acquisition. With practice, many motor skills (e.g., playing the piano, driving a car) can become largely automatic. This automaticity occurs because the cerebellum takes over much of the control, which allows the cortex to focus on activities requiring consciousness (e.g., thinking, problem solving).

Thalamus and Hypothalamus. Above the brain stem are two walnut-sized structures—the *thalamus* and *hypothalamus*. The thalamus acts as a bridge by sending inputs from the sense organs (except for smell) to the cortex. The hypothalamus is part of the ANS. It controls bodily functions needed to maintain homeostasis, such as body temperature, sleep, water, and food. The hypothalamus also is responsible for increased heart rate and breathing when we become frightened or stressed.

Amygdala. The *amygdala* (pronounced uh-MIG-dull-uh) is involved in the control of emotion and aggression (Presti, 2016). Incoming sensory inputs (except for smell, which travel straight to the cortex) go to the thalamus, which in turn relays the information to the appropriate area of the cortex and to the amygdala. The amygdala's function is to assess the harmfulness of sensory inputs. If it recognizes a potentially harmful stimulus, it signals the hypothalamus, which creates the emotional changes noted previously (e.g., increased heart rate and blood pressure).

Hippocampus. The *hippocampus* is the brain structure responsible for memory of the immediate past. How long is the immediate past? As we will see in Chapters 5 and 6, there is no objective criterion for what constitutes immediate and long-term (permanent) memory. Apparently the hippocampus helps establish information in long-term memory (which resides in the cortex) but maintains its role in activating that information as needed. Thus, the hippocampus may be involved in currently active (working) memory. Once information is fully encoded in long-term memory, the hippocampus may relinquish its role.

Corpus Callosum. Running along the brain (cerebrum) from front to back is a band of fibers known as the *corpus callosum*. It divides the cerebrum into two halves, or hemispheres, and connects them for neural processing. This is critical, because much mental processing occurs in more than one location in the brain and often involves both hemispheres.

Occipital Lobes. The *occipital lobes* of the cerebrum are primarily concerned with processing visual information. The occipital lobe also is known as the *visual cortex*. Visual stimuli are first received by the thalamus, which then sends these signals to the occipital lobes. Many functions that occur here involve determining motion, color, depth, distance, and other visual features. Once these determinations have occurred, the visual stimuli are compared to what is stored in memory to determine recognition (*perception*). An object that matches a stored pattern is recognized. When there is no match, then a new stimulus is encoded in memory. The visual cortex must communicate with other brain systems to determine whether a visual stimulus matches a stored pattern (Gazzaniga, Ivry, &

Mangun, 1998). The importance of visual processing in learning is highlighted by Joe in the opening vignette.

People can readily control their visual perception by forcing themselves to attend to certain features of the environment and to ignore others. If we are searching for a friend in a crowd, we can ignore a multitude of visual stimuli and focus only on those (e.g., facial features) that will help us determine whether our friend is present. Teachers apply this idea when they ask students to pay attention to visual displays and inform them of learning objectives at the start of the class.

Parietal Lobes. The *parietal lobes* at the top of the brain in the cerebrum are responsible for the sense of touch, and they help determine body position and integrate visual information. The parietal lobes have anterior (front) and posterior (rear) sections. The anterior part receives information from the body regarding touch, temperature, body position, and sensations of pain and pressure (Wolfe, 2010). Each part of the body has certain areas in the anterior part that receive its information and make identification accurate.

The posterior portion integrates tactile information to provide spatial body awareness, or knowing where the parts of your body are at all times. The parietal lobes also can increase or decrease attention to various body parts. For example, a pain in your leg will be received and identified by the parietal lobe, but if you are watching an enjoyable movie and are attending closely to that, you may not experience the pain in your leg.

Temporal Lobes. The *temporal lobes*, located on the side of the cerebrum, are responsible for processing auditory information. When an auditory input is received—such as a voice or other sound—that information is processed and transmitted to auditory memory to determine recognition. That recognition then can lead to action. When a teacher tells students to put away their books and line up at the door, that auditory information is processed and recognized, and then leads to the appropriate action.

Located where the occipital, parietal, and temporal lobes intersect in the cortex's left hemisphere is *Wernicke's area*, which allows us to comprehend speech and to use proper syntax when speaking. This area works closely with another area in the frontal lobe of the left hemisphere known as *Broca's area*, which is necessary for speaking. Although these key language processing areas are situated in the left hemisphere (but Broca's area is in the right hemisphere for some people, as explained later), many parts of the brain work together to comprehend and produce language. Language is discussed in greater depth later in this chapter.

Frontal Lobes. The *frontal lobes*, which lie at the front of the cerebrum, make up the largest part of the cortex. Their central functions are to process information relating to memory, planning, decision making, goal setting, and creativity. The frontal lobes also contain the primary motor cortex that regulates muscular movements.

It might be argued that the frontal lobes in the brain most clearly distinguish us from lower animals and even from our ancestors of generations past. The frontal lobes have evolved to assume ever more complex functions. They allow us to plan and make conscious decisions, solve problems, and converse with others. Further, these lobes allow us to be aware of our thinking and other mental processes, a form of *metacognition* (Chapter 7).

Running from the top of the brain down toward the ears is a strip of cells known as the *primary motor cortex*. This area controls the body's movements. If while dancing the "Hokey Pokey" you think, "put your right foot in," it is the motor cortex that directs you to put your right foot in. Each part of the body is mapped to a particular location in the motor cortex, so a signal from a certain part of the cortex leads to the proper movement being made.

In front of the motor cortex is Broca's area, which is the location governing the production of speech. This area is located in the left hemisphere for about 95% of people; for the other 5% (30% of left-handers), this area is in the right hemisphere (Wolfe, 2010). Not surprisingly, this area is linked to Wernicke's area in the left temporal lobe with nerve fibers. Speech is formed in Wernicke's area and then transferred to Broca's area to be produced (Wolfe, 2010).

The front part of the frontal lobe, or *prefrontal cortex*, is proportionately larger in humans than in other animals. It is here that the highest forms of mental activity occur (Evrard et al., 2016). Chapter 5 discusses how cognitive information processing associations are made in the brain. The prefrontal cortex is critical for these associations, because information received from the senses is related to knowledge stored in memory. In short, the seat of learning, and in turn the regulator of behavior, resides in the prefrontal cortex (D'Esposito & Postle, 2015). It also is the regulator of consciousness, allowing us to be aware of what we are thinking, feeling, and doing. As explained later, the prefrontal cortex seems to be involved in the regulation of emotions.

Table 2.1 summarizes the key functions of each of the major brain areas (Centre for Educational Research and Innovation, 2007; Jensen, 2005; Scalise & Felde, 2017; Wolfe, 2010). When reviewing this table, keep in mind that no part of the brain works independently. Rather, information (in the form of neural impulses) is rapidly transferred among areas of the brain. Although many brain functions are localized, different parts of the brain are involved in even simple tasks. It therefore makes little sense to label any brain function as residing in only one area, as brought out by Emma in the opening vignette.

Localization and Interconnections

We know much more about the brain's operation today than ever before, but the functions of the left and right hemispheres have been debated for a long time. Around 400 B.C., Hippocrates spoke of the duality of the brain (Wolfe, 2010). In 1870, researchers electrically stimulated different parts of the brains of animals and soldiers with head injuries (Cowey, 1998). They found that stimulation of certain parts of the brain caused movements in different parts of the body. The idea that the brain has a major hemisphere was proposed as early as 1874 (Binney & Janson, 1990).

In general, the left hemisphere governs the right visual field and side of the body, and the right hemisphere regulates the left visual field and side of the body. However, the two hemispheres are joined by bundles of fibers, the largest of which is the corpus callosum. Gazzaniga, Bogen, and Sperry (1962) demonstrated that language is controlled largely by the left hemisphere. These researchers found that when the corpus callosum was severed, patients who held an object out of sight in their left hands claimed they were holding nothing. Apparently, without the visual stimulus and because the left hand communicates with the right hemisphere, when this hemisphere received the input it could

Table 2.1
Key functions of areas of the brain.

Area	Key Functions
Cerebral cortex	Processes sensory information; regulates various learning and memory functions
Reticular formation	Controls bodily functions (e.g., breathing and blood pressure), arousal, sleep–wakefulness
Cerebellum	Regulates body balance, posture, muscular control, movement, motor skill acquisition
Thalamus	Sends inputs from senses (except for smell) to cortex
Hypothalamus	Controls homeostatic body functions (e.g., temperature, sleep, water, and food); increases heart rate and breathing during stress
Amygdala	Controls emotions and aggression; assesses harmfulness of sensory inputs
Hippocampus	Holds memory of immediate past and working memory; establishes information in long-term memory
Corpus callosum	Connects right and left hemispheres
Occipital lobe	Processes visual information
Parietal lobe	Processes tactile information; determines body position; integrates visual information
Temporal lobe	Processes auditory information
Frontal lobe	Processes information for memory, planning, decision making, goal setting, creativity; regulates muscular movements (primary motor cortex)
Broca's area	Controls production of speech
Wernicke's area	Comprehends speech; regulates use of proper syntax when speaking

not produce a name (because language is localized in the left hemisphere), and with a severed corpus callosum the information could not be transferred to the left hemisphere.

Brain research has identified other localized functions. Analytical thinking seems to be centered in the left hemisphere, whereas spatial, auditory, emotional, and artistic processing occurs in the right hemisphere (but the right hemisphere apparently processes negative emotions and the left hemisphere processes positive emotions; Ornstein, 1997). Music is processed better in the right hemisphere; directionality, in the right hemisphere; and facial recognition, the left hemisphere.

The right hemisphere also plays a critical role in interpreting contexts (Wolfe, 2010). For example, assume that someone hears a piece of news and says, "That's great!" This could mean the person thinks the news is wonderful or horrible. The context determines the correct meaning (e.g., whether the speaker is being sincere or sarcastic). Context can be gained from intonation, facial expressions and gestures, and knowledge of other elements in the situation. It appears that the right hemisphere is the primary location for assembling contextual information for a proper interpretation to be made.

Because functions are localized to some extent in brain sections, it is tempting to postulate that people who are highly verbal are dominated by their left hemisphere (left brained), whereas those who are more artistic and emotional are controlled by their right hemisphere (right brained). But this is a simplistic and misleading conclusion (Scalise & Felde, 2017), as the educators in the opening scenario realize. Although hemispheres have localized functions, they are connected and there is much passing of information (neural impulses) between them. Very little mental processing likely occurs only in one hemisphere (Ornstein, 1997). Further, we might ask which hemisphere governs individuals who are both highly verbal and emotional (e.g., impassioned speakers).

The hemispheres work in concert; information is available to both of them at all times. Speech offers a good example. If you are having a conversation with a friend, it is your left hemisphere that allows you to produce speech but your right hemisphere that provides the context and helps you comprehend meaning.

Neuroscientists do not agree about the extent of lateralization. Some argue that specific cognitive functions are localized in specific regions of the brain, whereas others believe that different regions have the ability to perform various tasks. This debate mirrors that in cognitive psychology (Chapters 5 and 6) between the traditional view that knowledge is locally coded and the parallel distributed processing view that knowledge is coded not in one location but rather across many memory networks (Bowers, 2009).

There is research evidence to support both positions. Different parts of the brain have different functions, but functions are rarely, if ever, completely localized in one section of the brain. This is especially true for complex mental operations, which depend on several basic mental operations whose functions may be spread out in several areas. Neuroscience researchers have shown, for example, that creativity does not depend on any single mental process and is not localized in any one brain region (Dietrich & Kanso, 2010). Studies employing fMRI have demonstrated that neural representations of stimuli in the cortex often are widely distributed (Rissman & Wagner, 2012), thus lending support to the idea that neural networks are highly connected. "Nearly any task requires the participation of both hemispheres, but the hemispheres seem to process certain types of information more efficiently than others" (Byrnes & Fox, 1998, p. 310). The practice of teaching to different sides of the brain (right brain, left brain) is not supported by empirical research (Scalise & Felde, 2017). Some applications of these points on interconnectedness and lateralization are given in Application 2.1.

Brain Research Methods

We know so much more today about the operation of the CNS than ever before, in part because of a convergence of interest in brain research among people in different fields. Historically, investigations of the brain were conducted primarily by researchers in medicine, the biological sciences, and psychology. Over the years, people in other fields have taken greater interest in brain research, believing that research findings might have implications for developments in their fields. Today we find educators, sociologists, social workers, counselors, government workers (especially those in the judicial system), and others interested in brain research. Funding for brain research also has increased, including by agencies that primarily fund non-brain–related research (e.g., education).

APPLICATION 2.1
Teaching to Both Brain Hemispheres

Brain research shows that much academic content is processed primarily in the left hemisphere, but that the right hemisphere processes context. A common educational complaint is that teaching is too focused on content with little attention to context. Focusing primarily on content produces student learning that may be unconnected to life events and largely meaningless. These points suggest that to make learning meaningful—and thereby involve both brain hemispheres and build more extensive neural connections—teachers should integrate content and context as much as possible.

Ms. Stone, a third-grade teacher, is doing a unit on butterflies. Children study material in books and on the Internet that shows pictures of different butterflies. To help connect this learning with context, she uses other activities. A local museum has a butterfly area, where butterflies live in a controlled environment. She takes her class to visit this so they can see the world of butterflies. A display is part of this exhibit, showing the different phases of a butterfly's life. These activities help children connect characteristics of butterflies with contextual factors involving their development and environment.

Mr. Marshall, a high school history teacher, knows that studying historical events in isolation is not meaningful and can be boring. Over the years, many world leaders have sought global peace. When covering in his U.S. history class President Woodrow Wilson's work to establish the League of Nations, Mr. Marshall draws parallels to the United Nations and contemporary ways that governments try to eliminate aggression (e.g., nuclear disarmament) to put the League of Nations into a context. Through class discussions, he has students relate the goals, structures, and problems of the League of Nations to current events and discuss how the League of Nations set the precedent for the United Nations and for worldwide vigilance of aggression.

Learning about psychological processes in isolation from real situations often leaves students wondering how the processes apply to people. When Dr. Brown covers Piagetian processes (e.g., egocentrism) in her undergraduate educational psychology course, she has students in their internships document behaviors displayed by children that are indicative of those processes. She does the same thing with other units in the course to ensure that the content learning is linked with contexts (i.e., psychological processes have behavioral manifestations).

Another reason for our increased knowledge is that there have been tremendous advances in technology for conducting brain research. Many years ago, the only way to perform brain research was to conduct an autopsy. Although examining brains of deceased persons has yielded useful information, this type of research cannot determine how the brain functions and constructs knowledge. Research investigating live brain functioning is needed to develop understanding about how the brain changes during learning and uses learned information to produce actions.

Table 2.2
Methods used in brain research.

Method	Description
X-ray	High-frequency electromagnetic waves used to determine abnormalities in solid structures (e.g., bones)
Computerized Axial Tomography (CAT) Scan	Enhanced images (three dimensions) used to detect body abnormalities (e.g., tumors)
Electroencephalograph (EEG)	Measures electrical patterns caused by movement of neurons; used to investigate various brain disorders (e.g., language and sleep)
Positron Emission Tomography (PET) Scan	Assesses gamma rays produced by mental activity; provides overall picture of brain activity but limited by slow speed and participants' ingestion of radioactive material
Magnetic Resonance Imaging (MRI)	Radio waves cause brain to produce signals that are mapped; used to detect tumors, lesions, and other abnormalities
Functional Magnetic Resonance Imaging (fMRI)	Performance of mental tasks fires neurons, causes blood flow, and changes magnetic flow; comparison with image of brain at rest shows responsible regions
Near-Infrared Optical Topography (NIR-OT)	Noninvasive technique for investigating higher-order brain functions in which near-infrared light is radiated on and penetrates the scalp, then is reflected by the cortex and passed back through the scalp

Techniques that have yielded useful information are discussed in the following section and summarized in Table 2.2. These are ordered roughly from least to most sophisticated.

X-ray. An *X-ray* consists of high frequency electromagnetic waves that can pass through nonmetallic objects where they are absorbed by body structures (Wolfe, 2010). The unabsorbed rays strike a photographic plate. Interpretation is based on light and dark areas (shades of gray). X-rays are two-dimensional and are most useful for solid structures, such as determining whether you have broken a bone. They do not work particularly well in the brain because it is composed of soft tissue, although X-rays can determine damage to the skull (a bone structure).

CAT Scan. The *CAT (computerized or computed axial tomography) scan* was developed in the early 1970s to increase the gradations in shades of gray produced by X-rays. CAT scans use X-ray technology but enhance the images from two to three dimensions. CAT scans are used to investigate tumors and other abnormalities, but, like X-rays, they do not provide detailed information about brain functioning.

EEG. The *EEG (electroencephalograph)* is an imaging method that measures electrical patterns created by the movements of neurons (Wolfe, 2010). Electrodes placed on the scalp detect neural impulses passing through the skull. The EEG technology magnifies the signals and records them on a monitor or paper chart (brain waves). Frequency of brain waves (oscillations) increase during mental activity and decrease during sleep. EEGs have proven useful to image certain types of brain disorders (e.g., epilepsy, language), as well as to monitor sleep disorders (Wolfe, 2010). EEGs provide valuable temporal information through *event-related potentials* (see the section Language Development), but they cannot detect the type of spatial information (i.e., where the activity occurs) that is needed to investigate learning in depth.

EEGs have been used to assess cognitive load (Chapter 5), or the demands placed on students' working memories while learning. Cognitive load is important; the goal is to reduce extraneous load not directly connected with learning so that learners can use their cognitive resources for learning. Newer wireless EEG technologies allow greater learner movements, reduce the size of the equipment, and can be applied to several learners at once (Antonenko, Paas, Grabner, & van Gog, 2010), thereby producing results more reflective of learners' actual cognitive processes while learning.

PET Scan. The *PET (positron emission tomography) scan* allows one to investigate brain activity while an individual performs tasks. The person is injected with a small dose of radioactive glucose, which the blood carries to the brain. While in the PET scanner the individual performs mental tasks. Those areas of the brain that become involved use more of the glucose and produce gamma rays, which are detected by the equipment. This leads to computerized color images (maps) being produced that show areas of activity.

Although PET scans represent an advance in brain imaging technology, there is a limit to how many sessions one can do and how many images can be produced at one time because the procedure requires ingesting radioactive material. Also, producing the images is a relatively slow process, so the speed with which neural activity occurs cannot be fully captured. Although the PET scan gives a good idea of overall brain activity, it does not show the specific areas of activity in sufficient detail (Wolfe, 2010).

MRI and fMRI. *Magnetic resonance imaging (MRI)* and *functional magnetic resonance imaging (fMRI)* are brain imaging techniques that address problems with PET scans. In an MRI, a beam of radio waves is fired at the brain. The brain is mostly water, which contains hydrogen atoms. The radio waves make the hydrogen atoms produce radio signals, which are detected by sensors and mapped onto a computerized image. The level of detail is superior to that of a CAT scan, and MRIs are commonly used to detect tumors, lesions, and other abnormalities (Wolfe, 2010).

The fMRI works much like the MRI, except that as persons perform mental or behavioral tasks the parts of the brain responsible fire neurons, which cause more blood to flow to these regions. The blood flow changes the magnetic field, so the signals become more intense. The fMRI scanner senses these changes and maps them onto a computerized image. This image can be compared to an image of the brain at rest to detect changes. The fMRI can capture brain activity as it occurs and where it occurs with second-to-second changes in blood flow (Pine, 2006); the fMRI can record four images per second (Wolfe, 2010). There is, however, some temporal disparity because blood flow changes can take several seconds to occur (Varma, McCandliss, & Schwartz, 2008).

Compared with other methods, the fMRI has many advantages. It does not require ingesting a radioactive substance. It works quickly and can measure activity precisely. It can record an image of a brain in a few seconds, which is much faster than other methods. And the fMRI can be repeated without problems.

Issues with brain technologies are that they must be used in artificial contexts (e.g., laboratories) with specialized equipment (e.g., CAT scan machines), which preclude their capturing learning in classrooms or other learning environments. These issues can be partially addressed by giving participants learning tasks during brain experiments or by subjecting them to the technology immediately after they have experienced different classroom contexts (Varma et al., 2008).

NIR-OT. *NIR-OT (near infrared optical topography)* is a newer noninvasive technique that has been used in brain research to investigate higher-level cognitive processing and learning. An optical fiber transmits a near-infrared light, which is radiated on the scalp. Some of that light penetrates to a depth of 30 mm. The cerebral cortex reflects the light and passes it back through the scalp, where it is detected by another optical fiber located near the point of penetration. NIR-OT measures concentrations of deoxygenated hemoglobin in the brain, which reflect brain activity (Centre for Educational Research and Innovation, 2007).

NIR-OT has many advantages over other methods. It can be employed in natural learning settings such as classrooms, homes, and workplaces. Its use has no mobility restrictions; participants move around freely. The NIR-OT analytical device is a mobile semiconductor. It can be used over longer periods of time with no serious side effects. And because the technology can be employed with multiple learners simultaneously, it can record brain changes as a consequence of social interactions.

The field of brain research is rapidly changing, and technologies are being developed and refined (e.g., wireless EEG, hand-held NIR-OT integrated circuit). In the future, we can expect to see techniques of greater sophistication that will allow learners greater mobility in natural learning environments, which will further pinpoint brain processes while learning occurs. The next section discusses the neurophysiology of learning, which addresses how the brain processes, integrates, and uses knowledge.

NEUROPHYSIOLOGY OF LEARNING

This section covering brain processing during learning uses as a frame of reference the information processing models discussed in Chapter 5. Brain processing during learning is complex (as the opening scenario shows), and what follows covers only the central elements. Readers who want detailed information about learning and memory from a neurophysiological perspective should consult other sources (Byrnes, 2012; Centre for Educational Research and Innovation, 2007; Ludvik, 2016; Presti, 2016; Wolfe, 2010).

Information Processing System

As explained in Chapter 5, key elements of the information processing system are sensory registers, working memory (WM), and long-term memory (LTM). The sensory registers receive inputs and hold them for a fraction of a second, after which they are discarded or channeled to WM. Most sensory inputs are discarded, since at any given time, we are bombarded with multiple inputs.

Earlier in this chapter, we saw that all sensory inputs (except for smells) go directly to the thalamus, where at least some of them then are sent to the appropriate part of the cerebral cortex for processing (e.g., brain lobes that process the appropriate sensory information). But the inputs are not sent in the same form in which they were received; rather, they are sent as neural "perceptions" of those inputs. For example, an auditory stimulus received by the thalamus will be transformed into the neural equivalent of the perception of that stimulus. This perception also is responsible for matching information to what already is stored in memory, a process known as *pattern recognition* (see Chapter 5). Thus, if the visual stimulus is the classroom teacher, the perception sent to the cortex will match the stored representation of the teacher and the stimulus will be recognized.

Part of what makes perception meaningful is that the brain's reticular activating system filters information to exclude trivial information and focus on important material (Wolfe, 2010). This process is adaptive because if we tried to attend to every input, we would never be able to focus on anything. There are several factors that influence this filtering. Perceived importance, such as teachers announcing that material is important (e.g., will be tested), is apt to command students' attention. Novelty attracts attention; the brain tends to focus on inputs that are novel or different from what might be expected. Another factor is intensity; stimuli that are louder, brighter, or more pronounced get more attention. Movement also helps to focus attention. Although these attentional systems largely operate unconsciously, it is possible to use these ideas for helping to focus students' attention in the classroom, such as by using bright and novel visual displays. Applications of these ideas to learning settings are given in Application 2.2.

APPLICATION 2.2
Arousing and Maintaining Students' Attention

Cognitive neuroscience research shows that various environmental factors can arouse and maintain people's attention. These factors include importance, novelty, intensity, and movement. As teachers plan instruction, they can determine ways to build these factors into their lessons and student activities.

Importance

Mrs. Peoples is teaching children to find main ideas in paragraphs. She wants children to focus on main ideas and not be distracted by interesting details. Children ask the question, "What is this story mostly about?" read the story, and ask the question again. They then pick out the sentence that best answers the question. Mrs. Peoples reviews the other sentences to show how they discuss details that may support the main idea but do not state it.

A middle school teacher is covering a unit on the state's history. There are many details in the text, and the teacher wants students to focus on key events and

(Continued)

APPLICATION 2.2 (*continued*)

persons who helped create the history. Before covering each section, the teacher gives students a list of key terms that includes events and persons. Students write a short explanatory sentence for each term.

Novelty

A fifth-grade teacher contacted an entomology professor at the local university who is an expert on cockroaches. The teacher took her class to his laboratory. There the students saw all types of cockroaches. The professor had various pieces of equipment that allowed students to see the activities of cockroaches firsthand, for example, how fast they move and what things they eat.

A high school tennis coach obtained a ball machine that sends tennis balls out at various speeds and arcs, which players then attempt to return. Rather than have players practice repetitively returning the balls, the coach sets up each session as a match (player versus machine) without the serves. If a player can successfully return the ball sent out from the ball machine, then the player gets the point; if not, the machine earns the point. Scoring follows the standard format (love-15-30-40-game).

Intensity

Many elementary children have difficulty regrouping in subtraction and incorrectly subtract the smaller from the larger number in each column. To help correct this error, Mr. Kincaid has students draw an arrow from the top number to the bottom number in each column before they subtract. If the number on top is smaller, students first draw an arrow from the top number in the adjacent column to the top number in the column being subtracted and then perform the appropriate regrouping. The use of arrows makes the order of operations more pronounced.

Ms. Lammaker wants her students to memorize the Gettysburg Address and recite it with emphasis in key places. She demonstrates the reading while being accompanied at a low volume by an instrumental version of "The Battle Hymn of the Republic." When she comes to a key part (e.g., "of the people, by the people, for the people"), she uses body and hand language and raises her inflection to emphasize certain words.

Movement

Studying birds and animals in books can be boring and does not capture their typical activities. An elementary teacher uses Internet sources and interactive videos to show birds and animals in their natural habitats. Students can see what their typical activities are as they hunt for food, take care of their young, and move from place to place.

Dr. Tsauro, an elementary methods instructor, works with her interns on their movements while they are teaching and working with children. Dr. Tsauro has each of her students practice a lesson with other students. As they teach, they are to move around and not simply stand or sit in one place at the front of the class. If they are using projected images, they are to move away from the screen. Then she teaches the students seat work monitoring, or how to move around the room effectively and check on students' progress as they are engaged in tasks individually or in small groups.

Brain research has helped to clarify attentional processes and differences seen in students with attention-deficit/hyperactivity disorder (ADHD). Attentional problems seen in these children include not paying close attention to details, difficulty in sustaining attention, and being easily distracted (Byrnes, 2012). MRI and fMRI studies have implicated certain brain areas including the prefrontal cortex, thalamus, and the area where the temporal, occipital, and parietal lobes join. Many of these same areas also have been implicated in WM deficits, which, not surprisingly, many children with ADHD have. Children with ADHD also often show problems with planning, strategic behavior, and self-regulation (executive functioning), which are affected by prefrontal cortex activity (Byrnes, 2012).

In summary, sensory inputs are processed in the sensory memories portions of the brain, and those that are retained long enough are transferred to WM. WM seems to reside in multiple parts of the brain but primarily in the prefrontal cortex of the frontal lobe (D'Esposito & Postle, 2015; Wolfe, 2010). As we will see in Chapter 5, information is lost from WM in a few seconds unless it is rehearsed or transferred to LTM. For information to be retained, there must be a neural signal to do so; that is, the information is deemed important and needs to be used.

A key aspect of the cognitive system is the brain's *executive function*. This function, which includes a group of activities, helps to manage the individual's goal attainment (Scalise & Felde, 2017). These activities are involved in planning, attention, self-control, monitoring, mental flexibility, and management of WM. Executive functioning, which relates positively to learning, is what keeps us task focused and goal directed. The concept bears some similarity to self-regulation (Chapter 10), although the latter also includes motivational processes. There are wide individual differences in students' executive functioning. Students with disabilities often show limitations in this area (Heward, Alber-Morgan, & Konrad, 2017).

The parts of the brain primarily involved in memory and information processing are the cortex and the medial temporal lobe (Wolfe, 2010). It appears that the brain processes and stores memories in the same structures that initially perceive and process information. At the same time, the particular parts of the brain involved in LTM vary depending on the type of information. In information processing theory, a distinction is made between declarative memory (facts, definitions, events) and procedural memory (procedures, strategies). Different parts of the brain are involved in using declarative and procedural information.

With declarative information, the sensory registers (e.g., visual, auditory) in the cerebral cortex receive the input and transfer it to the hippocampus and the nearby medial temporal lobe. Inputs are registered in much the same format as they appear (e.g., as a visual or auditory stimulus). The hippocampus is not the ultimate storage site; it acts as a processor and conveyor of inputs. As discussed in the next section, inputs that occur more often make stronger neural connections. With multiple activations, the memories form neural networks that become strongly embedded in the frontal and temporal cortexes. LTM for declarative information, therefore, appears to reside in the frontal and temporal cortex.

Much procedural information becomes automatized such that procedures can be accomplished with little or no conscious awareness (e.g., typing, riding a bicycle). Initial procedural learning involves the prefrontal cortex, the parietal lobe, and the cerebellum, which ensure that we consciously attend to the movements or steps and that these movements or steps are assembled correctly. With practice, these areas show less activity and other brain structures, such as the motor cortex, become more involved (Wolfe, 2010).

Cognitive neuroscience supports the idea that much can be learned through observation (Bandura, 1986; Chapter 4). Research shows that the cortical circuits involved in performing an action also respond when we observe someone else perform that action (van Gog, Paas, Marcus, Ayres, & Sweller, 2009).

With nonmotor procedures (e.g., decoding words, simple addition), the visual cortex is heavily involved. Repetition actually can change the neural structure of the visual cortex. These changes allow us to recognize visual stimuli (e.g., words, numbers) quickly without consciously having to process their meanings. As a consequence, many of these cognitive tasks become routinized. Conscious processing of information (e.g., stopping to think about what the reading passage means) requires extended activity in other parts of the brain.

But what if no meaning can be attached to an input? What if incoming information, although deemed important (such as by a teacher saying, "Pay attention"), cannot be linked with anything in memory? This situation necessitates creation of a new memory network, as discussed next.

Memory Networks

With repeated presentations of stimuli or information, neural networks can become strengthened such that the neural responses occur quickly. From a cognitive neuroscience perspective, *learning* involves forming and strengthening neural connections and networks (synaptic connections). This definition is similar to the definition of learning in current information processing theories (Chapter 5).

Hebb's Theory. The process by which these synaptic connections and networks are formed has been the study of scientific investigations for many years. Hebb (1949) formulated a neurophysiological theory of learning that highlights the role of two cortical structures: cell assemblies and phase sequences. A *cell assembly* is a structure that includes cells in the cortex and subcortical centers. Basically, a cell assembly is a neural counterpart of a simple association and is formed through frequently repeated stimulations. When the particular stimulation occurs again, the cell assembly is aroused. Hebb believed that when the cell assembly is aroused, it facilitates neural responses in other systems, as well as motor responses.

Hebb only could speculate on how cell assemblies formed, because in his time, the technology for examining brain processes was limited. Hebb felt that repeated stimulations led to the growth of synaptic knobs that increased the contact between axons and dendrites. With repeated stimulations, the cell assembly would be activated automatically, which facilitates neural processing.

A *phase sequence* is a series of cell assemblies. Cell assemblies that are stimulated repeatedly form a pattern or sequence that imposes some organization on the process. For example, we are exposed to multiple visual stimuli when we look at the face of a friend. One can imagine multiple cell assemblies, each of which covers a particular aspect of the face (e.g., left corner of the left eye, bottom of the right ear). By repeatedly looking at the friend's face, these multiple cell assemblies are simultaneously activated and become connected to form a coordinated phase sequence that orders the parts (e.g., so we do not transpose the bottom of the right ear onto the left corner of the left eye). The phase sequence allows the coordinated whole to be meaningfully and consciously perceived.

Neural Connections. Hebb's ideas, despite being formulated many years ago, are remarkably consistent with contemporary views on how learning occurs and memories are formed. As discussed in the next section on development, we are born with a large number of neural (synaptic) connections. Our experiences then work on this system. Connections are selected or ignored, strengthened or lost, and can be added and altered through new experiences (National Research Council, 2000).

It is noteworthy that the process of forming and strengthening synaptic connections (learning) changes the physical structure of the brain and alters its functional organization (National Research Council, 2000). Learning specific tasks produces localized changes in brain areas appropriate for the task, and these changes impose new organization on the brain. We tend to think that the brain determines learning, but in fact there is a reciprocal relationship because of the *plasticity* of the brain, or its capacity to change its structure and function as a result of experience (Centre for Educational Research and Innovation, 2007; Evrard & Ludvik, 2016; Presti, 2016; Scalise & Felde, 2017). Because of plasticity, the brain can remold and reshape itself. This is not accomplished through want or will but rather as a result of experiences. Through learning, people alter the physical structure of their brains, as well as their organization of neural connections. The adage "use it or lose it" seems appropriate.

Although brain research continues on this topic, available information indicates that memory is not formed completely at the time initial learning occurs. Rather, memory formation is a continuous process in which neural connections are adapted and stabilized over time (Wolfe, 2010). Each time knowledge passes from WM to LTM and then back to WM, the knowledge is modified, along with its affective content (discussed later). This knowledge transmission also leads to changes in brain structure and function. The process of stabilizing and strengthening neural (synaptic) connections is known as *consolidation* (Wang & Morris, 2010). The hippocampus appears to play a key role in consolidation, despite the fact that the hippocampus is not where memories are stored.

Which factors improve consolidation? Information processing theory postulates that organization, rehearsal, and elaboration impose structure (Chapter 5). Researchers have shown that the brain, far from being a passive receiver and recorder of information, plays an active role in storing and retrieving information (National Research Council, 2000).

In summary, it appears that stimuli or incoming information activates the appropriate brain portion and becomes encoded as synaptic connections. With repetition, these connections increase in number and become strengthened, which means they occur more automatically and communicate better with one another. Learning alters the specific regions of the brain involved in the tasks (National Research Council, 2000). Experiences are critical for learning, both with the environment (e.g., visual and auditory stimuli) and from one's mental activities (e.g., thoughts).

Given that the brain imposes some structure on incoming information, it is important that this structure help facilitate memory. We might say, then, that consolidation and memory are not sufficient to guarantee long-term learning. Rather, instruction should play a key role by helping to impose a desirable structure on the learning, a point noted by Emma and Claudia in the opening scenario. Applications of these ideas and suggestions for assisting learners to consolidate memories are given in Application 2.3.

APPLICATION 2.3
Teaching for Consolidation

Organization, rehearsal, and elaboration help the brain impose structure on learning and assist consolidation of neural connections in memory. Teachers can incorporate these ideas in various ways.

Organization

Ms. Standar's students are studying the American Revolution. Rather than ask them to learn many dates, she creates a timeline of key events and explains how each event led to subsequent events. Thus, she helps students chronologically organize the key events by relating them to events that they helped cause.

In her high school statistics course, Ms. Conwell organizes information about normally distributed data using the normal curve. On the curve she labels the mean and the standard deviations above and below the mean. She also labels the percentages of the area under portions of the curve so students can relate the mean and standard deviations to the percentages of the distribution. Using this visual organizer is more meaningful to students than is written information explaining these points.

Rehearsal

Mr. Luongo's elementary students will perform a Thanksgiving skit for parents. Students must learn their lines and their movements. He breaks the skit into subparts and works on one part each day then gradually merges the parts into a longer sequence. Students thus get plenty of rehearsal, including several rehearsals of the entire skit.

Mr. Gomez has his ninth grade English students rehearse their vocabulary words. For each word list, students write the word, the definition, and a sentence using the word. Students also write short essays every week, in which they try to incorporate at least five vocabulary words they have studied this year. This rehearsal helps to build memory networks with word spellings, meanings, and usage.

Elaboration

Elaboration is the process of expanding information to make it meaningful. Elaboration can help to build memory networks and link them with other relevant ones.

Mr. Jackson's students find precalculus difficult to link with other knowledge. Mr. Jackson surveys his students to determine their interests and what other courses they are taking. Then he relates precalculus concepts to these interests and courses. For example, for students taking physics he links principles of motion and gravity to conic sections (e.g., parabolas) and quadratic equations.

Ms. Kay's middle school students are applying critical thinking to personal responsibility issues. Students read vignettes and then discuss them. Rather than letting them simply agree or disagree with the story character's choices, she forces them to elaborate by addressing questions such as: How did this choice affect other people? What might have been the consequences if the character would have made a different choice? What would you have done and why?

Language Learning

The interaction of multiple brain structures and synaptic connections is seen clearly in language learning and especially in reading. Although contemporary technologies allow researchers to investigate real-time brain functioning as individuals acquire and use language skills, much brain research on language acquisition and use has been conducted on persons who have suffered brain injury and experienced some degree of language loss. Such research is informative of what functions are affected by injury to particular brain areas, but this research does not address language acquisition and use in children's developing brains.

Brain trauma studies have shown that the left side of the brain's cerebral cortex is central to reading and that the posterior (back) cortical association areas of the left hemisphere are critical for understanding and using language and for normal reading (Vellutino & Denckla, 1996). Reading dysfunctions often are symptoms of left posterior cortical lesions. Autopsies of brains of adolescents and young adults with a history of reading difficulties have shown structural abnormalities in the left hemispheres. Reading dysfunctions also are sometimes associated with brain lesions in the anterior (front) lobes—the area that controls speech—although the evidence much more strongly associates these dysfunctions with posterior lobe abnormalities. Since these results come from studies of persons who knew how to read (to varying degrees) and then lost some or all of the ability, we can conclude that the primarily left-sided areas of the brain associated with language and speech are critical for the maintenance of reading.

Keep in mind, however, that there is no one central area of the brain involved in reading. Rather, the various aspects of reading (e.g., letter and word identification, syntax, semantics) involve many localized and specialized brain structures and synaptic connections that must be coordinated to successfully read (Vellutino & Denckla, 1996). The section that follows examines how these interconnections seem to develop in normal readers and in those with reading problems. The idea is that coordinated reading requires the formation of *neural assemblies*, or collections of neural groups that have formed synaptic connections with one another (Byrnes, 2001). Neural assemblies seem conceptually akin to, although more complex than, Hebb's cell assemblies and phase sequences.

Results from neuroscience research show that specific brain regions are associated with orthographic, phonological, semantic, and syntactic processing required for reading (Byrnes, 2001). Orthographic (e.g., letters, characters) processing depends heavily on the primary visual area. Phonological processing (e.g., phonemes, syllables) is associated with the superior (upper) temporal lobes. Semantic processing (e.g., meanings) is associated with Broca's area in the frontal lobe and areas in the medial (middle) temporal lobe in the left hemisphere. Syntactic processing (e.g., sentence structure) also seems to occur in Broca's area.

Noted earlier were two key areas in the brain involved in language. Broca's area plays a major role in the production of grammatically correct speech. Wernicke's area (located in the left temporal lobe below the lateral fissure) is critical for proper word choice and elocution. Persons with deficiencies in Wernicke's area may use an incorrect word but one close in meaning (e.g., say "knife" when "fork" was intended).

Language and reading require the coordination of the various brain areas. Such coordination occurs through bundles of nerve fibers that connect the language areas to each other and to other parts of the cerebral cortex on both sides of the brain (Geschwind, 1998). The corpus callosum is the largest collection of such fibers, but there are others. Damage to or destruction of these fibers prevents the communication in the brain needed for proper language functioning, which can result in a language disorder. Brain researchers explore how dysfunctions operate and which brain functions continue in the presence of damage.

Recent research has shown the benefits on brain development of multiple language learning—an example of plasticity. Extensive study of a second language can result in growth in the hippocampus and in areas of the cortex governing higher-order reasoning (Kluger, 2013a). Other research has shown that multilingualism can lead to improvements in resolving conflicting ideas and multitasking (i.e., dividing and deploying attention resources to alternating sources of sensory input; Kluger, 2013a; Rothbart & Posner, 2015).

Language functioning is considered further in the following section, because it is intimately linked with brain development. For educators, knowing how the brain develops is important because developmental changes must be considered in planning instruction to ensure student learning.

BRAIN DEVELOPMENT

To this point we have focused on mature CNS functioning. Many educators, however, work with preschoolers, children, and adolescents. The topic of brain development is of interest not only in its own right but also because the educational implications for teaching and learning vary depending on the level of brain development. In the opening scenario, Bryan notes the importance of educators understanding brain development. This section discusses influential factors on development, the course of development, sensitive periods in development, the role of development in language acquisition and use, and the influence of technology.

Influential Factors

Although human brains are structurally similar, there are wide individual differences. Five influences on brain development are genetics, environmental stimulation, nutrition, steroids, and teratogens (Byrnes, 2001; Table 2.3). These influences begin during fetal development (Paul, 2010).

Table 2.3
Factors affecting brain development.

- Genetics
- Environmental stimulation
- Nutrition
- Steroids
- Teratogens

Genetics. The human brain differs in size and composition from those of other animals. Although the difference between the human genome and that of our closest animal relative (the chimpanzee) is only 1.23% (Lemonick & Dorfman, 2006), that difference and other genetic variations produce a species that can design and build bridges, compose music, write novels, solve complex equations, and so forth.

Human brains have a similar genetic structure, but they nonetheless differ in size and structure. Studies of monozygotic (one-egg) twins show that they sometimes develop brains that are structurally different (Byrnes, 2001). Genetic instructions determine the size, structure, and neural connectivity of the brain. Most of the time these differences yield normally functioning brains, but brain research continues to identify how certain genetic differences produce abnormalities.

Environmental Stimulation. Brain development requires stimulation from the environment. Prenatal development sets the stage for learning by developing a neural circuitry that can receive and process stimuli and experiences. Those experiences further shape the circuitry by adding and reorganizing synapses. For example, pregnant women who talk and sing to their babies may, through their speech and singing, help to establish neural connections in the babies (Wolfe, 2010). Brain development lags when experiences are missing or minimal. Although there are certain critical periods when stimulation can have profound effects (Jensen, 2005), research suggests that stimulation is important during the entire lifespan to ensure continued brain development.

Nutrition. Lack of good nutrition can have major effects on brain development, and the particular effects depend on when the poor nutrition occurs (Byrnes, 2001). Prenatal malnutrition, for example, slows the production and growth of neurons and glial cells. A critical period is between the fourth and seventh months of gestation when most brain cells are produced (Jensen, 2005). Later malnutrition slows how quickly cells grow in size and acquire a myelin sheath. Although the latter problem can be corrected with proper diet, the former cannot because too few cells have developed. This is why pregnant women are advised to avoid drugs, alcohol, and tobacco, maintain a good diet, and avoid stress (stress also causes problems for a developing fetus).

Steroids. *Steroids* refer to a class of hormones that affect several functions, including sexual development and stress reactions (Byrnes, 2001). Steroids can affect brain development in various ways. The brain has receptors for hormones. Such hormones as estrogen and cortisol will be absorbed and will potentially change brain structure during prenatal development. Excessive stress hormones can cause neurons to die. Researchers also have explored whether gender and sexual orientation differences arise in part due to differences in steroids. Although the evidence on the role of steroids in brain development is less conclusive than that for nutrition, steroids have the potential to affect the brain.

Teratogens. *Teratogens* are foreign substances (e.g., alcohol, viruses) that can cause abnormalities in a developing embryo or fetus (Byrnes, 2001). A substance is considered to be a teratogen only if research shows that a not unrealistically high level can affect brain development. For example, caffeine in small amounts may not be a teratogen, but it may become one when intake is higher. Teratogens can have effects on the development and interconnections of neurons and glial cells. In extreme cases (e.g., the rubella virus), they can cause birth defects.

Phases of Development

During prenatal development, the brain grows in size and structure, as well as in number of neurons, glial cells, and neural connections (synapses). Prenatal brain development is rapid because it occurs in nine months, and most cells are produced between months 4 and 7 (Jensen, 2005). Cells travel up the neural tube, migrate to various parts of the brain, and form connections. It is estimated that at its peak, the embryo generates a quarter of a million brain cells a minute.

At birth, the brain has over a million connections, which represent about 60% of the peak number of synapses that will develop over the lifetime (Jensen, 2005). Given these numbers, it is little wonder that prenatal development is so important. Changes that occur then can have far-reaching and permanent effects.

Brain development also occurs rapidly in infants. By the age of 2 years, a child will have as many synapses as an adult, and by the age of 3 years, the child will have billions more than an adult. Young children's brains are dense and have many complex neural connections and more than at any other time in life (Trawick-Smith, 2003).

In fact, young children have too many synapses. About 60% of babies' energy is used by their brains; in comparison, adult brains require only 20%–25% (Brunton, 2007). With development, children and adolescents lose far more brain synapses than they gain. By the time adolescents turn 18, they have lost about half of their infant synapses. Brain connections that are not used or needed simply disappear. This example of the "use it or lose it" strategy is desirable because connections that are used will be reinforced and consolidated, whereas those not used will be permanently lost.

By the age of 5 years, the child's brain has acquired a language and developed sensory motor skills and other competencies. The rapid changes of the first years have slowed, but the brain continues to add synapses. Neural networks are becoming more complex in their linkages. This process continues throughout development.

As noted by Bryan in the opening vignette, major changes occur during the teenage years when the brain undergoes structural alterations (Jensen, 2005). The frontal lobes, which handle abstract reasoning and problem solving, are maturing, and the parietal lobes increase in size. The prefrontal cortex, which controls judgments and impulses, matures slowly (Shute, 2009). There also are changes in neurotransmitters—especially *dopamine*—that can leave the brain more sensitive to the pleasurable effects of drugs and alcohol. There is a thickening of brain cells and massive reorganizations of synapses, which makes this a key time for learning. The "use it or lose it" strategy results in brain regions becoming strengthened through practice (e.g., practicing the piano thickens neurons in the brain region controlling the fingers; Wallis, 2004).

Given these widespread changes in their brains, it is not surprising that teenagers often make poor decisions and engage in high-risk behaviors involving drugs, alcohol, and sex. Instructional strategies need to take these changes into account. Applications of these ideas to instruction are given in Application 2.4.

APPLICATION 2.4
Teaching and Learning with Teenagers

The rapid and extensive changes that occur in teenagers' brains suggest that we not view teens as smaller versions of adults (or as young children either). Some suggestions for instruction with teens based on brain research follow.

Give Simple and Straightforward Directions

Mr. Glenn, who teaches 10th grade English, knows that his students' memories may not accommodate many ideas at once. For each novel students read, they must do a literary analysis that comprises several sections (e.g., plot summary, literary devices, analysis of a major character). Mr. Glenn reviews these sections carefully. For each, he explains what it should include and shows a sample or two.

Use Models

Students process information well when it is presented in multiple modes—visual, auditory, tactile. In her chemistry class, Ms. Carchina wants to ensure that students understand laboratory procedures. She explains and demonstrates each procedure she wants students to learn, then has students work in pairs to perform the procedure. As students work, she circulates among them and offers corrective feedback as needed.

Ensure That Students Develop Competence

Motivation theory and research show that students want to avoid appearing incompetent (Chapter 9). This is especially true during the teenage years when their senses of self are developing. Ms. Patterson teaches calculus, which is difficult for some students. Through quizzes, homework, and classwork, she knows which students are having difficulty. Ms. Patterson holds review sessions before school every day for her students, and she makes a point to urge students having difficulty to attend those sessions.

Incorporate Decision Making

The rapid development occurring in teens' brains means that their decision making often is flawed. They may base decisions on incomplete information or what they think will please their friends, and they may fail to think through potential consequences. Mr. Manley incorporates much decision making and many discussions of consequences into his marine science classes. Students study topics such as global warming and water pollution, and he presents them with case studies that they discuss (e.g., a ship's captain who wants to dump garbage at sea). He asks students questions that address topics such as the potential consequences of possible actions and other ways that the problem could be addressed.

Sensitive Periods

Some books on child rearing stress critical periods (e.g., the first two to three years of life), such that if certain experiences do not occur then, the child's development will suffer permanently. There is some truth to this statement, although the claim is overstated. It is more accurate to label them *sensitive periods*, which means that development

Table 2.4
Aspects of brain development
having sensitive periods.

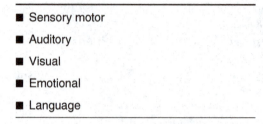

- Sensory motor
- Auditory
- Visual
- Emotional
- Language

proceeds well then but that further development can occur later. Five aspects of brain development for which there seem to be sensitive periods are language, emotions, sensory motor development, auditory development, and vision (Jensen, 2005; Table 2.4). Language and emotions are discussed elsewhere in this chapter; the remaining three are covered next.

Sensory Motor Development. The systems associated with vision, hearing, and motor movements develop extensively through experiences during the first two years of life. The vestibular system in the inner ear influences the senses of movement and balance and affects other sensory systems. Inadequate vestibular stimulation among infants and toddlers can lead to learning problems later (Jensen, 2005).

   Often, however, infants and toddlers are not in stimulating environments, especially those who spend much time in day care centers that provide mostly caregiving. Many children also do not receive sufficient stimulation outside of those settings, because they spend too much time in car seats, walkers, or in front of televisions. Allowing youngsters movement and even rocking them provides stimulation. About 60% of infants and toddlers spend an average of one to two hours per day watching television or videos (Courage & Setliff, 2009). Although young children can learn from these media, they do not do so easily. Children's comprehension and learning are enhanced when parents watch with them and provide descriptions and explanations (Courage & Setliff, 2009).

Auditory Development. The child's first two years are ideal for auditory development. By the age of 6 months, infants can discriminate most sounds in their environments (Jensen, 2005). In the first two years, children's auditory systems mature in terms of range of sounds heard and ability to discriminate among sounds. Problems in auditory development can lead to problems in learning language, because much language acquisition depends on children hearing the speech of others in their environments.

Vision. Vision develops largely during the first year of life and especially after the fourth month. Synaptic density in the visual system increases dramatically, including the neural connections regulating the perception of color, depth, movement, and hue. Proper visual development requires a visually rich environment where infants can explore objects and movements. Television and movies are poor substitutes. Although they provide color and movement, they are two-dimensional, and the developing brain needs depth. The action shown on television and in the movies often occurs too rapidly for infants to focus on properly (Jensen, 2005).

In short, the first two years of life are important for proper development of the sensory motor, visual, and auditory systems; and development of these systems is aided when infants are in a rich environment that allows them to experience movements, sights, and sounds. At the same time, brain development is a lifelong process; brains need stimulation after the age of 2 years. The brain's plasticity means that it continually is adding, deleting, and reorganizing synaptic connections and changing structurally. Researchers have shown that certain aspects of brain development occur more rapidly at certain times, but individuals of all ages benefit from stimulating environments.

Language Development

Previously we saw how certain functions associated with language operate in the brain. Although researchers have explored brain processes with different types of content involving various mental abilities, a wealth of research has been conducted on language acquisition and use. This is a key aspect of cognitive development and one that has profound implications for learning.

As stated earlier, much brain research on language has been conducted on persons who have suffered brain injury and experienced some degree of language loss. Such research is informative of what functions are affected by injury to particular brain areas, but these research investigations do not address language acquisition and use in children's developing brains.

Brain studies of developing children, while less common, have offered important insights into the development of language functions. Studies often have compared normally developing children with those who have difficulties learning in school. In place of the surgical techniques often used on brain-injured or deceased patients, these studies employ less invasive techniques such as those described earlier in this chapter. Researchers often measure *event-related potentials* (or *evoked potentials*), which are changes in brain waves that occur when individuals anticipate or engage in various tasks (Halliday, 1998).

Differences in event-related potentials reliably differentiate among below-average, average, and above-average children (Molfese et al., 2006). Children who are developing normally show extensive bilateral and anterior (front) cortical activation and accentuated left-sided activations in language and speech areas. In contrast to reading maintenance, it appears that reading development also depends on anterior activation, perhaps on both sides of the brain (Vellutino & Denckla, 1996). Other research shows that developing children who experience left-sided dysfunction apparently compensate to some extent by learning to read using the right hemisphere. The right hemisphere may be able to support and sustain an adequate level of reading, but it seems critical that this transition occurs prior to the development of language competence. Such assumption of language functions by the right hemisphere may not happen among individuals who have sustained left-hemisphere damage as adults.

A sensitive period in language development is between birth and age 5, during which children's brains develop most of their language capabilities. There is a rapid increase in vocabulary between the ages of 19 and 31 months (Jensen, 2005). The development of these language capabilities is enhanced when children are in language-rich environments where parents and others talk with children. This sensitive period for language development overlaps the one for auditory development between birth and age 2.

In addition to this period, language development also seems to be part of a natural process with a timetable. The auditory and visual systems develop capacities to supply input for the development of language. A parallel process may occur in language development with the capacity to perceive *phonemes*, which are the smallest units of speech sounds (e.g., the "b" and "p" sounds in "bet" and "pet"). Children learn or acquire phonemes when they are exposed to them in their environments; if phonemes are absent in their environments, then children do not acquire them. Thus, there may be a sensitive period in which synaptic connections are properly formed, but only if the environment provides the inputs. In short, children's brains may be "ready" ("prewired") to learn various aspects of language at different times in line with their levels of brain development (National Research Council, 2000).

Importantly for education, instruction can help to facilitate language development. Different areas of the brain must work together to learn language, such as the areas involved in seeing, hearing, speaking, and thinking (Byrnes, 2001). Acquiring and using language is a coordinated activity. People listen to speech and read text, think about what was said or what they read, and compose sentences to write or speak. This coordinated activity implies that language development should benefit from instruction that coordinates these functions; that is, experiences that require vision, hearing, speech, and thinking (see Application 2.5).

APPLICATION 2.5
Facilitating Language Development

Birth to age 5 represents a sensitive period for the development of language, but its acquisition and use are lifelong activities. Teachers can help develop the language skills of students of all ages. Instruction ideally should coordinate the component functions of seeing, hearing, thinking, and speaking.

A kindergarten teacher works with her students on learning phonemes. To help develop recognition of phonemes in "__at" words (e.g., mat, hat, pat, cat, sat), she has each of these words printed on a slide. The phoneme is printed in red and the "at" appears in black. She gives students practice by showing a slide, asking them to say the word, and then asking individual students to use the word in a sentence.

Mrs. O'Neal teaches her third graders animal names and spellings. She has a picture of each animal and its printed name on a slide, along with two to three interesting facts about the animal (e.g., where it lives, what it eats). She has children pronounce the animal's name several times and spell it aloud, then write a short sentence using the word. This is especially helpful for animal names that are difficult to pronounce or spell (e.g., giraffe, hippopotamus).

Ms. Kaiton, a middle school mathematics teacher, is working with her students on place value. Some students are having a lot of difficulty and cannot correctly order numbers from smallest to largest (e.g., .007, 7/100, seven tenths, 7). Ms. Kaiton has three large magnetic number lines, each ranging from 0 to 1 and broken into units

APPLICATION 2.5 (*continued*)

of tenths, hundredths, and thousandths. She asked students to put a magnetic bar on the appropriate number line (e.g., put the bar on the 7 of the hundredths line for 7/100). Then she broke the class into small groups of students, gave them problems, and asked them to use number lines to show where numbers fell so they could properly order them. Next she worked with them to convert all numbers to a common denominator (e.g., 7/10 = 70/100) and to place the markers on the same board (e.g., thousandths) so they could see the correct order.

Students in Mr. Bushnell's tenth-grade class learn about key documents in U.S. history (e.g., Declaration of Independence, Constitution, Bill of Rights). To appeal to multiple senses, he brought facsimile copies of these documents to class. Then he had students engage in role-playing where they read selections from the documents. Students were taught how to put emphasis at appropriate places while reading to make these passages especially distinctive.

Many students in Dr. Hua's child development course have difficulty comprehending and correctly using psychological terms (e.g., assimilation, satiation, zone of proximal development). He obtains videos that demonstrate these concepts (e.g., a child being administered Piagetian tasks) and gives students case studies that exemplify concepts, which students discuss in class. For example, in a case study illustrating satiation a student is repeatedly praised by a teacher. Finally, the student becomes satiated with praise and tells the teacher that she does not always have to tell him that he did well.

In summary, different areas of the brain participate in language development in normally developing children, although left-hemisphere contributions typically are more prominent than right-hemisphere ones. Over time, language functions are heavily subsumed by the left hemisphere. In particular, reading skill seems to require left-hemisphere control. But further research is needed before we fully understand the relationships between brain functions and developing language and reading competencies.

Like other aspects of brain development, language acquisition reflects the interaction between heredity and environment discussed in Chapter 1. The cultural experiences of infants and children will determine to a large extent which brain synapses they retain. If the culture stresses motor functions, then these should be strengthened; whereas if the culture stresses cognitive processes, then these will ascend. If young children are exposed to a rich linguistic environment stressing oral and written language, then their language acquisition will develop more rapidly than will the language capabilities of children in impoverished environments.

The implication for facilitating early brain development is to provide rich experiences for infants and young children, stressing perceptual, motor, and language functions. This is especially critical in the first years of life. These experiences should enhance the formation of synaptic connections and networks. Children who have suffered in utero (e.g., from mothers' drug or alcohol abuse), as well as those with developmental disabilities (e.g., retardation, autism), benefit from intervention in the first three years (Shore, 1997).

Influence of Technology

The brain's plasticity (or neuroplasticity) means that its neural connections are formed, strengthened, and weakened, based on experiences. In recent years, the rapid growth of technology and its influx into everyday lives have created a new set of experiences that heretofore were not present. We might ask how technology affects brain development.

Before addressing this question, we should consider how technology is used, especially by students. We live in an age of technological multitasking! There are desktop and laptop computers, phones, tablets, and other personal devices. It is not uncommon to use multiple devices simultaneously. A student may be using the Internet on a computer while e-mailing on a personal device and texting on a phone. The student may rapidly shift back and forth between these applications. For any single application, technology may present us with much information rapidly. Internet use, for example, is based on quick and often superficial reading and rapid following of links. Because texting is limited to short messages, one can send and receive several texts in a few minutes.

Living in an online environment can promote cursory reading, hurried and distracted thinking, and superficial learning (Carr, 2011). Although it is possible to think deeply and take one's time on the Internet, its structure does not encourage it. The Internet delivers sensory and cognitive stimuli that tend to be repetitive, interactive, and intensive. Users repeat the same or similar actions (e.g., following links) at high speed and often in response to cues. Some cues require physical responses (e.g., type, rotate screen), but others provide a lot of visual and auditory input. These activities tend to be rewarded; clicking links or answering messages gives quick responses and new inputs. The rapid feedback that often brings rewards encourages continued use.

As discussed in Chapter 5, our attention to stimuli is a limited resource. Heavy use of technology can bombard and overload our capacity to attend. Stimuli attended to are transferred to working memory for processing. When multiple stimuli impinge, working memory can become overloaded due to the high cognitive load (Chapter 5). This situation means that most information is lost since it is not adequately processed or connected with information in long-term memory. As Carr (2011) notes, the Internet seizes our attention only to scatter it. The resulting learning can be minimal. Information not rehearsed is lost, and it is easy not to rehearse in an online environment. Further, the knowledge that is retained may not be well connected with itself or knowledge in long-term memory.

Neuroscience researchers have investigated the components of *multitasking*, which requires aligning attention with various sources of sensory input (e.g., phones, computers). The executive attention network allows us to control and shift attention relevant to goals and to control distractions (Rothbart & Posner, 2015). This executive function also underlines *effortful control*, or voluntary control of behavior and emotions. It may be that multitaskers are more capable of displaying a greater breadth of attention than they are of focusing attention on one task at a time (Lin, 2009). Multitasking also involves working memory (WM; Chapter 5), which is affected by attention. Improvements in attention and WM can lead to neurons in the affected areas performing more efficiently (Rothbart & Posner, 2015).

From a neuroscience perspective, different cognitive activities show different patterns of brain activity. Small, Moody, Siddarth, and Bookheimer (2009) found differences in brain activity between book reading (which requires sustained attention and deep thought) and Internet use. Book reading led to activity in brain areas associated with language, memory, and visual processes. Web surfing, conversely, resulted in more brain activity in prefrontal areas associated with decision making and problem solving. Further, such brain "rewiring" (an example of plasticity) can occur with only a few hours of online use (Small & Vorgan, 2008).

These tasks work at cross-purposes. Evaluating links and making navigational choices requires mental coordination and decision making, which distract the brain from interpreting text or other information and thereby impede comprehension and retention. Although one can read deeply online, it is not easily compatible with doing so without distractions. Deep reading requires concentrated thought where we eliminate distractions and quiet the problem solving functions of the frontal lobes. When multiple devices are used at once, the distractions increase and the learning that occurs is apt to be fragmented.

There is, of course, nothing wrong with browsing and scanning. These are useful skills in many endeavors, including those outside of online environments. We often do not need to read or think deeply; rather, we want to get the gist of information or browse quickly to find the resources we desire. Neuroscience evidence shows benefits of Web browsing on the development of visual-spatial skills (Carr, 2011). As we work in a busy online environment, our neural circuits devoted to scanning, skimming, and multitasking are expanding and strengthening. But the downside is that if browsing and scanning become dominant modes—as opposed to operations we use less often—synapses devoted to thinking deeply and sustaining concentration may be weakening. From an evolutionary perspective, we might say that success in online environments promotes the survival of the busiest!

Another point to keep in mind is that long-term memories require consolidation of events that have been attended to and processed in working memory. Consolidation takes time to form strong memories. When too much information impinges rapidly, it is not properly consolidated and linked with existing knowledge in long-term memory. To grow, strengthen, and maintain synapses requires that students devote some time away from the rapid pace of online environments and think about what they have been learning. Consolidation continues to occur after exposure to information stops.

The use of technology is neither inherently good nor bad (Wolfe, 2010). An educational implication of neuroscience research is that to develop different cognitive brain functions requires students to engage in different activities. Scanning, problem solving, and decision making are useful skills, but so are reflective and meditative thinking and evaluating and interpreting information. Teachers can plan instructional activities that require different skills and ensure that students do not spend too much time on Web surfing and not enough on assembling knowledge into a coherent whole.

MOTIVATION AND EMOTIONS

Researchers have investigated how brain processes link with many different cognitive functions. They also have been concerned with the brain processes involved with noncognitive functions, such as motivation and emotions (Presti, 2016; Reeve & Lee, 2016). These functions are discussed in turn.

Motivation

In Chapter 9, *motivation* is defined as the process whereby goal-directed activities are instigated and sustained. Motivated actions include choosing to engage in tasks, expending physical and mental effort, and persisting in the face of difficulties. Chapter 9 also discusses various processes that have been shown to affect motivation, such as goals, self-efficacy, needs, values, and perceptions of control.

Contemporary theories posit that motivational processes have cognitive components. *Self-efficacy*, for example, refers to perceived capabilities to learn or perform behaviors at designated levels (Bandura, 1997). Self-efficacy is a cognitive belief. As such, it also has a neural representation of the kind discussed in this chapter. Although research is lacking in this area, we might expect that self-efficacy beliefs are represented in the brain as a neural network that links the domain being studied (e.g., solving fraction problems, comprehending text) with current sensory input. Other motivational processes also may be represented in synaptic networks, as might processes involved in self-regulated learning (Chapter 10). More research on motivation and self-regulation variables would help to bridge the gap between education and neuroscience.

From a cognitive neuroscience perspective, there are at least two kinds of neural counterparts of motivation. These involve rewards and motivational states.

Rewards. Rewards have a long history in motivation research. They are key components of behavior theories (Chapter 3), which contend that behaviors that are reinforced (rewarded) tend to be repeated in the future. Motivation represents an increase in the rate, intensity, or duration of behavior.

Cognitive and constructivist theories of motivation postulate that it is the expectation of reward, rather than the reward itself, that motivates behavior. Rewards can sustain motivation when they are given contingent on competent performance or progress in learning. Motivation may decline over time when people view the rewards as controlling their behavior (i.e., they are performing a task so that they can earn a reward). Further, new learning can occur rapidly when events run contrary to expectancies. Previous neural connections become disrupted and new ones form to reflect the new contingencies between responses and outcomes (Tucker & Luu, 2007).

Research shows that the brain has a system for processing rewards (Jensen, 2005; Reeve & Lee, 2016), but, like other brain functions, this one is complex. Many brain structures are involved, including the hypothalamus, prefrontal cortex, and amygdala. The brain produces its own rewards in the form of opiates that result in a natural high. This effect suggests that the brain may be predisposed toward experiencing and sustaining pleasurable outcomes. The expectation that one may receive a reward for competent or improved performance can activate this pleasure network (Reeve & Lee, 2016), which produces the neurotransmitter *dopamine*. It may be that the brain stores, as part of a neural network, the expectation of reward for performing the action. In fact, dopamine can be produced by the expectation of pleasure (anticipation of reward), as well as by the pleasure itself. Dopamine increases when there is a discrepancy between expected and realized rewards (e.g., one expects a large reward but receives a small one). The dopamine system can help people adjust their expectations, which is a type of learning (Varma et al., 2008).

Interestingly, addictive substances (e.g., drugs, alcohol) also increase the amount of dopamine (Lemonick, 2007b), which raises feelings of pleasure. Addiction may occur when repetitive use of addictive substances disrupts the normal balance of synaptic connections that control rewards, cognition, and memory.

The brain also can become satiated with rewards such that the expectation of a reward or the receipt of a reward does not produce as much pleasure as previously. It is possible that the expectation of a larger reward is needed to produce dopamine, and if that is not forthcoming, then the effect may extinguish. This point may help explain why a particular reward can lose its power to motivate over time.

Research is needed on whether other cognitive motivators—such as goals and the perception of learning progress—also trigger dopamine responses and thus have neuro-physiological referents. Since dopamine production is idiosyncratic, the same level of reward or expectation of reward will not motivate all students uniformly. This point suggests that additional brain processes are involved in motivation, which has practical implications for teaching. Teachers who plan to use rewards must learn what motivates each student and establish a reward system that can accommodate changes in students' preferences.

Motivational States. *Motivational states* are complex neural connections that include emotions, cognitions, and behaviors (Jensen, 2005). States change with conditions. If it has been several hours since we have eaten, then we likely are in a hunger state. We may be in a worried state if problems are pressing on us. If things are going well, we may be in a happy state. Similarly, a motivational state may include emotions, cognitions, and behaviors geared toward learning. Like other states, a motivational state is an integrated combination of mind, body, and behavior that ultimately links with a neural network of synaptic connections.

States are fluid; they are ever changing based on internal (e.g., thoughts) and external (e.g., environmental) events. Any given motivational state can strengthen, weaken, or change to another type of state. This changing nature of synaptic connections matches the nature of motivation (discussed in Chapter 9); that is, motivation is a process rather than an outcome. As a process, it is not steady but rather waxes and wanes. The key to learning is to maintain motivation within an optimal range.

Teachers intuitively understand the idea of motivational states. Their goal is to have students in a motivational state for learning. At any given moment, some students will be in that state, but others will be experiencing different states, including apathy, sadness, hyperactivity, and distraction. To change these states, teachers may have to first address the present states (e.g., attend to why Kira is sad) and then attempt to focus students' attention on the task at hand.

The integration of cognition, emotion, and behavior posited by neuroscience is important. The individual components will not lead to desirable learning. For example, students who believe they want to learn and are emotionally ready to do so nonetheless will learn little if they engage in no learning behavior. Likewise, motivated behavior without a clear cognitive focus on learning will be wasted activity. Students who are experiencing emotional stress yet want to learn and engage in learning actions are apt to find their learning less than maximal because emotions are thwarting synaptic connections from being formed and consolidated.

Emotions

The study of emotions is relevant to neuroscience (Scalise & Felde, 2017). *Emotions* are feelings or internal events that typically are short-lived and intense and have specific, salient causes (Forgas, 2000; Pekrun, 2006). They can be positive (e.g., enjoyment, hope, relief, pride, gratitude) or negative (e.g., anxiety, boredom, sadness, anger, jealousy). Individuals typically are aware of the cause of an emotion; for example, anger and disappointment after failing an exam.

Emotions are considered to be integral parts of learning and memory (Scalise & Felde, 2017). Emotional experiences may get stored in neural networks and LTM along with cognitive information; thus, these two become associated. When information subsequently is transferred from LTM back to WM for use, both the cognitive and emotional information may be altered during this phase and the subsequent transfer back to LTM. This continual brain reorganization can improve learning and memory.

But similar to the neurophysiological evidence for motivation, the operation of emotions in the CNS is not fully understood. Emotions have multiple components (Centre for Educational Research and Innovation, 2007). Mental (cognitive) processing occurs in response to incoming information. Physiological changes occur, such as an increase in blood pressure. Behaviors or impulses to act can be instigated. These three elements are not always coordinated. Physiological and behavioral responses may occur largely bypassing the mental processing (e.g., when one acts impulsively to save someone who is drowning). How this process operates and the conditions that affect it are the subject of current neurophysiological research (Scalise & Felde, 2017).

Network theory (Halgren & Marinkovic, 1995) postulates that emotional reactions consist of four overlapping stages: orienting complex, emotional event integration, response selection, and sustained emotional context. The orienting complex is an automatic response in which individuals direct their attention toward a stimulus or event and mobilize resources to deal with it. The orienting complex produces a neural response that is sent to other stages. In the emotional event integration stage, this stimulus or event is integrated with information in WM and LTM, such as information about the definition or meaning of the stimulus or event and the context.

In the third stage (response selection), the individual ascribes cognitive meaning to the stimulus or event, integrates this meaning with an affective component, identifies possible actions, and selects one. Finally, during the sustained emotional context stage, the individual's mood is linked with outputs of prior stages. Each stage is linked with specific neural areas. For example, sustained emotional context seems to be associated with neural firings in areas of the frontal lobe (Halgren & Marinkovic, 1995).

But emotions are more complex than this analysis, because the same event has the potential to arouse different emotions. The English language reflects this potential multiple triggering, as when one says after hearing a piece of news, "I didn't know whether to laugh or cry." Neuroscience research studies of emotion regulation show that the prefrontal cortex can regulate the amygdala (Heatherton, 2011). When the prefrontal cortex is regulating emotions, the amygdala shows decreased activity. Similar to much else about the brain, the regulation of emotions involves interactions between brain regions (Presti, 2016).

Another possibility is that emotional activity in the brain is different for primary and culturally based emotions (Byrnes, 2001). Primary emotions (e.g., fear, anger, surprise) may have an innate neural basis centered in the right hemisphere (which regulates much ANS functioning), whereas emotions that involve cultural meanings (e.g., statements made by people that can be interpreted in different ways) may be governed more by the left hemisphere with its language functions.

Emotions can help to direct attention, which is necessary for learning (Phelps, 2006). Information from the environment goes to the thalamus, where it is relayed to the amygdala and to the frontal cortex. The amygdala determines the emotional significance of the stimulus (Wolfe, 2010). This determination is facilitative, because it tells us whether to run, seek shelter, attack, or stay calm. The frontal cortex provides the cognitive interpretation of the stimulus, but this takes additional time. Part of what is meant by "emotional control" is not to simply react to the emotional significance (although when safety is an issue, that is desirable) but rather to delay action until the proper cognitive interpretation can be made.

In addition to their role in attention, emotions also influence learning and memory (Phelps, 2006). It appears that the hormones epinephrine and norepinephrine, which are secreted by the adrenal cortex to produce the autonomic responses involved in emotions, also enhance memory for the triggering stimulus or event in the temporal lobe of the brain (Wolfe, 2010). Conscious memory of emotional situations is consolidated better due to the actions of these hormones.

The point that emotions can enhance learning should not be interpreted as a recommendation that educators should make learning as stressful as possible. As we saw earlier, too much stress interferes with the formation and consolidation of neural networks. But a certain amount of stress can facilitate memory and learning (Scalise & Felde, 2017). In developing skills, learners may engage in blocked practice where they perform the same skills repeatedly (e.g., work several problems of the same type) or in interleaving where they perform different skills from task to task (e.g., work several problems where problem types keep changing). Because learners do not become bored, interleaving produces more stress, which can result in hormonal changes that strengthen synapses (Gregory, 2013).

Motivation and emotions can be used constructively to produce better learning. Teachers who lecture a lot engender little emotional involvement by students. But emotional interest should rise when teachers design activities that engage students in the learning. Activities such as role-playing, peer collaboration, searching the Internet, discussions, and demonstrations are likely to instigate greater motivation and emotions and lead to better learning than will teacher lecturing (Application 2.6).

Increasing emotion during learning is effective only up to a point. Too much emotion (e.g., high stress) for lengthy periods is not desirable because of all the negative side effects (e.g., increased blood pressure, compromised immune system). Students in prolonged stressful situations worry excessively, and the thoughts associated with worry thwart learning.

Negative effects brought on by stress or threats arise partly because of the hormone *cortisol*, which like epinephrine and norepinephrine is secreted by the adrenal glands (Lemonick, 2007a). Epinephrine and norepinephrine act quickly, and cortisol is a long-lasting backup. High amounts of cortisol in the body over long time periods can lead to deterioration of the hippocampus and a decline in cognitive functioning (Wolfe, 2010).

Cortisol also is critical during brain development. Infants bond emotionally with parents or caregivers. When babies experience stress, their levels of cortisol become elevated

APPLICATION 2.6
Involving Emotions in Learning

Mrs. Ortiz wants her elementary students to enjoy school, and she knows how important it is to arouse children's emotions for learning. She tries to link academic content to students' experiences so that their positive emotions associated with these experiences become associated with the learning. When her children read a story about a child who took a trip, she asks them to tell about when they took a trip to visit a relative, go on vacation, or so forth. When working on mathematical division, she asks children to think about something that was divided into parts (e.g., pizza, cake) so that several people could enjoy it.

Mr. LeTourneau wants his students to not only learn history but also experience the emotions involved in key events. Reading about events such as World War I and the Great Depression can devoid them of emotions, yet these and other events stirred strong emotions among those who lived then. He helps students express emotions they likely would have felt. For a role-playing on the Great Depression, one student played an unemployed person looking for work, and others played the roles of employers he visited asking for work. As each employer turned him down, the job seeker became more frustrated and finally began sobbing and saying, "All I want is a job so I can provide for my family. I hope my children never see this again in their lives!"

Dr. Smith-Burton understands that some students might view her elementary social studies methods course as dry and boring. To invoke her students' emotions, each week she has her students focus on one or two concepts to address in their school internships. For example, reading about learning can be dull, but seeing a child learn is exciting. As her students work with schoolchildren, they keep a log on the children's behaviors and reactions as they are learning. Her students report how excited they become when they are tutoring children and the children begin to show that they are learning. As one of her students reported, "I became so happy while working with Keenan when he said, 'Oh I get it,' and sure enough he did!"

in their bodies. Cortisol retards brain development because it reduces the number of synapses and leaves neurons vulnerable to damage (Trawick-Smith, 2003). In contrast, when babies form attachments and maintain them over time, cortisol levels do not become elevated (Gunnar, 1996). When attachments are secure, cortisol levels do not rise to dangerous levels even under stressful conditions. Thus, it is critical that young children believe that their parents or caregivers love them and are reliable caregivers.

In summary, we can see that motivation and emotions are integrally linked with cognitive processing, neural activities, and behaviors. Further, the evidence summarized in this section shows that when motivation and emotions are properly regulated, they can positively affect attention, learning, and memory. We now turn to the instructional applications of neuroscience for teaching and learning.

INSTRUCTIONAL APPLICATIONS

Relevance of Brain Research

Many educators view brain research with interest, because they believe that it might suggest ways to make educational materials and instruction compatible with how children process information and learn. But unfortunately, the history of behavioral science reflects a disconnect between brain research and learning theories. Learning theorists in various traditions, while acknowledging the importance of brain research, have tended to formulate and test theories independently of brain research findings. And there are no stellar examples of neuroscience research promoting more-effective teaching methods (Bowers, 2016).

This situation is changing. Educational researchers increasingly believe that understanding brain processes provides additional insights into the nature of learning and development (Byrnes & Fox, 1998). Indeed, some cognitive explanations for learning (e.g., activation of knowledge in memory, transfer of information from WM to LTM; Chapter 5) involve CNS processes, and brain psychology has begun to explain operations involved in learning and memory. Findings from brain research support many results obtained in research studies on learning and memory (Byrnes, 2012; Centre for Educational Research and Innovation, 2007). This point suggests that a profitable direction for research is to strike a balance between neuroscience and other disciplines such as learning (Schwartz, Lilienfeld, Meca, & Sauvigné, 2016).

It is unfortunate that some educators have overgeneralized results of brain research to make unwarranted instructional recommendations. Although brain functions are to some extent localized, there is much evidence that tasks require activity of both hemispheres and that their differences are more relative than absolute (Centre for Educational Research and Innovation, 2007). The identification of "right-brained" and "left-brained" students usually is based on informal observations rather than on scientifically valid and reliable measures and instruments. The result is that some educational methods are being used with students not because of proven effects on learning but, rather, because they presumably use students' assumed brain preferences.

Brain Myths

The complexity of brain research means that most people have difficulty understanding it. That, coupled with a general fascination with the brain, has yielded myths about the brain. Some myths that have relevance to instruction and learning are summarized in this section (Centre for Educational Research and Innovation, 2007; Table 2.5).

The most important learning occurs before the age of 3 years. It is true that, in the early years, children's brains are undergoing rapid increases (synaptogenesis) and consolidation (pruning) of synapses and that early stimulation can aid brain development and especially of language. But brain development never ceases. If it did, there would be no point in having our present educational system because it does not formally begin until age 5. What happens from birth to age 3 influences later development but does not completely determine it.

Table 2.5
Brain myths.

- The most important learning occurs before the age of 3 years
- There are critical periods for learning
- We use only 10% of our brains
- Men and women have different brains
- You can learn while you sleep
- People are right brained or left brained

There are critical periods for learning. There are times when learning is easier, but it is not critical that it occurs then. For example, the capability to reproduce sounds of a language (phonology, accent) and integrate them with grammar is optimal during childhood (Centre for Educational Research and Innovation, 2007). After that, people still can learn a language and vocabulary equally well as children. It is more accurate to say that there are sensitive periods for learning. Learning of different skills occurs across the lifespan.

We use only 10% of our brains. In one sense, that is true. Of our billions of brain cells, 10% are neurons; the remaining 90% are glial cells. Since neurons are involved in learning, we only use 10% of our brain cells directly for learning. But neuroscience research shows that 100% of the brain is always active and especially so compared with the rest of the body. Although the brain represents 2% of body weight, it consumes 20% of available energy (Centre for Educational Research and Innovation, 2007).

Men and women have different brains. There are some differences. Men's brains generally are larger, and the language areas of the brain are more strongly activated among women (Centre for Educational Research and Innovation, 2007). At times, cognitive terms are used that have no biological reality (e.g., a "male" brain better understands mechanics; a "female" brain communicates better). Neuroscience research does not show gender differences in developing neural networks during learning. Teachers are wise to treat all students as capable of learning.

You can learn while you sleep. This is every student's dream! But there is no neuroscience evidence to support it. Some research has shown that sleep may help memory of things learned just prior to going to sleep (Gais & Born, 2004). The learning occurs before sleep; sleep may help to consolidate the memory.

People are right brained or left brained. This issue is discussed in this chapter. Although there is localization of functions to some degree, crossover is the rule rather than the exception. In short, we use all of our brains for learning.

Educational Issues

Brain research, and CNS research in general, raises many issues relevant to education (Table 2.6). With respect to developmental changes, one issue involves the key role of

Table 2.6
Educational issues
relevant to brain research.

- Role of early education
- Complexity of cognitive processes
- Diagnosis of specific difficulties
- Multifaceted nature of learning

early education. That children's brains are super-dense implies that more neurons are not necessarily better. There likely is an optimal state of functioning in which brains have the "right" number of neurons and synapses—neither too many nor too few. Physical, emotional, and cognitive development involves the brain approaching its optimal state. Atypical development—resulting in developmental disabilities—may occur because this paring-down process does not proceed normally.

This molding and shaping process in the brain suggests that early childhood education is important. The developmental periods of infancy and preschool can set the stage for the acquisition of competencies needed to be successful in school (Byrnes & Fox, 1998). Early intervention programs (e.g., Head Start) have been shown to improve children's school readiness and learning, and many states have implemented preschool education programs. Brain research justifies this emphasis on early education.

A second issue is that instruction and learning experiences must be planned to take into account the complexities of cognitive processes such as attention and memory (Chapter 5). Neuroscience research has shown that attention is not a unitary process but, rather, includes many components (e.g., alerting to a change in the current state, localizing the source of the change). Memory is similarly differentiated into types, such as declarative and procedural. The implication is that educators cannot assume that a particular instructional technique "gains students' attention" or "helps them remember." Rather, we must be more specific about what aspects of attention that instruction will appeal to and what specific type of memory is being addressed.

A third issue involves remedying students' learning difficulties. Brain research suggests that the key to correcting deficiencies in a specific subject is to determine with which aspects of the subject the learner is having difficulty and then specifically address those. Mathematics, for example, includes such subcomponents as comprehension of written numbers and symbols, retrieval of facts, and the ability to write numbers. Reading comprises orthographic, phonological, semantic, and syntactic processes. To say that one is a poor reader does not diagnose where the difficulty lies. Only fine-tuned assessments can make that identification, and then a corrective procedure can be implemented that will address the specific deficiency. A general reading program that addresses all aspects of reading (e.g., word identification, word meanings) is analogous to a general antibiotic given to one who is sick; it may not be the best therapy. It is educationally advantageous to offer corrective instruction in those areas that require correction most. For example, cognitive strategy instruction in children's weaknesses can be combined with traditional reading instruction (Katzir & Paré-Blagoev, 2006).

The final issue concerns the complexity of learning theories. Brain researchers have shown that multifaceted theories of learning seem to capture the actual state of affairs better than do parsimonious models. There is much redundancy in brain functions, which accounts for the common finding that when an area of the brain known to be associated with a given function is traumatized, the function may not completely disappear (another reason why the "right-brain" and "left-brain" distinctions do not hold much credibility). Over time, theories of learning have become more complex. Classical and operant conditioning theories (Chapter 3) are much simpler than social cognitive theory, information processing theory, and constructivist theory (Chapters 4–8). These latter theories better reflect brain reality. This suggests that educators should accept the complexity of school learning environments and investigate ways that the many aspects of environments can be coordinated to improve teaching and student learning (Dubinsky et al. 2013).

Brain-Based Educational Practices

This chapter suggests some specific educational practices that facilitate learning and that are substantiated by brain research (Scalise & Felde, 2017). Byrnes (2001) contended that brain research is relevant to psychology and education to the extent that it helps psychologists and educators develop a clearer understanding of learning, development, and motivation; that is, it is relevant when it helps to substantiate existing predictions of learning theories.

In other chapters of this text, theories and research findings that suggest effective teaching and learning practices are reviewed. Table 2.7 lists some educational practices that are derived from learning theories and their effectiveness supported by both learning and brain research. In the opening vignette, we suspect that Emma and Claudia will be using these practices (among others). Application 2.7 gives examples of these applied in learning settings.

Problem-Based Learning. Problem-based learning is an effective learning method (Chapter 8). Problem-based learning engages students in learning and helps to motivate them. When students work in groups (peer collaboration; supported by constructivism), they also can improve their cooperative learning skills. Problem-based learning requires students to think creatively and bring their knowledge to bear in unique ways. It is especially useful for projects that have no one correct solution.

The effectiveness of problem-based learning is substantiated by brain research. With its multiple connections, the human brain is wired to solve problems (Scalise & Felde, 2017). Students who collaborate to solve problems become aware of new ways that

Table 2.7
Educational practices
substantiated by brain research.

- ■ Problem-based learning
- ■ Simulations and role-playing
- ■ Active discussions
- ■ Graphics
- ■ Positive climate

APPLICATION 2.7
Effective Educational Practices

There are many educational practices whose positive effects on learning are supported by both learning and brain research. Some important practices are problem-based learning, simulations and role-playing, active discussions, graphics, and positive climate.

Problem-Based Learning

Mr. Abernathy's eighth graders have studied their state's geography, including characteristics of the main regions and cities of the state. He divided the class into small groups to work on the following problem. A large company wants to open a facility in the state. Each small group of students is assigned a specific region in the state. The task for each group is to make a convincing argument for why the facility should be located in that region. Factors to be addressed include costs associated with locating in that area, accessibility to major highways and airports, availability of a labor force, quality of schools, nearness of higher education facilities, and support from the community. Students gather information from various sources (e.g., media center, Internet), prepare a poster with pictures and descriptions, and give a 10-minute presentation with slides supporting their position. Each member of a group has responsibility for one or more aspects of the project.

Simulations and Role-Playing

Mr. Barth's fifth-grade students have read *Freedom on the Menu* by Carole Boston Weatherford. This book tells the story of the Greensboro, North Carolina, lunch counter sit-ins in the 1960s as seen through the eyes of a young African American girl. Mr. Barth discusses this book with the students and probes them for how they thought it felt to these individuals to be discriminated against. He then organizes class simulations and role-plays so that students can see how discrimination can operate. For one activity, he selected the girls to be the leaders and the boys to follow their directions. For another activity, he only called on boys with blue eyes, and for a third activity, he moved all students with dark hair to the front of the room. Using these activities, he hoped that students would see and feel the unfairness of treating people differently based on characteristics that they cannot change.

Active Discussions

Ms. Carring's civics class has been studying U.S. presidential elections. U.S. presidents are elected by electoral votes. There have been occasions where presidents elected by gaining the necessary electoral votes have not had a majority (50%) of the popular vote or have actually had a lower popular-vote total than the losing candidate. Ms. Carring holds a class discussion on the topic, "Should U.S. presidents be elected by popular vote?" She facilitates the discussion by raising questions in response to points raised by students. For example, Candace argued that a popular vote better reflects the will of the people. Ms. Carring then asked whether, if we used only a popular vote, candidates would tend to focus on voters in heavily populated states (e.g., California, New York) and neglect voters in states with small populations (e.g., Montana, Vermont).

(Continued)

APPLICATION 2.7 (*continued*)

Graphics

Mr. Antonelli, a high school vocational instructor, has his students design a house, which they then will help to build with help from community members. The school system owns the land, a local contractor will pour the foundation, and a builder's supply company will donate the lumber and electrical and plumbing supplies. The students use computer graphics to design different house styles and interior layouts. The class considers these and decides on an exterior and interior design plan. They then work with Mr. Antonelli and the builder's supply company to determine what supplies and equipment they will need. Several community members volunteer to help students build the house, and after they finish it, the house is given to a local family selected by a community organization.

Positive Climate

Ms. Taylor teaches second grade in a school serving a high-poverty neighborhood. Many of her students live in single-parent homes, and over 80% of the students receive lunch for free or at a reduced cost. Ms. Taylor does many things to create a positive climate. Her classroom ("Taylor's Nest") is warm and inviting and has cozy corners where students can go to read. Each day she talks with all students individually to learn what is happening in their lives. Ms. Taylor has a teacher's aide and an intern from a local university in her class, so students get much individual attention. She has a private space ("Taylor's Corner") where she goes to talk privately with a student about any problems or stresses the student may be experiencing. She contacts the parents or guardians of her students to invite them to come to class and assist in any way that they can.

knowledge can be used and combined, which forms new synaptic connections. Further, problem-based learning is apt to appeal to students' motivation and engender emotional involvement, which also can create more extensive neural networks.

Simulations and Role-Playing. Simulations and role-playing have many of the same benefits as does problem-based learning. Simulations might occur via technology applications, in the regular class, or in special settings (e.g., museums). Role-playing is a form of modeling (Chapter 4) where students observe others. Both simulations and role-playing provide students with learning opportunities that are not ordinarily available. These methods have motivational benefits and command student attention. They allow students to engage with the material actively and invest themselves emotionally. Collectively, these benefits help foster learning.

Active Discussions. Many topics lend themselves well to student discussions. Students who are part of a discussion are forced to participate; they cannot be passive observers. This increased level of cognitive and emotional engagement leads to better learning. Further, by participating in discussions, students are exposed to new ideas and integrate these with their current conceptions. This cognitive activity helps build synaptic connections and new ways of using information.

Graphics. The human body is structured such that we take in more information visually than through all other senses (Wolfe, 2010). Visual displays help to foster attention, learning, and retention. The collective findings from learning and brain research support the benefits of graphics. Teachers who use graphics in their teaching and have students employ graphics (e.g., PowerPoint presentations, videos, demonstrations, drawings, concept maps, graphic organizers) capitalize on visual information processing and are apt to improve learning.

Positive Climate. We saw in the section on emotions that learning proceeds better when students have a positive attitude and feel emotionally secure. Conversely, learning is not facilitated when students are stressful or anxious, such as when they fear volunteering answers because the teacher becomes angry if their answers are incorrect. In Chapter 9 and elsewhere in this text, we discuss how students' positive beliefs about themselves and their environments are critical for effective learning. Brain research substantiates the positive effect that emotional involvement can have on learning and the building of synaptic connections. Teachers who create a positive classroom climate may find that behavior problems are minimized and that students become more invested in learning.

SUMMARY AND CRITIQUE

Chapter Summary

The neuroscience of learning is the science of the relation of the nervous system to learning and behavior. Although neuroscience research has been conducted for several years in medicine and the sciences, it recently has become of interest to educators because of the potential instructional implications of research findings. Neuroscience research addresses the central nervous system (CNS), which comprises the brain and spinal cord and regulates voluntary behavior, and the autonomic nervous system (ANS), which regulates involuntary actions.

The CNS is composed of billions of cells in the brain and spinal cord. There are two major types of cells: neurons and glial cells. Neurons send and receive information across muscles and organs. Each neuron is composed of a cell body, thousands of short dendrites, and one axon. Dendrites receive information from other cells; axons send messages to cells. Myelin sheath surrounds axons and facilitates the travel of signals. Axons end in branching structures (synapses) that connect with the ends of dendrites. Chemical neurotransmitters at the ends of axons activate or inhibit reactions in the contracted dendrites. This process allows signals to be sent rapidly across neural and bodily structures. Glial cells support the work of neurons by removing unneeded chemicals and dead brain cells. Glial cells also establish the myelin sheath.

The human adult brain (cerebrum) weighs about three pounds and is approximately the size of a cantaloupe. Its outer texture is wrinkled. Covering the brain is the cerebral cortex, a thin layer that is the wrinkled gray matter of the brain. The wrinkles allow the cortex to have more neurons and neural connections. The cortex has two hemispheres (left and right), each of which has four lobes (occipital, parietal, temporal, frontal). With some exceptions, the structure of the brain is roughly symmetrical. The cortex is the primary area involved in learning, memory, and processing of sensory information. Some other key areas of the brain are the brain stem, reticular formation, cerebellum, thalamus, hypothalamus, amygdala, hippocampus, corpus callosum, Broca's area, and Wernicke's area.

The brain's left hemisphere generally governs the right visual field, and vice versa. Many brain functions are localized to some extent. Analytical thinking seems to be centered in the left hemisphere, whereas spatial, auditory, emotional, and artistic processing occurs primarily in the right hemisphere. At the same time, many brain areas work together to process information and regulate actions. There is much crossover between the two hemispheres as they are joined by bundles of fibers, the largest of which is the corpus callosum.

The working together of multiple brain areas is seen clearly in language acquisition and use. The left side of the brain's cerebral cortex is central to reading. Specific brain regions are associated with orthographic, phonological, semantic, and syntactic processing required in reading. Wernicke's area in the left hemisphere controls speech comprehension and use of proper syntax when speaking. Wernicke's area works closely with Broca's area in the left frontal lobe, which is necessary for speaking. However, the right hemisphere is critical for interpreting context and thus the meaning of much speech.

Various technologies are used to conduct brain research. These include the X-ray, CAT scan, EEG, PET scan, MRI, fMRI, and NIR-OT. The field of brain research is changing rapidly, and new technologies of greater sophistication will continue to be developed.

From a neuroscientific perspective, learning is the process of building and modifying neural (synaptic) connections and networks. Sensory inputs are processed in the sensory memories portions of the brain; those that are retained are transferred to WM, which seems to reside in multiple parts of the brain but primarily in the prefrontal cortex of the frontal lobe. Under the control of the brain's executive function, information then may be transferred to LTM. Different parts of the brain are involved in LTM depending on the type of information (e.g., declarative, procedural). With repeated presentations of stimuli or information, neural networks become strengthened such that the neural responses occur quickly. Because of its *plasticity*, the brain changes as a result of learning. The process of stabilizing and strengthening synaptic connections is known as *consolidation*, and through consolidation the physical structure and functional organization of the brain is changed.

Influential factors on brain development are genetics, environmental stimulation, nutrition, steroids, and teratogens. During prenatal development, the brain grows in size, structure, and number of neurons, glial cells, and synapses. The brain develops rapidly in infants; young children have complex neural connections. As children lose brain synapses, those they retain depend partly on the activities they engage in. There seem to be sensitive periods during the first few years of life for the development of language, emotions, sensory motor functions, auditory capabilities, and vision. Early brain development benefits from rich environmental experiences and emotional bonding with parents and caregivers. Major changes also occur in teenagers' brains in size, structure, and number and organization of neurons.

Two neural counterparts of motivation involve rewards and motivational states. The brain seems to have a system for processing rewards and produces its own rewards in the form of opiates that result in a natural high. The brain may be predisposed toward experiencing and sustaining pleasurable outcomes, and the pleasure network can be activated by the expectation of reward. Motivational states are complex neural connections that include emotions, cognitions, and behaviors. It is important to maintain motivation for learning within an optimal range.

The operation of emotions in the CNS is complex. Emotional reactions consist of stages, such as orienting to the event, integrating the event, selecting a response, and sustaining the emotional context. Brain-linked emotional activity may differ for primary and culturally based emotions. Emotions can facilitate learning because they direct attention and influence learning and memory. Emotional involvement is desirable for learning; but when emotions become too strong, cognitive learning is impeded.

Findings from brain research support many results obtained in cognitive research studies on learning and memory. But it is important not to overgeneralize brain research findings through such labeling of students as right or left brained. Most learning tasks require activity of both hemispheres, and the differences between brain functions are more relative than absolute.

Brain research suggests that early education is important, instruction should take children's cognitive complexities into account, assessment of specific problems is necessary to plan proper interventions, and complex theories of learning capture the brain's operation better than do simpler theories. Some educational practices supported by brain research are problem-based learning, simulations and role-playing, active discussions, graphics, and a positive climate.

A summary of learning issues appears in Table 2.8.

Chapter Critique

Neuroscience is the science of brain development and operation; it is not a theory of learning. But educators and others concerned about learning are interested in neuroscience research because of its potential to provide explanations for learning and implications for teaching. To date, however, neuroscience research has had minimal impact on education.

Historically, the relevance of neuroscience to education was limited in various ways. Most neuroscience research was done using individuals who were deceased or who had cognitive or physical impairments. Neither of these allow valid generalization of findings to living learners who learn normally. The methodology of neuroscience also was limited to methods that required extensive equipment hookups, which is not conducive to studying learning in settings where it typically occurs.

Advances in technology are changing this picture. As equipment becomes more mobile, its capability to capture real-time learning increases. There also has been much more research conducted on individuals who are engaged in learning tasks.

Yet going from neuroscience to education requires a conceptual leap from neural processes to behavior because there is no one-to-one correspondence. For example, the same type of neural emotional processing can manifest itself behaviorally in different ways. To say how neural processes translate into behavior—which, as educators, we are concerned with—will require more extensive research.

It is not fair to neuroscience to draw implications of neuroscience research for teaching and learning. Instead, the best that we can say is that neuroscience research findings suggest that certain practices may be beneficial for teaching and learning. Then neuroscience findings can be validated by determining how consistent they are with learning research.

Table 2.8
Summary of learning issues.

How Does Learning Occur?

Learning involves the forming and strengthening of neural connections (synapses), a process known as consolidation. Repeated experiences help to strengthen connections and make neural firings and transmissions of information more rapid. Other factors that improve consolidation are organization, rehearsal, elaboration, and emotional involvement in learning.

How Does Memory Function?

Memory is not a unitary phenomenon. Instead, different areas of the brain are involved in working memory (WM) and long-term memory (LTM). Memory involves information being established so that neural connections are made and neural transmissions become automatic.

What Is the Role of Motivation?

The brain has a natural predisposition toward pleasurable outcomes and produces opiates to produce a natural high. This predisposition also seems to be triggered by the expectation of rewards. Motivational states are complex neural connections that include emotions, cognitions, and behaviors.

How Does Transfer Occur?

Transfer involves using information in new ways or in new situations. Transfer occurs when neural connections are formed between the learning and the new uses and situations. These connections are not made automatically. Students must learn them through experiences (e.g., teaching) or determine them on their own (e.g., through problem solving).

How Does Self-Regulated Learning Operate?

The processes involved in self-regulated learning (e.g., goals, assessment of goal progress, self-efficacy; Chapter 10) are cognitions that are represented in the same way that knowledge is represented; namely, by synaptic connections in the brain. Most of these self-regulatory activities likely reside in the brain's frontal lobe. Neural connections formed between self-regulatory activities and the task students are engaged in allow learners to self-regulate their learning.

What Are the Implications for Instruction?

Brain research suggests that early childhood education is important and that instruction and remediation must be specified clearly so that interventions can be tailored to specific needs. Activities that engage learners (e.g., discussions, role playing) and command and hold their attention (e.g., graphical displays) are apt to produce better learning.

And there are examples of consistency. Thus, both neuroscience and information processing contend that learning involves creating and modifying networks. This finding suggests for teaching and learning that we should strive to help students create these networks and ways to access them.

Another point to make is that, as educators, we should not ignore findings from neuroscience research but rather to keep ourselves informed about the important developments that are occurring in this discipline. Neuroscience has the potential to add extensively to our understanding of learning, motivation, emotion, and human development. These are topics with which educators should be highly concerned. As with other perspectives, it is not whether neuroscience is right or wrong but rather how it can help us provide a quality education for all learners.

REFLECTION QUESTIONS

- As an educator, what advice would you give to parents who were interested in their children's brain development and its effects on learning? Might your advice differ for parents of elementary children and those whose children are in high school?

- Some of the educational suggestions made based on brain research (e.g., right brain/left brain) are neuromyths: simplistic and misleading. We should, however, be able to use brain research findings to inform research and teaching practice and promote student learning. What do you believe are the major implications of brain research findings for educational research, teaching, and learning?

- The brain's executive function allows students to stay task focused and goal directed, which many students have difficulty doing. This chapter suggests that like other brain processes, executive functioning can be developed. What suggestions would you give to teachers to help them promote their students' executive functioning?

FURTHER READING

Byrnes, J. P. (2012). How neuroscience contributes to our understanding of learning and development in typically developing and special-needs students. In K. R. Harris, S. Graham, & T. Urdan (Eds.), *APA educational psychology handbook. Vol. 1: Theories, constructs, and critical issues* (pp. 561–595). Washington, DC: American Psychological Association.

Centre for Educational Research and Innovation (2007). *Understanding the brain: The birth of a learning science.* Paris: Organisation for Economic Co-operation and Development.

Presti, D. E. (2016). *Foundational concepts in neuroscience: A brain-mind odyssey.* New York: Norton.

Scalise, K., & Felde, M. (2017). *Why neuroscience matters in the classroom: Principles of brain-based instructional design for teachers.* Boston: Pearson Education.

Varma, S., McCandliss, B. D., & Schwartz, D. L. (2008). Scientific and pragmatic challenges for bridging education and neuroscience. *Educational Researcher, 37*(3), 140–152.

Wolfe, P. (2010). *Brain matters: Translating research into classroom practice* (2nd ed.). Alexandria, VA: ASCD.

3 Behaviorism

At the end of the school day at Park Lane Elementary, three teachers —Leo Battaglia, Shayna Brown, and Emily Matsui—leave the building together. Their conversation as they walk to the parking lot is as follows:

Leo: Boy, they were wild today. I don't know what got into them. Hardly anyone earned any points today.

Emily: What points, Leo?

Leo: I give points for good behavior, which they then can exchange for privileges, such as extra free time.

Emily: And it works?

Leo: Sure does. Keeps them working productively most days. But not today.

Shayna: Maybe they were thinking about spring break next week.

Leo: Perhaps. Lots of things can trigger wild behavior. How am I supposed to know what does? That's why I focus on the behavior.

Shayna: But sometimes we need to go beyond the behavior. For example, Sean's been acting out lately. If I just focused on his behavior, I would not have learned that his parents are getting divorced and he's blaming himself for it.

Leo: Isn't that why we have a counselor? Isn't that her job?

Shayna: Yes, but we have a role, too. We need to try to find out what's behind the behavior.

Leo: I understand what you're saying, but my system of rewards helps minimize the time I spend on classroom management issues.

Emily: Maybe you should use some of the time you save to try to understand the reasons for their behaviors.

Against the background of structuralism and functionalism (Chapter 1), behaviorism began its rise to become the leading psychological discipline of the first half of the twentieth century. John B. Watson (1878–1958), generally considered to be the founder and champion of behaviorism (Heidbreder, 1933; Hunt, 1993), believed that theories and research methods that dealt with the mind were unscientific. If psychology were to become a science, it had to structure itself along the lines of the physical sciences, which examined observable and measurable phenomena. Behavior was the proper material for psychologists to study (Watson, 1924). Introspection (Chapter 1) was unreliable; conscious experiences were not observable, and people having such experiences could not be trusted to report them accurately (Murray, Kilgour, & Wasylkiw, 2000).

Watson (1916) thought that Pavlov's conditioning model (discussed later in this chapter) was appropriate for building a science of human behavior. He was impressed with Pavlov's precise measurement of observable behaviors. Watson believed that Pavlov's model could account for diverse forms of learning and personality characteristics. For example, newborns are capable of displaying three emotions: love, fear, and rage (Watson, 1926a). Through Pavlovian conditioning, these emotions could become attached to stimuli to produce a complex adult life. Watson expressed his belief in the power of conditioning in this famous pronouncement:

> Give me a dozen healthy infants, well-formed, and my own specified world to bring them up in and I'll guarantee to take any one at random and train him to become any type of specialist I might select—a doctor, lawyer, artist, merchant-chief and, yes, even into beggar-man and thief, regardless of his talents, penchants, tendencies, abilities, vocations and race of his ancestors. (Watson, 1926b, p. 10)

Although Watson's research has little relevance for academic learning, he spoke and wrote with conviction, and his adamant views influenced psychology from around 1920 until the early 1960s (Hunt, 1993). His emphasis on the importance of the environment is readily seen in the ensuing work of Skinner (discussed later in this chapter; Horowitz, 1992).

This chapter covers behaviorism as expressed in behavior or conditioning theories of learning. The hallmark of conditioning theories is not that they deal with behavior (all theories do that) but rather that they explain learning in terms of environmental events. While not denying the existence of mental phenomena, these theories contend that such phenomena are not necessary to explain learning. In the opening scenario, Leo espouses a conditioning theory position.

The study of behaviorism is important because behavior theory principles have been widely and effectively employed to teach students adaptive behaviors that lead to better functioning in learning settings. While it is tempting to conclude from Leo's examples that behavior theory represents a system of bribery, that is not the case. The hallmark of behavior theories is linking desired behaviors with positive consequences, which is a goal of any theory that attempts to explain learning. The principles of behaviorism are well grounded in theory and research, even though other theories (e.g., social cognitive, information processing, constructivist) provide different explanations for the effects of behavioral consequences and have different implications for teaching.

The best-known behavior theory is B. F. Skinner's *operant conditioning*. Before discussing this theory, historical work on conditioning is presented to set the backdrop for Skinner's theory: Thorndike's connectionism, Pavlov's classical conditioning, and Guthrie's contiguous conditioning.

When you finish studying this chapter, you should be able to do the following:

■ Explain how behaviors are learned according to connectionism theory.

- Discuss some of Thorndike's contributions to educational practice.

- Explain how responses become conditioned, extinguished, and generalized, according to classical conditioning theory.

- Describe a process whereby an emotional response might become conditioned to an initially neutral object.

- Explain, using contiguous conditioning principles, how movements are combined to become an act.

- Describe Skinner's three-term contingency model of operant conditioning and provide examples.

- Define key operant conditioning concepts and exemplify how they might promote learning: positive and negative reinforcement, punishment, generalization, discrimination, shaping, and Premack principle.

- Explain how operant principles are reflected in educational applications: behavioral objectives, learning time, mastery learning, computer-based instruction, and contingency contracts.

CONNECTIONISM

Edward L. Thorndike (1874–1949) was a prominent psychologist whose *connectionism* theory of learning was dominant in the United States for a long time (Mayer, 2003). Unlike many early psychologists, he was interested in education and especially learning, transfer, individual differences, and intelligence (Hilgard, 1996; McKeachie, 1990). He applied an experimental approach when measuring students' achievement outcomes. His impact on education is reflected in the Thorndike Award, the highest honor given yearly by the Division of Educational Psychology of the American Psychological Association for distinguished contributions to educational psychology.

Trial-and-Error Learning

Thorndike's major work is the three-volume series *Educational Psychology* (Thorndike, 1913a, 1913b, 1914). He postulated that the most fundamental type of learning involves the forming of associations (*connections*) between sensory experiences (perceptions of stimuli or events) and neural impulses (responses) that manifest themselves behaviorally. He believed that learning often occurs by *trial and error* (selecting and connecting).

Thorndike began studying learning with a series of experiments on animals (Thorndike, 1911). Animals in problem situations try to attain a goal (e.g., obtain food, reach a destination). From among the many responses they can perform, they select one, perform it, and experience the consequences. The more often they make the same response to a stimulus, the more firmly that response becomes connected to that stimulus. For example, a cat in a cage can open an escape hatch by pushing a stick. After a series of random responses, the cat eventually escapes by pushing the stick. Over trials, the cat reaches the goal (escape) more quickly and makes fewer errors prior to responding correctly. A typical plot of results is shown in Figure 3.1.

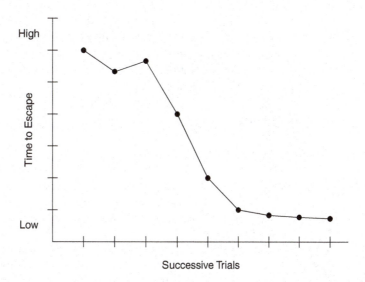

Figure 3.1
Incremental performance over trials exemplifying Thorndike's trial-and-error learning.

High

Time to Escape

Low

Successive Trials

Trial-and-error learning occurs gradually (incrementally). Connections are formed through repetition; conscious awareness is not necessary. Animals do not catch on or have insight. Thorndike understood that human learning is more complex because people engage in learning involving connecting ideas, analyzing, and reasoning (Thorndike, 1913b). Nonetheless, the similarity in research results from animal and human studies led Thorndike to explain complex learning with elementary learning principles. An educated adult possesses millions of stimulus–response connections.

Principles of Learning

Laws of Exercise and Effect. Thorndike's basic ideas about learning are embodied in the Laws of Exercise and Effect. The *Law of Exercise* has two parts: The *Law of Use*—a response to a stimulus strengthens their connection; the *Law of Disuse*—when a response is not made to a stimulus, the connection's strength is weakened (forgotten). The longer the time interval before a response is made, the greater is the decline in the connection's strength.

The Law of Effect emphasizes the *consequences* of behavior: Responses resulting in satisfying (rewarding) consequences are learned; responses producing annoying (punishing) consequences are not learned (Thorndike, 1913b). This is a functional account of learning because satisfiers (responses that produce desirable outcomes) allow individuals to adapt to their environments.

Other Principles. Thorndike's (1913b) theory included other principles relevant to education. The *Law of Readiness* states that when one is prepared (ready) to act, to do so is rewarding and not to do so is punishing. If one is hungry, responses that lead to food are in a state of readiness, whereas other responses not leading to food are not in a state of readiness. If one is fatigued, it is punishing to be forced to exercise. Applying this idea to learning, we might say that when students are ready to learn a particular action (in terms of developmental or skill level), then behaviors that foster this learning will be rewarding. When students are not ready to learn or do not possess prerequisite skills, then attempting to learn is punishing and a waste of time.

The principle of *associative shifting* refers to a situation in which responses made to a particular stimulus eventually are made to a different stimulus if, on repeated trials, there are small changes in the nature of the stimulus. To teach students to divide a two-digit number into a four-digit number, we first teach them to divide a one-digit number into a one-digit number and then gradually add more digits to the divisor and dividend.

The principle of *identical elements* affects *transfer (generalization),* or the extent that strengthening or weakening of one connection produces a similar change in another connection (Hilgard, 1996; Thorndike, 1913b; see Chapter 7). Transfer occurs when situations have identical (highly similar) elements and call for similar responses. Thorndike and Woodworth (1901) found that practicing a skill in a specific context did not improve one's ability to transfer that skill. Thus, training on estimating the area of rectangles does not advance learners' ability to estimate the areas of triangles, circles, and irregular figures. Skills should be taught with different types of content for students to understand how to apply them (Application 3.1).

Revisions. Thorndike revised the Laws of Exercise and Effect after other research evidence did not support them (Thorndike, 1932). Thorndike discarded the Law of Exercise when he found that simple repetition of a situation does not necessarily "stamp in" responses. In the absence of feedback, people may be unlikely to perform the same behavior because they are unsure whether it is correct.

APPLICATION 3.1
Facilitating Transfer

Thorndike suggested that drilling students on a specific skill does not help them master it nor does it teach them how to apply the skill in different contexts.

When teachers instruct students how to use map scales, they also must teach them to calculate miles from inches. Students become more proficient if they actually apply the skill on various maps and create maps of their own surroundings than if they are just given problems to solve.

Elementary teachers work with students on liquid and dry measurement. Having the students use a recipe to measure ingredients and create a food item is more meaningful than using pictures, charts, or filling cups with water or sand.

In teacher education courses, having students observe and assist in classrooms is more meaningful than reading about and watching videos on teaching and learning.

With respect to the Law of Effect, Thorndike originally thought that the effects of satisfiers (rewards) and annoyers (punishments) were opposite but comparable, but research showed this was not the case. Rather, rewards strengthened connections, but punishment did not necessarily weaken them (Thorndike, 1932). Instead, connections are weakened when alternative connections are strengthened.

Punishment suppresses responses, but they are not forgotten. Punishment is not an effective means of altering behavior because it does not teach students correct behaviors but rather informs them of what not to do.

Thorndike and Education

As a professor of education at Teachers College, Columbia University, Thorndike wrote books that addressed topics such as educational goals, learning processes, teaching methods, curricular sequences, and techniques for assessing educational outcomes (Hilgard, 1996; Mayer, 2003; Thorndike, 1906, 1912; Thorndike & Gates, 1929). Some of Thorndike's many contributions to education are discussed next.

Principles of Teaching. Teachers should help students form good habits. As Thorndike (1912) noted:

- Form habits. Do not expect them to create themselves.
- Beware of forming a habit that must be broken later.
- Do not form two or more habits when one will do as well.
- Other things being equal, have a habit formed in the way in which it is to be used. (pp. 173–174)

The last principle cautions against teaching content that is removed from its applications. Students need to understand how to apply knowledge and skills they acquire. Uses should be learned in conjunction with the content.

Sequence of Curricula. A skill should be introduced (Thorndike & Gates, 1929):

- At the time or just before the time when it can be used in some serviceable way
- At the time when the learner is conscious of the need for it as a means of satisfying some useful purpose
- When it is most suited in difficulty to the ability of the learner
- When it will harmonize most fully with the level and type of emotions, tastes, instinctive and volitional dispositions most active at the time
- When it is most fully facilitated by immediately preceding learnings and when it will most fully facilitate learnings which are to follow shortly. (pp. 209–210)

These principles conflict with typical content placement in schools, where content is segregated by subject (e.g., social studies, mathematics). But Thorndike and Gates (1929) urged that knowledge and skills be taught across multiple subjects (Application 3.2). For example, forms of government are appropriate topics not only in social studies but also in English (how governments are reflected in literature) and foreign language (government structure in other countries).

Thorndike's views on the sequence of curricula suggest that learning should be integrated across subjects. In the fall, Mrs. Woleska prepared a unit on pumpkins for her second-grade class. The students study the significance of pumpkins to the American colonists (history), where pumpkins are grown (geography), and the varieties of pumpkins grown (agriculture). They measure and chart the various sizes of pumpkins (mathematics), carve the pumpkins (art), plant pumpkin seeds and study their growth (science), and read and write stories about pumpkins (language arts). This approach provides a meaningful and integrated experience for children.

In developing a history unit on the Civil War, Ms. Parks went beyond covering factual material and incorporated comparisons from other wars, attitudes and feelings of the populace during that time period, biographies and personalities of individuals involved in the war, and the impact the war had on the United States at that time and in the future. In addition, she worked with other teachers in the middle school to expand the unit by examining the terrain of major battlefields (geography), weather conditions during major battles (science), and the emergence of literature (language arts) and creative works (art, music, drama) during that time period.

Mental Discipline. *Mental discipline* is the view that learning certain subjects (e.g., the classics, mathematics) enhances general mental functioning better than learning other subjects. Mental discipline was a popular view during Thorndike's time. He tested this idea with 8,500 students in grades 9 to 11 (Thorndike, 1924). Students were given intelligence tests a year apart, and their programs of study that year were compared to determine whether certain courses were associated with greater intellectual gains. The results provided no support for mental discipline. Students who had greater ability to begin with made the best progress regardless of what they studied.

So rather than assuming that some subject areas improve students' mental abilities better than others, we should assess how different subject areas affect students' ability to think and achievement-related outcomes (e.g., interests, goals). Thorndike's influential research led educators to redesign curricula away from the mental discipline idea.

CLASSICAL CONDITIONING

Events in the United States in the early 20th century helped establish psychology as a science and learning as a legitimate field of study. At the same time, there were important developments in other countries. One of the most significant was the work of Ivan Pavlov (1849–1936), a Russian physiologist who won the Nobel Prize in 1904 for his body of work on digestion (Tallis, 2014).

Pavlov's legacy to learning theory was his work on *classical conditioning* (Hunt, 1993; Pavlov, 1927, 1928; Windholz, 1997). While Pavlov was the director of the physiological laboratory at the Institute of Experimental Medicine in Petrograd, he noticed that dogs often would salivate at the sight of the attendant bringing them food or at the sound of the attendant's footsteps. The attendant was not a natural stimulus for the reflex of salivating; rather, the attendant acquired this power by being associated with food.

Basic Processes

Classical conditioning is a multistep procedure that initially involves presenting an *unconditioned stimulus (UCS)*, which elicits an *unconditioned response (UCR)*. Pavlov presented a hungry dog with meat powder (UCS), which caused the dog to salivate (UCR). To condition the animal requires repeatedly presenting an initially neutral stimulus immediately before presenting the UCS. Pavlov often used a ticking metronome as the neutral stimulus. In the early trials, the ticking of the metronome produced no salivation. Eventually, the dog salivated in response to the ticking metronome prior to the presentation of the meat powder. The metronome had become a *conditioned stimulus (CS)* that elicited a *conditioned response (CR)* similar to the original UCR (Table 3.1). Repeated nonreinforced presentations of the CS (i.e., without the UCS) cause the CR to diminish in intensity and disappear, a phenomenon known as *extinction* (Larrauri & Schmajuk, 2008; Pavlov, 1932b).

Spontaneous recovery may occur after a time lapse in which the CS is not presented and the CR presumably extinguishes. If the CS then is presented and the CR returns, we say that the CR spontaneously recovered from extinction. Pairings of the CS with the UCS can restore the CR to full strength. The fact that CS–CR pairings can be instated without great difficulty suggests that extinction does not involve unlearning of the associations (Redish, Jensen, Johnson, & Kurth-Nelson, 2007).

Generalization means that the CR occurs to stimuli similar to the CS (Figure 3.2). Once a dog is conditioned to salivate in response to a metronome ticking at 70 beats per minute, it also may salivate in response to a metronome ticking faster or slower, as well as to ticking clocks or timers. The more dissimilar the new stimulus is to the CS or the fewer elements that they share, the less generalization occurs (Harris, 2006).

Discrimination is the complementary process that occurs when the dog learns to respond to the CS but not to other, similar stimuli. To train discrimination, an experimenter might pair the CS with the UCS and also present other, similar stimuli without the UCS. If the CS is a metronome ticking at 70 beats per minute, it is presented with the UCS,

Table 3.1 Classical conditioning procedure.	Phase	Stimulus		Response
	1	UCS (food powder)	→	UCR (salivation)
	2	CS (metronome), then UCS (food powder)	→	UCR (salivation)
	3	CS (metronome)	→	CR (salivation)

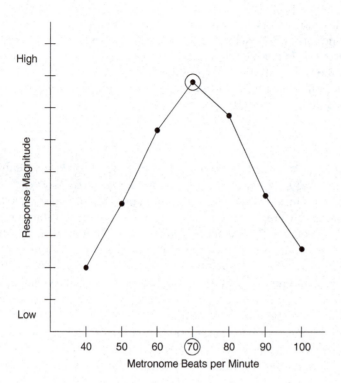

Figure 3.2
Generalization curve showing decreased magnitude of conditioned response as a function of increased dissimilarity with the conditioned stimulus.

whereas other cadences (e.g., 50 and 90 beats per minute) are presented but not paired with the UCS.

Once a stimulus becomes conditioned, it can function as a UCS and *higher-order conditioning* can occur (Pavlov, 1927). If a dog has been conditioned to salivate at the sound of a metronome ticking at 70 beats per minute, the ticking metronome can function as a UCS for higher-order conditioning. A new neutral stimulus (such as a buzzer) can be sounded for a few seconds, followed by the ticking metronome. If, after a few trials, the dog begins to salivate at the sound of the buzzer, the buzzer has become a second-order CS. Conditioning of the third order involves the second-order CS serving as the UCS and a new neutral stimulus being paired with it. Conditioning beyond the third order is difficult (Pavlov, 1927).

Higher-order conditioning is complex and not well understood (Rescorla, 1972). The concept might help to explain why some social phenomena (e.g., test failure) can cause conditioned emotional reactions, such as stress and anxiety. Early in life, failure may be a neutral event, but it usually becomes associated with disapproval from significant others (e.g., parents, teachers) that may be an UCS eliciting anxiety. Through conditioning, failure can elicit anxiety. Cues associated with the situation also can become conditioned stimuli. Students may feel anxious when they walk into a room where they will take a test or when a teacher passes out a test.

CSs capable of producing CRs are called *primary signals*. People have a *second signal system*—language—that greatly expands the potential for conditioning (Windholz, 1997).

Words or thoughts are labels denoting events or objects and can become CSs. Thinking about a test or listening to a teacher discuss a forthcoming test may cause anxiety. Thus, the linguistic representations or meanings of tests can produce anxiety.

Informational Variables

Pavlov believed that conditioning is an automatic process that occurs with repeated CS–UCS pairings and that nonpairings extinguish the CR. In humans, however, conditioning can occur rapidly, sometimes after only a single CS–UCS pairing. Repeated nonpairings of the CS and UCS may not extinguish the CR. Extinction seems highly context dependent (Bouton, Nelson, & Rosas, 1999). Reponses may stay extinguished in the same context, but when the setting is changed, CRs may recur. Further, conditioning cannot occur between any two variables. Within any species, responses can be conditioned to some stimuli but not to others. Conditioning depends on the compatibility of the stimulus and response with species-specific reactions (Hollis, 1997). These findings call into question Pavlov's description of conditioning.

Research subsequent to Pavlov has shown that conditioning depends less on the CS–UCS pairing and more on the extent that the CS conveys information about the likelihood of the UCS occurring (Rescorla, 1972, 1976). Assume that one stimulus always is followed by a UCS and another stimulus sometimes is followed by it. The first stimulus should result in conditioning because it reliably predicts the onset of the UCS. It even may not be necessary to pair the CS and UCS; conditioning can occur by simply telling people that they are related (Brewer, 1974). Likewise, repeated CS–UCS nonpairings may not be necessary for extinction; telling people the contingency is no longer in effect can reduce or extinguish the CR.

An explanation for these results is that people form *expectations* concerning the probability of the UCS occurring (Rescorla, 1987). For a stimulus to become a CS, it must convey information to the individual about the time, place, quantity, and quality of the UCS. Even when a stimulus is predictive, it may not become conditioned if another stimulus is a better predictor. Rather than conditioning being automatic, it appears to be mediated by cognitive processes. If people do not realize there is a CS–UCS link, conditioning does not occur. When no CS–UCS link exists, conditioning can occur if people believe it does. Although this contingency view of conditioning may not be entirely accurate (Papini & Bitterman, 1990), it provides a different explanation for conditioning than Pavlov's and highlights its complexity.

Conditioned Emotional Reactions

Pavlov (1932a, 1934) applied classical conditioning principles to abnormal behavior (e.g., neuroses). His views were speculative and unsubstantiated, but classical conditioning principles have been applied by others to condition emotional reactions.

Watson claimed to demonstrate the power of emotional conditioning in the well-known Little Albert experiment (Watson & Rayner, 1920). Albert was an infant who showed no fear of a white rat when he was tested between the ages of 8 and 11 months. The conditioning involved a hammer being struck against a steel bar behind Albert as he reached out for the rat. "The infant jumped violently and fell forward, burying his face in the mattress" (p. 4). This sequence was immediately repeated. One week later, when the rat was presented, Albert began to reach out but then withdrew his hand. The previous week's conditioning was apparent. Tests over the next few days showed that Albert reacted emotionally to the rat's presence. There also was generalization of fear to a rabbit, dog, and fur coat. When Albert was retested a month later with the rat, he showed a mild emotional reaction.

This controversial study is widely cited as showing how conditioning can produce emotional reactions (Powell, Digdon, Harris, & Smithson, 2014), but there are questions about the study's validity and credibility. Recent evidence suggests that Albert may have been neurologically impaired (Bartlett, 2012). With this deficit, his reactions to the white rat would not be typical of a healthy child. Albert died at the age of 6 years of hydrocephalus (Beck, Levinson, & Irons, 2009), a condition he apparently had from birth. He never learned to walk or talk and had vision problems. Other research dispels these details about Albert but concludes that Watson and Rayner exaggerated the effectiveness of their conditioning procedure (Powell et al., 2014). In short, drawing conclusions from this study and generalizing its results are problematic. The influence of conditioning usually is not as powerful as that claimed by Watson and Rayner (Harris, 1979). Attempts to replicate Watson and Rayner's findings were not uniformly successful (Valentine, 1930a).

A more reliable means of producing emotional conditioning is with *systematic desensitization*, which is often used with individuals who possess debilitating fears (Wolpe, 1958; see Application 3.3). Desensitization comprises three phases. In the first phase, a therapist and client jointly develop an anxiety hierarchy of several situations graded from least to most anxiety producing for the client. For a test-anxious student, low-anxiety situations might be hearing a test announcement in class and gathering together materials to study. Situations of moderate anxiety might be studying the night before the test and walking into class on the day of the test. High-anxiety situations could include receiving the test and not knowing the answer to a question.

APPLICATION 3.3
Emotional Conditioning

Principles of classical conditioning seem relevant to some emotions. Children entering kindergarten or first grade may be fearful. At the beginning of the school year, primary teachers might develop procedures to help desensitize the fears. Visitation sessions allow students to meet their teachers and other students and to see their classrooms. On the first few days of school, teachers might plan fun but relatively calm activities involving students getting to know their teachers, classmates, rooms, and school buildings. Students could tour the buildings, return to their rooms, and draw pictures. They might talk about what they saw. Students can be taken to offices to meet the principal and other staff members. They also could play name games in which they introduce themselves and then try to recall names of classmates.

These activities represent an informal desensitization procedure. For some children, cues associated with the school serve as stimuli eliciting anxiety. The fun activities elicit pleasurable feelings, which are incompatible with anxiety. Pairing fun activities with cues associated with school may cause the latter to become less anxiety producing.

Education students may be anxious about teaching an entire class. Anxieties should be lessened when students spend time in classrooms and gradually assume more responsibility for instruction. Pairing classroom and teaching experiences with formal study can desensitize fears related to being responsible for children's learning.

Some drama students have stage fright. Drama teachers might work with students to lessen these anxieties by practicing more on the actual stage and by opening up rehearsals to allow others to watch. Performing in front of others can help diminish their fears.

In the second phase, the client learns to relax by imagining pleasant scenes (e.g., lying on a beach) and cuing relaxation (saying "relax"). In the third phase, the client, while relaxed, imagines the lowest (least anxious) scene on the hierarchy. This may be repeated several times, after which the client imagines the next scene. Treatment proceeds up the hierarchy until the client can imagine the most anxiety-producing scene without feeling anxious. If the client reports anxiety while imagining a scene, the client drops back down the hierarchy to a scene that does not produce anxiety. Treatment may require several sessions.

Desensitization involves counterconditioning. The relaxing scenes that one imagines (UCS) produce relaxation (UCR). Anxiety-producing cues (CS) are paired with the relaxing scenes. Relaxation is incompatible with anxiety. By initially pairing a weak anxiety cue with relaxation and by slowly working up the hierarchy, all of the anxiety-producing cues eventually should elicit relaxation (CR).

Desensitization is an effective procedure that can be accomplished in a therapist's or counselor's office. It does not require the client to perform the activities on the hierarchy. A disadvantage is that the client must be able to imagine scenes, and people differ in their ability to form mental images. Desensitization also requires the skill of a professional therapist or counselor and should not be attempted by anyone unskilled in its application.

CONTIGUOUS CONDITIONING

Acts and Movements

Edwin R. Guthrie (1886–1959), a prominent behavioral psychologist, postulated learning principles based on associations (Guthrie, 1940). These principles reflect the idea of *contiguity* of stimuli and responses:

> A combination of stimuli which has accomplished a movement will on its recurrence tend to be followed by that movement. (Guthrie, 1952, p. 23)

Movements are discrete behaviors, whereas *acts* are large-scale classes of movements that produce an outcome. Playing the piano and using a computer are acts that include many movements. A particular act may be accompanied by a variety of movements; the act may not specify the movements precisely. In basketball, shooting a basket (an act) can be accomplished with various movements.

Contiguity learning implies that a behavior in a situation will be repeated when that situation recurs (Guthrie, 1959); however, contiguity learning is selective. At any given moment, a person is confronted with many stimuli. Only a few stimuli are selected, and associations are formed between them and responses. The contiguity principle also applies to memory. Verbal cues are associated with stimulus conditions or events at the time of learning (Guthrie, 1952). *Forgetting* involves new learning and is due to interference in which an alternative response is made to an old stimulus.

Guthrie's theory contends that learning occurs through pairing of stimulus and response. Guthrie (1942) also discussed the strength of the pairing, or *associative strength*:

> A stimulus pattern gains its full associative strength on the occasion of its first pairing with a response. (p. 30)

This *all-or-none* principle of learning rejects the notion of frequency, as embodied in Thorndike's original Law of Exercise (Guthrie, 1930). Although Guthrie did not suggest that people learn complex behaviors (e.g., how to solve equations or write research papers) by performing them once, he believed that initially one or more movements become associated. Repetition of a situation adds movements, combines movements into acts, and establishes the act under different environmental conditions.

Practice links the various movements involved in the acts of solving equations and writing research papers. The acts themselves may have many variations (types of equations and papers) and ideally should transfer—students should be able to solve equations and write papers in different contexts. Guthrie accepted Thorndike's notion of identical elements. Behaviors should be practiced in the exact situations (e.g., class, home) in which they will be called for.

Guthrie believed that responses do not need to be rewarded to be learned. Rather, learning requires close pairing in time between stimulus and response (contiguity). Guthrie (1952) disputed Thorndike's Law of Effect because satisfiers and annoyers are effects of actions; therefore, they cannot influence learning of previous connections but only subsequent ones. Rewards might help to prevent *unlearning* (forgetting) because they prevent new responses from being associated with stimulus cues.

Contiguity is a central feature of school learning. Flashcards help students learn arithmetic facts. Students learn to associate a stimulus (e.g., 4×4) with a response (16). Foreign-language words are associated with their English equivalents, and chemical symbols are associated with their element names.

Habit Formation and Change

Guthrie's ideas are relevant to habit formation and change. *Habits* are learned dispositions to repeat past responses (Wood & Neal, 2007). Because habits are behaviors established to many cues, teachers who want students to behave well in school should link school

Table 3.2
Guthrie's methods for breaking habits.

Method	Explanation	Example
Threshold	Introduce weak stimulus. Increase stimulus, but keep it below threshold value that will produce unwanted response.	Introduce academic content in short blocks of time for children. Gradually increase session length, but not to a point where students become frustrated or bored.
Fatigue	Have student make unwanted response repeatedly in presence of stimulus.	Give student a stack of paper and have student make each sheet into a plane.
Incompatible response	In presence of stimulus, have student make response incompatible with unwanted response.	Pair cues associated with media center with reading rather than talking.

rules with many cues. "Treat others with respect," needs to be linked with the classroom, computer lab, halls, cafeteria, gymnasium, auditorium, and playground. By applying this rule in each of these settings, students' respectful behaviors toward others become habitual. If students believe they have to practice respect only in the classroom, respecting others will not become a habit.

The key to changing behavior is to "find the cues that initiate the action and to practice another response to these cues" (Guthrie, 1952, p. 115). Guthrie identified three methods for altering habits: threshold, fatigue, and incompatible response (Table 3.2 and Application 3.4).

APPLICATION 3.4
Breaking Habits

Guthrie's contiguity principle offers practical suggestions for how to break habits. One application of the threshold method involves the time young children spend on academic activities. Young children have short attention spans, which limits how long they can sustain work on one activity. Most class activities are scheduled to last no longer than 30–40 minutes. However, at the start of the school year, attention spans quickly wane for many children. To apply Guthrie's theory, at the start of the year, a teacher might limit activities to 15–20 minutes. Over the next few weeks,

the teacher gradually increases the time students spend working on a single activity.

The threshold method also can be applied to teaching printing. When children first learn to form letters, their movements are awkward, and they lack fine motor coordination. The distances between lines on a page are purposely wide so children can fit the letters into the space. If paper with narrower lines were initially introduced, students' letters would spill over the borders and students might become frustrated. Once students can form letters within the wider lines, they can use paper

(Continued)

APPLICATION 3.4 (*continued*)

with narrower lines to help them refine their skills.

Teachers need to be judicious when using the fatigue method because of potential negative consequences. Jason likes to make paper airplanes and sail them across the room. His teacher might remove him from the classroom, give him a large stack of paper, and tell him to start making paper airplanes. After Jason has made several airplanes, the activity should lose its attraction, and paper will no longer be a cue for him to make airplanes.

Some students like to race around the gym when they first enter their physical education class. To employ the fatigue method, the physical education teacher might just let these students keep running after the class has begun. Soon they should tire and quit running.

The incompatible response method can be used with students who talk and misbehave in the media center. Reading is incompatible with talking. The media center teacher might ask the students to find interesting books and read them while in the center. Assuming that the students find the books enjoyable, the media center will, over time, become a cue for selecting and reading books rather than for talking with other students.

A social studies teacher has some students who regularly do not pay attention in class. The teacher realized that using many slides while lecturing was boring. Soon the teacher began to incorporate other elements into each lesson, such as experiments, video clips, and debates, in an attempt to involve students and raise their interest in the course.

In the *threshold method*, the cue (stimulus) for the habit to be changed (the undesired response) is introduced at such a weak level that it does not elicit the response; it is below the threshold level of the response. Gradually the stimulus is introduced at greater intensity until it is presented at full strength. Were the stimulus introduced at its greatest intensity, the response would be the behavior that is to be changed (the habit). For example, some children react to the taste of spinach by refusing to eat it. To alter this habit, parents might introduce spinach in small bites or mixed with a food that the child enjoys. Over time, the amount of spinach the child eats can be increased.

In the *fatigue method*, the cue for engaging in the behavior is transformed into a cue for avoiding it. The stimulus is introduced at full strength, and the individual performs the undesired response until he or she becomes satiated. The stimulus becomes a cue for not performing the response. To alter a child's behavior of repeatedly throwing toys, parents might make the child throw toys until it is no longer fun (some limits are needed!). To break college students' from continually checking their phones they might use their phones without stopping until they get tired of it and stop.

In the *incompatible response* method, the cue for the undesired behavior is paired with a response incompatible with the undesired response; that is, the two responses cannot be performed simultaneously. The response to be paired with the cue must be more attractive to the individual than the undesired response. The stimulus becomes a cue for performing the alternate response. To stop snacking while watching TV, people should keep their hands busy (e.g., sew, paint, work on puzzles). Over time, watching TV becomes a cue for engaging in an activity other than snacking. Systematic desensitization (described earlier) also makes use of incompatible responses.

Punishment is ineffective in altering habits (Guthrie, 1952). Punishment following a response cannot affect the stimulus–response association. Punishment given while a behavior is being performed may disrupt or suppress the habit but not change it. Punishment does not establish an alternate response to the stimulus. It is better to alter negative habits by replacing them with desirable ones (i.e., incompatible responses).

Guthrie's theory does not include cognitive processes. Although it is not a viable learning theory today, its emphasis on contiguity is timely because current theories stress contiguity and much learning involves it. Cognitive theories predict that learning requires understanding the relationship between a stimulus (situation, event) and the appropriate response. Guthrie's ideas about changing habits provide general guidance for developing better habits.

OPERANT CONDITIONING

A well-known behavior theory is *operant conditioning*, formulated by B. F. (Burrhus Frederic) Skinner (1904–1990). Beginning in the 1930s, Skinner published a series of papers on laboratory studies with animals in which he identified the components of operant conditioning. He summarized this early work in his influential book, *The Behavior of Organisms* (Skinner, 1938).

Skinner applied his ideas to human functioning. Early in his career, he became interested in education and developed teaching machines and programmed instruction. *The Technology of Teaching* (Skinner, 1968) addresses instruction, motivation, discipline, and creativity. In 1948, he published *Walden Two*, which describes how behavioral principles can be applied to create a utopian society. Skinner (1971) addressed the problems of modern life and advocated applying a behavioral technology to the design of cultures in *Beyond Freedom and Dignity*. Skinner and others have applied operant conditioning principles to school learning and discipline, child development, language acquisition, social behaviors, mental illness, medical problems, substance abuse, and vocational training (DeGrandpre, 2000; Morris, 2003).

As a young man, Skinner aspired to be a writer (Skinner, 1970):

> I built a small study in the attic and set to work. The results were disastrous. I frittered away my time. I read aimlessly, built model ships, played the piano, listened to the newly-invented radio, contributed to the humorous column of a local paper but wrote almost nothing else, and thought about seeing a psychiatrist. (p. 6)

Skinner became interested in psychology after reading Pavlov's (1927) *Conditioned Reflexes* and Watson's (1924) *Behaviorism*. His subsequent career had a profound impact on the psychology of learning.

Despite Skinner's admission that he failed as a writer (Skinner, 1970), he became a prolific writer who channeled his literary aspirations into scientific writing that spanned six decades (Lattal, 1992). His dedication to his profession is evident in his giving an invited address at the American Psychological Association convention eight days before he died (Holland, 1992; Skinner, 1990). The association honored him with a special issue of its monthly journal, *American Psychologist* (American Psychological Association, 1992). Although his theory has been discredited by current learning theorists because it cannot adequately explain higher-order and complex forms of learning (Bargh & Ferguson, 2000), his influence continues as operant conditioning principles are commonly applied to enhance student learning and behavior (Morris, 2003). In the opening scenario, for example, Leo espouses operant conditioning principles to address student misbehavior. Emily and Shayna, on the other hand, argue for the importance of cognitive factors.

Conceptual Framework

This section discusses the assumptions underlying operant conditioning, how it reflects a functional analysis of behavior, and the implications of the theory for the prediction and control of behavior. Operant conditioning theory is complex (Dragoi & Staddon, 1999); its principles most relevant to human learning are covered in this chapter.

Scientific Assumptions. Pavlov viewed behavior as a manifestation of neurological functioning. Hull (1943), another influential behavior theorist, similarly viewed learning as the process of establishing neurological reactions in response to need situations. Skinner (1938) did not deny the existence of neurological responses but believed a psychology of behavior can be understood without reference to neurological or other internal events.

He raised similar objections to the unobservable processes and entities proposed by cognitive views of learning (Overskeid, 2007). *Private events* are internal responses accessible only to the individual and can be studied through people's verbal reports, which are forms of behavior (Skinner, 1953). Skinner did not deny the existence of attitudes, beliefs, opinions, desires, and other forms of self-knowledge (he, after all, had them) but, rather, qualified their role.

People experience their bodies, not consciousness or emotions; thus, internal reactions are responses to internal stimuli (Skinner, 1987). A further problem with internal processes is that translating them into language is difficult, because language does not completely capture the dimensions of an internal experience (e.g., pain). Much of what is called "knowing" involves using language (verbal behavior). Thoughts are types of behavior that are brought about by other stimuli (environmental or private) and that give rise to responses (overt or covert). When private events are expressed as overt behaviors, their role in a functional analysis can be determined.

Functional Analysis of Behavior. Skinner (1953) referred to his theory as a *functional analysis*:

> The external variables of which behavior is a function provide for what may be called a causal or functional analysis. We undertake to predict and control the behavior of the individual organism. This is our "dependent variable"—the effect for which we are to find the cause. Our "independent variables"—the causes of behavior—are the external conditions of which behavior

is a function. Relations between the two—the "cause-and-effect relationships" in behavior—are the laws of a science. (p. 35)

Learning is "the reassortment of responses in a complex situation"; *conditioning* refers to "the strengthening of behavior which results from reinforcement" (Skinner, 1953, p. 65). There are two types of conditioning: Type S and Type R. *Type S* is Pavlovian conditioning, characterized by the pairing of the reinforcing (unconditioned) stimulus with another (conditioned) stimulus. The S calls attention to the importance of the stimulus in eliciting a response from the organism. The response made to the eliciting stimulus is known as *respondent behavior*.

Although Type S conditioning may explain conditioned emotional reactions, most human behaviors are emitted in the presence of stimuli rather than automatically elicited by them. Responses are controlled by their consequences, not by antecedent stimuli. This type of behavior, which Skinner termed *Type R* to emphasize the response aspect, is *operant behavior* because it operates on the environment to produce an effect.

> If the occurrence of an operant is followed by presentation of a reinforcing stimulus, the strength is increased. . . . If the occurrence of an operant already strengthened through conditioning is not followed by the reinforcing stimulus, the strength is decreased. (Skinner, 1938, p. 21)

We might think of operant behavior as "learning by doing," and, in fact, much learning occurs when we perform behaviors (Lesgold, 2001). Unlike respondent behavior—which, prior to conditioning, does not occur—the probability of occurrence of an operant is never zero because the response must be made for reinforcement to be provided. Reinforcement changes the likelihood or rate of occurrence of the response. Operant behaviors act upon their environments and become more or less likely to occur because of reinforcement.

Basic Processes

This section examines the basic processes in operant conditioning: reinforcement, extinction, primary and secondary reinforcers, the Premack principle, punishment, schedules of reinforcement, generalization, and discrimination.

Reinforcement. *Reinforcement* is responsible for response strengthening—increasing the rate of responding or making responses more likely to occur. A reinforcer (or *reinforcing stimulus*) is any stimulus or event following a response that leads to response strengthening. Reinforcers are defined based on their effects, which do not depend upon mental processes such as consciousness, intentions, or goals (Schultz, 2006). Because reinforcers are defined by their effects, they cannot be determined in advance.

> The only way to tell whether or not a given event is reinforcing to a given organism under given conditions is to make a direct test. We observe the frequency of a selected response, then make an event contingent upon it and observe any change in frequency. If there is a change, we classify the event as reinforcing to the organism under the existing conditions. (Skinner, 1953, pp. 72–73)

Reinforcers are situationally specific: They apply to individuals at given times under specific conditions. What is reinforcing to Maria during reading now may not be during mathematics now or reading later. Despite this specificity, stimuli or events that reinforce behavior can be predicted (Skinner, 1953). Students typically find reinforcing such events as teacher praise, free time, privileges, stickers, and high grades. Nonetheless, one never can know for certain whether a consequence is reinforcing until it is presented after a response and we see whether behavior changes.

The basic operant model of conditioning is the *three-term contingency:*

$$S^D \rightarrow R \rightarrow S^R$$

A *discriminative stimulus* (S^D) sets the occasion for a response (R) to be emitted, which is followed by a *reinforcing stimulus* (S^R, or *reinforcement*). The reinforcing stimulus is any stimulus (event, consequence) that increases the probability the response will be emitted in the future when the discriminative stimulus is present. In terms that are easier to remember, we can label this the *A–B–C* model:

$$A \text{ (Antecedent)} \rightarrow B \text{ (Behavior)} \rightarrow C \text{ (Consequence)}$$

Positive reinforcement involves presenting a stimulus, or adding something to a situation, following a response, which increases the future likelihood of that response occurring in that situation. A *positive reinforcer* is a stimulus that, when presented following a response, increases the future likelihood of the response occurring in that situation. In the opening scenario, Leo uses points as positive reinforcers for good behavior (Table 3.3).

Negative reinforcement involves removing a stimulus, or taking something away from a situation following a response, which increases the future likelihood that the response will occur in that situation. A *negative reinforcer* is a stimulus that, when removed by a response, increases the future likelihood of the response occurring in that situation. Some stimuli that often function as negative reinforcers are bright lights, loud noises, alarms, criticism, annoying people, and low grades, because behaviors that remove them tend to be reinforcing. If you are sitting next to a chatty student in a large class, moving to another seat away from this student may be negatively reinforcing. Positive and negative

Table 3.3
Reinforcement and punishment processes.

Discriminative Stimulus	Response	Reinforcing (Punishing) Stimulus
Positive Reinforcement (Present positive reinforcer)		
T* asks question	L* volunteers	T says to L, "That's good"
Negative Reinforcement (Remove negative reinforcer)		
T asks question	L volunteers	T says L does not have to do homework
Punishment (Present negative reinforcer)		
T asks question	L misbehaves	T assigns L homework
Punishment (Remove positive reinforcer)		
T asks question	L misbehaves	T says L will miss free time

*T refers to teacher and L to learner.

reinforcement have the same effect: They increase the likelihood that the response will be made in the future in the presence of the stimulus.

To illustrate these processes (Table 3.3), assume that a teacher is holding a question-and-answer session with the class. The teacher asks a question (S^D or A), after which some students raise their hands. The teacher calls on a student volunteer who gives the correct answer (R or B) and says to the student, "That's good" (S^R or C). If volunteering by this student increases, saying "That's good" is a positive reinforcer and this is an example of positive reinforcement because volunteering increased. Now assume that, after a student gives the correct answer, the teacher tells the student he or she does not need to do the homework. If volunteering by this student increases, homework is a negative reinforcer, and this is an example of negative reinforcement because removing the homework increased volunteering. Application 3.5 gives other examples of positive and negative reinforcement.

A common positive reinforcer is praise (e.g., "Good job!"); however, praise is not the same as feedback informing students how they performed. When the two are combined (e.g., "Good job! Your answer is correct."), it is difficult to know which had the stronger effect on subsequent behavior. A danger in combining the two is that with corrective feedback (e.g., "Good job! But you still need to work on this part."), students may attend more to the praise and miss the part needing correction (Hattie, 2012). If praise is used in

---

APPLICATION 3.5
Positive and Negative Reinforcement

Teachers can use positive and negative reinforcement to motivate students to master skills and spend more time on task. For example, while teaching concepts in a science unit, Mrs. Davos might ask students to answer questions shown on a slide. She also might set up activity centers around the room that involve hands-on experiments related to the lesson. Students circulate and complete the experiments contingent on their successfully answering the questions (positive reinforcement). This contingency reflects the Premack Principle of providing the opportunity to engage in a more valued activity (experiments) as a reinforcer for engaging in a less valued one (completing questions). Students who complete 80% of the questions correctly and who participate in a minimum of two experiments do not have to complete homework. This would function as negative reinforcement if students perceive homework as a negative reinforcer.

A middle school counselor working with Penny to improve classroom behavior could have each of her teachers rate her class behavior for that day as acceptable or unacceptable. For each "acceptable," Penny receives 1 minute to work on a computer (positive reinforcement for Penny). At the end of the week, Penny can use the earned computer time following lunch. Further, if she earns a minimum of 15 minutes in the lab, she does not have to take a behavior note home to be signed by parents (this assumes Penny perceives a behavior note as a negative reinforcer).

conjunction with correction, it is best to ensure that students understand what they need to improve.

Extinction. *Extinction* involves the decline of response strength due to nonreinforcement. Students who raise their hands in class but never get called on may stop raising their hands. People who send many e-mails to the same individual but never receive a reply eventually may quit sending e-mails to that person.

How rapidly extinction occurs depends on the *reinforcement history* (Skinner, 1953). Extinction occurs quickly if few preceding responses have been reinforced. Responding is much more durable with a lengthier history of reinforcement. Extinction is not the same as forgetting. Responses that extinguish can be performed but are not because of lack of reinforcement. In the preceding examples, the individuals still know how to raise their hands and how to send e-mails. Forgetting involves a true loss of conditioning over time in which the opportunities for responding have not been present.

Primary and Secondary Reinforcers. Stimuli such as food, water, and shelter are called *primary reinforcers* because they are necessary for survival. *Secondary reinforcers* are stimuli that become conditioned through their association with primary reinforcers. A child's favorite milk glass becomes secondarily reinforcing through its association with milk (a primary reinforcer). A secondary reinforcer that becomes paired with more than one primary reinforcer is a *generalized reinforcer*. People work long hours to earn money (a generalized reinforcer), which they use to pay for many other reinforcers (e.g., food, housing, TVs, vacations).

Operant conditioning explains the development and maintenance of much social behavior with generalized reinforcers. Children may behave in ways to draw adults' attention. Attention is reinforcing because it is paired with primary reinforcers from adults (e.g., food, water, protection). Important educational generalized reinforcers are teachers' praise, high grades, privileges, honors, and degrees. These reinforcers often are paired with other generalized reinforcers, such as approval (from parents and friends) and money (a college degree leads to a good job).

Premack Principle. Recall that we label a behavioral consequence as reinforcing only after we apply it and see how it affects future behavior. It seems troubling that we must use common sense or trial and error in choosing reinforcers because we cannot know in advance whether a consequence will function as a reinforcer.

Premack (1962, 1971) described a means for ordering reinforcers that allows prediction. The *Premack Principle* says that the opportunity to engage in a more valued activity reinforces engaging in a less valued activity, where "value" is defined in terms of the amount of responding or time spent on the activity in the absence of reinforcement. If a contingency is arranged such that the value of the second (contingent) event is higher than the value of the first (instrumental) event, an increase will be expected in the probability of occurrence of the first event (the reward assumption). If the value of the second event is lower than that of the first event, the likelihood of occurrence of the first event ought to decrease (the punishment assumption).

Suppose that a child is allowed to choose between working on an art project, going to the media center, reading a book, or using a computer. Over the course of 10 such choices, the child works on an art project once, goes to the media center 3 times, never reads a book, and uses a computer 6 times. For this child, the opportunity to use a computer is valued the most. To apply the Premack Principle, a teacher might say to the child, "After you finish reading this book, you can use a computer." Empirical evidence supports Premack's ideas, especially with respect to the reward assumption (Dunham, 1977).

The Premack Principle offers guidance for selecting effective reinforcers: Observe what people do when they have a choice, and order those behaviors in terms of likelihood. The order is not permanent, since the value of reinforcers can change. Any reinforcer, when applied often, can result in *satiation* and lead to decreased responding. Teachers who employ the Premack Principle need to check students' preferences periodically by observing them and asking what they like to do. Determining in advance which reinforcers are likely to be effective in a situation is critical in planning behavioral change.

Punishment. *Punishment* decreases the future likelihood of responding to a stimulus. Punishment may involve withdrawing a positive reinforcer or presenting a negative reinforcer following a response, as shown in Table 3.3. Assume that during a question-and-answer session, a student misbehaves when the teacher asks a question (and maybe is not watching) (teacher asks question = S^D or A; misbehavior = R or B). The teacher spots the misbehavior and assigns the student homework (S^R or C). If the student stops misbehaving, assigning homework operates as a negative reinforcer, and this is an example of punishment because assigning the homework decreased misbehavior. But note that from the teacher's perspective, this is an example of negative reinforcement (misbehavior = S^D or A; assigning homework = R or B; end of misbehavior = S^R or C). Since the teacher was negatively reinforced, the teacher may be likely to assign homework in the future in response to student misbehavior.

Instead of assigning homework, assume that the teacher takes away the student's free time. If the student's misbehavior stops, free time operates as a positive reinforcer, and this is an example of punishment because the loss of free time stops the misbehavior. As before, the cessation of student misbehavior is negatively reinforcing for the teacher.

Punishment *suppresses* a response but does not eliminate it; when the threat of punishment is removed, the punished response may return. The effects of punishment are complex (Skinner, 1953). Spanking a child for misbehaving may produce guilt and fear, which can suppress misbehavior. If the child misbehaves in the future, the conditioned guilt and fear may reappear and stop the child from misbehaving. Punishment also conditions responses that lead one to escape or avoid punishment. Students whose teacher criticizes incorrect answers soon learn to avoid volunteering answers. Punishment can condition maladaptive behaviors, because punishment does not teach how to behave more productively. Punishment can further hinder learning by creating a conflict such that the individual vacillates between responding one way or another. If a teacher sometimes criticizes students for incorrect answers and sometimes does not, students never know when criticism is forthcoming. Such variable behavior can have emotional by-products (e.g., fear, anger) that interfere with learning.

Table 3.4
Alternatives to punishment.

Alternative	Example
Change the discriminative stimuli	Move misbehaving student away from other misbehaving students.
Allow the unwanted behavior to continue	Have student who stands when he or she should be sitting continue to stand.
Extinguish the unwanted behavior	Ignore minor misbehavior so that it is not reinforced by teacher attention.
Condition an incompatible behavior	Reinforce learning progress, which occurs only when student is not misbehaving.

Common school punishments are loss of privileges, removals from the classroom, in- and out-of-school suspensions, and expulsions (Maag, 2001). Yet there are alternatives to punishment (Table 3.4). One is to *change the discriminative stimuli* for negative behavior. For example, a student seated in the back of the room may misbehave. Teachers can change the discriminative stimuli by moving the disruptive student to the front of the class. Another alternative is to *allow the unwanted behavior to continue* until the perpetrator becomes satiated, which is similar to Guthrie's fatigue method. A parent may allow a child throwing a tantrum to continue to throw it until he or she becomes fatigued. A third alternative is to *extinguish an unwanted behavior* by ignoring it. This may work well with minor misbehaviors (e.g., students whispering to one another), but when classrooms become disruptive, teachers need to act in other ways. A fourth alternative is to *condition incompatible behavior* with positive reinforcement. Teacher praise for productive work habits helps condition those habits. The primary advantage of this alternative over punishment is that it shows the student how to behave adaptively.

Schedules of Reinforcement. Schedules refer to when reinforcement is applied (Ferster & Skinner, 1957; Skinner, 1938). A *continuous schedule* involves reinforcement for every correct response. This may be desirable for a short period while skills are being acquired. Continuous reinforcement helps to ensure that incorrect responses are not learned.

An *intermittent schedule* involves reinforcing some but not all correct responses. Intermittent reinforcement is common in classrooms, because usually it is not possible for teachers to reinforce each student for every correct or desirable response. Students are not called on every time they raise their hands, are not praised after working each problem, and are not constantly told they are behaving appropriately.

Intermittent schedules are defined in terms of time or number of responses. An *interval schedule* involves reinforcing the first correct response after a specific time period. In a *fixed-interval (FI) schedule*, the time interval is constant from one reinforcement to the next. An FI5 schedule means that reinforcement is delivered for the first response made after 5 minutes. Students who receive 30 minutes of free time every Friday (contingent on good behavior during the week) are operating under a fixed-interval schedule.

In a *variable-interval (VI) schedule*, the time interval varies from occasion to occasion around some average value. A VI5 schedule means that on the average, the first correct response after 5 minutes is reinforced, but the time interval varies (e.g., 2, 3, 7, or 8 minutes). Students who receive 30 minutes of free time (contingent on good behavior) on an average of once a week, but not necessarily on the same day each week, are operating under a variable-interval schedule.

A *ratio schedule* depends on the number of correct responses or rate of responding. In a *fixed-ratio (FR) schedule*, every *n*th correct response is reinforced, where *n* is constant. An FR10 schedule means that every 10th correct response receives reinforcement. In a *variable-ratio (VR) schedule*, every *n*th correct response is reinforced, but the value varies around an average number *n*. A teacher may give free time after every fifth workbook assignment is completed (FR5) or periodically around an average of five completed assignments (VR5).

Reinforcement schedules produce characteristic patterns of responding, as shown in Figure 3.3. Ratio schedules often produce higher response rates than interval schedules, but a limiting factor is fatigue due to rapid responding. Fixed-interval schedules produce a scalloped pattern. Responding drops off immediately after reinforcement but picks up toward the end of the interval between reinforcements. The variable-interval schedule produces a steady rate of responding. Unannounced quizzes operate on variable-interval schedules and help keep students studying regularly. Intermittent schedules are more resistant to extinction than continuous schedules: When reinforcement is discontinued, responding continues for a longer time if reinforcement has been intermittent rather than continuous. The durability of intermittent schedules can be seen in people's persistence at such events as playing slot machines, fishing, and shopping for bargains.

Figure 3.3
Patterns of responding under different reinforcement schedules. *Note:* VR = variable ratio; FR = fixed ratio; FI = fixed interval; VI = variable interval.

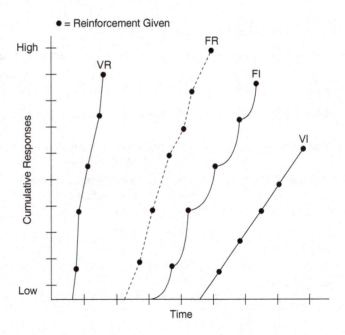

Generalization. Once a certain response occurs regularly to a given stimulus, the response also may occur to other stimuli. Generalization (Skinner, 1953) seems to be a problem for operant theory, because a response should not be made in a situation in which it never has been reinforced. Skinner explained generalization by noting that people perform many behaviors that lead to the final (reinforced) response. These component behaviors are often part of the chains of behavior of different tasks and therefore are reinforced in different contexts. When people are in a new situation, they are likely to perform the component behaviors, which produce an accurate response or rapid acquisition of the correct response.

For example, students with good academic habits typically come to class, attend to and participate in the activities, take notes, do the required reading, and keep up with the assignments. These component behaviors produce high achievement and grades. When such students begin a new class, it is not necessary that the content be similar to previous classes in which they have been enrolled. Rather, the component behaviors have received repeated reinforcement and thus are likely to generalize to the new setting.

Generalization, however, does not occur automatically. O'Leary and Drabman (1971) noted that generalization "must be programmed like any other behavioral change" (p. 393). One problem with many behavior modification programs is that they change behaviors but the new behaviors do not generalize outside the training context. O'Leary and Drabman (1971) offer suggestions on ways to facilitate generalization (Table 3.5 and Application 3.6).

Discrimination. *Discrimination*, the complementary process to generalization, involves responding differently (in intensity or rate) depending on the stimulus or features of a situation. Although teachers want students to generalize what they learn to other situations,

Table 3.5
Suggestions for facilitating generalization.

Parental Involvement:	Involve parents in behavioral change programs.
High Expectations:	Convey to students that they are capable of performing well.
Self-Evaluation:	Teach students to monitor and evaluate their behaviors.
Contingencies:	Withdraw artificial contingencies (e.g., points), and replace with natural ones (privileges).
Participation:	Allow students to participate in specifying behaviors to be reinforced and reinforcement contingencies.
Academics:	Provide a good academic program because many students with behavior problems have academic deficiencies.
Benefits:	Show students how behavioral changes will benefit them by linking changes to activities of interest.
Reinforcement:	Reinforce students in different settings to reduce discrimination between reinforced and nonreinforced situations.
Consistency:	Prepare teachers in inclusion classes to continue to reinforce behaviors of students who have been in special education classes.

APPLICATION 3.6
Generalization

Generalization can advance skill development across subject areas. Finding main ideas in text is relevant to language arts, social studies, mathematics (word problems), and other content areas. A language arts teacher might provide students with a strategy for finding main ideas. Once students master this strategy, the teacher explains how to modify its use for other academic subjects and asks students to think of uses. By teaching the strategy well in one domain and facilitating potential applications in other domains, teachers save much time and effort because they do not have to teach the strategy in each content area.

Teaching expected behaviors (e.g., walking in the hall, raising a hand to speak) can also be generalized. For example, if all seventh-grade teachers decide to have students use the same academic planner, it could be explained in one class. Then students can be asked to use the same planner in each of their other classes, adapting entries as needed.

they also want them to respond discriminately. In solving mathematical word problems, teachers might want students to adopt a general problem-solving approach comprising steps such as determining the given and the needed information, drawing a picture, and generating useful formulas. Teachers also want students to learn to discriminate problem types (e.g., area, time-rate-distance, interest rate). Being able to identify quickly the type of problem enhances students' successes.

Teaching discrimination requires that desired responses be reinforced and unwanted responses extinguished by nonreinforcement. Teachers can highlight similarities and differences among similar content and provide for periodic reviews to ensure that students discriminate properly and apply correct problem–solution methods.

Errors can be disruptive and produce learning of incorrect responses, which suggests that students' errors should be minimized. But eliminating all errors may not be desirable. Students who learn to deal with errors adaptively subsequently persist longer on difficult tasks than do students who have experienced errorless learning (Dweck, 1975; Chapter 9).

Behavior Change

Reinforcement can be given for correct responses only when people know what to do. Often, however, operant responses do not exist in final, polished form. If teachers wait to deliver reinforcement until learners emit the proper responses, many learners would never receive reinforcement because they do not acquire the responses. This section discusses how behavior change occurs in operant conditioning, which has important implications for learning.

Successive Approximations (Shaping). The operant conditioning method of behavioral change is *shaping*, or differential reinforcement of successive approximations to the desired form or rate of behavior (Morse & Kelleher, 1977). To shape behavior:

- Identify what the student can do now (initial behavior)
- Identify the desired behavior
- Identify potential reinforcers in the student's environment
- Break the desired behavior into small substeps to be mastered sequentially
- Move the student from the initial behavior to the desired behavior by successively reinforcing each approximation to the desired behavior

Shaping is learning by doing with corrective feedback. A natural instance of shaping can be seen in a student attempting to shoot a basketball from a point on the court. The first shot falls short of the basket. The student shoots harder the second time, and the ball hits the backboard. The student does not shoot quite as hard the third time, and the ball hits the right rim and bounces off. On the fourth attempt, the student shoots as hard as the third attempt but aims left. The ball hits the left rim and bounces off. Finally, the student shoots just as hard but aims slightly to the right, and the ball goes into the basket. Gradually the shot is honed to an accurate form.

Shaping might be applied with a student who can work on a task for only a few minutes before becoming distracted. The goal is to shape the student's behavior so she can work uninterrupted for 30 minutes. Initially the teacher delivers a reinforcer when the student works productively for 2 minutes. After a few successful 2-minute intervals, the criterion for reinforcement is raised to 3 minutes. Assuming that she works uninterrupted for a few 3-minute periods, the criterion is raised to 4 minutes. This process continues to the goal of 30 minutes as long as the student reliably performs at the criterion level. If the student encounters difficulty at any point, the criterion for reinforcement decreases to a level at which she can perform successfully.

Chaining. Most human actions are complex and include several three-term contingencies (*A–B–C*) linked successively. For example, shooting a basketball requires dribbling, turning, getting set in position, jumping, and releasing the ball. Each response alters the environment, and this altered condition serves as the stimulus for the next response. *Chaining* is the process of producing or altering some of the variables that serve as stimuli for future responses (Skinner, 1953). A chain consists of a series of operants, each of which sets the occasion for further responses.

Consider a student solving an algebraic equation (e.g., $2x - 10 = 4$). The -10 serves as the S^D, to which the student makes the appropriate response (R, add 10 to both sides of the equation). This new equation ($2x = 14$) is the S^R and also the S^D for the next response (divide both sides of the equation by 2) to solve the equation ($x = 7$). This stimulus serves as the S^D to move to the next equation. Operations within each equation constitute a chain, and the entire problem set constitutes a chain.

Chains are similar to Guthrie's acts, whereas three-term contingencies resemble movements. Many chains are integrated sequences such that successful implementation of the chain defines a skill. When skills are well honed, execution of the chain occurs automatically. Riding a bicycle consists of several discrete acts, yet an accomplished rider executes these with little or no conscious effort. Such automaticity is evident often in cognitive skills (e.g., reading, solving mathematical problems).

Behavior Modification

Behavior modification (or *behavior therapy*) refers to the systematic application of behavior principles to facilitate adaptive behaviors. Behavior modification has been employed with adults and children in such diverse contexts as classrooms, counseling settings, prisons, and mental hospitals. It has been used to treat phobias, dysfunctional language, disruptive behaviors, negative social interactions, poor child rearing, and low self-control (Becker, 1971; Keller & Ribes-Inesta, 1974). Lovaas (1977) successfully employed behavior modification to teach language to children with autism. Classroom applications are given in Application 3.7.

Techniques. Behavior modification requires reinforcement of desired behaviors and extinction of undesired ones. Punishment is rarely employed, but when it is used, it more often involves removing a positive reinforcer rather than presenting a negative reinforcer.

A program of change involves addressing some key issues. Which behaviors should be decreased (i.e., are maladaptive), and which should be increased (i.e., are desirable)? What environmental contingencies maintain undesirable behaviors or reduce the likelihood of performing more adaptive responses? What environmental features can be altered to change behavior?

APPLICATION 3.7
Behavior Modification

Behavior modification for disruptive students is difficult because such students may display few appropriate responses to be positively reinforced. Ms. Tiebout has been having problems with Erik, who pushes and shoves other students when the class gets in line to go somewhere. When the class is going only a short distance, Ms. Tiebout informs Erik that if he stays in line without pushing and shoving, he will be the line leader on the way back to the class; however, if he pushes or shoves, he immediately will be removed from the line. This procedure can be repeated until Erik can handle short distances. Ms. Tiebout then can allow him to walk with the class

for progressively longer distances until he can behave in line for any distance.

Sarah, another child in Ms. Tiebout's class, frequently turns in messy work (e.g., dirty, torn, barely readable). Ms. Tiebout might use generalized reinforcers such as special stickers (exchangeable for various privileges) to help Sarah. Ms. Tiebout might tell her that she can earn one sticker if she turns in a paper that is clean, another sticker if it is not torn, and a third sticker if the writing is neat. Once Sarah begins to make improvements, Ms. Tiebout gradually can move the rewards to other areas for improvement (e.g., correct work, finishing work on time).

The first step in establishing a behavior change program is to define the problem in behavioral terms. For example, the statement, "Keith is out of his seat too often," refers to overt behavior that can be measured: One can keep a record of the amount of time that Keith is out of his seat. General expressions referring to unobservables (e.g., "Keith has a bad attitude") do not allow for objective problem definition.

The next step is to determine the reinforcers maintaining undesirable behavior. Perhaps Keith is getting teacher attention only when he gets out of his seat. A simple plan is to have the teacher attend to Keith while he is seated and engaged in academic work and to ignore him when he gets out of his seat. If the amount of times that Keith is out of his seat decreases, teacher attention is a positive reinforcer.

A behavior modification program might employ such generalized reinforcers as points that students exchange for *backup reinforcers*, such as tangible rewards, free time, or privileges. Having more than one backup ensures that at least one will be effective for each student at all times. A behavioral criterion must be established to earn reinforcement. The five-step shaping procedure (discussed previously) can be employed. The criterion is initially defined at the level of initial behavior and progresses in small increments toward the desired behavior. A point is given to the student each time the criterion is satisfied. To extinguish any undesirable behavior by Keith, the teacher should not give him too much attention if he gets out of his seat but rather should inform him privately that because he has not satisfied the criterion, he will not earn a point.

Punishment is used infrequently but may be needed when behavior becomes so disruptive that it cannot be ignored (e.g., fighting). A common punishment is *time out from reinforcement.* During time out, the student is removed from the class social context. There the student continues to engage in academic work without peer social interaction or the opportunity to earn reinforcement. Another punishment is to remove positive reinforcers (e.g., free time, recess, privileges) for misbehavior.

Critics have argued that behavior modification shapes quiet and docile behaviors (Winett & Winkler, 1972). Although too much noise may disrupt learning, it is not necessary to have a quiet classroom at all times. Some noise from social interactions can facilitate learning. The use of behavior modification is inherently neither good nor bad. It can produce overly quiet classrooms or promote social interactions (Strain, Kerr, & Ragland, 1981). Like the techniques themselves, the goals of behavior modification need to be thought out carefully by those implementing the procedures.

Positive Behavior Supports. Positive behavior supports reflect several principles from operant conditioning and are designed to produce behavior change. Dysfunctional behaviors are instigated by environmental stimuli (cues) and maintained by reinforcement. A child who misbehaves, for example, might get attention from teacher and peers. To the extent that the attention is reinforcing, operant conditioning theory predicts that the child will be more likely to misbehave in the future in the presence of the discriminative stimuli (e.g., teachers, peers) to do so.

Positive behavior supports refer to components of a system to identify and remediate problem behaviors (Sugai & Horner, 2002). It is essentially a problem-solving and teaching approach to managing problem behaviors. Initially an assessment is conducted, which describes problem behaviors and the contexts in which they occur, as well as the reinforcers that are maintaining them. Then a support plan is developed in which children are taught more productive behaviors (i.e., academic, social, communication, self-management) and reinforcement contingencies are established.

Three levels of positive behavior supports may be established: primary, secondary, and tertiary. Primary prevention strategies are used schoolwide for all students. Such strategies include effective teaching practices, use of corrective feedback, and reinforcement systems (e.g., privileges for desirable behaviors). Secondary strategies are used for students who do not respond well to primary strategies. They may be part of an intervention used individually or in groups, such as social skills training and tutoring. Students who continue to respond inappropriately may receive tertiary strategies at school and at home. The strategies may be incorporated into an intervention plan.

Some common positive behavior support strategies include those emphasized by operant conditioning, such as changing environmental cues (e.g., moving student to another seat), extinction (ignore behavior), positive reinforcement for appropriate behavior, desensitization, time out, and teaching of productive behaviors. Research evaluating the effectiveness of positive behavior supports shows that the strategies typically result in improved student behavior (Bear & Manning, 2014), which is necessary for good self-management, social functioning, and academic achievement.

Cognitive Behavior Modification. Researchers also have incorporated cognitive elements into behavior modification procedures. In *cognitive behavior modification*, learners' thoughts (when verbalized) function as discriminative and reinforcing stimuli. Learners may verbally instruct themselves what to do and then perform the appropriate behavior. Cognitive behavior modification techniques often are applied with students with handicaps (Hallahan, Kneedler, & Lloyd, 1983) and are used to reduce hyperactivity and aggression (Robinson, Smith, Miller, & Brownell, 1999). Meichenbaum's (1977) *self-instructional training* is an example of cognitive behavior modification (see Chapter 4).

Contemporary Perspective

With their emphasis on observable events, behavior theories seem mechanistic: Set the proper stimuli in the environment, and the responses will occur. Although people experience internal events (e.g., thoughts, feelings), these are not necessary to explain behavior.

These assumptions have been repeatedly challenged, especially by cognitive theorists. But it is not necessary to completely reject behavior theories in favor of cognitive ones. As noted in this chapter, behavior principles can be applied without wholly subscribing to conditioning theories. For example, establishing a conducive learning environment and reinforcing students for learning are desirable regardless of one's theoretical perspective.

There is increasing evidence that principles of conditioning do not operate in a completely mechanistic fashion. Recall the research by Rescorla (1987) showing that for classical conditioning to occur, people must form expectations—which are cognitive beliefs—about the likelihood of the UCS following the CS. CSs that are good predictors of UCSs are most apt to produce conditioning.

Recent research also has investigated the nature of voluntary acts. Skinner (1953) contended that operant behaviors were voluntary behaviors emitted in the presence of discriminative stimuli. When followed by reinforcement, the probability of occurrence of such operants increases in the future in the presence of these discriminative stimuli.

The notion of voluntary acts seems incompatible with operant conditioning because these acts imply a degree of learner choice and control. Another issue is that there can be variability among operants since presumably not all possible variations will have been reinforced for a given individual. For example, a student who seeks teacher attention (a positive reinforcer) could conceivably engage in different acts such as perform well, misbehave, get sick, fall on the floor, and the like—not all of which may been reinforced in the past.

Neuringer and Jensen (2010) addressed this concern by proposing that voluntary acts (operants) are intentional and goal directed. In line with Skinner's contention, they predict that reinforcers and discriminative stimuli affect the form and rate of operants, but they also contend that reinforcers and discriminative stimuli influence the variability of operants, which can range from patterned and repetitive (and therefore predictable) to random (and therefore unpredictable). These predictions, which Neuringer and Jensen support with research, mean that if variability in responding is reinforced, people may act one way now and differently later. By imposing a measure of volition onto operant conditioning, the analysis by Neuringer and Jensen gives operant conditioning at least a bit of a cognitive flavor.

This behavior theory interpretation of voluntary acts has implications for education since it suggests that variability in actions can be reinforced and made more likely to occur. There are many situations in teaching and learning where teachers desire variability in student responses; for example, in problem solving, creative thinking, and brainstorming. Regardless of whether the analysis by Neuringer and Jensen is fully accurate, it seems desirable for teachers to reinforce students who demonstrate variability, which might encourage this type of thinking.

INSTRUCTIONAL APPLICATIONS

Skinner (1954, 1961, 1968, 1984) wrote extensively on how his ideas can be applied to education. He believed there was too much aversive control. Although students rarely receive corporal punishment, they often work on assignments not because they want to learn or because they enjoy them but rather to avoid punishments such as teacher criticism, loss of privileges, and trips to the principal's office.

A second concern is that reinforcement occurs infrequently and often not at the proper time. Teachers attend to each student for only a few minutes each day. While students are engaged in learning, minutes can elapse between when they finish an assignment and when they receive teacher feedback. Consequently, students may learn incorrectly, which means that teachers must spend additional time giving corrective feedback.

A third point is that the scope and sequence of curricula do not ensure that all students acquire skills. Students do not learn at the same pace. To cover all the material, teachers may move to the next lesson before all students have mastered the previous one.

Skinner contended that these and other issues cannot be addressed by paying teachers more money (although they would like that!), lengthening the school day and year, raising standards, or toughening teacher certification requirements. Rather, he recommended better use of instructional time. Since it is unrealistic to expect students to move through the curriculum at the same rate, individualizing instruction will improve efficiency.

Skinner believed that teaching required properly arranging reinforcement contingencies. Instruction is more effective when (1) teachers present the material in small steps, (2) learners actively respond rather than passively listen, (3) teachers give feedback immediately following learners' responses, and (4) learners move through the material at their own pace. Regardless of one's theoretical perspective, these are sound instructional points.

The basic process of instruction involves shaping. The goal of instruction (desired behavior) and the students' initial behavior are identified. Substeps (behaviors) leading from the initial behavior to the desired behavior are formulated. Each substep represents a small modification of the preceding one. Students are moved through the sequence using various approaches including demonstrations, small-group work, and individual seat work. Students actively respond to the material and receive immediate feedback.

This instructional approach involves specifying learners' present knowledge and desired objectives in terms of what learners do. Desired behaviors often are specified as behavioral objectives (discussed shortly). Individual differences are taken into account by beginning instruction at learners' present performance levels and allowing them to progress at their own rates. Given the assembly-line culture that is prevalent in many educational systems (i.e., all students work on the same material at the same time), these goals seem impractical: Teachers would have to begin instruction at different points and cover material at different rates for individual students. However, with advances in technology, individualized computer-based instruction can circumvent these problems as curricula and assessments are adaptive (discussed later).

The remainder of this section describes some instructional applications that incorporate behavioristic principles. Not all of these applications are derived from Skinner's or other behavior theories covered in this chapter, but they all reflect key ideas of behavior theory.

Behavioral Objectives

Behavioral objectives are clear statements of the intended student outcomes of instruction. Objectives can range from general to specific. General or vague objectives such as "improve student awareness" can be satisfied by different kinds of student behaviors. Conversely, objectives that are too specific and document every minute change in student behavior are time consuming to write and can cause teachers to lose sight of the most important learning outcomes. Optimal objectives fall somewhere between these extremes (Application 3.8).

A behavioral objective describes what students do when demonstrating their achievements and how teachers know what students are doing (Mager, 1962). Four parts of a good objective are:

APPLICATION 3.8
Behavioral Objectives

As teachers prepare lesson plans, it is important that they decide on specific behavioral objectives and plan activities to assist students in mastering these objectives. Instead of an art teacher planning a lesson with the objective, "Have students complete a pen drawing of the front of the building," the teacher should decide on the major objective for the students to master. Is it to use a pen or to draw the front of the school building? The objective may be better stated as follows: "Have the students draw the major lines of the front of the building in correct perspective (materials/medium: drawing paper, pens)."

A kindergarten teacher writes that she wants "Students to go to art, music, and physical education in an orderly fashion." For that age child, it would be better if the teacher would develop a more specific objective; for example, "Students should move to other classrooms by walking in a line without talking and by keeping their hands to themselves."

1. The specific group of students
2. The actual behaviors students are to perform as a consequence of instructional activities
3. The conditions or contexts in which the students are to perform the behaviors
4. The criteria for assessing student behaviors to determine whether objectives have been met

A sample objective with the parts identified is:

Given eight addition problems with fractions of unlike denominators (3), fourth-grade students (1) will write the correct sums (2) for at least seven of them (4).

Behavioral objectives should specify the important learning outcomes, which aid in lesson planning and testing to assess learning. Formulating objectives also helps teachers decide what content students can master. Given unit-teaching objectives and a fixed amount of time to cover them, teachers can decide which objectives are most important and focus on them. Although objectives for lower-level learning outcomes (e.g., remember, understand) are generally easier to specify, good behavioral objectives can be written to assess higher-order outcomes (e.g., analyze, evaluate) as well.

Students given behavioral objectives have better verbatim recall of verbal information compared with students not provided with objectives (Hamilton, 1985). Objectives may cue students to process the information at the appropriate level; when students are given objectives requiring recall, they engage in rehearsal and other strategies that facilitate that type of recall. Research also shows that providing students with objectives does not enhance learning of material unrelated to the objectives (Duchastel & Brown, 1974), which suggests that students may concentrate on learning material relevant to the objectives and disregard other material.

The effect of objectives on learning depends on students' prior experience with them and on how important they perceive the information to be. Training in using objectives or familiarity with criterion-based instruction leads to better learning compared to the absence of such training or familiarity. When students can determine on their own what material is important to learn, providing objectives does not facilitate learning. Informing students of the objectives seems to be more important when students do not know what material is important. Muth, Glynn, Britton, and Graves (1988) also found that text structure can moderate the effect of objectives on learning. Information in a prominent position (e.g., early in a text or highlighted) is recalled well, even when objectives are not provided.

Learning Time

Operant theory predicts that environmental variables affect students' learning. One such variable is learning time.

Carroll (1963, 1965, 1989) formulated a model of school learning that places primary emphasis on time spent learning. Students successfully learn to the extent that they spend the amount of time they need to learn. *Time* means academically engaged time, or time spent paying attention and trying to learn. Although time is an environmental (observable) variable, this definition is cognitive because it goes beyond a simple behavioral indicator of clock time. Within this framework, Carroll postulated factors that influence how much time learning requires and how much time is actually spent learning.

Time Needed for Learning. One influence on the time a student needs to learn is *aptitude for learning the task*. Learning aptitude depends on the amount of prior task-relevant learning and on personal characteristics such as abilities and attitudes. A second influence is *ability to understand instruction*. This variable relates to instructional method; for example, some learners comprehend verbal instruction well, whereas others benefit more from visual presentations.

A third influence is *quality of instruction*, or how well the task is organized and presented to learners. Quality includes what learners are told about what they will learn and how they will learn it, the extent to which they have adequate contact with the content to be learned, and how much prerequisite knowledge is acquired prior to learning the task. The lower the quality of instruction, the more time learners require to learn.

Time Spent in Learning. How much time the student spends learning depends on the *time allowed for learning*. School curricula include so much content that time allotted for a particular type of learning is less than optimal for some students. When teachers cover material with the entire class at once (i.e., the assembly-line culture), some learners are more likely to experience difficulty grasping it and require additional instruction. When students are grouped by ability levels, the amount of time devoted to different content varies depending on the ease with which students learn.

A second influence is the *time the learner is willing to spend learning*. Even when learners are given ample time to learn, they may not spend that time working productively. Whether due to low interest, high perceived task difficulty, or other factors, students may not be motivated to persist at a task for the amount of time they require to learn it. Carroll incorporated these factors into a formula to estimate the degree of learning for any student on a given task:

degree of learning = time spent in learning/time needed for learning

Ideally, students spend as much time as they need to learn (degree of learning = 1.0), but learners typically spend either more time (degree of learning > 1.0) or less time (degree of learning < 1.0) than they require.

Carroll's model highlights the importance of academic engaged time required for learning and the factors influencing time spent and time needed to learn. The model incorporates valid psychological principles but only at a general level as instructional or motivational factors. It does not explore cognitive engagement in depth. Mastery learning researchers, by systematically investigating the time variable, have provided greater specificity (discussed in the next section).

Many educators have decried the way that learning time is misspent (Zepeda & Mayers, 2006). Time is central to current discussions on ways to maximize student achievement. Research supports the idea that time is essential for learning. When students are given more time to learn content, their conceptual understanding increases (American Educational Research Association, 2007). Further, the No Child Left Behind Act of 2001 greatly expanded the role of the federal government in elementary and secondary education (Shaul & Ganson, 2005). Although the act did not specify how much time was to be devoted to instruction, its requirements for student achievement and its accountability standards, combined with critics calling for better use of time, have led school systems to re-examine their use of time to ensure better student learning.

One consequence is that many secondary schools have changed from the traditional six-hour schedule to *block scheduling*. Although there are variations, many use the A/B block, in which classes meet on alternate days for longer periods per day. Presumably block scheduling allows teachers and students to explore content in greater depth than is possible with the traditional shorter class periods (e.g., 50 minutes).

Given that block scheduling still is relatively new, there is not a lot of research assessing its effectiveness. In their review, Zepeda and Mayers (2006) found that block scheduling may improve school climate and students' grade point averages, but studies show inconsistent results for student attendance and scores on standardized tests. As block scheduling becomes more common, we can expect additional research that may clarify these inconsistencies.

Another means for increasing time for learning is through out-of-school programs, such as after-school programs and summer school. Compared with research on block scheduling, research on the effects of out-of-school programs shows greater consistency. Lauer et al. (2006) found positive effects for such programs on students' reading and mathematics achievement; effects were larger for programs with enhancements (e.g., tutoring). Mahoney, Lord, and Carryl (2005) found benefits of after-school programs on children's academic performances and motivation; results were strongest for children rated as highly engaged in the after-school program's activities. Consistent with Carroll's model, we might conclude that out-of-school programs are successful to the extent that they focus on academic learning and provide supports to encourage it.

Technology also can help alleviate the problem of students not spending enough time engaged in learning. Blended learning combines fact-to-face with online instruction. Computer software that can adapt to student differences provides additional time to students who require it. Carroll's model needs some modification to move beyond the face-to-face context on which it is based. The hope is that adaptive programming will help move educational thinking beyond the idea that all students learn at the same rate and require equal amounts of time to learn.

Mastery Learning

Carroll's model predicts that if students vary in aptitude for learning a subject and if all receive the same amount and type of instruction, their achievement will differ. If the amount and type of instruction vary depending on individual differences among learners, then each student has the potential to demonstrate mastery.

These ideas form the basis of *mastery learning* (Anderson, 2003; Bloom, 1976; Bloom, Hastings, & Madaus, 1971). Mastery learning incorporates Carroll's ideas into a systematic instructional plan that includes defining mastery, planning for mastery, teaching for mastery, and grading for mastery (Block & Burns, 1977). Mastery learning contains cognitive elements, although its formulation seems more behavioral in nature compared with many current cognitive theories.

To *define mastery*, teachers prepare a set of objectives and a final (summative) exam. Level of mastery is established (e.g., where *A* students typically perform under traditional instruction). Teachers break the course into learning units mapped against course objectives.

Planning for mastery means teachers plan instruction to include corrective feedback (formative evaluation). Such evaluation typically takes the form of unit mastery assessments that set mastery at a given level (e.g., 90%). Corrective instruction, which is used with students who fail to master aspects of the unit's objectives, is given in small-group study sessions, individual tutorials, and supplemental content.

At the outset of *teaching for mastery*, teachers orient students to the mastery procedures and provide instruction using the entire class, small groups, or individual activities. Teachers give the formative test and certify which students achieved mastery. Students who fall short might work in small groups reviewing troublesome content, often with the aid of peer tutors who have mastered it. Teachers allow students time to work on remedial content, along with homework. *Grading for mastery* includes a summative (end-of-course) test. Students who score at or above the course mastery performance level receive *A* grades; lower scores are graded accordingly.

The emphasis on student abilities as determinants of learning may seem uninteresting given that abilities generally do not change much as a result of instructional interventions. Bloom (1976) also stressed the importance of *alterable variables* of schooling: cognitive entry behaviors (e.g., student skills and cognitive processing strategies at the outset of instruction), affective characteristics (e.g., interest, motivation), and specific factors influencing the quality of instruction (e.g., student participation, type of corrective feedback). Instructional interventions can improve these variables.

Although many studies have shown that mastery learning is effective (Zimmerman & DiBenedetto, 2008), other studies have yielded mixed results. For example, Block and Burns (1977) found mastery learning more effective than traditional forms of instruction. With college students, Péladeau, Forget, and Gagné (2003) obtained results showing that mastery learning improved students' achievement, long-term retention, and attitudes toward the course and subject matter. Kulik, Kulik, and Bangert-Drowns (1990) examined more than 100 evaluations of mastery learning programs and found positive effects on academic performances and course attitudes among college, high school, and upper-grade elementary school learners. They also found that mastery learning may increase the time students spend on instructional tasks. In contrast, Bangert, Kulik, and Kulik (1983) found weaker support for mastery learning programs. They noted that mastery-based instruction was more effective at the college level than at lower levels. Its effectiveness undoubtedly depends on the proper instructional conditions (e.g., planning, teaching, grading) being established (Kulik et al., 1990).

Students participating in mastery instruction often spend more time in learning compared with learners in traditional classes (Block & Burns, 1977). Given that time is at a premium in schools, much mastery work must be accomplished outside of regular school hours (i.e., such as with online learning). Most studies show smaller effects of mastery instruction on affective outcomes (e.g., interest in and attitudes toward the subject matter) than on academic outcomes.

Anderson (1976) found that when remedial students gained experience with mastery instruction, they gradually required less extra time to attain mastery because their entry-level skills improved. These results imply cumulative benefits of mastery learning. There remains, however, the question of how much practice is enough (Péladeau et al., 2003). Too much repetitive practice might decrease motivation and thereby hinder learning. Examples of mastery learning are given in Application 3.9.

APPLICATION 3.9
Mastery Learning

A mastery learning approach can be beneficial in certain learning environments. In a remedial reading group for secondary students, a well-organized mastery learning program—such as in a computer-based learning environment—would allow students to progress at their own rates. Students motivated to make rapid progress are not slowed down by this type of instruction, as might happen if they are placed in a traditional learning format. A key requirement is to allow for a progression of activities from easier to more difficult. The program should have checkpoints at which the students interact with the teacher so that their progress is evaluated and reteaching provided if needed.

Young children enter school with a wide range of experiences and abilities. Mastery learning can help teachers deal effectively with the varying abilities and developmental levels. Mastery learning techniques can be implemented by using learning centers and small groups. Children

APPLICATION 3.9 (*continued*)

can be placed in the different centers and groups according to their current levels. Then they can move through the various levels at their own rates.

Mastery learning also can build students' self-efficacy for learning (Chapter 4). As they perceive their progress in completing units, they are apt to believe they are capable of further learning. Enhancing self-efficacy is particularly important with learners who have encountered learning difficulties and doubt their capabilities to learn, as well as for young children with limited experiences and skills.

Differentiated Instruction

Differentiated instruction refers to instructional activities tailored to individual student needs. Differentiated instruction eliminates the problem of instructional activities occurring too rapidly or slowly for learners. In this section, historical work is discussed, followed by recent developments.

Historical Work. Historically, one type of differentiated instruction was *programmed instruction (PI)*, or instructional materials developed in accordance with operant conditioning principles of learning (O'Day, Kulhavy, Anderson, & Malczynski, 1971). In the 1920s, Sidney Pressey designed machines to use primarily for testing. Students were presented with multiple-choice questions, and they pressed a button corresponding to their choice. If students responded correctly, the machine presented the next choice; if they responded incorrectly, the error was recorded and they continued to respond to the item.

Skinner revived Pressey's machines in the 1950s and modified them to incorporate instruction (Skinner, 1958). These teaching machines presented students with material in small steps (frames). Each frame required learners to make an overt response. Material was carefully sequenced and broken into small units to minimize errors. Students received immediate feedback on the accuracy of each response. They moved to the next frame when their answer was correct. When it was incorrect, supplementary instruction was provided. Although errors occurred, the programs were designed to minimize errors and ensure that learners typically succeeded (Benjamin, 1988).

There are many benefits when students generally perform well, but as noted earlier, research suggests that preventing errors may not be desirable. Dweck (1975) found that an occasional failure increased persistence on difficult tasks more than did constant success. Further, constant success is not as informative of one's capabilities as is occasionally having difficulty because the latter highlights what one can and cannot do. This is not to suggest that teachers should let students fail but rather that under the proper circumstances, students can benefit from tasks structured so that they occasionally encounter difficulty.

PI did not require the use of a machine; a book by Holland and Skinner (1961) is an example of PI. Current instructional programs are more elaborate than the early PI ones.

Today most PI is computerized and is a type of *computer-based instruction* (*CBI*; discussed later).

PI reflected several learning principles (O'Day et al., 1971). Behavioral objectives specified what students should perform on completion of the instruction. Units were subdivided into sequenced frames, each of which presented a small bit of information and a test item to which learners responded. Although a lot of content might have been included in the program, the frame-to-frame increments were small. Learners worked at their own pace and responded to questions as they worked through the program. Responses might have required learners to supply words, provide numerical answers, or choose which of several statements best describes the idea being presented. Feedback depended on the learner's response. If the learner was correct, the next item was given. If the learner answered incorrectly, additional information was presented and the item was tested in slightly different form.

There were two types of programs—linear and branching—distinguished according to how they treat learner errors. In a *linear program*, all students proceeded in the same sequence but not necessarily at the same rate. Regardless of whether they responded correctly to a frame, they moved to the next frame where they received feedback on the accuracy of their answer. Programs minimized errors by covering the same material in more than one frame and by prompting student responses.

In a *branching program*, students' movement depended on how they answered the questions (Figure 3.4). Those who learned quickly skipped frames and bypassed much of the repetition of linear programs, whereas slower learners received additional instruction. A potential disadvantage was that branching programs may not have provided sufficient repetition to ensure that all students learned concepts well.

Some researchers found that linear and branching programs promoted student learning equally well and that PI was as effective as conventional classroom teaching (Bangert et al., 1983; Lange, 1972). PI seemed especially useful with students who demonstrated skill deficiencies; working through programs provided remedial instruction and practice. PI also was useful for independent study on a topic.

Contemporary Developments. Until it was supplanted by the Internet, CBI was the most common application of computer learning in schools (Jonassen, 1996). Studies investigating CBI in college courses show beneficial effects on students' achievement and attitudes (Kulik, Kulik, & Cohen, 1980). Several CBI features are firmly grounded in learning theory and research. Computers command students' attention and provide immediate feedback, which can be of a type typically not given in class (e.g., how present performances compare with prior performances to highlight progress). Computers can individualize content and rate of presentation. Information about students' skills and prior responses can be stored. Through advances in technology, learning can be adapted to individual students' needs in multiple ways, such that they move through learning units with personalized frames (Webley, 2013).

Even simple forms of personalization can be beneficial. Students can enter information about themselves, parents, and friends, which is then included in the instruction. Research shows that personalization can produce higher achievement (Anand & Ross, 1987;

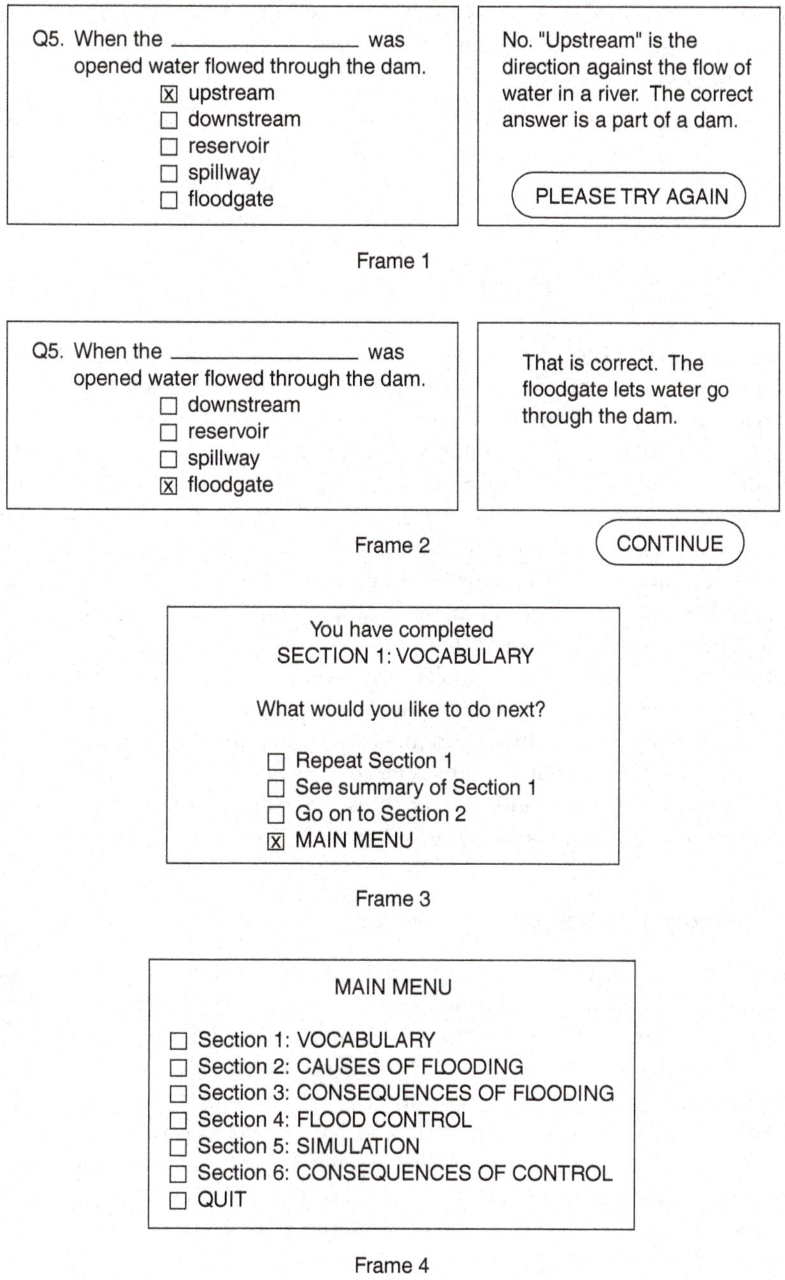

Q5. When the _____ was
    opened water flowed through the dam.
        ☒ upstream
        ☐ downstream
        ☐ reservoir
        ☐ spillway
        ☐ floodgate

No. "Upstream" is the
direction against the flow of
water in a river. The correct
answer is a part of a dam.

(PLEASE TRY AGAIN)

Frame 1

Q5. When the _____ was
    opened water flowed through the dam.
        ☐ downstream
        ☐ reservoir
        ☐ spillway
        ☒ floodgate

That is correct. The
floodgate lets water go
through the dam.

(CONTINUE)

Frame 2

You have completed
SECTION 1: VOCABULARY

What would you like to do next?

    ☐ Repeat Section 1
    ☐ See summary of Section 1
    ☐ Go on to Section 2
    ☒ MAIN MENU

Frame 3

MAIN MENU

    ☐ Section 1: VOCABULARY
    ☐ Section 2: CAUSES OF FLOODING
    ☐ Section 3: CONSEQUENCES OF FLOODING
    ☐ Section 4: FLOOD CONTROL
    ☐ Section 5: SIMULATION
    ☐ Section 6: CONSEQUENCES OF CONTROL
    ☐ QUIT

Frame 4

Figure 3.4
Frames from a branching program.

Ross, McCormick, Krisak, & Anand, 1985). Anand and Ross (1987) gave elementary children instruction in dividing fractions according to one of three problem formats (abstract, concrete, personalized):

> (Abstract) There are three objects. Each is cut in half. In all, how many pieces would there be?
>
> (Concrete) Billy had three candy bars. He cut each of them in half. In all, how many pieces of candy did Billy have?
>
> (Personalized for Joseph) Joseph's teacher, Mrs. Williams, surprised him on December 15 when she presented Joseph with three candy bars. Joseph cut each one of them in half so that he could share the birthday gift with his friends. In all, how many pieces of candy did Joseph have? (pp. 73–74)

The personalized format led to better learning and transfer than the abstract format and to more positive attitudes toward instruction than the concrete format.

Advances in technology have greatly increased the instructional and assessment differentiation capabilities of computer-based systems. *Computer-adaptive systems* are those that deliver instruction or assessment items based on how students respond. Thus, the system will give material or items at a given difficulty level. If students respond correctly, the system provides new material or more-difficult items. If students respond incorrectly, the computer provides review material or easier items. The system therefore adapts to students' responses by providing material or items matched to the assessment-determined level of achievement (Popham, 2014).

Although this methodology looks behavioral, computer-based systems typically are developed and researched by individuals holding a cognitive or constructivist theoretical orientation. It is not simply how students respond; a critical issue is why they respond as they do. The focus is on determining students' levels of thinking about the content being learned or tested. Research on students' thinking and understanding moves far beyond the behavior theory emphasis on students' responses.

Contingency Contracts

A *contingency contract* is an agreement between teacher and student specifying what work the student will accomplish and the expected outcome (reinforcement) for successful performance (Homme, Csanyi, Gonzales, & Rechs, 1970). A contract can be made verbally, although it usually is written. Teachers can devise the contract and ask if the student agrees with it. If teacher and student formulate it jointly, students may feel more committed to fulfilling the contract's terms. When people participate in goal selection, they tend to be more committed to attaining the goal than when they are excluded from the selection process (Locke & Latham, 2002).

Contracts specify goals or expected outcomes in terms of particular behaviors to be displayed. The "contingency" is the expected outcome, which often can be reduced to, "If you do this, then you will receive that." The behaviors should be specific—for example, "I will complete problems 1–30 in math with at least 90% accuracy," or "I will stay in my seat during reading period." General behaviors (e.g., "I will work on my math" or "I will behave appropriately") are unacceptable. With young children, time frames should be brief; however, objectives can cover more than one time, such as successive 30-minute periods

---

APPLICATION 3.10
Contingency Contracts

A contingency contract represents a systematic application of reinforcement principles to change behavior. It can be used to improve any behavior, such as completing assignments, behaving appropriately in class, and participating in discussions. When developing a contract, a teacher should make sure that the reinforcer is something that interests and motivates the students.

Mrs. Lauter has tried unsuccessfully to apply several motivational techniques to encourage James, a student in her class, to complete assignments in language arts. She and James might jointly develop a contract to address the inappropriate behaviors. They should discuss the problem, identify the desired behavior, and list the consequences and time frame for fulfilling the terms of the contract. A sample contract might be as follows:

Contract for the Week of January 9–13

I will complete my language arts assignments with 80% accuracy in the time allotted during class. If I complete my assignments, I will be allowed to participate in a learning center activity. If I do not complete my assignments, I will miss recess and complete them then.

Monday:
_____ Completed _____ Not completed
Tuesday:
_____ Completed _____ Not completed
Wednesday:
_____ Completed _____ Not completed
Thursday:
_____ Completed _____ Not completed
Friday:
_____ Completed _____ Not completed

Bonus: If I complete my assignments at least three of the five days, I will receive computer time for 30 minutes on Friday afternoon.

_____   _____
Student   Teacher
Signature/Date   Signature/Date

---

or during each social studies period for one week. Contracts may include academic and nonacademic behaviors (Application 3.10).

Developing contracts with students and monitoring progress is time consuming. Fortunately, most learners do not require contracts to behave appropriately or accomplish work. Contracts seem especially helpful as a means of assisting students to engage more productively in activities. A lengthy, long-term assignment can be subdivided into a series of short-term goals with due dates. This type of plan helps students keep up with the work and turn in material on time.

Contracts are based on the principle that goals that are specific, temporally close at hand, and difficult but attainable maximize performance (Schunk, 2012). Contracts also convey information to students about their progress in completing the task. Such information on progress raises student motivation and achievement (Locke & Latham, 2002). Contracts should promote achievement if they reinforce student progress in learning or in accomplishing more on-task behavior.

SUMMARY AND CRITIQUE

Chapter Summary

Behaviorism—as reflected in conditioning theories—dominated the psychology of learning for the first half of the twentieth century. Behavior theories explain learning in terms of environmental events. Mental processes are not necessary to explain the acquisition, maintenance, and generalization of behavior.

The theories of Thorndike, Pavlov, and Guthrie helped to establish the psychology of learning as a legitimate area of study. These theories differ, but each views learning as a process of forming associations between stimuli and responses. Thorndike believed that responses to stimuli are strengthened when followed by satisfying consequences. Pavlov experimentally demonstrated how stimuli could be conditioned to elicit responses by being paired with other stimuli. Guthrie hypothesized that a contiguous relation between stimulus and response established their pairing. Although these theories are no longer viable in their original form, many of their principles are evident in current learning theories.

Operant conditioning—the learning theory formulated by B. F. Skinner—is based on the assumption that features of the environment (stimuli, situations, events) serve as cues for responding. Reinforcement strengthens responses and increases their future likelihood of occurring when the stimuli are present. It is not necessary to refer to underlying physiological or mental states to explain behavior.

The basic operant conditioning model is a three-term contingency involving a discriminative stimulus (antecedent), response (behavior), and reinforcing stimulus (consequence). The consequences of behaviors determine the likelihood that people will respond to environmental cues. Consequences that are reinforcing increase behavior; consequences that are punishing decrease behavior. Some other important operant conditioning concepts are extinction, generalization, discrimination, primary and secondary reinforcers, reinforcement schedules, and the Premack Principle.

Shaping—a process for altering behavior—involves reinforcing successive approximations of the desired behavior toward its desired form or frequency of occurrence. Complex behaviors are formed by chaining together simple behaviors in successive three-term contingencies. Behavior modification programs have been commonly applied in diverse contexts to promote adaptive behaviors.

Operant principles have been applied to many aspects of teaching and learning. These principles can be seen in applications involving behavioral objectives, learning time, mastery learning, computer-based instruction, and contingency contracts. Research evidence often shows positive effects of these applications on student achievement. Regardless of theoretical orientation, one can apply behavioral principles to facilitate student learning and achievement. A summary of the learning issues (Chapter 1) for conditioning theories appears in Table 3.6.

Chapter Critique

Behaviorism has many solid points to offer for the scientific study of learning. Few would dispute the basic premises that we learn by association and that reinforcements and

Table 3.6
Summary of learning issues.

How Does Learning Occur?

The basic model of operant learning is expressed by the three-term contingency: $S^D \rightarrow R \rightarrow S^R$, or $A \rightarrow B \rightarrow C$. A response (B) is performed in the presence of a discriminative stimulus (A) and is followed by a reinforcing stimulus (C). The likelihood of the R being performed in the future in the presence of that S^D is increased. To build complex behaviors requires shaping, which consists of chains of three-term contingencies where gradual approximations to the desired form of behavior are successively reinforced. Factors affecting learning are developmental status and reinforcement history. For conditioning to occur, one must have the physical capabilities to perform the behaviors. The responses that one makes in given situations depend on what one has been reinforced for doing in the past.

How Does Memory Function?

Memory is not explicitly addressed by conditioning theories. These theories do not study internal processes. Responses to given stimuli are strengthened through repeated reinforcement. This response strengthening accounts for present behavior.

What Is the Role of Motivation?

Motivation is an increase in the quantity or rate of behavior. No internal processes such as emotions are used to explain motivation. The increase in quantity or rate can be explained in terms of reinforcement history. Certain schedules of reinforcement produce higher rates of responding than others.

How Does Transfer Occur?

Transfer, or generalization, occurs when one responds in an identical or similar fashion to stimuli other than the ones that were used in conditioning. At least some of the elements in the transfer setting must be similar to those in the conditioning setting for transfer to occur.

How Does Self-Regulated Learning Operate?

As discussed in Chapter 10, operant conditioning construes self-regulated behavior as choosing among alternative actions, often by deferring an immediate reinforcer in favor of a different and usually greater future reinforcer. The key processes are self-monitoring, self-instruction, and self-reinforcement. One decides which behaviors to regulate, establishes discriminative stimuli for their occurrence, receives instruction, monitors performance and determines whether it matches the standard, and administers reinforcement.

What Are the Implications for Instruction?

Learning requires establishing responses to discriminative stimuli. Practice is needed to strengthen responses. Complex skills can be established by shaping progressive, small approximations to the desired behavior. Instruction should have clear, measurable objectives, proceed in small steps, and deliver reinforcement. Mastery learning, computer-based instruction, and contingency contracts are useful ways to promote learning.

---

punishments affect associations. Other behavioral concepts—such as extinction, generalization, discrimination, and reinforcement schedules—have been substantiated by learning research. The wide range of applications underscores the applied potential of behavioral principles.

At the same time, there are many troubling issues with behaviorism. The basic principles were developed largely in research with animals. A question is the extent of the generalization possible. Humans are much more complex given their capacity for language, problem solving, and higher-level thinking. A theory developed from research on animals cannot postulate cognitive or affective processes, which humans possess and which other research shows play critical roles in learning. The generality of conditioning principles has been challenged by cognitive and constructivist theorists who contend that by ignoring cognitive and affective processes, conditioning theories offer an incomplete account of human learning. Stimuli and reinforcement may explain some human learning, but much research shows that to explain learning—and especially higher-order and complex learning—we must take into account people's thoughts, beliefs, and feelings. The fact that newer behavior theory perspectives retain basic behavioral principles but interject some cognitive elements such as volition is a further testament to the inadequacy of conditioning theories to explain human learning.

Another point of contention is the assumption that errors or difficulties in learning are problematic. It is true that learning proceeds faster when learners do not make errors, but this text makes it clear that learning difficulties can have salutary effects so long as learners persist and adopt better strategies. Conquering difficulties helps build learners' sense of self-efficacy, which has important motivational consequences. Further, researchers have shown that learning can occur rapidly and without actually performing the actions, which calls into question the ideas that learners must perform actions and be reinforced for small improvements in performance.

A key point is that it is possible to adopt methods of conditioning theories without adopting the conditioning theory explanation of their effects. Although it is undoubtedly true that learners perform behaviors for which they previously have been reinforced (behavior theory explanation), they also form expectations such that they expect to continue to do well if they act accordingly (cognitive explanation). It is this belief that drives future behavior.

Behaviorism was a dominant theory for many years and served an important role by instigating much research into learning processes. Today, however, cognitive and constructivist accounts have supplanted behaviorism in the study of learning. It is these accounts to which the remainder of this text is devoted.

REFLECTION QUESTIONS

- Behavior theories conceive of learning as an incremental process in which responses gradually become strengthened (or more likely to occur) through frequent pairings with stimuli and reinforcers. This incremental view contrasts with what might be called an all-or-none view in which learning occurs suddenly and strengthening or the likelihood of occurrence increases rapidly rather than gradually. Can you think of types of learning that seem to reflect the all-or-none perspective? The incremental view? Which type of learning is more common in your students? What are the implications for teaching of each view?

■ A key provision of Skinner's ideas about instruction is that learners experience success. An ideal instructional sequence is one in which learners make no errors (or only a few). Skinner contended that errors reinforce improper behavior and are wasteful because teachers must take time to correct behaviors. Do you agree with Skinner that success-only learning always is desirable? Or are there times when making errors or experiencing some difficulty learning has benefits?

■ Computer-based instruction seems to reflect many principles of behavior theory, but a central purpose of it is to gain insight into students' thinking processes. What design features of computer-based instruction seem necessary to be able to explore students' thinking and understanding? What types of data should these features yield so that information can be gained about students' cognitive and constructivist processes?

FURTHER READING

Hattie, J. (2012). Know thy impact. *Educational Leadership, 70*(1), 18–23.

Mayer, R. E. (2003). E. L. Thorndike's enduring contributions to educational psychology. In B. J. Zimmerman & D. H. Schunk (Eds.), *Educational psychology: A century of contributions* (pp. 113–154). Mahwah, NJ: Erlbaum.

Morris, E. K. (2003). B. F. Skinner: A behavior analyst in educational psychology. In B. J. Zimmerman & D. H. Schunk (Eds.), *Educational psychology: A century of contributions* (pp. 229–250). Mahwah, NJ: Erlbaum.

Windholz, G. (1997). Ivan P. Pavlov: An overview of his life and psychological work. *American Psychologist, 52,* 941–946.

Wood, W., & Neal, D. T. (2007). A new look at habits and the habit-goal interface. *Psychological Review, 114,* 843–863.

Zimmerman, B. J., & DiBenedetto, M. K. (2008). Mastery learning and assessment: Implications for students and teachers in an era of high-stakes testing. *Psychology in the Schools, 45,* 206–216.

4 Social Cognitive Theory

The girls' tennis team at Westbrook High School is practicing after school. The team has played a few matches; they are playing well, but improvements are needed. Coach Sandra Martin is working with Donnetta Awalt. Donnetta's overall game is good, but lately she has been hitting many of her backhands into the net. Coach Martin asks Donnetta to hit backhands to her as she hits balls to Donnetta.

Donnetta:	This is impossible. I just can't do it.
Coach Martin:	Sure you can. You've been able to hit backhands before, and you will again.
Donnetta:	Then what should I do?
Coach Martin:	You're swinging downward during your backhand, which means you'll hit the ball into the net a lot. We need for you to develop more of an upward swing. Come over here please, and I'll demonstrate (Coach Martin demonstrates Donnetta's swing and then an upward swing and points out the differences). Now you try it, slowly at first. Do you feel the difference?
Donnetta:	Yes. But from where should I start my swing? How far back and how low down?
Coach Martin:	Watch me again. Adjust your grip like this before hitting a backhand (Coach Martin demonstrates grip). Get into position, about like this relative to the ball (Coach Martin demonstrates). Now start your backhand like this (Coach Martin demonstrates) and bring it through like this (Coach Martin demonstrates). You see you're swinging upward, not downward.
Donnetta:	Okay, that feels better (practices). Can you hit some to me?
Coach Martin:	Sure. Let's try it, slowly at first; then we'll pick up speed (they practice for several minutes). That's good. I'll give you a book and a video. These show and explain what I've been saying.

Donnetta: Thanks, I will. I really felt I couldn't do this anymore, so I've been trying to avoid hitting backhands in matches. But now I'm feeling more confident.

Coach Martin: That's good. Keep thinking like that and practicing and you'll do great!

The preceding chapter focused on conditioning theories (behaviorism), which held sway in the field of learning for the first half of the twentieth century. Beginning in the late 1950s and early 1960s, these theories were challenged on many fronts. Their influence waned to the point where today the prevailing theoretical perspectives are cognitive and constructivist.

One of the major challenges to behaviorism came from studies on observational learning conducted by Albert Bandura and his colleagues. A central finding of this research was that people could learn new actions by observing others perform them. Observers did not have to perform the actions at the time of learning. Reinforcement was not necessary for learning to occur. These findings disputed central assumptions of conditioning theories.

The focus of this chapter is on Bandura's (1986, 1997, 2001) *social cognitive theory*, which stresses the idea that much human learning occurs in a social environment. By observing others (models), people acquire knowledge, rules, skills, strategies, beliefs, and attitudes. Individuals also learn from models the usefulness and appropriateness of behaviors and the consequences of modeled behaviors, and they act in accordance with beliefs about their capabilities and the expected outcomes of their actions. The opening scenario portrays an instructional application of modeling.

By stressing the importance of the social environment, social cognitive theory underscores the key point that learning is highly context dependent. Although we can and do learn by ourselves, most learning situations include social elements such as classrooms, peers, colleagues, groups, schools, and communities. Further, social cognitive theory's emphasis on modeling is integral to many forms of teaching. The idea of demonstrating and explaining skills to be learned is captured at all educational levels with diverse skills and contexts (e.g., face-to-face, online).

The conceptual framework of social cognitive theory is discussed, along with its underlying assumptions about the nature of human learning and behavior. A significant portion of the chapter is devoted to modeling processes. The various influences on learning and performance are described, and motivational influences are discussed with special emphasis on the critical role of self-efficacy. Some instructional applications that reflect social cognitive learning principles are provided.

When you finish studying this chapter, you should be able to do the following:

- Describe and exemplify the process of triadic reciprocal causality.

- Distinguish between enactive and vicarious learning and between learning and performance.

- Explain the role of self-regulation in social cognitive theory.

- Define and exemplify three functions of modeling.

- Discuss the processes of observational learning.

- Explain the various factors that affect observational learning and performance.

- Discuss the motivational properties of goals, outcome expectations, and values.

- Define self-efficacy and explain its causes and effects in learning settings.
- Discuss how features of models (e.g., peers, multiple, coping) affect self-efficacy and learning.

- Describe some educational applications that reflect social cognitive theoretical principles.

CONCEPTUAL FRAMEWORK FOR LEARNING

Albert Bandura was born in Alberta, Canada, in 1925. He received his doctorate in clinical psychology from the University of Iowa, where he was influenced by Miller and Dollard's (1941) *Social Learning and Imitation* (discussed later in this chapter). After moving to Stanford University in the 1950s, Bandura began a research program exploring the influences on social behavior. He believed that the behavior theories in vogue at that time (e.g., operant conditioning) offered incomplete explanations of the acquisition and performance of prosocial and deviant behaviors:

> Indeed, most prior applications of learning theory to issues concerning prosocial and deviant behavior . . . have suffered from the fact that they have relied heavily on a limited range of principles established on the basis of, and mainly supported by, studies of animal learning or human learning in one-person situations. (Bandura & Walters, 1963, p. 1)

Bandura formulated a comprehensive theory of observational learning that he has expanded to encompass acquisition and performance of diverse skills, strategies, and behaviors. Social cognitive principles have been applied to the learning of cognitive, motor, social, and self-regulation skills, as well as to the topics of violence (live, filmed), moral development and behavior, education, health, societal values, and terrorism (Zimmerman & Schunk, 2003).

Bandura is a prolific writer. Beginning with the book *Social Learning and Personality Development*, written in 1963 with Richard Walters, he has authored several other books, including *Principles of Behavior Modification* (1969), *Aggression: A Social Learning Analysis* (1973), *Social Learning Theory* (1977b), *Social Foundations of Thought and Action: A Social Cognitive Theory* (1986), *Self-Efficacy: The Exercise of Control* (1997), and *Moral Disengagement: How People Do Harm and Live With Themselves* (2016). Bandura extended his original theory to address ways people seek control over important events of their lives through self-regulation of their thoughts and actions. The basic processes involve setting goals; judging anticipated outcomes of actions; evaluating progress toward goals; and self-regulating thoughts, emotions, and actions. As Bandura (1986) explained:

> Another distinctive feature of social cognitive theory is the central role it assigns to self-regulatory functions. People do not behave just to suit the preferences of others. Much of their behavior is motivated and regulated by internal standards and self-evaluative reactions to their own actions. After personal standards have been adopted, discrepancies between a performance and the standard against which it is measured activate evaluative self-reactions, which serve to influence subsequent behavior. An act, therefore, includes among its determinants self-produced influences. (Bandura, 1986, p. 20)

Social cognitive theory makes assumptions about learning and performance of behaviors (Schunk, 2012). These assumptions address the reciprocal interactions among persons, behaviors, and environments; enactive and vicarious learning (i.e., how learning occurs); the distinction between learning and performance; and the role of self-regulation.

Reciprocal Interactions

Bandura (1982a, 1986, 2001) discussed human behavior within a framework of *triadic reciprocality*, or reciprocal interactions among behavioral, environmental, and personal variables such as cognitions (Figure 4.1). These interacting determinants can be illustrated using *perceived self-efficacy* (a personal variable), or beliefs about one's capabilities to organize and implement actions necessary to learn or perform behaviors at designated levels (Bandura, 1982b, 1986, 1997). With respect to the interaction of self-efficacy and behavior, researchers have shown that self-efficacy influences such achievement behaviors as choice of tasks, persistence, effort expenditure, and skill acquisition (person → behavior; Schunk, 2012; Schunk & DiBenedetto, 2016). In the opening scenario, Donnetta's low self-efficacy for hitting backhands led her to avoid hitting them. In turn, students' actions modify their self-efficacy. As students work on tasks, they observe their progress toward their learning goals (e.g., completing assignments, finishing sections of a term paper). Such progress indicators convey to students that they are capable of performing well and enhance their self-efficacy for continued learning (behavior → person).

Research on students with learning disabilities has demonstrated the interaction between self-efficacy and environmental factors. Many such students hold a low sense of self-efficacy for performing well (Licht & Kistner, 1986). Individuals in students' social environments may react to students based on attributes typically associated with students with learning disabilities (e.g., low self-efficacy) rather than on the individuals' actual capabilities (person → environment). These individuals may judge such students as less capable than students without disabilities and hold lower academic expectations for them, even in content areas where students with learning disabilities are performing adequately (Bryan & Bryan, 1983). In turn, feedback can affect self-efficacy (environment → person). When a teacher or parent tells a student, "I know you can do this," the student likely will feel more confident about succeeding.

Students' behaviors and classroom environments influence one another in many ways. Consider a typical instructional sequence in which a teacher presents information and asks students to direct their attention to a slide. Environmental influence on

Figure 4.1
Triadic reciprocality model of causality.
Source: Based on *Social Foundations of Thought and Action* by A. Bandura, © 1986. Pearson Education, Inc. Upper Saddle River, NJ.

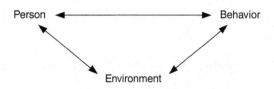

behavior occurs when students look at the slide without much conscious deliberation (environment → behavior). Students' behaviors often alter the instructional environment. If a teacher asks questions and students give the wrong answers, the teacher may reteach some points rather than continue the lesson (behavior → environment).

The model portrayed in Figure 4.1 does not imply that the directions of influence are always the same. At any given time, one factor may predominate. When environmental influences are weak, personal factors predominate. For instance, students allowed to write a report on a topic of their choosing will select one they enjoy. However, a person caught in a burning house is apt to evacuate quickly; the environment dictates the behavior.

Much of the time, the three factors interact. As a teacher presents a lesson to the class, students think about what the teacher is saying (environment influences cognition—a personal factor). Students who do not understand raise their hands to ask a question (cognition influences behavior). The teacher reviews the content (behavior influences environment). Eventually the teacher gives students work to accomplish (environment influences cognition, which influences behavior). As students work on the task, they believe they are performing it well (behavior influences cognition). They decide they like the task, ask the teacher if they can continue to work on it, and are allowed to do so (cognition influences behavior, which influences environment).

Enactive and Vicarious Learning

In social cognitive theory:

> Learning is largely an information processing activity in which information about the structure of behavior and about environmental events is transformed into symbolic representations that serve as guides for action. (Bandura, 1986, p. 51)

Learning occurs either *enactively* by doing or *vicariously* by observing models (e.g., live, symbolic, electronic) perform (Schunk, 2012).

Enactive learning involves learning from the consequences of one's actions. Behaviors that result in successful consequences are retained; those that lead to failures are refined or discarded. Behavior theories also say that people learn by doing, but social cognitive theory provides a different explanation. Skinner (1953) noted that cognitions may accompany behavioral change but do not influence it (Chapter 3). Rather than strengthening behaviors as postulated by conditioning theories, social cognitive theory contends that behavioral consequences serve as sources of information and motivation. Consequences inform people of the accuracy or appropriateness of behavior. People who succeed at a task or are rewarded understand that they are performing well. When people fail or are punished, they know that they are doing something wrong and may try to correct the problem. Consequences also motivate people. People strive to learn behaviors they value and believe will have desirable consequences, whereas they avoid learning behaviors that are punished or otherwise not satisfying. People's cognitions, rather than consequences, affect learning.

Much human learning occurs vicariously, or without overt performance by the learner, at the time of learning. Common sources of vicarious learning are observing or listening to models who are live (appear in person), symbolic or nonhuman (e.g., talking animals, cartoon characters), electronic (e.g., television, computer, DVD), or in print (e.g., books, magazines). Vicarious sources accelerate learning over what would be possible if people had to perform every behavior for learning to occur. Vicarious sources also save people from personally experiencing negative consequences. We learn that poisonous snakes are dangerous through teaching by others, reading books, watching films, and so forth, rather than by experiencing the unpleasant consequences of their bites!

Learning complex skills typically occurs through a combination of observation and performance (Schunk, 2012). Students observe teacher models explain and demonstrate skills, then practice them. This sequence is evident in the opening scenario, where Coach Martin explains and demonstrates and Donnetta observes and practices. Through observation, students may learn some components of a complex skill and not others. Practice gives teachers and coaches opportunities to provide corrective feedback to help students perfect their skills. As with enactive learning, response consequences from vicarious sources inform and motivate observers. Observers are more apt to learn modeled behaviors leading to successes than those resulting in failures. When people believe that modeled behaviors are useful, they attend carefully to models and mentally rehearse the behaviors.

Learning and Performance

Unlike behavior theories, social cognitive theory differentiates learning from performance of previously learned behaviors. Although much learning occurs by doing, we learn a great deal by observing, often in the absence of a goal or reinforcement (vicarious learning). Whether we ever perform what we learn depends on factors such as our motivation, interest, incentives to perform, perceived need, physical state, social pressures, and type of competing activities. Reinforcement, or the belief that it will be forthcoming, affects performance rather than learning.

Some school activities (e.g., review sessions) involve performance of previously learned skills, but much time is spent learning. By observing teacher and peer models, students acquire knowledge they may not demonstrate at the time of learning. For example, students might learn in school that skimming is a useful procedure for acquiring the gist of a passage and might learn a strategy for skimming, but may not employ that knowledge to promote learning until they read at home.

Self-Regulation

A key assumption of social cognitive theory is that people desire "to control the events that affect their lives" and to perceive themselves as agents (Bandura, 1997, p. 1). This sense of *agency* manifests itself in intentional acts, cognitive processes, and affective processes (Bandura, 2006). *Perceived self-efficacy* (discussed later in this chapter) is a central process affecting one's sense of agency. Other key processes (also discussed in this chapter) are outcome expectations, values, goal setting, self-evaluation of goal progress, and cognitive modeling and self-instruction.

Central to this conception of personal agency is *self-regulation*—or the process whereby individuals activate and sustain behaviors, cognitions, and affects—which are systematically oriented toward the attainment of goals (Zimmerman, 2000, 2013). By striving to self-regulate important aspects of their lives, individuals attain a greater sense of personal agency. In learning situations, self-regulation requires that learners have choices, for example, in what they do and how they do it. Choices are not always available to learners, as when teachers control many aspects by giving students an assignment and spelling out the parameters. When all or most task aspects are controlled, it is accurate to speak of external regulation or regulation by others. The social cognitive theoretical perspective on self-regulation is covered in greater depth in Chapter 10.

MODELING PROCESSES

Modeling—a critical component in social cognitive theory—refers to behavioral, cognitive, and affective changes deriving from observing one or more models (Rosenthal & Bandura, 1978; Schunk, 1987, 2012; Zimmerman, 2013). Historically, modeling was equated with *imitation*, but modeling is a more inclusive concept. Some historical work is covered next to provide a background against which the significance of modeling research by Bandura and others can be appreciated.

Theories of Imitation

Throughout history, people have viewed imitation as an important means of transmitting behaviors (Rosenthal & Zimmerman, 1978). The ancient Greeks used the term *mimesis* to refer to learning through observation of the actions of others and of abstract models exemplifying literary and moral styles. Other perspectives on imitation relate it to instinct, development, conditioning, and instrumental behavior (Table 4.1).

Instinct. At the beginning of the twentieth century, the dominant scientific view was that people possessed a natural instinct to imitate the actions of others (James, 1890; Tarde, 1903). James believed that imitation was largely responsible for socialization, but he did not explain the process by which imitation occurs. McDougall (1926) restricted his definition of imitation to the instinctive copying by one person of the actions of another.

The instinct notion was discarded by behaviorists because it assumed the existence of an internal drive (and possibly a mental image) intervening between a stimulus (action

Table 4.1
Theories of imitation.

View	Assumptions
Instinct	Observed actions elicit an instinctive drive to copy those actions.
Development	Children imitate actions that fit with existing cognitive structures.
Conditioning	Behaviors are imitated and reinforced through shaping. Imitation becomes a generalized response class.
Instrumental behavior	Imitation becomes a secondary drive through repeated reinforcement of responses matching those of models. Imitation results in drive reduction.

of another person) and response (copying of that action). Watson (1924) believed that people's behaviors labeled "instinctive" resulted largely from training and therefore were learned.

Development. Piaget (1962) believed that human development involved the acquisition of *schemes (or schemas)*, which are cognitive structures that underlie and make possible organized thought and action. Thoughts and actions are not synonymous with schemes but rather are overt manifestations of schemes. Schemes available to individuals determine how they react to events. Schemes reflect prior experiences and comprise one's knowledge at any given time.

Schemes presumably develop through maturation and experiences slightly more advanced than one's existing cognitive structures. Imitation is restricted to activities corresponding to existing schemes. Children may imitate actions they understand, but they should not imitate actions incongruent with their cognitive structures. Development, therefore, precedes imitation.

This view limits the potential of imitation to create and modify cognitive structures. Further, there is little empirical support for this position (Rosenthal & Zimmerman, 1978). In an early study, Valentine (1930b) found that infants could imitate actions within their capabilities that they had not previously performed. Infants showed a strong tendency to imitate unusual actions commanding attention. The imitation was not always immediate, and actions often had to be repeated before infants would imitate them. The individual performing the original actions was important: Infants were most likely to imitate their mothers. These and results from subsequent research show that imitation is not a simple reflection of developmental level but rather may serve an important role in advancing development (Rosenthal & Zimmerman, 1978).

Conditioning. Behavior theorists construe imitation in terms of conditioned responses. For example, Skinner's (1953) operant conditioning theory treats imitation as a generalized response class (Chapter 3). In the three-term contingency ($S^D \rightarrow R \rightarrow S^R$), a modeled act serves as the S^D (discriminative stimulus). Imitation occurs when an observer performs the same response (R) and receives reinforcement (S^R). This contingency becomes established early in life. For example, a parent makes a sound ("Dada"), the child imitates, and the parent delivers reinforcement (smile, hug). Once an imitative response class is conditioned, it can be maintained on an intermittent reinforcement schedule. Children imitate the behaviors of models (e.g., parents, friends) as long as the models remain discriminative stimuli for reinforcement.

A limitation of this view is that one can imitate only those responses one can perform, but much research shows that diverse types of behaviors can be acquired through observation (Rosenthal & Zimmerman, 1978). Another limitation concerns the need for reinforcement to produce and sustain imitation. Research by Bandura and others shows that observers learn from models in the absence of reinforcement to models or observers (Bandura, 1986). Reinforcement primarily affects learners' performance of previously learned responses rather than new learning.

Instrumental Behavior. Miller and Dollard (1941) proposed an elaborate theory of imitation, or *matched-dependent behavior*, which contends that imitation is instrumental learned behavior because it leads to reinforcement. Matched-dependent behavior is matched to (the same as) that of the model and depends on, or is elicited by, the model's action. Initially the imitator responds to behavioral cues in trial-and-error fashion, but eventually the imitator performs the correct response and is reinforced. Responses performed by imitators previously were learned.

This conception of imitation was an important advance, but it has problems. New responses are not created through imitation; rather, imitation represents performance of learned behaviors. This perspective cannot account for learning through imitation, for delayed imitation (i.e., when imitators perform the matching responses some time after the actions are performed by the model), or for imitated behaviors that are not reinforced (Bandura & Walters, 1963). This narrow conception of imitation is restricted to imitative responses corresponding closely to those portrayed by models.

Functions of Modeling

Bandura (1986) distinguished three key functions of modeling: response facilitation, inhibition/disinhibition, and observational learning (Table 4.2).

Response Facilitation. People learn many skills and behaviors that they do not perform because they lack motivation to do so. *Response facilitation* refers to modeled actions that serve as social prompts for observers to behave accordingly. Consider an elementary teacher who has set up an attractive display in a corner of the classroom. When the first students enter in the morning, they spot the display and immediately go to look at it. When other students enter the room, they see a group in the corner, so they, too, move to the corner to see what everyone is looking at. Several students together serve as a social prompt for others to join them, even though the latter may not know why the others are gathered.

Response facilitation effects are common. Have you ever seen a group of people looking in one direction? This can serve as a cue for you to look in the same direction. Response facilitation does not reflect learning because people already know how to perform the behaviors. Rather, the models serve as cues for observer's actions. Observers gain information about the appropriateness of behavior and may be motivated to perform the actions if models receive positive consequences.

Table 4.2
Functions of modeling.

Function	Underlying Process
Response facilitation	Social prompts create motivational inducements for observers to model the actions ("going along with the crowd").
Inhibition and disinhibition	Modeled behaviors create expectations in observers that they will experience similar consequences should they perform the actions.
Observational learning	Processes include attention, retention, production, and motivation.

Response facilitation modeling may occur without conscious awareness. Chartrand and Bargh (1999) found evidence for a *chameleon effect*, whereby people nonconsciously mimic behaviors and mannerisms of people in their social environments. Simply perceiving behavior may trigger a response to act accordingly.

Inhibition/Disinhibition. Observing a model can strengthen or weaken inhibitions to perform behaviors previously learned. *Inhibition* occurs when models are punished for performing certain actions, which in turn stops or prevents observers from acting accordingly. *Disinhibition* occurs when models perform threatening or prohibited activities without experiencing negative consequences, which may lead observers to perform the same behaviors. Inhibitory and disinhibitory effects on behavior occur because the modeled displays convey to observers that similar consequences are probable if they perform the modeled behaviors. Such information also may affect emotions (e.g., increase or decrease anxiety) and motivation.

Teachers' actions can inhibit or disinhibit classroom misbehavior. Unpunished student misbehavior may prove disinhibiting: Students who observe modeled misbehavior not punished might start misbehaving themselves. Conversely, misbehavior in other students may be inhibited when a teacher disciplines one student for misbehaving. Observers are more likely to believe that they, too, will be disciplined if they continue to misbehave and are spotted by the teacher.

Inhibition and disinhibition are similar to response facilitation in that behaviors reflect actions people already have learned. One difference is that response facilitation generally involves behaviors that are socially acceptable, whereas inhibited and disinhibited actions often have moral or legal overtones (i.e., involve breaking rules or laws) and have accompanying emotions (e.g., fears).

Observational Learning. Observational learning through modeling occurs when observers display new behaviors that, prior to exposure to the modeled behaviors, have a zero probability of occurrence even when motivation is high (Bandura, 1969). A key mechanism is the information conveyed by models to observers of ways to produce new behaviors (Rosenthal & Zimmerman, 1978). In the opening scenario, Donnetta needed to learn (or relearn) the correct procedure for hitting a backhand. Observational learning comprises four processes: attention, retention, production, and motivation (Bandura, 1986; see Table 4.3).

Observer *attention* is necessary so that relevant events are meaningfully perceived. At any given moment one can attend to many activities. Characteristics of the model and the observer influence one's attention to models. Task features can command attention, especially unusual size, shape, color, or sound. Teachers often make modeling more distinctive with bright colors and oversized features. Attention also is influenced by perceived functional value of modeled activities. Modeled activities that observers believe are important and likely to lead to rewarding outcomes command greater attention. Students believe that most teacher activities are highly functional because they are intended to enhance student learning. Learners also are apt to believe that their teachers are highly competent, which enhances attention. Factors that promote the perception of model competence are modeled actions that lead to success and symbolic indicators of competence, such as one's title or position.

Table 4.3
Processes of observational learning.

Process	Activities
Attention	Student attention is directed by accentuating relevant task features, subdividing complex activities into parts, using competent models, and demonstrating usefulness of modeled behaviors.
Retention	Retention is increased by rehearsing information to be learned, coding in visual and symbolic form, and relating new material to information previously stored in memory.
Production	Behaviors produced are compared to one's conceptual (mental) representation. Feedback helps to correct deficiencies.
Motivation	Consequences of modeled behaviors inform observers of functional value and appropriateness. Consequences motivate by creating outcome expectations and raising self-efficacy.

Retention requires cognitively organizing, rehearsing, coding, and transforming modeled information for storage in memory (see Chapter 5). Although the retention process is not specified in depth, social cognitive theory postulates that a modeled display can be stored as an image, in verbal form, or both (Bandura, 1977b). *Rehearsal,* or the mental review of information, serves a key role in retention. Bandura and Jeffery (1973) found benefits of coding and rehearsal. Adults were presented with complex modeled movement configurations. Some participants coded these movements at the time of presentation by assigning to them numerical or verbal designators. Other participants were not given coding instructions but were told to subdivide the movements to remember them. In addition, participants either were or were not allowed to rehearse the codes or movements following presentation. Both coding and rehearsal enhanced retention of modeled events; individuals who coded and rehearsed showed the best recall.

Production involves translating visual and symbolic conceptions of modeled events into overt behaviors. Many actions may be learned by simply observing them; subsequent production by observers indicates learning. Rarely, however, are complex behaviors learned solely through observation. Learners often will acquire a rough approximation of a complex skill by observing modeled demonstrations (Bandura, 1977b). They refine skills with practice, corrective feedback, and reteaching.

Problems in producing modeled behaviors arise not only because information is inadequately coded but also because learners experience difficulty translating coded information in memory into overt action. For example, a child may have a basic understanding of how to tie shoelaces but not be able to translate that knowledge into behavior. Teachers who suspect that students are having trouble demonstrating what they have learned may need to test students in different ways.

Motivation influences observational learning because people are more likely to engage in attention, retention, and production of modeled actions when they believe these actions are important. Children's and adults' learning from models is not a mere reflection of the modeled actions they observe (Koenig & Sabbagh, 2013). Rather, learners cognitively process what they observe and form expectations about anticipated outcomes of actions based on consequences experienced by them and models (Bandura, 1997). They perform those actions they believe will result in rewarding outcomes and avoid acting in ways they believe will be responded to negatively (Schunk, 1987). Even young children's modeling of actions is affected not only by whether the model's goal is attained but also by how reliably the modeled actions lead to the goal (Schulz, Hooppell, & Jenkins, 2008).

Persons also act based on their values, performing activities they value and avoiding those they find unsatisfying, regardless of the consequences to themselves or others. People forgo money, prestige, and power when they believe activities they must engage in to receive these rewards are unethical (e.g., questionable business practices). Teachers promote motivation in various ways, including making learning interesting, relating material to student interests, having students set goals and monitor goal progress, providing feedback indicating increasing competence, and stressing the value of learning (Chapter 9).

Cognitive Skill Learning

Observational learning expands the range and rate of learning over what could occur through shaping (Chapter 3), where each response must be performed and reinforced. Modeled portrayals of cognitive skills are standard features in classrooms. A teacher explains and demonstrates the skills to be acquired, after which students receive guided practice while the teacher checks for student understanding. Skills are retaught if students experience difficulty. When the teacher is satisfied that students have a basic understanding, they may engage in independent practice while the teacher monitors their work (Application 4.1).

Many features of instruction incorporate models, and much research shows that people of various ages, including young children, learn skills and strategies by observing models (Horner, 2004; Schulz et al., 2008). Observing tutoring sessions can benefit observers' learning (Muldner, Lam, & Chi, 2014). Students who observe tutoring sessions subsequently demonstrate greater collaborative engagement in learning and long-term retention than do students who do not observe tutoring (Craig, Chi, & VanLehn, 2009). Two especially germane applications of modeling to instruction are cognitive modeling and self-instruction.

Cognitive Modeling. *Cognitive modeling* is a procedure developed several years ago, which incorporates modeled explanation and demonstration with verbalization of the model's thoughts and reasons for performing given actions (Meichenbaum, 1977; Zimmerman, 2013). Coach Martin used cognitive modeling with Donnetta. In teaching division skills, a teacher might verbalize the following in response to the problem $276 \div 4$:

> First, I have to decide what number to divide 4 into. I take 276, start on the left, and move toward the right until I have a number the same as or larger than 4. Is 2 larger than 4? No. Is 27 larger than 4? Yes. So my first division will be 4 into 27. Now I need to multiply 4 by a number that will give an answer the same as or slightly smaller than 27. How about 5? $5 \times 4 = 20$. No, too small. Let's try 6. $6 \times 4 = 24$. Maybe. Let's try 7. $7 \times 4 = 28$. No, too large. So 6 is correct.

Cognitive modeling can include other types of statements. Errors may be built into the modeled demonstration to show students how to recognize and cope with them. Self-reinforcing statements (e.g., "I'm doing well") also are useful, especially with students who encounter difficulties learning and doubt their capabilities to perform well.

Researchers have substantiated the useful role of cognitive modeling and shown that modeling combined with explanation produces better learning than does explanation alone (Rosenthal & Zimmerman, 1978). In an early study, Schunk (1981) compared the effects of cognitive modeling with those of didactic instruction on children's long-division self-efficacy and achievement. Children lacking division skills received instruction and practice. In the cognitive modeling condition, students observed an adult model explain and demonstrate division operations while applying them to sample problems. In the didactic instruction condition, students reviewed instructional material that explained and demonstrated the operations, but they were not exposed to models. Cognitive modeling enhanced children's division achievement better than did didactic instruction.

Self-Instruction. *Self-instruction* has been used to teach students to regulate their learning activities (Meichenbaum, 1977). In an early study, Meichenbaum and Goodman (1971) incorporated cognitive modeling into self-instructional training with impulsive second graders in a special-education class. The procedure included:

APPLICATION 4.1
Teacher Modeling

Teachers often incorporate modeled demonstrations into lessons to teach students skills such as solving mathematical problems, identifying main ideas in text, writing topic sentences, using power tools safely, and executing basketball maneuvers. Modeled demonstrations can be used to teach elementary schoolchildren how to head their papers properly. Ms. Longanecker might draw on the board a sketch of the paper students are using. She then can review the heading procedure step by step, explaining and demonstrating how to complete it.

In a high school biology class, Mrs. Rollacci models how to study for a test. Working through a chapter, she explains and demonstrates how to locate and summarize the major terms and points for each section.

In a middle school life skills class, students can learn how to insert a sleeve into a garment through modeled demonstrations. The teacher might begin by describing the process and then use visual aids to portray the procedure. The teacher could conclude the presentation by demonstrating the process at a sewing machine.

Some students in Dr. Zicklin's graduate methods course have been coming to his office after class with questions about how to present their findings from their research projects. During the next class, he uses a research project he completed to demonstrate how one might present findings to a group. He uses handouts and slides to illustrate ways to present data.

A drama teacher can model various performance skills while working with students as they practice a play. The teacher can demonstrate desired voice inflections, mood, volume, and body movements for each character in the play.

- *Cognitive modeling:* Adult tells child what to do while adult performs the task.
- *Overt guidance:* Child performs under direction of adult.
- *Overt self-guidance:* Child performs while self-instructing aloud.
- *Faded overt self-guidance:* Child whispers instructions while performing task.
- *Covert self-instruction:* Child performs while guided by inner silent speech.

Self-instruction often is used to slow down children's rate of performing. An adult model used the following statements during a line-drawing task:

> Okay, what is it I have to do? You want me to copy the picture with the different lines. I have to go slow and be careful. Okay, draw the line down, down, good; then to the right, that's it; now down some more and to the left. Good, I'm doing fine so far. Remember go slow. Now back up again. No, I was supposed to go down. That's okay, just erase the line carefully. . . . Good. Even if I make an error I can go on slowly and carefully. Okay, I have to go down now. Finished. I did it. (Meichenbaum & Goodman, 1971, p. 117)

Note that in this example the model makes a mistake and shows how to deal with it. This is an important form of learning for students who may become frustrated and quit easily following errors. Meichenbaum and Goodman (1971) found that cognitive modeling slowed down response times, but that the self-instructions decreased errors.

Self-instruction has been used with a variety of tasks and types of students. It is especially useful for students with learning disabilities (Wood, Rosenberg, & Carran, 1993) and for teaching students to work strategically. In teaching reading comprehension, the preceding instructions might be modified as follows: "What is it I have to do? I have to find the topic sentence of the paragraph. The topic sentence is what the paragraph is about. I start by looking for a sentence that sums up the details or tells what the paragraph is about" (McNeil, 1987, p. 96). Statements for coping with difficulties ("I haven't found it yet, but that's all right") can be built into the modeled demonstration.

Motor Skill Learning

Although it is not a theory of motor skill learning, social cognitive theory postulates that such learning involves constructing a mental model that provides the conceptual representation of the skill for response production and serves as the standard for correcting responses subsequent to receiving feedback (Bandura, 1986; McCullagh, 1993; Weiss, Ebbeck, & Wiese-Bjornstal, 1993). The conceptual representation is formed by transforming observed sequences of behaviors into visual and symbolic codes to be cognitively rehearsed. Individuals usually have a mental model of a skill before they attempt to perform it. For example, by observing tennis players, individuals construct a mental model of such activities as the serve, volley, and backhand. These mental models are rudimentary in that they require feedback and correction to be perfected, but they allow learners to perform approximations of the skills at the outset of training. In the opening scenario, Donnetta needed to construct a mental model of a backhand. In the case of novel or complex behaviors, learners may have no prior mental model and need to observe modeled demonstrations before attempting the behaviors.

This social cognitive perspective differs from other motor learning explanations in that the latter place greater emphasis on error correction after acting and postulate different memory mechanisms to store information and evaluate accuracy (McCullagh, 1993). Social cognitive theory also highlights the role of personal cognitions (e.g., goals, expectations) in the development of motor skills (Application 4.2).

A problem in motor skill learning is that learners cannot observe aspects of their performances that lie outside their field of vision. People who are swinging a golf club, hitting a tennis serve, kicking a football, throwing a baseball, or hurling a discus, cannot observe many aspects of these sequences. Not being able to see what one is doing requires one to rely on kinesthetic feedback and compare it with one's conceptual representation. The absence of visual feedback makes learning difficult.

Carroll and Bandura (1982) exposed learners to models performing a motor skill and then asked them to reproduce the pattern. The experimenters gave some learners concurrent visual feedback of their performances by running a video camera and allowing them to observe their real-time performances on a monitor. Other learners did not receive visual feedback. When visual feedback was given before learners formed a mental model of the motor behavior, it had no effect on performance. Once learners had an adequate model in mind, visual feedback enhanced their accurate reproduction of the modeled behaviors. Visual feedback eliminated discrepancies between their conceptual models and their actions once the former were in place.

Researchers also have examined the efficacy of using models to teach motor skills. Weiss (1983) compared the effects of a silent model (visual demonstration) with those of a verbal model (visual demonstration plus verbal explanation) on the learning of a six-part motor skill obstacle course. Older children (ages 7 through 9 years) learned equally well with either model; younger children (ages 4 through 6 years) learned better with the verbal model. Perhaps the addition of the verbalizations created a cognitive model that helped to maintain children's attention and assisted with coding of information in memory. Weiss and Klint (1987) found that children in visual-model and no-model conditions who

---

APPLICATION 4.2
Motor Skill Learning

Observational learning is useful for learning motor skills. To teach students to dribble a basketball, physical education teachers might begin with skill exercises, such as standing stationary and bouncing the ball and moving and bouncing the ball with each step. After introducing each skill leading to the final sequence, teachers can demonstrate slowly and precisely what the students are to perform. Students then should practice that skill. If they have difficulty on a particular step, teachers can repeat the modeled demonstration before the students continue practicing.

For high school students to successfully learn a dance to perform in the spring musical, the teacher needs to demonstrate and slowly progress toward putting the dance to music. The teacher may break up the dance, working on each step separately, gradually combining steps and eventually putting all the various steps together with the music.

verbally rehearsed the sequence of actions learned the motor skills better than children who did not verbally rehearse. Collectively these results suggest that verbalization may facilitate motor skill learning.

INFLUENCES ON LEARNING AND PERFORMANCE

Observing models does not guarantee that learning will occur or that learned behaviors will be performed later. Several factors influence vicarious learning and performance of learned behaviors (Table 4.4). Developmental status, model prestige and competence, and vicarious consequences are discussed here; outcome expectations, goal setting, values, and self-efficacy are discussed in sections that follow.

Developmental Status of Learners

Learning depends heavily on developmental factors (Wigfield, Tonks, & Klauda, 2016), and these include students' abilities to learn from models (Bandura, 1986). Research shows that children as young as 6–12 months can perform behaviors displayed by models

Table 4.4
Factors affecting observational learning and performance.

Characteristic	Effects on Modeling
Developmental status	Improvements with development include longer attention and increased capacity to process information, use strategies, compare performances with memorial representations, and adopt intrinsic motivators.
Model prestige and competence	Observers pay greater attention to competent, high-status models. Consequences of modeled behaviors convey information about functional value. Observers attempt to learn actions that they believe they will need to perform.
Vicarious consequences	Consequences to models convey information about behavioral appropriateness and probable outcomes of actions. Valued consequences motivate observers. Similarity in attributes or competence signals appropriateness and heightens motivation.
Outcome expectations	Observers are more likely to perform modeled actions that they believe are appropriate and will result in rewarding outcomes.
Goal setting	Observers are more likely to attend to models who demonstrate behaviors that help observers attain goals.
Values	Observers are more likely to attend to models who display behaviors that the observers believe are important and find satisfying.
Self-efficacy	Observers attend to models when they believe they are capable of learning or performing the modeled behavior. Observation of similar models affects self-efficacy ("If they can do it, I can too").

(Nielsen, 2006), and peer modeling is effective with preschoolers (Ledford & Wolery, 2013); however, young children have difficulty attending to modeled events for long periods and distinguishing relevant from irrelevant cues. Information processing functions such as rehearsing, organizing, and elaborating (see Chapter 5) improve with development. Older children have a more extensive knowledge base to help them comprehend new information and are more capable of using memory strategies. Young children may encode modeled events in terms of physical properties (e.g., a ball is round, it bounces, you throw it), whereas older children often represent information visually or symbolically.

With respect to production, information acquired through observation cannot be performed if children lack the requisite physical capabilities. Production also requires translating into action information stored in memory, comparing performance with memorial representation, and correcting performance as necessary. The ability to self-regulate one's actions for longer periods increases with development. Motivational inducements for action also vary depending on development. Young children are motivated by the immediate consequences of their actions. As children mature, they are more likely to perform modeled actions consistent with their goals and values (Bandura, 1986).

Model Prestige and Competence

Modeled behaviors vary in perceived usefulness. Behaviors that successfully deal with the environment command greater attention than those that do so less effectively. People attend to a model in part because they believe they might face the same situation themselves and they want to learn the necessary actions to succeed. Students attend to a teacher because the teacher prompts them but also because they believe they will have to demonstrate the same skills and behaviors. Donnetta attends to her coach because the coach is an expert tennis player and because Donnetta knows she needs to improve her game. Children and adults are more likely to attend to competent models (Wood, Kendal, & Flynn, 2013).

Model competence is inferred from the outcomes of modeled actions (success, failure) and from symbols that denote competence such as membership in a group (Wood et al., 2013). An important attribute is prestige. Models who have gained distinction are more apt to command attention than those of lower prestige. Attendance usually is higher at a talk given by a well-known person than by one who is less known. In most instances, high-status models have ascended to their positions because they are competent. Their actions have greater functional value for observers, who are apt to believe that rewards will be forthcoming if they act accordingly.

Parents and teachers are high-status models for most children. The scope of adult influence on children's modeling can generalize to many domains. Although teachers are important models in the development of children's intellect, their influence typically spreads to such other areas as social behaviors, educational attainments, dress, and mannerisms. The effects of model prestige often generalize to areas in which models have no particular competence, such as when adolescents adopt the dress and products touted by prominent entertainers in commercials. Modeling becomes more prevalent with development, but even young children are highly susceptible to adult influence (Wood et al., 2013; Application 4.3).

APPLICATION 4.3
Model Attributes

People attend to models partly because they believe they may have to face the same situations themselves. Effective use of model prestige and competence can help motivate secondary students to attend to and learn from lessons.

If the use of alcohol is a problem in a university, school personnel might deliver a program on alcohol education and abuse (prevention, treatment) to include persons from outside the school. Influential speakers would be recent college graduates, persons who have successfully overcome problems with alcohol including current students, and those who work with alcohol abusers. The relative similarity in age of the models to the students, coupled with the models' personal experiences, should make the models appear highly competent. Such individuals might have more impact on the students than literature or lessons taught by university staff (e.g., counselors).

At the elementary school level, using peers to help teach academic skills can promote learning and self-efficacy among the learners. Children may identify with other children who have had the same difficulties. A teacher has four students in her class who are having trouble learning to divide. She pairs these four students with other students who formerly had trouble dividing but now understand how to divide. A child explaining to a classmate how to solve a division problem will do so in a way that the classmate can understand.

Vicarious Consequences to Models

Vicarious consequences to models can affect observers' learning and performance of modeled actions. Students who observe models rewarded for their actions are more likely to attend to the models, rehearse and code their actions for retention, and be motivated to perform the same actions. Thus, vicarious consequences serve to *inform* and *motivate* (Bandura, 1986).

Information. The consequences experienced by models convey information to observers about the types of actions most likely to be effective. Observing competent models perform actions that result in success conveys information to observers about the sequence of actions one should use to succeed. By observing modeled behaviors and their consequences, people form beliefs concerning which behaviors will be rewarded and which will be punished.

In a classic demonstration, Bandura, Ross, and Ross (1963) exposed children to live aggressive models, filmed aggression, or aggression portrayed by cartoon characters. The models, who pummeled a Bobo doll by hitting, throwing, kicking, and sitting on it, were neither rewarded nor punished, which most likely conveyed to the observers that the modeled behaviors were acceptable. Children subsequently were allowed to play with a Bobo doll. Compared with youngsters not exposed to aggression, children who viewed aggressive models displayed significantly higher levels of aggression. The type of aggressive model (live, filmed, cartoon) made no difference in children's level of aggression.

Similarity to models is important (Schunk, 1987, 2012; Wood et al., 2013). The more alike observers are to models, the greater is the probability that observers will consider similar actions socially appropriate for them to perform. Most social situations are structured so that behavioral appropriateness depends on factors such as age, gender, or status. Modeled tasks with which observers are unfamiliar or those that are not immediately followed by consequences may be highly influenced by model similarity.

Some research shows that children are more likely to attend to and learn from models of the same gender, whereas other research suggests that model gender has a greater effect on performance than on learning (Bandura & Bussey, 2004; Perry & Bussey, 1979). Benenson, Quinn, and Stella (2012), for example, found with young children that, compared with girls, boys were more likely to affiliate with familiar, same-gender peers. Children learn from models of both genders and categorize behaviors as appropriate for both or as more appropriate for members of one gender. Model gender, therefore, seems important as a conveyor of information about task appropriateness. When children are uncertain about the gender appropriateness of a modeled behavior, they may model peers of the same gender because they are more likely to think that those actions are socially acceptable.

Model–observer similarity in age is important when children perceive the actions of same-age peers to be more appropriate for themselves than the actions of younger or older models (Schunk, 1987; Wood et al., 2013). Brody and Stoneman (1985) found that in the absence of competence information, children were more likely to model the actions of same-age peers. When children were provided with competence information, modeling was enhanced by similar competence regardless of model age.

Although children learn from models of any age (Schunk, 1987), peers and adults use different teaching strategies. Peers often use nonverbal demonstrations and link instruction to specific items (e.g., how to do it); adults typically employ more verbal instruction stressing general principles and relate information to be learned to other material (Ellis & Rogoff, 1982). Peer instruction may be especially beneficial with students who have experienced learning problems and with those who have difficulty processing verbal information.

The highest degree of model–observer similarity occurs when one is one's own model (*self-modeling*), which has been used to develop social, vocational, motor, cognitive, and instructional skills (Bellini & Akullian, 2007; Dowrick, 1983, 1999; Hartley, Bray, & Kehle, 1998; Hitchcock, Dowrick, & Prater, 2003). In a typical procedure, one's performance is recorded, and he or she subsequently views the recording. Observing a self-modeled performance is a form of review and is especially informative for skills one cannot watch while performing (e.g., gymnastics). Viewing video feedback of a skillful performance conveys that one is capable of learning and can continue to make progress, which raises self-efficacy (Fukkink, Trienekens, & Kramer, 2011).

Schunk and Hanson (1989b) found benefits of self-modeling during acquisition of arithmetic (fraction) skills. Children received instruction and problem-solving practice. Self-modeling students' problem-solving performances were video recorded, and they subsequently viewed the recordings; others were video recorded but not shown the recordings until after the study was completed (to control for effects of recording); and students in a third condition were not video recorded (to control for effects of participation).

Self-modeling children scored higher on self-efficacy for learning, motivation, and posttest self-efficacy and achievement. Researchers found no differences between mastery self-model students who viewed recordings of their successful problem solving and self-model children whose recordings portrayed gradual improvement in skill acquisition, which supports the point that the perception of progress or mastery can build efficacy (Schunk & DiBenedetto, 2016).

Motivation. Observers who see models rewarded may become motivated to act accordingly. Perceived similarity enhances these motivational effects, which depend in part on self-efficacy (Bandura, 1982b, 1997). By observing similar others succeed, students are apt to believe that if others can succeed, they can as well. Such motivational effects are common in classrooms. Learners who observe other students performing a task well may be motivated to try their best.

Of particular importance is the observation of persistence and effort that leads to success (Schunk & Mullen, 2013). Seeing others succeed with effort and receiving praise from teachers may motivate observing peers to work harder. Students may become more motivated by watching similar others succeed than by those who they believe are superior in competence.

But vicarious success will not sustain behavior over long periods. Although motivation is boosted when students observe teachers giving praise and high grades to others for hard work and good performances, motivation is sustained over time when students believe their own efforts are leading to better performances.

MOTIVATIONAL PROCESSES

Among the important influences on enactive and vicarious learning and on performance of learned behaviors are observers' goals, outcome expectations, values, and self-efficacy. This section covers the first three; self-efficacy is addressed in the next section.

Goals

Much human behavior sustained over long periods in the absence of immediate external incentives depends on goal setting and self-evaluations of progress. A *goal* reflects one's purpose and refers to quantity, quality, or rate of performance (Locke & Latham, 2002). *Goal setting* involves establishing a standard or objective to serve as the aim of one's actions. People can set their own goals, or goals can be established by others (parents, teachers, supervisors).

Goals were a central feature of Tolman's (1932, 1951, 1959) theory of *purposive behaviorism*. His experiments resembled those of Thorndike and Skinner (Chapter 3) because they dealt with responses to stimuli under varying environmental conditions. But he disagreed with conditioning theorists over their view of behavior as a series of stimulus–response connections. He contended that learning is more than the strengthening of responses to stimuli, and he recommended a focus on *molar behavior*—a large sequence of goal-directed behavior.

The "purposive" aspect of Tolman's (1932) theory refers to his belief that behavior is goal directed. Stimuli in the environment (e.g., objects, paths) are means to goal attainment. They cannot be studied in isolation; rather, entire behavioral sequences must be studied to understand why people engage in particular actions. High school students whose goal is to attend a leading university study hard in their classes. By focusing only on the studying, researchers miss the purpose of the behavior. The students do not study because they have been reinforced for studying in the past (i.e., by getting good grades). Rather, studying is a means to intermediate goals (e.g., learning, high grades), which, in turn, enhance the likelihood of acceptance to the university.

Tolman qualified his use of "purposive" by noting that it is defined objectively. The behavior of people and animals is goal oriented. They act "as if" they are pursuing a goal and have chosen a means for attainment. Thus, Tolman went well beyond simple stimulus–response associations to discuss underlying cognitive mechanisms.

Social cognitive theory contends that goals enhance learning and performance through their effects on perceptions of progress, self-efficacy, and self-evaluations (Bandura, 1988, 1997; Locke & Latham, 1990, 2002; Schunk, 2012). Initially, people must make a *commitment* to attempt to attain their goals because goals do not affect performance without commitment. As they work on the task, they compare their current performances with goals. Positive self-evaluations of progress help sustain motivation (Huang, Zhang, & Broniarczyk, 2012). Motivational effects depend heavily on self-efficacy (Schunk & DiBenedetto, 2016). A perceived discrepancy between present performance and the goal may create dissatisfaction, which can enhance effort.

Goals motivate people to exert effort necessary to meet task demands and persist over time (Locke & Latham, 2002). Goals also direct attention to relevant task features and behaviors to be performed, and they can affect how learners process information. Goals give people "tunnel vision" to focus on the task, select task-appropriate strategies, and decide on the effectiveness of their approach, all of which are likely to raise performance.

But goals, by themselves, do not automatically enhance learning and motivation. Rather, the properties of specificity, proximity, and difficulty enhance self-perceptions, motivation, and learning (Locke & Latham, 2002; Nussbaum & Kardash, 2005; Application 4.4 and Table 4.5).

Table 4.5
Goal properties and their effects.

Goal Property	Effects on Behavior
Specificity	Goals with specific standards of performance increase motivation and raise self-efficacy because goal progress is easy to gauge.
Proximity	Proximal goals increase motivation and self-efficacy and are especially important for young children who may not divide a long-term goal into a series of short-term goals.
Difficulty	Challenging but attainable goals raise motivation and self-efficacy better than easy or hard goals.

APPLICATION 4.4
Goal Properties

Goal properties are easily incorporated into lessons. In his fourth-grade class, Mr. Zumbreski introduced a new spelling unit by stating the following goal:

> Of our 20 words this week, I know that all of you will be able to learn to spell the first 15. We are going to work in class on these words, and I expect you to do the same at home. With our work at school and at home, I know that all of you will be able to spell these words correctly by Friday. The last five words are more difficult. These will be our bonus words.

This goal is specific, but for some children, it is distant and might be viewed as too difficult. To ensure that all students achieve the overall goal, Mr. Zumbreski sets short-term goals each day: "Today we are going to work on these five words. By the end of class time, I know that you will be able to spell these five words." Children should view the daily goals as easier to attain than the weekly goal. To further ensure goal attainment, he will make sure that the 15 words selected for mastery by Friday challenge the students but are not overly difficult.

A teacher working with students on keyboarding might establish a words-per-minute goal for students to reach by the end of the semester:

> Students, this semester I know that all of you will be able to learn keyboarding. Some of you, because of other experiences or talents, will be able to type faster, but I know that all of you will be able to enter at least 30 words per minute with no mistakes by the end of the semester.

To help students achieve this goal, the teacher might set weekly short-term goals. The first week the goal might be 10 words per minute with no mistakes, the second week 12 words per minute, and so forth, increasing the number each week.

Specificity. Goals that incorporate specific standards of performance are more likely to enhance learning and activate self-evaluations than are general goals (e.g., "Do your best;" Locke & Latham, 2002). Specific goals boost task performance by providing more information about how much effort is required to succeed, and they promote self-efficacy because it is easy to evaluate progress toward an explicit goal. It is better for college students to set a goal of reading a specified number of pages in a text than a goal of reading some pages.

Much research attests to the effectiveness of specific goals in raising performance (Bandura, 1988; Locke & Latham, 1990, 2002; Schunk, 2012). Schunk (1983b) provided children with instruction and practice solving long-division problems. During the sessions, some children received a specific goal denoting the number of problems to complete; others had a general goal to work productively. Within each condition, half of the children received social comparative information on the number of problems that peers completed (which matched the session goal) to convey that goals were attainable. Goals raised self-efficacy; goals plus comparative information led to the highest self-efficacy and achievement.

Schunk (1984a) compared the effects of goals with those of rewards. Children received long-division instruction and practice over sessions. Some were offered rewards based on the number of problems completed, others pursued goals (number of problems to complete), and children in a third condition received rewards and goals. The three conditions promoted motivation during the sessions; rewards plus goals resulted in the highest division self-efficacy and achievement. Combining rewards with goals provided children with two sources of information to use in gauging learning progress.

Proximity. Goals are distinguished by how far they project into the future. Proximal, short-term goals are closer at hand, are achieved quicker, and result in greater motivation than more temporally distant, long-term goals (Locke & Latham, 2002). Motivation increases as people get close to attaining the goal (Huang et al., 2012). Although benefits of proximal goals are found regardless of developmental status, short-term goals are needed with children because they have short time frames of reference and are not fully capable of representing distant outcomes in thought (Bandura & Schunk, 1981). Proximal goals fit well with lesson planning as teachers plan activities around blocks of time, such as when teachers ask children to complete 10 problems (specific) in 15 minutes (proximal). Setting a short-term goal (e.g., next 1–2 hours) to complete an assignment is more motivating than setting aside the entire evening to complete it.

Bandura and Schunk (1981) gave children subtraction instruction with practice opportunities over seven sessions. Children received seven packets of material. Some pursued a proximal goal of completing one packet each session; a second group received a distant goal of completing all packets by the end of the last session; a third group was given a general goal of working productively. Proximal goals led to the highest motivation during the sessions, as well as the highest subtraction self-efficacy, achievement, and intrinsic interest (based on the number of problems solved during a free-choice period). The distant goal resulted in no benefits compared with the general goal. Manderlink and Harackiewicz (1984) found that proximal and distant goals did not differentially affect adults' performances on word puzzles, but proximal goals led to higher expectations of goal attainment and perceived competence.

Difficulty. Goal difficulty refers to the level of task proficiency required as assessed against a standard. Individuals expend greater effort to attain a difficult goal than an easy one (Locke & Latham, 2002); however, difficulty level and performance do not bear an unlimited positive relationship to each other. Difficult goals do not enhance performance in the absence of needed skills. Self-efficacy also is important. Learners who think they cannot reach a goal hold low self-efficacy, do not commit to attempting the goal, and work half-heartedly. Motivating goals are those perceived as difficult but attainable.

Schunk (1983c) gave children a difficult (but attainable) or an easier goal of completing a given number of long-division problems during each instructional session. To prevent students from believing goals were too difficult, the teacher gave half of each group attainment information ("You can work 25 problems"); the other half received social comparative information indicating that similar peers completed that many. Difficult goals enhanced motivation; children who received difficult goals and attainment information displayed the highest self-efficacy and achievement.

Self-Set Goals. Researchers have found that allowing students to set their goals enhances self-efficacy and learning, perhaps because self-set goals produce high goal commitment. Schunk (1985) provided subtraction instruction to sixth graders with learning disabilities. Some set daily performance goals, others had comparable goals assigned, and a third group worked without goals. Self-set goals led to the highest judgments of confidence for attaining goals, self-efficacy for solving problems, and subtraction achievement. Children in the two goal groups demonstrated greater motivation during the instructional sessions than did those without goals.

Hom and Murphy (1985) put college students who were high or low in achievement motivation in self-set or assigned-goal conditions. Self-set participants decided how many anagrams they could solve; assigned-goal participants were given comparable goals. Students high in achievement motivation performed equally well under the two goal conditions; self-set goals enhanced the performances of students low in achievement motivation. College students benefit from regularly setting their own goals for studying and completing assignments.

Goal Progress Feedback. *Goal progress feedback* provides information about progress toward goals (Hattie & Timperley, 2007). Such feedback, which is especially valuable when people cannot derive reliable information on their own, should raise self-efficacy, motivation, and achievement when it informs people that they are competent and can continue to improve by working diligently. Higher self-efficacy sustains motivation when people believe that continued effort will allow them to attain their goals. Once individuals attain goals, they are likely to set new goals (Schunk, 2012). College students who assess their progress while pursuing goals are apt to remain motivated to complete them.

Schunk and Rice (1991) taught students who had experienced reading difficulties a strategy to answer comprehension questions. Children were given a product goal of answering questions, a process goal of learning to use the strategy, or a process goal plus progress feedback that conveyed they were making progress toward their goal of learning to use the strategy to answer questions. Following the instruction, goal-plus-feedback children demonstrated higher reading self-efficacy and achievement than did learners assigned to the process and product goal conditions. Schunk and Swartz (1993a, 1993b) obtained comparable results in writing achievement with average-achieving and academically gifted elementary schoolchildren. Self-efficacy and achievement gains generalized across types of writing tasks and maintained themselves over time.

Outcome Expectations

Outcome expectations are personal beliefs about the anticipated outcomes of actions (Schunk & Zimmerman, 2006). Outcome expectations were among the first cognitive variables to be included in explanations of learning. Tolman (1932, 1949) defined *field expectancies* as involving relations between stimuli ($S_1 - S_2$) or among a stimulus, response, and stimulus ($S_1 - R - S_2$). Relations between stimuli concern what stimulus is apt to follow what other stimulus; for example, thunder follows lightning. In three-term relations, people develop the belief that a certain response to a given stimulus produces a certain result. If one's goal is to get to a roof (S_2), the sight of the ladder (S_1) could lead one to think, "If I place this ladder against the house (R), I can get to the roof." This is similar to Skinner's (1953; Chapter 3) three-term contingency except that Tolman conceived of this type of relation as reflecting a cognitive expectancy.

Field expectancies helped people form *cognitive maps*, or internal plans comprising expectancies of which actions are needed to attain goals. People follow signs to a goal; they learn meanings rather than discrete responses. People use their cognitive maps to determine the best course of action to attain a goal.

Tolman tested his ideas in an ingenious series of experiments (Tolman, Ritchie, & Kalish, 1946a, 1946b). In one study, rats were trained to run an apparatus, shown in Figure 4.2 (Maze 1). Subsequently, the apparatus was replaced with one in which the original path was blocked. Conditioning theories predict that animals will choose a path close to the original one, as shown in Figure 4.2 (Maze 2a). In fact, rats most frequently chose a path following the direction in which they originally found food (Maze 2b). These results supported the idea that the animals formed a cognitive map of the location of the food and responded based on that map rather than on prior responses to stimuli.

Social cognitive theory contends that people form outcome expectations based on their personal experiences (Bandura, 1986, 1997). Individuals act in ways they believe will be successful and attend to models who teach them valued skills. Outcome expectations sustain behaviors over long periods when people believe their actions eventually will produce success. In new situations, people are apt to engage in actions that were successful in previous situations because they believe that similar consequences will follow.

Outcome expectations can refer to external outcomes ("If I try my best on this exam, I will make a good grade on it") or to internal ones ("If I try my best on this exam, I will feel good about myself"). An important type of outcome expectation relates to progress in skill learning ("If I try my best, I will become a better reader"). Students who believe they are making little or no progress in learning may become demoralized and lackadaisical. Progress in academic learning often occurs slowly, and students notice little day-to-day change. For example, learners may improve their skills to read longer and more difficult passages, find main ideas, draw inferences, and read for details, but progress is slow. Teachers can inform students of their reading comprehension progress when it is not immediately apparent.

The influential role of outcome expectations was demonstrated in an early study by Shell, Murphy, and Bruning (1989). College students completed measures of reading and writing self-efficacy, outcome expectancies, and achievement. The self-efficacy assessment asked students to rate their competencies to perform various reading and writing tasks (e.g., letter from a friend, employment application, short fiction story). For the outcome expectancy measure, students judged the importance of reading and writing for achieving such life goals as getting a job, being financially secure, and being happy.

Self-efficacy and outcome expectancies related positively to achievement in reading and writing. In both domains, self-efficacy was more strongly related to achievement than outcome expectancies. This study also showed that the expectancy beliefs for each domain

Figure 4.2
Experimental arrange-
ment to study expectancy
learning.
Source: Adapted from "Studies in
Spatial Learning," by E. C. Tolman,
B. F. Ritchie, and D. Kalish, 1946,
Journal of Experimental Psychology,
36, pp. 13–24.

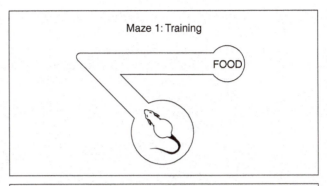

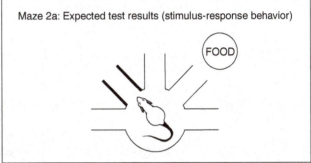

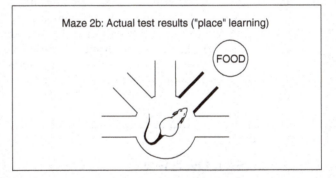

related significantly to achievement in the other domain, which suggests that teachers'
attempts to improve students' self-efficacy and outcome expectations in one literacy area
may generalize to others.

Values

Value refers to the perceived importance or usefulness of learning (Wigfield et al., 2016).
An important premise of social cognitive theory is that individuals' actions reflect their
value preferences (Bandura, 1986). Learners do things that bring about what they desire
and work to avoid outcomes that are inconsistent with their values. Learners are motivated
to learn and perform when they deem that learning or performance important.

Values can be assessed against external and internal standards. There are many reasons why students might value high grades. Making As and the honor roll may bring them recognition (i.e., from parents and teachers) and acceptances at universities. But high grades also can produce internal satisfaction, as when students feel proud of their work and a sense of accomplishment. Such internal satisfaction also occurs when learners act in accordance with their ethical beliefs.

Values are covered in more depth in Chapter 9 because they figure prominently in theories of motivation. Values are intimately linked with the other motivational processes discussed here: goals, outcome expectations, and self-efficacy. For example, assume that Larissa's family has moved and that Larissa (a fifth grader) is starting at a new school. One of her goals is to make new friends. She values friendships; she enjoys spending time with other children and sharing on a personal level with them (she has no siblings). She believes that if she is nice to other children that they will be nice to her and may become her friends (positive outcome expectations). Although she is initially shy in her new school, she has made new friends before and feels reasonably self-efficacious about doing so again. Larissa observes the actions of her new peers to learn what types of things they like to do. She interacts with her peers in ways that she believes will lead to friendships, and as she begins to develop new friends, her social self-efficacy becomes strengthened.

An important part of a teacher's job is to determine students' value preferences and especially if any of these reflect stereotypes or cultural differences. Research by Wigfield and Eccles (1992) showed some stereotypes among adolescents: Boys valued mathematics more, whereas girls placed greater emphasis on English. Mickelson (1990) contended that perceived racial inequalities can result in some minority students devaluing school achievement. Teachers are responsible for promoting achievement values in all students, such as by teaching students how to set goals and assess their progress, showing students how their achievement results in positive outcomes, and building learners' self-efficacy.

SELF-EFFICACY

Conceptual Overview

Self-efficacy (or *efficacy expectations*) is a key variable in social cognitive theory and refers to personal beliefs about one's capabilities to learn or perform actions at designated levels (Bandura, 1977a, 1977b, 1986, 1993, 1997). Self-efficacy is a belief about what one is capable of doing; it is not the same as knowing what to do. In gauging self-efficacy, individuals assess their skills and their capabilities to translate those skills into actions. Self-efficacy is critical for promoting a sense of *agency* in people that they can bring about important outcomes in their lives (Bandura, 1997, 2001). Although self-efficacy often is discussed in terms of individuals, it also applies to groups. *Collective self-efficacy* refers to perceptions of the capabilities of the group to produce outcomes (see section on collective teacher efficacy later in this chapter).

Self-efficacy and outcome expectations do not have the same meaning (Schunk & Zimmerman, 2006). Self-efficacy refers to perceptions of one's capabilities to produce actions; outcome expectations involve beliefs about the anticipated outcomes of those actions. For example, Jeremy may believe that if he correctly answers the teacher's questions, the teacher will praise him (positive outcome expectation). He also may value praise from the teacher. But he may not attempt to answer the teacher's questions if he doubts his capabilities to answer them correctly (low self-efficacy).

Despite self-efficacy and outcome expectations being conceptually distinct, they often are related (Schunk, 2012). Students who typically perform well have confidence in their learning capabilities and expect (and usually receive) positive outcomes for their efforts. At the same time, there is no necessary relation between self-efficacy and outcome expectations. Even students with high self-efficacy for learning may expect a low grade as an outcome if they think that the teacher does not like them.

Although some evidence indicates that perceptions of self-efficacy generalize to different tasks (Smith, 1989), theory and research suggest that self-efficacy is primarily domain specific (Pajares, 1996, 1997; Schunk & DiBenedetto, 2016). Thus, it is meaningful to speak of self-efficacy for drawing inferences from text, performing chemical experiments, solving quadratic equations, running certain times at track events, performing computer operations, searching the Internet, and so on. Smith and Fouad (1999) found that self-efficacy, goals, and outcome expectations are specific to subject areas and show little generalization across areas. Self-efficacy might transfer to new situations, however, when learners believe that the same skills will produce success. Learners who feel self-efficacious about outlining in English class also may feel confident about outlining in science class, and their self-efficacy may motivate them to construct an outline in science.

Self-efficacy is distinguished from *self-concept* (Pajares & Schunk, 2002; Schunk & DiBenedetto, 2016), which refers to one's collective self-perceptions formed through experiences with and interpretations of the environment and which depends heavily on reinforcements and evaluations by significant others (Shavelson & Bolus, 1982; Wylie, 1979). Self-efficacy refers to perceptions of specific capabilities; self-concept is one's general self-perception that includes self-efficacy in different areas (Schunk & Zimmerman, 2006; see Chapter 9).

Self-efficacy depends in part on student abilities. In general, high-ability students feel more efficacious about learning compared with low-ability students; however, self-efficacy is not another name for ability. Collins (1982) identified high-, average-, and low-ability students in mathematics. Within each level, she found students of high and low self-efficacy. She gave students problems to solve, and told them they could rework those they missed. Ability was positively related to achievement, but regardless of ability level, students with high self-efficacy solved more problems correctly and chose to rework more problems they missed than those with low self-efficacy.

Self-efficacy can have diverse effects in achievement settings (Bandura, 1993; Pajares, 1996, 1997; Schunk, 2012; Schunk & DiBenedetto, 2016). Self-efficacy can influence choice of activities. Students with low self-efficacy for learning may avoid attempting tasks; those who judge themselves efficacious should participate more eagerly. Self-efficacy also can affect effort expenditure, persistence, and learning. Students who feel efficacious about learning generally expend greater effort and persist longer than students who doubt their capabilities, especially when they encounter difficulties. In turn, these behaviors promote learning.

People acquire information about their self-efficacy from their performances, observations of models (vicarious experiences), forms of social persuasion, and physiological indexes (e.g., heart rate, sweating). Actual performances offer the most valid information for assessing efficacy. Successes generally raise efficacy and failures lower it, although an occasional failure (success) after many successes (failures) should not have much effect.

Students acquire much self-efficacy information through knowledge of how others perform. Perceptions of *similarity* to others are used in making many social judgments (Olson & Dweck, 2009), and they are important cues for gauging self-efficacy (Schunk & DiBenedetto, 2016). Observing similar others succeed raises observers' self-efficacy and motivates them to try the task because they believe that if others can succeed, they can as well. At the same time, a vicarious increase in self-efficacy can be negated by subsequent personal failures. Students who observe peers fail may believe they lack the competence to succeed, which can dissuade them from attempting the task. Donnetta experienced some increase in self-efficacy from watching her coach demonstrate the backhand, but her doing it without hitting into the net is a more potent influence.

Students often receive persuasive information from teachers that they possess the capability to perform well (e.g., "You can do it"). Although positive feedback enhances self-efficacy, this increase will not endure for long if students subsequently perform poorly. Learners also acquire some self-efficacy information from physiological symptoms they experience. They may interpret emotional symptoms (e.g., sweating, trembling) to mean that they are not capable of learning. When learners notice they are experiencing less stress in response to academic demands, they may feel more efficacious for mastering the task.

Information acquired from these sources does not influence self-efficacy automatically; for example, successfully performing a task does not guarantee higher self-efficacy. Rather, this information is cognitively appraised (Bandura, 1982b, 1993, 1997). Appraisal is an inferential process in which persons weigh and combine the contributions of personal, behavioral, and environmental factors. In forming self-efficacy beliefs, students consider factors such as perceptions of their ability, effort expended, task difficulty, teacher assistance, and number and pattern of successes and failures (Bandura, 1981, 1997; Schunk, 2012).

Self-Efficacy in Achievement Contexts

Self-efficacy is germane to academic learning. Researchers have found support for the hypothesized effects of self-efficacy on choice, effort, persistence, and achievement (Pajares, 1996, 1997; Schunk & DiBenedetto, 2016). Self-efficacy is related as well to career choices. Betz and Hackett (1981, 1983; Hackett & Betz, 1981) found that although there are structural and social influences on career choices, self-efficacy is an important mediator of these external influences and has a direct bearing on career choices. In addition, gender differences that emerge in vocational choices are due to differences in self-efficacy. Women are more self-efficacious for careers traditionally held by women than for careers traditionally held by men, whereas men's self-efficacy is less dependent on career gender typing.

Self-efficacy is strongly related to effort and task persistence (Bandura & Cervone, 1983, 1986; Schunk & DiBenedetto, 2016). Individuals with high self-efficacy beliefs are likely to exert effort in the face of difficulty and persist at a task when they have the requisite skills. There is, however, some evidence that self-doubts may foster learning when students have not previously acquired the skills. As Bandura (1986) noted, "Self-doubt creates the impetus for learning but hinders adept use of previously established skills" (p. 394). Salomon (1984) found that students high in self-efficacy were more likely to be cognitively engaged in learning when the task was perceived as difficult but less likely to be effortful and less cognitively engaged when the task was deemed easy. Besides the quantity of effort, the quality of effort (deeper cognitive processing and general cognitive engagement) has been linked to self-efficacy (Graham & Golan, 1991). Pintrich and De Groot (1990) showed that junior high students high in self-efficacy were more likely to report using cognitive and self-regulatory learning strategies.

With respect to achievement and cognitive performance, Schunk (1982a, 1982b, 1983a, 1983b, 1983c, 1983d, 1984a, 1984b, 1996) found in a series of experimental studies that self-efficacious students mastered various academic tasks better than students with weaker self-efficacy. Students' computer self-efficacy relates positively to their success in computer-based learning environments (Moos & Azevedo, 2009). Self-efficacy is a significant predictor of learning and achievement even after prior achievement and cognitive skills are taken into account (Schunk, 1981, 1982a). Results of a meta-analysis by Beaudoin and Desrichard (2011) showed that memory self-efficacy related positively to memory performance.

In summary, self-efficacy is an important influence on motivation and achievement (Multon, Brown, & Lent, 1991; Pajares, 1996, 1997; Schunk & DiBenedetto, 2016; Valentine, DuBois, & Cooper, 2004). Students with a strong sense of self-efficacy for learning are apt to be more motivated to do so and consequently achieve at higher levels (Schunk & DiBenedetto, 2016; see discussion of growth mindset in Chapter 9).

Self-efficacy is assumed to be more situationally specific, dynamic, fluctuating, and changeable than the more static and stable measures of self-concept and general self-competence (Schunk & Pajares, 2002). One's self-efficacy for a specific task might fluctuate while one is engaged with the task due to the individual's preparation, physical condition (sickness, fatigue), and affective mood, as well as external conditions such as the nature of the task (length, difficulty) and social milieu (general classroom conditions). In contrast, other views of self-competence view it more globally (e.g., mathematical competence) and are less concerned with instability of beliefs. In measuring self-efficacy, therefore, it is important to link it specifically with the key processes and capabilities underlying successful performance in the domain being assessed (Bruning, Dempsey, Kauffman, McKim, & Zumbrunn, 2013).

The reciprocal interaction between personal and environmental factors can be seen clearly with social and self variables. Social (environmental) factors can affect many self (personal) variables, such as learners' goals, self-efficacy, outcome expectations, attributions, self-evaluations of learning progress, and self-regulatory processes. In turn, self influences can affect social environments, as when learners decide they need more instruction on a skill and seek out qualified teachers (Schunk, 1999).

Achievement variables such as perceived goal progress, motivation (e.g., choice of activities, effort, persistence), and learning are affected by social and self influences. In turn, learner actions affect these factors. As students work on tasks, they evaluate their learning progress. Perceptions of progress, which can be facilitated by feedback about progress, substantiate their self-efficacy for learning, which sustains motivation and learning (Hattie & Timperley, 2007; Schunk & DiBenedetto, 2016).

A key process is the *internalization* of social variables to self influences. Learners transform information acquired from the social environment into mechanisms of self-regulation (Chapter 10). With increased skill acquisition, this social-to-self transformation process becomes a bidirectional interactive process as learners alter and adjust their social environments to further enhance their achievement (Schunk, 1999).

Models and Self-Efficacy

Children readily emulate proficient models in their environments (e.g., parents, teachers, coaches, peers; Wood et al., 2013). These models also serve as important sources of information for gauging self-efficacy.

Adult Models. Research shows that exposing students to adult models influences their self-efficacy for learning and performing well. Zimmerman and Ringle (1981) had children observe a model unsuccessfully attempt to solve a puzzle for a long or short time and verbalize statements of confidence or pessimism, after which children attempted to solve the puzzle. Observing a confident but nonpersistent model raised self-efficacy; children who observed a pessimistic but persistent model lowered their self-efficacy. Relich, Debus, and Walker (1986) found that exposing low-achieving children to models explaining mathematical division and providing them with feedback stressing the importance of ability and effort positively affected self-efficacy.

Schunk (1981) showed that both cognitive modeling and didactic instruction by adults raised self-efficacy; however, cognitive modeling led to greater gains in division skill and to more accurate perceptions of capabilities as these children's self-efficacy judgments corresponded more closely to their actual performances. Students who received only didactic instruction overestimated what they could do. Regardless of treatment condition, self-efficacy related positively to persistence and achievement. Bandura, Barbaranelli, Caprara, and Pastorelli (1996) found that parents' academic aspirations for their children affected both children's academic achievements and their self-efficacy.

Peer Models. One way to raise self-efficacy is to use *coping models*, who initially demonstrate fears and skill deficiencies but gradually improve their performance and self-efficacy. Coping models illustrate how determined effort and positive self-thoughts overcome difficulties. In contrast, *mastery models* demonstrate faultless performance and high confidence from the outset (Schunk & Hanson, 1985). Coping models may enhance observers' perceived similarity to models and self-efficacy for learning better than mastery models among students who are more likely to view the initial difficulties and gradual progress of coping models as more similar to their typical performances than the rapid learning of mastery models.

Children who had experienced difficulties learning subtraction with regrouping watched videos portraying a peer mastery model, a peer coping model, a teacher model, or no model (Schunk & Hanson, 1985). In the peer-model conditions, an adult teacher provided instruction, after which the peer solved problems. The peer mastery model easily grasped operations and verbalized positive achievement beliefs reflecting high self-efficacy and ability, low task difficulty, and positive attitudes. The peer coping model initially made errors and verbalized negative achievement beliefs but gradually performed better and verbalized coping statements (e.g., "I need to pay attention to what I'm doing"). Eventually, the coping model's problem-solving behaviors and verbalizations matched those of the mastery model. Teacher-model children observed videos portraying only the teacher providing instruction; no-model children did not view videos. All children judged self-efficacy for learning to subtract and received instruction and practice over sessions.

Observing a peer model raised self-efficacy and achievement more than observing a teacher model or no model; the teacher-model condition promoted these outcomes better than no model. The mastery and coping conditions led to similar outcomes. Possibly children focused more on what the models had in common (task success) than on their differences. Children may have thought about their prior successes in subtraction without regrouping and concluded that if the model could learn, they could as well.

Another important variable is *number of models*. Compared with a single model, multiple models increase the probability that observers will perceive themselves as similar to at least one of the models. Students who might easily discount the successes of a single model may be swayed by observing several successful peers and believe that if all these models can learn, they can as well. Notice in the opening scenario that Donnetta's coach served as a model, and Coach Martin gave Donnetta materials portraying backhands demonstrated by other models.

Schunk, Hanson, and Cox (1987) investigated the effects of single and multiple coping and mastery models with a task (fractions) on which children had experienced few prior successes. Viewing a single coping model or multiple coping or mastery models enhanced children's self-efficacy and achievement better than viewing a single mastery model.

Schunk and Hanson (1989a) further explored variations in perceived similarity by having average-achieving children view one of three types of peer models. Mastery models easily grasped arithmetic operations and verbalized positive beliefs (e.g., "I know I can do this one"). Coping-emotive models initially experienced difficulties and verbalized negative statements (e.g., "I'm not very good at this"), after which they verbalized coping statements (e.g., "I'll have to work hard on this one") and displayed coping behaviors; eventually they performed as well as mastery models. Coping-alone models performed in identical fashion to coping-emotive models but never verbalized negative beliefs.

Coping-emotive models led to the highest self-efficacy for learning. Mastery and coping-alone children perceived themselves as equal in competence to the model; coping-emotive children viewed themselves as more competent than the model. The belief that one is more talented than an unsuccessful model can raise self-efficacy and motivation. The three conditions promoted self-efficacy and achievement equally well, which shows that actual task experience outweighed initial effects due to watching models.

Peer models can increase prosocial behaviors. Strain et al. (1981) taught peers to initiate social play with withdrawn children by using verbal signals (e.g., "Let's play blocks") and motor responses (handing child a toy). Training peer initiators is time consuming but effective because methods of remedying social withdrawal (prompting, reinforcement) require nearly continuous teacher involvement. Application 4.5 discusses some additional uses of peer models.

APPLICATION 4.5
Building Self-Efficacy with Peer Models

Observing similar peers performing a task increases students' self-efficacy for learning. This idea is applied when a teacher selects certain students to solve mathematics problems while class members observe. By demonstrating success, the peer models help raise observers' self-efficacy for performing well. If skill levels in a class vary considerably, the teacher might pick peer models at different levels of ability. Students in the class are more likely to perceive themselves as similar in competence to at least one of the models.

Peers who readily master skills may help teach skills to observing students but may not have much impact on the self-efficacy of those students who experience learning difficulties. For the latter, students who learn more slowly may be excellent models. Mr. Riordian's history class has been learning about Civil War battles. Because so many battles occurred, learning about all of them has been difficult for some of the students. He places students into three groups: Group 1—students who mastered the material easily; Group 2—students who have been working hard and are gradually

developing mastery; and Group 3—students who still are having difficulty. He pairs Groups 2 and 3 for peer tutoring, figuring that Group 2 students will be good models for Group 3 students.

Teachers can point out the concentration and hard work of peer models. For instance, as an elementary teacher moves about the room monitoring students' work, she provides learners with social comparative information (e.g., "See how well Kevin is working? I'm sure that you can work just as well"). Teachers need to ensure that learners view the comparative performance level as one they can attain; judicious selection of referent students is necessary.

Peers also can enhance students' self-efficacy during small-group work. Successful groups are those in which each member has some responsibility and members share rewards based on their collective performance. The use of such groups helps to reduce negative ability-related social comparisons by students experiencing learning difficulties. Teachers need to select tasks carefully because unsuccessful groups do not raise self-efficacy.

Motor Skills

Researchers have shown that self-efficacy predicts the acquisition and performance of motor skills (Bandura, 1997; Poag-DuCharme & Brawley, 1993; Wurtele, 1986). Gould and Weiss (1981) found benefits due to model similarity. College women viewed a similar model (female student with no athletic background) or dissimilar model (male physical education professor) perform a muscular endurance task. Students who viewed the similar model performed the task better and judged self-efficacy higher than those who observed the dissimilar model. Regardless of treatment condition, self-efficacy related positively to performance.

George, Feltz, and Chase (1992) replicated these results using female college students and models performing a leg-extension endurance task. Students who observed nonathletic male or female models extended their legs longer and judged self-efficacy higher than those who observed an athletic model. Among these unskilled observers, model ability was a more important similarity cue than model gender.

Bandura and Cervone (Bandura & Cervone, 1983) showed how feedback was important during motor skill acquisition. College students operated an ergometer by alternatively pushing and pulling arm levers that resisted their efforts. Some participants pursued a goal of increasing performance by 40% over the baseline, others were told they had increased their performance by 24%, those in a third condition received goals and feedback, and control-group participants received neither goals nor feedback. Goals combined with feedback improved performance most and instilled self-efficacy for goal attainment, which predicted subsequent effort.

In follow-up research (Bandura & Cervone, 1986), participants received a goal of 50% improvement over baseline. Following their performance, they received false feedback indicating they achieved an increase of 24%, 36%, 46%, or 54%. Self-efficacy was lowest for the 24% group and highest for the 54% condition. After students set goals for the next session and performed the task again, effort expenditure related positively to goals and self-efficacy across all conditions.

Poag-DuCharme and Brawley (1993) found that self-efficacy predicted individuals' involvement in community-based exercise programs. Self-efficacy was assessed for performing in-class activities and for overcoming barriers to exercising and scheduling problems. Self-efficacy related positively to the initiation and maintenance of regular exercise. In similar fashion, Motl and colleagues (Motl, Dishman, Saunders, Dowda, & Pate, 2007; Motl et al., 2005) have shown that self-efficacy for overcoming barriers to exercise predicted physical exercise by adolescent girls. These results suggest that promoting exercise requires attention to developing individuals' self-efficacy for coping with potential problems in scheduling and engagement.

Teacher Self-Efficacy

Self-efficacy is relevant to teachers as well as students (Fives & Buehl, 2016; Schunk & DiBenedetto, 2016; Woolfolk-Hoy, Hoy, & Davis, 2009). *Teacher* (or *instructional*) *self-efficacy* refers to personal beliefs about one's capabilities to help students learn (Schunk & DiBenedetto, 2016). Teacher self-efficacy should influence teachers' activities, effort, and persistence with students. Teachers with low self-efficacy may avoid planning activities—to include using technology for instruction—they believe exceed their capabilities, not persist with students having difficulties, expend little effort to find materials, and not reteach content in ways students might understand better. Teachers with higher self-efficacy are more apt to develop challenging activities, help students succeed, and persevere with students who have problems learning. These motivational effects on teachers enhance student achievement. Teachers with higher self-efficacy also show stronger commitment to their work (Chan, Lau, Nie, Lim, & Hogan, 2008). Ashton and Webb (1986) found that teachers with higher self-efficacy were likely to have a positive classroom environment, support students' ideas, and address students' needs. Teacher self-efficacy was a significant predictor of student achievement.

Not surprisingly, more-experienced teachers tend to have higher self-efficacy (Wolters & Daugherty, 2007). These researchers also found that teacher self-efficacy related positively to their efforts to create classroom mastery goal structures emphasizing learning progress and overcoming challenges (see Chapter 9). Teacher self-efficacy has been shown to positively predict job satisfaction (Collie, Shapka, & Perry, 2012). Feltz, Chase, Moritz, and Sullivan (1999) showed that the same predictions for teacher self-efficacy also applied to coaches.

Researchers have investigated the dimensions of teacher efficacy that relate best to student learning. Ashton and Webb (1986) distinguished *teaching efficacy*, or outcome expectations about the consequences of teaching in general, from *personal efficacy*, defined as self-efficacy to perform particular behaviors to bring about given outcomes. As noted earlier, self-efficacy and outcome expectations often are related but need not be. A teacher might have a high sense of personal efficacy but lower teaching efficacy if he or she believes that most student learning is due to home and environmental factors outside of the teacher's control. Other research suggests that teacher self-efficacy reflects an internal–external distinction: internal factors represent perceptions of personal influence and power and external factors relate to perceptions of influence and power of elements that lie outside the classroom (Guskey & Passaro, 1994).

Goddard, Hoy, and Woolfolk Hoy (2000) discussed *collective teacher efficacy*, or perceptions of a group of teachers in a school that their efforts as a whole will positively affect students. Collective teacher efficacy requires support from administrators who facilitate improvement by creating an environment free of roadblocks, and it seems critical for effective school reform.

The role of collective teacher efficacy may depend on the level of organizational coupling (Henson, 2002). Collective teacher efficacy may not predict outcomes in loosely knit schools; individual self-efficacy may be a better predictor. This situation may occur in some secondary schools where coupling, if present, resides at the departmental level rather than at the whole-school level. Conversely, elementary schools typically are closely coupled, and the collective efficacy of the school's teachers may predict student outcomes.

Goddard et al. (2000) discussed the process whereby collective teacher efficacy can affect student learning. The same four sources of self-efficacy information affect collective efficacy: performance attainments, vicarious experiences, social persuasion, and physiological indicators. Collective efficacy is apt to be strengthened when teachers successfully work together to implement changes, learn from one another and from other successful schools, receive encouragement for change from administrators and professional development sources, and work together to cope with difficulties and alleviate stress (Goddard, Hoy, & Woolfolk Hoy, 2004). As collective teacher efficacy is strengthened, teachers continue to improve opportunities for students.

Caprara, Barbaranelli, Borgogni, and Steca (2003) found that teachers' collective efficacy beliefs bore a positive relation to their job satisfaction. Further, collective efficacy depends on teachers believing that others (e.g., principals, staff, parents, students) are working diligently to fulfill their obligations. Retaining teachers in the profession—a critical priority given the teacher shortage in many areas—will be aided by creating an environment in which teachers' self-efficacy is fostered and their efforts lead to positive changes.

An important challenge for pre- and in-service teacher education programs is to develop methods for increasing teachers' self-efficacy by incorporating efficacy-building sources. Internships where students work with teacher mentors provide actual performance success plus expert modeling. Teacher models not only teach observers skills but also build their self-efficacy for succeeding in the classroom (Application 4.6).

Health and Therapeutic Activities

Researchers have shown that self-efficacy predicts health and therapeutic behaviors (Bandura, 1997; Maddux, 1993; Maddux, Brawley, & Boykin, 1995; Maes & Gebhardt, 2000). Self-efficacy correlates positively with controlled smoking (Godding & Glasgow, 1985), positively with longest period of smoking cessation (DiClemente, Prochaska, & Gilbertini, 1985), negatively with temptation to smoke (DiClemente et al., 1985), and positively with weight loss (Bernier & Avard, 1986). Love (1983) found that self-efficacy to resist bulimic behaviors correlated negatively with binging and purging. Bandura (1994) discussed the role of self-efficacy in the control of HIV infection.

In DiClemente's (1981) study, individuals who had recently quit smoking judged their self-efficacy to avoid smoking in situations of varying stress levels; they were surveyed months later to determine maintenance. Maintainers judged self-efficacy higher than those who relapsed. Self-efficacy was a better predictor of future smoking than was smoking history or demographic variables. People tended to relapse in situations where they had judged their self-efficacy low for avoiding smoking.

Researchers have investigated how well self-efficacy predicts therapeutic behavioral changes (Bandura, 1991). In one study (Bandura, Adams, & Beyer, 1977), adults with

---

APPLICATION 4.6
Teacher Self-Efficacy

Teacher self-efficacy is developed in the same ways as among students. An effective means of building self-efficacy is to observe someone model specific teaching behaviors. A new elementary teacher might observe his or her mentor teacher implement the use of learning centers before the new teacher introduces the same activity. By observing the mentor, the new teacher acquires skill and self-efficacy for being able to implement the centers.

Self-efficacy in beginning teachers also may be aided by observing second- and third-year teachers successfully perform actions; new teachers may perceive greater similarity between themselves and other relatively new teachers than between themselves and more-experienced teachers.

Practicing helps to develop skills and also builds self-efficacy. Music teachers will increase their self-efficacy for teaching pieces to the class by practicing those pieces until they know them well and feel confident about working with students. Teachers should learn to use a new computer application well before they introduce it to their classes so they will feel self-efficacious about teaching their students to use it.

Becoming more knowledgeable about a particular subject increases self-efficacy for discussing the subject more accurately and completely. College instructors should review the work of significant researchers for each major topic area included in the course discussions. Such reviews help instructors provide students with information beyond what is in the text and builds instructors' self-efficacy for effectively teaching the content.

snake phobias received a participant modeling treatment in which a therapist initially modeled a series of progressively more threatening encounters with a snake. After clients jointly performed the various activities with the therapist, they were allowed to perform on their own. Compared with clients who only observed the therapist model the activities and with those who received no training, participant-modeling clients demonstrated the greatest increases in self-efficacy and approach behaviors toward the snake. Regardless of treatment, self-efficacy for performing tasks was highly related to clients' actual behaviors. In a related study, Bandura and Adams (1977) found participant modeling superior to systematic desensitization (Chapter 3). These results support Bandura's (1982b, 1997) contention that performance-based treatments combining modeling with practice produce higher self-efficacy and greater behavioral change.

The development and maintenance of healthy lifestyles often have been explained in terms of prescriptive medical management, but increasingly researchers and practitioners are emphasizing collaborative self-management (Bandura, 2005). The latter includes many of the social cognitive processes described in this chapter: self-monitoring of health-related behaviors, goals and self-efficacy for attaining them, self-evaluation of progress, and self-motivating incentives and social supports for healthy lifestyles (Maes & Karoly, 2005).

This view of health and wellness reflects Bandura's (2005) agentic perspective on human functioning described at the start of this chapter. Successful lifestyle change that is maintained over time requires that people feel self-efficacious for managing their own activities and controlling events that affect their lives. Self-efficacy affects whether people think in positive or negative ways, how they motivate themselves and persist during difficulties, how they handle their emotions and especially during periods of stress, how resilient they are to setbacks, and what choices they make at critical times (Benight & Bandura, 2004).

In summary, research evidence shows that self-efficacy predicts diverse outcomes such as smoking cessation, pain tolerance, athletic performance, assertiveness, coping with feared events, recovery from heart attack, and sales performance (Bandura, 1986, 1997). Self-efficacy is a key variable influencing career choices (Lent, Brown, & Hackett, 2000), and children's self-efficacy affects the types of occupations in which they believe they can succeed (Bandura, Barbaranelli, Caprara, & Pastorelli, 2001).

INSTRUCTIONAL APPLICATIONS

Many ideas in social cognitive theory lend themselves well to instruction and student learning. Instructional applications involving models and self-efficacy, worked examples, and tutoring and mentoring reflect social cognitive principles.

Models and Self-Efficacy

Observational learning through modeling is stressed by social cognitive theory. Teacher models facilitate learning and provide self-efficacy information. Students who observe teachers explain and demonstrate concepts and skills are apt to learn and believe that they are capable of further learning. Teachers also provide persuasive self-efficacy information to students. When teachers introduce lessons by stating that all students can learn and that by working diligently they will master the new skills, they instill in students self-efficacy for learning, which is substantiated as learners successfully complete the task. Teachers should ensure that their instructions to students (e.g., "keep your work area tidy") are consistent with their own actions (teacher's work area is tidy).

In similar fashion, peer models can promote student motivation and learning. Relative to teachers, peers may be more focused on "how to do it," which improves learning in observers. Further, observing a similar peer succeed instills a vicarious sense of self-efficacy for learning in observers, which is validated as they perform well (Schunk, 2012). When using peers, it helps to choose models such that each student can relate to at least one. This may mean using multiple peer models, where the peers represent varying levels of skill. An excellent example of using both adult and peer models during instruction is *reciprocal teaching* (discussed in Chapter 7).

To determine which instructional methods to use, teachers can gauge their effects on students' self-efficacy as well as on their learning. It may be that a method that produces learning does not enhance self-efficacy very well. For example, providing students with extensive assistance is apt to aid their learning, but it will not do much for students' self-efficacy for learning or performing well on their own. As Bandura (1986, 1997) recommended, periods of self-directed mastery, where students practice skills independently, are needed.

Competent models teach skills, but similar models can enhance self-efficacy. Having the best mathematics student in the class demonstrate operations may teach skills to the observers, but many of the latter students may not feel efficacious because they may believe that they never will be as good as the model. Top students often serve as tutors for less-capable students, which may improve learning but should be accompanied by periods of independent practice to build self-efficacy (see Tutoring and Mentoring section).

Pre-service teachers' self-efficacy can be developed through teacher preparation that includes internships with teachers—especially those with whom they share some similarities—where the pre-service teachers observe and practice teaching skills. For in-service teachers, continuing professional development helps them learn new strategies to use in challenging situations, such as how to foster learning in students with varying abilities, how to work with students with limited English proficiency, and how to involve parents in their children's learning. By removing impairments to teaching (e.g., excess paperwork), administrators allow teachers to focus on curricular improvement and student learning (see Application 4.6).

Worked Examples

Worked examples are graphic portrayals of problem solutions (Atkinson, Derry, Renkl, & Wortham, 2000). Worked examples present step-by-step problem solutions (Bokosmaty, Sweller, & Kalyuga, 2015), often with accompanying diagrams or sound (narration). A worked example provides a model—with accompanying explanation—that illustrates how a proficient problem solver would proceed. Learners study worked examples before they attempt to solve problems themselves. Worked examples are often used in instruction in mathematics and science, although their use need not be confined to these disciplines. Researchers have identified a *worked-example effect* (Chen, Kalyuga, & Sweller, 2015; van Gog, Paas, & Sweller, 2010), or the advantage for learning and transfer from studying worked examples before solving problems compared with problem solving alone.

The theoretical underpinnings for worked examples derive from information processing theory, especially principles involving working memory (Chapter 7). But worked examples also reflect many principles of social cognitive theory (van Gog & Rummel, 2010). Worked examples incorporate cognitive models and demonstration plus explanation. As with other complex forms of observational learning, students do not learn how to solve a particular problem but rather general skills and strategies that they can use to solve a wider class of problems. Worked examples also have motivational benefits. They may help to raise self-efficacy in learners who, after reviewing worked examples, believe they understand the model and can apply the skills and strategies (Schunk, 2012).

Certain principles should be kept in mind when using worked examples. It is better to use more than one mode of presentation than a single mode. Thus, a worked example might include textual (words, numbers), graphical (arrows, charts), and aural (sounds) information. But too much complexity can overload learners' attention and working memory. Research also shows that two examples are better than a single one, two varied examples are better than two examples of the same type, and intermixing practice with worked examples produces better learning than if all examples are presented first followed by practice (Atkinson et al., 2000). An algebra teacher teaching a lesson on solving equations in one unknown might present two worked examples of the form $4x + 2 = 10$, after which students solve problems. Then the teacher might present two worked examples of the form $x \div 2 + 1 = 5$, after which students solve problems of this type. The worked examples could be accompanied by graphics and sound, as in interactive computer-based learning environments.

Tutoring and Mentoring

Tutoring and mentoring incorporate several principles of social cognitive theory. *Tutoring* refers to a situation in which one or more persons serve as the instructional agents for another, usually in a specific subject or for a particular purpose (Stenhoff & Lignugaris/ Kraft, 2007). When peers are the instructional agents, tutoring is a form of peer-assisted learning (Rohrbeck, Ginsburg-Block, Fantuzzo, & Miller, 2003; Chapter 8).

Tutors serve as instructional models for tutees by explaining and demonstrating skills, operations, and strategies that tutees are to learn. Both adults and children can be effective tutors for children. As noted earlier, however, there may be some motivational benefits that result from peer tutors. Effective peer tutors are those whom tutees perceive as similar to themselves except that tutors are farther along in their skill acquisition. The perception of similarity may lead tutees to believe that if the tutors could learn, they can as well, which can raise tutees' self-efficacy and motivation. Peer tutoring typically has benefits for learning and achievement (Leung, 2015; see discussion of peer tutoring in Chapter 8).

Researchers also have examined the effects of tutoring on tutors. Similar to the results of instructional self-efficacy, tutors with higher self-efficacy for tutoring are more apt to exert effort, tackle difficult material, and persist longer with tutees than are tutors with lower self-efficacy (Roscoe & Chi, 2007). There also is evidence that tutoring can enhance tutors' motivation and self-efficacy (Roscoe & Chi, 2007).

Mentoring refers to interactions between more-experienced mentors and less-experienced mentees (or protégés), where mentors provide career (instrumental) and psychosocial (relational) knowledge, advice, and support (Eby, Rhodes, & Allen, 2007; Fletcher & Mullen, 2012). The overall goal of mentoring is to help people function effectively in their professional and personal lives. Ideally, mentoring incorporates mutual learning and engagement between the mentor and protégé. Mentoring is, therefore, a fuller and deeper educational experience than tutoring. While tutoring emphasizes content instruction within a short time period, mentoring typically involves modeled counsel and guidance over a longer time (Johnson, 2007).

Mentoring is common at various levels of education, such as in learning communities, inquiry and writing groups, university–school partnerships, staff development, higher education, and peer coaching (Mullen, 2005). In higher education, mentoring often occurs between senior and junior faculty members or between professors and students. In this context, mentoring ideally becomes a developmental relationship where more-experienced professors share their expertise and invest time with less-experienced professors or students to nurture their achievement and self-efficacy (Johnson, 2007; Mullen, 2011).

Mentoring reflects many social cognitive principles and can have instructional and motivational benefits (Schunk & Mullen, 2013). Protégés learn skills and strategies that help them succeed in their environments from mentors who model, explain, and demonstrate these skills and strategies. Protégés who perceive themselves as similar in important ways to mentors may develop higher self-efficacy for being successful through their interactions with mentors. Similar to motivation and self-regulated learning, mentoring emphasizes goal-directed activity over time (Schunk & Mullen, 2013). Mentoring of doctoral students has been shown to improve their self-regulation, self-efficacy, motivation, and achievement (Mullen, 2011). Mentors also can learn and refine their skills through their interactions with their protégés, which could raise their self-efficacy for continuing to succeed. Consistent with social cognitive theory, the mentoring relationship can result in benefits for both parties (Schunk & Mullen 2013).

SUMMARY AND CRITIQUE

Chapter Summary

Social cognitive learning theory contends that people learn from their social environments. In Bandura's theory, human functioning is viewed as a series of reciprocal interactions among personal, behavioral, and environmental factors. Learning is an information processing activity in which knowledge is cognitively represented as symbolic representations that are guides for action. Learning occurs enactively through actual performances and vicariously by observing models, listening to instructions, and engaging with print or electronic content. The consequences of behavior are especially important. Behaviors that result in successful consequences are retained; those that lead to failures are discarded.

Social cognitive theory presents an agentic perspective of human behavior: Persons can learn to set goals and self-regulate their cognitions, emotions, behaviors, and environments in ways to facilitate attainment of those goals.

Historical perspectives on imitation do not fully capture the range and influence of modeling. Bandura and colleagues have shown how modeling greatly expands the range and rate of learning. Various modeling effects are distinguished: inhibition and disinhibition, response facilitation, and observational learning. Observational learning through modeling expands the learning rate, as well as the amount of knowledge acquired. Subprocesses of observational learning are attention, retention, production, and motivation.

According to social cognitive theory, observing a model does not guarantee learning or later ability to perform the behaviors. Rather, models provide information about probable consequences of actions and motivate observers to act accordingly. Factors influencing learning and performance are developmental status of learners, prestige and competence of models, and vicarious consequences to models.

Among the important motivational influences on learning are goals, outcome expectations, values, and self-efficacy. Goals enhance learning through their effects on perceived progress, self-efficacy, and self-evaluations. As people work on a task, they compare their progress with their goal. The perception of progress raises self-efficacy and sustains motivation. Goal properties of specificity, proximity, and difficulty enhance self-perceptions and motivation, as do self-set goals and goals for which people make a commitment to attain.

Outcome expectations (perceived consequences of behavior) affect learning and motivation because people strive to attain desired outcomes and shun undesirable ones. People also act in concert with their values, working towards outcomes that they find self-satisfying.

Self-efficacy, or one's perceived capabilities of learning or performing behaviors at designated levels, is not the same as knowing what to do. Self-efficacy affects choice of activities, effort, persistence, and achievement. People gauge their self-efficacy based on their performance attainments, vicarious consequences to models, forms of persuasion, and physiological indicators. Actual performances provide the most reliable information for assessing self-efficacy. Instructional self-efficacy and collective self-efficacy, which have been studied with teachers, bear a positive relation to student learning and achievement.

Researchers have found support for Bandura's theory in a variety of contexts involving cognitive, social, motor, health, instructional, and self-regulatory skills. Self-efficacy has been shown to predict behavioral change with different types of participants (e.g., adults, children) in various settings. This research also has shown that learning of complex skills occurs through a combination of enactive and vicarious learning. Observers acquire an approximation of the skill by observing models. Subsequent practice of the skill allows teachers to provide corrective feedback to learners. With additional practice, learners refine and internalize self-regulatory skills and strategies. Important instructional applications of social cognitive theory involve models and self-efficacy, worked examples, tutoring, and mentoring.

A summary of learning issues appears in Table 4.6.

Table 4.6
Summary of learning issues.

How Does Learning Occur?

Learning occurs enactively (by doing) and vicariously (by observing, reading, and listening). Much school learning requires a combination of vicarious and enactive experiences. Observational learning greatly expands the scope of human learning possible. Observational learning consists of four processes: attention, retention, production, and motivation. A major contribution of social cognitive theory is its emphasis on learning from the social environment.

How Does Memory Function?

Social cognitive researchers have not investigated in depth the role of human memory. Social cognitive theory predicts that memory includes information stored as images or symbols.

What Is the Role of Motivation?

Key motivational processes are goals, values, and expectations. People set goals for learning and assess progress against goals. Values reflect what persons find self-satisfying and believe are important. Expectations are of two types. Outcome expectations refer to the expected outcomes of actions. Self-efficacy (efficacy expectations) refers to one's perceived capabilities for learning or performing tasks at designated levels. The belief that one is making goal progress substantiates self-efficacy and motivates one to continue learning.

How Does Transfer Occur?

Transfer is a cognitive phenomenon. It depends on people believing that certain actions in new or different situations are socially acceptable and will be met with favorable outcomes. Learners' self-efficacy also can facilitate transfer.

How Does Self-Regulated Learning Operate?

In the classical view, self-regulation consists of three processes: self-observation, self-judgment, and self-reaction. This view has been broadened to a cyclical model that includes activities before, during, and after task engagement. Social cognitive theory stresses goals, self-efficacy, attributions, learning strategies, and self-evaluations. These processes reciprocally interact with one another such that goal attainment can lead to the adoption of new goals.

What Are the Implications for Instruction?

The use of modeling is highly recommended. Effective instruction begins with social influences, such as models, and gradually shifts to self-influences as learners internalize skills and strategies. It is important to determine how instruction affects not only learning but also learners' self-efficacy. Students should be encouraged to set goals and assess goal progress. Teachers' self-efficacy affects instruction because efficacious teachers help promote student learning better. Social cognitive principles also are reflected in worked examples, tutoring, and mentoring.

Chapter Critique

Social cognitive theory has made many contributions to the study of learning. Its central premise that learning depends heavily on the social environment is embraced by many conceptions of teaching and learning. Learning principles are not context free; they operate within social conditions, and these must be taken into account to adequately understand learning.

A major contribution of the theory is its theoretical explanation of and research on observational learning through modeling. Modeling is a central process for teaching diverse skills with learners of all ages. When used profitably, modeling can greatly enhance learning.

As Bandura expanded his original theory, he included the important role played by self-efficacy. This variable affects the motivational outcomes of choices, effort, and persistence, which in turn lead to better learning. With its emphasis on self-efficacy and other motivational variables such as goals and outcome expectations, social cognitive theory underscores the pivotal role played by motivation in learning. Further refinements of the theory have resulted in a social cognitive conceptualization of self-regulation, which is intimately linked with learning.

Although social cognitive theory has had a profound influence on the study of learning, it is not without its shortcomings. The role of memory is under-specified in the theory. Social cognitive researchers tend to invoke information processing principles (Chapters 5–7). The process whereby verbal and visual inputs become learned also is not specified in depth. Although there is developmental research employing social cognitive theory, clearly more research is needed to determine children's acquisition of capabilities to attend to and learn from models and the processes involved in developing self-efficacy.

Social cognitive theory was initially formulated largely as a reaction to the behavioral theories that were prominent in the middle of the twentieth century. With added research and theoretical refinements by Bandura and others, social cognitive theory has grown appreciably more cognitive in its focus. We can expect this trend to continue as social cognitive researchers tackle issues in diverse social learning environments including schools, homes, and communities.

REFLECTION QUESTIONS

- Social cognitive theory predicts that human functioning depends on reciprocal interactions between personal, behavioral, and environmental variables. Some of these influences seem obvious (e.g., how a personal belief can affect behavior), whereas others do not (e.g., how an environmental variable can affect behavior independently of personal variables). This conception suggests multiple ways that teachers can help to improve students' learning. How might teachers try to improve students' learning through personal, behavioral, and environmental variables?

- Bandura's early research investigated the operation of modeling. His research and research by others identified characteristics of models that promote observational learning; for example, competence, perceived similarity, credibility. But it seems that some of these characteristics conflict with one another. For example, teachers are competent but may not be similar to students in many ways (e.g., age, gender, educational level, socioeconomic status). Given this situation, do you think there is a general set of effective model characteristics, or do they vary according to the context? If they vary with the context, can you think of some specific situations and explain who would be the best models in those situations?

■ Teacher self-efficacy is affected by the same factors that influence student self-efficacy: performance accomplishments, vicarious experiences, social persuasion, and physiological indicators. Suppose you were a school principal who desired to promote self-efficacy in teachers. What types of experiences would you provide to ensure that teachers gained positive self-efficacy information from multiple sources? Try to address both individual and collective teacher self-efficacy.

FURTHER READING

Bandura, A. (1986). *Social foundations of thought and action: A social cognitive theory.* Englewood Cliffs, NJ: Prentice Hall.

Bandura, A. (1997). *Self-efficacy: The exercise of control.* New York: Freeman.

Goddard, R. D., Hoy, W. K., & Woolfolk Hoy, A. (2004). Collective efficacy beliefs: Theoretical developments, empirical evidence, and future directions. *Educational Researcher, 33*(3), 3–13.

Locke, E. A., & Latham, G. P. (2002). Building a practically useful theory of goal setting and task motivation: A 35-year odyssey. *American Psychologist, 57,* 705–717.

Schunk, D. H. (2012). Social cognitive theory. In K. R. Harris, S. Graham, & T. Urdan (Eds.), *APA educational psychology handbook. Vol 1: Theories, constructs, and critical issues* (pp. 101–123). Washington, DC: American Psychological Association.

Schunk, D. H., & DiBenedetto, M. K. (2016). Self-efficacy theory in education. In K. R. Wentzel & D. B. Miele (Eds.), *Handbook of motivation at school* (2nd ed., pp. 34–54). New York: Routledge.

Zimmerman, B. J., & Schunk, D. H. (2003). Albert Bandura: The scholar and his contributions to educational psychology. In B. J. Zimmerman & D. H. Schunk (Eds.), *Educational psychology: A century of contributions* (pp. 431–457). Mahwah, NJ: Erlbaum.

5 Information Processing Theory: Encoding and Storage

Cass Paquin, a middle school mathematics teacher, seemed sad when she met with her team members Don Jacks and Fran Killian.

Don: What's the matter, Cass? Things got you down?

Cass: They just don't get it. I can't get them to understand what a variable is. "*X*" is a mystery to them.

Fran: Yes, "*x*" is too abstract for kids.

Don: It's abstract to adults too. "*X*" is a letter of the alphabet, a symbol. I've had the same problem. Some seem to pick it up, but many don't.

Fran: In my master's program, they teach that you have to make learning meaningful. People learn better when they can relate the new learning to something they know. "*X*" has no meaning in math. We need to change it to something the kids know.

Cass: Such as what—cookies?

Fran: Well, yes. Take the problem $4x + 7 = 15$. How about saying: 4 times how many cookies plus 7 cookies equals 15 cookies? That way the kids can relate "*x*" to something tangible—real. Then "*x*" won't just be something they memorize how to work with. They'll associate "*x*" with things that can take on different values, such as cookies.

Don: That's a problem with a lot of math—it's too abstract. When kids are little, we use real objects to make it meaningful. We cut pizzas into pieces to illustrate fractions. Then, when they get older, we stop doing that and use abstract symbols most of the time. Sure, they have to know how to use those symbols, but we should try to make the concepts meaningful.

Cass: Yes. I've fallen into that trap—teach the material like it is in the book. I need to try to relate the concepts better to what the kids know and what makes sense to them.

Information processing theory focuses on how people attend to environmental events, construct and encode information to be learned and relate it to knowledge in memory, store new knowledge in memory, and retrieve it as needed (Mayer, 2012; Radvansky & Ashcraft, 2014). Information processing is not a single theory; it is a generic name applied to theoretical perspectives dealing with the sequence and execution of cognitive events. Furthermore, there is no one dominant theory, and researchers disagree about aspects of current theories (Matlin, 2009). In part, this situation may be due to the influence on information processing by advances in other domains including psychology, communications, technology, and neuroscience.

Much early information processing research was conducted in laboratories and dealt with phenomena such as eye movements, recognition and recall times, attention to stimuli, and interference in perception and memory. Later research has explored learning, memory, problem solving, visual and auditory perception, cognitive development, and artificial intelligence. Despite a healthy research literature, information processing principles have not always lent themselves readily to school learning, curricular structure, and instructional design. This situation does not imply that information processing has little educational relevance, only that many potential applications are yet to be developed. Fortunately, researchers increasingly are applying principles to educational settings involving such subjects as reading, mathematics, and science. The participants in the opening scenario are discussing meaningfulness, a key aspect of information processing.

Initially, this chapter discusses the assumptions of information processing, historical influences, and early information processing models. The bulk of the chapter is devoted to explicating a contemporary generic model comprising component processes of attention, perception, working memory, and storage in long-term memory. Chapter 6 continues this discussion by covering retrieval of knowledge from long-term memory, along with related topics such as transfer and imagery.

When you finish studying this chapter, you should be able to do the following:

- Discuss the major assumptions of information processing and some historical influences on contemporary theory: verbal learning, Gestalt theory, the two-store memory model, and levels of processing.

- Describe the major components of a contemporary generic information processing model: attention, perception, working memory, and long-term memory.

- Distinguish different views of attention, and explain how attention affects learning.

- Discuss how information enters sensory registers and is perceived.

- Describe the operation of working memory to include storage and transformation of knowledge.

- Explain the major factors that influence encoding.

- Define propositions and spreading activation, and explain their roles in encoding of long-term memory information.

- Discuss the differences between declarative and procedural knowledge.

- Identify information processing principles inherent in instructional applications involving advance organizers, the conditions of learning, and cognitive load.

EARLY INFORMATION PROCESSING PERSPECTIVES

Assumptions

Information processing theorists challenge a central tenet of behaviorism (Chapter 3) that learning involves merely forming associations between stimuli and responses. Information processing theorists do not reject associations, because they postulate that forming associations between bits of knowledge helps facilitate their acquisition and storage in memory. These theorists are less concerned with external conditions and focus more on internal (mental) processes that intervene between stimuli and responses. Learners are active seekers and processors of information. Unlike behaviorists, who said that people respond when stimuli impinge on them, information processing theorists contend that people select and attend to features of the environment, construct and rehearse knowledge, relate new information to previously acquired knowledge, and organize and transform knowledge to make it meaningful (Mayer, 2012).

Information processing theories differ in their views on which cognitive processes are important and how they operate, but these theories make common assumptions. One is that information processing occurs in phases that intervene between receiving a stimulus and producing a response. A corollary is that the form of information, or how it is represented mentally, differs depending on the phase. There is debate about whether the phases are part of a larger memory system or are qualitatively different from one another.

Another assumption is that information processing is analogous to computer processing, at least metaphorically. The human system functions similarly to a computer: It receives information, stores it in memory, and retrieves it as necessary. Cognitive processing is remarkably efficient; there is little waste or overlap. Researchers differ in how far they extend this analogy. For some, the computer analogy is nothing more than a metaphor. Others employ computers to simulate thinking and other human activities. The field of *artificial intelligence* is concerned with programming computers to engage in activities such as thinking, using language, and solving problems (Chapter 7).

Researchers also assume that information processing is involved in all cognitive activities: perceiving, rehearsing, constructing, problem solving, remembering, forgetting, and imaging (Matlin, 2009; Mayer, 2012; Terry, 2009). Information processing, which extends beyond human learning as traditionally delineated, has memory as its focus (Surprenant & Neath, 2009). This chapter is concerned primarily with those information processes most germane to learning. The remainder of this section discusses some key historical influences on contemporary information processing theory: verbal learning, Gestalt theory, the two-store (dual) memory model, and levels of processing.

Verbal Learning

Stimulus–Response Associations. The impetus for research on verbal learning derived from the work of Ebbinghaus (Chapter 1), who construed learning as gradual strengthening of associations between verbal stimuli (words, nonsense syllables). With repeated pairings, the response *dij* became more strongly connected with the stimulus *wek*. Other responses also could become connected with *wek* during learning of a list of paired nonsense syllables, but these associations became weaker over trials.

Ebbinghaus showed that three factors affected the ease or speed of learning a list of items: their *meaningfulness;* the *degree of similarity* between them; and the *length of time* separating study trials (Terry, 2009). Words (meaningful items) are learned more readily than nonsense syllables. With respect to similarity, the more alike items are to one another, the harder they are to learn. Similarity in meaning or sound can cause confusion. An individual asked to learn several synonyms such as *gigantic, huge, mammoth,* and *enormous* may fail to recall some of these but instead may recall words similar in meaning but not on the list (*large, behemoth*). With nonsense syllables, confusion occurs when the same letters are used in different positions (*xqv, khq, vxh, qvk*). The length of time separating study trials can vary from short (*massed practice*) to longer (*distributed practice*). When interference is probable (see Chapter 6), distributed practice yields better learning (Underwood, 1961).

Learning Tasks. Verbal learning researchers commonly employed three types of learning tasks: serial, paired-associate, and free-recall. In *serial learning,* people recall verbal stimuli in the order in which they were presented. Serial learning is involved in such school tasks as memorizing a poem or the ordered steps in a procedure. Results of many serial learning studies typically yield a *serial position curve* (Figure 5.1). Words at the beginning and end of the list are readily learned, whereas middle items require more trials for learning. The serial position effect may arise due to differences in distinctiveness of the various positions.

Figure 5.1
Serial position curve showing errors in recall as a function of item position.

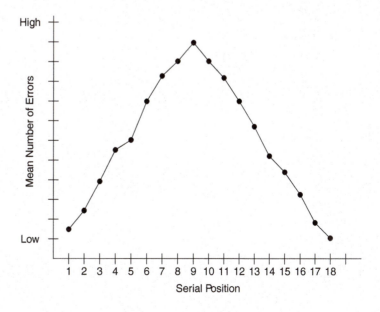

People must remember not only the items but also their positions in the list. The ends of a list are more distinctive and therefore "better" stimuli than the middle positions of a list.

In *paired-associate learning*, one stimulus is provided for one response item (e.g., *cat-tree, boat-roof, bench-dog*). Participants respond with the correct response upon presentation of the stimulus. Paired-associate learning has three aspects: discriminating among the stimuli, learning the responses, and learning which responses accompany which stimuli. Researchers have debated the process by which paired-associate learning occurs and the role of cognitive mediation. Originally it was assumed that learning was incremental and that each stimulus–response association was gradually strengthened. This view was supported by the typical learning curve (Figure 5.2). The number of errors people make is high at the beginning, but errors decrease with repeated presentations of the list.

Research by Estes (1970) and others suggested a different perspective. Although list learning improves with repetition, learning of any given item is *all-or-none*: The learner either knows the correct association or does not. Over trials, the number of learned associations increases. Learners often impose their organization to make material meaningful rather than simply memorizing responses. They may use cognitive mediators to link stimulus words with their responses. For the pair *cat-tree*, one might picture a cat running up a tree or think of the sentence, "The cat ran up the tree." When presented with *cat*, one recalls the image or sentence and responds with *tree*. Researchers have shown that verbal learning is more complex than originally believed (Terry, 2009).

In *free-recall learning*, learners are presented with a list of items and recall them in any order. Free recall lends itself well to organization imposed by learners to facilitate memory (Sederberg, Howard, & Kahana, 2008). During recall, learners typically group words presented apart on the original list. Groupings often are based on similar meaning or membership in the same category (e.g., animals, fruits, vegetables). Such *categorical clustering* shows that words recalled together tend to be associated under normal conditions, either

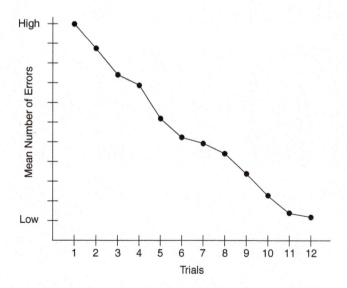

Figure 5.2
Learning curve showing errors as a function of study trials.

to one another directly (e.g., *pear-apple*) or to a third word (*fruit*). A cognitive explanation is that individuals learn both the words presented and their categories. The category names serve as mediators: When asked to recall, learners retrieve category names and then their members.

Free recall often shows primacy (first words recalled better) and recency (last words recalled better) effects (Laming, 2010). Primacy effects presumably occur because the first words receive extra rehearsals. Recency effects may occur because the last words still are in learners' working memories.

Verbal learning research identified the course of acquisition and forgetting of verbal material. At the same time, the idea that associations could explain learning of verbal material was simplistic. This became apparent when researchers moved beyond simple list learning to more meaningful learning from text. One might question the relevance of learning lists of nonsense syllables or words paired in arbitrary fashion. In school, verbal learning occurs within meaningful contexts—for example, word pairs (e.g., states and their capitals, English translations of foreign language words), ordered phrases and sentences (e.g., poems, songs), and meanings for vocabulary words. With the advent of information processing theory, many of the ideas propounded by verbal learning theorists were discarded or substantially modified. Researchers increasingly address learning and memory of context-dependent verbal material (Bruning, Schraw, & Norby, 2011).

Gestalt Theory

Gestalt theory was an early cognitive view of perception that challenged many assumptions of behaviorism. Although Gestalt theory in its original form no longer is viable, it offers important principles that are found in current conceptions of perception and learning (Wagemans et al., 2012a, 2012b).

The Gestalt movement began with a group of psychologists in early 20th-century Germany. In 1912, Max Wertheimer wrote an article on apparent motion (Wagemans et al., 2012a). The article was significant among German psychologists but had no influence in the United States, where the Gestalt movement had not yet begun. The subsequent publication in English of Kurt Koffka's *The Growth of the Mind* (1924) and Wolfgang Köhler's *The Mentality of Apes* (1925) helped the Gestalt movement spread to the United States. Many Gestalt psychologists, including Wertheimer, Koffka, and Köhler, eventually emigrated to the United States, where they applied their ideas to psychological phenomena.

In a typical demonstration of the apparent motion perceptual phenomenon, two lines close together are exposed successively for a fraction of a second with a short time interval between each exposure. An observer sees not two lines but rather a single line moving from the line exposed first toward the line exposed second. The timing of the demonstration is critical. If the time interval between exposures of the two lines is too long, the observer sees the first line and then the second but no motion. If the interval is too short, the observer sees two lines side by side but no motion.

This apparent motion is known as the *phi phenomenon* and demonstrates that subjective experiences cannot be explained by referring to the objective elements involved (Wagemans et al., 2012a). Observers perceive movement even though none occurs. Phenomenological experience (apparent motion) differs from sensory experience (exposure of lines). The attempt to explain these types of phenomena led Wertheimer to challenge psychological explanations of perception as the sum of one's sensory experiences because these explanations did not take into account the unique wholeness of perception.

Meaningfulness of Perception. Imagine that Rebecca is 5 feet tall. When we view Rebecca at a distance, our retinal image is much smaller than when we view her up close. Yet we know that Rebecca is 5 feet tall regardless of how far away she is. Although the perception (retinal image) varies, the meaning of the image remains constant.

The German word *Gestalt* translates as "form," "figure," "shape," or "configuration." A Gestalt is an integrated form—a whole greater than the sum of its parts (Wagemans et al., 2012b). The essence of Gestalt psychology is that objects or events are viewed as organized wholes (Köhler, 1947/1959). The basic organization involves a figure (what one focuses on) against a ground (the background). What is meaningful is the configuration, not the individual parts (Koffka, 1922). A tree is not a random collection of leaves, branches, roots, and trunk; it is a meaningful configuration of these elements. When viewing a tree, people typically do not focus on individual elements but rather on the whole. The human brain transforms objective reality into mental events organized as meaningful wholes. This capacity to view things as wholes is an inborn quality, although perception is modified by experience and training (Köhler, 1947/1959; Leeper, 1935).

Gestalt theory originally applied to perception, but when its European proponents came to the United States, they found an emphasis on learning. In the Gestalt view, learning is a cognitive phenomenon involving reorganizing experiences into different perceptions of things, people, or events (Koffka, 1922, 1926). Much human learning is *insightful*, which means that the transformation from ignorance to knowledge occurs rapidly. When confronted with a problem, individuals figure out what is known and what needs to be determined. They then think about possible solutions. Insight occurs when people suddenly "see" how to solve the problem.

Gestalt theorists disagreed with Watson and other behaviorists about the role of consciousness (Chapter 3). In Gestalt theory, meaningful perception and insight occur only through conscious awareness. Gestalt psychologists also disputed the idea that complex phenomena can be broken into elementary parts. Behaviorists stressed associations—the whole is equal to the sum of the parts. Gestalt psychologists felt that the whole loses meaning when it is reduced to individual components. In the opening scenario, "*x*" lacks meaning unless it can be related to broader categories. Interestingly, Gestalt psychologists agreed with behaviorists in objecting to introspection, but for a different reason. Behaviorists viewed it as an attempt to study consciousness; Gestalt theorists felt it was inappropriate because it tried to separate meaning from perception. Gestalt theory holds that perception is meaningful.

Principles of Organization. Gestalt theory postulates that people use principles to organize their perceptions. Some of the most important principles are figure–ground relation, proximity, similarity, common direction, simplicity, and closure (Figure 5.3; Koffka, 1922; Köhler, 1926, 1947/1959).

The principle of *figure–ground relation* postulates that any perceptual field may be subdivided into a figure against a background. Such salient features as size, shape, color, and

Figure 5.3
Examples of Gestalt
principles.

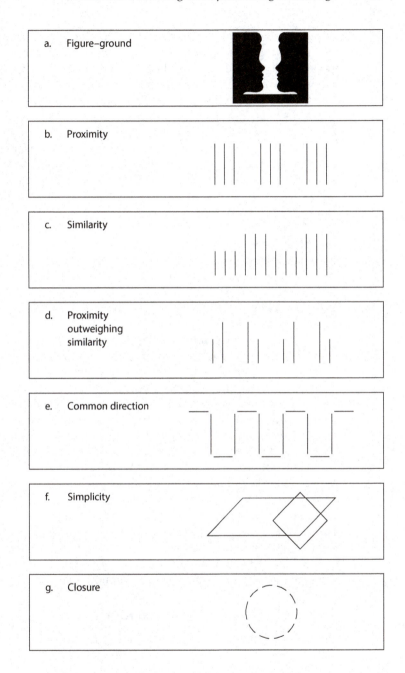

pitch distinguish a figure from its background. When figure and ground are ambiguous, perceivers may alternatively organize the sensory experience one way and then another (Figure 5.3a).

The principle of *proximity* states that elements in a perceptual field are viewed as belonging together according to their closeness to one another in space or time. Most people will view the lines in Figure 5.3b as three groups of three lines each, although other ways of perceiving this configuration are possible. This principle of proximity also is involved in the perception of speech. People hear (organize) speech as a series of words or phrases separated with pauses. When people hear unfamiliar speech sounds (e.g., different languages), they have difficulty discerning pauses.

The principle of *similarity* means that elements similar in aspects such as size or color are perceived as belonging together. Viewing Figure 5.3c, people tend to see a group of three short lines, followed by a group of three long lines, and so on. Proximity can out-weigh similarity; when dissimilar stimuli are closer together than similar ones (Figure 5.3d), the perceptual field tends to be organized into four groups of two lines each.

The principle of *common direction* implies that elements appearing to constitute a pattern or flow in the same direction are perceived as a figure. The lines in Figure 5.3e are most likely to be perceived as forming a distinct pattern. The principle of common direction also applies to an alphabetic or numeric series in which one or more rules define the order of items. Thus, the next letter in the series *abdeghjk* is *m,* as determined by the rule: Beginning with the letter *a* and moving through the alphabet sequentially, list two letters and omit one.

The principle of *simplicity* states that people organize their perceptual fields in simple, regular features and tend to form good Gestalts comprising symmetry and regularity. This idea is captured by the German word *Pragnanz,* which, roughly translated, means "meaningfulness" or "precision." Individuals are most likely to see the visual patterns in Figure 5.3f as one geometrical pattern overlapping another rather than as several irregularly shaped geometric patterns. The principle of *closure* means that people fill in incomplete patterns or experiences. Despite the missing lines in the pattern shown in Figure 5.3g, people tend to complete the pattern and see a meaningful picture.

Although Gestalt concepts can help to explain our perceptions, the principles are general and do not address actual perceptual mechanisms. To say that individuals perceive similar items as belonging together does not explain how they perceive items as similar in the first place. Gestalt principles are illuminating but vague and not explanatory. Furthermore, research does not support some Gestalt predictions. Kubovy and van den Berg (2008) found that the joint effect of proximity and similarity was equal to the sum of their separate effects, not greater than it, as Gestalt theory predicts. Information processing principles are clearer and explain perception better.

Two-Store (Dual) Memory Model

An early information processing model formulated by Atkinson and Shiffrin (1968, 1971) exemplified the possibilities of the new cognitive theoretical perspective (Lehman & Malmberg, 2013). This model proposed two types of information storage: short and long term. Information processing begins when a stimulus (e.g., visual, auditory) impinges on one or more senses (e.g., hearing, sight, touch). The appropriate *sensory register* receives the input and holds it briefly in sensory form. It is here that *perception (pattern recognition)* occurs, which is the process of assigning meaning to a stimulus input. This typically does not involve naming because naming takes time and information stays in the sensory register for only a fraction of a second. Rather, perception involves matching an input to known information.

The sensory register transfers information to *short-term memory (STM)*, which corresponds roughly to awareness or what one is conscious of at a given moment. STM is limited in capacity. Miller (1956) proposed that it holds seven plus or minus two chunks (units) of information. A chunk is a meaningful item: a letter, word, number, or common expression (e.g., "bread and butter"). STM also is limited in duration; for chunks to be retained, they must be rehearsed (repeated). Without rehearsal, information is lost after a few seconds. With development, children are able to hold more and larger chunks of information in memory (Cowan et al., 2010).

While information is in STM, related knowledge in *long-term memory (LTM)*, or permanent memory, is activated and placed in STM to be integrated with the new information. To name all the state capitals beginning with the letter *A*, students recall the names of states—perhaps by region of the country—and scan memory for the names of their capital cities. When students who do not know the capital of Maryland learn "Annapolis," they can store it with "Maryland" in LTM.

It is debatable whether information is lost from LTM (i.e., forgotten). Some researchers contend that it can be, whereas others say that failure to recall reflects a lack of good retrieval cues rather than forgetting. If Sarah cannot recall her third-grade teacher's name (Mapleton), she might be able to if given the hint, "Think of trees." Regardless of theoretical perspective, researchers agree that information remains in LTM for a long time (see Chapter 6).

Control (executive) processes regulate the flow of information throughout the information processing system. Rehearsal is an important control process that occurs in STM. For verbal material, rehearsal takes the form of repeating information aloud or subvocally. Other control processes include coding (putting information into a meaningful context—an issue being discussed in the opening scenario), imaging (visually representing information), implementing decision rules, organizing information, monitoring level of understanding, and using retrieval, self-regulation, and motivational strategies.

The two-store model was a major advance in the field of information processing. Researchers showed that the two-store model could account for many research results. One of the most consistent research findings is that when people have a list of items to learn, they tend to recall best the initial items (*primacy effect*) and the last items (*recency effect*), as portrayed in Figure 5.1. As noted earlier, initial items receive the most rehearsal and are transferred to LTM, whereas the last items are still in STM at the time of recall. Middle items are recalled the most poorly because they are no longer in WM at the time of recall (having been pushed out by subsequent items), they receive fewer rehearsals than initial items, and they are not properly stored in LTM.

Other research suggested, however, that learning may be more complex than the basic two-store model stipulates (Baddeley, 1998). One problem is that this model does not fully specify how information moves from one stage of processing to another. Control processes are central to the model because they manipulate information to serve task demands (Lehman & Malmberg, 2013); however, the notion of control processes is vague. We might ask: Why do some inputs proceed from the sensory registers into STM and others do not? Which mechanisms decide that information has been rehearsed long enough and transfer it into LTM? How is information in LTM selected to be activated? Another concern is that this model seems best suited to handle verbal material. How nonverbal representation occurs with material that may not be readily verbalized, such as modern art and well-established skills, is not clear.

The model also is vague about what really is learned. Consider people learning word lists. With nonsense syllables, they have to learn the words themselves and the positions in which they appear. When they already know the words, they must only learn the positions; for example, "cat" appears in the fourth position, followed by "tree." People must take into account their purpose in learning and modify learning strategies accordingly. What mechanism controls these processes?

Whether all components of the system are used at all times is also an issue. STM is useful when people are acquiring knowledge and need to relate incoming information to knowledge in LTM. But we do many things automatically: get dressed, walk, ride a bicycle, respond to simple requests (e.g., "Do you have the time?"). For many adults, reading (decoding) and simple arithmetic computations are automatic processes that place little demand on cognitive processes. Such automatic processing may not require STM. How does automatic processing develop, and what mechanisms govern it?

These and other issues not addressed well by the two-store model (e.g., the role of motivation in learning and the development of self-regulation) have led to alternative models and modifications to the original model (Matlin, 2009; Nairne, 2002; Radvansky & Ashcraft, 2014). Next we examine levels (or depth) of processing.

Levels (Depth) of Processing

Levels (depth) of processing theory conceptualizes memory according to the type of processing that information receives rather than its location (Craik, 1979; Lockhart, Craik, & Jacoby, 1976; Surprenant & Neath, 2009). This view does not incorporate stages or structural components such as STM or LTM (Surprenant & Neath, 2009). Rather, it proposes different ways to process information (such as levels or depth at which it is processed): physical (surface), acoustic (phonological, sound), semantic (meaning). These three levels are dimensional, with physical processing being the most superficial (such as "*x*" as a symbol devoid of meaning as discussed by the teachers in the introductory scenario) and semantic processing being the deepest. For example, suppose you are reading, and the next word is *wren*. This word can be processed on a surface level (e.g., it is not capitalized), a phonological level (rhymes with *den*), or a semantic level (small bird). Each level represents a more elaborate (deeper) type of processing than the preceding level; processing the meaning of *wren* expands the information content of the item more than acoustic processing, which expands content more than surface-level processing.

These three levels have some conceptual overlap with the sensory register, STM, and LTM of the two-store model. Both views contend that processing becomes more elaborate with succeeding stages or levels. Unlike the two-store model, the levels of processing theory does not assume that the three types of processing constitute stages. In levels of processing, one does not have to move to the next process to engage in more elaborate processing; depth of processing can vary within a level. *Wren* can receive low-level semantic processing (small bird) or more extensive semantic processing (how it is similar to and different from other birds).

Another difference between the two information processing models concerns the order of processing. The two-store model assumes information is processed first by the sensory register, then by STM, and finally by LTM. The levels of processing theory does not make a sequential assumption. To be processed at the meaning level, information does not have to be first processed at the surface and sound levels (beyond what processing is required for information to be received; Lockhart et al., 1976).

The two models also have different views of how type of processing affects memory. In levels of processing, the deeper the level at which an item is processed, the better the memory, because the memory trace is more ingrained. The teachers in the opening scenario are concerned about how they can help students process algebraic information at a deeper level. Once an item is processed at a particular point within a level, additional processing at that point should not improve memory. In contrast, the two-store model contends that memory can be improved with additional processing of the same type. This model predicts that the more a list of items is rehearsed, the better it will be recalled.

Some research evidence supports levels of processing. Craik and Tulving (1975) presented individuals with words. As each word was presented, they were given a question to answer. The questions were designed to facilitate processing at a particular level. For surface processing, people were asked, "Is the word in capital letters?" For phonological processing, they were asked, "Does the word rhyme with *train?*" For semantic processing, "Would the word fit in the sentence, 'He met a _____ in the street'?" The time people spent processing at the various levels was controlled. Their recall was best when items were processed at a semantic level, next best at a phonological level, and worst at a surface level. These results suggest that forgetting is more likely with shallow processing and is not due to loss of information from WM or LTM.

The levels of processing theory implies that student understanding is better when material is processed at deeper levels. Glover, Plake, Roberts, Zimmer, and Palmere (1981) found that asking students to paraphrase ideas while they read essays significantly enhanced recall compared with activities that did not draw on previous knowledge (e.g., identifying key words in the essays). Instructions to read slowly and carefully did not assist students during recall.

Despite these positive findings, the levels of processing theory has problems. One concern is whether semantic processing always is deeper than the other levels. The sounds of some words (*kaput*) are at least as distinctive as their meanings ("ruined"). In fact, recall depends not only on level of processing but also on type of recall task. Morris, Bransford, and Franks (1977) found that, given a standard recall task, semantic coding produced better results than rhyming coding; however, given a recall task emphasizing rhyming, asking rhyming questions during coding produced better recall than semantic questions. Moscovitch and Craik (1976) proposed that deeper processing during learning results in a higher potential memory performance, but that potential will be realized only when conditions at retrieval match those during learning.

Another concern with the levels of processing theory is whether additional processing at the same level produces better recall. Nelson (1977) gave participants one or two repetitions of each stimulus (word) processed at the same level. Two repetitions produced better recall, contrary to the levels of processing hypothesis. Other research shows that additional rehearsal of material facilitates retention, recall, and automaticity of processing (Anderson, 1990; Jacoby, Bartz, & Evans, 1978).

A final issue concerns the nature of a level. Investigators have argued that the notion of depth is fuzzy, both in its definition and measurement (Surprenant & Neath, 2009; Terry, 2009). As a result, we do not know how processing at different levels affects learning and memory (Baddeley, 1978; Nelson, 1977). Time is a poor criterion of level because some surface processing (e.g., "Does the word have the following letter pattern: consonant-vowel-consonant-consonant-vowel-consonant?") can take longer than semantic processing ("Is it a type of bird?"). Neither is processing time within a given level indicative of deeper processing (Baddeley, 1978, 1998). A lack of clear understanding of levels (depth) limits the usefulness of this perspective. We now turn to a contemporary perspective on information processing.

CONTEMPORARY INFORMATION PROCESSING MODEL

A contemporary, generic model of information processing is shown in Figure 5.4. This model bears some similarity to the original Atkinson and Shiffrin (1968, 1971) model, but there are important differences. Based on years of research, the current model reflects key refinements in the operation of the information processing system. This section gives an overview of the model; greater explanation is provided in the sections that follow.

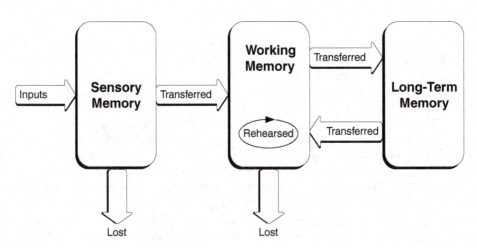

Figure 5.4
Contemporary information processing model.

Unlike the earlier model, the current one is not a stage model. There are phases of information processing such as perceiving and integrating new knowledge into LTM, but the system is dynamic, and rapid shifting among processes is the norm rather than the exception. A second difference is that STM has been dropped as a separate memory in favor of working memory (WM). WM better reflects the dynamic nature of information processing and its interrelated functions with perception and LTM.

Third, the control processes have been dropped. Contemporary information processing theory addresses cognitive and motivational factors—such as goals, beliefs, and values— that focus learners' attention and help them construct and process information in line with their goals, beliefs, and values (Mayer, 2012).

Finally, the contemporary model is less mechanistic and emphasizes the active construction and transformation of knowledge by learners (Mayer, 2012). Learners do not simply react to stimuli that impinge upon them but rather seek information that helps them learn. The current model reflects, in short, a large degree of learner control and self-regulation (see Chapter 10).

The model assumes that information in memory begins as environmental sensory input. Sensory memory only holds information for milliseconds—long enough for the stimulus trace to be processed further. At any moment, a lot of information is bombarding our sensory memories. Most of it is discarded, as much as 99% (Wolfe, 2010). This is desirable as most of it is irrelevant.

Inputs received by sensory memories, except for smells, are sent to the thalamus and then to the specific parts of the cortex designed to process those inputs (see Chapter 2). At this early stage of processing, inputs are transformed from sensory information to perceptions that include meanings. A visual stimulus, for example, goes from being a visual light beam to "light from a flashlight."

Next information is processed in WM. Perceptions are worked on (e.g., rehearsed, thought about) and integrated with information in LTM. Information that receives sufficient attention and rehearsal is processed for transfer to LTM; information that is not adequately processed is lost. Although WM functions may occur in different parts of the brain, the primary area seems to be the prefrontal cortex of the frontal lobe (Wolfe, 2010).

Information that is sufficiently constructed and processed is integrated with knowledge in LTM. Such consolidation occurs by forming or adapting existing neural networks or by strengthening existing ones. The process is dynamic because while WM is integrating with LTM, it also is receiving new sensory inputs. The process also involves much coordination between information processing phases, and a major goal of education is to help learners develop their abilities to coordinate (Schwartz & Goldstone, 2016).

Current information processing theories emphasize learner control. As Mayer (2012) explains: "Meaningful learning occurs when people engage in appropriate cognitive processing during learning, including selecting relevant information, organizing it into coherent mental representations, and integrating representations with each other and with relevant knowledge activated from long-term memory" (p. 89). Compared with earlier views that emphasized knowledge acquisition, contemporary theories stress transformation: knowledge construction by learners or co-construction if others (e.g., teacher, peers) participate in the process (Mayer, 2012). The sections that follow provide elaborated descriptions of the processes discussed so far.

ATTENTION

The word *attention* is heard often in educational settings. *Attention* refers to concentrated mental activity that focuses on a limited amount of information in sensory memory and WM (Matlin, 2009). Teachers and parents complain that students do not pay attention to instruction or directions. (This does not seem to be the problem in the opening scenario; rather, the issue involves meaningfulness of processing.) Even high-achieving students do not always attend to instructionally relevant events. Sights, sounds, smells, tastes, and sensations bombard us; we cannot and should not attend to them all. Because our attentional capabilities are limited, attention can be construed as the process of selecting some of many potential inputs.

Alternatively, attention can refer to a limited human resource expended to accomplish one's goals by powering (i.e., mobilizing and maintaining) cognitive processes (Radvansky & Ashcraft, 2014). Attention is not a bottleneck in the information processing system through which only so much information can pass. Rather, it describes a general limitation on the entire human information processing system.

Although attention always is important, it is not always conscious. Attending to environmental inputs is necessary for them to enter the sensory registers. Some of this attention is conscious, as when learners direct their attention to computer screens. But much is not consciously driven (Dijksterhuis & Aarts, 2010); it is not possible to direct our attention to the multiple inputs that simultaneously impinge on us. And attention is not always selective; our reticular activating systems filter these stimuli, mostly without conscious awareness (Wolfe, 2010). Attention becomes more conscious with increased processing once inputs get to WM (Hübner, Steinhauser, & Lehle, 2010).

The focus here is on conscious attention, which is necessary for learning. Conscious attention affects rehearsal in WM and the processes involved in integrating knowledge into LTM, such as elaboration and organization. This section suggests ways that teachers can help focus students' attention for learning—which, although primarily involving conscious attention, also can help direct the more unconscious aspects of students' attention to inputs relevant to learning.

Theories of Attention

Researchers have explored how people select inputs for attending. In *dichotic listening* tasks, people wear headphones and receive different messages in each ear. They are asked to "shadow" one message (report what they hear); most can do this quite well. In an early study, Cherry (1953) investigated what happened to the unattended message. He found that listeners knew when it was present, whether it was a human voice or a noise, and when it changed from a male to a female voice. They typically did not know what the message was, what words were spoken, which language was being spoken, or whether words were repeated.

Broadbent (1958) proposed a model of attention known as *filter (bottleneck) theory*. In this view, incoming information from the environment is held briefly in a sensory system. Based on their physical characteristics, pieces of information are selected for further processing by the perceptual system. Information not acted on by the perceptual system is filtered out—not processed beyond the sensory system. Attention is selective because of the bottleneck—only some messages receive further processing. In dichotic listening studies, filter theory proposes that listeners select a channel based on their instructions. They know some details about the other message because the physical examination of information occurs prior to filtering.

Subsequent work by Treisman (1960, 1964) identified problems with filter theory. Treisman found that during dichotic listening experiments, listeners routinely shifted their attention between ears depending on the location of the message they were shadowing. If they were shadowing the message coming into their left ear, and if that message suddenly shifted to the right ear, they continued to shadow the original message and not the new message coming into the left ear. Selective attention depends not only on the physical location of the stimulus but also on its meaning.

Treisman (1992; Treisman & Gelade, 1980) proposed a *feature-integration* theory. Sometimes we distribute attention across many sensory inputs, each of which receives low-level processing. At other times, we focus on a particular sensory input, which is more cognitively demanding. Rather than blocking out messages, attention simply makes them less salient than those being attended to. Information inputs initially are subjected to different tests for physical characteristics and content. Following this preliminary analysis, one input may be selected for attention.

Treisman's model is problematic in the sense that much analysis must precede attending to an input, which is puzzling because presumably the original analysis involves some conscious attention. Norman (1976) proposed that all inputs are attended to in sufficient fashion to activate a portion of LTM. At that point, one input is selected for further attention based on the degree of activation, which depends on the context. An input is more likely to be attended to if it fits into the context established by prior inputs. While people read, for example, many outside stimuli impinge on their sensory system, yet they attend to the printed symbols.

In Norman's view, stimuli activate portions of LTM, but attention involves more complete activation. Neisser (1967) suggested that preattentive processes are involved in head and eye movements (e.g., refocusing attention) and in guided movements (e.g., walking, driving). Preattentive processes are automatic—people implement them without conscious mediation. In contrast, attentional processes are deliberate and require conscious activity. In support of this point, Logan (2002) postulated that attention and categorization occur together. As an object is attended to, it is categorized based on information in memory. Attention, categorization, and memory (WM and LTM) are three aspects of deliberate, conscious cognition. Such cognition is important for sustained attention, or maintenance of attention over long periods (Radvansky & Ashcraft, 2014).

Attention and Learning

Sustained attention is critical for learning. In learning to distinguish letters, a child learns the distinctive features: To distinguish *b* from *d*, students must attend to the position of the vertical line on the left or right side of the circle, not to the mere presence of a circle attached to a vertical line. To learn from a teacher, students must attend to the teacher's voice and actions and ignore other inputs. To develop reading comprehension skills, students must attend to the printed words and ignore such irrelevancies as page size and color.

Learners consciously allocate attention to activities as a function of motivation and self-regulation (Kanfer & Ackerman, 1989; Kanfer & Kanfer, 1991). As skills become established, information processing requires less conscious attention. In learning to work multiplication problems, students must attend to each step in the process and check their computations. Once students learn multiplication tables and the algorithm, working problems becomes more automatic.

Differences in the ability to control attention are associated with student age, hyperactivity, and learning problems. Sustained attention is difficult for young children, as is attending to relevant rather than irrelevant information. Children also have difficulty switching attention rapidly from one activity to another. Training programs can help improve children's attention (Wass, Scerif, & Johnson, 2012). The ability to control attention contributes to the improvement of WM (Swanson, 2008). It behooves teachers to forewarn students of the attentional demands required to learn content. Outlines and study guides can serve as advance organizers and cue learners about the types of information that will be important. While students are working, teachers can use prompts, questions, and feedback to help students remain focused on the task (Meece, 2002).

Attention deficits are associated with learning problems. Students with hyperactivity are characterized by excessive motor activity, distractibility, and low academic achievement. They have difficulty focusing and sustaining attention on academic material. They may be unable to block out irrelevant stimuli, which overloads their WMs. Sustaining attention requires that students work in a strategic manner and monitor their level of understanding. Normal achievers and older children sustain attention better than do low achievers and younger learners on tasks requiring strategic processing (Short, Friebert, & Andrist, 1990).

Executive control is the capability to maintain attentional control (Randall, Oswald, & Beier, 2014). This means maintaining attention on task-relevant information and not attending to task-irrelevant information. Executive control of attention is an important component of self-regulation (Chapter 10). Children who have difficulties with executive attentional control are apt to show learning difficulties.

Teachers can identify attentive students by noting their eye focus, their ability to begin working on cue (after directions are completed), and physical signs (e.g., writing, keyboarding) indicating they are engaged in work. But physical signs alone may not be sufficient; strict teachers can keep students sitting quietly even though students may not be engaged in classwork.

Teachers can promote student attention to relevant material through the design of classroom activities (Application 5.1). Eye-catching displays or actions at the start of lessons engage student attention. Teachers who move around the classroom help sustain student attention on the task. Other suggestions for focusing and maintaining student attention are given in Table 5.1.

Meaning and Importance

We are more likely to attend to inputs that have meaning than to those with less meaning (Wolfe, 2010). When sensory inputs enter WM, it attempts to find related information in LTM. If nothing relevant can be found, attention is likely to wane and be directed toward other inputs. The important role of meaningfulness in learning is exemplified in the opening vignette and discussed later in this chapter.

APPLICATION 5.1
Maintaining Student Attention

Various practices help keep classrooms from becoming predictable and repetitive, which decreases attention. Teachers can vary their presentations, materials used, student activities, and personal qualities such as dress and mannerisms. Lesson formats for young children should be kept short. Teachers can sustain a high level of activity through student involvement and by moving about to check on student progress.

As Ms. Keeling begins a language arts activity in her third-grade class, she asks students to point to the location of the activity in their books. She varies how she introduces activities: Sometimes she organizes students into small groups, whereas at other times, they work individually. She also varies how students' answers are checked. Students might use hand signals or respond in unison, or individual students can answer and explain their answers. As students independently complete the exercise, she moves about the room, checks students' progress, and assists those having difficulty learning or maintaining task focus.

A music teacher might increase student attention by using vocal exercises, singing certain selections, using instruments to complement the music, and adding movement to instruments. The teacher might combine activities or vary their sequence. Small tasks also can be varied to increase attention, such as the way a new music selection is introduced. The teacher might play the entire selection, then model by singing the selection, and then involve the students in the singing. Alternatively, for the last activity the teacher could divide the selection into parts, work on each of the small sections, and then combine these sections to complete the full selection.

Perceived importance also can help direct and sustain conscious attention. In reading, for example, students are more likely to recall important text elements than less important

Table 5.1
Ways to focus and maintain student attention.

Device	Implementation
Signals	Signal to students at the start of lessons or when they are to change activities.
Movement	Move while presenting material to the whole class. Move around the room while students are engaged in seat work.
Variety	Use different materials and teaching aids. Use gestures. Do not speak in a monotone.
Interest	Introduce lessons with stimulating material. Appeal to students' interests at other times during the lesson.
Questions	Ask students to explain a point in their own words. Stress that they are responsible for their own learning.

ones (Grabe, 1986). Both good and poor readers locate important material and attend to it for longer periods (Ramsel & Grabe, 1983; Reynolds & Anderson, 1982). What distinguishes these readers is subsequent processing and comprehension. Perhaps poor readers, being more preoccupied with basic reading tasks (e.g., decoding), become distracted from important material and do not process it adequately for retention and retrieval. While attending to important material, good readers may be more apt to rehearse it, make it meaningful, and relate it to knowledge in LTM, all of which improve comprehension (Resnick, 1981).

The importance of text material can affect subsequent recall through differential attention (R. Anderson, 1982). Text elements apparently are processed at some minimal level so importance can be assessed. Based on this evaluation, the text element either is dismissed in favor of the next element (unimportant information) or receives additional attention (important information). Assuming attention is sufficient, the types of processing students engage in are likely to differ, which can affect comprehension. Better readers engage in automatic text processing more often than poorer readers.

PERCEPTION

Perception (or pattern recognition) refers to attaching meaning to environmental inputs received through the senses. For an input to be perceived, it must register in one or more of the sensory registers and be transferred to the appropriate brain structure. The input then is compared to knowledge in LTM. Sensory registers and the comparison process are discussed in this section.

Sensory Registers

Environmental inputs are received through the senses: vision, hearing, touch, smell, and taste. Each sense has its own register (or memory) that holds information briefly in the same form in which it is received (Wolfe, 2010). Information stays in the sensory register (memory) for less than 0.25 seconds (Mayer, 2012). Some sensory input is transferred to WM for further processing. Other input is lost and replaced by new input. The sensory registers operate in parallel fashion because several senses can be engaged simultaneously and independently of one another. The two sensory memories that have been most extensively explored are *iconic* (vision) and *echoic* (hearing).

In a typical experiment to investigate iconic memory, a researcher presents learners with rows of letters briefly (e.g., 50 milliseconds) and asks them to report as many as they remember. They commonly report only four to five letters from an array. Early work by Sperling (1960) provided insight into iconic memory. Sperling briefly presented learners with rows of letters and then cued them to report letters from a particular row. Sperling estimated that, after exposure to the array, they could recall about nine letters. Sensory memory could hold more information than was previously believed, but while participants were recalling letters, the traces of other letters quickly faded. Sperling also found that recall was poorer when there was more time between the end of a presentation of the array and the beginning of recall. This finding supports the idea that the loss of a stimulus from a sensory register involves *trace decay*. Sakitt (1976; Sakitt & Long, 1979) argued that the icon is located in the rods of the eye's retina. It is debatable whether the icon is a memory store or a persisting image.

There is evidence for an echoic memory similar in function to iconic memory (Matlin, 2009). Early studies (e.g., Darwin, Turvey, & Crowder, 1972) yielded results comparable to Sperling's (1960). Research participants heard three or four sets of recordings simultaneously and then were asked to report one. Findings showed that echoic memory is capable of holding more information than can be recalled. Similar to iconic information, traces of echoic information rapidly decay following removal of stimuli. The echoic decay is not quite as rapid as the iconic, but periods beyond 2 seconds between cessation of stimulus presentation and onset of recall produce poorer recall.

LTM Comparisons

Perception occurs through bottom-up (data-driven) and top-down (conceptually driven) processing (Radvansky & Ashcraft, 2014). In *bottom-up processing*, inputs received by sensory registers are transferred to WM for comparisons with information in LTM to assign meanings beyond the physical properties. Environmental inputs have tangible physical properties. Assuming normal color vision, everyone who looks at a yellow tennis ball will recognize it as a yellow object, but only those familiar with tennis will recognize it as a tennis ball. The types of information people have acquired account for the different meanings they assign to objects.

Perception is affected not only by objective characteristics but also by prior experiences and expectations. *Top-down processing* refers to the influence of our knowledge and beliefs on perception (Radvansky & Ashcraft, 2014). Motivation also is important. Perception is affected by what we wish and hope to perceive (Balcetis & Dunning, 2006). We often perceive what we expect and fail to perceive what we do not expect. Have you ever thought you heard your name spoken, only to realize that another name was being called? While waiting to meet a friend at a public place or to pick up an order in a restaurant, you may hear your name because you expect to hear it. Also, people may not perceive things whose appearance has changed or that occur out of context. You may not recognize persons from work or school you meet at the beach because you do not expect to see them dressed in beach attire. Top-down processing often occurs with ambiguous stimuli or those that register briefly (e.g., a stimulus spotted in the "corner of the eye").

An information processing theory of perception is *template matching*, which holds that people store *templates*, or miniature copies of stimuli, in LTM. When they encounter a stimulus, they compare it with existing templates and identify it if a match is found. This view is appealing but problematic. People would need millions of templates stored in LTM to recognize everyone and everything in their environment. Such a large stock would exceed the brain's capability. Template theory also does a poor job of accounting for stimulus variations. Chairs, for example, come in all sizes, shapes, colors, and designs; hundreds of templates would be needed just to perceive a chair.

The problems with templates can be solved by assuming that they can have some variation. Prototype theory addresses this. *Prototypes* are abstract forms that include the basic ingredients of stimuli (Matlin, 2009; Rosch, 1973). Prototypes are stored in LTM and are compared with encountered stimuli that are subsequently identified based on the prototype they match or resemble in form, smell, sound, and so on. Some research supports the existence of prototypes (Franks & Bransford, 1971; Posner & Keele, 1968; Rosch, 1973).

A major advantage of prototypes over templates is that each stimulus has only one prototype instead of countless variations; thus, identification of a stimulus should be easier because comparing it with several templates is not necessary. One issue with prototypes concerns the amount of acceptable stimulus variability; that is, how closely a stimulus must match a prototype to be identified as an instance of that prototype.

A variation of the prototype model involves *feature analysis* (Radvansky & Ashcraft, 2014). One learns the critical features of stimuli and stores these in LTM as images or verbal codes (Markman, 1999). When an input enters the sensory register, its features are compared with memorial representations. If enough of the features match, the stimulus is identified. For a chair, the critical features may be legs, seat, and a back. Many other features (e.g., color, size) are irrelevant. Any exceptions to the basic features need to be learned (e.g., bleacher and beanbag chairs that have no legs). Unlike the prototype analysis, information stored in memory is not an abstract representation of a chair but rather a set of critical features. One advantage of feature analysis is that each stimulus does not have just one prototype, which partially addresses the concern about the amount of acceptable variability. There is empirical research support for feature analysis (Matlin, 2009).

Regardless of how LTM comparisons are made, research evidence supports the idea that perception depends on bottom-up and top-down processing (Matlin, 2009; Resnick, 1985). In reading, for example, bottom-up processing analyzes features and builds a meaningful representation to identify stimuli. Beginning readers typically use bottom-up processing when they encounter letters and new words and attempt to sound them out. People also use bottom-up processing when experiencing unfamiliar stimuli (e.g., handwriting).

But reading would proceed slowly if all perception required analyzing features in detail. In top-down processing, individuals develop expectations regarding perception based on the context. Skilled readers build a mental representation of the context while reading and expect certain words and phrases in the text (Resnick, 1985). Effective top-down processing depends on extensive prior knowledge. We now turn to a discussion of encoding, a key process that occurs in WM.

ENCODING

Encoding refers to the process of putting new incoming information into the information processing system and preparing it for integration and storage in LTM. Once an input has been attended to, processed by sensory memory, and perceived, it enters WM. This section discusses WM and the influences on encoding.

Working Memory (WM)

WM is our memory of immediate consciousness, or the information that currently is held in one's mind (Cowan, 2014). Although WM functions may occur in different parts of the brain depending on the task to be performed, its primary activity seems to reside in the prefrontal cortex of the frontal lobe (Gazzaniga et al., 1998; Wolfe, 2010). Some researchers (e.g., Baddeley, 2012) distinguish WM from STM, with the latter referring to the temporary storage of information and the former to storage and manipulation of knowledge. WM is "working" because it manages, manipulates, and transforms information from STM and LTM (Fenesi, Sana, Kim, & Shore, 2015). In this text, the term "WM" is used because both WM and sensory memory are of short-term duration.

WM performs two critical functions: maintenance and retrieval (Baddeley, 1998, 2007. 2012; Radvansky & Ashcraft, 2014; Unsworth & Engle, 2007). Incoming information is maintained in an active state for a short time and is worked on by being rehearsed or related to information retrieved from LTM. As you read, WM holds for a few seconds the last words or sentences you read. You might try to remember a particular point by repeating it several times (rehearsal) or by asking how it relates to a topic discussed earlier (relate to information in LTM). As another example, assume that a student is multiplying 45 by 7. WM holds these numbers (45 and 7), along with the product of 5 and 7 (35), the number carried (3), and the answer (315). The information in WM ($5 \times 7 = ?$) is compared with activated knowledge in LTM ($5 \times 7 = 35$). Also activated in LTM is the multiplication algorithm, and these procedures direct the student's actions.

WM often functions as a conduit for information to be transferred to or integrated with knowledge in LTM. But sometimes WM is the final destination for information, especially information that we use immediately. For example, if a friend verbalizes to you a phone number to call, you hold it in WM long enough to enter it on your phone. In this case, LTM is essentially "outsourced" to your phone.

The contemporary perspective on WM expands upon the limited conception of STM in early models, which was viewed primarily as a storage site. In current WM theories, WM both maintains and processes information (Barrouillet, Portrat, & Camos, 2011).

Research has provided a reasonably detailed picture of the operation of WM. WM is *limited in duration*: If not acted upon quickly, information in WM is lost. In a classic study (Peterson & Peterson, 1959), participants were presented with a nonsense syllable (e.g., *khv*), after which they performed an arithmetic task before attempting to recall the syllable. The purpose of the arithmetic task was to prevent learners from rehearsing the syllable, but because the numbers did not have to be stored, they did not interfere with storage of the syllable in WM. The longer participants spent on the distracting activity, the poorer was their recall of the nonsense syllable. These findings imply that WM is fragile; information is quickly lost if not learned well. If in the preceding example you were distracted before entering the number in your phone, you may not be able to recall it.

WM also is *limited in capacity*: It can hold only a small amount of information. Miller (1956) suggested that the capacity of WM is seven plus or minus two items, where items are such meaningful units as words, letters, numbers, and common expressions. One can increase the amount of information by *chunking*, or combining information in a meaningful fashion. The phone number 555-1960 consists of seven items, but it can easily be chunked into two items as follows: "Triple 5 plus the year Kennedy was elected president."

Sternberg's (1969) research on *memory scanning* provides insight into how information is retrieved from WM. Participants were presented rapidly with a small number of digits that did not exceed the capacity of WM. They then were given a test digit and were asked whether it was in the original set. Because the learning was easy, participants rarely made errors; however, as the original set increased from two to six items, the time to respond increased about 40 milliseconds per additional item. Sternberg concluded that people retrieve information from active memory by successively scanning items.

Baddeley (1998, 2001, 2012) developed a WM model that includes a phonological loop, visuo-spatial sketch pad, and central executive (Figure 5.5). The phonological loop processes auditory (speech-based) information and keeps it active through rehearsal. The visuo-spatial sketch pad is responsible for establishing and maintaining visual information (images). Presumably there are additional sensory functions performed in WM (i.e., taste, smell, touch), but the visual and auditory have received the most research attention. The central executive is essentially a controller of attention. This is critical for learning, since much learning requires sustained task attention.

The *central executivee* directs the processing of information in WM, as well as the movement of knowledge into and out of WM (Baddeley, 1998, 2001, 2012). The middle part of Figure 5.5 is a type of *episodic buffer*, where information from multiple modalities can be integrated. This area acts as a buffer when it links the information in WM, as well as WM with perception and LTM (Baddeley, 2012).

In addition to focusing attention, the central executive divides attention as needed between two or more inputs (e.g., visual and auditory) and controls switching between tasks when necessary (Baddeley, 2012). The central executive also interfaces with LTM and is goal directed; it selects information relevant to people's plans and intentions from the sensory registers. Information deemed important is rehearsed. Rehearsal can maintain information in WM and improve recall (Baddeley, 2001; Rundus, 1971).

Environmental or self-generated cues activate a portion of LTM, which then is more accessible to WM. This activated memory holds a representation of events occurring recently, such as a description of the context and the content. It is debatable whether active memory constitutes a separate memory store or merely an activated portion of LTM. Some researchers also have postulated that WM is not a separate memory but rather the activated portion of LTM (Cowan, 1999; Schweppe & Rummer, 2014). In this activation view, rehearsal keeps information in WM. In the absence of rehearsal, information is lost with the passage of time (Nairne, 2002). There is high interest in the operation of WM, and researchers continue to explore its processes (Baddeley, 2012; Davelaar, Goshen-Gottstein, Ashkenazi, Haarmann, & Usher, 2005).

Figure 5.5
Model of working memory.
(Baddeley, 1998)

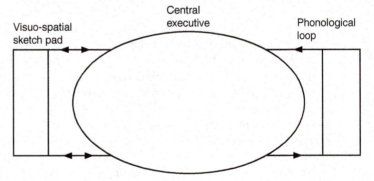

WM plays a critical role in learning. Compared with normally achieving students, those with mathematical and reading disabilities show poorer WM operation (Andersson & Lyxell, 2007; Mastropieri & Scruggs, 2018; Pimperton & Nation, 2014; Swanson, 2016). Like other information processing functions, WM improves with development (Simmering, 2012). Executive processing of information becomes more efficient (Swanson, 2011). The capacity for maintenance (e.g., rehearsal) develops (Gaillard, Barrovillet, Jarrold, & Camos, 2011; Jarrold & Hall, 2013), as does the capability to keep goals in mind (Marcovitch, Boseovski, Knapp, & Kane, 2010). The executive function of WM bears a positive relation to problem solving (Chapter 7; Swanson & Fung, 2016).

A key instructional implication is not to overload students' WMs by presenting too much material at once or too rapidly (see the section on Cognitive Load later in this chapter). Where appropriate, teachers can present information visually and verbally to ensure that students retain it in WM sufficiently long enough to further cognitively process it (e.g., relate to information in LTM). Although the capacity of WM is limited (Cowan, Rouder, Blume, & Saults, 2012), its capacity can be improved through training (Schwaighofer, Fischer, & Bühner, 2015), such as by using span tasks where learners are asked to recall increasingly longer lists. The attentional control processes of WM also can be enhanced through training (Shipstead, Redick, & Engle, 2012).

Influences on Encoding

Encoding begins in WM and is accomplished by constructing new knowledge that is meaningful and then integrating it with knowledge in LTM. Although information need not be meaningful to be learned—one unfamiliar with geometry could memorize the Pythagorean theorem without understanding what it means—meaningfulness improves learning and retention.

Attending to and perceiving stimuli do not ensure that information processing will continue. Many things teachers say in class go unlearned (even though students attend to the teacher and the words are meaningful) because students do not continue to process the information in WM and encode it. Important factors that influence encoding are elaboration and organization (Figure 5.4), which help to form schemas.

Elaboration. *Elaboration* is the process of expanding upon new information by adding to it or linking it to what one knows. Elaborations assist encoding and retrieval because they link the to-be-remembered information with other knowledge. Recently learned information is easier to access in this expanded memory network. Even when the new information is forgotten, people often can recall the elaborations (Anderson, 1990). As the introductory vignette illustrates, a problem that many students have in learning algebra is that they cannot elaborate the material because it is abstract and does not easily link with other knowledge.

Rehearsing information keeps it in WM but does not necessarily elaborate it. A distinction can be drawn between *maintenance rehearsal* (repeating information over and over) and *elaborative rehearsal* (relating new information to something already known). Students learning U.S. history can simply repeat "D-Day was June 6, 1944," or they can elaborate it by relating it to something they know (e.g., In 1944, Roosevelt was elected president for the fourth time). With development, children become more proficient at elaborative rehearsal, which is desirable because it leads to better recall than maintenance rehearsal (Lehmann & Hasselhorn, 2010).

Mnemonic strategies (see Chapter 10) elaborate information in different ways. Once such strategy is to form the first letters into a meaningful sentence. For example, to remember the order of the planets from the sun you might learn the sentence, "*My very educated mother just served us nectarines,*" in which the first letters correspond to those of the planets (*M*ercury, *V*enus, *E*arth, *M*ars, *J*upiter, *S*aturn, *U*ranus, *N*eptune). You recall the sentence and then reconstruct planetary order based on the first letters.

Students may be able to devise elaborations, but if they cannot, they do not need to labor needlessly when teachers can provide effective elaborations. To assist storage in memory and retrieval, elaborations must make sense. Elaborations that are too unusual may not be remembered. Precise, sensible elaborations facilitate memory and recall.

Organization. Gestalt theory and research showed that well-organized material is easier to learn and recall (Katona, 1940). Miller (1956) argued that learning is enhanced by classifying and grouping bits of information into organized chunks. Memory research demonstrates that even when items to be learned are not organized, people often impose organization on the material, which facilitates recall (Matlin, 2009). Organized material improves memory because items are linked to one another systematically. Recall of one item prompts recall of items linked to it. Organization is effective for encoding among children and adults (Basden, Basden, Devecchio, & Anders, 1991).

One way to organize material is to use a hierarchy into which pieces of information are integrated. Figure 5.6 shows a sample hierarchy for animals. The animal kingdom as a

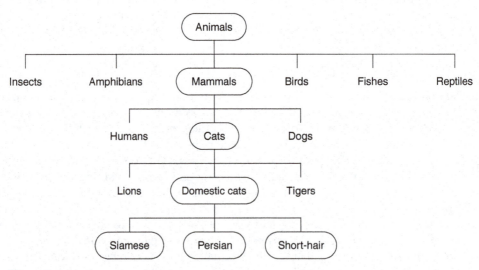

Figure 5.6
Memory network with hierarchical organization.

whole is on top, and underneath are the major categories (e.g., mammals, birds, reptiles). Individual species are found on the next level, followed by breeds.

Other ways of organizing information include the use of mnemonic strategies (Chapter 10) and mental imagery (Chapter 6). Mnemonics enable learners to enrich or elaborate material, such as by forming the first letters of words to be learned into an acronym, familiar phrase, or sentence (Matlin, 2009). Some mnemonic techniques employ imagery; in remembering two words (e.g., *honey* and *bread*), one might imagine them interacting with each other (honey on bread). Using audiovisuals in instruction can improve students' imagery.

Schemas. Elaboration and organization help to form schemas. A *schema* (plural *schemas* or *schemata*) is a structure that organizes large amounts of information into a meaningful system. Schemas include our generalized knowledge about situations (Matlin, 2009). Schemas are plans we learn and use during our environmental interactions. Larger units are needed to organize propositions representing bits of information into a coherent whole (Anderson, 1990). Schemas assist us in generating and controlling routine sequential actions (Cooper & Shallice, 2006).

In a classic study, Bartlett (1932) found that schemas aid in comprehending information. A participant read a story about an unfamiliar culture, after which this person reproduced it for a second participant, who reproduced it for a third participant, and so on. By the time the story reached the 10th person, its unfamiliar context had been changed to one that participants were familiar with (e.g., a fishing trip). Bartlett found that as stories were repeated, they changed in predictable ways. Unfamiliar information was dropped, a few details were retained, and the stories became more like participants' experiences. They altered incoming information to fit their pre-existing schemas.

Any well-ordered sequence can be represented as a schema. One type of schema is "going to a restaurant." The steps consist of activities such as being seated at a table, looking over a menu, ordering food, being served, having dishes picked up, receiving a bill, leaving a tip, and paying the bill. Schemas are important because they indicate what to expect in a situation. People recognize a problem when reality and schema do not match. Have you ever been in a restaurant where one of the expected steps did not occur (e.g., you received a menu, but no one returned to take your order)?

Common educational schemas involve laboratory procedures, studying, and comprehending stories. When given material to read, students activate the type of schema they believe is required. If students are to read a passage and answer questions about main ideas, they may periodically stop and quiz themselves on what they believe are the main points (Resnick, 1985). Schemas have been investigated extensively in research on reading and writing (McVee, Dunsmore, & Gavelek, 2005).

Schemas assist encoding because they help elaborate new knowledge and integrate it into an organized, meaningful structure. When learning material, students attempt to fit information into the schema's spaces. Less important or optional schema elements may not be learned. In reading works of literature, students who have formed the schema for a tragedy can fit the characters and actions of the story into the schema. They expect to find elements such as good versus evil, human frailties, and a dramatic

APPLICATION 5.2
Schemas

Teachers can increase learning by helping students develop schemas. A schema is helpful when learning can occur by applying an ordered sequence of steps. An elementary teacher might teach the following schema to his or her children to assist their reading of unfamiliar words:

- Read the word in the sentence to see what might make sense.
- Look at the beginning and ending of the word—reading the beginning and the ending is easier than the whole word.
- Think of words that would make sense in the sentence and that would have the same beginning and ending.
- Sound out all the letters in the word.
- If these steps do not help identify the word, look it up in a dictionary.

With some modifications, this schema can be used by students of any age.

Teachers might help their students learn to use a schema to locate answers to questions listed at the end of chapters, such as the following:

- Read through all of the questions.
- Read the chapter completely once.
- Reread the questions.
- Reread the chapter slowly and mark a section that seems to fit with one of the questions.
- Go back and match each question with an answer.
- When you find the answer, write it and the question on your paper.
- If you cannot find an answer, use your index to locate key words in the question.
- If you still cannot locate the answer, ask the teacher for help.

denouement. When these events occur, they are fit into the schema students have activated for the story (Application 5.2).

Schemas may facilitate recall independently of their benefits on encoding. Anderson and Pichert (1978) presented college students with a story about two boys skipping school. Students were advised to read it from the perspective of either a burglar or a home buyer; the story had elements relevant to both. Students recalled the story and later recalled it a second time. For the second recall, half of the students were advised to use their original perspective and the other half the other perspective. On the second recall, students recalled more information relevant to the second perspective but not to the first perspective and less information unimportant to the second perspective that was important to the first perspective. Kardash, Royer, and Greene (1988) also found that schemas exerted their primary benefits at the time of recall rather than at encoding. Collectively, these results suggest that at retrieval, people recall a schema and attempt to fit elements into it. This reconstruction may not be accurate but will include most schema elements. *Production systems* (discussed later) bear some similarity to schemas.

LONG-TERM MEMORY: STORAGE

Although our knowledge about LTM is limited because we do not have a window into the brain, neuroscience and psychological research has painted a reasonably consistent picture of the storage process. The characterization of LTM in this chapter involves a structure with knowledge being represented as locations or nodes in networks, with networks connected (associated) with one another. Note the similarity between these cognitive networks and the neural networks discussed in Chapter 2. When discussing networks, we deal primarily with declarative knowledge and procedural knowledge. Conditional knowledge is covered in Chapter 7, along with metacognitive activities that monitor and direct cognitive processing. It is assumed that most knowledge is stored in LTM in verbal codes, but the role of imagery also is addressed in Chapter 6.

Propositions

The Nature of Propositions. Propositions are the basic units of knowledge and meaning in LTM (Anderson, 1990; Kosslyn, 1984). A *proposition* is the smallest unit of information that can be judged true or false (Radvansky & Ashcraft, 2014). Each of the following is a proposition:

- The Declaration of Independence was signed in 1776.
- $2 + 2 = 4$.
- Aunt Frieda hates turnips.
- I'm good in math.
- The main characters are introduced early in a story.

These sample propositions can be judged true or false. Note, however, that people may disagree on their judgments. Carlos may believe that he is bad in math, but his teacher may believe that he is very good. The criterion for a proposition is not objective truth but rather whether a true or false judgment is possible.

The exact nature of propositions is not well understood. Although they can be thought of as sentences, it is more likely that they are meanings of sentences. Research supports the point that we store information in memory as propositions rather than as complete sentences. Kintsch (1974) gave participants sentences to read that were of the same length but varied in the number of propositions they contained. The more propositions contained in a sentence, the longer it took participants to comprehend it. This finding implies that, although students can generate the sentence, "The Declaration of Independence was signed in 1776," what they most likely have stored in memory is a proposition containing only the essential information (Declaration of Independence—signed—1776). With certain exceptions (e.g., memorizing a poem), it seems that people usually store meanings rather than precise wordings.

Propositions form networks that are composed of individual nodes or locations. Nodes can be thought of as individual words, although their exact nature is unknown but probably abstract. For example, students taking a history class likely have a "history class" network comprising such nodes as "text," "teacher," "location," "name of student sitting on their left," and so forth.

Propositional Networks. Propositions are formed according to a set of rules. Researchers disagree on which rules constitute the set, but they generally believe that rules combine nodes into propositions and, in turn, propositions into higher-order structures or *networks*, which are sets of interrelated propositions.

Anderson's *ACT theory* (Anderson, 1990, 1993, 1996, 2000; Anderson et al., 2004; Anderson, Reder, & Lebiere, 1996; Anderson, Zhang, Borst, & Walsh, 2016) proposes an *ACT-R (Adaptive Control of Thought-Rational)* network model of LTM with a propositional structure. ACT-R is a model of cognitive architecture that attempts to explain how all components of the mind work together to produce coherent cognition (Anderson et al., 2004). A proposition is formed by combining two nodes with a *subject–predicate link,* or association; one node constitutes the subject and another node the predicate. Examples are (implied information in parentheses): "Fred (is) rich" and "Shopping (takes) time." A second type of association is the *relation–argument link,* where the relation is verb (in meaning) and the argument is the recipient of the relation or what is affected by the relation. Examples are "eat cake" and "solve puzzles." Relation arguments can serve as subjects or predicates to form complex propositions. Examples are "Fred eat(s) cake," and "solv(ing) puzzles (takes) time."

Propositions are interrelated when they share a common element. Common elements allow people to solve problems, cope with environmental demands, draw analogies, and so on. Without common elements, transfer would not occur; all knowledge would be stored separately, and information processing would be slow. One would not recognize that knowledge relevant to one domain is also relevant to other domains.

Figure 5.7 shows an example of a propositional network. The common element is "cat" because it is part of the propositions, "The cat walked across the front lawn," and "The cat caught a mouse." One can imagine that the former proposition is linked with other propositions relating to houses, whereas the latter is linked with propositions about mice.

Evidence suggests that propositions are organized in hierarchical structures. Collins and Quillian (1969) showed that people store information at the highest level of generality. For example, the LTM network for "animal" would be stored at the highest level with such facts as "moves" and "eats." Under this category would come such species as "birds" and "fish." Stored under "birds" are "has wings," "can fly," and "has feathers" (although there are exceptions—chickens are birds but they do not fly). The fact that birds eat and move

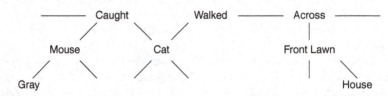

Figure 5.7
Sample propositional network.

is not stored at the level of "bird" because that information is stored at the higher level of animal. Collins and Quillian found that retrieval times increased the farther apart concepts were stored in memory.

The hierarchical organization idea has been modified by research showing that information is not always hierarchical. Thus, "collie" is closer to "mammal" than to "animal" in an animal hierarchy, but people are quicker to agree that a collie is an animal than to agree that it is a mammal (Rips, Shoben, & Smith, 1973).

Furthermore, familiar information may be stored both with its concept and at the highest level of generality (Anderson, 1990). If you have a bird feeder and you often watch birds eating, you might have "eat" stored with both "birds" and "animals." This finding does not detract from the central idea that propositions are organized and interconnected. Although some knowledge may be hierarchically organized, much information is probably organized in a less systematic fashion in propositional networks.

Storage of Knowledge

Declarative Knowledge. The major types of knowledge are declarative and procedural (Figure 5.4). *Declarative knowledge*, or knowing that something is the case, includes facts, beliefs, opinions, generalizations, theories, hypotheses, and attitudes and beliefs about oneself, others, and world events (Gupta & Cohen, 2002; Paris, Lipson, & Wixson, 1983). It is acquired when a new proposition is stored in LTM, usually in a related propositional network (Anderson, 1990). ACT theory postulates that declarative knowledge is represented in chunks comprising the basic information plus related categories (Anderson, 1996; Anderson, Reder, & Lebiere, 1996).

The storage process operates as follows. First, the learner receives new information, such as when the teacher makes a statement or the learner reads a sentence. Next, the new information is parsed into one or more propositions in the learner's WM. At the same time, related propositions in LTM are activated. The new propositions are associated with the related propositions in WM through the process of spreading activation (discussed in the following section). As this point, learners might generate additional propositions. Finally, all the new propositions—those received and those generated by the learner—are stored together in LTM (Hayes-Roth & Thorndyke, 1979).

Figure 5.8 illustrates this process. Assume that a teacher is presenting a unit on the U.S. Constitution and says to the class, "The vice president of the United States serves as president of the Senate but does not vote unless there is a tie." This statement may activate other propositional knowledge stored in students' memories relating to the vice president (e.g., elected with the president, becomes president when the president dies or resigns, can be impeached for crimes of treason) and the Senate (e.g., 100 members, two elected from each state, 6-year terms). Putting these propositions together, the students should infer that the vice president would vote if 50 senators voted for a bill and 50 voted against it.

Storage problems can occur when students have no pre-existing propositions with which to link new information. Students who have not heard of the U.S. Constitution or do not know what a constitution is will draw a blank when they hear the word for the first time. Conceptually meaningless information can be stored in LTM, but students learn

Statement:
"The vice president of the United States serves as president of the Senate but does not vote unless there is a tie."

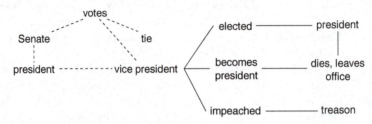

Figure 5.8
Storage of declarative knowledge.
Note: Dotted lines represent new knowledge; solid lines indicate knowledge in long-term memory.

better when new information is related to something they know. Showing students a copy of the U.S. Constitution or relating it to something they have studied (e.g., Declaration of Independence) gives them a referent to link with the new information.

Even when students have studied related material, they may not automatically link it with new information. Often the links need to be made explicit. When discussing the function of the vice president in the Senate, teachers could remind students of the composition of the U.S. Senate and the other roles of the vice president. Propositions sharing a common element are linked in LTM only if they are active in WM simultaneously. This point helps to explain why students might fail to see how new material relates to old material, even though the link is clear to the teacher. Instruction that best establishes propositional networks in learners' minds incorporates review, organization of material, and reminders of things they know but are not thinking of now.

As with many memory processes, meaningfulness, organization, and elaboration facilitate storing information in memory. Meaningfulness is important because meaningful information can be easily associated with pre-existing information in memory. Consequently, less rehearsal is necessary, which saves space and time spent in WM. The students being discussed in the opening scenario are having a problem making algebra meaningful, and the teachers express their frustration at not teaching the content in a meaningful fashion.

A study by Bransford and Johnson (1972) provides a dramatic illustration of the role of meaningfulness in storage and comprehension. Consider the following passage:

> The procedure is actually quite simple. First you arrange things into different groups. Of course, one pile may be sufficient depending on how much there is to do. If you have to go somewhere else due to lack of facilities that is the next step, otherwise you are pretty well set. It is important not to overdo things. That is, it is better to do too few things at once than too many. In the short run this may not seem important, but complications can easily arise. A mistake can be expensive as well. At first the whole procedure will seem complicated. Soon, however, it will become just another facet of life. It is difficult to foresee any end to the necessity for this task in the immediate future, but then one never can tell. After the procedure is completed one

arranges the materials into different groups again. Then they can be put into their appropriate places. Eventually they will be used once more and the whole cycle will then have to be repeated. However, that is part of life. (p. 722)

Without prior knowledge this passage is difficult to comprehend and store in memory because relating it to existing knowledge in memory is hard to do. However, knowing that it is about "washing clothes" makes remembering and comprehension easier. Bransford and Johnson found that students who knew the topic recalled about twice as much as those who were unaware of it. The importance of meaningfulness in learning has been demonstrated in many research studies (e.g., Anderson, 1990; Mayer, 2012).

Organization facilitates storage because well-organized material is easier to relate to pre-existing memory networks than is poorly organized material (Anderson, 1990). To the extent that material can be organized into a hierarchical arrangement, it provides a ready structure to be accepted into LTM. For example, Kauffman and Kiewra (2010) found that presenting information to be learned in the form of a matrix (i.e., a two-dimensional cross-classification table where topics are compared on one or more categories) facilitated college students' memory storage and retrieval. Without an existing LTM network, creating a new LTM network is easier with well-organized information than with poorly organized information.

Elaboration improves storage because it helps learners relate information to something they know (Radvansky & Ashcraft, 2014). Through spreading activation, the elaborated material may be quickly linked with information in memory. For example, a teacher might be discussing the Mt. Etna volcano. Students who can elaborate that knowledge by relating it to their personal knowledge of volcanoes (e.g., Mt. St. Helens) will be able to associate the new and old information in memory and better retain the new material.

Spreading Activation. *Spreading activation* helps to explain how new information is linked to knowledge in LTM (Anderson, 1983, 1984, 1990, 2000). The underlying principles are as follows (Anderson, 1984):

- Human knowledge can be represented as a network of nodes, where nodes correspond to concepts and links to associations among these concepts.
- The nodes in this network can be in various states that correspond to their levels of activation. More active nodes are processed "better."
- Activation can spread along these network paths by a mechanism whereby nodes can cause their neighboring nodes to become active. (p. 61)

Anderson (1990) cited the example of an individual presented with the word *dog*. This word is linked with such other concepts in the individual's LTM as *bone, cat,* and *meat*. In turn, each of these concepts is linked to other concepts. The activation of *dog* in LTM will spread beyond *dog* to linked concepts, with the spread lessening with concepts farther away from *dog* (e.g., giraffe).

Spreading activation is based on the idea that memory structures vary in their *activation level* (Anderson, 1990). In this view, we do not have separate memory structures or phases but rather one memory with different activation states. Information may be in an active or inactive state. When active, the information can be accessed quickly. The active state is maintained as long as information is attended to. Without attention, the activation level will diminish, in which case the information can be activated when the memory is reactivated (Collins & Loftus, 1975).

Active information can include information entering the information processing system and information that has been stored in memory (Baddeley, 1998). Regardless of the source, active information either is currently being processed or can be processed rapidly. Active material is roughly synonymous with WM, but the former category is broader than the latter. WM includes information in immediate consciousness, whereas active memory includes that information plus material that can be accessed easily. For example, if I am visiting Aunt Frieda and we are admiring her flower garden, that information is in WM, but other information associated with Aunt Frieda's yard (trees, shrubs, dog) may be in an active state.

Rehearsal allows information to be maintained in an active state (Anderson, 1990). As with WM, only a limited amount of memory can be active at a given time. As one's attention shifts, activation level changes.

Experimental support for the existence of spreading activation was obtained by Meyer and Schvaneveldt (1971). These investigators used a reaction time task that presented participants with two strings of letters and asked them to decide whether both were words. Words associatively linked (*bread, butter*) were recognized faster than words not linked (*nurse, butter*).

Spreading activation results in a larger portion of LTM being activated than knowledge immediately associated with the content of WM. Activated information stays in LTM unless it is deliberately accessed, but this information is more readily accessible to WM. Spreading activation also facilitates transfer of knowledge to different domains. Transfer depends on propositional networks in LTM being activated by the same cue, so students recognize that knowledge is applicable in the domains.

One advantage of activation level is that it can explain retrieval of information from memory. By dispensing with the notion of memory phases, the model eliminates the potential problem of transferring information. Activation decreases with the passage of time, unless rehearsal keeps the information activated (Nairne, 2002).

At the same time, activation level has not escaped the dual-store model's problems because it too dichotomizes the information system (active-inactive). We also have the problem of the strength level needed for information to pass from one state to another. Thus, we intuitively know that information may be partially activated (e.g., a word on the "tip of your tongue"—you know it but cannot recall it), so we might ask how much activation is needed for material to be considered active. These concerns notwithstanding, activation level and spreading activation offer important insights into the processing of information.

Schemas. Propositional networks represent small pieces of knowledge. Schemas (or schemata) are large networks that represent the structure of objects, persons, and events (Anderson, 1990). Structure is represented with a series of "slots," each of which corresponds to an attribute. In the schema or slot for *houses*, some attributes (and their values) might be as follows: material (wood, brick), contents (rooms), and function (human dwelling). Schemas are hierarchical; they are joined to superordinate ideas (building) and subordinate ones (roof).

Brewer and Treyens (1981) found research support for the underlying nature of schemas. Individuals were asked to wait in an office for a brief period, after which they were brought into a room where they wrote down everything they could recall about the office. Recall reflected the strong influence of a schema for *office*. They correctly recalled the office having a desk and a chair (typical attributes) but not that the office contained a skull (nontypical attribute). Books are a typical attribute of offices; although the office had no books, many persons incorrectly recalled books.

Schemas are important for teaching and transfer (Matlin, 2009). Once students learn a schema, teachers can activate this knowledge when they teach any content to which the schema is applicable. Suppose an instructor teaches a general schema for describing geographical formations (e.g., mountain, volcano, glacier, river). The schema might contain the following attributes: height, material, and activity. Once students learn the schema, they can employ it to categorize new formations they study. In so doing, they would create new schemata for the various formations.

Procedural Knowledge. *Procedural knowledge*, or knowledge of how to perform cognitive activities (Anderson, 1990; Gupta & Cohen, 2002; Hunt, 1989; Paris et al., 1983), is central to much school learning. We use procedural knowledge to solve mathematical problems (e.g., algorithms), summarize information, skim passages, use the Internet, and perform laboratory techniques.

Procedural knowledge may be stored in networks as verbal codes and images, much the same way as declarative knowledge is stored. ACT theory posits that procedural knowledge is stored as a production system (Anderson, 1996; Anderson, Reder, & Lebiere, 1996). A *production system* (or *production*) is a network of condition–action sequences (rules), in which the condition is the set of circumstances that activates the system and the action is the set of activities that occurs (Anderson, 1990; Andre, 1986; see next section). Production systems seem conceptually similar to neural networks (discussed in Chapter 2).

Production Systems and Connectionist Models

Production systems and connectionist models provide paradigms for examining the operation of cognitive learning processes (Anderson, 1996, 2000; Radvansky & Ashcraft, 2014). To date, there has been little research on connectionist models that is relevant to education. Additional sources provide further information about these models (Bourne, 1992; Farnham-Diggory, 1992; Matlin, 2009).

Production Systems. ACT—an activation theory—specifies that a production system (or production) is a network of condition–action sequences (rules), in which the condition is a set of circumstances that activates the system and the action is the set of activities that occurs (Anderson, 1990, 1996, 2000; Anderson, Reder, & Lebiere, 1996; Andre, 1986). A production consists of *if–then statements*: *If* statements (the condition) include the goal and test statements and *then* statements are the actions. As an example:

- IF I see two numbers and they must be added,
- THEN decide which is larger and start with that number and count up to the next one. (Farnham-Diggory, 1992, p. 113)

Although productions are forms of procedural knowledge that can have conditions attached to them, they also include declarative knowledge.

Learning procedures for performing skills often occurs slowly (J. Anderson, 1982). First, learners represent a sequence of actions in terms of declarative knowledge. Each step in the sequence is represented as a proposition. Learners gradually drop out individual cues and integrate the separate steps into a continuous sequence of actions. For example, children learning to add a column of numbers will perform each step slowly, possibly even verbalizing it aloud. As they become more skillful, adding becomes part of an automatic, smooth sequence that occurs rapidly and without deliberate, conscious attention. *Automaticity* is a central feature of many cognitive processes (e.g., attention, retrieval) (Moors & De Houwer, 2006). When processes become automatic, this allows the processing system to devote itself to complex parts of tasks (Chapter 7).

A major constraint on skill learning is the size limitation of WM (Baddeley, 2001). Procedures would be learned quicker if WM could simultaneously hold all the declarative knowledge propositions. Because it cannot, students must combine propositions slowly and periodically stop and think (e.g., "What do I do next?"). WM contains insufficient space to create large procedures in the early stages of learning. As propositions are combined into small procedures, the latter are stored in WM simultaneously with other propositions. In this fashion, larger productions are gradually constructed.

These ideas explain why skill learning proceeds faster when students can perform the prerequisite skills (i.e., when they become automatic). When the latter exist as well-established productions, they are activated in WM at the same time as new propositions to be integrated. In learning to solve long-division problems, students who know how to multiply simply recall the procedure when necessary; it does not have to be learned along with the other steps in long division. Although this does not seem to be the problem in the opening scenario, learning algebra is difficult for students with basic skill deficiencies (e.g., addition, multiplication), because even simple algebra problems become difficult to answer correctly. Many children with reading disabilities may lack the capability to effectively process and store information at the same time (de Jong, 1998).

In some cases, specifying the steps in detail is difficult. For example, thinking creatively may not follow the same sequence for each student. Teachers can model creative thinking to include such self-questions as, "Are there any other possibilities?" Whenever steps can be specified, teacher demonstrations of the steps in a procedure, followed by student practice, are effective.

One problem with the learning of procedures is that students might view them as lockstep sequences to be followed regardless of whether they are appropriate. Gestalt psychologists showed how *functional fixedness*, or an inflexible approach to a problem, hinders problem solving (Duncker, 1945; Chapter 7). Adamantly following a sequence while learning may assist its acquisition, but learners also need to understand the circumstances under which other methods are more efficient.

Sometimes students overlearn skill procedures to the point that they avoid using alternative, easier procedures. At the same time, there are few, if any, alternatives for many of the procedures students learn (e.g., decoding words, adding numbers, determining subject–verb agreement). Overlearning these skills to the point of automatic production becomes an asset to students and makes it easier to learn new skills (e.g., drawing inferences, writing term papers) that require mastery of these basic skills.

One might argue that teaching problem-solving or inference skills to students who are deficient in basic mathematical facts and decoding skills, respectively, makes little sense. Research shows that poor grasp of basic number facts is related to low performance on complex arithmetic tasks (Romberg & Carpenter, 1986), and slow decoding relates to poor comprehension (Calfee & Drum, 1986). Not only is skill learning affected, but self-efficacy (Chapter 4) suffers as well (Schunk & DiBenedetto, 2016).

Practice is essential to instate basic procedural knowledge. In the early stages of learning, students require corrective feedback highlighting the portions of the procedure they implemented correctly and those requiring modification. Often students learn some parts of a procedure but not others. As students gain skill, teachers can point out their progress in solving problems quicker or more accurately.

Transfer of procedural knowledge occurs when the knowledge is linked in LTM with different content. Transfer is aided by having students apply the procedures to the different content and altering the procedures as necessary. General problem-solving strategies (Chapter 7) are applicable to varied academic content. Students learn about their generality by applying them to different subjects (e.g., reading, mathematics).

Productions are relevant to cognitive learning, but several issues need to be addressed. ACT theory posits a single set of cognitive processes to account for diverse phenomena (Matlin, 2009). This view conflicts with other cognitive perspectives that delineate different processes depending on the type of learning (Shuell, 1986). For example, Rumelhart and Norman (1978) identified three types of learning. *Accretion* involves encoding new information in terms of existing schemata; *restructuring* (schema creation) is the process of forming new schemata; and *tuning* (schema evolution) refers to the slow modification and refinement of schemata that occur when using them in various contexts. These involve different amounts of practice: much for tuning and less for accretion and restructuring.

ACT is essentially a computer program designed to simulate learning in a coherent manner. As such, it may not address the range of factors involved in human learning. One issue concerns how people know which production to use in a given situation, especially if situations lend themselves to different productions being employed. Productions may be ordered in terms of likelihood, but a means for deciding what production is best given the circumstance must be available. Also of concern is the issue of how productions are altered. For example, if a production does not work effectively, do learners discard it, modify it, or retain it but seek more evidence? What is the mechanism for deciding when and how productions are changed?

Another concern relates to Anderson's (1983, 1990) claim that productions begin as declarative knowledge. This assumption seems too strong given evidence that this sequence is not always followed (Hunt, 1989). Because representing skill procedures as pieces of declarative knowledge is essentially a way station along the road to mastery, one might question whether students should learn the individual steps. The individual steps eventually will not be used, so time may be better spent allowing students to practice them.

Finally, one might question whether production systems, as generally described, are nothing more than elaborate stimulus–response (S–R) associations. Propositions (bits of procedural knowledge) become linked in memory and formed into networks so that when one piece is cued, others also are activated. Anderson (1983) acknowledged the associationist nature of productions but believes they are more advanced than simple

S–R associations because they incorporate goals. In support of this point, ACT associations are analogous to neural network connections (Chapter 2). Perhaps, as is the case with behavior theories, ACT can explain performance better than it can explain learning. These and other questions (e.g., the role of motivation) need to be addressed better to establish the usefulness of productions in education better.

Connectionist Models. *Connectionist models* (or *connectionism*, but not to be confused with Thorndike's connectionism discussed in Chapter 3; Baddeley, 1998; Farnham-Diggory, 1992; Matlin, 2009; Smith, 1996) represent a more recent line of theorizing about complex cognitive processes. Like productions, connectionist models represent computer simulations of learning processes. These models link learning to neural system processing where impulses fire across synapses to form connections (Chapter 2). It is assumed that higher-order cognitive processes are formed by connecting many basic elements such as neurons (Anderson, 1990, 2000; Anderson, Reder, & Lebiere, 1996; Bourne, 1992). Connectionist models include distributed representations of knowledge (i.e., spread out over a wide network), parallel processing (many operations occur at once), and interactions among large numbers of simple processing units (Siegler, 1989). Connections may be at different stages of activation (Smith, 1996) and linked to input into the system, output, or one or more in-between layers.

Rumelhart and McClelland (1986) described a system of *parallel distributed processing* (*PDP*). This model is useful for making categorical judgments about information in memory. These authors provided an example involving two gangs and information about gang members, including age, education, marital status, and occupation. In memory, the similar characteristics of each individual are linked. For example, Members 2 and 5 would be linked if they both were about the same age, married, and engaged in similar gang activities. To retrieve information about Member 2, we could activate the memory unit with the person's name, which in turn would activate other memory units. The pattern created through this spread of activation corresponds to the memory representation for the individual. Borowsky and Besner (2006) described a PDP model for making lexical decisions (e.g., deciding whether a stimulus is a word).

Connectionist units bear some similarity to productions in that both involve memory activation and linked ideas. At the same time, differences exist. In connectionist models, all units are alike, whereas productions contain conditions and actions. Units are differentiated in terms of pattern and degree of activation. Another difference is that whereas productions are governed by rules, connectionism has no set rules. Neurons "know" how to activate patterns, although we may provide a rule to label the sequence (e.g., rules for naming patterns activated; Farnham-Diggory, 1992).

One problem with the connectionist approach is explaining how the system knows which of the many units in memory to activate and how these multiple activations become linked in integrated sequences. This process seems straightforward in the case of well-established patterns; for example, neurons "know" how to react to a ringing phone, a cold wind, and a teacher announcing, "Everyone pay attention!" With less-established patterns, the activations may be problematic. We also might ask how neurons become self-activating in the first place. This question is important because it helps to explain the role of connections in learning and memory. Although the notion of connections seems plausible and grounded in what we know about neurological functioning (Chapter 2), to date, this model has been more useful in explaining perception rather than learning and problem solving. The latter applications are critical for education.

These recent advances call increased attention to the idea that cognitive processing is complex and that unlike earlier information processing conceptions that postulated a linear stage-like progression, parallel processing of multiple inputs can occur. This is a type of "multitasking"; an example of several cognitive processes operating simultaneously (Radvansky & Ashcraft, 2014). Such multitasking should not be surprising, given that inputs can affect different parts of the brain that can be activated in concert (Chapter 2). Future cognitive and neuroscience research should help us better understand this complexity.

INSTRUCTIONAL APPLICATIONS

Information processing principles increasingly have been applied to educational settings. Three instructional applications that reflect these principles are advance organizers, conditions of learning, and cognitive load.

Advance Organizers

Advance organizers are broad statements presented at the outset of lessons that help to connect new material with prior learning (Mayer, 1984). Organizers direct learners' attention to important concepts to be learned, highlight relationships among ideas, and link new material to what students know (Faw & Waller, 1976). Organizers also can be maps that are shown with accompanying text (Verdi & Kulhavy, 2002). It is assumed that learners' LTMs are organized such that inclusive concepts subsume subordinate ones. Organizers provide information at high (inclusive) levels. The better organization promotes memory storage (Radvansky & Ashcraft, 2014).

The historical basis of organizers derives from Ausubel's (1963, 1977, 1978; Ausubel & Robinson, 1969) theory of *meaningful reception learning*. Learning is meaningful when new material bears a systematic relation to relevant concepts in LTM; that is, new material expands, modifies, or elaborates information in memory. Meaningfulness also depends on personal variables such as age, background experiences, socioeconomic status, and educational background.

Ausubel advocated deductive teaching: General ideas are taught first, followed by specific points. This requires teachers to help students break ideas into smaller, related points and to link new ideas to similar content in memory. In information processing terms, the aims of the model are to expand propositional networks in LTM by adding knowledge and to establish links between networks.

Advance organizers can be expository or comparative. *Expository organizers* provide students with new knowledge needed to comprehend the lesson. Expository organizers include concept definitions and generalizations. *Concept definitions* state the concept, a superordinate concept, and characteristics of the concept. In presenting the concept "warm-blooded animal," a teacher might define it (i.e., animal whose internal body temperature remains relatively constant), relate it to superordinate concepts (i.e., animal kingdom), and give its characteristics (e.g., birds, mammals). *Generalizations* are broad statements of general principles from which hypotheses or specific ideas are drawn. A generalization appropriate for the study of terrain would be: "Less vegetation grows at higher elevations." Teachers can present examples of generalizations and ask students to think of others.

Comparative organizers introduce new material by drawing analogies with familiar material. Comparative organizers activate and link networks in LTM. If a teacher were giving a unit on the body's circulatory system to students who have studied communication systems, the teacher might relate the circulatory and communication systems with relevant concepts such as the source, medium, and target. For comparative organizers to be effective, students must have a good understanding of the material used as the basis for the analogy. Learners also must perceive the analogy easily. Difficulty perceiving analogous relationships impedes learning.

Organizers can promote learning and, because they help students relate content to a broader set of experiences, may facilitate transfer (Ausubel, 1978; Faw & Waller, 1976; Mautone & Mayer, 2007). Maps are especially effective organizers and lend themselves well to infusion in lessons via technology (Verdi & Kulhavy, 2002). Some examples of organizers are given in Application 5.3.

APPLICATION 5.3
Advance Organizers

Advance organizers help students connect new material with prior learning. Ms. Lowery, a fourth-grade teacher, is teaching her students how to develop paragraphs. The students have been writing descriptive sentences. Ms. Lowery projects the students' sentences onto a screen and uses them as an organizer to show how to put sentences together to create a paragraph.

Mr. Oronsco, a middle school teacher, employed an organizer during geography. He began a lesson on landforms (surfaces with characteristic shapes and compositions) by reviewing the definition and components of geography concepts previously discussed. He wanted to show that geography includes elements of the physical environment, human beings and the physical environment, and different world regions and their ability to support human beings. To do this, Mr. Oronsco initially focused on elements of the physical environment and then moved to landforms. He discussed types of landforms (e.g., plateaus, mountains, hills) by showing mock-ups and asking students to identify key features of each landform. This approach gave students an overall framework or outline into which they could integrate new knowledge about the components.

Dr. Kidd, a science instructor at a university, has been teaching the effects of blood disorders. She began by reviewing the basic parts of blood (e.g., plasma, white and red cells, platelets). Then she covered the various categories of blood disease (e.g., anemia, bleeding and bruising, leukemia, bone marrow disease). The students can build on this outline by exploring the diseases in the different categories and by studying the symptoms and treatments for each condition.

Conditions of Learning

Gagné (1985) formulated an applied (instructional) theory that reflects information processing principles and highlights the *conditions of learning*, or the circumstances that prevail
when learning occurs (Ertmer, Driscoll, & Wager, 2003). Two steps are critical. The first
is to *specify the type of learning outcome*; Gagné identified five major types (discussed
later). The second is to *determine the events of learning*, or factors that make a difference
in instruction.

Learning Outcomes The five types of learning outcomes are (Gagné, 1984): intellectual
skills, verbal information, cognitive strategies, motor skills, and attitudes (Table 5.2).

Intellectual skills include rules, procedures, and concepts. They are forms of procedural knowledge or productions. This type of knowledge is employed in speaking, writing,
reading, solving mathematical problems, and applying scientific principles to problems.

Verbal information, or declarative knowledge, is knowledge that something is the
case. Verbal information involves facts or meaningfully connected prose recalled verbatim (e.g., words to a poem or the "Star Spangled Banner"). Schemas are forms of verbal
information.

Cognitive strategies are executive control processes. They include information processing skills such as attending to new information, rehearsing information, elaborating, using
LTM retrieval strategies, and problem solving (Chapter 7).

Motor skills are developed through gradual improvements in the quality (smooth-
ness, timing) of movements attained through practice. Whereas intellectual skills can
be acquired quickly, motor skills develop gradually with continued, deliberate practice
(Ericsson, Krampe, & Tesch-Römer, 1993). Practice conditions differ: Intellectual skills are
practiced with different examples, whereas motor-skill practice involves repetition of the
same muscular movements.

Attitudes are internal beliefs that influence actions and reflect characteristics such as
generosity, honesty, and commitment to healthy living. Teachers can arrange conditions
for learning intellectual skills, verbal information, cognitive strategies, and motor skills, but
attitudes are learned indirectly through experiences and exposures to live and symbolic
(televised, videotaped) models.

Table 5.2
Learning outcomes in Gagné's theory.

Learning Outcomes	
Type	**Examples**
Intellectual skills	Rules, procedures, concepts
Verbal information	Facts, dates
Cognitive strategies	Rehearsal, problem solving
Motor skills	Hitting a ball, juggling
Attitudes	Generosity, honesty, fairness

Learning Conditions. The five types of learning outcomes differ in their conditions. *Internal conditions* are prerequisite skills and cognitive processing requirements; *external conditions* are environmental stimuli that support the learner's cognitive processes. One must specify as completely as possible both types of conditions when designing instruction.

Internal conditions are learners' current capabilities (knowledge in LTM). Instructional cues from teachers and materials activate relevant LTM knowledge (Gagné & Glaser, 1987). External conditions differ as a function of the learning outcome and the internal conditions. To teach students a classroom rule, a teacher might verbalize and visually display it. To teach students a strategy for checking their comprehension, a teacher might explain and demonstrate the strategy and give students practice and feedback on its effectiveness. Proficient readers are instructed differently from those with decoding problems. Each phase of instruction is subject to alteration as a function of learning outcomes and internal conditions.

Learning Hierarchies. *Learning hierarchies* are organized sets of intellectual skills. The highest element in a hierarchy is the *target skill*. To devise a hierarchy, one begins at the top and asks what skills the learner must perform prior to learning the target skill or what skills are immediate prerequisites for the target skill. Then one asks the same question for each prerequisite skill, continuing down the hierarchy until one arrives at the skills the learner can perform now (Dick & Carey, 1985; Merrill, 1987; Figure 5.9).

Hierarchies are not linear orderings of skills. One often must apply two or more prerequisite skills to learn a higher-order skill with neither of the prerequisites dependent on the other. Nor are higher-order skills necessarily more difficult to learn than lower-order ones. Some prerequisites may be difficult to acquire; once learners have mastered the lower-order skills, learning a higher-order one may seem easier.

Phases of Learning. *Instruction* is a set of external events designed to facilitate internal learning processes. Table 5.3 shows the nine phases of learning grouped into the three categories (Gagné, 1985).

Table 5.3
Gagné's phases of learning.

Category	Phase
Preparation for learning	Attending
	Expectancy
	Retrieval
Acquisition and performance	Selective perception
	Semantic encoding
	Retrieval and responding
	Reinforcement
Transfer of learning	Cueing retrieval
	Generalizability

Figure 5.9
Sample learning hierarchy.

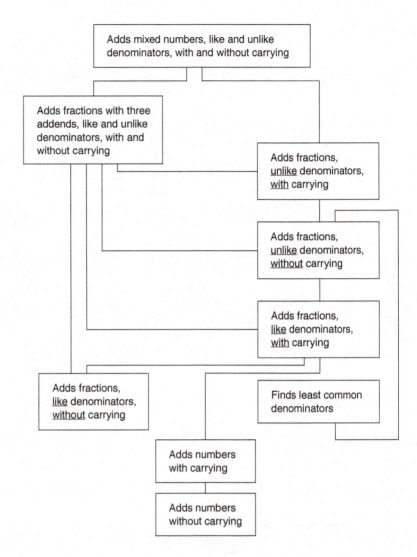

Preparation for learning includes introductory learning activities. During *attending*, learners focus on stimuli relevant to content to be learned (e.g., audiovisuals, written materials, teacher-modeled behaviors). The learner's *expectancy* orients the learner to the goal (learn a motor skill, learn to reduce fractions). During retrieval of relevant information from LTM, learners activate the portions relevant to the topic studied (Gagné & Dick, 1983).

The main phases of learning are *acquisition* and *performance*. *Selective perception* means that the sensory registers recognize relevant stimulus features and transfer them to WM. *Semantic encoding* is the process whereby new knowledge is transferred to LTM. During *retrieval and responding*, learners retrieve new information from memory and make a response demonstrating learning. *Reinforcement* refers to feedback that confirms the accuracy of a student's response and provides corrective information as necessary.

Transfer of learning phases include cueing retrieval and generalizability. In *cueing retrieval*, learners receive cues signaling that previous knowledge is applicable in that situation. When solving word problems, for instance, a mathematics teacher might inform learners that their knowledge of right triangles is applicable. *Generalizability* is enhanced by providing learners the opportunity to practice skills with different content and under different circumstances (e.g., homework, distributed review sessions).

These nine phases are equally applicable for the five types of learning outcomes. Gagné and Briggs (1979) specified types of instructional events that might accompany each phase (Table 5.4). Instructional events enhancing each phase depend on the type of outcome. Instruction proceeds differently for intellectual skills than for verbal information.

One issue is that developing learning hierarchies can be difficult and time consuming. The process requires expertise in the content domain to determine the successive prerequisite skills—the scope and sequence of instruction. Even a seemingly simple skill may have a complex hierarchy if learners must master several prerequisites. For skills with less well-defined structures (e.g., creative writing), developing a hierarchy may be difficult. Another issue is that the system allows for little learner control because it prescribes how learners should proceed, which could negatively affect learner motivation. Instructional technology that allows learners greater control over their activities may help override this possibility. These issues notwithstanding, the theory offers solid suggestions for ways to apply information processing principles to the design of instruction (Ertmer et al., 2003).

Cognitive Load

Cognitive load refers to the demands placed on the information processing system and in particular on WM (Mayer, 2012; Paas, van Gog, & Sweller, 2010; Sweller, 2010; Winne & Nesbit, 2010). The capacity of WM is limited. Because information processing takes time and involves multiple cognitive processes, at any given time, only a limited amount of information can be held in WM, transferred to LTM, rehearsed, and so forth.

Table 5.4
Instructional events accompanying learning phases (Gagné).

Phase	Instructional Event
Attending	Inform class that it is time to begin.
Expectancy	Inform class of lesson objective and type and quantity of performance to be expected.
Retrieval	Ask class to recall subordinate concepts and rules.
Selective perception	Present examples of new concept or rule.
Semantic encoding	Provide cues for how to remember information.
Retrieval and responding	Ask students to apply concept or rule to new examples.
Reinforcement	Confirm accuracy of students' learning.
Cueing retrieval	Give short quiz on new material.
Generalizability	Provide special reviews.

Cognitive load theory takes these processing limitations into account in the design of instruction (DeLeeuw & Mayer, 2008; Paas & Ayres, 2014; Paas & Sweller, 2012; Schnotz & Kürschner, 2007). There are two types of cognitive load. *Intrinsic cognitive load* refers to the demands placed on WM by the unalterable properties of the knowledge to be acquired. *Extrinsic* (or *extraneous*) *cognitive load* is a burden on WM caused by unnecessary content, distractions, or difficulties with the instructional presentation (Bruning et al., 2011). Some researchers also speak of *germane cognitive load,* which includes intrinsic load plus necessary extraneous load due to situational factors (e.g., monitoring of attention; Feldon, 2007).

For example, in learning key trigonometric relationships (e.g., sine, tangent), a certain cognitive load (intrinsic) is inherent in the material to be learned; namely, developing knowledge about the ratios of sides of a right triangle. Extraneous load would include information in instruction not relevant to the content to be learned, such as irrelevant features of pictures used. Teachers who give clear presentations help to minimize extraneous load.

In similar fashion, Mayer (2012) distinguished three types of cognitive processing demands. *Essential processing* refers to cognitive processing necessary to mentally represent material in WM (similar to intrinsic load). *Extraneous processing* (similar to extrinsic load) refers to processing not necessary for learning and which wastes cognitive capacity. *Generative processing* is deeper cognitive processing that attempts to make sense of the material, such by organizing it and relating it to prior knowledge.

A key idea is that instructional methods should decrease extraneous cognitive load so that existing resources can be devoted to learning (van Merriënboer & Sweller, 2005). The use of scaffolded assistance should be beneficial (van Merriënboer, Kirschner, & Kester, 2003). Initially the scaffold helps learners acquire skills that they would be unlikely to acquire without the assistance. The scaffolding helps to minimize the extrinsic load so learners can focus their resources on the intrinsic demands of the learning. As learners develop a schema to work with the information, the scaffolded assistance can be phased out.

Another suggestion is to use simple-to-complex sequencing of material (van Merriënboer et al., 2003), in line with Gagné's theory. Complex learning is broken into simple parts that are acquired and combined into a larger sequence. This procedure minimizes extrinsic load, so learners can focus their cognitive resources on the learning at hand.

A third suggestion is to use authentic tasks in instruction. Reigeluth's (1999) *elaboration theory,* for example, requires identifying conditions that simplify performance of the task and then beginning instruction with a simple but authentic case (e.g., one that might be encountered in the real world). Tasks that have real-world significance do not require learners to engage in extraneous processing to understand the context. It is more meaningful, for example, for students to determine the sine of the angle formed by joining a point 40 feet from the school's flagpole to the top of the pole than it is to solve comparable trigonometric problems in a textbook.

These considerations also suggest the use of collaborative learning. As intrinsic cognitive load increases, learning becomes less effective and efficient (Kirschner, Paas, & Kirschner, 2009). With greater task complexity, dividing the cognitive processing demands across individuals reduces load on learners. These ideas fit well with the constructivist emphasis on peer collaboration (Chapter 8). Some examples are provided in Application 5.4.

APPLICATION 5.4
Reducing Unnecessary Cognitive Load

Student learning will be best when instruction minimizes extraneous load. Ms. Watson, a high school English teacher, knows that locating symbolic elements in novels can prove taxing to many students. To help minimize extraneous load, she introduces only one symbolic element at a time, explains it, and asks students to try to find examples of it in only a few pages of the novel. By focusing their attention only on one element in a small subset of the novel, students do not feel overwhelmed by the demands of the task and their need to pay careful attention.

Ms. Anton, an elementary teacher, has students who have difficulty writing descriptive paragraphs. She breaks the task into parts so as to not impose a great extraneous load. First she has students write down what features of the object they want to describe in their paragraph. Then she asks them to write one sentence for each feature.

When they are finished, she tells them to review their paragraphs and revise them as needed, making sure the paragraphs are clear and well organized.

Students in Professor Lauphar's undergraduate educational psychology course have to do a group project where they design an ideal learning environment that addresses several concepts covered in the course (e.g., learning, motivation, assessment). Dr. Lauphar forms small groups of four students each and sets a timeline of when various aspects of the project are to be completed. Students meet in the groups and set their own timelines for when they will complete their research and reconvene as a group. By breaking the task into subparts and by reviewing the content areas over the course of the semester, students do not experience excessive extraneous load and can focus their attention and efforts on the immediate task at hand.

SUMMARY AND CRITIQUE

Chapter Summary

Information processing theories focus on attention, perception, encoding, storage, and retrieval of knowledge. Information processing has been influenced by advances in communications, computer technology, and neuroscience.

Important historical influences on contemporary information processing views are verbal learning, Gestalt psychology, the two-store model, and levels of processing. Verbal learning researchers used serial learning, free recall, and paired-associate tasks. A number of important findings were obtained from verbal learning research. Free-recall studies showed that organization improves recall and that people impose their own organization when none is present. Gestalt theorists stressed the role of organization in perception and learning.

The two-store (dual) memory model was an early information processing model that posited stages of processing: sensory registers, perception, short-term memory, long-term memory. Levels of processing conceived of information processing in terms of depth, where information processed at deeper levels was more likely to be stored in memory and recalled.

A contemporary information processing model posits that information processing occurs in phases. Information enters through the sensory registers. Although there is a register for each sense, most research has been conducted on the visual and auditory registers. At any one time, only a limited amount of information can be attended to. Attention may act as a filter or a general limitation on capacity of the human system. Inputs attended to are perceived by being compared in WM with information in LTM.

When information enters WM, it can be retained through rehearsal and linked with related information in LTM. Information is not automatically encoded in LTM; rather, it is constructed and transformed before integration into LTM. Encoding is facilitated through organization, elaboration, and schemas. The central executive of WM controls its interface with perception and LTM.

Attention and perception processes involve critical features, templates, and prototypes. Whereas WM is limited in capacity and duration, LTM appears to be very large. The basic unit of knowledge is the proposition, and propositions are organized in networks. Major types of knowledge are declarative and procedural. Large bits of procedural knowledge may be organized in production systems. Networks further are linked in connectionist fashion through spreading activation.

Although much early research on information processing was basic in nature and conducted in experimental laboratories, researchers increasingly are conducting research in applied settings and especially on learning of academic content. Three instructional applications that reflect information processing principles involve advance organizers, the conditions of learning, and cognitive load.

A summary of learning issues for information processing theory appears at the end of Chapter 6.

Chapter Critique

Beginning in the 1960s, information processing theory emerged as a contrast to behavior theory. The theoretical predictions of information processing theory, combined with many research results, showed that behavior theory did not provide an adequate explanation for learning and memory. Rather, cognition played a major role in what individuals encoded in memory.

Information processing theory has made major contributions to the study of learning and memory. Furthermore, its predictions are remarkably consistent with evidence from neuroscience research. It now seems apparent, for example, that people form networks of related knowledge in memory that can be linked with one another. WM has been shown to be remarkably complex, performing functions related to maintaining information, relating it to knowledge in LTM, and directing the storage and integration of new knowledge in LTM. Similarly, the processes of attention and perception have been studied extensively.

Historically information processing researchers were more concerned with basic research, and there was little application to applied contexts such as education. This situation has changed in the last several years as researchers now tackle issues related to how students learn and retain and apply knowledge they acquire in educational contexts. Cognitive processes involved in attention, perception, and memory have high relevance to education.

Although information processing research has advanced in many ways, there remain issues to address. A key issue is what directs the movement of information through the system. Explanations of mechanisms to account for this movement, such as executive functions, seem under-developed theoretically. Another issue is that information processing theory assigns a prominent role to forming associations. Although these are cognitive associations, the mechanism shares some similarities with that postulated by behavior theory. Additional research is needed to elucidate the process whereby cognitive associations are formed and to differentiate this process from that involved in forming behavioral associations.

Advances continue to be made in this field, especially in the compatibility of theory and research with the field of neuroscience. Further development along these lines will undoubtedly occur, and the results should be of great benefit to both researchers and practitioners who seek ways to improve students' cognitive processing during learning and memory.

REFLECTION QUESTIONS

- Information processing theory postulates the existence of several cognitive processes including attention, perception, rehearsal, organization, encoding, and retrieval. A central question is: What is responsible for the flow of information through the system? In other words, why does information get processed? What mechanism or process do you think is responsible for information processing? Is it innate or learned? If this mechanism or process is innate, can education improve its operation? If education can improve the operation of an innate process or if this process is learned, then what are some effective ways to enhance its functioning?

- Information processing theory predicts that meaningfulness improves the encoding of knowledge. From a theoretical perspective, why is meaningful knowledge easily encoded? How does meaningful knowledge compare with non-meaningful knowledge in memory? What do meaningful and non-meaningful memory networks look like? From an applied perspective, how might teachers improve the meaningfulness of information for students? What are some instructional practices that might improve it?

- Cognitive load refers to the demands placed on the information processing system and especially working memory. Cognitive load has major instructional implications. When cognitive load becomes too great—either from external conditions or from the difficulty of the material to be learned—students' learning and memory suffer. What are some practical suggestions you might make to teachers for ways to reduce cognitive load and thereby improve learning? How might your suggestions differ depending on the developmental levels of the learners? For example, what might you suggest for teachers of elementary, middle school, high school, and postsecondary learners?

FURTHER READING

Anderson, J. R. (1996). ACT: A simple theory of complex cognition. *American Psychologist, 51*, 355–365.

Baddeley, A. D. (2012). Working memory: Theories, models, and controversies. *Annual Review of Psychology, 63*, 1–29.

Cowan, N. (2014). Working memory underpins cognitive development, learning, and education. *Educational Psychology Review, 26*, 197–223.

Gagné, R. M. (1985). *The conditions of learning* (4th ed.). New York: Holt, Rinehart & Winston.

Mayer, R. E. (2012). Information processing. In K. R. Harris, S. Graham, & T. Urdan (Eds.), *APA handbook of educational psychology. Vol. 1: Theories, constructs, and critical issues* (pp. 85–99). Washington, DC: American Psychological Association.

Surprenant, A. M., & Neath, I. (2009). *Principles of memory.* New York: Taylor & Francis.

van Merriënboer, J. J. G., & Sweller, J. (2005). Cognitive load theory and complex learning: Recent developments and future directions. *Educational Psychology Review, 14*, 331–351.

6 Information Processing Theory: Retrieval and Forgetting

Terrill Sharberg, a professor of education, is teaching an educational psychology course for graduate students. All of the students are educators—current or former teachers, administrators, or professional staff members. This week's class is devoted to remembering and forgetting. Several of the students have stories to tell.

Marcia: My students return after semester break, and they can hardly remember anything we studied before the break.

Silas: I see that sometimes after a long holiday weekend.

JoEllen: I spend so much class time on review. I wish I could cut back.

Jeff: The teachers in my school have their students periodically review computer modules on the content.

Terrill: What you're describing is common. Forgetting occurs, but continual review takes time and shouldn't be necessary so often. We're going to study how to apply principles of information processing theory to student learning to improve retention and recall.

JoEllen: Yes, Dr. Sharberg, but we have so much to cover, and I feel sorry for the kids. They can't remember everything.

Terrill: No, they can't. But that's not the goal. There are lots of things we can do as educators to improve retention and retrieval to decrease forgetting.

Jeff: I want to have a workshop on this topic for my teachers. They need help. They're frustrated.

Terrill: Well, teaching to promote retention takes more effort, but it's worth it because it should decrease time spent on reviews and reteaching, not to mention improve teachers' and students' motivation and make learning more enjoyable.

Chapter 5 discussed how information is received, constructed, and transformed for encoding as knowledge in LTM. The process is complex. It begins with learners attending to inputs so that these register, are perceived, and are processed by WM. The WM processing includes elaborating and organizing information and integrating it with knowledge in LTM. Through this processing, new memory networks are created, and existing ones are modified and enriched.

Practically speaking, however, such learning is useless if learners subsequently cannot access knowledge in LTM and thereby put it to further use. *Forgetting* refers to the loss of information from memory or to the inability to retrieve information. Forgetting often has no serious consequences. When we forget something, we may ask someone, look it up on the Internet, and so forth. Unless you plan to be a contestant on *Jeopardy!* that requires factual recall, most of what we forget in the course of a day poses no risk to life, liberty, or the pursuit of happiness!

But, as the opening vignette shows, forgetting causes problems in education. Teachers cannot move to more-advanced content if students do not remember the basic prerequisite knowledge. Reviews and reteaching take valuable class time. It is a frustrating experience for teachers as well as for students, who may become bored spending time on reviews. Learning should be exciting so that students and teachers remain motivated.

The focus of this chapter is on retrieval. Compared with only a few years ago, we now know much more about how knowledge is stored in memory and retrieved. We also know techniques that are effective in helping learners store knowledge in LTM so that it is easier to retrieve. Effective storage of knowledge facilitates not only retrieval but also transfer of knowledge to new situations.

The next section discusses processes that individuals use to retrieve information from LTM. The chapter then covers theories of forgetting and influences on forgetting. Given that forgetting occurs, relearning becomes necessary; this topic is addressed, along with how testing may affect learning and retrieval. Much of what we have discussed up to now has involved verbal memory, but visual memory is covered to include the benefits it provides for learning. The key educational topic of transfer is discussed including theoretical perspectives and types of transfer. Educational applications involving encoding-retrieval similarity, retrieval-based learning, and teaching for transfer are described.

When you finish studying this chapter, you should be able to do the following:

- Explain the information processes used to retrieve information from LTM including elaboration and spreading activation.

- Describe encoding specificity and why it benefits retrieval.

- Explain how language comprehension exemplifies information processes involved in storage and retrieval of knowledge.

- Define interference and distinguish between retroactive and proactive interference.

- Discuss an information processing perspective on forgetting.

- Define visual memory and explain why it can promote learning.

- Distinguish the different types of transfer and explain why transfer is important for learning.

- Discuss the components necessary for students to transfer use of learning strategies.

- Explain the relevance of information processing principles in educational applications involving encoding-retrieval similarity, retrieval-based learning, and teaching for transfer.

LONG-TERM MEMORY: RETRIEVAL

Retrieval Processes

Retrieval is a key aspect of information processing and actually can help promote learning (Blunt & Karpicke, 2014; Grimaldi & Karpicke, 2014; Karpicke & Grimaldi, 2012). This section discusses the theory and processes involved in retrieval.

Retrieval Strategies. What happens when a student is asked the question, "What does the vice president of the United States do in the Senate?" (see Chapter 5). According to retrieval theories, the question enters the student's WM and is broken into units of meaning (propositions). The process by which this occurs has a neurological basis and is not well understood, but available evidence indicates that information activates associated knowledge in memory networks through *spreading activation* to determine the answer to the question. If the answer is found, it is constructed into a sentence and verbalized to the questioner or into motor patterns to be written. If the activated propositions do not answer the query, activation spreads until the answer is located. When insufficient time is available for spreading activation to locate the answer, students may make an educated guess (Anderson, 1990).

Much cognitive processing occurs automatically. We routinely remember our address, phone number, Social Security number, and close friends' names. People often are unaware of the steps taken to answer a question. However, when people must judge several activated propositions to determine whether the propositions properly answer the question, they are more aware of the process.

Because knowledge is encoded as propositions, retrieval proceeds even though the information to be retrieved does not exist in exact form in memory. If a teacher asks whether the vice president would vote on a bill when the initial vote was 51 for and 49 against, students could retrieve the proposition that the vice president votes only in the event of a tie. By implication, the vice president would not vote. Processing like this, which involves construction, takes longer than when a question requires knowledge coded in memory in the same form, but students should respond correctly assuming they activate the relevant propositions in LTM. The same process is involved in transfer (discussed later in this chapter); for example, students learn a rule (e.g., the Pythagorean theorem in mathematics) and recall and apply it to solve problems they have never seen before.

Encoding Specificity. Retrieval depends on the manner of encoding. According to the *encoding specificity hypothesis* (Brown & Craik, 2000; Thomson & Tulving, 1970), the manner in which knowledge is encoded determines which retrieval cues will effectively activate that knowledge. In this view, the best retrieval occurs when retrieval cues match or resemble those present during learning, a condition known as *encoding-retrieval similarity* (Baddeley, 1998; Suprenant & Neath, 2009).

There is experimental evidence supporting encoding specificity. When people are given category names while they are encoding specific instances of the categories, they recall the instances better if they are given the category names at recall than if not given the names (Matlin, 2009). A similar benefit is obtained if they learn words with associates and then are given the associate names at recall. Brown (1968) gave students a partial list of U.S. states to read; others read no list. Subsequently all students recalled as many states as they could. Students who received the list recalled more of the states on the list and fewer states not on it.

Encoding specificity also includes context. In an early study (Godden & Baddeley, 1975), scuba divers learned a word list either on shore or underwater. On a subsequent free recall task, learners recalled more words when they were in the same environment as the one in which they learned the words than when they were in the other environment. It seems that context cues are linked with content, and memory is more accessible when the context cues are activated (Radvansky & Ashcraft, 2014).

Encoding specificity can be explained in terms of spreading activation among propositional networks. Cues associated with material to be learned are linked in LTM with the material at the time of encoding. During recall, presentation of these cues activates the relevant portions in LTM. In the absence of the same cues, recall depends on recalling individual propositions. Because the cues lead to spreading activation (not the individual propositions or concepts), recall is facilitated by presenting the same cues at encoding and recall. Other evidence suggests that retrieval is guided in part by expectancies about what information is needed and that people may distort inconsistent information to make it coincide with their expectations (Hirt, Erickson, & McDonald, 1993).

Retrieval of Declarative Knowledge. Declarative knowledge often is processed automatically, but that is no guarantee that it will be integrated with relevant information in LTM and subsequently retrieved. We can see this inadequate retrieval in the scenario at the start of this chapter. Meaningfulness, elaboration, and organization enhance the potential for declarative information to be effectively processed and retrieved. Application 6.1 provides classroom examples.

Meaningfulness improves retrieval. Nonmeaningful information will not activate information in LTM and will be lost unless students rehearse it repeatedly until it becomes established in LTM, perhaps by forming a new propositional network. One also can connect the sounds of new information, which are devoid of meaning, to other similar sounds. The word *constitution*, for example, may be linked phonetically with other uses of the word stored in learners' memories (e.g., *Constitution Avenue*).

Meaningful information is more likely to be retained because it easily connects to propositional networks. In the opening scenario in Chapter 5, one suggestion offered is to relate algebraic variables to tangible objects with which learners are familiar to give the algebraic variables some meaning. Meaningfulness not only promotes learning, but it also saves time. Propositions in WM take time to process; Simon (1974) estimated that each new piece of information takes 10 seconds to encode, which means that only six new pieces of information can be processed in a minute. Even when information is meaningful, much knowledge is lost before it can be encoded. Although every piece of incoming information is not important and some loss usually does not impair learning, students typically retain little information even under the best circumstances.

When we elaborate, we add to information being learned with examples, details, inferences, or anything that serves to link new and old information. A learner might elaborate the role of the vice president in the Senate by thinking through the roll call and, when there is a tie, having the vice president vote.

APPLICATION 6.1
Organizing Information by Networks

Teachers enhance learning when they develop lessons that assist students to link new information with knowledge in memory. Information that is meaningful, elaborated, and organized is more readily integrated into LTM networks and retrieved.

A teacher planning a botany unit on the reproduction of different species of plants might start by reviewing common plant knowledge that students have stored in their memories (e.g., basic structure, conditions necessary for growth). As the teacher introduces new information, students examine familiar live plants that reproduce differently to make the experience more meaningful. Factual information to be learned can be elaborated by providing visual drawings and written details

regarding the reproductive processes. For each live plant examined, students can organize the new information by creating outlines or charts to show the means of reproduction.

An art teacher planning a design unit might start by reviewing the various elements of color, shape, and texture. As the teacher introduces new techniques related to placement, combination of the various elements, and balance as it relates to the whole composition, manipulatives of various shapes, colors, and textures are provided for each student to use in creating different styles. The students can use the manipulatives to organize the elements and media they want to include in each of their design compositions.

Elaboration facilitates learning because it is a form of rehearsal: By keeping information active in WM, elaboration increases the likelihood that information will be permanently stored in LTM. This facilitates retrieval, as does the fact that elaboration establishes links between old and new information. Students who elaborate the role of the vice president in the Senate link this new information with what they know about the Senate and the vice president. Well-linked information in LTM, often stored as schemas, is easier to recall than poorly linked information (Stein, Littlefield, Bransford, & Persampieri, 1984; Surprenant & Neath, 2009).

Although elaboration promotes storage and retrieval, it also takes time. It takes longer to comprehend sentences requiring elaboration than it does to comprehend sentences not requiring elaboration (Haviland & Clark, 1974). For example, the following sentences require drawing an inference that Marge took her credit card to the grocery store: "Marge went to the grocery store," and "Marge charged her groceries." The link is clarified in the following sentences: "Marge took her credit card to the grocery store," and "Marge used her credit card to pay for her groceries." Making explicit links between adjoining propositions assists encoding and retention.

An important aspect of learning is deciding on the importance of information. Not all learned information needs to be elaborated. Comprehension is aided when students elaborate only the most important aspects of text. Elaboration aids retrieval by providing alternate paths along which activation can spread, so that if one path is blocked, others are available (Anderson, 2000). Elaboration also provides additional information from which answers can be constructed, such as when students must answer questions with information in a different form from that of the learned material.

In general, almost any type of elaborative rehearsal assists encoding and retrieval (Radvansky & Ashcraft, 2014); however, some elaborations are more effective than others. Activities such as taking notes and asking how new information relates to what one knows build propositional networks. Effective elaborations link propositions and stimulate accurate recall.

Organization takes place by breaking information into parts and specifying relationships between parts. In studying U.S. government, organization might involve breaking government into three branches (executive, legislative, judicial), breaking each of these into subparts (e.g., functions, agencies), and so on. Older students employ organization more often, but elementary children are capable of using organizational principles (Meece, 2002). For example, children studying leaves may organize them by size, shape, and edge pattern.

Retrieval theories postulate that organization improves retrieval by linking relevant information so that when retrieval is cued, spreading activation accesses the relevant propositions in LTM. Teachers routinely organize material, but student-generated organization is also effective for retrieval. Instruction on organizational principles assists learning. Consider a schema for understanding stories with four major attributes: setting, theme, plot, and resolution (Rumelhart, 1977). The setting ("Once upon a time . . . ") places the action in a context. The theme is then introduced, which consists of characters who have certain experiences and goals. The plot traces the actions of the characters to attain their goals. The resolution describes how the goal is reached or how the characters adjust to not attaining the goal. By describing and exemplifying these phases of a story, teachers help students learn to identify them on their own.

Sound instruction can help students develop better retrieval skills. For example, *explicit instruction* is a systematic approach in which students are clearly informed about the purpose and importance of the learning, given explanations and demonstrations of the skills, and provided with guided and independent practice opportunities (Archer & Hughes, 2011). As teachers convey the objectives and lesson openers to stimulate motivation, they can help students use retrieval of knowledge that will be needed in the new lesson. During the explanation and demonstration, teachers model the new skills (see Chapter 4) to include a strategy for retrieving needed knowledge from LTM. While students engage in guided practice, teachers can cue them as necessary to retrieve needed knowledge (e.g., "What have we worked on that also involved rectangles?"). Independent practice is the time when learners hone their skills and integrate the new learning of knowledge and skills with declarative and procedural knowledge in LTM for future retrieval.

Retrieval of Procedural Knowledge. Retrieval of procedural knowledge is similar to that of declarative knowledge. Retrieval cues trigger associations in memory, and the process of spreading activation activates and recalls relevant knowledge. Thus, if students are told to perform a procedure in chemistry laboratory frequently, they will cue that production in memory, retrieve it, and implement it.

Often retrieval of both declarative and procedural knowledge is necessary. While adding fractions, students use procedures (i.e., convert fractions to their lowest common denominator, add numerators) and declarative knowledge (addition facts). During reading comprehension, some processes operate as procedures (e.g., decoding, monitoring comprehension), whereas others involve declarative knowledge (e.g., word meanings, functions of punctuation marks). People typically employ procedures to acquire declarative knowledge, such as using mnemonic techniques to remember declarative knowledge (see Chapter 10). Having declarative information is typically a prerequisite for successfully implementing procedures. To solve for roots using the quadratic formula, students must know multiplication facts.

Declarative and procedural knowledge vary tremendously in scope. Individuals possess declarative knowledge about the world, themselves, and others; they understand procedures for accomplishing diverse tasks. Declarative and procedural knowledge are different in that *procedures transform information.* Such declarative statements as "$2 \times 2 = 4$" and "Uncle Fred smokes smelly cigars" change nothing, but applying the long-division algorithm to a problem changes an unsolved problem into a solved one.

Another difference is in speed of processing. Retrieval of declarative knowledge often is slow and conscious. Even assuming people know the answer to a question, they may have to think for some time to answer it. For example, consider the time needed to answer "Who was the U.S. president in 1867?" (Andrew Johnson). In contrast, once procedural knowledge is established in memory, it is retrieved quickly and often automatically. Skilled readers decode printed text automatically; they do not have to consciously reflect on what they are doing. Processing speed distinguishes skilled from poor readers (de Jong, 1998). Once you learned how to multiply, you did not have to think about what steps to follow to solve problems.

The differences in declarative and procedural knowledge have implications for teaching and learning. Students may have difficulty with a particular content area because they lack domain-specific declarative knowledge or because they do not understand the prerequisite procedures. Discovering which is deficient is a necessary first step for planning remedial instruction. Not only do deficiencies hinder learning, they also produce low self-efficacy (Chapter 4). Students who understand how to divide but do not know multiplication facts become demoralized when they often obtain incorrect answers.

False Memory. An area that has seen a fair amount of research attention is *false memory*, or memory of something that did not happen (Gallo, 2010). We all "remember" things that actually never happened. False memory highlights many points raised in this chapter. Retrieval from LTM never is automatic, but, rather, when we retrieve, we also reconstruct and transform. Associated knowledge may become combined such that what we retrieve is partially true and partially not. In a sense, such composite memory occurs frequently.

Research on false memory suggests why some eyewitness memory is flawed (Gallo, 2010). Further, researchers have shown that memory can be distorted by later events (Loftus, 2003, 2004). For example, asking people to retrieve information in the context of posing leading questions has been shown to distort memory (Loftus, 2003, 2004). These points support the notion that when memories are retrieved, they are transformed and reconsolidated with knowledge that makes sense given the context. It thus is little wonder that students often mix up knowledge when they retrieve it.

Language Comprehension

The process of language comprehension illustrates storage and retrieval of information in LTM (Carpenter, Miyake, & Just, 1995; Corballis, 2006; Matlin, 2009). Language comprehension is highly relevant to school learning and especially in light of the increasing numbers of students in U. S. schools who are English language learners (Fillmore & Valadez, 1986; Ford, 2016; Hancock, 2001; Padilla, 2006).

Comprehending spoken and written language represents a problem-solving process involving domain-specific declarative and procedural knowledge (Anderson, 1990). Language comprehension has three major components: perception, parsing, and utilization. *Perception* involves attending to and recognizing an input; sound patterns are translated into words in WM. *Parsing* means mentally dividing the sound patterns into units of meaning. *Utilization* refers to the disposition of the parsed mental representation: storing it in LTM if it involves learning, giving an answer if it is a question, asking a question if it is not comprehended, and so forth. This section covers parsing and utilization; perception was discussed in Chapter 5 (Application 6.2).

Parsing. Linguistic research shows that people understand the grammatical rules of their language, even though they usually cannot verbalize them (Clark & Clark, 1977; Matlin, 2009). Beginning with the work of Chomsky (1957), researchers have investigated the role of

---

APPLICATION 6.2
Language Comprehension

Students presented with confusing or vague information may misconstrue it or relate it to the wrong context. Teachers should present information clearly and concisely and ensure that students have adequate background information to build networks and schemata.

Mrs. Lineahan plans to present a social studies unit comparing city life with country life, but she wonders whether many of her fourth-grade students will have difficulty comprehending the unit because they never have seen a farm or heard words such as *silo, milking, sow,* and *livestock.*

Mrs. Lineahan can produce better student understanding by providing farm-related experiences: take a field trip to a farm; show videos illustrating farm life; and bring in farm materials such as seeds and plants. As students become familiar with farms, they will be better able to comprehend spoken and written communication about farms.

Young children may have difficulty following directions. Their limited use and understanding of language may cause them to interpret certain words or phrases differently than intended. For instance, if a

(Continued)

teacher said to a small group of children playing in a "dress-up" center, "Let's get things tied up so we can work on our next activity," the teacher might return to find children tying clothes together instead of cleaning up! Or a teacher might say, "Make sure you color this whole page," to children working with crayons. Later the teacher may discover that some children took a single crayon and colored the entire page from top to bottom instead of using various colors to color the items on the page. Teachers must explain, demonstrate, and model what they want children to do. Then they can ask the children to repeat in their own words what they think they are supposed to do.

deep structures containing prototypical representations of language structure. For example, the English language contains a deep structure for the pattern "noun 1–verb–noun 2," which allows us to recognize these patterns in speech and interpret them as "noun 1 did verb to noun 2" (e.g., "Jake dropped the ball"). Deep structures may be represented in LTM as productions. Chomsky postulated that the capacity for acquiring deep structures is innately human, although which structures are acquired depends on the language of one's culture.

Parsing includes more than just fitting language into productions. When people are exposed to language, they recall from LTM knowledge about the context into which they integrate new knowledge. A central point is that *all communication is incomplete*. Speakers do not provide all information relevant to the topic being discussed. Rather, they omit the information listeners are most likely to know (Clark & Clark, 1977). For example, suppose Sam meets Kira and Kira remarks, "You won't believe what happened to me at the concert!" Sam is most likely to activate propositional knowledge in LTM about concerts. Then Kira says, "As I was finding my seat . . . " To comprehend this statement, Sam must know that one purchases a ticket with an assigned seat. Kira did not tell Sam these things because she assumed he knew them.

Effective parsing requires using knowledge and drawing inferences (Resnick, 1985). When exposed to verbal communication, individuals access information from LTM about the situation. This information exists in LTM as propositional networks hierarchically organized as schemas. Networks allow people to understand incomplete communications. Consider the following sentence: "I went to the grocery store and saved five dollars with coupons." Knowledge that people buy merchandise in grocery stores and that they can redeem coupons to reduce costs enables listeners to comprehend this sentence. The missing information is filled in with knowledge in memory.

People often misconstrue communications because they construct missing information with the wrong context. When given a vague passage about four friends getting together for an evening, music students interpreted it as a description of playing music, whereas physical education students described it as an evening of playing cards (Anderson, Reynolds, Schallert, & Goetz, 1977). The interpretative schemas salient in people's minds are used to comprehend problematic passages. Interpretations of communications become more reliable with development as children realize both the literal meaning of a message and its intent (Beal & Belgrad, 1990).

That spoken language is incomplete can be shown by decomposing communications into propositions and identifying how propositions are linked. Consider this example (Kintsch, 1979):

> The Swazi tribe was at war with a neighboring tribe because of a dispute over some cattle. Among the warriors were two unmarried men named Kakra and his younger brother Gum. Kakra was killed in battle.

Although this passage seems straightforward, analysis reveals at least 11 distinct propositions:

1. The Swazi tribe was at war.
2. The war was with a neighboring tribe.
3. The war had a cause.
4. The cause was a dispute over some cattle.
5. Warriors were involved.
6. The warriors were two men.
7. The men were unmarried.
8. The men were named Kakra and Gum.
9. Gum was the younger brother of Kakra.
10. Kakra was killed.
11. The killing occurred during battle.

Even this propositional analysis is incomplete. Propositions 1 through 4 link together, as do Propositions 5 through 11, but a gap occurs between 4 and 5. To supply the missing link, one might have to change Proposition 5 to "The dispute involved warriors." When much material has to be inferred, WM can become overloaded and comprehension suffers (Paas et al., 2010; Sweller, 2010).

Just and Carpenter (1992) formulated a *capacity theory of language comprehension*, which postulates that comprehension depends on WM capacity. Elements of language (e.g., words, phrases) become activated in WM and are operated on by other processes. If the total amount of activation available to the system is less than the amount required to perform a comprehension task, then cognitive load is high (see Chapter 5) and some of the activation maintaining older elements will be lost (Carpenter et al., 1995). Elements comprehended at the start of a lengthy sentence may be lost by the end. Production-system rules presumably govern activation and the linking of elements in WM.

We see the application of this model in parsing of ambiguous sentences or phrases (e.g., "The soldiers warned about the dangers . . . "; MacDonald, Just, & Carpenter, 1992). Although alternative interpretations of such constructions initially may be activated, the duration of maintaining them depends on WM capacity. Persons with large WM capacities maintain the interpretations for quite a while, whereas those with smaller capacities typically maintain only the most likely (although not necessarily correct) interpretation. With increased exposure to the context, comprehenders can decide which interpretation is correct.

In building representations, people include important information and omit details. These *gist representations* include propositions most germane to comprehension. Listeners' ability to make sense of a text depends on what they know about the topic.

When the appropriate network or schema exists in listeners' memories, they employ a production that extracts the most central information to fill the slots in the schema. Comprehension proceeds slowly when a network must be constructed because it does not exist in LTM.

Stories exemplify how schemas are employed. Stories have a prototypical schema that includes setting, initiating events, internal responses of characters, goals, attempts to attain goals, outcomes, and reactions (Black, 1984; Rumelhart, 1975, 1977; Stein & Trabasso, 1982). When hearing a story, people construct a mental model of the situation by recalling the story schema and gradually fitting information into it (Bower & Morrow, 1990; Surprenant & Neath, 2009). Some categories (e.g., initiating events, goal attempts, consequences) are nearly always included, but others (internal responses of characters) may be omitted (Mandler, 1978; Stein & Glenn, 1979). Comprehension proceeds quicker when schemas are easily activated. People recall stories better when events are presented in the expected order (i.e., chronological) rather than in a nonstandard order (i.e., flashback). Early home literacy experiences that include exposure to books relate positively to the development of listening comprehension (Sénéchal & LeFevre, 2002).

Utilization. Utilization refers to what people do with the communications they receive. For example, if the communicator asks a question, listeners retrieve information from LTM to answer it. In classrooms, students link the communication with related information in LTM.

To use sentences properly, as speakers intend them, listeners must encode three pieces of information: speech act, propositional content, and thematic content. A *speech act* is the speaker's purpose in uttering the communication, or what the speaker is trying to accomplish with the utterance (Austin, 1962; Searle, 1969). Speakers may be conveying information to listeners, commanding them to do something, requesting information from them, promising them something, and so on. *Propositional content* is information that can be judged true or false. *Thematic content* refers to the context in which the utterance is made. Speakers make assumptions about what listeners know. On hearing an utterance, listeners infer information not explicitly stated but germane to how it is used. The speech act and propositional and thematic contents are most likely encoded with productions.

As an example of this process, assume that Ms. Gravitas is discussing history and questioning students about text material. She might ask, "What was Churchill's position during World War II?" The speech act is a request and is signaled by the sentence beginning with "what." The propositional content refers to Churchill's position during World War II; it might be represented in memory as follows: Churchill–Prime Minister–Great Britain–World War II. The thematic content refers to what the teacher left unsaid; the teacher assumes students have heard of Churchill and World War II. Thematic content also includes the classroom question-and-answer format. The students understand that they will be asked questions.

Of special importance is how students encode assertions. When teachers utter an assertion, they are conveying to students they believe the stated proposition is true. If Ms. Gravitas said, "Churchill was the Prime Minister of Great Britain during World War II," she is conveying her belief that this assertion is true. Students record the assertion with related information in LTM.

Speakers may facilitate the process whereby people relate new assertions with information in LTM by employing the *given-new contract* (Clark & Haviland, 1977), a type of implicit understanding. Given information should be readily identifiable, and new information should be unknown to the listener. We might think of the given-new contract as a production. In integrating information into memory, listeners identify given information, access it in LTM, and relate new information to it. For the given-new contract to enhance utilization, given information must be readily identified by listeners. When given information is not readily available because it is not in listeners' memories or has not been accessed in a long time, using the given-new production is difficult.

Language comprehension is a central component of information processing, communication, listening, and literacy. Habit 5 of Covey's (1989) *Seven Habits of Highly Effective People* is "Seek first to understand, then to be understood," which emphasizes listening. Listening is intimately linked with high achievement. A student who is a good listener is rarely a poor reader. Among college students, measures of listening comprehension may be indistinguishable from those of reading comprehension (Miller, 1988).

There are many students who have language processing disorders. School-based professionals who identify, evaluate, and provide therapeutic services to these students are *speech-language pathologists*. Their primary goal is to help remedy learners' speech and language problems and thereby help them achieve their maximum communication potential (Heward, Alber-Morgan, & Konad, 2017).

Treatments for language disorders are varied (Heward et al., 2017), but they share the common element of helping students process language more effectively. Professionals may work with students one-to-one or in groups; the latter have the added benefit of peer language modeling and support. Some therapists use didactic, structured formats with targeted speech and language behaviors prompted and reinforced; others are less structured and attend to other aspects such as children's interests and motivation. Some use naturalistic contexts as might be found in children's environment where conversations occur. Regardless of the context, interventions must take into account that communication is interactive and interpersonal and involves information processes of attention, perception, WM, and LTM.

FORGETTING

Forgetting involves the loss of knowledge from memory or the inability to retrieve knowledge. Researchers disagree about whether information is lost from memory or whether it still is present but cannot be retrieved because it has been distorted, the retrieval cues are inadequate, or other information is interfering with its recall. Forgetting has been studied experimentally since the time of Ebbinghaus (Chapter 1). Before presenting an information processing perspective on forgetting, some historical work on interference is discussed.

Interference Theory

One of the contributions of verbal learning research (Chapter 5) was the *interference theory of forgetting*. According to this theory, learned associations are never completely forgotten. Forgetting results from competing associations that lower the probability of the correct association being recalled; that is, other material becomes associated with the original stimulus (Postman, 1961). The problem lies in retrieving information from memory rather than in memory itself.

Two types of interference were experimentally identified (Table 6.1). *Retroactive interference* occurs when new verbal associations make remembering prior associations difficult. *Proactive interference* refers to older associations that make newer learning more difficult.

To demonstrate retroactive interference, an experimenter might ask two groups of individuals to learn Word List A. Group 1 then learns Word List B, while group 2 engages in a competing activity (e.g., counting backward from 100) to prevent rehearsal of List A. Both groups then attempt to recall List A. Retroactive interference occurs if the recall of Group 2 is better than that of Group 1. For proactive interference, Group 1 learns List A while Group 2 does nothing. Both groups then learn List B and attempt to recall List B. Proactive interference occurs if the recall of Group 2 surpasses that of Group 1.

Retroactive and proactive interference occur often in school. Retroactive interference is seen among students who learn words with regular spellings and then learn words that are exceptions to spelling rules. If, after some time, they are tested on the original words, they might alter the spellings to those of the exceptions. Proactive interference is evident among students taught first to multiply and then to divide fractions. When subsequently tested on division, they may simply multiply without first inverting the second fraction. Developmental research shows that proactive interference decreases between the ages of 4 and 13 (Kail, 2002). Application 6.3 offers suggestions for dealing with interference.

Interference theory represented an important step in specifying memory processes. Early theories of learning postulated that learned connections leave a memory "trace" that weakens and decays with nonuse. Skinner (1953; Chapter 3) did not postulate an internal memory trace but suggested that forgetting results from lack of opportunity to respond due to the stimulus being absent for some time. Each of these views has shortcomings. Although some decay may occur (discussed later), the memory trace notion is vague and difficult to verify experimentally. The nonuse position holds at times, but exceptions do exist; for example, being able to recall information after many years of nonuse (e.g., names

Table 6.1
Interference and forgetting.

Task	Retroactive Interference		Proactive Interference	
	Group 1	**Group 2**	**Group 1**	**Group 2**
Learn	A	A	A	—
Learn	B	—	B	B
Test	A	A	B	B

Note: Each group learns the task to some criterion of mastery. The "—" indicates a period of time in which the group is engaged in another task that prevents rehearsal but does not interfere with the original learning. Interference is demonstrated if Group 2 outperforms Group 1 on the test.

APPLICATION 6.3
Interference in Teaching and Learning

Proactive and retroactive interference occur often in teaching and learning. Teachers cannot completely eliminate interference, but they can minimize its effects by recognizing areas in the curriculum that easily lend themselves to interference. For example, students learn to subtract without regrouping and then to subtract with regrouping. Ms. Hastings often finds that when she gives her third-grade students review problems requiring regrouping, some students do not regroup. To minimize interference, she teaches students the underlying rules and principles and has them practice applying the skills in different contexts. She points out similarities and differences between the two types of problems

and teaches students how to decide whether regrouping is necessary. Frequent reviews help to minimize interference.

When spelling words are introduced at the primary level, words often are grouped by phonetic similarities (e.g., *crate, slate, date, state, mate, late*); however, when children learn certain spelling patterns, it may confuse them as they encounter other words (e.g., *weight* or *wait* rather than *wate*; *freight* rather than *frate*). Ms. Hastings provides additional instruction regarding other spellings for the same sounds and exceptions to phonetic rules along with periodic reviews over time. These practices should help alleviate confusion and interference among students.

---

of some of your elementary school teachers) is not unusual. Interference theory surmounts these problems by postulating how information in memory becomes confused with other information. It also specifies a research model for investigating these processes.

Tulving (1974) postulated that forgetting represents *inaccessibility of information* due to improper retrieval cues. Information in memory does not decay, become confused, or get lost. Rather, the memory trace is intact but cannot be accessed. Memory of information depends on the trace being intact and on having adequate retrieval cues. Perhaps you cannot remember your phone number from when you were a child. You may not have forgotten it; the memory is submerged because your current environment is different from that of years ago and the cues associated with your old phone number—your house, street, neighborhood—are absent. This principle of *cue-dependent forgetting* also is compatible with the common finding that people perform better on recognition than on recall tests. From a cue-dependent perspective, they should perform better on recognition tests because more retrieval cues are provided; in recall tests, they must supply their own cues.

In line with this point, forgetting can be a function of an encoding specificity mismatch where retrieval cues do not match the encoded meanings (Ceci, Fitneva, & Williams, 2010). Providing students with more retrieval cues enhances the likelihood that one of these will align with the encoded information. Other research on interference suggests that interference occurs (e.g., people confuse elements) when the same cognitive schema or plan is used on multiple occasions (Thorndyke & Hayes-Roth, 1979; Underwood, 1983).

Interference has been implicated in *retrieval-induced* forgetting, or forgetting of some knowledge in memory due to retrieval of other knowledge (Jonker, Seli, & MacLeod, 2013; Radvansky & Ashcraft, 2014). Retrieval-induced forgetting may result from inhibition that reduces the accessibility of nontarget items that interfere with retrieval of target items (Murayama, Miyatsu, Buchli, & Storm, 2014). Retrieval-induced forgetting is thus facilitative because it allows us to recall knowledge needed, but such forgetting may be enduring such that the suppressed knowledge may be difficult to recall later. Interference theory continues to provide a viable framework for investigating forgetting (Brown, Neath, & Chater, 2007; Oberauer & Lewandowsky, 2008).

Information Processing

From an information processing perspective and supported by neuroscience research, *interference* refers to a blockage of the spread of activation across memory networks (Anderson, 1990). For various reasons, when people attempt to access information in memory, the activation process is thwarted. Although the mechanism blocking activation is not well understood, theory and research suggest various causes of interference.

One factor that can affect whether structures are activated is the *strength of original encoding*. Information that originally is strongly encoded through frequent rehearsal or extensive elaboration is more likely to be accessed than information that originally is weakly encoded.

A second factor is the number of *alternative network paths* down which activation can spread (Anderson, 1990). Information that can be accessed via many routes is more likely to be remembered than information that is only accessible via fewer paths. For example, if I want to remember the name of Aunt Frieda's parakeet (Mr. T), I should associate that with many cues, such as my friend Mr. Thomas, the fact that when Mr. T spreads his wings it makes the letter *T*, and the idea that his constant chirping taxes my tolerance. Then, when I attempt to recall the name of the parakeet I can access it via my memory networks for Aunt Frieda and for parakeets. If these fail, then I still have available the networks for my friends, the letter *T*, and things that tax my tolerance. In contrast, if I associate only the name "Mr. T" with the bird, then the number of alternative paths available for access is fewer, and the likelihood of interference is greater.

A third factor is the *amount of distortion or merging of information*. We have discussed the memory benefits of organizing, elaborating, and making information meaningful by relating it to what we know. Whenever we engage in these practices, we change the nature of information, and in some cases, we merge it with other information or subsume it under more-general categories. Such merging and subsumption facilitate *meaningful reception learning* (Ausubel, 1963, 1968; see Chapter 5). Sometimes, however, such distortion and merging may cause interference and make recall more difficult than if information is remembered on its own. When we attempt to recall knowledge, we may fill in gaps with what makes sense. These distortions are in fact meaningful.

Interference is an important cause of forgetting, but it is unlikely that it is the only one (Anderson, 1990). It appears that some information in LTM decays systematically with the passage of time and independently of any interference. Wickelgren (1979) traced systematic decay of information in time intervals ranging from 1 minute to 2 weeks. Information decays rapidly at first with decay gradually tapering off. Researchers find little forgetting after 2 weeks. However, the best evidence for decay is found in memories that are time bound; namely, sensory memory and WM (Surprenant & Neath, 2009)

The position that forgetting occurs because of decay is difficult to affirm or refute. Explanations given for decay often are vague (Surprenant & Neath, 2009). Failure to recall even with extensive cuing does not unequivocally support a decay position because it still is possible that the appropriate memory networks were not activated. Similarly, the fact that the decay position posits no psychological processes responsible for forgetting (rather only the passage of time) does not refute the position. Memory traces include both perceptual features and reactions to the experiences (Estes, 1997). Decay or changes in one or both cause forgetting and memory distortions. Furthermore, the decay process may be neurological. Synaptic connections weaken with lack of use in the same way that muscles do (Chapter 2).

Decay is commonly cited as a reason for forgetting (Nairne, 2002). You may have learned French in high school but now, some years later, cannot recall many vocabulary words. You might explain that as, "I haven't used it for so long that I've forgotten it." And forgetting is beneficial. Were we to remember everything we have ever learned, our memories would be so overcrowded that new learning would be difficult. Forgetting is facilitative when it rids us of knowledge that we have not used and thus may not be important, analogous to your discarding things that you no longer need. Forgetting leads people to act, think, judge, and feel differently than they would in the absence of forgetting. Forgetting has profound effects on teaching and learning (Application 6.4).

APPLICATION 6.4
Minimizing Forgetting of Academic Learning

Forgetting is a problem when learned knowledge is needed for new learning. To help students retain important information and skills, teachers might do the following:

- Engage in periodic reviews of important knowledge and skills using authentic tasks.
- Structure classwork and homework so that they reinforce previously learned skills.
- During vacation breaks, have students complete online modules that reinforce knowledge and skills.
- When introducing a new lesson or unit, review previously learned material needed for mastering the new material.

When Mrs. Baitwick-Smith introduces long division, some third graders have forgotten how to regroup in subtraction, which can slow the new learning. She spends a little time reviewing subtraction—especially problems requiring regrouping—as well as quizzing students on multiplication and simple division facts. She also gives homework that reinforces the same skills.

Ms. Zhang, a physical education teacher, is teaching a basketball unit over several days. At the start of each class, she reviews the skills taught in the previous class before she introduces the new skill. Periodically she spends an entire class period reviewing all the skills

(Continued)

(e.g., dribbling, passing, shooting, playing defense) that the students have been working on up to that point. They then apply all of these skills in the games that Ms. Zhang organizes.

In Professor Astoolak's graduate seminar, students have been assigned an application paper that focuses on motivation techniques. During the semester, she introduced various motivational theories. Many students have forgotten some key principles of the theories. To help the students prepare for writing their papers, she spends part of one class period reviewing the major motivation theories. Then she divides students into small groups and has each group write a brief summary of one of the theories with some classroom applications. After working in small groups, each group shares its findings with the entire class.

RELEARNING

Memory Savings

Relearning is learning material for the second or subsequent time after it previously had been learned (i.e., had satisfied the criteria of learning as stated in Chapter 1). Relearning is a common phenomenon and occurs daily for all of us. The opening vignette exemplifies relearning that occurs in school settings.

But relearning is more than just a common human activity; it also strikes to the heart of the issue about whether knowledge, once encoded in LTM, is there permanently or whether it can be lost. Recall from Chapter 1 the research by Ebbinghaus on memory. He relearned material some time after the original learning and calculated the savings score, or the amount of time or number of trials necessary to relearn as a percentage of the amount of time or number of trials necessary for original learning. The result that relearning is easier than new learning has been obtained in other research studies (Bruning et al., 2011).

Since relearning is easier than new learning, it suggests that at least some knowledge in LTM may not be permanently lost. Forgetting is said to occur when knowledge cannot be retrieved, perhaps because of inadequate retrieval cues, retrieval conditions not matching those of original learning, and so forth. Relearning research suggests that we may not forget but rather retain in LTM more knowledge than we can recall, recognize, or otherwise retrieve.

From the perspective of information processing theory, it is not clear why relearning is more efficient than new learning. It may be that memory network traces are retained, so that when people relearn they reconstruct these memories. Neuroscience research (Chapter 2) shows that networks respond to use, so when people do not use them, they become weakened but not necessarily lost (Wolfe, 2010).

As with new learning, relearning proceeds better with distributed practice (regular shorter sessions) than with massed practice (irregular more-intense sessions; Bruning et al., 2011). Perhaps the distributing of relearning allows memory networks to strengthen in such a way that they become established better.

Effect of Testing

Another factor that can affect relearning is testing. The role of testing in accountability was discussed in Chapter 1. There is much pressure on schools today to ensure that students learn requisite skills and meet learning standards and outcomes. This emphasis can create a negative view of testing among educators, parents, and students.

A *testing effect* occurs when taking tests or quizzes enhances learning and retention such that scores on the final test are higher than if prior testing had not occurred (Bruning et al., 2011). Retrieving the knowledge helps to strengthen the memory of the retrieved knowledge (Rowland, 2014). This effect has been observed with different types of content (Karpicke & Aue, 2015), and with learners of various ages including children as young as first graders (Lipowski, Pyc, Dunlosky, & Rawson, 2014). The testing effect suggests that some learning occurs while students are being tested, presumably because they recall and rehearse material and relate it in new ways to other knowledge. What also is interesting, however, is that taking a test can have a stronger effect on retention than spending the same amount of time restudying the content (Bruning et al., 2011). Roediger and Karpicke (2006) found that on a test a week after learning, students who studied and were tested during original learning outperformed those who only had studied the content.

Being tested while one is learning forces one to retrieve knowledge. It may be that the testing requires learners to organize and elaborate material better, and these transformations lead to better long-term retention and relearning. Also, the retrieval practiced during learning is done under similar conditions as that done during subsequent testing, so we should expect positive transfer from the original learning context to the later testing one. Conversely, research studies have yielded mixed results on whether the benefits of testing on facts transfers to application-type questions (Pan, Gopal, & Rickard, 2016). Transfer is discussed later in this chapter.

This benefit should not be construed as an argument for more testing in schools. But educators who are aware of the potential advantage can design curricula to use testing not just for accountability but also as a means to promote learning. The judicious use of quizzes and tests may help alleviate some of the need for reviews lamented by the educators in the opening vignette.

VISUAL MEMORY

Chapters 5 and 6 focus primarily on verbal memory—the memory of words and meanings. But another type is visual memory (Matlin, 2009). In fact, people often remember information better in visual rather than in verbal form, and memory is enhanced when information is presented in both forms (Sadoski & Paivio, 2001).

Visual memory (or *visual imagery* or *mental imagery*) refers to mental representations of visual/spatial knowledge including physical properties of the objects or events represented. Visual memory should not be confused with a visual *learning style* (Chapter 11), which refers to an individual's stable and preferred means of organizing and processing information. All learners with normal visual capabilities possess visual memories, but only some may be characterized as possessing a visual learning style. This section discusses how knowledge is represented visually and individual differences in visual memory capabilities.

Representation of Visual Information

Visual stimuli that are attended to are held briefly in veridical (true) form in the sensory register and then are transferred to WM. Recall from Chapter 5 that in

Visual memory has been valued as far back as the time of the ancient Greeks. Plato felt that thoughts and perceptions are impressed on the mind as a block of wax and are remembered as long as the images last (Paivio, 1970). Simonides, a Greek poet, believed that images are associative mediators. He devised the *method of loci* as a memory aid (Chapter 10). In this method, information to be remembered is paired with locations in a familiar setting.

Visual imagery also has been influential in discoveries. Shepard (1978) described Einstein's *Gedanken experiment* that marked the beginning of the relativistic reformulation of electromagnetic theory. Einstein imagined himself traveling with a beam of light (186,000 miles per second), and what he saw corresponded neither to light nor to anything described by Maxwell's equations in classical electromagnetic theory. Einstein reported that he typically thought in terms of images and only reproduced his thoughts in words and mathematical equations once he conceptualized the situation visually. The German chemist Kekulé supposedly had a dream in which he visualized the structure of benzene, and Watson and Crick apparently used mental rotation to break the genetic code.

In contrast to images, propositions are discrete representations of meaning not resembling their referents in structure. The expression "New York City" no more resembles the city than virtually any three words picked at random from a dictionary. An image of New York City containing skyscrapers, stores, people, and traffic is more similar in structure to its referent. The same contrast is evident for events. Compare the sentence, "The black dog ran across the lawn," with an image of this scene.

Visual memory is a controversial topic (Matlin, 2009). A central issue is how closely visual images resemble actual pictures: Do they contain the same details as pictures or are they fuzzy pictures portraying only highlights? The visual pattern of a stimulus is perceived when its features are linked to a LTM representation. This implies that images can only be as clear as the LTM representations. To the extent that images are the products of people's perceptions, images are likely to be incomplete representations of stimuli. There is evidence that people construct images in memory and then reconstruct them during retrieval (Surprenant & Neath, 2009), both of which cause distortion.

Support for the idea that people use visual memory to represent spatial knowledge comes from studies where participants were shown pairs of two-dimensional pictures, each of which portrayed a three-dimensional object (Cooper & Shepard, 1973; Shepard & Cooper, 1983). The task was to determine if the two pictures in each pair portrayed the same object. The solution strategy involved mentally rotating one object in each pair until it matched the other object or until the individual decided that no amount of rotation would yield an identical object. Reaction times were a direct function of the number of mental rotations needed. Although these and other data suggest that people employ images to represent knowledge, they do not directly address the issue of how closely images correspond to actual objects.

To the extent that students use visual memory to represent spatial and visual knowledge, imagery is germane to educational content involving concrete objects. When teaching a unit about different types of rock formations (e.g., mountains, plateaus, ridges), an instructor could show pictures of the various formations and ask students to imagine them. In geometry, imagery could be employed when dealing with mental rotations. Pictorial illustrations improve students' learning from texts (Carney & Levin, 2002; see Application 6.5 for more examples).

APPLICATION 6.5
Using Visual Memory in Classrooms

Visual memory can improve student learning. One application involves instructing students on three-dimensional figures (e.g., cubes, spheres, cones) to include calculating their volumes. Verbal descriptors and two-dimensional diagrams are also used, but actual models of the figures greatly enhance teaching effectiveness. Allowing students to hold the shapes fosters their visual understanding of the concept of volume.

Visual memory can be applied in physical education. When students are learning an exercise routine accompanied by music, the teacher can model in turn each portion of the routine initially without music, after which students visualize what they saw. The students then perform each part of the routine. Later the teacher can add music to the individual portions.

For an elementary language arts unit involving writing a paragraph that gives directions for performing a task or making something, a teacher might ask his or her students to think about and picture the individual steps (e.g., of making a peanut butter and jelly sandwich). Once students finish, they can visualize each step while writing it down.

Art teachers can use visual memory to teach students to follow directions. The teacher might give the following directions orally and write them on the board: "Visualize on a piece of art paper a design including four circles, three triangles, and two squares, with some of the shapes overlapping one another." The teacher might ask the following questions to ensure that students are using visual memory: "How many circles do you see?" "How many triangles?" "How many squares?" "Are any of the shapes touching? Which ones?"

A dance teacher might have students listen to the music to which they will be performing. Then the students could imagine themselves dancing, visualizing every step and movement. The teacher also might ask students to visualize where they and their classmates are on the stage as they dance.

An American history teacher took his classes to a Civil War battlefield and had them imagine what it must have been like to fight a battle at that site. Later in class, he had students construct with technology a map that duplicated the site and then create visual scenarios for what could have happened as the Union and Confederate forces fought.

Researchers increasingly are studying the role of visualizations in learning. A *visualization* is a nonverbal symbolic or pictorial illustration such as a graph, realistic diagram, or picture (Höffler, 2010). A *dynamic visualization* is one that portrays change, such as a video and animation. Höffler reported that learners with low spatial ability seem better supported by dynamic rather than non-dynamic visualizations. Further, segmenting a dynamic visualization (showing in pieces with interspersed pauses) may help to reduce extraneous cognitive load (see Chapter 5), which can help students better process the representation (e.g., encode and store in LTM; Spanjers, van Gog, & van Merriënboer, 2010).

Evidence shows that people also can use visual memory with abstract dimensions. Kerst and Howard (1977) asked students to compare pairs of cars, countries, and animals on the concrete dimension of size and on an appropriate abstract dimension (e.g., cost, military power, ferocity). The abstract and concrete dimensions yielded similar results: As items became more similar, reaction times increased. For instance, comparing the sizes of a bobcat and an elephant is easier than comparing the sizes of a rhinoceros and a hippopotamus. How participants imagined abstract dimensions or whether they even used visual memory is not clear. Perhaps they represented abstract dimensions in terms of propositions, such as by comparing the United States and Jamaica on military power using the proposition, "(The) United States (has) more military power (than) Jamaica." Knowledge maps, which are pictorial representations of linked ideas, aid student learning (O'Donnell, Dansereau, & Hall, 2002).

Visual Memory and LTM

Although researchers agree that visual memory is part of WM, they disagree about whether images are retained in LTM (Kosslyn & Pomerantz, 1977; Matlin, 2009; Pylyshyn, 1973). *Dual-code theory* directly addresses this issue (Clark & Paivio, 1991; Paivio, 1971, 1978, 1986). LTM has two means of representing knowledge: A *verbal system* incorporating knowledge expressed in language and an *imaginal system* storing visual and spatial information. These systems are interrelated—a verbal code can be converted into an imaginal code and vice versa—but important differences exist. The verbal system is suited for abstract information, whereas the imaginal system can be used to represent concrete objects or events.

The experiments by Cooper and Shepard (1973) and by Shepard and Cooper (1983; described earlier in this section) support the utility of imagery and offer indirect support for the dual-code theory. Other supporting evidence comes from research showing that when recalling lists of concrete and abstract words, people recall concrete words better than abstract ones (Terry, 2009). According to dual-code theory. concrete words can be coded verbally and visually, whereas abstract words usually are coded only verbally. At recall, people draw on both memory systems for the concrete words, but only the verbal system for the abstract words. Other research on imaginal mnemonic mediators supports the dual-code theory (Chapter 10).

In contrast, *unitary theory* postulates that all information is represented in LTM in verbal codes (propositions). Images in WM are reconstructed from verbal LTM codes. Indirect support for this notion comes from Mandler and Johnson (1976) and Mandler and Ritchey (1977). As with verbal material, people employ schemas while acquiring visual information. They remember scenes better when elements are in a typical pattern; memory is poorer when elements are disorganized. Meaningful organization and elaboration of information into schemas improve memory for scenes much as they do for verbal material. This finding suggests the operation of a common process regardless of the form of information presented.

This debate notwithstanding, using concrete materials and pictures enhances memory (Terry, 2009). Such instructional tools as manipulatives, audiovisual aids, and computer graphics facilitate learning. Although concrete devices are undoubtedly more important for young children because they lack the cognitive capability to think in abstract terms, students of all ages benefit from information presented in multiple modes.

Individual Differences

How much people actually use visual memory varies as a function of cognitive development. Kosslyn (1980) proposed that children are more likely to use visual memory to remember and recall information than adults, who rely more on verbal representation. Kosslyn gave children and adults statements such as, "A cat has claws," and "A rat has fur." The task was to determine accuracy of the statements. Kosslyn reasoned that adults could respond quicker because they could access the propositional information from LTM, whereas children would have to recall the image of the animal and scan it. To control for adults' better information processing in general, some adults were asked to scan an image of the animal, whereas others were free to use any strategy.

Adults were slower to respond when given the imagery instructions than when free to choose a strategy, but no difference was found for children. These results suggest that children use visual memory even when they are free to do otherwise, but they do not address whether children cannot use verbal information (because of cognitive limitations) or whether they can but choose not to because for them visual memory is more effective.

Use of visual memory also depends on effectiveness of performing two types of component processes. One type helps to activate stored memories of parts of images, whereas the other reconstructs the parts into the proper configuration. These processes may be localized in different parts of the brain. Individual differences in imagery can result because people differ in how effectively this dual processing occurs (Kosslyn, 1988).

The use of visual memory by people of any age depends on what is to be imagined. Concrete objects are more easily imagined than abstractions. But the use of visual memory may be partially lost with development, perhaps because verbal representation replaces visual thinking. It also is possible that adults retain the capacity to form clear images but do not routinely do so because their verbal systems can represent more information. Although the capacity to use visual memory can be improved, many adults do not try to develop it.

TRANSFER

Transfer refers to knowledge being applied in new ways, in new situations, or in familiar situations with different content. Transfer also explains how prior learning affects subsequent learning. Transfer is involved in new learning when students retrieve their prior relevant knowledge and experiences (National Research Council, 2000). Without the cognitive capability for transfer, all learning would be situationally specific, and much instructional time would be spent reteaching skills in different contexts.

There are different types of transfer. *Positive transfer* occurs when prior learning facilitates subsequent learning. Learning how to drive a car with standard transmission should facilitate learning to drive other cars with standard transmission. *Negative transfer* means that prior learning interferes with subsequent learning or makes it more difficult. Learning to drive a standard transmission car might have a negative effect on subsequently learning to drive a car with automatic transmission because one might try to hit the non-existent clutch and shift gears while the car is moving, which could ruin the transmission. *Zero transfer* means that one type of learning has no noticeable influence on subsequent learning. Learning to drive a standard transmission car should have no effect on learning to operate a computer.

Current cognitive and constructivist conceptions of learning highlight the complexity of transfer (Phye, 2001; Taatgen, 2013). Although some forms of simple skill transfer seem to occur automatically, much transfer requires higher-order thinking skills and beliefs about the usefulness of knowledge. As such, transfer often does not occur (Perkins & Salomon, 2012). This section begins with a brief overview of historical perspectives on transfer, followed by a discussion of contemporary views and the relevance of transfer to school learning.

Historical Views

Historical views of transfer explained it in terms of identical elements, mental discipline, and generalization. These are discussed in turn.

Identical Elements. Behavior (conditioning) theories (Chapter 3) stress that transfer depends on identical elements or similar features (stimuli) among situations. Thorndike (1913b) contended that transfer occurs when situations have identical elements (stimuli) and call for similar responses. A clear and known relation must exist between the original and transfer tasks, as is often the case between classroom/tasks and homework.

This view is intuitively appealing. Students who learn to solve the problem $602 - 376 = ?$ are apt to transfer that knowledge and also solve the problem $503 - 287 = ?$ We might ask, however, what the elements are and how similar they must be to be considered identical. In subtraction, do the same types of numbers need to be in the same column? Elementary teachers know that students who can solve the problem $42 - 37 = ?$ will not necessarily be able to solve the problem $7428 - 2371 = ?$, even though the former problem is contained within the latter one. Findings such as this call into question the validity of identical elements. Furthermore, even when identical elements exist, students must recognize them. If students believe no commonality exists between situations, no transfer should occur. The identical elements position, therefore, is inadequate to explain all transfer.

Mental Discipline. The *mental discipline* doctrine (Chapter 3) holds that learning certain subjects (e.g., mathematics, the classics) enhances general mental functioning and facilitates learning of new content better than does learning other subjects. This view was popular in Thorndike's day and periodically re-emerges in the form of recommendations for basic or core skills, knowledge, and courses (e.g., Hirsch, 1987).

Research by Thorndike (1924) provided no support for the mental discipline idea (Chapter 3). Instead, Thorndike concluded that what facilitates new learning is students' beginning level of mental ability. Students who were more intelligent when they began a course gained the most from the course. The intellectual value of studies reflects not how much they improve students' ability to think but rather how they affect students' interests and goals.

Generalization. Skinner's (1953) operant conditioning theory proposed that transfer involves *generalization* of responses from one discriminative stimulus to another. For example, students might be taught to put their books in their desks when the bell rings. When students go to another class, putting books away when the bell rings might generalize to the new setting.

The notion of generalization, like identical elements, has intuitive appeal. Surely some transfer occurs through generalization, and it may even occur automatically. Students who are punished for misbehavior in one class may not misbehave in other classes. Once drivers learn to stop their cars at a red light, then that response will generalize to other red lights regardless of location, weather, time of day, and so forth.

Nonetheless, the generalization position has problems. As with identical elements, we can ask what features of the situation are used to generalize responses. Situations share many common features, yet we respond only to some of them and disregard others. We respond to the red light regardless of many other features in the situation. At the same time, we might be more likely to run a red light when no other cars are around or when we are in a hurry. Our response is not fixed but rather depends on our cognitive assessment of the situation. The same can be said of other situations where generalization does not occur automatically. Cognitive processes are involved in most generalization as people determine whether responding in similar fashion is appropriate in that setting. The generalization position, therefore, is incomplete because it neglects the role of cognitive processes.

Contemporary Perspectives

An information processing perspective contends that transfer involves activating knowledge in memory networks. It requires that knowledge bits be cross-referenced (linked) in memory (Anderson, 1990). The more links between forms of knowledge in memory, the likelier that activating one form of knowledge will cue other forms in memory. Such links can be made within and between networks.

In other words, transfer depends on students recognizing the common "deep" structure between the learning and transfer contexts, especially when the "surface" structures of the situations may differ (Chi & VanLehn, 2012). Information in memory networks involving deep structure will facilitate transfer when learners recognize that structure in the transfer context.

The same process is involved in transfer of procedural knowledge and productions (Bruning et al., 2011). Transfer occurs when knowledge and productions are linked in LTM with different content. Students must also believe that productions are useful in various situations. Transfer is aided by the uses of knowledge being stored with the knowledge itself. For example, learners may possess a production for skimming text. This may be linked in memory with other reading procedures (e.g., finding main ideas, sequencing) and may have various uses stored with it (e.g., skimming web page text to get the gist, skimming memos to determine meeting place and time). The more links in LTM and the more uses stored with skimming, the better the transfer. Such links are formed by having students practice skills in various settings and by helping them understand the uses of knowledge. The general aspects of production rules (similar to "deep" structures) promote transfer (Taatgen, 2013). These general aspects are developed by combining task-specific features that learners accumulate over different experiences.

This cognitive description of transfer fits much of what we know about cued knowledge. Where more LTM links are available, accessing information in different ways is possible. We may not be able to recall the name of Aunt Martha's dog by thinking about her (cuing the "Aunt Martha" network), but we might be able to recall the name by thinking about (cuing) breeds of dogs ("collie"). Such cuing is reminiscent of the experiences we periodically have of not being able to recall someone's name until we think about that person from a different perspective or in a different context.

But we still do not know much about how such links form. Links are not automatically made simply by pointing out uses of knowledge to students or having them practice skills in different contexts (National Research Council, 2000). The next section discusses different forms of transfer, which are governed by different conditions.

Other perspectives on transfer also stress cognitive and constructivist elements. Nokes-Malach and Mestre (2013) proposed that transfer is a problem-solving process that requires sense making. When confronted with a new situation, individuals activate knowledge based on their interpretation of what is needed in the current environment. They generate and evaluate a solution, and repeat the process if the solution is not successful. At all points along the way, learners employ *sense making*, or determining whether the task goals have been accomplished based on coordination of prior knowledge with information about the environment and the task.

Perkins and Salomon (2012) formulated a detect-elect-connect model of transfer. Learners detect a potential relation between the new situation and prior learning, elect to pursue it, and connect the two in meaningful ways. Motivation is important, both to help learners engage in transfer and thwart competing distractions.

Types of Transfer

Transfer is not a unitary phenomenon but rather is complex (Barnett & Ceci, 2002; Table 6.2). One distinction is between near and far transfer (Royer, 1986). *Near transfer* occurs when situations overlap a great deal, such as between the stimulus elements during instruction and those present in the transfer situation. An example is when fraction skills are taught and then students are tested on the content in the same format in which it was taught. In contrast, *far transfer* involves a transfer context much different from that in which original learning occurred. An example is applying fraction skills in an entirely different setting without explicitly being told to do so. Thus, students might have to add parts of a recipe ($\frac{1}{2}$ cup milk and $\frac{1}{4}$ cup water) to determine the amount of liquid without being told the task involves fractions.

Table 6.2
Types of transfer.

Type	Characteristics
Near	Much overlap between situations; original and transfer contexts are highly similar
Far	Little overlap between situations; original and transfer contexts are dissimilar
Literal	Intact skill or knowledge transfers to a new task
Figural	Use of some aspects of general knowledge to think or learn about a problem, such as with analogies or metaphors
Low road	Transfer of well-established skills in spontaneous and possibly automatic fashion
High road	Transfer involving abstraction through an explicit conscious formulation of connections between situations
Forward reaching	Abstracting behavior and cognitions from the learning context to one or more potential transfer contexts
Backward reaching	Abstracting in the transfer context features of the situation that allow for integration with previously learned skills and knowledge

Another distinction is between literal and figural transfer. *Literal transfer* involves transfer of an intact skill or knowledge to a new task (Royer, 1986). Literal transfer occurs when students use fraction skills in and out of school. *Figural transfer* refers to using some aspect of our general knowledge to think or learn about a particular problem. Figural transfer often involves using analogies, metaphors, or comparable situations. Figural transfer occurs when students encounter new learning and employ the same study strategies that they used to master prior learning in a related area. Figural transfer requires drawing an analogy between the old and new situations and transferring that general knowledge to the new situation.

Although some overlap exists, forms of transfer involve different types of knowledge. Near transfer and literal transfer involve primarily declarative knowledge and mastery of basic skills. Far transfer and figurative transfer involve declarative and procedural knowledge, as well as conditional knowledge concerning the types of situations in which the knowledge may prove useful (Royer, 1986).

Salomon and Perkins (1989) distinguished low-road from high-road transfer. *Low-road transfer* refers to transfer of well-established skills in a spontaneous and perhaps automatic fashion. In contrast, *high-road transfer* is abstract and mindful; it "involves the explicit conscious formulation of abstraction in one situation that allows making a connection to another" (Salomon & Perkins, 1989, p. 118).

Low-road transfer occurs with skills and actions that have been practiced extensively in varied contexts. The behaviors tend to be performed automatically in response to characteristics of a situation that are similar to those of the situation in which they were acquired. Examples are learning to drive a car and then driving a different but similar car, brushing one's teeth with a regular toothbrush and with an electric toothbrush, or solving algebra problems at school and at home. At times the transfer may occur with little conscious awareness of what one is doing. The level of cognitive activity increases when some aspect of the situation differs and requires attention. For example, most people have little trouble accommodating to features in rental cars. When features differ (e.g., the headlight control works differently or is in a different position from what one is used to), people have to learn these new features.

High-road transfer occurs when students learn a rule, principle, prototype, schema, and so forth, and then use it in a more general sense than how they learned it. Transfer is mindful because students do not apply the rule automatically. Rather, they examine the new situation and decide what strategies will be useful to apply. Abstraction is involved during learning and later when students perceive basic elements in the new problem or situation and decide to apply the skill, behavior, or strategy. Low-road transfer primarily involves declarative knowledge, and high-road transfer uses productions and conditional knowledge to a greater extent.

Salomon and Perkins (1989) distinguished two types of high-road transfer—forward reaching and backward reaching—according to where the transfer originates. *Forward-reaching transfer* occurs when one abstracts behavior and cognitions from the learning context to one or more potential transfer contexts. For example, while students are studying precalculus, they might think about how some of the material (e.g., limits) might be pertinent in calculus. Another example is while being taught in a class how a parachute works, students might think about how they will use the parachute in actually jumping from an airplane.

Forward-reaching transfer is proactive and requires self-monitoring of potential contexts and uses of skills and knowledge. To determine potential uses of precalculus, for example, learners must be familiar with other content knowledge of potential contexts in which knowledge might be useful. Forward-reaching transfer is unlikely when students have little knowledge about potential transfer contexts.

In *backward-reaching transfer*, students abstract in the transfer context features of the situation that allow for integration with previously learned ideas (Salomon & Perkins, 1989). While students are working on calculus problems, they might try to think of any situations in precalculus that could be useful for solving the calculus problems. Students who have difficulty learning new material employ backward-reaching transfer when they think back to other times when they experienced difficulty and ask what they did in those situations (e.g., seek help from friends, conduct a web search, reread the text, talk with the teacher). They then might be apt to implement one of those solutions in hopes of remedying their current difficulty. Analogical reasoning (Chapter 7) might involve backward-reaching transfer, as students apply steps from the original problem to the current one. Consistent with the effects of analogical reasoning on learning, Gentner, Loewenstein, and Thompson (2003) found that analogical reasoning enhanced transfer, especially when two original cases were presented together.

From an information processing perspective, transfer involves linked knowledge in LTM such that the activation of one item by WM can cue other items. Presumably low-road transfer is characterized by relatively automatic cuing. A central distinction between the two forms is degree of mindful abstraction, or the volitional, metacognitively guided employment of non-automatic processes (Salomon & Perkins, 1989). Mindful abstraction requires that learners do not simply act based on the first possible response but rather that they examine situational cues, define alternative strategies, gather information, and seek new connections between information. LTM cuing is not automatic with high-road transfer but rather deliberate and can result in links being formed in LTM as individuals think of new ways to relate knowledge and contexts.

Anderson, Reder, and Simon (1996) contended that transfer is more likely when learners attend to the cues that signal the appropriateness of using a particular skill. They then will be more apt to notice those cues on transfer tasks and employ the skill. In this sense, the learning and transfer tasks share symbolic elements. These shared elements are important in strategy transfer.

Strategy Transfer

Transfer applies to strategies as well as to skills and knowledge (Phye, 2001). An unfortunate finding of much research is that students learn strategies and apply them effectively but fail to maintain their use over time or generalize them beyond the instructional setting (Clerc, Miller, & Cosnefroy, 2014). This is a common issue encountered in problem solving (Chapter 7; Jonassen & Hung, 2006). Many factors impede strategy transfer, including not understanding that the strategy is appropriate for different settings, not understanding how to modify its use with different content, believing that the strategy is not as useful for performance as other factors (e.g., time available), thinking that the strategy takes too much effort, or not having the opportunity to apply the strategy with new material (Clerc et al., 2014; Dempster & Corkill, 1999; Pressley et al., 1990; Schunk & Rice, 1993).

Phye (1989, 1990, 1992, 2001; Phye & Sanders, 1992, 1994) developed a model for enhancing strategy transfer and conducted research testing its effectiveness. During the initial acquisition phase, learners receive instruction and practice to include assessment of their metacognitive awareness of the uses of the strategy. A later retention phase includes further practice on training materials and recall measures. The third transfer phase occurs when participants attempt to solve new problems that have different surface characteristics but that require the same solution strategy practiced during training. Phye also stressed the role of learner motivation for transfer and ways to enhance motivation by showing learners uses of knowledge. Motivation is a critical influence on transfer (Perkins & Salomon, 2012; Pugh & Bergin, 2006).

In one of Phye's studies, adults worked on verbal analogy problems. Some participants received corrective feedback during trials that consisted of identifying the correct solutions, whereas others were given advice concerning how to solve analogies. All students judged confidence in the correctness of solutions they generated. During training, corrective feedback was better than advice in promoting transfer of problem-solving skills; however, on a delayed transfer task, no difference occurred between conditions. Regardless of condition, confidence in problem-solving capabilities (analogous to self-efficacy; see Chapter 4) bore a positive relation to actual performance. Butler, Godbole, and Marsh (2013) found that providing feedback that included an explanation of the correct answer produced better transfer than did feedback that only included the correct answer.

In addition to knowledge of the strategy, transfer requires knowledge of the uses of the strategy, which is facilitated when learners explain the strategy as they learn it

APPLICATION 6.6
Facilitating Transfer

Ms. DiGiorgio helps her elementary students build on the knowledge they already have learned. She has her students recall the major points of each page of a story in their reading book before they write a summary paragraph about the story. She also reviews with them how to develop a complete paragraph. Building on former learning helps her children transfer knowledge and skills to a new activity.

In preparing for a class discussion about influential presidents of the United States, Mr. Neufeldt asks his high school students to list presidents who they feel had a major impact on American history. He instructs them to rely not only on what has been discussed in class but also on knowledge they have from previous courses or other readings and research they have done. He encourages students to pull the information together from the class discussion and incorporate the former learning into the learning that occurs from the new material.

(Crowley & Siegler, 1999). Feedback about how the strategy helps improve performance facilitates strategy retention and transfer (Phye & Sanders, 1994; Schunk & Swartz, 1993a, 1993b). Research results highlight the link between strategy transfer and information processing and the key roles played by practice, corrective feedback, and motivation. It also underscores the point that teaching students self-regulated learning strategies can facilitate transfer (Fuchs et al., 2003; Fuchs, Fuchs, Finelli, Courey, & Hamlett, 2004; Chapter 10). Application 6.6 has suggestions for ways to facilitate transfer.

INSTRUCTIONAL APPLICATIONS

Information processing principles increasingly have been applied to school learning settings. This section describes retrieval applications: encoding-retrieval similarity, retrieval-based learning, and teaching for transfer.

Encoding-Retrieval Similarity

There are memory benefits from encoding specificity, or when learning conditions at retrieval match as closely as possible those present during encoding. The term "encoding specificity" omits "retrieval," which can convey the erroneous impression that encoding is the most important process and that once encoding occurs, retrieval will happen. Suprenant and Neath (2009) underscore the importance of retrieval and present an encoding-retrieval principle of memory, which states that memory depends heavily on the relation between the conditions at encoding and those at retrieval. This relation is referred to as *encoding-retrieval similarity*.

An instructional implication of encoding-retrieval similarity is to have the same or similar context at retrieval that was present at encoding. For example, students who learn in a computer-based learning environment (e.g., online) might be tested in the same environment. Students who learn to solve algebra problems written in particular formats might be tested with similar problems. The prediction is that the similarity between encoding and retrieval conditions should facilitate memory and performance.

But as we have seen in this chapter, transfer is important. Educators want students to be able to transfer their skills beyond the conditions present at encoding and retrieve them under different conditions. Teachers can facilitate transfer by helping students encode a reminder that they can subsequently retrieve and that will promote further retrieval. For example, if students are learning a strategy for comprehending written text, the teacher might label this strategy "the steps," then tell students that when they have to answer comprehension questions to think of "the steps." Such a reminder should cue retrieval of the strategy's steps for comprehension.

The educators in the opening vignette lament the need for many reviews because students seem to forget so much, even over long weekends. It is possible that students have not forgotten the content but rather cannot retrieve it due to inadequate cues. Providing more cues at retrieval may help lessen the need for reviews. Under what conditions did students learn the material? Did they work individually or in groups? Whole class or small groups? Computer-based learning environment? What content was associated with the original learning? When students return from a long break, teachers can cue not only the content learned but also the conditions under which students learned it. For example, a teacher might remind students that they studied this content last week Thursday afternoon, where they worked in small groups on computers studying environmental pollution.

Retrieval-Based Learning

Retrieval often is thought of as an end product of learning (encoding) because retrieval happens after learning occurs. But retrieval also can affect learning directly and indirectly (Karpicke & Grimaldi, 2012). Retrieval influences learning directly because when we retrieve knowledge, we alter it and enhance our capability to reconstruct that knowledge in the future. Indirect retrieval effects on learning occur when retrieval affects other variables that, in turn, can influence learning. For example, when an instructor asks you a question in class, you attempt to retrieve knowledge, and the success of your retrieval gives you feedback about how well you know the material. Such feedback may motivate you to study harder and may affect your self-efficacy for performing well in the class.

There are many ways that teachers use retrieval to promote learning, including class questions and discussions, tests, and quizzes. Yet the opening vignette shows that teachers do not like to engage in so many review sessions, and few teachers would advocate for more testing. Quizzes without grades can be given for students to check their levels of understanding, perhaps at the end of learning sessions. But there are other ways to effectively use retrieval as a learning process.

One means is to have students use retrieval when they study. Students may believe that studying involves mostly reading, but studying also can include frequent times when students stop reading and attempt to recall what they have read. The recall is a form of active rehearsal. Studying plus retrieval produces superior learning compared with studying alone (Karpicke & Grimaldi, 2012).

Another suggestion is to have students construct concept maps that link with networks of related concepts in memory. Students can do this as they work in class or study on their own. Teachers can facilitate this process by asking students to construct maps that reflect not only concepts directly related to one another but also those requiring inferences (e.g., the example used earlier about when the vice president would vote in the Senate).

Students may not be aware of the potential benefits of retrieval on learning, which suggests that teaching students retrieval strategies (e.g., self-cuing) may be helpful. Retrieval is a key process of academic studying stressed by self-regulated learning researchers (Chapter 10). An abundance of research shows that students can be taught self-regulated learning strategies and can transfer them outside of the learning context to improve their academic performances (Zimmerman & Schunk, 2011).

Some other effective ways to build retrieval into learning settings include reciprocal teaching (Chapter 8) and computer-based learning methods (Chapter 7). Computer-based systems can be programmed to guide students' retrieval (Karpicke & Grimaldi, 2012). For example, the system has students engage in repeated retrieval, but the study decisions are made by the system rather than the student. This type of arrangement takes into account individual student differences, as some students will benefit more from greater retrieval opportunities than will others.

Retrieval-based learning can have motivational effects (Chapter 9). Students who can retrieve knowledge are apt to experience heightened self-efficacy for performing well (Chapter 4; Schunk & DiBenedetto, 2016). The belief that they have learned may strengthen their self-efficacy and motivate them to continue to apply themselves to learn.

Teaching for Transfer

Although there are different forms of transfer, they often work in concert. While students complete a task, some behaviors may transfer automatically, whereas others may require mindful application. For example, assume that Jeff is writing a short paper. In thinking through the organization, Jeff might employ high-road, backward-reaching transfer by thinking about how he organized papers in previous, similar situations. Many aspects of the task, including word choice and spellings, will occur automatically (low-road transfer). As Jeff writes, he also might think about how this information could prove useful in other settings. Thus, if the paper is on some aspect of the Civil War, Jeff might think of how to use this knowledge in history class. Salomon and Perkins (1989) cited an example involving chess masters, who accumulate a repertoire of configurations from years of play. Although some of these may be executed automatically, expert play depends on mindfully analyzing play and potential moves. It is strategic and involves high-road transfer.

In some situations, low-road transfer could involve a good degree of mindfulness. With regard to strategy transfer, even minor variations in formats, contexts, or requirements can make transfer problematic among students, especially among those who experience learning problems (Borkowski & Cavanaugh, 1979). Conversely, some uses of analogical reasoning can occur with little conscious effort if the analogy is relatively clear. A good rule is never to take transfer for granted; it must be directly addressed.

This raises the issue of how teachers might encourage transfer in students. A major goal of teaching is to promote long-term retention and transfer (Halpern & Hakel, 2003). We know that having students practice skills in varied contexts and ensuring that they understand different uses for knowledge builds links in LTM (Anderson, Reder, & Simon, 1996). Homework is a mechanism for transfer because at home students practice and refine skills learned in school. Although the direction of the influence is not clear, researchers have found a positive relation between homework and student achievement with the relation being stronger in grades 7–12 than in grades K–6 (Cooper, Robinson, & Patall, 2006).

Another way to facilitate transfer is to have students engage in small-group learning that emphasizes inquiry and project-based learning. Compared with individual learning, small groups have been shown to promote knowledge acquisition, comprehension, problem solving, metacognition, and motivation (O'Donnell, 2006; Pai, Sears, & Maeda, 2015). Interacting with others can promote a deep understanding of content, which relates to better transfer (Chi & VanLehn, 2012). In support of these points, Pai et al. (2015) conducted a review of research and found that small-group learning promoted transfer and that this benefit did not depend on whether the groups were more or less structured (e.g., with group goals and individual roles and accountability).

But students do not automatically transfer strategies for the reasons noted earlier. Practice addresses some of these concerns, but not others. Cox (1997) recommended that as students learn in many contexts, they should determine what they have in common. Complex skills, such as comprehension and problem solving, will probably benefit most from this situated cognition approach (Griffin, 1995). Motivation also should be addressed (Pugh & Bergin, 2006). Teachers may need to provide students with explicit motivational feedback that links strategy use with improved performance and provides information about how the strategy will prove useful in that setting. Studies show that such motivational feedback enhances strategy use, academic performance, and self-efficacy for performing well (Schunk & Rice, 1993).

Learners also can establish academic goals (a motivational variable), the attainment of which requires careful deliberation and use of available resources. By cuing students at appropriate times, teachers may help them use relevant knowledge in new ways. Teachers might ask a question such as, "What do you know that might help you in this situation?" Such cuing tends to be associated with greater generation of ideas. Teachers can serve as models for transfer. Modeling strategies that bring related knowledge to bear on a new situation encourages students to seek ways to enhance transfer in both forward- and backward-reaching fashion and feel more efficacious about doing so. Working with children in grades 3–5 during mathematical problem solving, Rittle-Johnson (2006) found that having children explain how answers were arrived at and whether they were correct promoted transfer of problem-solving strategies.

SUMMARY AND CRITIQUE

Chapter Summary

Retrieval is a key component of information processing. Retrieval is the successful result of encoding but also can facilitate learning. When learners have to retrieve knowledge, the appropriate cues enter WM and activate LTM networks through spreading activation.

For verbal knowledge, the learner's WM constructs a response when the knowledge is obtained. Memory search continues until knowledge is retrieved. An unsuccessful search yields no information. Much retrieval occurs automatically.

Certain conditions affect the efficacy of retrieval. One is encoding specificity or encoding-retrieval similarity: Retrieval proceeds best when retrieval cues and conditions match those present at encoding. Other conditions that facilitate retrieval are elaboration, meaningfulness, and organization of knowledge in LTM. Presumably these conditions promote spreading activation and access by learners of needed memory networks.

An area that illustrates the storage and retrieval of information in LTM is language comprehension, which involves perception, parsing, and utilization. Communications are incomplete; speakers omit information they expect that listeners will know. Effective language comprehension requires that listeners possess adequate propositional knowledge and schemas and understand the context. To integrate information into memory, listeners identify given information, access it in LTM, and relate new information to it. Language comprehension is a central aspect of literacy and relates strongly to academic success—especially in subjects that require extensive reading.

Even when knowledge is encoded, it may be forgotten. Forgetting refers to the loss of information from memory or the failure to access it. Failure to retrieve may result from decay of information or interference. Factors that facilitate retrieval and lessen the chance of forgetting are the strength of the original encoding, the number of alternative memory networks, and the amount of distortion or merging of information. Retrieval always involves some amount of re-construction of knowledge as learners access information in LTM.

Because forgetting occurs, relearning often is necessary. Research evidence shows that relearning typically is easier than new learning, which suggests that some amount of knowledge in LTM is not forgotten but rather difficult to access. The savings score indicates the amount of time or number of trials necessary for relearning as a percentage of the amount of time or number of trials necessary for original learning. A testing effect occurs when taking tests or quizzes enhances learning and retention such that scores on the final test are higher than if prior testing had not occurred. Although this is not an argument for more testing of students, research supports the point that testing seems to facilitate retention and relearning and perhaps better than additional studying. To lessen evaluative pressures, teachers can give students non-graded quizzes at the end of learning sessions.

Much evidence exists for information being stored in memory in verbal form (meanings), but there also is evidence for visual memory. Visual/spatial knowledge is stored as an analog representation: It is similar but not identical to its referents. Dual-code theory postulates that the imaginal system primarily stores concrete objects and events and the verbal system stores more abstract information expressed in language. Conversely, images may be reconstructed in WM from verbal codes stored in LTM. Developmental evidence shows that children are more likely than adults to represent knowledge as images, but visual memory can be developed in persons of any age.

Transfer is a complex phenomenon. Historical views include identical elements, mental discipline, and generalization. From a cognitive perspective, transfer involves activation of memory networks and occurs when knowledge is linked. Distinctions are drawn between near and far, literal and figural, and low-road and high-road transfer. Some forms of transfer may occur automatically, but much is conscious and involves abstraction and recognizing underlying structures. Providing students with feedback on the usefulness of skills and strategies makes transfer more likely to occur.

The importance of retrieval and transfer for learning suggests some educational applications. Three that are pertinent involve encoding-retrieval specificity, retrieval-based learning, and teaching for transfer.

A summary of learning issues for information processing theory appears in Table 6.3.

Table 6.3
Summary of learning issues.

How Does Learning Occur?

Learning, or encoding, occurs when information is stored in LTM. Information initially enters the information processing system through a sensory register after it is attended to. It then is transferred to WM and perceived by being compared with information in LTM. This information can stay activated, be transferred to LTM, or be lost. Factors that help encoding are meaningfulness, elaboration, organization, and links with schema structures.

How Does Memory Function?

Memory is a key component of the information processing system. There is debate about how many memories there are. The classical model postulated two memory stores: short- and long-term. Contemporary theory posits a WM and a LTM, although WM may be an activated portion of LTM. The information processing system receives and transforms new information and through associative networks links it with knowledge that is retrieved from LTM and then stores it in LTM.

What Is the Role of Motivation?

Relative to other learning theories, motivation has received less attention by information processing theories. Learners presumably engage their cognitive processes to support attainment of their goals. Motivational processes such as goals and self-efficacy likely are represented in memory as verbal codes embedded in networks. The central executive, which directs WM activities, also seems to have motivational properties.

How Does Transfer Occur?

Transfer occurs through the process of spreading activation in memory, where information is linked to other information such that recall of certain knowledge can produce recall of related knowledge. It is important that learning cues be attached to knowledge so that the learning may be linked with different contexts, skills, or events.

How Does Self-Regulated Learning Operate?

Key self-regulation processes are goals, learning strategies, production systems, and schemas (Chapter 10). Information processing theories contend that learners can direct their information processing during learning.

What Are the Implications for Instruction?

Information processing theories emphasize the transformation and flow of information through the cognitive system. It is important that information be presented in such a way that students can relate the new information to known information (meaningfulness) and that they understand the uses for the knowledge. These points suggest that learning be structured so that it builds on existing knowledge and can be clearly comprehended by learners. Teachers also should provide advance organizers and cues that learners can use to recall information when needed and that minimize extraneous cognitive load. It also is important to use instructional activities that include retrieval and that help students learn ways to transfer knowledge to new contexts.

Chapter Critique

The topics covered in this chapter—retrieval, forgetting, transfer and others—are of key educational importance. Curricula are established under the assumption that learners will acquire knowledge and improve their skills, then be able to retrieve knowledge and use it in ways beyond those addressed during original learning. Unfortunately, this situation often does not occur, making research on these topics even more significant.

The information processing literature on retrieval and transfer offers some clear implications for ways to foster meaningful learning by students and help them determine when to use knowledge in different contexts. Additional research in authentic learning settings will promote understanding among educators.

Retrieval-based learning is a newer topic that fits well with information processing theory and neuroscience research. In education, retrieval often becomes associated with testing, and the current emphasis on testing and accountability makes one loathe to suggest additional testing. But there are ways to use retrieval in non-testing contexts (e.g., non-graded quizzes, discussions and question-and-answer sessions), and researchers need to explore these other contexts with different types of content to determine their effectiveness.

Visual learning often has been neglected in favor of verbal learning, but the evidence seems strong that individuals can learn in both modes and that representing knowledge in multiple forms may produce more meaningful retention. Because visual learning becomes less prominent with development, it behooves educators to stress that to help learners maintain their capabilities to represent knowledge visually.

Special consideration should be given to language comprehension. The situation in education is critical with increasing numbers of students who are English language learners. Language comprehension is relevant to both information processing and neuroscience, and future research from both theoretical positions can promote understanding and have implications for effective instruction for these learners.

REFLECTION QUESTIONS

■ Researchers have shown that retrieval is not only a memory process but also can facilitate learning. Retrieval involves reconstructing and transforming knowledge, which can strengthen and expand memory networks. A key issue involves the educational implications for teaching and learning. The most obvious form of retrieval occurs during testing. But for test-weary students and teachers, the idea of more testing to improve learning seems unacceptable. Can you think of some other ways that retrieval might be used in teaching to improve learning?

■ The importance of transfer for learning cannot be emphasized enough. Without transfer, or the right type of transfer, learning would be inefficient and repetitive. Transfer is one of the pillars of curriculum design. Given the theoretical considerations discussed in this chapter, what do you believe facilitates and hinders transfer? What are some instructional methods that seem to be well designed to promote transfer? And how might these methods be adapted to be appropriate for learners at various developmental levels?

■ Information processing research is not representative of schooling when it uses learning tasks (e.g., word lists), participants (e.g., intelligent and motivated college students who are at the peak of their learning capabilities), settings (e.g., laboratories), and techniques (e.g., short sessions) that bear little relevance to life in schools. The question can be raised about how generalizable information processing research findings are to schools that have meaningful tasks, participants of all ability and achievement levels, an environment where learning typically takes place, and techniques involving teaching and teacher–student interactions. What do you think we can generalize from information processing research to school settings? What are the implications of information processing theory and research for teaching and learning in school?

FURTHER READING

Butler, A. C., Godbole, N., & Marsh, E. J. (2013). Explanation feedback is better than correct answer feedback for promoting transfer of learning. *Journal of Educational Psychology, 105*, 290–298.

Chi, M. T. H., & VanLehn, K. A. (2012). Seeing deep structure from the interactions of surface features. *Educational Psychologist, 47*, 177–188.

Höffler, T. N. (2010). Spatial ability: Its influence on learning with visualizations—a meta-analytic review. *Educational Psychology Review, 22*, 245–269.

Karpicke, J. D., & Grimaldi, P. J. (2012). Retrieval-based learning: A perspective for enhancing meaningful learning. *Educational Psychology Review, 24*, 401–418.

Rowland, C. A. (2014). The effect of testing versus restudy on retention: A meta-analytic review of the testing effect. *Psychological Bulletin, 140*, 1432–1463.

Taatgen, N. A. (2013). The nature and transfer of cognitive skills. *Psychological Review, 120*, 439–471.

7 Cognitive Learning Processes

Meg LaMann, the principal of Franklin U. Nikowsky Middle School, was holding a faculty meeting. The school's teachers had participated recently in a professional development session on helping students learn problem solving and critical thinking skills. Meg asked the teachers for feedback on the session.

Tina Lawrance, one of the more outspoken teachers in the school, spoke first. "Well, Meg, I thought the presenters had lots of good things to say and suggestions for developing skills in the students. But you know what the problem is. We don't have time to do any of this. We're too crunched with covering what we need to so that the kids are ready for the state tests. And besides, those tests cover mostly low-level factual information, not what you need problem solving for. So, realistically, I don't see how I'll use much of what I learned yesterday."

Piper Rowland spoke up next. "That's right, Meg. I thought it was wonderful information. And surely our kids would benefit from learning some of these strategies. But if we neglect the basic skills to teach this stuff and our test results fall, we'll hear about it. I don't know what to do."

Meg replied, "I hear you and have the same concern. But I don't think we need to work on problem solving and critical thinking in everything we teach. There are facts and basic skills to be learned. But sometimes we don't think enough about how we might incorporate problem solving into our instruction. I think we all can do that.

Tina said, "I agree, Meg. What about some time set aside periodically to work on problem-solving skills?"

"You heard what the presenters said," replied Meg. "Problem solving and critical thinking are best taught in the context of regular learning. That way the kids see how they can apply these skills as they're learning math, English, science, social studies, and so on. The stand-alone thinking skills programs are less effective, and the kids usually don't apply those skills outside of the training setting."

"I'm willing to work on this more in social studies," said Tina.

"And I will in math," replied Piper. "I just hope the test scores don't fall."

"Don't worry about the test scores," said Meg. "I'll address that if it becomes an issue."

The teachers made a concerted effort to incorporate suggestions they learned from the session into their teaching for the rest of the school year. The end-of-grade test scores for the school rose by a small amount.

At the start of the next academic year, the school held a "walk the schedule" night for parents and students. Several parents told Meg how much they appreciated the teachers working more on problem solving. One parent remarked, "Those strategies are great, not just for school but for other things. I'm working with my son now, having him set goals for what he needs to do, check his progress, and so on." Another parent told Meg, "My daughter loves the new emphasis on problem solving. She says that school now isn't so boring and is more like its initials—FUN!"

Previous chapters covered cognitive theories of learning: social cognitive (Chapter 4) and information processing (Chapters 5 and 6). This chapter extends this cognitive perspective to the operation of key processes during learning. Following a discussion of skill acquisition, metacognition is covered, which is central to learning. Subsequent sections address concept learning, problem solving, critical thinking and creativity, cognition and technology, and instructional applications.

There is debate among professionals on the extent that the cognitive processes discussed in this chapter are involved in most, if not all, learning. Problem solving, for example, has been proposed as the central process in learning (Anderson, 1993), whereas other views limit its application to settings where specific conditions prevail (Chi & Glaser, 1985). Teachers generally agree on the importance of concept learning, problem solving, critical thinking, creativity, and metacognition, and educators recommend that these topics be incorporated into instruction (Pressley & McCormick, 1995). The opening vignette describes a schoolwide effort to integrate problem solving and critical thinking into the curriculum. The processes discussed in this chapter are integral components of complex types of learning that occur in school subjects such as reading, writing, mathematics, and science.

When you finish studying this chapter you should be able to do the following:

- Distinguish between general and specific skills, and discuss how they work together in the acquisition of competence.

- Describe the novice-to-expert research methodology.

- Explain why metacognition is important for learning, and discuss variables affecting it.

- Distinguish properties of concepts, and explain models of concept learning and conceptual change.

- Explain the differences between various methods for solving problems.

- Describe problem solving from an information processing perspective.

- Explain the differences between critical thinking, reasoning, and creativity, and describe ways to help develop these skills in students.

- Discuss key features of computer-based learning environments, online social media, and distance learning, and how these technologies may affect learning.

- Describe some instructional applications involving worked examples, problem solving, and mathematics.

SKILL ACQUISITION

Developing proficiency in any domain represents a process of skill acquisition. The next section examines issues relevant to the acquisition of general and specific skills.

General and Specific Skills

Skills may be differentiated according to degree of specificity. *General skills* apply to a wide variety of disciplines; *specific skills* are useful only in certain domains. For example, problem solving and critical thinking are general skills because they are useful in acquiring a range of cognitive, motor, and social skills, whereas factoring polynomials and solving square-root problems involve specific skills because they have limited mathematical applications.

Acquisition of general skills facilitates learning in many ways. Bruner (1985, pp. 5–6) noted that tasks such as "learning how to play chess, learning how to play the flute, learning mathematics, and learning to read the sprung rhymes in the verse of Gerard Manley Hopkins" are similar in that they involve attention, memory, and persistence.

But each type of skill has unique features. Bruner (1985) contended that views of learning are not unambiguously right or wrong; rather, they can be evaluated only in light of such conditions as the nature of the task to be learned, the type of learning to be accomplished, and the characteristics that learners bring to the situation. The many differences between tasks, such as learning to balance equations in chemistry and learning to balance on a beam in gymnastics, require different processes to explain learning.

Domain specificity is defined in various ways. Ceci (1989) used the term to refer to discrete declarative knowledge structures (Chapter 5). Other researchers include procedural knowledge and view specificity as pertaining to the usefulness of knowledge (Perkins & Salomon, 1989). The issue is not one of proving or disproving one position because we know that both general strategies and domain-specific knowledge are involved in learning (Nandagopal & Ericsson, 2012; Voss, Wiley, & Carretero, 1995). Rather, the issue is one of specifying the extent to which a given type of learning involves general and specific skills, what those skills are, and what course their acquisition follows. Thinking of skill specificity ranging along a continuum is preferable, as Perkins & Salomon (1989) explained:

> General knowledge includes widely applicable strategies for problem solving, inventive thinking, decision making, learning, and good mental management, sometimes called autocontrol, autoregulation, or metacognition. In chess, for example, very specific knowledge (often called local knowledge) includes the rules of the game as well as lore about how to handle innumerable specific situations, such as different openings and ways of achieving checkmate. Of intermediate generality are strategic concepts, like control of the center, that are somewhat specific to chess but that also invite far-reaching application by analogy. (p. 17)

Ohlsson (1993) advanced a model of skill acquisition through practice that comprises three subfunctions: generate task-relevant behaviors, identify errors, and correct errors. This model includes both general and task-specific processes. As learners practice, they monitor their progress by comparing their current state to their prior knowledge. This is a general strategy, but as learning occurs, it becomes increasingly adapted to specific task conditions. Errors often are caused by applying general procedures inappropriately

(Ohlsson, 1996), but prior domain-specific knowledge helps learners detect errors and identify the conditions that caused them. With practice and learning, therefore, general methods become more specialized.

Problem solving is useful for learning skills in many content areas, but task conditions often require specific skills for the development of expert performance (Tricot & Sweller, 2014). Research shows that expert problem solvers often use general strategies when they encounter unfamiliar problems and that asking general metacognitive questions (e.g., "What am I doing now?" "Is it getting me anywhere?") facilitates problem solving (Perkins & Salomon, 1989). Despite these positive results, general principles often do not transfer (Pressley et al., 1990; Schunk & Rice, 1993). Transfer requires combining general strategies with factors such as instruction on self-monitoring and practice in specific contexts. Motivation also is important (Nandagopal & Ericsson, 2012). The goal in the opening vignette is that once students learn general strategies, they will be able to adapt them to specific settings and motivated to do so.

In short, expert performance requires much domain knowledge (Lajoie, 2003; Nandagopal & Ericsson, 2012; Tricot & Sweller, 2014). It requires a rich knowledge base that includes the facts, concepts, and principles of the domain, coupled with general learning strategies that can be applied to different domains and that may have to be tailored to each domain. One would not expect strategies such as seeking help and monitoring goal progress to operate in the same fashion in disparate domains (e.g., calculus and pole vaulting). At the same time, general strategies are useful for coping with atypical problems in different domains regardless of one's overall level of competence in the domain (Perkins & Salomon, 1989). These findings imply that students need to be well grounded in basic content-area (domain) knowledge (Ohlsson, 1993), as well as in general problem-solving (this chapter) and self-regulatory strategies (Chapter 10). Application 7.1 provides suggestions for integrating the teaching of general and specific skills.

Novice-to-Expert Research Methodology

With the growth of cognitive (Chapters 4–6) and constructivist (Chapter 8) views of learning, researchers moved away from viewing learning as changes in responses due to differential reinforcement (Chapter 3) and became interested in exploring students' beliefs and thought processes during learning. The focus of learning research has shifted accordingly.

To investigate academic learning, some researchers have used a *novice-to-expert methodology* that reflects the following steps:

- Identify the skill to be learned.
- Find an expert (i.e., one who performs the skill well) and a novice (one who knows something about the task but performs it poorly).
- Determine how the novice can be moved to the expert level as efficiently as possible.

This methodology is intuitively plausible. The basic idea is that if you want to understand how to become more skillful in an area, closely study someone who performs that skill well (Bruner, 1985). In so doing, you can learn what knowledge is needed, what procedures and strategies are useful, how to handle difficult situations, and how to correct mistakes. The model has many real-world counterparts and is reflected in mentoring, apprenticeships, and on-the-job training (Fletcher & Mullen, 2012).

APPLICATION 7.1
Integrating the Teaching of General and Specific Skills

Teachers can help students learn general skills and strategies to increase students' success in various domains, while also stressing the skills that are needed for learning within a specific domain.

Mr. Thomson might work with his fifth-grade students on the general strategy of goal setting to complete assignments. In reading, he might help students determine how to finish reading two chapters in a book by the end of the week. The students might establish a goal to read a certain number of pages or subsections each day of the week. Because the goal comprises more than just reading pages, he also must teach specific comprehension skills, such as locating main ideas and reading for details. He can have students use goal setting in mathematics;

they might decide how many problems or activities to do each day to complete a particular unit by the end of the week. Specific skills that come into play in this context are determining what the problem is asking for, representing the problem, and knowing how to perform the computations.

In physical education, students may use goal setting to master skills, such as working toward running a mile in 6 minutes. The students begin by running the mile and recording their times, after which they set a goal to decrease the running time by a certain amount every week. Motor and endurance skills must be developed to successfully meet the goal. Such skills are most likely to be specific to the context of running a mile in a good time.

Much of the knowledge on how more- and less-proficient persons differ in a domain comes from research based in part on assumptions of this methodology (VanLehn, 1996). Compared with novices, expert performers have more-extensive domain knowledge, have better understanding of what they do not know, spend more time initially analyzing problems, and solve them quicker and more accurately (Lajoie, 2003). Research also has identified differences in the stages of skill acquisition. Conducting such research is labor intensive and time consuming because it requires studying learners over time, but it yields rich results.

Bear in mind, however, that this model is descriptive rather than explanatory: It describes what learners do but does not explain why they do it. The model also tacitly assumes that a fixed constellation of skills exists that constitutes expertise in a given domain, but this is not always the case. With respect to teaching, Sternberg and Horvath (1995) argued that no one standard exists; rather, expert teachers resemble one another in prototypical fashion. This makes sense given our experiences with master teachers who typically differ in several ways.

Finally, the model does not automatically suggest teaching methods. As such, it may have limited usefulness for classroom teaching and learning. Explanations for learning and corresponding teaching suggestions should be firmly grounded in theories and identify important personal and environmental factors, which are emphasized in this and other chapters in this book.

Expert–Novice Differences in Science

Science is a good domain to explore expert–novice differences in scientific expertise. Researchers also have investigated students' construction of scientific knowledge and the implicit theories and reasoning processes that they use during problem solving and learning (Linn & Eylon, 2006; Voss et al., 1995; White, 2001; C. Zimmerman, 2000; Chapter 8).

Expert performers in science differ from novices in quantity and organization of knowledge. Experts possess more domain-specific knowledge and are more likely to organize it in hierarchies, whereas novices often demonstrate little overlap between scientific concepts.

Chi, Feltovich, and Glaser (1981) had expert and novice problem solvers sort physics textbook problems on any basis they wanted. Novices classified problems based on superficial features (e.g., apparatus); experts classified the problems based on the principle needed to solve the problem. Experts and novices also differed in declarative knowledge memory networks. "Inclined plane," for example, was related in novices' memories with descriptive terms such as "mass," "friction," and "length." Experts had these descriptors in their memories but also had stored principles of mechanics (e.g., conservation of energy, Newton's force laws). The experts' greater knowledge of principles was organized with descriptors subordinate to principles.

Novices often use principles erroneously to solve problems. McCloskey and Kaiser (1984) posed the following question to college students:

> A train is speeding over a bridge that spans a valley. As the train rolls along, a passenger leans out of a window and drops a rock. Where will it land?

About one third of the students said the rock would fall straight down (Figure 7.1). They believed that an object pushed or thrown acquires a force but that an object being carried by a moving vehicle does not acquire a force, so it drops straight down. The analogy the students made was with a person standing still who drops an object, which falls straight down. The path of descent of the rock from the moving train is, however, parabolic. The idea that objects acquire force is erroneous because objects move in the same direction and at the same speed as their moving carriers. When the rock is dropped, it continues to move forward with the train until gravity pulls it down. Novices generalized their basic knowledge and arrived at an erroneous solution.

As discussed later in this chapter, another difference between novice and expert performers concerns the use of problem-solving strategies (Larkin, McDermott, Simon, & Simon, 1980; White & Tisher, 1986). When confronted with scientific problems, novices often use a means–ends analysis, determining the goal of the problem and deciding which formulas might be useful to reach that goal. They work backward and recall formulas containing quantities in the target formula. If they become uncertain how to proceed, they may abandon the problem or attempt to solve it based on their current knowledge.

Experts first recognize the problem format, then work forward toward intermediate subgoals, and use that information to reach the ultimate goal. Experience in working scientific problems builds knowledge of problem types. Experts often automatically recognize familiar problem features and carry out necessary productions. Even when they

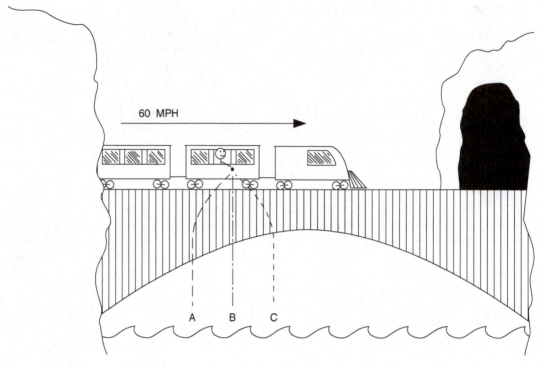

60 MPH

A   B   C

Figure 7.1
Possible answers to falling rock problem.

are less certain about how to solve a problem, experts begin with some information given in the problem and work forward to the solution. Notice that the last step experts take is often novices' first step. Klahr and Simon (1999) contended that the process of scientific discovery is a form of problem solving and that the general heuristic approach is much the same across domains.

METACOGNITION

Information processing theories contend that inputs are received into WM, rehearsed, organized and elaborated, linked with relevant information in LTM, and stored in LTM. We might ask why any of these activities happen. Especially during learning—when processing is not automatic—we need an explanation for why the system processes information. For example, what determines how much rehearsal takes place? How is relevant information selected in LTM? How do people know what knowledge is required in different situations?

Metacognition provides answers to some of these questions. *Metacognition*, or cognition about cognition (Flavell, 1985), refers to the deliberate conscious control of cognitive activity (Brown, 1980; Matlin, 2009). Metacognition is, essentially, people's awareness of their own cognitive processes (Rhodes & Tauber, 2011). Before discussing how metacognitive processes help to integrate information processing, the topic of conditional knowledge will be addressed, because this type of knowledge is part of metacognition.

Conditional Knowledge

Declarative and procedural knowledge refer to knowledge of facts and procedures, respectively (Chapter 5). *Conditional knowledge* is knowledge about when and why to employ forms of declarative and procedural knowledge (Paris et al., 1983). Possessing requisite declarative and procedural knowledge to perform a task does not guarantee students will perform it well. Students reading a social studies text may know what to do (read a chapter), know the meanings of vocabulary words (declarative knowledge), and know how to read for understanding (procedural knowledge). But they might skim the chapter. As a consequence, they perform poorly on a quiz.

This type of situation is common. In this example, conditional knowledge includes knowing when skimming is appropriate. One might skim a magazine article or a web page for the gist, but skimming should not be used to comprehend textual content.

Conditional knowledge helps students select and employ declarative and procedural knowledge to attain goals. To decide to read a chapter carefully and then do it, students should believe that careful reading is appropriate for the task at hand; that is, this strategy has functional value because it will allow them to comprehend the material.

Learners who do not possess conditional knowledge about when and why skimming is valuable will employ it at inappropriate times. If they believe it is valuable for all reading tasks, they may indiscriminately employ it unless otherwise directed. If they believe it has no value, they may never use it unless directed.

Conditional knowledge may be represented in LTM in networks and linked with the declarative and procedural knowledge to which it applies. Conditional knowledge actually is a form of declarative knowledge because it is "knowledge that"—for example, knowledge that skimming is valuable to get the gist of a passage and knowledge that summarizing text is valuable to derive greater understanding. Conditional knowledge also is included in procedures: Skimming is valuable as long as I can get the gist; but if I find that I am not getting the gist, I should abandon skimming and read more carefully. The three types of knowledge are summarized in Table 7.1.

Conditional knowledge is an integral part of self-regulated learning (Zimmerman & Schunk, 2011; Chapter 10). Self-regulated learning requires that students decide which learning strategy to use prior to engaging in a task (B. Zimmerman, 2000). While students are engaged in a task, they assess task progress (e.g., their level of comprehension) using metacognitive processes. When comprehension problems are detected, students alter their strategy based on conditional knowledge of what might prove more effective. Researchers also have shown that computer-based learning environments can serve as metacognitive tools for fostering students' self-regulated learning (Azevedo, 2005a, 2005b).

Table 7.1
Comparison of types of knowledge.

Type	Knowing	Examples
Declarative	That	Historical dates; number facts; episodes—what happened when; task features (e.g., stories have a plot and setting); beliefs (e.g., "I am good in math")
Procedural	How	Mathematical algorithms; reading strategies (e.g., skimming, scanning, summarizing); goal setting (e.g., breaking long-term goals into subgoals)
Conditional	When, Why	Skim web pages to get the gist in little time; read texts carefully for understanding

Metacognition and Learning

Metacognition comprises related sets of skills (Dimmitt & McCormick, 2012). One must understand what skills, strategies, and resources a task requires. Included in this cluster are finding main ideas, rehearsing information, forming associations or images, using memory techniques, organizing material, taking notes or underlining, and using test-taking techniques. One also must know how and when to use these skills and strategies and apply them to ensure the task is completed successfully. These monitoring activities include checking level of understanding, predicting outcomes, evaluating the effectiveness of efforts, planning activities, deciding how to budget time, and revising or switching to other activities to overcome difficulties (Baker & Brown, 1984). Collectively, metacognitive activities reflect the planned and strategic application of declarative, procedural, and conditional knowledge to tasks (Schraw & Moshman, 1995). Metacognitive skills contribute to the development of critical thinking and problem solving (Dimmitt & McCormick, 2012; Kuhn, 1999; discussed later in this chapter), and metacognition is a central aspect of self-regulated learning (Azevedo, 2009; Efklides, 2006; Chapter 10).

Metacognition is involved during all phases of learning (Efklides, 2006). Before learning, students may experience feelings of familiarity, difficulty, knowing, interest, and liking, as well as judgments about the best strategy to use and time needed for learning. While engaged in the task, learners' metacognitive processes may comprise feelings of difficulty, estimated effort and time needed for task completion, and judgments about strategy effectiveness. During pauses or when the learning task is complete, students may experience feelings of confidence, satisfaction, and liking of the task, as well as cognitive estimates of solution accuracy.

Metacognitive skills develop slowly (Dimmitt & McCormick, 2012). Young children are not fully aware of which cognitive processes various tasks involve. For example, they may not understand that disorganized passages are harder to comprehend than organized ones or that passages containing unfamiliar material are more difficult than those composed of familiar material (Baker & Brown, 1984). Dermitzaki (2005) found that second graders used metacognitive strategies but that their use bore little relation to children's actual self-regulatory activities. Monitoring is employed more often by older children and adults than by young children; however, older children and adults do not always monitor their comprehension and often are poor judges of how well they have comprehended text (Baker, 1989). Relative to regular learners, gifted students tend to show enhanced metacognitive capabilities (Snyder, Nietfeld, & Linnenbrink-Garcia, 2011).

At the same time, young children are cognitively capable of monitoring their activities on simple tasks (Kuhn, 1999). Learners are more likely to monitor their activities on tasks of intermediate difficulty as opposed to easy tasks (where monitoring may not be necessary) or on very difficult tasks (where one may not know what to do or may quit working).

Metacognition begins to develop around ages 5 to 7 and continue throughout the time children are in school, although within any age group there is much variability (Flavell, 1985; Flavell, Green, & Flavell, 1995). Preschool children are capable of learning some strategic behaviors (Kail & Hagen, 1982), but as a result of schooling, children develop the awareness they can control what they learn by the strategies they use (Duell, 1986). Flavell and Wellman (1977) hypothesized that children form generalizations concerning how their actions influence the environment; for example, they learn "what works" for them to promote school achievement. This is especially true with memory strategies, perhaps because much school success depends on memorizing information (Application 7.2).

Variables Influencing Metacognition

Metacognitive awareness is influenced by variables associated with learners, tasks, and strategies.

Learner Variables. Learners' levels of development influence their metacognition (Alexander, Carr, & Schwanenflugel, 1995). Older children understand their own memory abilities and limitations better than younger children do. With development, children can more accurately gauge when they have learned material well enough to recall it.

Learners' abilities to monitor how well they have done on a memory task also vary. Older children are more accurate in judging whether they have recalled all items they were to recall. Wellman (1977) presented children with pictures of objects and asked them to name the objects. If children could not name them, they were asked whether they would recognize the name. Compared with kindergartners, third graders were more accurate at predicting which object names they would be able to recognize.

Another important variable is the implicit theory of intelligence (or ability) that the individual holds. Students differ in whether they view intelligence as a fixed quality (i.e., one that cannot change) or as an incremental one that can be developed (Dweck, 1999; see Chapter 9). Miele, Son, and Metcalf (2013) presented third and fifth graders with texts in easy- or difficult-to-read fonts. Children who ascribed to a fixed theory of intelligence were less likely than those holding an incremental theory to interpret difficult encoding of the text as increasing mastery and more likely to report lower comprehension as their perceived effort increased. These results suggest that children's theories of intelligence may affect their metacognitive judgments.

Task Variables. Knowing the relative difficulty of different forms of learning and retrieving from memory various types of information are parts of metacognitive awareness. Although

APPLICATION 7.2
Metacognition

Students can develop better metacognitive skills. A teacher working with students on listening comprehension might include situations such as listening to an enjoyable story, a set of explicit directions, and a social studies lecture. For each situation, the teacher could ask students why they would listen in that setting; for example, enjoyment and general theme (stories), specific elements (directions), facts and concepts (social studies). Then the teacher could ask the students to retell the story in their own words, visualize the directions, and take notes. To foster conditional knowledge, the teacher can discuss with students the various listening techniques that seem most appropriate for each situation.

A teacher helping students improve their memory skills might give them a list of items to memorize. The teacher could teach them to reconstruct the list of items given partial cues. The students might be encouraged to explore various memorization techniques such as putting the items into categories, visualizing a picture that contains the items, associating the items with a familiar setting or task, using acronyms that include the first letter of each item, and creating a jingle, poem, or song that incorporates the items. Then the teacher could help each student determine which techniques work best for him or her.

kindergartners and first graders believe that familiar or easily named items are easier to remember, older children are better at predicting that categorized items are easier to recall than conceptually unrelated items (Duell, 1986). Older children are more likely to believe that organized stories are easier to remember than disorganized pieces of information. With respect to the goal of learning, sixth graders know better than second graders that students should use different reading strategies depending on whether the goal is to recall a story word for word or in their own words (Myers & Paris, 1978).

Some school tasks do not require much metacognition because they can be handled routinely. Part of the issue in the opening vignette is to use more tasks that require metacognition, with a corresponding decrease in low-level learning that can be accomplished easily.

Strategy Variables. Metacognition depends on the strategies learners employ. Children as young as ages 3 and 4 can use memory strategies to remember information, but their ability to use strategies improves with development. Older children are able to state more ways that help them remember things. Regardless of age, children are more likely to think of external things (e.g., write a note) than internal ones (e.g., think about doing something). Students' use of memory strategies such as rehearsal and elaboration also improves with development (Duell, 1986).

Although many students are capable of using metacognitive strategies, they may not know which strategies aid learning and LTM retrieval, and they may not employ those that are helpful (Zimmerman & Martinez-Pons, 1990). Simply generating a strategy does not guarantee its use. This *utilization deficiency* is more common in younger children (Justice, Baker-Ward, Gupta, & Jannings, 1997) and appears to stem from children's understanding of how a strategy works. Older learners understand that the intention to use a strategy leads to strategy use, which produces an outcome. Younger children typically have only partial understanding of the links between intentions, actions, and outcomes. Such understanding develops between the ages of 3 and 6 (Wellman, 1990).

Teaching metacognitive strategies can promote learners' motivation and learning. In the context of problem solving in science, eighth-grade students were taught to use metacognitive strategies for planning (identifying a goal and a strategy for attaining it), monitoring of progress toward the goal, and evaluating the effectiveness of the problem-solving strategy (Zepeda, Richey, Ronevich, & Nokes-Malach, 2015). Compared with a control condition that received instructional materials, the metacognitive training improved students' learning, motivation, and accuracy of metacognitive judgments.

Task, strategy, and learner variables typically interact when students engage in metacognitive activities. Learners consider the type and length of material to be learned (task), the potential strategies to be used (strategy), and their skill at using the various strategies (learner). If learners think that note taking and underlining are good strategies for identifying main points of a technical article and if they believe they are good at underlining but poor at taking notes, they likely will decide to underline. As Schraw and Moshman (1995) noted, learners construct metacognitive theories that include knowledge and strategies that they believe will be effective in a given situation. Such metacognitive knowledge is critical for self-regulated learning (Dinsmore, Alexander, & Loughlin, 2008; Chapter 10).

Metacognition and Epistemic Thinking

In recent years, researchers increasingly explored the role of metacognition in epistemic thinking. Recall the discussion in Chapter 1 on *epistemology*, or the study of the origin, nature, limits, and methods of knowledge. Epistemology essentially is one's theory of knowledge (Greene, Sandoval, & Bråten, 2016)—that is, about the nature and limits of knowing. Individuals' personal epistemologies are guided by their *epistemic thinking*, which includes cognitive and metacognitive processes. As we have seen in previous chapters, cognition includes such mental processes as attending, perceiving, remembering, and reasoning. Metacognition involves such meta-processes as monitoring and control of cognition and evaluating one's knowledge acquisition. Epistemic thinking comprises epistemic cognition and epistemic metacognition (Barzilai & Zohar, 2016).

Metacognition is an integral aspect of epistemic thinking. Epistemic thinking is central when individuals are engaged in learning because this type of thinking involves learners' beliefs about how they learn. In a study by Barzilai and Zohar (2016), university students read scientific passages that contained partially conflicting information. While students read and studied the sources, they verbalized aloud, and verbalizations were recorded and transcribed. The results showed that about half of learners' verbalizations involved epistemic issues including planning, monitoring, and evaluating the sources—for example, planning information gathering, monitoring consistency with prior information, and evaluating changes to knowledge and understanding.

As with other forms of metacognition, epistemic metacognition is subject to developmental influences. Initially children develop the understanding of a theory of mind, which means they understand that the mind exists and that people have different knowledge and beliefs (Barzilai & Zohar, 2016). Later they develop an understanding that the same information can be interpreted in different ways. They also integrate into their vocabularies such epistemic terms as "know" and "deny." Like metacognition in general, epistemic metacognition increases in both quality and quantity throughout the early school years (Bryce & Whitebread, 2012).

Epistemic metacognition can be improved through instruction. Teachers might introduce epistemic vocabulary terms and question students' assertions (e.g., "How do you know?"). They also can model and explain epistemic strategies, such as ways to evaluate evidence. Students working collaboratively to apply epistemic thinking can foster metacognitive skills in one another (Barzilai & Zohar, 2016).

Metacognition and Behavior

Understanding which skills and strategies help us learn and remember information is necessary but not sufficient to enhance our achievement. Even students who are aware of what helps them learn do not consistently engage in metacognitive activities for various reasons. In some cases, metacognition may be unnecessary because the material is easily learned. Learners also might be unwilling to invest the effort to employ metacognitive activities. The latter are tasks in their own right; they take time and effort. Learners may not understand fully that metacognitive strategies improve their performances, or they may believe they do but that other factors, such as time spent or effort expended, are more important for learning (Borkowski & Cavanaugh, 1979; Flavell & Wellman, 1977; Schunk & Rice, 1993).

Metacognitive activities improve achievement, but the fact that students often do not use them presents a quandary for educators. Students need to be taught a menu of activities ranging from those applying to learning in general (e.g., determining the purpose in learning) to those applying to specific situations (e.g., underlining important points in text), and they need to be encouraged to use them in various contexts. Although the *what* component of learning is important, so are the *when, where*, and *why* of strategy use. Teaching the *what* without the latter will only confuse students and could prove demoralizing; students who know what to do but not when, where, or why to do it might hold low self-efficacy for performing well (Chapter 4).

Learners often need to be taught basic declarative or procedural knowledge along with metacognitive skills (Duell, 1986). Students need to monitor their understanding of main ideas, but the monitoring is pointless if they do not understand what a main idea is or how to find one. Students must be encouraged to employ metacognitive strategies—this is one of the implications of the discussion at the Nikowsky Middle School—and given opportunities to apply what they have learned outside of the instructional context. Students also need feedback on how well they are applying a strategy and how strategy use improves their performance (Schunk & Rice, 1993; Schunk & Swartz, 1993a). A danger of teaching a metacognitive strategy in conjunction with a single task is that students will see the strategy as applying only to that task or to highly similar tasks, which does not foster transfer. It is desirable to use multiple tasks to teach strategies.

Metacognition and Reading

Metacognition is relevant to reading because it is involved in understanding and monitoring reading purposes and strategies (Barzilai & Zohar, 2016; Dimmitt & McCormick, 2012). Beginning readers often do not understand the conventions of printed material: In the English language, one reads words from left to right and top to bottom. Beginning and poorer readers typically do not monitor their comprehension or adjust their strategies accordingly (Baker & Brown, 1984). Compared with younger and less-skilled readers, older and skilled readers are better at comprehension monitoring (Alexander et al., 1995).

Metacognition comes into play when learners set goals, evaluate goal progress, and make necessary corrections (McNeil, 1987). Skilled readers do not approach all reading tasks identically. They determine their goal: find main ideas, read for details, skim, get the gist, and so on. They then use a strategy they believe will accomplish the goal. When reading skills are highly developed, these processes may occur automatically.

While reading, skilled readers check their progress. If their goal is to locate important ideas, and if after reading a few pages they have not located any important ideas, they are apt to reread those pages. If they encounter a word they do not understand, they try to determine its meaning from context or consult a dictionary rather than continue reading.

Developmental research evidence indicates a trend toward greater recognition and correction of comprehension deficiencies (Alexander et al., 1995). Younger children recognize comprehension failures less often than do older children. Younger children who are good comprehenders may recognize a problem but may not employ a strategy to solve it (e.g., rereading). Older children who are good comprehenders recognize problems and employ correction strategies.

Children develop metacognitive abilities through interactions with others (Chapter 8). Adults (e.g., parents, teachers) help guide children through solution steps, reminding them of their goal and assisting them plan how to reach their goal. An effective teaching procedure includes informing children of the goal, making them aware of information relevant to the task, arranging a situation conducive to problem solving, and reminding them of their goal progress.

Strategy instruction programs generally have been successful in helping students learn strategies and maintain their use over time (Pressley & Harris, 2006). Brown and her colleagues advocated that strategy training incorporate practice in use of skills, instruction in how to monitor outcomes of one's efforts, and feedback on when and where a strategy may be useful (Brown, 1980; Brown, Palincsar, & Armbruster, 1984).

Palincsar and Brown (1984) identified seventh graders with poor comprehension skills. They trained students in self-directed summarizing (review), questioning, clarifying, and predicting. Summarizing included stating what had happened in the text and also served as a self-test on the content. Questioning was directed at determining what main idea question a teacher or test might ask about that material. Clarifying was used when portions of the text were unclear and students could not adequately summarize. Predicting was used when text cues signaled forthcoming information.

Researchers taught these activities as part of an interactive dialogue between teacher and student known as *reciprocal teaching*. During the lessons, an adult teacher met with students. Initially the teacher modeled the activities. The teacher and students read a passage, after which the teacher asked a question that a teacher or test might ask, summa-rized the content, clarified troublesome points, and predicted future content. Following the teacher's modeled demonstration, the teacher and students took turns being the teacher. At first, students had difficulty assuming the role of teacher; the teacher often had to con-struct paraphrases and questions for students. Eventually students became more capable of following the procedure and implementing the four activities.

Compared with a condition in which students received instruction on locating informa-tion in text, reciprocal teaching led to greater comprehension gains, better maintenance over time, and better generalization to classroom comprehension tests. Students exposed to reciprocal teaching also showed greater improvements in quality of summaries and ques-tions asked. The maintenance and generalization results are important because changes brought about by strategy training programs may not maintain themselves or generalize to other tasks (Phye, 2001).

The following dialogue occurred between teacher (T) and student (S) early in the training program (Palincsar & Brown, 1984).

> The snake's skeleton and parts of its body are very flexible—something like a rubber hose with bones. A snake's backbone can have as many as 300 vertebrae, almost 10 times as many as a human's. These vertebrae are connected by loose and rubbery tissues that allow easy movement. Because of this bendable, twistable spinal construction, a snake can turn its body in almost any direction at almost any point.

S: Like, if a snake is turning around, he wouldn't break any bones because he is flexible.

T: And the reason he is so flexible is . . .

S: If someone stepped on his tail, he wouldn't be able to move unless he was flexible.

T: Okay. That explains why it would be helpful to be so flexible, but what makes the snake so flexible? I think that is an important part of the summary.

S: So he can move faster?

T: That is another reason for being flexible. Let me do a summary for you. Sara [the student] is right. The most important thing we have learned is that snake[s are] very flexible. The reason they can bend so easily is that they have so many little bones in their backbones and each of them can move separately, making the snake very flexible. Does that make sense? (p. 142)

The last statement by the teacher is a modeled demonstration of summarization.

There are other reading programs that incorporate strategy instruction and teach students to self-regulate. For example, the *Self-Regulated Strategy Development* program combines strategy instruction with instruction in self-regulation (e.g., self-monitoring, self-instructions, goal setting, self-reinforcement; Graham & Harris, 2003; Harris, Graham, & Santangelo, 2013; Mason, 2004). This program has proven to be effective with children with learning disabilities and reading problems.

Concept-Oriented Reading Instruction (CORI) incorporates cognitive strategy instruc-tion on the strategies of activating background knowledge, questioning, searching for information, summarizing, organizing graphically, and identifying story structure (Guthrie et al., 2004; Guthrie, Wigfield, & Perencevich, 2004; Wigfield et al., 2016). CORI has shown to be effective in raising students' reading comprehension.

Motivation plays a critical role in reading comprehension. Guthrie, Wigfield, and VonSecker (2000) integrated reading strategy instruction with science content and found significant benefits on students' motivation compared with traditional instruction emphasizing coverage of material. Student interest presumably was heightened with the real-world use of effective reading strategies. The CORI program also incorporates motivational practices such as goal setting and giving students choices. Compared with strategy instruction alone, Guthrie et al. (2004) found that CORI led to greater benefits in comprehension, motivation, and use of strategies.

Other research shows that motivational factors affect reading outcomes. Meece and Miller (2001) found that task-mastery goals predicted students' use of learning strategies in reading instruction. After reviewing a large number of studies, Blok, Oostdam, Otter, and Overmaat (2002) concluded that computer-assisted instruction was effective in beginning reading instruction. It is possible that the motivational benefits of computers may aid in the development of early reading skill. Morgan and Fuchs (2007) examined 15 studies and obtained a positive correlation between children's reading skills and motivation and also obtained evidence suggesting that skills and motivation can affect one another.

The increase in the number of English language learners in U.S. schools has necessitated expansion of programs for them. For English instruction, students often are placed in immersion or second language programs. In immersion programs, students learn English in an all-English–speaking classroom with formal or informal support when they have difficulties. In second language programs, students receive instruction in reading and possibly other subjects in their native languages. Students often transition to English instruction around grade 2 or 3. Slavin and Cheung (2005) compared immersion with second language programs and found an advantage of second language programs on students' reading competencies; however, the number of studies in their review was small, and longitudinal studies are needed to determine long-term effects.

CONCEPT LEARNING

The Nature of Concepts

Cognitive learning processes are involved in concept learning. *Concepts* are labeled sets of objects, symbols, or events that share common characteristics, or critical attributes. A concept is a mental construct or representation of a category that allows one to identify examples and nonexamples of the category. Concepts may involve concrete objects (e.g., "table," "chair," "cat") or abstract ideas (e.g., "love," "democracy," "wholeness"). There are many types of concepts (for a detailed review, see Medin, Lynch, & Solomon, 2000). *Concept learning* refers to forming representations to identify attributes, generalize them to new examples, and discriminate examples from nonexamples.

Early studies by Bruner, Goodnow, and Austin (1956) explored the nature of concepts. Learners were presented with boxes portraying geometrical patterns. Each pattern could be classified using four different attributes: number of stimuli (one, two, three), shape (circle, square, cross), color (red, green, black), and number of borders on the box (one, two, three). The task was to identify the concept represented in different subsets of the boxes.

The configuration of features in a concept-learning task can be varied to yield different concepts. A *conjunctive concept* is represented by two or more features (e.g., two red circles). Other features (number of borders) are not relevant. A *disjunctive concept* is represented by one of two or more features; for example, two circles of any color or one red circle. A *relational concept* specifies a relationship between features that must be present, such as the number of objects in the figure must outnumber the number of borders (type of object and color are unimportant).

Bruner et al. (1956) found that learners formulated a hypothesis about the rule underlying the concept. Rules can be expressed in if-then form. A rule classifying a pet cat might be: "If it is domesticated, has four legs, fur, whiskers, a tail, is relatively small, purrs, and vocalizes 'meow,' then it is a cat." Although exceptions exist, this rule will accurately classify cats most of the time. Generalization occurs when the rule is applied to a variety of cats.

Bruner et al. (1956) found that people tend to form rules quickly. For any given concept, they retain the rule as long as it correctly identifies instances and noninstances of the concept and they modify it when it fails to do so. Learners acquire concepts better (i.e., confirm the rule underlying the concept) when they are presented with *positive instances*, or examples of the concept. Learning is much slower with *negative (non-) instances*.

The *features analysis theory* of concept learning derives from the work of Bruner and others and postulates that concepts involve rules that define the critical features, or the intrinsic (necessary) attributes of the concept (Gagné, 1985; Smith & Medin, 1981). Through experiences with the concept, one formulates a rule that satisfies the conditions and retains the rule as long as it functions effectively.

This view predicts that different instances of a concept should be recognized equally quickly because each instance is judged against critical features, but this is not always the case. Most people find some instances of a category (e.g., a dolphin is a mammal) more difficult to verify than others (e.g., a dog is a mammal). This highlights the problem that many concepts cannot be defined precisely in terms of a set of critical attributes.

A second perspective is *prototype theory* (Rosch, 1973, 1975, 1978). A *prototype* is a generalized image of the concept, which may include only some of the concept's defining attributes. When confronted with an instance, one recalls the most likely prototype from LTM and compares it to the instance to see if they match. Prototypes may include some nondefining (optional) attributes. In information processing terms, prototypes may be thought of as *schemas* (Andre, 1986), or organized forms for the knowledge we have about a particular concept (Chapter 5).

Research supports the prototype theory prediction that instances closer to the prototype (e.g., prototype = "bird"; instances = "robin," "sparrow") are recognized quicker than those less typical (e.g., "owl," "ostrich"; Rosch, 1973). One concern is that prototype theory implies that people would store thousands of prototypes in LTM, which would consume much more space than rules. A second concern is that learners easily could construct incorrect prototypes if they are allowed to include some nondefining characteristics and not all necessary ones.

Combining the features analysis and prototype positions is possible. Given that prototypes include critical features, we might employ prototypes to classify instances of concepts that are typical (Andre, 1986). For instances that are ambiguous, we may employ critical feature analysis, which might modify the list of critical features to incorporate the new features.

Children's understandings of concepts change with development and experience. There are multiple ways that conceptual change can occur (Chinn & Samarapungavan, 2009), including when learners recognize that rules pertinent in one domain also seem applicable to another domain (Ohlsson, 2009). Children in transition about the meaning of a concept may simultaneously keep a prior hypothesis in mind as they are developing a revised one (Goldin-Meadow, Alibali, & Church, 1993). This interpretation is consistent with Klausmeier's position, which is discussed next.

A testing effect (see Chapter 6) also can promote conceptual change. Jensen, McDaniel, Woodard, and Kummer (2014) found with college students that taking quizzes and exams regularly improved students' higher-order conceptual understanding.

Concept Attainment

Theory and research suggest various ways to learn and modify concepts (Chinn & Samarapungavan, 2009). One way to develop prototypes is to be exposed to a typical instance of the concept that reflects the classic attributes (Klausmeier, 1992). A second way is by abstracting features from two or more examples; for birds, features might be "feathers," "two legs," "beak," and "flies," although not every feature applies to every member of the class. Prototypes are refined and expanded when one is exposed to new examples of the concept; thus, "lives in the jungle" (parrot) and "lives by the ocean" (seagull).

Gagné's (1985) theory (Chapter 5) includes concepts as a central form of learning. Learners initially must have basic prerequisite capabilities to discriminate among stimulus features (i.e., distinguish relevant from irrelevant features).

In Gagné's (1985) view, concept learning involves a *multistage sequence*. First, the stimulus feature is presented as an instance of the concept along with a noninstance. The learner confirms the ability to make the discrimination. In the next (generalization) stage, the learner identifies instances and noninstances. Third, the stimulus feature—which is to become the concept—is varied and presented along with noninstances. Concept attainment is verified by asking for identification of several instances of the class using stimuli not previously employed in learning. Throughout the process, correct responses are reinforced, and contiguity learning occurs (Chapter 3) by presenting several instances of the concept in close association.

Klausmeier (1990, 1992) developed and tested a model of concept attainment. This model postulates a four-stage sequence: concrete, identity, classificatory, and formal. Competence at each level is necessary for attainment at the next level. The process of concept attainment represents an interaction of development, informal experience, and formal education.

At the *concrete level*, learners can recognize an item as the same one previously encountered when the context or spatial orientation in which it was originally encountered remains the same. This level requires learners to attend to the item, discriminate it as different from its surroundings on the basis of one or more defining attributes, represent it in memory as a visual image, and retrieve it from LTM to compare it with a new image and determine that it is the same item. Thus, a learner might learn to recognize an equilateral triangle and discriminate it from a right or isosceles triangle.

The *identity level* is characterized by recognizing an item as the same one previously encountered when the item is observed from a different perspective or in a different modality. This stage involves the same processes as at the concrete level, as well as the process of generalization. Thus, the learner will be able to recognize equilateral triangles in different orientations or positions on a page.

The *classificatory level* requires that learners recognize at least two items as being equivalent. Additional generalization is involved; in the case of equilateral triangles, this involves recognizing a smaller and larger equilateral triangle as equivalent. The process continues until the learner can recognize examples and nonexamples; at this stage, however, the learner may not understand the basis for classification (e.g., equality of side length and angles). Being able to name the concept is not necessary at this level, but, as in the preceding stages, it can facilitate concept acquisition.

The final *formal level* requires the learner to identify examples and nonexamples of the concept, name the concept and its defining attributes, define the concept, and specify the attributes that distinguish it from closely related concepts (i.e., three equal sides and angles). Mastery of this stage requires the learner to implement classificatory-level cognitive processes and a set of higher-order thinking processes involving hypothesizing, evaluating, and inferring.

This stage model has instructional implications for learners at various points in development. Instruction can be spread over several grades in which concepts are periodically revisited at higher levels of attainment. Young children initially are provided with concrete referents, and with development become able to operate at more abstract cognitive levels. For example, young children may learn the concept of "honesty" by seeing specific examples (e.g., not stealing, giving back something that is not yours), but with development they can understand the concept in more abstract and complex terms (e.g., recognize honest feedback by a supervisor of a worker's performance; discuss benefits of honesty).

Teaching of Concepts

Teaching concepts is a key instructional activity, and the theory and research covered in this section have implications for instructional planning and activities. For example, Tennyson (1980, 1981) developed a model of concept teaching based on empirical research. This model includes the following steps (Tennyson & Park, 1980):

- Determine the structure of the concept to include superordinate, coordinate, and subordinate concepts, and identify the critical and variable attributes (e.g., features that can legitimately vary and not affect the concept).
- Define the concept in terms of the critical attributes, and prepare several examples with the critical and variable attributes.
- Arrange the examples in sets based on the attributes, and ensure that the examples have similar variable attributes within any set containing examples from each coordinate concept.

■ Order and present the sets in terms of the divergence and difficulty of the examples, and order the examples within any set according to the learner's current knowledge.

Most concepts can be represented in a hierarchy with *superordinate* (higher) and *subordinate* (lower) concepts. For any given concept, similar concepts may be at roughly the same level in the hierarchy; these are known as *coordinate* concepts. For example, the concept "domestic cat" has "cat family" and "mammal" as superordinate concepts, the various breeds (short hair, Siamese) as subordinate concepts, and other members of the cat family (lion, jaguar) as coordinate concepts. The concept has critical attributes (e.g., paws, teeth) and variable attributes (e.g., hair length, eye color). A *set* comprises examples and nonexamples (e.g., dog, squirrel) of the concept.

Although the concept should be defined with its critical attributes before examples and nonexamples are given, presenting a definition does not ensure that students will learn the concept. Examples should differ widely in variable attributes, and nonexamples should differ from examples in a small number of critical attributes at once. This mode of presentation prevents students from overgeneralizing (classifying nonexamples as examples) and undergeneralizing (classifying examples as nonexamples).

Pointing out relationships among examples is an effective way to foster generalization. One means is by using *concept (knowledge) maps,* or diagrams that represent ideas as node-link assemblies (Nesbit & Adesope, 2006). O'Donnell et al. (2002) showed that learning is facilitated with knowledge maps where ideas are interlinked. Nesbit and Adesope (2006) found that concept maps improved students' knowledge retention. Application 7.3 contains suggestions for teaching concepts.

The optimal number of examples to present depends on such concept characteristics as number of attributes and degree of abstractness of the concept. Abstract concepts (e.g., love, kindness) usually have fewer tangible examples than concrete concepts (e.g., dog, train), and examples of the former may be difficult for learners to grasp. Concept learning also depends on learner attributes such as age and prior knowledge (Tennyson & Park, 1980). Older students learn better than younger ones, and students with more relevant knowledge outperform those lacking such knowledge.

In teaching concepts, it is helpful to present examples that differ in optional attributes but have relevant attributes in common so that the latter can be clearly pointed out, along with the irrelevant dimensions. In teaching the concept "right triangle," for example, the size is irrelevant, as is the direction it faces. One might present right triangles of various sizes pointing in different directions. Using worked examples is an effective cognitive instructional strategy (Atkinson et al., 2000; see Chapter 4 and later in this chapter).

Not only must students learn to generalize right triangles, but they also must learn to distinguish them from other triangles. To foster concept discrimination, teachers should present negative instances that clearly differ from positive instances. As students' skills develop, they can be taught to make finer discriminations. The suggestions shown in Table 7.2 are helpful in teaching students to generalize and discriminate among concepts.

This model requires a careful analysis of the taxonomic structure of a concept. Structure is well specified for many concepts (e.g., the animal kingdom), but for many others—especially abstract concepts—the links with higher- and lower-order concepts, as well as with coordinate concepts, may be problematic.

APPLICATION 7.3
Teaching of Concepts

Concept learning involves identifying attributes, generalizing them to new examples, and discriminating examples from nonexamples. Using superordinate, coordinate, and subordinate concepts and critical and variable attributes to present the concept should help students learn.

A kindergarten teacher presenting a unit on identifying and distinguishing shapes (e.g., circle, square, rectangle, oval, triangle, diamond) might initially have children group objects alike in shape and identify critical attributes (e.g., a square has four straight sides; the sides are the same length) and variable attributes (squares, rectangles, triangles, and diamonds have straight sides but a different number of sides of different lengths and arranged in different ways). The teacher might then focus on a particular shape by presenting different examples representing each shape so children can compare attributes with those of other shapes. As for content progression, the teacher might introduce shapes familiar to students (e.g.,

circle and square) before moving to less common ones (e.g., parallelogram).

Ms. Lautter introduced a unit on mammals by having her elementary students sort a list of various animals into the major animal groups. Then the students discussed the major differences between the animal groups. After reviewing these facts, she focused on the amphibian group by teaching the physical characteristics and by reviewing other attributes such as eating habits and the ideal environment and climate.

Mr. Whitehurst, a history teacher, showed a slide portraying the various immigrant groups that settled in the United States. After reviewing the time periods when each group immigrated, he and the students discussed the reasons why each group came, where they predominantly settled in the country, and what types of trades they practiced. Then they described the impact of each group separately and collectively on the growth of the United States.

Table 7.2
Generalizing and discriminating concepts.

Step	Examples
Name concept	Chair
Define concept	Seat with a back for one person
Give relevant attributes	Seat, back
Give irrelevant attributes	Legs, size, color, material
Give examples	Easy chair, high chair, beanbag chair
Give nonexamples	Bench, table, stool

Motivational Processes

Pintrich, Marx, and Boyle (1993) contended that conceptual change also involves *motivational processes* (e.g., goals, expectations, needs). These authors argued that four conditions are necessary for conceptual change to occur. First, dissatisfaction with one's current conceptions is needed; change is unlikely if people feel their conceptions are accurate or useful. Second, the new conception must be intelligible—people must understand a conception in order to adopt it. Third, the new conception must be plausible—learners must understand how it fits with other understandings of how it might be applied. Finally, they must perceive the new conception as fruitful—being able to explain phenomena and suggesting new areas of investigation or application.

Motivational processes enter at several places in this model. For example, research shows that students' goals direct their attention and effort, and their self-efficacy relates positively to motivation, use of effective task strategies, and skill acquisition (Schunk, 2012). Furthermore, students who believe that learning is useful and that task strategies are effective display higher motivation and learning (Pressley et al., 1990; Schunk & Rice, 1993). Goals, self-efficacy, and self-evaluations of competence have been shown to promote learning and self-regulation in such domains as reading comprehension, writing, mathematics, and decision making (Pajares, 1996; Schunk & DiBenedetto, 2016; Schunk & Swartz, 1993a; Wood & Bandura, 1989; Zimmerman & Bandura, 1994). High self-efficacy and interest are positively related to conceptual change (Cordova, Sinatra, Jones, Taasoobshivazi, & Lombardi, 2014). We see in the opening vignette that the shift toward more problem solving actually improved students' motivation for learning.

In short, the literature suggests that conceptual change involves an interaction of students' cognitions and motivational beliefs (Pintrich et al., 1993), which has implications for teaching. Rather than simply help learners construct knowledge, teachers must take students' pre-existing ideas into account when planning instruction and ensure that instruction includes motivation for learning.

These ideas are highly applicable to science, where knowledge is constructed by learners rather than simply transmitted (Driver, Asoko, Leach, Mortimer, & Scott, 1994; Linn & Eylon, 2006). An interesting issue is how students develop scientific misconceptions and simplistic scientific models (Windschitl & Thompson, 2006). An important task is to help students challenge and correct misconceptions (Sandoval, 1995). Although some research shows that conceptual change can occur in the absence of cognitive conflict (Ramsburg & Ohlsson, 2016), experiences that produce cognitive conflict can be helpful (Mayer, 1999; Sandoval, 1995; Williams & Tolmie, 2000). This might entail having students engage in hands-on activities (e.g., problem-based learning) and work with others (e.g., in discussions) to interpret their experiences through selective questioning (e.g., "Why do you think that?" "How did you figure that?"). This approach fits well with the Vygotskian emphasis on social influences on knowledge construction (Chapter 8).

Although science has many themes that ought to be interesting, studying science holds little interest for many students. Motivation and learning benefit from hands-on instruction and links to aspects of students' lives. For example, to increase interest motion can be linked to the path of soccer balls, electricity to DVD players, and ecology to community recycling programs. Using illustrations and diagrams helps students understand scientific concepts (Carlson, Chandler, & Sweller, 2003; Hannus & Hyönä, 1999), although some students may need to be taught how to study illustrations.

PROBLEM SOLVING

One of the most important types of information processing that occurs during learning is problem solving (National Research Council, 2000). Problem solving has been studied for a long time, but interest in the topic has grown in recent years with the ascendance of cognitive and constructivist learning theories. Some theorists consider problem solving to be the key process in learning, especially in domains such as science and mathematics (Anderson, 1993). "Problem solving" and "learning" are not synonymous, but the former often is involved in the latter—especially when learners engage in self-regulated learning (Chapter 10) and when learning involves challenges and nonobvious solutions. In the opening vignette, Meg recommends more emphasis on problem solving.

A *problem* exists when there is a "situation in which you are trying to reach some goal, and must find a means for getting there" (Chi & Glaser, 1985, p. 229). The problem may be to answer a question, compute a solution, find information using the Internet, locate an object, secure a job, teach a student, and so on. *Problem solving* refers to people's efforts to achieve a goal for which they do not have an automatic solution.

Regardless of content area and complexity, all problems have certain commonalities. A problem has an initial state—the problem solver's current status or level of knowledge, as well as a goal, or what the problem solver is attempting to attain. Most problems also require the solver to break the goal into subgoals that, when mastered (usually sequentially), result in goal attainment. Finally, a problem requires performing operations (cognitive and behavioral activities) on the initial state and the subgoals, which alter the nature of those states (Anderson, 1990; Chi & Glaser, 1985).

Given this definition, not all learning activities include problem solving. For example, problem solving likely is not involved when students' skills become so well established that they automatically execute actions to attain goals, which happens with many skills in different domains. Problem solving also may not occur in low-level (possibly trivial) learning, where students know what to do to learn. This seems to be an issue at Nikowsky Middle School, as teachers are focusing on basic skills needed for the tests. At the same time, students learn new skills and new uses for previously learned skills, so most school learning could involve problem solving at some point.

Problem solving skills can be developed. Encouraging young children's tool use (i.e., using a tool such as a rake to obtain objects) facilitates their problem solving (Keen, 2011), as does teaching them schemas with problem-solving strategies (Peltier & Vannest, 2017). With development, students' problem solving benefits more from concrete visual representations, or illustrations of real-life elements, than from abstract representations during instruction (Moreno, Ozogul, & Reisslein, 2011). This section initially examines some historical perspectives and then discusses contemporary views.

Historical Perspectives

Two historical perspectives on problem solving are examined as a backdrop to current cognitive views: trial and error, and insight.

Trial and Error. Thorndike's (1913b) research with cats (Chapter 3) required problem solving; the problem was how to escape from the cage. Thorndike conceived of problem solving as *trial and error*. The animal was capable of performing certain behaviors in the cage. From this behavioral repertoire, the animal performed one behavior and experienced the consequences. After a series of random behaviors, the cat made the response that opened the hatch leading to escape. With repeated trials, the cat made fewer errors before performing the escape behavior, and the time required to solve the problem diminished. The escape behavior (response) became connected to cues (stimuli) in the cage.

We use trial and error to solve problems when we simply perform actions until one works. But trial and error is not reliable and often not effective. It can waste time, may never result in a solution, may lead to a less-than-ideal solution, and can have negative effects. In desperation, a teacher might use a trial-and-error approach by trying different reading materials with Kayla until she begins to read better. This approach might be effective but also might expose her to materials that prove frustrating and thereby slow her reading progress.

Insight.   Problem solving often is thought to involve *insight*, or the sudden awareness of a likely solution. Wallas (1921) studied great problem solvers and formulated a four-stage model as follows:

- *Preparation:* A time to learn about the problem and gather information that might be relevant to its solution.
- *Incubation:* A period of thinking about the problem, which may also include putting the problem aside for a time.
- *Illumination:* A period of insight when a potential solution suddenly comes into awareness.
- *Verification:* A time to test the proposed solution to ascertain whether it is correct.

Wallas's stages were descriptive and not subjected to empirical verification. Hélie and Sun (2010) presented a more detailed, process-oriented conceptualization of the incubation and illumination stages. Gestalt psychologists (Chapter 5) also postulated that much human learning was insightful and involved a change in perception. Learners initially thought about the ingredients necessary to solve a problem. They integrated these in various ways until the problem was solved. When learners arrived at a solution, they did so suddenly and with insight.

Many problem solvers report having moments of insight; Watson and Crick had insightful moments in discovering the structure of DNA (Lemonick, 2003). An important educational application of Gestalt theory was in the area of problem solving, or *productive thinking* (Duncker, 1945; Luchins, 1942; Wertheimer, 1945). The Gestalt view stressed the role of *understanding*—comprehending the meaning of some event or grasping the principle or rule underlying performance. In contrast, rote

APPLICATION 7.4
Role of Understanding in Learning

Teachers want students to understand concepts rather than simply memorize how to complete tasks. Gestalt psychologists believed that an emphasis on drill and practice, memorization, and reinforcement resulted in trivial learning and that understanding was achieved by grasping rules and principles underlying concepts and skills.

Teachers often use hands-on experiences to help students understand the structure and principles involved in learning. In biology, students might memorize what a cross section of a bean stem looks like under a microscope, but they may have difficulty conceptualizing the structures in the living organism. Mock-ups assist student learning. A large, hands-on model of a bean stem that can be taken apart to illustrate the internal structures should enhance student understanding of the stem's composition and how the parts function. Computer technology also may show the same thing.

Talking about child care in a high school family studies class is not nearly as beneficial as the hour students spend each week with children in a day care center and applying what they have been studying.

In discussing the applications of learning theories, it is preferable that students see firsthand the utilization of techniques that enhance learning. To gain understanding when students in an educational psychology course observe in classrooms, they list examples of situations to include which learning principles are evident.

memorization—although used often by students—was inefficient and rarely used in life outside of school (Application 7.4).

Research by Katona (1940) demonstrated the utility of rule learning compared with memorization. In one study, participants were asked to learn number sequences (e.g., 816449362516941). Some learned the sequences by rote, whereas others were given clues to aid learning (e.g., "Think of squared numbers"). Learners who determined the rule for generating the sequences retained them better than those who memorized.

Rules lead to better learning and retention than memorization because rules give a simpler description of the phenomenon so less information must be learned. In addition, rules help organize material. To recall information, one recalls the rule and then fills in the details. In contrast, memorization entails recalling more information. Memorization generally is inefficient because most situations have some organization (Wertheimer, 1945). Problems are solved by discovering the organization of the situation and the relationship of the elements to the problem solution. By arranging and rearranging elements, learners eventually gain insight into the solution.

Köhler (1925, 1926) did well-known work on problem solving with apes on the island of Tenerife during World War I. In one experiment, Köhler put a banana just out of reach of an ape in a cage; the ape could fetch the banana by using a long stick or by putting two sticks together. Köhler concluded that problem solving was insightful: Animals surveyed the situation, suddenly "saw" the means for attaining the goal, and tested the solution. The apes' first problem-solving attempts failed as they tried different ineffective strategies (e.g., throwing a stick at the banana). Eventually they saw the stick as an extension of their arms and used it accordingly.

A barrier to problem solving is *functional fixedness*, or the inability to perceive different uses for objects or new configurations of elements in a situation (Duncker, 1945). In a classic study, Luchins (1942) gave individuals problems that required them to obtain a given amount of water using three jars of different sizes. Persons from ages 9 to adult easily learned the formula that always produced the correct amount. Intermixed in the problem set were some problems that could be solved using a simpler formula. Persons generally continued to apply the original formula. Cuing them that there might be an easier solution led some to discover the simpler methods, although many persisted with the original formula. This research shows that when students do not understand a phenomenon, they may blindly apply a known algorithm and fail to understand that easier methods exist. This procedure-bound nature of problem solving can be overcome when different procedures are emphasized during instruction (Chen, 1999).

Gestalt theory had little to say about how problem-solving strategies are learned or how learners could be taught to be more insightful. Wertheimer (1945) believed that teachers could aid problem solving by arranging elements of a situation so that students would be more likely to perceive how the parts relate to the whole. But such general advice may not be helpful for teachers.

Heuristics

A common way to solve problems is to use *heuristics*, which are general methods for solving problems that employ principles (rules of thumb) that usually lead to a solution (Anderson, 1990). There are a number of general heuristics that have seen widespread applications with students to help them solve problems and learn better. For example, for reading comprehension, a common method is *SQ4R*: *S*urvey—*Q*uestion—*R*ead—*R*ecite—*R*elate—*R*eview. Students initially survey (scan) a passage and ask themselves questions, after which they read the passage, recite key points, relate those to what they already know, and finally review the entire passage.

Polya's (1945/1957) list of mental operations involved in problem solving is as follows:

- Understand the problem.
- Devise a plan.
- Carry out the plan.
- Look back.

Understanding the problem involves asking such questions as "What is the unknown?" and "What are the data?" It often helps to draw a diagram representing the problem and the given information. In devising a plan, one tries to find a connection between the data and the unknown. Breaking the problem into subgoals is useful, as is thinking of a similar problem and how that was solved (i.e., use analogies). The problem may need to be restated. While carrying out the plan, checking each step to ensure it is being properly implemented is important. Looking back means examining the solution: Is it correct? Is there another means of attaining it?

Bransford and Stein (1984) formulated a similar heuristic known as IDEAL:

■ *I*dentify the problem.
■ *D*efine and represent the problem.
■ *E*xplore possible strategies.
■ *A*ct on the strategies.
■ *L*ook back and evaluate the effects of your activities.

Creative problem solving involves problems that require creative solutions because the potential solutions may not be known. In these situations, it is important to attempt to construct different task representations and generate alternative solutions. These problems cannot be solved by an analytical step-by-step process; for example, how do I get a student in my class more engaged in learning? How can I maintain my academic motivation when I feel overwhelmed and stressed? Such problems benefit from thoughtful reflection on possible courses of action and not rushing to attain closure (see section on creativity later in this chapter).

General heuristics are most useful when one is working with unfamiliar content (Andre, 1986). They are less effective in a familiar domain, because as domain-specific knowledge develops, students increasingly use it. General heuristics have an instructional advantage: They can help students become systematic problem solvers. Although the heuristic approach may appear to be inflexible, there actually is flexibility in how steps are carried out. For many students, a heuristic will be more systematic than their current problem-solving approaches and will lead to better solutions.

Problem-Solving Strategies

Newell and Simon (1972) proposed an information processing model of problem solving that included a problem space with a beginning state, a goal state, and possible solution paths leading through subgoals and requiring application of operations. The problem solver forms a mental representation of the problem and performs operations to reduce the discrepancy between the beginning and goal states.

The first step in problem solving is to form a mental representation. Similar to Polya's first step (understand the problem), representation requires translating known information into a model in memory. The internal representation consists of propositions, and possibly images, in WM. The problem also can be represented externally (e.g., on paper or computer). Information in WM activates related knowledge in LTM, after which the solver selects a problem-solving strategy. As people solve problems, they evaluate their progress and often alter their initial representation and activate new knowledge, especially if their strategy does not succeed.

The problem representation determines what knowledge is activated in memory and, consequently, how easy the problem is to solve (Holyoak, 1984). If solvers incorrectly represent the problem by not considering all aspects or by adding too many constraints, the search process is unlikely to identify a good solution path (Chi & Glaser, 1985). No matter how clearly solvers subsequently reason, they will not reach a correct solution unless they form a new representation. Not surprisingly, problem-solving training programs typically devote a lot of time to the representation phase (Andre, 1986).

As we saw with skills (discussed earlier), problem-solving strategies can be general or specific. *General strategies* can be applied to problems in several domains regardless of content; *specific strategies* are useful only in a particular domain. For example, breaking a complex problem into subproblems (subgoal analysis) is a general strategy applicable to problems such as writing a term paper, choosing an academic major, and deciding where to live. Conversely, tests that one might perform to classify laboratory specimens are task specific. The professional development given to Nikowsky's teachers probably included general and specific strategies.

General strategies are useful when one is working on problems where solutions are not immediately obvious. Useful general strategies are generate-and-test, means–ends analysis, analogical reasoning, and brainstorming. The first three are discussed here; brainstorming is covered later in this chapter. These general strategies are less useful than domain-specific strategies when working with highly familiar content. Some examples of problem solving in learning contexts are given in Application 7.5.

APPLICATION 7.5
Problem Solving

Students can improve their problem-solving skills. When middle school students solve mathematical word problems, Mr. Quinn encourages them to state each problem in their own words, draw a sketch, decide what information is relevant, and state the ways they might solve the problem. These and other similar questions help focus students' attention on important task aspects and guide their thinking:

- What information is important?
- What information is missing?
- Which formulas are necessary?
- What is the first thing to do?

Another way to assist students is to encourage them to view a problem from varying perspectives. In a world history class, high school students discussed how to categorize major wartime figures (e.g., Churchill, Hitler). They determined different ways these individuals could be categorized, such as by personality type, political makeup of their countries, goals of the war, and the effects that their leadership and goals had. This exercise illustrates different ways to organize information, which aids problem solving.

Teachers also can teach strategies. In a geography lesson, students might be given the following problem: "Pick a state (not your own) that you believe could attract new residents, and create a poster depicting the most important attributes of that state." A working backward strategy could be taught as follows:

Goal: Create a poster depicting the state's important attributes.

Subgoal: Decide how to portray the attributes in a poster.

Subgoal: Decide which attributes to portray.

Subgoal: Decide which state to pick.

Initial Subgoal: Decide which attributes attract new residents.

(Continued)

APPLICATION 7.5 (*continued*)

To attain the initial subgoal, students could collaborate in small groups to determine which factors attract people to a state. They then could conduct research to check on which states possess these attributes. Students could reconvene to discuss the attributes of different states and decide on one. They then would decide which attributes to portray in the poster and how to portray them, after which they would create their poster and present it to the class.

When students are developing problem-solving skills, teachers might want to give clues rather than answers. A teacher working with younger children on categorizing might give the children a word list of names of animals, colors, and places to live. Children are most likely to experience some difficulty categorizing the names. The teacher could provide clues such as, "Think of how the words go together. How are *horse* and *lion* alike? How are *pink* and *house* different?

Generate-and-Test. Generate-and-test is a useful strategy when a limited number of problem solutions can be tested to see if they attain the goal (Resnick, 1985). This strategy works best when multiple solutions can be ordered in terms of likelihood, and at least one solution is apt to solve the problem.

As an example, assume that you walk into a room and flip the light switch, but the light does not come on. Possible causes include: the bulb is burned out; the electricity is turned off; the switch is broken; the lamp socket is faulty; the circuit breaker is tripped; or the wiring has a short. You will probably generate and test the most likely solution (replace the bulb); if this does not solve the problem, you may generate and test other likely solutions. Although content does not need to be highly familiar, some knowledge is needed to use this method effectively. Prior knowledge establishes the hierarchy of possible solutions; current knowledge influences solution selection. Thus, if you notice no lights on in your neighborhood you would suspect that the power is off.

Means–Ends Analysis. To use *means–ends analysis*, one compares the current situation with the goal and identifies the differences between them (Resnick, 1985). Subgoals are set to reduce the differences. One performs operations to accomplish the first subgoal, at which point the process is repeated until the goal is attained.

Newell and Simon (1972) studied means–ends analysis and formulated the General Problem Solver (GPS)—a computer simulation program. GPS breaks a problem into subgoals, each representing a difference from the current state. GPS starts with the most important difference and uses operations to eliminate that difference. In some cases, the operations must first eliminate another difference that is prerequisite to the more important one.

Means-ends analysis is a powerful problem-solving heuristic. When subgoals are properly identified, means–ends analysis will likely solve the problem. One drawback is that with complex problems, means–ends analysis can create a heavy cognitive load for WM because one may have to keep track of several subgoals. Forgetting a subgoal thwarts problem solution.

Means–ends analysis can proceed from the goal to the initial state (*working backward*) or from the initial state to the goal (*working forward*). In working backward, one starts

Figure 7.2
Means-ends analysis applied to a geometry problem.

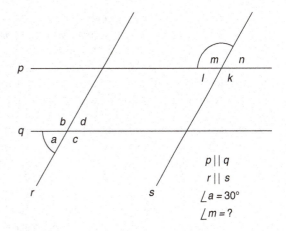

$p \| q$
$r \| s$
$\angle a = 30°$
$\angle m = ?$

with the goal and asks what subgoals are necessary to accomplish it. One then asks what is necessary to attain these subgoals and so forth, until the initial state is reached. To work backward, therefore, one plans a series of moves, each designed to attain a subgoal. Successfully working backward requires a fair amount of knowledge in the problem domain to determine goal and subgoal prerequisites.

Working backward may be used to prove geometric theorems. One starts by assuming that the theorem is true and then works backward until the postulates are reached. A geometric example is shown in Figure 7.2. The problem is to solve for angle *m*. Working backward, students realize that they need to determine angle *n*, because angle m = 180° – angle *n* (straight line = 180°). Continuing to work backward, students understand that because the parallel lines intersect, the corresponding angle *d* on line *q* equals angle *n*. Drawing on their geometric knowledge, students determine that angle *d* = angle *a*, which is 30°. Thus, angle *n* = 30°, and angle *m* = 180°–30° = 150°.

As another example of working backward, suppose that Jay has a term paper due in three weeks. The last step before turning it in is to proofread it (do the day before the paper is due). The step before that is to type and print the final copy (allow one day). Before that, Jay makes final revisions (one day), revises the paper (three days), and types and prints the draft copy (one day). Continuing to work backward, Jay might allow five days to write the draft, one day to outline, three days for research, and one day to decide on a topic. For Jay to allow a total of 17 days to spend in part working on the paper, he needs to begin four days from today.

A second type of means–ends analysis is working forward, sometimes referred to as *hill climbing* (Matlin, 2009; Mayer, 1992). The problem solver starts with the current situation and alters it in the hope of moving closer to the goal. Several alterations usually are necessary to attain the goal. One danger is that working forward sometimes proceeds based on superficial problem analysis. Although each step represents an attempt to attain a necessary subgoal, one can easily veer off on a tangent or arrive at a dead end because typically one cannot see many alternatives ahead but rather only the next step (Matlin, 2009).

As an example of a working forward strategy, consider students in a laboratory who have various substances in jars. Their goal is to label the substances in their jars. To do so, they perform a series of tests on the substances, which, if correctly done, will result in a solution. This represents a working forward strategy because each test moves students closer to their goal of classifying their substances. The tests are ordered, and the results show what the substances are not, as well as what they might be. To prevent students from going off on the wrong track, the teacher sets up the procedure carefully and ensures that students understand how to perform the tests.

Analogical Reasoning. Another general problem-solving strategy is to use *analogical reasoning*, which involves drawing an analogy between the problem situation (the target) and a situation with which one is familiar (the base or source; Anderson, 1990; Chen, 1999; Hunt, 1989). One works the problem through the familiar domain and then relates the solution to the problem situation (Holyoak & Thagard, 1997). Analogical reasoning involves accessing the familiar domain's network in LTM and mapping it onto (relating it to) the problem situation in WM (Halpern, Hansen, & Riefer, 1990). Successful application requires that the familiar situation be structurally similar to the problem situation, although the situations may differ in surface features (e.g., one might involve the solar system and the other molecular structures). The subgoals in this approach are relating the steps in the original (familiar) domain to those in the transfer (problem) area. Students often use the analogy method to solve problems in textbooks. Examples are worked in the text (familiar domain); then students relate these steps to the problems they must solve.

Gick and Holyoak (1980, 1983) demonstrated the power of analogical problem solving. They presented learners with a difficult medical problem and, as an analogy, a solved military problem. Simply giving them the analogical problem did not automatically prompt them to use it. However, giving them a hint to use the military problem to solve the medical problem improved problem solving. Gick and Holyoak also found that giving students two analog stories led to better problem solving than giving one story, but what did not enhance problem solving was having them summarize the analog story, giving them the principle underlying the story while they read it, or providing them with a diagram illustrating the problem-solution principle. These results suggest that in an unfamiliar domain, students need guidance for using analogies and that multiple examples increase the likelihood of students' linking at least one example to the problem to be solved.

To be most effective, analogical problem solving requires good knowledge of the familiar and problem domains. Students often have enough difficulty using analogies to solve problems even when the solution strategy is highlighted. With inadequate knowledge, students are unlikely to see the relation between the problem and the analogue. Even assuming good knowledge, the analogy is most likely to fail when the familiar and problem domains are conceptually dissimilar. Learners may understand how fighting a battle (the military problem) is similar to fighting a disease (the medical problem), but they may not grasp other analogies (e.g., fighting a corporate takeover attempt).

Developmental evidence indicates that, despite its difficulties, children can employ analogical reasoning (Siegler, 1989). Teaching analogies to children—including those with learning disabilities—can improve their subsequent problem solving (Grossen, 1991). The use of case studies and case-based reasoning can help develop analogical thinking (Kolodner, 1997). Effective techniques for using analogies include having the teacher and child verbalize the solution principle that underlies the original and transfer problems, prompting children to recall elements of the original problem's causal structure, and presenting the two problems such that the causal structures proceed from most to least obvious (Crisafi & Brown, 1986). Other suggestions include using similar original and transfer problems, presenting several similar problems, and using pictures to portray causal relations.

This is not to suggest that all children can learn to use analogies well. The task is difficult, and children often draw inappropriate analogies. Compared with older students, younger ones require more hints, are more apt to be distracted by irrelevant perceptual features, and process information less efficiently (Crisafi & Brown, 1986). Children's success depends on their knowledge about the original problem and their skill at encoding and making mental comparisons, which show wide individual differences (Richland, Morrison, & Holyoak, 2006). Children learn problem-solving strategies better when they observe and explain them than when they merely observe (Crowley & Siegler, 1999).

Analogical problem solving is useful in teaching. Teachers often have students in their classes whose native language is not English. Teaching each student in his or her native language is impossible. Teachers might relate this problem to teaching students who have difficulty learning. With the latter students, teachers would proceed slowly, use concrete experiences whenever possible, and provide much individual instruction. They might try the same tactics with English language learners while simultaneously teaching them English words and phrases so they can keep up with the other students in class.

This analogy is appropriate because many students with learning problems and those who are learning English have difficulties in the classroom. Other analogies might be inappropriate. Unmotivated students also have learning difficulties. Using them for the analogy, the teacher might offer the English language learners rewards for learning. This solution may not be effective because the issue with English language learners likely is instructional rather than motivational.

Problem Solving and Learning

According to an information processing theory (Anderson, 1990, 1993, 2000), problem solving involves the acquisition, retention, and use of production systems, which are networks of condition–action sequences (rules) in which the conditions are the sets of circumstances that activate the system and the actions are the sets of activities that occur (Chapter 5). A production system consists of if–then statements. If statements (the condition) include the goal and test statements; then statements are the actions.

Productions are forms of procedural knowledge that include declarative knowledge and the conditions under which these forms are applicable. In problem solving, declarative knowledge includes problem-solving steps that are retrieved and adapted to the current problem (Anderson & Fincham, 2014). Productions are represented in LTM as propositional networks and are acquired in the same fashion as other procedural knowledge. Productions also are organized hierarchically with subordinate and superordinate productions. To solve two equations with two unknowns, one first represents one unknown in terms of the second unknown (subordinate production), after which one solves for the second unknown (production) and uses that value to solve for the first unknown (superordinate production).

Productions can be general or specific. Specific productions apply to content in well-defined areas. In contrast, heuristics are general productions because they apply to diverse content. A means–ends analysis might be represented as follows (Anderson, 1990):

IF the goal is to transform the current state into the goal state and D is the largest difference between the states

THEN set as subgoals

1. To eliminate the difference D
2. To convert the resulting state into the goal state. (p. 243)

A second production will then need to be employed with the if–then statement, "If the goal is to eliminate the difference D." This sequence continues until the subgoals have been identified at a specific level; then domain-specific rules are applied. In short, general productions are broken down until the level at which domain-specific knowledge is applied. Production systems offer a means of linking general with specific problem-solving procedures. Other problem-solving strategies (e.g., analogical reasoning) also can be represented as productions.

School learning that is highly regulated may not require problem solving. Problem solving is not applicable when students have a goal and a clear means for attaining it. Problem solving becomes more important when teachers move away from regimented instruction and encourage more original and critical thinking by students (National Research Council, 2000). A classroom climate where students are encouraged to tackle new problems and test novel solutions supports problem solving (Wüstenberg, Greiff, Vainikainen, & Murphy, 2016). This is what the teachers at Nikowsky worked on after their meeting with Meg.

Experts and Novices

As with skill acquisition, researchers have identified differences between novice and expert problem solvers (Anderson, 1990, 1993; Bruning et al., 2011; Resnick, 1985). One difference involves the demands made on WM. Expert problem solvers do not activate large amounts of potentially relevant information; they identify key features of the problem, relate these to background knowledge, and generate one or a small number of potential solutions (Mayer, 1992). Experts reduce complex problems to a manageable size by separating the problem space from the larger task environment, which includes the domain of facts and knowledge within which the problem is embedded (Newell & Simon, 1972). Coupled with the fact that experts can hold more information in WM (Chi, Glaser, & Farr, 1988), this reduction process retains relevant information, discards irrelevant information, fits within the limits of WM without causing excessive cognitive load, and is accurate enough to allow a solution.

Experts often employ a working forward strategy by identifying the problem format and generating an approach to fit it (Mayer, 1992). This typically entails breaking the problem into parts and solving the parts sequentially (Bruning et al., 2011). Novice problem solvers, however, often attempt problem solving in piecemeal fashion, in part because of the poorer organization in their memories. They may use trial and error or try to work backward from what they are trying to find to the problem givens—an ineffective strategy if they are unaware of the substeps needed (Mayer, 1992). Their means–ends analyses often are based on surface features of problems. In mathematics, novices generate formulas from memory when confronted with word problems. Trying to store too much information in WM causes excessive cognitive load (Kalyuga, Renkl, & Paas, 2010).

Experts and novices appear to be comparably versed in knowledge of general problem-solving strategies (Elstein, Shulman, & Sprafka, 1978; Simon, 1979). Such generalized knowledge structures are essential for problem solving (Kalyuga et al., 2010). But expert performers have more extensive and better-organized LTM domain-specific knowledge (Chi et al., 1981). The greater amount of knowledge experts can use in solving problems, the more likely they are to solve them and the better their memory organization facilitates efficiency.

Qualitative differences are evident in how knowledge is structured in memory (Chi, Glaser, & Rees, 1982). Experts' knowledge is more hierarchically organized. Experts tend to classify problems according to "deep structure," whereas novices rely more on surface features (Hardiman, Dufresne, & Mestre, 1989). Teaching novices to recognize deep features improves their performances.

Novices typically respond to problems in terms of how they are presented; experts reinterpret problems to reveal an underlying structure, one that most likely matches their own LTM network (Resnick, 1985). Novices attempt to translate the given information directly into formulas and solve for the missing quantities. Rather than generate formulas, experts may initially draw diagrams to clarify the relations among problem aspects. They often construct a new version of the problem. By the time they are ready to perform calculations, they usually have simplified the problem and perform fewer calculations than novices. While working, experts monitor their performances better to assess goal progress and the value of the strategy they are using.

Finally, experts spend more time planning and analyzing. They are more thoughtful and do not proceed until they have a strategy in mind. Experienced teachers spend more time planning, as well as more time exploring new classrooms, than do less-experienced teachers (Moore, 1990). Such planning makes strategy implementation easier.

In summary, compared with novices, experts:

- Possess more declarative knowledge
- Have better hierarchical organization of knowledge
- Spend more time planning and analyzing
- Recognize problem formats more easily
- Represent problems at a deeper level
- Monitor their performances more carefully
- Understand better the value of strategy use

CRITICAL THINKING, REASONING, AND CREATIVITY

In addition to metacognition, concept learning, and problem solving, complex cognitive processes include those involved in critical thinking, reasoning, and creativity.

Critical Thinking

The educators in the opening vignette struggled with how to incorporate more critical thinking into the curriculum. *Critical thinking* is reflective cognitive activity focused on deciding what to do or what to believe (Ennis, 1987). Critical thinking involves how to think rather than what to think. It is, essentially, better or deeper thinking.

Unlike problem solving that is focused on obtaining a solution to a problem, critical thinking is focused on understanding the nature of the problem. Problem solving also tends to be focused on specific domains (e.g., science, mathematics), whereas critical thinking may occur at a more general level (e.g., the effects of pollution) and may cut across multiple domains (Bruning et al., 2011).

Critical thinking may, of course, include aspects of problem solving. We may want not only to understand the effects of pollution but also to generate some solutions to the problems it creates. However, as generally construed, critical thinking does not require decisions or solutions, rather only more complete understanding.

Investigators have proposed various components of critical thinking. Four that seem important are knowledge, inference, evaluation, and metacognition (Bruning et al., 2011; Halpern, 1998). Some knowledge of the issue being considered helps individuals ask questions and judge new information or perspectives. Knowledge of strategies as discussed in this and other chapters can help focus the direction critical thinking takes. As a result of engaging in critical thinking, people acquire new knowledge.

Inference refers to making connections between two or more units of knowledge (Bruning et al., 2011). Making inferences helps people understand issues better and at deeper levels. Later in this chapter, two types of inference processes are discussed: deductive and inductive reasoning.

Evaluation refers to processes such as analyzing, judging, and weighing evidence. By analyzing, we identify and select information that seems relevant to the issue at hand. Judging serves to assess the credibility of information or evidence and can help eliminate bias. Weighing means that we compare information we have and organize it into a fashion that makes sense to us.

Metacognition is a key aspect of critical thinking (Byrnes & Dunbar, 2014). Earlier we saw that metacognition was "thinking about thinking." Metacognitive activities help us monitor our thought processes and reflect on the adequacy of the conclusions we draw. Through metacognitive activities, we may decide that we have thought about an issue sufficiently or conversely that we are not ready to make a decision because we need more information.

Lastly, because critical thinking necessitates time and effort, it requires motivation (Byrnes & Dunbar, 2014). To think critically, you must engage in cognitive processing beyond that required for comprehension and may have to spend extra time to gain more information (e.g., read additional articles to be able to properly evaluate a claim). Many of the motivational processes relevant to learning (Chapter 9) undoubtedly come into play.

Critical thinking can be improved (Abrami et al., 2015). It requires a certain amount of knowledge of the domain under consideration such as science and social studies (Byrnes & Dunbar, 2014). Students also benefit from instruction and practice in critical thinking skills (e.g., evaluation). Abrami et al. (2015) conducted a meta-analysis of critical thinking research studies and found that exposing students to authentic (real-life) issues was important through use of role playing, applied problem solving, case studies, and simulations. Also important was the opportunity for discussions. One-to-one mentoring by teachers or peers seemed to promote the effects of authentic tasks and discussions. Learning environments that include these features can help to develop critical thinking.

Reasoning

Reasoning refers to the mental processes involved in generating and evaluating logical arguments (Anderson, 1990). Reasoning yields a conclusion from thoughts, percepts, and assertions (Johnson-Laird, 1999) and involves working through problems or issues to explain why something happened or what will happen (Hunt, 1989). There are general reasoning skills, as well as skills applicable to particular domains such as historical reasoning (van Drie & van Boxtel, 2008). General reasoning skills include clarification, basis, inference, and evaluation (Ennis, 1987; Quellmalz, 1987; Table 7.3 and Application 7.6). Note the partial overlap of some of these with critical thinking skills.

Clarification. *Clarification* requires identifying and formulating questions, analyzing elements, and defining terms. These skills involve determining which elements in a situation are important, what they mean, and how they are related. At times, scientific questions are posed, but at other times, students must develop questions such as, "What is the problem, hypothesis, or thesis?" Clarification corresponds to the representation phase of problem solving; students define the problem to obtain a clear mental representation. Little productive reasoning occurs without a clear problem statement.

Basis. People's conclusions about a problem are supported by information from personal observations, statements by others, and previous inferences. Judging the credibility of a source is important. In so doing, one must distinguish between fact, opinion, and reasoned judgment. Assume that a suspect armed with a gun is apprehended near the scene of a murder. That the suspect had a gun when arrested is a fact. Laboratory tests on the gun, bullets, and victim lead to the reasoned judgment that the gun was used in the crime. Someone investigating the case might be of the opinion that the suspect is the murderer.

Inference. Scientific reasoning proceeds inductively or deductively. *Inductive reasoning* refers to developing general rules, principles, and concepts from observations and knowledge of specific examples (Pellegrino, 1985). It requires determination of a model and its associated rules of inference (Hunt, 1989). People reason inductively when they extract similarities and

Table 7.3
Reasoning skills.

Skill	Definition	Sample Questions
Clarification	Identifying and formulating questions, analyzing elements, defining terms	"What do I know?" "What do I need to figure out?"
Basis	Determining source(s) of support for conclusions about a problem	"Is this a fact or opinion?" "What is the source of this information?"
Inference	Reasoning inductively from specific cases to general principles or deductively from general principles to specific cases	"What do these diverse examples have in common?" (induction) "How can I apply these general rules to this example?" (deduction)
Evaluation	Using criteria to judge adequacy of a problem solution	"Do I need more information?" "Is my conclusion reasonable?"

APPLICATION 7.6
Reasoning

Students can learn how to ask questions to produce an accurate mental representation of a problem and reason about it. A teacher might give elementary students objects to classify according to shape. To help students identify, clarify, and reason about the problem, the teacher could ask questions such as:

- What have you been asked to do?
- What items do you have?
- What are some of the shapes you know?
- Does it matter if the items are different colors?
- Does it matter if some of the items are little and some are big?
- Does it matter if some of the items are soft and some are hard?
- What do you think you will do with the items you have?

Students verbalize what information they need to use and what they are supposed to do with that information. Each time the teacher works with students in solving a problem, the teacher can help them

generate questions to determine what information is important for solving the problem.

A medical researcher working with a group of interns gives them information about a virus, and their task is to identify the virus. To assist the students in the identification process, the instructor might generate a list of questions similar to the following:

- What effect does the virus have on blood cells?
- What effect does the virus have on human tissue?
- How quickly does the virus appear to grow, and under what conditions does it grow?
- What does the virus do when exposed to warmth?
- What does the virus do when exposed to cold?
- What does the virus do when exposed to moisture?
- What does the virus do in an airtight environment?
- What reaction does the virus have when exposed to various drugs?

differences among specific objects and events and arrive at generalizations, which are tested by applying them to new experiences. Individuals retain their generalizations as long as they are effective, and they modify them when they experience conflicting evidence.

Some of the more common types of tasks used to assess inductive reasoning are *classification, concept,* and *analogy problems.* Consider the following analogy (Pellegrino, 1985):

sugar : sweet : lemon : _____
yellow sour fruit squeeze tea

To solve this analogy, the learner initially mentally represents critical attributes of each term in the analogy. She activates networks in LTM involving each term, which contain critical attributes of the terms to include subordinate and superordinate concepts. Next, she compares the features of the first pair to determine the link. "Sweet" is a property of sugar that involves taste. She then searches the "lemon" network to determine which of the five features listed corresponds in meaning to "lemon" as "sweet" does to "sugar." Although all five terms are most likely stored in her "lemon" network, only "sour" directly involves taste.

Children begin to display basic inductive reasoning around age 8. With development, children can reason faster and with more complex material. This occurs because their LTM networks become more complex and better linked, which in turn reduces the burden on the WM. To help foster inductive thinking, teachers might use a guided discovery approach (Chapter 8) in which children learn different examples and try to formulate a general rule. For example, children may collect leaves and formulate some general principles involving stems, veins, sizes, and shapes of leaves from different trees. Or teachers might pose a problem such as "Why does metal sink in water but metal ships float?" Rather than tell students how to solve the problem, the teacher might provide materials and encourage them to formulate and test hypotheses as they work on the task. Phye (1997; Klauer & Phye, 2008) discussed effective teaching methods and programs that have been used to teach inductive reasoning to students.

Deductive reasoning refers to applying inference rules to a formal model of a problem to decide whether specific instances logically follow. When individuals reason deductively, they proceed from general concepts (premises) to specific instances (conclusions) to determine whether the latter follow from the former. A deduction is valid if the premises are true and if the conclusion follows logically from the premises (Johnson-Laird, 1985, 1999).

Linguistic and deductive reasoning processes are intimately linked (Falmagne & Gonsalves, 1995; Polk & Newell, 1995). One type of deduction problem is the *three-term series* (Johnson-Laird, 1972). For example,

> If Karen is taller than Tina, and
> If Mary Beth is not as tall as Tina, then
> Who is the tallest?

The problem-solving processes employed with this problem are similar to those discussed previously. Initially one forms a mental representation of the problem, such as K > T, MB < T. One then works forward by combining the propositions (K > T > MB) to solve the problem. Developmental factors limit children's proficiency in solving such problems. Children may have difficulty keeping relevant problem information in WM and may not understand the language used to express the relationships.

Another type of deductive reasoning problem is the *syllogism*. Syllogisms are characterized by two premises and a conclusion containing the words *all, no,* or *some,* such as, "All As are Bs" and "Some As are not Bs" (Khemlani & Johnson-Laird, 2012). The following are sample premises:

> All university professors are teachers.
> Some graduate students are not teachers.
> No undergraduate student is a teacher.

A sample syllogism is as follows:

> All the students in Ken's class are good in math.
> All students who are good in math will attend college.
> (Therefore) All the students in Ken's class will attend college.

Researchers debate what mental processes people use to solve syllogisms, including whether they use heuristics, rules of inference, or diagrams (e.g., Venn; Khemlani & Johnson-Laird, 2012). For example, using inference rules we might believe that a syllogism is true only if there is no way to interpret the premises to imply the opposite of the conclusion; that is, a syllogism is true unless an exception to the conclusion can be found.

In information processing terms, people may learn the rules (e.g., the *modus ponens* rule governs "if *p* then *q*" statements) and then match instances to the rules. Or individuals may use content-specific rules, which can be expressed as productions such that specific instances trigger the production rules. Thus, a production may involve all cars and may be triggered when a specific car ("my brand X") is encountered.

Solving syllogisms also might depend on semantic procedures that search for interpretations of the premises that are counterexamples to conclusions. According to this view, people construct one or more mental models for the assertions they encounter (interpretations of the premises); the models differ in structure and are used to test the logic of the situation. Students may repeatedly re-encode the problem based on information; thus, deduction largely is a form of verbal reasoning (Polk & Newell, 1995). Johnson-Laird and colleagues (Johnson-Laird, 1999; Johnson-Laird, Byrne, & Schaeken, 1992; Johnson-Laird, Byrne, & Tabossi, 1989) have extended this semantic analysis to various classes of inferences (e.g., those involving *if, or, and, not,* and multiple quantifiers). Further research will help clarify these processes and determine instructional implications.

Evaluation. *Evaluation* involves using criteria to judge the adequacy of a problem solution. In evaluating, students ask questions such as, "Are the data sufficient to solve the problem?" "Do I need more information?" and "Are my conclusions based on facts, opinions, or reasoned judgments?" Evaluation also involves deciding what ought to happen next—that is, formulating hypotheses about future events assuming that one's analysis is correct so far.

Deductive reasoning also can be affected by content apart from the logic. Wason (1966) put four cards (showing *A B 2 3*) in front of participants. They were told that each card contained a letter on one side and a number on the other, and they were given a conditional rule: "If a card has *A* on one side, then it has *2* on the other." Their task was to select the cards that needed to be turned over to determine whether the rule was true. Although most participants picked the *A* card and many also chose the *2*, few picked the *3*; however, it must be turned over because if there is an *A* on the other side, then the rule is false. When the content was changed to an everyday generalization (e.g., letter = hair color, number = eye color, *A* = blond hair, *2* = blue eyes), most people made the correct selections (Wason & Johnson-Laird, 1972). These results speak to the importance of not assuming generalization in reasoning but rather giving students experience working with different types of content.

Metacognition is a central component of reasoning (Thompson, Turner, & Pennycook, 2011). Learners monitor their efforts to ensure that questions are properly posed, that data from adequate sources are available and used to draw inferences, and that relevant criteria are employed in evaluation. Teaching reasoning requires instruction in general and domain-specific skills and in metacognitive strategies. Cognitive load also seems important (Chapter 5). Reasoning is difficult if multiple sources of information must be processed simultaneously, which taxes WM. Carlson et al. (2003) found that students' science performance benefited from two procedures designed to reduce cognitive load: diagrams and instructions that minimized the amount of information to be processed simultaneously.

Creativity

Creativity (or *creative thinking*) is closely aligned with other topics covered in this chapter. The features that distinguish creativity from other cognitive processes involve novelty and value (or appropriateness). Creative thinking involves the development of a novel idea, problem solution, or product that is of value and appropriate for the individual or larger social group (Hennessey & Amabile, 2010). Beyond these two criteria, researchers disagree about the necessary or desirable components of creativity.

Like problem solving, creativity deals with generating solutions; however, problem solving does not require that solutions be novel. They may be tried and true methods, just not those thought of previously by the problem solver. Creative thinking deals with outcomes that are valued and appropriate, but creative thinking does not require that one generate solutions, only that one consider an issue more thoroughly.

Creativity is not a single phenomenon; there are different forms. One distinction is between Big C creativity and little c creativity (Hennessey & Amabile, 2010). Big C creativity is eminent creativity, or a rare type that produces major breakthroughs and products and that has significant effects on others. While that type is newsworthy and often garners awards for the creator, it is much less common than little c creativity or that which occurs in everyday life and involves problem solving and ways to adapt to situations (e.g., creative ways to plan activities). In line with information processing theory, creativity also is at work in the construction of knowledge and linking knowledge with other knowledge in LTM networks. Regardless of the type, creativity seems dependent on the combining of concepts in new or unusual ways.

A key question is whether students can learn to be more creative. Like other cognitive processes, creativity capabilities can be improved. Creativity depends heavily on the knowledge that one brings to the situation (Sweller, 2009). The more knowledge one has about the area, the likelier one is to engage in creative thinking. Teaching divergent thinking (or spontaneous thinking with the goal of generating many different ideas) seems to benefit creativity as opposed to convergent thinking (i.e., more disciplined thinking focused on narrowing possible solutions), and there is evidence that creativity is enhanced when learners work in groups rather than individually (Hennessey & Amabile, 2010). And unlike many cognitive capabilities, creative thinking can stay strong throughout one's life (Kluger, 2013b). There are countless examples of high creativity by persons who were octogenarians or older, such as Frank Lloyd Wright, Grandma Moses, and Benjamin Franklin.

Creativity also can be affected by motivational factors. Intrinsic motivation (see Chapter 9) facilitates creativity, whereas extrinsic motivation may not. Researchers have explored whether rewarding students for creative thinking leads to increases in it. Although the research literature is not consistent on this issue (Joussemet & Koestner, 1999), results of a meta-analysis of research studies found that rewards given contingent on creative performance lead to increases in creativity (Byron & Khazanchi, 2012). It also helps to provide students with instructions to think creatively (Hennessey & Amabile, 2010).

The Creative Problem Solving (CPS) model is a generic framework (Treffinger, 1985; Treffinger & Isaksen, 2005). This model comprises three major components: understanding the challenge, generating ideas, and preparing for action (Treffinger, 1995; Treffinger & Isaksen, 2005). Metacognitive components (e.g., planning, monitoring, modifying behavior) are present throughout the process.

Understanding the challenge begins with a general goal or direction for problem solving. After important data (e.g., facts, opinions, concerns) are obtained, a specific goal or question is formulated. The hallmark of generating ideas is divergent thinking to produce options for attaining the goal. Preparing for action includes examining promising options and searching for sources of assistance and ways to overcome resistance.

Brainstorming is a general problem-solving strategy that is useful for formulating possible problem solutions (Isaksen & Gaulin, 2005; Mayer, 1992; Osborn, 1963), and it is positively linked with enhanced creativity (Sweller, 2009). The steps in brainstorming are as follows:

- Define the problem.
- Generate as many solutions as possible without evaluating them.
- Decide on criteria for judging potential solutions.
- Use these criteria to select the best solution.

Successful brainstorming requires that participants withhold criticism and evaluation of ideas until after all ideas are generated. In addition, participants may generate ideas that build onto one another. Thus, "wild" and unusual ideas should be encouraged (Mayer, 1992).

The amount of knowledge one has about the problem domain affects the success of brainstorming because better domain knowledge allows one to generate more potential solutions and criteria for judging their feasibility (Sweller, 2009). Brainstorming can be used individually, although the group interaction usually leads to more solutions.

Brainstorming lends itself well to many instructional and administrative decisions made in schools. It is most useful for generating many varied—and possibly some unique—ideas (Isaksen & Gaulin, 2005). Assume that a new school principal finds low staff morale. Staff members agree that better communication is needed. The grade-level leaders meet with the principal, and the group arrives at the following potential solutions: Hold a weekly meeting with staff, send out a weekly (electronic) bulletin, post notices on a bulletin board, hold weekly meetings with grade-level leaders (after which they meet with teachers), send e-mail informational messages frequently, make announcements over the public address system. The group formulates two criteria: (a) minimally time-consuming for teachers and (b) minimally disrupting to classes. With the criteria in mind, they decide that the principal should send out a weekly bulletin and frequent e-mail messages and meet with grade-level leaders as a group. Although these will take time, meetings between the principal and grade-level leaders will be more focused than those between the principal and the entire staff.

COGNITION AND TECHNOLOGY

In the last several years, there has been a rapid expansion of technology in instruction through electronic, distance, and online learning (Bernard et al., 2009; Brown, 2006; Campbell, 2006; Clark, 2008; Larreamendy-Joerns & Leinhardt, 2006; Li & Ma, 2010; Ng, 2015; Roblyer, 2006; Thorne & May, 2017). Technology often is equated with equipment (e.g., computers), but its meaning is much broader. *Technology* refers to the designs and environments that engage learners (Ertmer, 1999; Jonassen, Peck, & Wilson, 1999). Research on the effects of technology on learning is increasing, as are efforts to remove barriers to infusing technology into instruction.

We have witnessed a tremendous increase in forms of digital technologies including learning management systems, social networking sites, instant messengers, cloud-based storage and creation services, and educational resource sites (Ng, 2015). Technology has the potential to facilitate instruction in ways that formerly were unimaginable. Today's students can experience simulations of environments and events that they never could in regular classes, receive instruction from and communicate with others at long distances, and interact with large knowledge bases and expert tutoring systems. The use of classroom clickers keeps students attentive and engaged in the class activities.

A challenge for researchers is to determine how technology affects learners' cognitive processes during encoding, retention, transfer, problem solving, and so forth. This section focuses on the role that technology plays in learning. This material is not a practical guide on how to use technology in education. Readers interested in in-depth applications of technology should consult other sources (e.g., Brown, 2006; Carrington & Robinson, 2009; Ng, 2015; Roblyer, 2006; Seo, Pellegrino, & Engelhard, 2012). The following sections examine the role on learning of CBLEs, online social media, and distance (online) learning—three popular uses of technology in education.

Computer-Based Learning Environments

Researchers are interested in the roles that computer technologies play in teaching and learning (Van der Kleij, Feskens, & Eggen, 2015). Much research has been conducted in *computer-based learning environments* (*CBLEs*) Azevedo, Taub, & Mudrick, 2018; Li & Ma, 2010; Reimann & Bannert, 2018). Although computer-based learning is not a theory, it is important to know whether computers improve learning and help develop complex cognitive processing.

It is tempting to evaluate CBLEs by comparing them to environments not involving computers, but such comparisons can be misleading because other factors (e.g., authenticity of the content, teacher–student/student–student interactions) also may differ. Rather than focusing on this issue, it is better to examine the types of cognitive processing that can occur in CBLEs and from other technological applications.

Jonassen et al. (1999) presented a dynamic perspective on the role of technology in learning. The maximum benefits of technology derive when it energizes and facilitates thinking and knowledge construction. In this conceptualization, technology can serve the functions shown in Table 7.4. The technological applications relevant to learning described in this section are differentially effective in accomplishing these functions.

Table 7.4
Functions of technology.

- *Tool* to support knowledge construction
- *Information vehicle* for exploring knowledge to support learning by constructing
- *Context* to support learning by doing
- *Social medium* to support learning by conversing
- *Intellectual partner* to support learning by reflecting

(Jonassen et al., 1999)

Technology always should be used in support of instructional goals and not because it is available and educators believe they should use it. The effectiveness of technology depends on how well it complements instructional goals and practices. Results of a meta-analysis of research studies showed that students in classes where technology was used scored about 12 percentage points higher in achievement compared with students in classes where technology was not used to enhance learning (Tamim, Bernard, Borokhovski, Abrami, & Schmid, 2011). Other research also shows a slight but consistent advantage in achievement for students in classes where technology was used (Ng, 2015). However, research studies show much variability between classes, most likely due to how well technology was integrated with instruction. A meta-analysis of research on one-to-one programs (where each student has access to a computer) revealed benefits on information literacy and achievement, especially for students from lower socio-economic backgrounds who otherwise might have little if any access (Zheng, Warschauer, Lin, & Chang, 2016).

Computer-Based Instruction. Until it was supplanted by the Internet, *computer-based instruction* (CBI) (or CAI—*computer-assisted instruction*) was the most common application of computer learning in schools (Jonassen, 1996). CBI is often used for drills and tutorials (Chapter 3), which present information and feedback to students and respond based on students' answers.

Several CBI features are firmly grounded in learning theory and research. The material can command students' attention and provide immediate response feedback. Feedback can be of a type not often given in the classroom, such as how individual students' present performances compare with their prior performances to show progress in learning. In their review of research studies on CBLEs, Van der Kleij et al. (2015) found that elaborated feedback (i.e., proving explanations) led to better learning than did feedback only providing correct answers.

Another advantage of CBI is that many programs allow personalization; students enter information about themselves, parents, and friends, which is then included in the instructional presentation. Some evidence suggests that personalization can produce higher achievement than other formats (Anand & Ross, 1987). Personalizing instruction may improve meaningfulness and facilitate integration of content into LTM networks. Knowledge construction should be aided with familiar referents.

CBI also can be used for more-complex learning through tutoring by *expert systems*, or large computer programs that contain the knowledge and cognitive (thinking) processes of experts (Azevedo et al., 2018; Graesser, Conley, & Olney, 2012). Expert systems represent an application of *artificial intelligence*, which refers to computer programs that simulate human cognitive processes and learning. Such systems can, for example, help students become better self-regulated learners by teaching them how to plan and monitor learning and use effective learning strategies (Schraw, 2010), and also can be used for collaborative problem solving (Järvelä & Hadwin, 2013; see Chapter 10). Unlike classic CBI that is answer based (i.e., student enters an answer and computer gives feedback on its correctness), intelligent tutoring systems are process based. Thus, the system may prompt for what method the student wants to use to solve a problem and then may engage in a dialogue with the student regarding the method to use. The system gives hints and feedback on each step in the process.

Reviews of research on the effects of intelligent tutoring systems on students' learning generally are positive. Ma, Adesope, Nesbit, and Liu (2014) found that intelligent tutoring systems led to higher achievement compared with large-group instruction, textbooks/workbooks, and non-intelligent tutoring systems CBI. Results of a meta-analysis of studies with college students showed that intelligent tutoring systems had a positive effect on learning (Steenbergen-Hu & Cooper, 2014). A review by Kulik and Fletcher (2016) found that intelligent tutoring systems raised student achievement from the 50th to the 75th percentile. Based on a research review, VanLehn (2011) found that intelligent tutoring systems were comparable to human tutoring in their effects on student learning. Adding worked examples to intelligent tutors helps to decrease instructional time and promote learning compared with the tutor alone, perhaps because worked examples decrease extraneous cognitive load (Salden, Koedinger, Renkl, Aleven, & McLaren, 2010).

One common problem is that students may use ineffective methods in CBI with resulting piecemeal learning. Such learning violates the idea that learning should be meaningful and linked with knowledge in LTM. Students who are taught effective study strategies (e.g., organizing, summarizing) show corresponding achievement gains (Jairam & Kiewra, 2010).

Simulations. *Simulations* represent real or imaginary situations that cannot be brought into the learning setting. Examples are programs simulating the flights of aircraft, underwater expeditions, and life in a fictional city. Learners can build memory networks better when they have tangible referents during learning.

As a type of computer-based environment, simulations seem well suited for discovery and inquiry learning (Chapter 8). In their review of studies using computer simulations in discovery learning, de Jong and van Joolingen (1998) concluded that simulations were more effective than traditional instruction in inculcating students' "deep" (intuitive) cognitive processing.

For simulations to be effective, it is essential that they not create excessive cognitive load for learners (see Chapter 5). Splitting the content onto two successive screens rather than displaying all of it on one screen benefits learning and transfer (Lee, Plass, & Homer, 2006). Mayrath, Nihilani, and Robinson (2011) found that a voice tutorial reduces extraneous cognitive load better than a text tutorial and leads to greater transfer. The higher cognitive load of the text may result from learners splitting their visual attention between two sources of information.

Simulations also may be beneficial for developing problem-solving skills. Similar to the results for CBI, Moreno and Mayer (2004) found that personalized messages from an on-screen agent during simulations improved retention and problem solving better than did nonpersonalized messages. Woodward, Carnine, and Gersten (1988) found that the addition of computer simulations to structured teaching produced problem-solving gains for special-education high school students compared with traditional instruction alone. The authors noted, however, that the mechanism producing these results was unclear, and the results may not generalize to stand-alone computer simulations.

Games. *Games* are systems where players engage in rule-based artificial conflicts that lead to quantifiable outcomes (Plass, Hamer, & Kinzer, 2015; Salen & Zimmerman, 2004). Games are designed to create an enjoyable learning context by linking material with sport, adventure, or fantasy. Games can emphasize thinking skills and problem solving but also can be used to teach content (e.g., basketball game to teach fractions).

Games also may influence learning by increasing motivation (Nietfeld, 2018). Motivation is greater when an *endogenous* (natural) relationship exists between the content and the means ("special effects") by which the game or simulation presents the content (Lepper & Hodell, 1989). Fractions are endogenously related to a basketball game, for example, when students are asked to determine how much of the court is covered by players dribbling down the floor. Such an endogenous relationship enhances meaningfulness and LTM coding and storage. In many games and simulations, however, the relation between content and means is arbitrary, such as when a student's correct response to a question produces fantasy elements (e.g., cartoon characters). When the relation is arbitrary, the game does not produce better learning than traditional instruction, although the former may be more interesting.

Another issue is that games have many interesting features that potentially can overload learners' WMs and distract them from learning content. Focusing learners' attention on the relevant content can promote learning and transfer beyond the learning context. Fiorella and Mayer (2012) found benefits on learning and transfer from providing students worksheets that directed their attention to relevant features of the game and summarized its underlying principles.

In the last few years, research has increased on the role of games in student learning and achievement (Nietfeld, 2018). Results of a meta-analysis of research studies (Clark, Tanner-Smith, & Killingsworth, 2016) revealed that digital games enhanced student learning relative to non-game contexts. Granic, Lobel, and Engels (2014) reviewed research on interactive video games and found benefits on several student outcomes including attention, resilience, mood management, and prosocial behavior. It seems imperative that for games to benefit learning, their design should take into account known principles from cognitive and motivation theories (Plass et al., 2015).

Multimedia. *Multimedia* refers to technology that combines the capabilities of various media such as computers, film, video, sound, music, and text (Roblyer, 2006). Multimedia learning occurs when students interact with information presented in more than one mode (e.g., words, pictures, video streaming).

The effectiveness of multimedia for learning depends on learners' WMs. As information is presented in multiple modalities, the phonological loop (verbal information), visuospatial sketch pad (visual and spatial information), episodic buffer (temporary storage of multimodal information), and central executive (monitoring and coordinating functions and interface with LTM) are engaged (Baddeley, 1998; Schüler, Scheiter, & van Genuchten, 2011; see Chapter 5). As WM only can handle so much information at once, instruction should optimize cognitive demands so that load is not excessive. Effective multimedia learning requires that students select the relevant information, integrate and organize it into a coherent representation in WM, and integrate this representation with existing LTM knowledge (Lee et al., 2006).

Multimedia learning has important implications for teaching because it offers many possibilities for infusing technology into instruction (Roblyer, 2006). Research evidence provides some support for the benefits of multimedia for learning (Moos, 2018). An analysis of early research showed that multimedia enhanced students' problem solving and transfer (Mayer, 1997); however, effects were strongest for students with little prior knowledge and high spatial ability. Dillon and Gabbard (1998) also concluded from their review that multimedia effects depended in part on ability: Students with lower general ability had the greatest difficulty. Multimedia may be especially advantageous on tasks requiring rapid searching through information.

Researchers have investigated the conditions favoring learning from multimedia. When verbal and visual information (e.g., narration and animation) is combined during instruction, students benefit from dual coding (Adesope & Nesbit, 2012; Mayer & Johnson, 2008). The simultaneous presentation helps learners form connections between words and pictures because they are in WM at the same time (Mayer, Moreno, Boire, & Vagge, 1999), although the dual modalities have the potential to create excessive cognitive load. Multimedia may facilitate learning better than tailoring media to individual student differences (Reed, 2006). By using different media, teachers increase the likelihood that at least one type will be effective for every student, but it is important that the media do not add interesting but irrelevant information (Mayer, Heiser, & Lonn, 2001).

Various instructional devices can assist multimedia learning. Among those shown by research are: forming mental images of information presented in text (Leopold & Mayer, 2015); observing an instructor draw diagrams while listening to an explanation (Fiorella & Mayer, 2016); having single elements of pictures named in an accompanying audio (Glaser & Schwan, 2015); providing text signals that emphasize the structure of the content and its relationship to other material (Mautone & Mayer, 2001); using personalized messages (i.e., informal, conversational) that address students and make them feel like participants in the lesson (Kartal, 2010; Mayer, Fennell, Farmer, & Campbell, 2004; Moreno & Mayer, 2000); generating self-explanations for the phenomena presented (Eysink et al., 2009); allowing learners to exercise control over the pace of instruction (Mayer & Chandler, 2001); including animations with movement and simulations (Mayer & Moreno, 2003); being able to interact with an on-screen speaker (Mayer, Dow, & Mayer, 2003); taking a practice test on the material (Johnson & Mayer, 2009); and being exposed to a human rather than a machine-generated speaker (Mayer, Sobko, & Mantone, 2003).

Maximal benefits of multimedia require that some logistical and administrative issues be addressed. Interactive capabilities are expensive to develop and produce, although they are very effective (Moreno & Mayer, 2007). Costs may prohibit many school systems from purchasing components. Interactive video may require additional instruction time because it presents more material and requires greater student time. But interactive multimodal learning environments provide great potential for increasing students' motivation (Scheiter & Gerjets, 2007). The greater amount of learner control that is possible yields better benefits on learning and can foster self-regulation (Azevedo, 2005b; Chapter 10).

Multimedia are an integral component of *flipped classrooms*, which reverse the typical classwork–homework model. In a flipped classroom, content is studied at home from multimedia (e.g., online videos that the instructor has posted); the next class session focuses on discussion and other activities based on the homework and that explores concepts at a deeper level. Although research on flipped classrooms is in its infancy, initial results suggest that these arrangements can promote better learning than traditional ones (Ng, 2015). To date, however, most research has been at the postsecondary level.

Despite potential issues involving costs and technological skills needed, the use of multimedia can benefit student learning, and research increasingly is showing that this technology can help to develop students' self-regulated learning (Azevedo, 2005a, 2005b; Azevedo & Cromley, 2004; Azevedo, Guthrie, & Siebert, 2004; Moos, 2018). Further research is needed on multimedia's effects on motivation and how to link it with a sequence of acquiring self-regulatory skills (e.g., social influence to self-influence; Zimmerman & Tsikalas, 2005; Chapter 10).

E-learning. *E-learning* refers to learning through electronically delivered means. The term often is used to refer to any type of electronic communication (e.g., videoconferencing, e-mail); however, here it is used in the narrower sense of online (Internet, web-based) instruction. E-learning is learning mediated through technology.

The Internet is a wonderful resource for information, but the relevant issue here is its role in learning. On the surface, the Internet has advantages. Web-based instruction provides students with access to more resources in less time than is possible in traditional ways; however, more resources do not automatically mean better learning. The latter is accomplished only if students acquire new skills, such as methods for conducting research on a topic or critical thinking about the accuracy of material. Building automated prompts into web-based instruction (e.g., "Now would be a good time to ask yourself if you have collected all the important information;" Kauffman, 2004, p. 149) increases students' meta-cognitive activity and leads to higher achievement (Kauffman, Ge, Xie, & Chen, 2008). Further, guiding learners' web-based searches results in higher self-efficacy, performance, and satisfaction than does allowing learners to self-guide their searches (Debowski, Wood, & Bandura, 2001), which can prove frustrating for some students. Useful are virtual peda-gogical agents (e.g., tutors with human-like bodies), which can focus students' learning and enhance their motivation for learning (Krämer & Bente, 2010). Web resources also can promote learning when students take information from the Web and incorporate it into classroom activities (e.g., discovery learning; Chapter 8).

Teachers can assist the development of students' Internet skills with scaffolding (Chapter 8). Students must be taught search strategies (e.g., ways to use browsers), but teachers also might conduct the initial web search and provide students with names of helpful websites. Having students take online notes and self-monitor their performances also help promotes student achievement (Kauffman, Zhao, & Yang, 2011). Applications involving technology in classroom instruction are given in Application 7.7.

A danger in students using the Internet is that the large array of information avail-able could increase cognitive load on WM, thereby hindering students' searches. Provid-ing instructional guidance helps to minimize extraneous load (Kalyuga, 2007). So much information also can inculcate the belief among learners that everything is important and reliable. Students then may engage in "associative writing" by trying to include too much information in reports and papers. To the extent that e-learning helps teach students the higher-level skills of analysis and synthesis, they will acquire strategies for determining what is important and merging information into a coherent product.

APPLICATION 7.7
Technology and Learning

Technological applications can be applied effectively to help improve student learning. Two high school classes worked together to develop a Civil War computer simulation. The classes flipped a coin to determine which class would be the Union and which the Confederacy. The students in each class then studied the battles of the Civil War and looked for information about the terrain, the weather at the time of each battle, the number of soldiers involved, and the leadership abilities of the individuals in charge. The students in both classes then simulated the battles on the computer, interacting with each other, using the data, trying to see if they might change the outcome of the original battle. When students made a strategic move, they had to defend and support their move with historical data.

A college professor uses streaming video on the Web to have her students study and reflect on educational psychology principles applied in classrooms. As students observe the video of an elementary class lesson, they stop the video and enter responses to relate educational practices to psychological principles they have been discussing in class. Then students are able to interact with other students and with her to share thoughts on the lesson observed. She also has a fictional classroom set up on a website. She poses questions to her students (e.g., "How might the teacher use authentic assessment in science?"), after which they go to the website, read and reflect, and construct a response that is distributed to her and all students. Thus, everyone can respond and interact with others.

Ms. Tarkinton uses technology for creative writing with her elementary students. She starts a story on the computer entitled, "The Adventures of Ms. Tarkinton's Class." Children have the opportunity to add to the story as often as they wish. At the end of the month, they print the story and read it aloud in class. The computer-based environment provides a unique means for constructing a story collaboratively.

Online Social Media

Online social media are Internet tools used to collaborate, communicate, and distribute information (the "social web"). The use of social media in education has increased dramatically in recent years (Kimmerle, Moskaliuk, Oeberst, & Cress, 2015; Ng, 2015). Four categories of online social media that have relevance to education are communication, collaboration, multimedia, and virtual world (Seo et al., 2012).

The primary purpose of communication tools (e.g., Facebook, LinkedIn) is to facilitate interactions among users. Instructional examples include instructors posting class notes, students completing group homework, and students posting and reviewing online reflections (Seo et al., 2012). The collaboration category includes wikis, blogs, and social bookmarking. A wiki is a platform for group work; students can collaborate on a project and compose and edit it. Wikis are popular tools for writing tasks (Kimmerle et al., 2015). Blogs include running dialogue between instructors and students on issues or questions. With social bookmarking, students bookmark selected web pages to create a collection of related pages, or resource for a specific topic area (Seo et al., 2012). Multimedia tools (e.g., YouTube, Skype) provide materials for students to study before and after classes, tutorials and educational videos, and interactive group projects (Seo et al., 2012). Virtual world media (e.g., Second Life) provide a platform for synchronous learning. Instructors and students can interact with one another without being physically present, and instructors can meet with students during virtual office hours (Seo et al., 2012).

These and other online social media have revolutionized the way that people interact with one another. The primary interest here is how use of social media might affect learning. Online social media tools have several features that are positively associated with learning. They greatly facilitate the dissemination of information. By presenting knowledge in multiple modes (e.g., in verbal and visual forms), they allow encoding of knowledge in dual formats, which can enhance development of memory networks and subsequent retrieval from LTM (Chapters 5 and 6). By allowing multiple users simultaneously, online social media can promote collaboration, which is emphasized by social cognitive and constructivist theories (see Chapters 4 and 8). Collaboration is essential for peer-assisted learning (Chapter 8). Further, students perceive online social media positively, which implies that they are motivated to use them (Chapter 9).

Research on online social media is in its infancy, and most applications of social media in education have not explored the full potential of these media for learning (Kimmerle et al., 2015). At this time, therefore, it is difficult to validly assess their effects on learning. Kirshner and Karpinski (2010) found that college students who had Facebook accounts had lower grade point averages and spent fewer hours studying than students who did not have accounts. However, additional research is needed because Facebook primarily is used by students as a social medium rather than for course learning. Research evidence shows that online social media use promotes student participation and collaboration (Carrington, 2009; Kimmerle et al., 2015), which are important for group learning such as occurs in problem-based learning. As social media become better established in educational programs, researchers should be able to reliably evaluate their effects on student learning.

Today's students use online social media frequently. They tend to be comfortable using these tools and learn new technological applications easily. On this count, therefore, teachers would be wise to tap into this student resource. We must keep in mind that online social media, like other forms of technology, should not be the center of learning but rather complement instructional objectives (Seo et al., 2012). If course objectives suggest that an online social media tool can create an excellent learning environment for students, then teachers have an opportunity to try this application. If nothing else, the introduction of some variety into teaching may prove motivating for students (Chapter 9).

Distance Learning

Distance learning (distance education) occurs when instruction that originates in one location is transmitted to students at one or more remote sites. It is a type of independent study. Interactive capabilities allow two-way feedback and discussions to become part of the online learning experience. Distance learning saves time, effort, and money because instructors and students do not have to make long journeys to classes. Universities, for example, can recruit students from a wide geographical area. There is less concern about the students traveling great distances to attend classes. School districts can conduct in-service programs by transmitting from a central site to all of the schools. Distance learning sacrifices face-to-face contact with instructors, although if two-way interactive video is used, the interactions are real-time (synchronous). In their review of distance education programs, Bernard et al. (2004) found their effects on student learning and retention comparable to those of traditional instruction. Effects for synchronous instruction favored classroom instruction, whereas distance education was more effective for asynchronous applications (involving lag time).

Another networking application is the *electronic bulletin board (conference)*. People networked with computers can post messages, but taking part in a discussion (chat) group can be more important for learning. Participants ask questions and raise issues, as well as respond to the comments of others. A fair amount of research has examined whether such exchanges facilitate writing skill acquisition (Fabos & Young, 1999). Whether this asynchronous means of telecommunication exchange promotes learning any better than face-to-face interaction is problematic because much of the early research is conflicting or inconclusive (Fabos & Young, 1999); however, the review by Bernard et al. (2004) suggests that distance education may be more effective with asynchronous learning. Telecommunication has the benefit of convenience in that people can respond at any time, not just when they are gathered together. The receptive learning environment may indirectly promote learning.

Being forms of *computer-mediated communication (CMC)*, distance learning and computer conferencing greatly expand the possibilities for learning through social interaction. Further research is needed to determine whether personal characteristics of learners and types of instructional content can affect students' learning and motivation.

Web-based (online) learning is commonly incorporated into traditional instruction as a *blended model* of instruction (i.e., some face-to-face instruction and the rest online). Web-based learning also is useful in conjunction with multimedia projects. In many teacher preparation programs, pre-service teachers use the Web to obtain resources and then selectively incorporate these into multimedia projects as part of lesson designs.

In their review of online courses, Tallent-Runnels et al. (2006) found that students liked moving at their own pace, students with more computer experience expressed greater satisfaction, and asynchronous communication facilitated in-depth discussions. Distance education that incorporates interactions (student–student, student–teacher, student–content) helps to increase student achievement (Bernard et al., 2009). Other types of interactions (e.g., wikis, blogs) also may be useful. Infusing multimedia presentations into distance education increases its personalization and thus makes it more akin to face-to-face instruction (Larreamendy-Joerns & Leinhardt, 2006), which may increase student motivation.

Attempting to compare online with traditional courses is difficult because there are so many differences, one of which is that online courses have tended to enroll more non-traditional and White American students. This demographic is changing as online courses become more prevalent, which will permit better assessment of online learning outcomes and environmental characteristics that facilitate learning.

INSTRUCTIONAL APPLICATIONS

Several instructional applications have been given in this chapter for the principles covered. This section describes three additional applications that reflect many of the principles discussed: worked examples, problem solving, and mathematics.

Worked Examples

Worked examples (see Chapter 4) present step-by-step problem solutions and often include accompanying diagrams. They portray an expert's problem-solving model for learners to study before they begin to emulate it. Researchers have shown that studying worked examples promotes learning better than does simply solving problems (Atkinson et al., 2000; Wittwer & Renkl, 2010).

Worked examples reflect Anderson's ACT-R theory (Lee & Anderson, 2001) and are especially appropriate for complex forms of learning, such as algebra, physics, and geometry (Atkinson et al., 2000; Atkinson, Renkl, & Merrill, 2003). Applying the novice–expert model, researchers have found that experts typically focus on deeper (structural) aspects of problems, whereas novices more often deal with surface features. Worked examples seem most beneficial with students in the early stages of skill acquisition; as learners become more proficient solving problems enhances skills better (Salden et al., 2010).

The applicability of worked examples is seen in the four-stage model of skill acquisition within the ACT-R framework (Anderson, Fincham, & Douglass, 1997; Chapter 5). In stage 1, learners use analogies to relate examples to problems to be solved. In stage 2, they develop abstract declarative rules through practice. During stage 3, performance becomes quicker and smoother as aspects of problem solution become automatized. By stage 4, learners have in memory many types of problems and can retrieve the appropriate solution strategy quickly when confronted with a problem. Use of worked examples is best suited for stage 1 and early stage 2 learners. During later stages, people benefit from practice to hone their strategies, although even at advanced stages, studying solutions of experts can be helpful.

A key instructional issue is how to integrate the components of an example, such as diagram, text, and aural information. It is imperative that a worked example not overload the learner's WM (create excessive cognitive load), which multiple sources of information presented simultaneously can do. Stull and Mayer (2007) found that providing graphic organizers (similar to worked examples) produced better problem-solving transfer than did allowing learners to construct their own, which may have produced high cognitive load (Chapter 5). Other evidence shows that worked examples can reduce cognitive load (Renkl, Hilbert, & Schworm, 2009).

Research supports the prediction that dual presentation (e.g., verbal and visual) facilitates learning better than single-mode presentation (Atkinson et al., 2000; Mayer, 1997). This result is consistent with dual-coding theory (Paivio, 1986; Chapter 6), with the caveat that too much complexity is not desirable. Similarly, examples intermixed with subgoals help create deep structures and facilitate learning.

Examples that include multiple presentation modes should be unified so that learners' attention is not split across nonintegrated sources. Aural and verbal explanations should indicate to which aspect of the example they refer, so learners do not have to search on their own. Subgoals should be clearly labeled and visually isolated in the overall display.

A second instructional issue concerns how examples should be sequenced. Research supports the conclusions that two examples are superior to a single one, that varied examples are better than two of the same type, and that intermixing different examples with practice (*interleaved practice*) is more effective than a lesson that presents examples followed by practice problems (Atkinson et al., 2000; Rohrer, Dedrick, & Stershic, 2015). Gradually fading out worked examples in an instructional sequence is associated with better student transfer of learning (Atkinson et al., 2003).

Chi, Bassok, Lewis, Reimann, and Glaser (1989) found that students who provided *self-explanations* while studying examples subsequently achieved at higher levels compared with students who did not self-explain. Presumably the self-explanations helped students understand the deep structure of the problems and thereby encode it more meaningfully. Self-explanation also is a type of rehearsal, and the benefit of rehearsal on learning is well established. Thus, students should be encouraged to self-explain while studying worked examples, such as by verbalizing subgoals.

Another issue is that worked examples can produce passive learning since learners may process them superficially. Including interactive elements, such as by providing prompts or leaving gaps that learners must complete, leads to more active cognitive processing and learning (Atkinson & Renkl, 2007). Animations also are helpful (Wouters, Paas, & van Merriënboer, 2008).

In summary, there are several features that when incorporated with worked examples help learners create cognitive schemas to facilitate subsequent achievement (Table 7.5). These instructional strategies are best employed during the early stages of skill learning. Through practice, the initial cognitive representations should evolve into the refined schemas that experts employ.

Problem Solving

The links between learning and problem solving suggest that students can learn heuristics and strategies and become better problem solvers (Bruning et al., 2011). In addition, for

Table 7.5
Using worked examples in instruction.

- Present examples in close proximity to problems students will solve.
- Present multiple examples showing different types of problems.
- Present information in different modalities (aural, visual).
- Indicate subgoals in examples.
- Ensure that examples present all information needed to solve problems.
- Teach students to self-explain examples, and encourage self-explanations.
- Allow sufficient practice on problem types so students refine skills.

information to be linked in memory, it is best to integrate problem solving with academic content (as Meg recommended in the opening vignette) rather than to teach problem solving with stand-alone programs. Nokes, Dole, and Hacker (2007) showed that heuristics instruction can be infused into classroom teaching without sacrificing students' content learning.

Andre (1986) listed several suggestions that are derived from theory and research and that are useful for training students in problem-solving skills.

- *Provide students with metaphorical representations.* A concrete analogical passage given to students prior to an instructional passage facilitates learning from the target passage.
- *Have students verbalize during problem solving.* Verbalization of thoughts during problem solving can facilitate problem solutions and learning.
- *Use questions.* Ask students questions that require them to practice concepts they have learned; many such questions may be necessary.
- *Provide examples.* Give students worked examples showing application of problem-solving strategies. Students may have difficulty seeing on their own how strategies apply to situations.
- *Coordinate ideas.* Show how productions and knowledge relate to one another and in what sequence they might need to be applied.
- *Use discovery learning.* Discovery learning often facilitates transfer and problem solving better than expository teaching. Discovery may force students to generate rules from examples. The same can be accomplished through expository teaching, but discovery may lend itself better to certain content (e.g., science experiments).
- *Give a verbal description.* Providing students with a verbal description of the strategy and its rules for application can be helpful.
- *Teach learning strategies.* Learners may need assistance in using effective learning strategies. As discussed in Chapter 10, strategies help learning and problem solving (Montague, Krawec, Enders, & Dietz, 2014).
- *Use small groups.* A number of studies have found that small-group learning helps develop students' problem-solving skills. Group members must be held accountable for their learning, and all students must share in the work.
- *Maintain a positive psychological climate.* Psychological factors are important to effective problem solving. Minimize excessive anxiety among students and help to create a sense of self-efficacy among students for improving their skills (Chapter 4).

Another instructional suggestion is to phase in problem solving, which may be especially helpful with students who have little experience with it. This can be done by using worked examples (Atkinson et al., 2003; Renkl & Atkinson, 2003; discussed in this section). Mathematics texts, for example, often state a rule or theorem, followed by one or more worked examples. Students then solve comparable problems by applying the steps from the worked examples (a type of analogical reasoning). Renkl and Atkinson (2003) recommend reliance on examples in the early stages of learning, followed by a transition to problem solving as students develop skills. This process also helps to minimize demands on WM's cognitive load (Chapter 5). Thus, the transition might proceed as follows. Initially a complete example is given, then an example where one step is omitted. With each succeeding example an additional step is omitted until the learners reach independent problem solving.

Problem-based learning (PBL; Hmelo-Silver, 2004), or case-based learning, offers another instructional application. In this approach, students work in groups on a problem that does not have one correct answer. Students identify what they need to know to solve the problem. Teachers act as facilitators by providing assistance but not answers. PBL has been shown to be effective in teaching problem-solving and self-regulation skills, although much research has been conducted in medical and gifted education (Evenson, Salisbury-Glennon, & Glenn, 2001; Hmelo-Silver, 2004). PBL is useful for the exploration of meaningful problems. Because it is time consuming, teachers need to consider its appropriateness given the instructional goals.

Mathematics

Mathematics has been a fertile area of cognitive and constructivist research (Ball, Lubienski, & Mewborn, 2001; Carr, 2012; National Research Council, 2000; Newcombe et al., 2009; Schoenfeld, 2006). This content area also lends itself well to many of the topics covered in this chapter including problem solving, metacognition, and reasoning. Researchers have explored how learners construct knowledge, how experts and novices differ, the role of motivation, and which methods of instruction are most effective (Schoenfeld, 2006). Growth in mathematics achievement depends on not only cognitive but also motivational variables such as perceived control, self-efficacy, and intrinsic motivation (Murayama, Pekrun, Lichtenfeld, & vom Hofe, 2013; Schunk & Richardson, 2011).

A distinction typically is made between mathematical *computation* (use of rules, procedures, and algorithms) and *concepts* (problem solving and use of strategies). Computational and conceptual problems require students to implement procedures involving rules and algorithms. The difference between these two categories lies in how explicitly the problem tells students which operations to perform. The following are computational problems.

- $26 + 42 = ?$
- $5x + 3y = 19$
  $7x - y = 11$

Solve for x and y.

- What is the length of the hypotenuse of a right triangle with sides equal to 3 and 4 inches?

Although students are not explicitly told what to do in problems 2 and 3, recognition of the problem format and knowledge of procedures lead them to perform the correct operations.

Now contrast those problems with the following:

- Alex has 20 coins composed of dimes and quarters. If the quarters were dimes and the dimes were quarters, he would have 90 cents more than he has now. How much money does Alex have?

- If a passenger train takes twice as long to pass a freight train after it first overtakes the freight train as it takes the two trains to pass when going in opposite directions, how many times faster than the freight train is the passenger train?
- When she hikes, Shana can average 2 mph going uphill and 6 mph going downhill. If she goes uphill and downhill and spends no time at the summit, what will be her average speed for an entire trip?

These word problems do not explicitly tell students what to do, but they require computations no more difficult than those needed in the first set. Solving word problems involves recognizing their problem formats, generating appropriate productions, and performing the computations.

This is not to suggest that conceptual expertise is better than computational proficiency, because deficiencies in either area cause problems. Understanding how to solve a problem but not being able to perform the computations results in incorrect answers, as does being computationally proficient but not being able to conceptualize problems.

Computational Problems. The earliest computational skill children use is *counting* (Resnick, 1985). Children count objects on their fingers and in their heads using a strategy. The *sum model* involves setting a hypothetical counter at zero, counting in the first addend in increments of one, and then counting in the second addend to arrive at the answer. For the problem "2 + 4 = ?" children might count from 0 to 2 and then count out 4 more. A more efficient strategy is to set the counter at the first addend (2) and then count in the second addend (4) in increments of one. Still more efficient is the *min model*: Set the counter at the larger of the two addends (4) and then count in the smaller addend (2) in increments of one (Romberg & Carpenter, 1986).

These types of invented procedures are successful. Children and adults often construct procedures to solve mathematical problems. Errors generally are not random but rather reflect *buggy algorithms*, or systematic mistakes in thinking and reasoning (Brown & Burton, 1978). Buggy algorithms reflect the constructivist assumption that students develop procedures based on their interpretation of experiences (Chapter 8). A common mistake in subtraction is to subtract the smaller number from the larger number in each column, regardless of direction, as follows:

$$
\begin{array}{cc}
53 & 602 \\
-27 & -274 \\
\hline
34 & 472
\end{array}
$$

Mathematical bugs may develop when students encounter new problems and incorrectly generalize procedures. In subtraction without regrouping, for example, students subtract the smaller number from the larger one column by column. It is easy to see how they could generalize this procedure to problems requiring regrouping. Buggy algorithms are durable and can instill in students a false sense of self-efficacy (Chapter 4), perhaps because their computations produce answers.

Another source of computational difficulties is poor declarative knowledge of number facts. Many children do not know basic facts, have difficulty retrieving facts, and show deficiencies in numerical processing (Geary, 2011; Geary, Hoard, Byrd-Craven, Nugent,

& Numtee, 2007). Until facts become established in LTM through practice, children count or compute answers. Speed of fact retrieval from memory relates directly to overall mathematical achievement in students from elementary school through college (Royer, Tronsky, Chan, Jackson, & Marchant, 1999). Computational skill improves with development, along with WM and LTM capabilities (Mabbott & Bisanz, 2003). Effective functioning of the central executive of WM (see Chapter 5) predicts mathematical achievement (Geary, 2011). Computational problem solving also improves when students use written rather than mental calculations, especially on complex problems (Hickendorff, van Putten, Verhelst, & Heiser, 2010).

Many difficulties in computation result from using overly complex but technically correct productions to solve problems. Such procedures produce correct answers, but because they are complex, the risk of computational errors is high. The problem 256 divided by 5 can be solved by successively subtracting 5 from 256 and counting the number of subtractions. This procedure, while technically correct, is inefficient and has a high probability of error.

Learners initially represent computational skill as declarative knowledge in a network. Facts concerning the different steps (e.g., in the algorithm) are committed to memory through mental rehearsal and overt practice. The procedure that guides performance at this stage is general; for example: "If the goal is to solve this division problem, then apply the method the teacher taught us." With added practice, the declarative representation changes into a domain-specific procedural representation and eventually becomes automated. Early counting strategies are replaced with more-efficient rule-based strategies (Hopkins & Lawson, 2002). At the automatic stage, learners quickly recognize the problem pattern (e.g., division problem, square root problem) and implement the procedure without much conscious deliberation.

Conceptual Problem Solving. Conceptual problem solving requires students to accurately represent the problem including the given information and the goal and then select and apply a strategy (Mayer, 1985, 1999). Translating a problem from its linguistic representation to a mental representation is often difficult (Bruning et al., 2011). The more abstract the language, the more difficult the text comprehension and the lower the likelihood of solution (Cummins, Kintsch, Reusser, & Weimer, 1988). Students who have difficulty comprehending show poorer recall of information and lower performance. Younger children often have difficulty translating abstract linguistic representations.

Translation also requires good declarative and procedural knowledge. Solving the earlier problem about Alex with 20 coins requires knowledge that dimes and quarters are coins, that a dime is one tenth ($0.10) of $1, and that a quarter is one fourth ($0.25) of $1. This declarative knowledge needs to be coupled with procedural understanding that dimes and quarters are variables such that the number of dimes plus the number of quarters equals 20.

One reason experts translate problems better is that their knowledge is better organized in LTM; the organization reflects the underlying structure of the subject matter (Romberg & Carpenter, 1986). Experts overlook surface features of a problem and analyze it in terms of the operations required for solution. Novices are swayed more by surface features. Silver (1981) found that good problem solvers organized problems according to the process required for solution, whereas poor problem solvers were more likely to group problems with similar content (e.g., money, trains).

Novices often adopt a working-backward strategy, beginning with the goal and working their way back to the givens. This is a good heuristic useful in the early stages of learning when learners have acquired some domain knowledge but are not competent enough to recognize problem formats quickly, but experts often work forward. They identify the problem type and select the appropriate procedure to solve the problem. Hegarty, Mayer, and Monk (1995) found that successful problem solvers translated the problem into a mental model in which the numbers in the problem statement were tied to their variable names. In contrast, less successful solvers were more likely to combine the numbers in the problem with the arithmetic operations primed by the key words (e.g., addition is the operation linked with the key word "more"). The latter strategy is based on surface features, whereas the former strategy is linked better with meanings.

Experts develop sophisticated procedural knowledge for classifying mathematical problems according to type. High school algebra problems fall into roughly 20 general categories, such as motion, current, coins, and interest/investment (Mayer, 1992). These categories can be aggregated into six major groups. For example, the amount-per-time group includes motion, current, and work problems. These problems are solvable with the general formula: amount = rate $\times$ time. The development of mathematical problem-solving expertise depends on classifying a problem into the correct group and then applying the strategy.

Verbalizing steps in problem solving aids the development of proficiency (Gersten et al., 2009). Fyfe, Rittle-Johnson, and DeCaro (2012) found that providing feedback on strategies and outcomes to learners as they engaged in exploratory problem solving prior to instruction promoted achievement but only for students who had low knowledge of domain-specific strategies. The feedback may have helped them identify errors and look for alternative strategies to use. Application 7.8 discusses teaching problem solving.

APPLICATION 7.8
Mathematical Problem Solving

Teachers use various ways to help students improve their skills on conceptual problems. As students solve mathematical word problems, they can state each problem in their own words, draw a sketch, decide what information is relevant, and state the ways they might solve the problem. A middle school teacher could use these and other similar questions to help focus her students' attention on important task aspects and guide their thinking:

- What information is important?
- What information is missing?
- Which formulas are necessary?
- What is the first thing to do?

SUMMARY AND CRITIQUE

Chapter Summary

Complex cognitive processes are involved in much human learning. Developing competence in an academic domain requires knowledge of the facts, principles, and concepts of that domain, coupled with general strategies that can be applied across domains and specific strategies that pertain to each domain. Research has identified many differences between expert and novice performers in a given domain.

Metacognition is the deliberate, conscious control of mental activities. Metacognition includes knowledge and monitoring activities designed to ensure that tasks are completed successfully. Conditional knowledge, or knowing when and why to employ declarative and procedural knowledge, is part of metacognitive activity. Metacognition begins to develop around ages 5 to 7 and continues throughout schooling. One's metacognitive awareness depends on task, strategy, and learner variables. Learners benefit from instruction on metacognitive activities.

Concept learning involves higher-order processes of forming mental representations of critical attributes of categories. Current theories emphasize analyzing features and forming hypotheses about concepts (feature analysis), as well as forming generalized images of concepts that include only some defining features (prototypes). Prototypes may be used to classify typical instances of concepts, and feature analysis may be used for less typical ones. Models of concept acquisition and teaching have been proposed, and motivational processes also are involved in conceptual change.

Problem solving consists of an initial state, a goal, subgoals, and operations performed to attain the goal and subgoals. Researchers have investigated the mental processes of learners as they solve problems and the differences between expert and novice solvers. Problem solving may occur through trial and error, insight, and using heuristics. These general approaches can be applied to academic content. From an information processing perspective, problem solving requires forming a mental representation of the problem and applying sets of rules (production systems) to solve it. With well-defined problems where potential solutions can be ordered in likelihood, a generate-and-test strategy is useful. For difficult or less well-defined problems, means–ends analysis (working backward or forward) or analogical reasoning may be used.

Critical thinking, reasoning, and creativity are related but distinct cognitive processes. Critical thinking is used to develop better understanding of problems or issues. Reasoning involves generating and evaluating logical arguments. It requires that learners work through problems to determine why something happened or what might happen. Creativity yields products or outcomes that are novel and valued by the larger community. Brainstorming—especially in groups—may help foster creative thinking.

Technology continues to increase in importance in learning and instruction. Three areas that have seen rapid growth are computer-based learning environments, online social media, and distance learning. Applications involving computer-based environments include computer-based instruction, simulations, games, multimedia, and e-learning. Online social media facilitate communication and collaboration among learners and have other benefits that may enhance student learning. Distance learning may involve two-way feedback and synchronous discussions, or online (web-based) asynchronous instruction. Many courses utilize a blended model with some face-to-face and some online instruction. Research shows benefits of using technology on metacognition, deep processing, and problem solving.

Some applications of the topics in this chapter involve worked examples, problem solving, and mathematics. Worked examples present problem solutions in step-by-step fashion and often include accompanying diagrams. Worked examples incorporate many features that facilitate learners' problem solving. Problem-solving instruction is more effective when it is clearly linked with academic content. Other suggestions include giving learners worked examples, providing verbal descriptions, and using small group learning. Children display early mathematical competence with counting. Computational skills require algorithms and declarative knowledge. Students often overgeneralize procedures (buggy algorithms). With conceptual problems, students acquire knowledge of problem types through experience and apply increasingly more-effective strategies.

Chapter Critique

The topics covered in this chapter have the common element of requiring complex cognitive processing. Historically there has been less research conducted on these topics than on other information processing topics such as attention, WM, encoding, and retrieval. Consequently, we know less about how complex cognitive processing occurs, which means there are fewer implications from the research findings for educational practices.

Another educational issue is that, although this chapter's topics are viewed by educators as important, they tend to receive less attention than learning basic skills and topics on required courses of study. An emphasis on accountability means that topics such as problem solving and creativity often receive little educational attention. Further, when such topics are covered, they may be done in special programs (e.g., creativity programs) rather than as part of the regular curriculum (e.g., covering creativity during social studies learning). As such, students may not understand how to apply critical thinking, problem solving, creativity, and so forth, in the context of their regular content classes.

Further research attention also is needed on the role that motivation plays as students solve problems, think critically and creatively, engage in reasoning, and the like. There has been some motivational research addressing this issue (e.g., role of motivation in conceptual change), but clearly much more is needed. Teachers attempting to inculcate these skills in their students also likely need to address motivational variables covered in Chapter 9 such as goals, self-efficacy, interest, and values.

The use of educational technology continues to expand at a rapid rate, and there is good evidence that use of technology can improve student learning. Students are comfortable using technology and learn applications quickly. Its potential to improve collaboration and the processes described in this chapter (e.g., problem solving, critical thinking) is underexplored, but we should expect continued research emphasis in the future with direct implications for teaching and learning.

REFLECTION QUESTIONS

■ Metacognition is an important type of cognitive processing that research shows promotes learning. Yet many students seem to engage in little metacognition, either because they are unaware of various metacognitive strategies or for other reasons (e.g., motivational). How might teachers attempt to help their students become more metacognitively active while engaged in learning?

■ Educators extol the value of such student processes as problem solving, critical thinking, creativity, and reasoning; however, educational curricula and student activities often emphasize lower-level outcomes such as acquisition of facts and procedures. What are some ways that teachers can infuse problem solving, critical thinking, creativity, and reasoning into lessons and instructional activities?

■ Technology offers many opportunities to facilitate student learning. Even young children can use technology effectively and often are familiar with some forms of technology when they begin schooling. In particular, technology may be especially effective in developing social collaboration among students, including those at a distance. How might technology be used to foster collaboration and learning at different student developmental levels (elementary, middle school, high school)?

FURTHER READING

Byrnes, J. P., & Dunbar, K. N. (2014). The nature and development of critical-analytic thinking. *Educational Psychology Review, 26*, 477–493.

Clark, D. B., Tanner-Smith, E. E., & Killingsworth, S. S. (2016). Digital games, design, and learning: A systematic review and meta-analysis. *Review of Educational Research, 86*, 79–122.

Hennessey, B. A., & Amabile, T. M. (2010). Creativity. *Annual Review of Psychology, 61*, 569–598.

Isaksen, S. G., & Gaulin, J. P. (2005). A reexamination of brainstorming research: Implications for research and practice. *Gifted Child Quarterly, 49*, 315–329.

Kulik, J. A., & Fletcher, J. D. (2016). Effectiveness of intelligent tutoring systems: A meta-analytic review. *Review of Educational Research, 86*, 42–78.

Lajoie, S. P. (2003). Transitions and trajectories for studies of expertise. *Educational Researcher, 32*(8), 21–25.

Seo, K. K., Pellegrino, D. A., & Engelhard, C. (Eds.) (2012). *Designing problem-driven instruction with online social media*. Charlotte, NC: Information Age Publishing.

8 Constructivism

Ms. Rahn, a sixth-grade middle school science teacher, is sitting at a table with four students. They are about to perform an experiment on the physical properties of matter called the "mystery substance experiment." On the table are the following materials: mixing bowl, 16 ounces of cornstarch, measuring cup, bottles of water, spoon, scissors, plate, and paper towels.

Ms. Rahn:	Okay, we're ready to begin. Jenna, empty the box of cornstarch into the bowl. Can you tell me, what do you notice about the cornstarch? What does it look like?
Trevor:	It's soft and powdery.
Ali:	It's whiteish.
Ms. Rahn:	Touch it with your fingers. What does it feel like? Does it have an odor?
Matt:	It's soft, sort of flaky like. No odor.
Ms. Rahn:	Yes, all of those things. Okay, now, Trevor, fill the measuring cup with one cup of water, and slowly pour it into the bowl. Put your hand inside the bowl and mix it up. What does it feel like?
Trevor:	Clumpy, wet, gooey.
Ms. Rahn:	What does it look like?
Ali:	Like a paste or something like that.
Ms. Rahn:	Yes, it does. Now reach down into the bowl, and grab a bunch of it. Let it rest in your hand. What happens to it?
Matt:	It's dripping down.
Ms. Rahn:	Pick up a handful and squeeze it. What does it feel like?
Jenna:	It gets hard, but it's still gooey.
Ms. Rahn:	What happens to the liquid oozing out?
Ali:	It's dripping down through my fingers.
Ms. Rahn:	Grab another handful and give it a squeeze. Let it rest in your hand. As some falls between your fingers, have your partner try cutting it with a scissors. Can you cut it?
Trevor:	Yes! That's so weird!

Ms. Rahn:	Take a spoonful and drop it onto the plate. Touch it. What does it feel like?
Ali:	Hard! Like Silly Putty.
Ms. Rahn:	Tip the plate sideways. What happens?
Jenna:	It's dripping like water. But it doesn't feel wet!
Ms. Rahn:	Poke it with your finger. What happens?
Matt:	It goes in, but it doesn't stick to my finger.
Ms. Rahn:	Now go back to the bowl. Push your fingers slowly through until you touch the bottom of the bowl. What do you notice?
Jenna:	It gets thicker as you go deeper. It feels hard.
Ms. Rahn:	So what is this substance? Is it a solid or a liquid?
Ali:	It's a solid. It's hard.
Matt:	No, it's a liquid because when you lift it, it drips, and gooey stuff comes out.
Ms. Rahn:	Could it be both, a liquid and a solid?
Trevor:	I think it is.

Constructivism is a psychological and philosophical perspective contending that individuals form or construct much of what they learn and understand (O'Donnell, 2012). It reflects a rationalist approach to the study of learning (see Chapter 1). A major influence on constructivism is theory and research in human development, especially the theories of Piaget and Vygotsky (discussed in this chapter). The emphasis that these theories place on the role of knowledge construction is central to constructivism.

Over the past several years, constructivism increasingly has been applied to learning and teaching. The history of learning theory reveals a shift away from environmental influences and toward human factors as explanations for learning. Cognitive theorists and researchers (Chapters 4–7) disputed the claim of behaviorism (Chapter 3) that stimuli, responses, and consequences were adequate to explain learning. Cognitive theories place great emphasis on learners' information processing as a central cause of learning. Despite the elegance of cognitive learning theories, some researchers believe that these theories fail to capture the complexity of human learning. This point is underscored by the fact that some cognitive perspectives use behavioral terminology such as the "automaticity" of performance and "forming connections" between items in memory.

Many contemporary learning researchers have shifted toward a stronger focus on learners. Rather than talk about how knowledge is acquired, they speak of how it is constructed. Although these researchers differ in their emphasis on factors that affect learning and learners' cognitive processes, the theoretical perspectives they espouse may be loosely grouped and referred to as constructivism. Learners' constructions of understandings are evident in the opening vignette.

Just as there is no one information processing theory, there is no one constructivist theory. Constructivist perspectives differ in how they view the process of construction. Some constructivist theories focus heavily on cognitive processes, detailing how the construction process operates within individual learners.

These views, which are exemplified by the theories of Piaget, Bruner, and the neo-Piagetians, are *cognitive constructivist* (or *individual constructivist*) perspectives. Other researchers are more concerned with how learners working together construct knowledge and with the role of sociocultural variables. *Social constructivist* theories include those that emphasize groups and sociocultural factors. The social constructivist perspective is exemplified in this chapter with Vygotsky's theory and with theoretical principles involving other topics in this chapter such as situated cognition and socially mediated learning.

This chapter begins by providing an overview of constructivism to include a description of its key assumptions and the different types of constructivist theories. The next section covers cognitive constructivism to include the theories of Piaget, the Neo-Piagetians, and Bruner. The sociocultural theory of Vygotsky is discussed to include its central points relevant to learning. The critical roles of private speech and socially mediated learning are explained. The chapter concludes with a discussion of constructivist learning environments and instructional applications that reflect principles of constructivism.

When you finish studying this chapter, you should be able to do the following:

- Discuss the major assumptions and various types of constructivism.

- Summarize the major processes in Piaget's theory that are involved in learning and some implications for instruction.

- Describe key differences between Piagetian and Neo-Piagetian theories.

- Discuss the types of knowledge representation proposed by Bruner and what is meant by the "spiral curriculum."

- Explain the key principles of Vygotsky's sociocultural theory and implications for teaching in the zone of proximal development.

- List how private speech can affect learning and the benefits of socially mediated learning.

- List the key features of constructivist learning environments, the major components of the APA learner-centered principles, and how teachers can become more reflective and thereby enhance student learning.

- Describe how discovery learning, inquiry teaching, and discussions and debates can be structured to reflect constructivist principles.

ASSUMPTIONS AND PERSPECTIVES

An important influence on the development of constructivism was the questioning by many researchers and practitioners of some of classic information processing theory's assumptions about learning and instruction. These individuals believed that these assumptions did not completely explain students' learning and understanding. According to Greeno (1989), some questionable assumptions were:

- Thinking resides in the mind rather than in interaction with persons and situations.
- Learning and thinking processes are relatively uniform across persons, and some situations foster higher-order thinking better than others.

■ Thinking derives from knowledge and skills developed in formal instructional settings more than on general conceptual competencies that result from one's experiences and innate abilities.

Early constructivists did not accept these assumptions because of evidence that thinking takes place in contexts and that cognitions are largely constructed by individuals as a function of their experiences in these contexts (Bredo, 1997). Constructivist accounts of learning and development highlight the contributions of individuals to what is learned. Social constructivist models further emphasize the importance of social interactions in acquisition of skills and knowledge. The next section further examines what constructivism is, its assumptions, and its forms.

Overview

What Is Constructivism? There is no single definition of constructivism (Harlow, Cummings, & Aberasturi, 2006). Strictly speaking, constructivism is not a theory but rather an *epistemology*, or philosophical explanation about the nature of knowing and learning (Hyslop-Margison & Strobel, 2008; Simpson, 2002). A theory is a scientifically valid explanation for learning (Chapter 1). Theories allow for hypotheses to be generated and tested. Constructivism does not propound that learning principles exist and are to be discovered and tested, but rather that learners create their own learning. Readers who are interested in exploring the historical and philosophical roots of constructivism are referred to Bredo (1997) and Packer and Goicoechea (2000).

Nonetheless, constructivism makes general predictions that can be tested. Although these predictions are general and open to different interpretations (e.g., what does it mean that learners construct their own learning?), they can be the focus of research.

Constructivist theorists reject the notion that scientific truths exist and await discovery and verification. They argue that no statement can be assumed to be true but rather should be viewed with reasonable doubt. The world can be mentally constructed in many different ways, so no theory has a lock on the truth. This is true even for constructivism: There are many varieties, and no one version should be assumed as more correct than any other (Simpson, 2002).

Rather than viewing knowledge as truth, constructivists construe it as a working hypothesis. Knowledge is not imposed from outside people but rather formed inside them. A person's constructions are true to that person but not necessarily to anyone else. This is because people construct knowledge based on their beliefs and experiences in situations (Cobb & Bowers, 1999), which differ from person to person. All knowledge, then, is subjective, personal, and a product of our cognitions (Simpson, 2002). Learning is situated in contexts (Bredo, 2006).

Assumptions. Constructivism highlights the interaction of persons and situations in the acquisition and refinement of skills and knowledge (Bredo, 2016; Cobb & Bowers, 1999). Constructivism contrasts with conditioning theories that stress the influence of the environment on the person, as well as with information processing theories that place the locus of learning within the mind with less attention to the context in which it occurs.

Constructivism shares with social cognitive theory the assumption that persons, behaviors, and environments interact in reciprocal fashion (Bandura, 1986, 1997).

A key assumption of constructivism is that people are active learners and develop knowledge for themselves (Simpson, 2002). To understand material well, learners must discover the basic principles, as the students in the opening vignette were striving to do. Constructivists differ in the extent to which they ascribe this function entirely to learners. Some believe that mental structures come to reflect reality, others believe that the individual's mental world is the only reality, and still others lie somewhere in between (Bredo, 2016). Constructivists also differ in how much they ascribe the construction of knowledge to social interactions with teachers, peers, parents, coaches, and the like (Bredo, 1997).

Many of the principles, concepts, and ideas discussed in this text reflect the idea of constructivism, including cognitive processing, expectations, values, and perceptions of self and others. Thus, although constructivism seems to be a recent arrival on the learning scene, its basic premise that learners construct understandings underlies many learning principles. This is the epistemological (way-of-knowing) aspect of constructivism.

Constructivism has affected theory and research in learning and development, and also has influenced educational thinking about curriculum and instruction. It underlies the emphasis on the integrated curriculum in which students study a topic from multiple perspectives. For example, in studying hot-air balloons, students might read about them, write about them, learn new vocabulary words, visit one (hands-on experience), study the scientific principles involved, draw pictures of them, and learn songs about them. Constructivist ideas also are found in many professional standards and affect design of curriculum and instruction, such as the learner-centered principles developed by the American Psychological Association (discussed later).

Another constructivist assumption is that teachers should not teach in the traditional sense of delivering instruction to a group of students. Rather, they should structure situations such that learners become actively involved with content through manipulation of materials and social interaction. How the teacher in the opening vignette structured the lesson allowed students to construct their understandings of what was happening. Activities include observing phenomena, collecting data, generating and testing hypotheses, and working collaboratively with others. Classes visit sites outside of the classroom. Teachers from different disciplines plan the curriculum together. Students are taught to be self-regulated learners by setting goals, monitoring and evaluating progress, and going beyond basic requirements by exploring interests (Bruning et al., 2011).

Perspectives

As noted in this chapter, there are different constructivist perspectives (Table 8.1; Bruning et al., 2011; Phillips, 1995). *Exogenous constructivism* refers to the idea that the acquisition of knowledge represents a reconstruction of structures that exist in the external world. This view posits a strong influence of the external world on knowledge construction, such as by experiences, teaching, and exposure to models. Knowledge is accurate to the extent it reflects that reality. Some aspects of contemporary information processing theories reflect this notion (e.g., schemas, memory networks; Chapter 5).

Table 8.1
Perspectives on constructivism.

Perspective	Premises
Exogenous	The acquisition of knowledge represents a reconstruction of the external world. The world influences beliefs through experiences, exposure to models, and teaching. Knowledge is accurate to the extent it reflects external reality.
Endogenous	Knowledge derives from previously acquired knowledge and not directly from environmental interactions. Knowledge is not a mirror of the external world; rather, it develops through cognitive abstraction.
Dialectical	Knowledge derives from interactions between persons and their environments. Constructions are neither invariably tied to the external world nor wholly the workings of the mind. Rather, knowledge reflects the outcomes of mental contradictions that result from one's interactions with the environment.

In contrast, *endogenous constructivism* emphasizes the coordination of cognitive actions (Bruning et al., 2011). Mental structures are created from earlier structures, not directly from environmental information; therefore, knowledge is not a mirror of the external world acquired through experiences, teaching, or social interactions. Knowledge develops through the cognitive activity of abstraction and follows a generally predictable sequence. Piaget's (1970) theory of cognitive development (discussed later) fits this framework.

Between these extremes lies *dialectical constructivism*, which holds that knowledge derives from interactions between persons and their environments. Constructions are not invariably bound to the external world nor are they wholly the result of the workings of the mind; rather, they reflect the outcomes of mental contradictions that result from interactions with the environment. This perspective has become closely aligned with many contemporary theories. For example, it is compatible with Bandura's (1986) social cognitive theory (Chapter 4) and with many motivation theories (Chapter 9). The developmental theories of the Neo-Piagetians, Bruner, and Vygotsky (discussed later) also reflect this framework. Within any of these three constructivist perspectives, whether the theory is more cognitive or social depends on how much emphasis it places on the role of sociocultural variables in affecting one's constructions.

Each of these perspectives has merit and is potentially useful for research and teaching. Exogenous views are appropriate when we are interested in determining how accurately learners perceive the structure of knowledge within a domain. The endogenous perspective is relevant to explore how learners develop from novices through greater levels of competence (Chapter 7). The dialectical view is useful for designing interventions to challenge children's thinking and for research aimed at exploring the effectiveness of social influences such as exposure to models and peer collaboration.

Situated Cognition

A core premise of constructivism is that cognitive processes (including thinking and learning) are situated (occur) in physical and social contexts (Cobb & Bowers, 1999;

Greeno & the Middle School Mathematics Through Applications Project Group, 1998). *Situated cognition* (or *situated learning*) involves relations between a person and a situation (Greeno, 1989).

The idea of person–situation interaction is not confined to constructivism. Most contemporary theories of learning and development assume that beliefs and knowledge are formed as people interact in situations. Research in a variety of disciplines—including cognitive psychology, social cognitive learning, and content domains (e.g., reading, mathematics)—shows that thinking involves an extended reciprocal relation with the context (Bandura, 1986; Cobb & Bowers, 1999; Greeno, 1989).

Research results highlight the importance of exploring situated cognition as a means of understanding the development of competence in domains such as literacy, mathematics, and (as we see in the opening scenario) science (Cobb, 1994; Cobb & Bowers, 1999; Driver et al., 1994; Chapter 7). Situated cognition also is relevant to motivation (Chapter 9). As with learning, motivation is not an entirely internal state as posited by classical views or wholly dependent on the environment as predicted by reinforcement theories (Chapter 3). Rather, motivation depends on cognitive activity in interaction with sociocultural and instructional factors, which include language and forms of assistance such as scaffolding (Sivan, 1986; van de Pol, Volman, & Beishuizen, 2010).

Situated cognition addresses the intuitive notion that many processes interact to produce learning. We know that motivation and instruction are linked: Good instruction can raise motivation for learning, and motivated learners seek effective instructional environments (Schunk & DiBenedetto, 2016). A situated cognition perspective also leads researchers to explore cognition in authentic learning contexts such as schools, workplaces, and homes, many of which involve mentoring or apprenticeships.

Researchers have found that situated learning is effective. Griffin (1995), for example, compared traditional (in-class) instruction on map skills with a situated learning approach in which college students received practice in the actual environments depicted on the maps. The situated learning group performed better on a map-skill assessment. Although Griffin found no benefit of situated learning on transfer, the results of situated learning studies should be highly generalizable to similar contexts.

Situated cognition also is relevant to beliefs about how learning occurs (Greeno & the Middle School Mathematics Through Applications Project Group, 1998). Students exposed to a certain procedure for learning a subject experience situated cognition for that method; in other words, this content is learned in this way. For example, if students repeatedly receive mathematics instruction taught in didactic fashion by a teacher explaining and demonstrating, followed by their engaging in independent problem solving at their desks, then mathematics learning is apt to become situated in this context. The same students might have difficulty adjusting to a new teacher who favors using guided discovery (as done by the teacher in the opening lesson) by collaborative peer groups.

The instructional implication is that teaching methods should reflect the outcomes we desire in our learners. If we are trying to teach them inquiry skills, the instruction must incorporate inquiry activities. The method and the content must be properly situated.

Situated cognition fits well with the constructivist idea that context is an inherent part of learning. Nonetheless, extending the idea of situated learning too far may be erroneous. As Anderson, Reder, and Simon (1996) showed, there is plenty of empirical evidence for

APPLICATION 8.1
Constructivism and Teaching

Constructivism emphasizes integrated curricula and having teachers use materials in such a way that learners become actively involved. Mr. Rotaub implements various constructivist ideas in his fourth-grade classroom using integrated units. In the fall, he presents a unit on pumpkins. In social studies, children learn where pumpkins are grown and about the products made from pumpkins. They also study the uses of pumpkins in history and the benefits of pumpkins to early settlers.

He takes his class on a field trip to a pumpkin farm, where they learn how pumpkins are grown. Each student selects a pumpkin and brings it back to class. The pumpkin becomes a valuable learning tool.

In mathematics, the students estimate the size and weight of their pumpkins and then measure and weigh them. They establish class graphs by comparing all the pumpkins by size, weight, shape, and color. The children also estimate the number of seeds they think one pumpkin has, and then they count the seeds when Mr. Rotaub cuts it open. For art, they design a shape for the carving of a pumpkin, and then he carves it. In language arts, they write a story about pumpkins. They also write a thank-you letter to the pumpkin farm. For spelling, Mr. Rotaub uses words that they have used in the study of pumpkins. These examples illustrate how the study of pumpkins is integrated across the curriculum.

contextual independence of learning and transfer of learning between contexts. We need more information about which types of learning occur best when they are firmly linked to contexts and when it is better to teach broader skills and show how they can be applied in different contexts. Application 8.1 gives constructivist applications to teaching and learning.

In the next section we begin the discussion of cognitive constructivism. To this end, the perspectives of Piaget, the Neo-Piagetians, and Bruner are covered. While not ignoring sociocultural processes, these perspectives place strong emphasis on cognition as students construct knowledge.

PIAGET'S THEORY OF COGNITIVE DEVELOPMENT

Piaget's theory of cognitive development reflects the fundamental ideas of constructivism and presents an alternative to information processing theory, which contends that cognitive development is characterized by higher quality and increasingly complex cognitive processing. Piaget's theory is concerned with knowing, or how people acquire knowledge. It is not a theory of learning, although it has relevance to the study of learning.

Piaget's theory is complex; a complete summary is beyond the scope of this text. Interested readers should consult other sources (Brainerd, 2003; Furth, 1970; Ginsburg & Opper, 1988; Piaget, 1952, 1970; Piaget & Inhelder, 1969; Wadsworth, 1996). This section presents a concise overview of the major points relevant to constructivism and learning.

Although Piaget's theory currently is not a leading theory of cognitive development, it remains important and has several useful implications for instruction and learning.

Developmental Processes

Equilibration. According to Piaget, cognitive development depends on four factors: biological maturation, experience with the physical environment, experience with the social environment, and equilibration. The first three are self-explanatory, but their effects depend on the fourth. *Equilibration* refers to a biological drive to produce an optimal state of equilibrium (or *adaptation*) between cognitive structures and the environment (Duncan, 1995). Equilibration is the central factor and the motivating force behind cognitive development. It coordinates the actions of the other three factors and makes internal mental structures and external environmental reality consistent with each other.

To illustrate the role of equilibration, consider 6-year-old Allison riding in a car with her father on a freeway. They are going 65 mph, and about 100 yards in front of them is a car. They have been following this car for some time, and the distance between them stays the same. Her dad points to the car and asks Allison, "Which car is going faster, our car or that car, or are we going the same speed?" Allison replies that the other car is going faster. When her dad asks why, she replies, "Because it's in front of us." If her dad then said, "We're actually going the same speed," this would create a conflict for Allison. She believes the other car is going faster, but she has received conflicting environmental input.

To resolve this conflict, Allison can use one of the two component processes of equilibration: assimilation and accommodation. *Assimilation* refers to fitting external reality to the existing cognitive structure. When we interpret, construe, and frame, we alter the nature of reality to make it fit our cognitive structure. To assimilate the information, Allison might alter reality by believing that her dad is teasing her or perhaps at that moment the two cars are going the same speed but that the other car had been going faster beforehand.

Accommodation refers to changing internal structures to make them consistent with external reality. We accommodate when we adjust our ideas to make sense of reality. To accommodate her belief system (structures) to the new information, she might believe her dad without understanding why or she might change her belief system to include the idea that all cars in front of them are going the same speed as they are.

Assimilation and accommodation are complementary processes. As reality is assimilated, structures are accommodated.

Stages. Piaget concluded from his research that children's cognitive development passes through a fixed sequence. The pattern of operations that children can perform may be thought of as a level or *stage*. Each level or stage is defined by how children know and view the world. Piaget's and other stage theories make certain assumptions:

■ Stages are discrete, qualitatively different, and separate. Progression from one stage to another is not a matter of gradual blending or continuous merging.
■ The development of cognitive structures is dependent on preceding development.

■ Although the order of structure development is invariant, the age at which one may be in a particular stage and the rate that one passes through it will vary from person to person. Stages should not be equated with ages. It is not the age that defines a stage but rather the type of cognitive processing that occurs.

Table 8.2 shows how Piaget characterized his stage progression. Much has been written on these stages and an extensive research literature exists on them. The stages are only briefly described here; interested readers should consult other sources (Brainerd, 2003; Meece, 2002; Wadsworth, 1996).

In the *sensorimotor* stage, children's actions are spontaneous and represent an attempt to understand the world. Understanding is rooted in present action; for example, a ball is for throwing and a bottle for sucking. The period is characterized by rapid change; a two-year-old is cognitively far different from an infant. Children actively equilibrate, albeit at a primitive level. Cognitive structures are constructed and altered, and the motivation to do this is internal. The notion of *effectance motivation* (*mastery motivation*; Chapter 9) is relevant to sensorimotor children. By the end of the sensorimotor period, children have attained sufficient cognitive development to progress to new conceptual-symbolic thinking characteristic of the preoperational stage (Wadsworth, 1996).

Preoperational children are able to imagine the future and reflect on the past, although they remain heavily perceptually oriented in the present. They are apt to believe that 10 coins spread out in a row are more than 10 coins in a pile. They also are unable to think in more than one dimension at a time; thus, if they focus on length, they are apt to think a longer object (a yardstick) is bigger than a shorter one (a brick) even though the shorter one is wider and deeper. Preoperational children demonstrate *irreversibility*; that is, once things are done, they cannot be changed (e.g., a box flattened cannot be remade into a box). They have difficulty distinguishing fantasy from reality. Cartoon characters appear as real as people. The period is one of rapid language development. Another characteristic is that children become less *egocentric*: They realize that others may think and feel differently than they do.

The *concrete operational* stage is characterized by remarkable cognitive growth and is a formative one in schooling, because it is when children's language and basic skills acquisition accelerate dramatically. Children begin to show some abstract thinking, although it typically is defined by properties or actions (e.g., honesty is returning money to the person who lost it). Concrete operational children display less egocentric thought, and language increasingly becomes social. *Reversibility* in thinking is acquired along with classification and seriation—concepts essential for the acquisition of mathematical skills.

Table 8.2
Piaget's stages of cognitive development.

Stage	Approximate Age Range (Years)
Sensorimotor	Birth to 2
Preoperational	2 to 7
Concrete operational	7 to 11
Formal operational	11 to adult

Concrete operational thinking no longer is dominated by perception; children draw on their experiences and are not always swayed by what they perceive.

The *formal operational* stage extends concrete operational thought. No longer is thought focused exclusively on tangibles; children are able to think about hypothetical situations. Reasoning capabilities improve, and children can think about multiple dimensions and abstract properties. Egocentrism emerges in adolescents' comparing reality to the ideal; thus, they often show idealistic thinking.

Piaget's stages have been criticized on different grounds. One issue is that children often grasp ideas and are able to perform operations earlier than Piaget found. Another is that cognitive development across domains typically is uneven; rarely does a child think in same-stage-typical ways across all topics (e.g., mathematics, science, history). This also is true for adults; the same topic may be understood quite differently. For example, some adults may think of baseball in preoperational terms ("Hit the ball and run"), others might think of it in a concrete operational sense ("What do I do in different situations?"), and some can reason using formal operational thought (e.g., "Explain why a curve ball curves"). As a general framework, however, the stages describe the thought patterns that tend to co-occur, which is useful knowledge for educators, parents, and others who work with children.

Mechanisms of Learning. Equilibration is an internal process (Duncan, 1995). As such, cognitive development can occur only when *disequilibrium* or *cognitive conflict* exists. An event must occur that produces a disturbance in the child's cognitive structures so that the child's beliefs do not match the observed reality. Equilibration seeks to resolve the conflict through assimilation and accommodation.

Piaget felt that development would proceed naturally through regular interactions with the physical and social environments. The impetus for developmental change is internal. Environmental factors are extrinsic; they can influence development but not direct it. This point has profound implications for education because it suggests that teaching may have little impact on development. Teachers can arrange the environment to cause conflict, but how any particular child resolves the conflict is not predictable.

Cognitive development occurs, then, when children experience cognitive conflict and engage in assimilation or accommodation to construct or alter internal structures. Importantly, however, the conflict should not be too great because this will not trigger equilibration. Learning (cognitive change) will be optimal when the conflict is small and especially when children are in transition between stages. Information must be partially understood (assimilated) before it can promote structural change (accommodation). Environmental stimulation to facilitate change should have negligible effect unless the critical stage transitions have begun so that the conflict can be successfully resolved via equilibration. Thus, cognitive change is limited by developmental level (Brainerd, 2003).

The research evidence on cognitive conflict is not overwhelmingly supportive of Piaget's position (Zimmerman & Blom, 1983a, 1983b). Rosenthal and Zimmerman (1978) summarized research studies showing that preoperational children can master concrete operational tasks through teaching involving verbal explanations and modeled demonstrations. According to the theory, this should not happen unless the children are in stage transition, at which time cognitive conflict would be at a reasonable level.

The stagelike changes in children's thinking seem to be linked to more gradual changes in attention and cognitive processing (Meece, 2002). Children may not demonstrate Piagetian stage understanding for various reasons, including not attending to the relevant stimuli, improperly encoding information, not relating information to prior knowledge, or using ineffective means to retrieve information (Siegler, 1991). When children are taught to use cognitive processes more effectively, they often can perform tasks at higher cognitive levels.

Piaget's theory is constructivist because it assumes that children construct and then impose their concepts on the world to know and make sense of it. These concepts are not inborn; rather, children acquire them through their normal experiences. Information from the physical and social environments is not automatically received but rather is processed according to the child's prevailing mental structures. Children make sense of their environments and construct reality based on their capabilities at the present time. With experience, these basic concepts develop into more sophisticated views.

Implications for Instruction

Piaget contended that cognitive development could not be taught, although researchers have shown that it can be accelerated. Piaget's theory seems to underestimate the potential of teaching, but the theory and research have implications for instruction (Table 8.3).

Understand Cognitive Development. Teachers will benefit when they understand at what levels their students are functioning. All students in a class should not be expected to operate at the same level. Many Piagetian tasks are easy to administer (Wadsworth, 1996). Teachers can try to ascertain levels and gear their teaching accordingly. Students who seem to be in stage transition may benefit from teaching at the next higher level, because the conflict will not be too great for them.

Keep Students Active. Piaget decried passive learning. Children need rich environments that allow for active exploration and hands-on activities. This arrangement facilitates active construction of knowledge.

Create Cognitive Conflict. Development occurs only when environmental inputs do not match students' cognitive structures. Material should not be readily assimilated but not too difficult to preclude accommodation. Cognitive conflict also can be created by allowing students to solve problems and arrive at wrong answers. Nothing in Piaget's theory says that children always have to succeed; teacher feedback indicating incorrect answers can promote disequilibrium.

Table 8.3
Implications of Piaget's theory for education.

- Understand cognitive development.
- Keep students active.
- Create cognitive conflict.
- Provide social interaction.

At all grades, teachers need to know how their students are thinking so they can introduce cognitive conflict at a reasonable level, where students can resolve it through assimilation and accommodation. Teachers at the early elementary levels, for example, are apt to have students who operate at both the preoperational and concrete operational levels, which means that one lesson will not suffice for any particular unit. Furthermore, because some children will grasp operations more quickly than others, teachers need to build enrichment activities into their lessons.

Teachers at later elementary and middle grades levels include lesson components that require basic understanding and also those that necessitate abstract reasoning. For example, they may incorporate activities that require factual answers, as well as activities that have no right or wrong answers but that require students to think abstractly and construct their ideas through reasoned judgments based on data. For students who are not fully operating at the formal operational level, the components requiring abstract reasoning may produce desired cognitive conflict and enhance a higher level of thinking. For students who already are operating at a formal operational level, the reasoning activities will continue to challenge them.

Provide Social Interaction. Although Piaget's theory does not place great emphasis on the influence of social interaction on cognitive development, the social environment nonetheless can affect development. Activities that provide social interactions are useful. Learning that others have different points of view can help children become less egocentric. Application 8.2 discusses ways that teachers can help to foster cognitive development.

NEO-PIAGETIAN THEORIES

Assumptions

Piaget's theory contends that cognitive development proceeds through a series of stages that are qualitatively different from one another. Some researchers have questioned whether development proceeds in such an orderly, stagelike progression (Flavell, 1985). Another issue is that equilibration seems inadequate to explain all aspects of cognitive development (Siegler, 1991).

Advances in information processing theory and research (Chapters 5–7) have shown that stagelike changes in children's thinking are causally linked to quantitative changes in children's information processes, especially attention and memory (WM, LTM). For example, children may fail to perform some Piagetian tasks (e.g., conservation) because they do not attend to the relevant dimensions such as length and height. They also may not properly encode information or relate information in WM to that in LTM. Available evidence suggests that children's performances on Piagetian tasks can be improved when children are taught to use information processes more effectively (Meece, 2002). Such evidence has led many developmental psychologists to move away from Piagetian theory and to more fully embrace information processing.

Yet other theorists believe that a stage theory of cognitive development—such as Piaget's—may be viable with some modifications. Neo-Piagetian theorists retain the basic premises and assumptions of Piaget's theory while incorporating information processing. In essence, Neo-Piagetian theories retain the structural changes postulated by Piaget but link them with the development of cognitive strategies and memory processes (Case & Mueller, 2001; Fischer & Bidell, 1991; Morra, Gobbo, Morini, & Sheese, 2008; Pascual-Leone, 1970).

Neo-Piagetian theories make several assumptions (Morra et al., 2008). One is that cognitive development depends on brain development. Children are cognitively capable of doing what their brain development will allow. WM capacity, for example, increases with development, as does the capability for sustained attention. Until these capabilities adequately mature, children's cognitive development will be limited. Neo-Piagetian theories propose that brain development will restrict children's capabilities for thinking and reasoning.

Another assumption is that capabilities develop within specific domains. Piaget's theory contends that the maturation of thinking capabilities should extend to a wide variety of disciplines; that is, have generality across domains. But development proceeds unevenly, and children can show wide variation in their thinking in different domains. For example, they may show more advanced thinking in mathematics and science and less advanced thinking in language arts. Neo-Piagetians propose that children do not pass through a single series of stages but rather multiple series of stages that relate to particular domains (Morra et al., 2008).

Related to this point is the assumption that children acquire specific cognitive strategies and concepts related to various content areas. Although general thinking skills (e.g., critical thinking, reasoning) develop, these are acquired in specific contexts. Thus, historical reasoning is not the same as mathematical reasoning. Students learn skills for thinking about content; they do not acquire general skills that they simply adapt to different contexts.

A fourth assumption is that teaching and instruction can affect cognitive development more than Piaget believed. Neo-Piagetians accept Piaget's belief that informal interactions can promote development, but they also believe that development can be enhanced through teaching. This point is highlighted nicely by Case's instructional model, which is described in the next section.

Case's Instructional Model

Case (1978a, 1978b, 1981) formulated a structural stage model of development to account for changes in cognitive information processing capabilities. Case's stages (approximate age ranges) and their defining characteristics are (Meece, 2002):

- Sensory motor (birth to 1.5 years)—mental representations linked to physical movements
- Relational (1.5 to 5 years)—relations coordinated along one dimension (e.g., weight is heavy or light)

- Dimensional (5 to 11 years)—relations coordinated along two dimensions (e.g., height and weight compared)
- Abstract (11 to 18.5 years)—use of abstract reasoning

Structural changes (i.e., movement to new stages) are linked with the development of cognitive strategies and memory processes. Cognitive development includes the acquisition of efficient strategies for processing information. Development produced an increase in the size of WM. As strategies become more efficient and automatic, they consume less WM space, which frees space for acquiring new strategies.

Case emphasized providing instruction to help learners process information more automatically. One first identifies the learning goal and the steps through which learners must proceed to reach the goal. During instruction, demands on WM are reduced by not presenting too much new material at once and by breaking each complex step into simpler steps.

This process can be illustrated with missing addend problems of the form $4 + \_\_ = 7$ (Case, 1978b, p. 214). The required steps are as follows:

- Read symbols from left to right.
- Note that quantity to be found is one of the two addends.
- Decide that the known addend must be subtracted from the known total.
- Note and store value of the given addend.
- Note and store value of the total.
- Perform the subtraction.

Children commonly make two types of strategy errors in solving the problem just given. One is that they give either 4 or 7 as the answer, seemingly by first looking at the symbols and reading one of them, then copying this symbol as the answer. The other is that they add the two given numbers to get 11 by performing the following strategy:

- Look at and store the first symbol.
- Count out that many (on fingers).
- Look at and store the second symbol.
- Count out that many.
- Count out the total number.
- Write this number as the answer.

To show children that their strategies are incorrect, a teacher might use faces. A full face is placed on one side of an equal sign and a half face on the other. Children see that these faces are not the same. Then a full face is portrayed on one side of the equal sign and two half faces on the other side, where one half face has markings on it and the other is blank. Children fill in the markings on the blank half to make it the same as the full face. Eventually numerical symbols are introduced to replace the faces.

Case (1978a) cited evidence showing that the previous method is more effective than either structured practice or traditional instruction. Case's model has been applied to the design of instruction and other areas such as assessment and early childhood education (Case, 1993). One drawback is the time required to diagnose, analyze, and plan. The model may be most useful for students requiring remedial assistance because such learners tend to use inefficient strategies and have WM limitations.

We now turn to Bruner's theory of cognitive growth. Bruner's and Piaget's theories are cognitive constructivist because they posit that people form or construct much of what they learn and understand.

BRUNER'S THEORY OF COGNITIVE GROWTH

Jerome Bruner's theory of cognitive growth does not link changes in development with cognitive structures as Piaget's does (Lutkehaus & Greenfield, 2003). Rather, Bruner's theory highlights the various ways that children represent knowledge. The theory has implications for teaching and learning.

Knowledge Representation

According to Bruner (1964), "The development of human intellectual functioning from infancy to such perfection as it may reach is shaped by a series of technological advances in the use of mind" (p. 1). These technological advances depend on increasing language facility and exposure to systematic instruction (Bruner, 1966). As children develop, their actions are constrained less by immediate stimuli. Cognitive processes (e.g., thoughts, beliefs) mediate the relationship between stimulus and response so that learners can maintain the same response in a changing environment or perform different responses in the same environment, depending on which is more adaptive.

People represent knowledge in three ways, which emerge in a developmental sequence: enactive, iconic, and symbolic (Bruner, 1964; Bruner, Olver, & Greenfield, 1966). These modes are not structures, but rather involve different forms of cognitive processing (i.e., functions; Table 8.4).

Enactive representation involves motor responses, or ways to manipulate the environment. Actions such as riding a bicycle and tying a knot are represented largely in muscular actions. Stimuli are defined by the actions that prompt them. Among toddlers, a ball (stimulus) is represented as something to throw and bounce (actions).

Iconic representation refers to action-free mental images. Children acquire the capability to think about objects that are not physically present. They mentally transform objects and think about their properties separately from what actions can be performed with the objects. Iconic representation allows one to recognize objects.

Table 8.4
Bruner's modes of knowledge representation.

Mode	Type of Representation
Enactive	Motor responses; ways to manipulate objects and aspects of the environment
Iconic	Action-free mental images; visual properties of objects and events that can be altered
Symbolic	Symbol systems (e.g., language, mathematical notation) remote and arbitrary

Symbolic representation uses symbol systems (e.g., language, mathematical notation) to encode knowledge. Such systems allow one to understand abstract concepts (e.g., the *x* variable in 3x − 5 = 10) and to alter symbolic information as a result of verbal instruction. Symbolic systems represent knowledge with remote and arbitrary features. The word "Philadelphia" looks no more like the city than a nonsense syllable (Bruner, 1964).

The symbolic mode is the last to develop and quickly becomes the preferred mode, although people maintain the capability to represent knowledge in the enactive and iconic modes. One might experience the feel of a tennis ball, form a mental picture of it, and describe it in words. The primary advantage of the symbolic mode is that it allows learners to represent and transform knowledge with greater flexibility and power than is possible with the other modes (Bruner, 1964).

Spiral Curriculum

That knowledge can be represented in different ways suggests that teachers should vary instruction depending on learners' developmental levels. Before children can comprehend abstract mathematical notation, they can be exposed to mathematical concepts and operations represented enactively (with blocks) and iconically (in pictures). Bruner emphasized teaching as a means of prompting cognitive development. To say that a particular concept cannot be taught because students will not understand it really is saying that students will not understand the concept the way teachers plan to teach it. Instruction should be differentiated to match children's cognitive capabilities.

Bruner (1960) proposed that any content can be taught in meaningful fashion to learners of any age:

> [O]ur schools may be wasting precious years by postponing the teaching of many important subjects on the ground that they are too difficult. . . . The foundations of any subject may be taught to anybody at any age in some form. . . . The basic ideas that lie at the heart of all science and mathematics and the basic themes that give form to life and literature are as simple as they are powerful. To be in command of these basic ideas, to use them effectively, requires a continual deepening of one's understanding of them that comes from learning to use them in progressively more complex forms. It is only when such basic ideas are put in formalized terms as equations or elaborated verbal concepts that they are out of reach of the young child, if he has not first understood them intuitively and had a chance to try them out on his own. (pp. 12–13)

Bruner's proposition has been misinterpreted to mean that learners of any age can be taught anything, which is not true. Bruner recommended that content be revisited: Concepts initially should be taught in a simple fashion so children can understand them and represented in a more complex fashion with development. Such revisiting creates a spiral curriculum: We return to teaching the same concepts, but the learning is different (e.g., more complex or nuanced). In literature, children may be able to understand intuitively the concepts of "comedy" and "tragedy" (e.g., "comedies are funny and tragedies are sad") even though they cannot verbally describe them in literary terms. With development, students read, analyze, and write papers on comedies and tragedies. Students should address topics at increasing levels of complexity as they move through the curriculum, rather than encountering a topic only once.

Bruner's theory is constructivist because it assumes that at any age, learners assign meaning to stimuli and events based on their cognitive capabilities and experiences with the social and physical environments. Bruner's modes of representation bear some similarity to the operations that students engage in during Piaget's stages (i.e., senso-rimotor–enactive, concrete operational–iconic, formal operational–symbolic), although Bruner's is not a stage theory. Bruner's theory also allows for concepts to be mentally represented in multiple modes simultaneously: An adolescent knows how to throw a basketball, can visualize its appearance, and can compute its circumference with the formula $c = \pi d$.

In summary, the implications of Bruner's theory are as follows:

- Represent content in multiple modalities
- Periodically review content in increasing complexity
- Devise ways to help learners at all ages meaningfully understand content

Application 8.3 gives some examples of Bruner's ideas applied to teaching and learning.

APPLICATION 8.3
Modes of Knowledge Representation

Bruner's theory elaborates ways that students can represent knowledge and recommends revisiting learning through a spiral curriculum. A good application is found in mathematics. Before students can comprehend abstract mathematical notation, teachers must ensure that students understand the concepts enactively and iconically. Ms. Braxton, a third-grade teacher, works with second- and fourth-grade teachers as she prepares her math units for the year. She wants to ensure that students understand previous concepts before tackling new ones, and she introduces ideas that will be further developed during the next year. When introducing multiplication to her third graders, she first reviews addition and counting by multipliers (e.g., 2, 4, 6, 8; 4, 8, 12, 16). Then she has the students work with manipulatives

(enactive representation), and she provides visual (iconic) representation of multiplication. Eventually she presents problems in symbolic mode (e.g., $4 \times 2 = ?$).

Ms. Cannon, a ninth-grade English teacher, examines curriculum guides and meets with middle school teachers to determine what material has been covered. As she develops units, she starts the first lesson with a review of the material that students studied previously and asks students to share what they can recall. Once she evaluates the mastery level of the students, she is able to build on the unit and add new material. She strives to employ all modes of knowledge representation in her teaching: enactive—role-playing, dramatization; iconic—pictures, videos; symbolic—print materials, websites.

VYGOTSKY'S SOCIOCULTURAL THEORY

A prime example of social constructivist theory is that proposed by Vygotsky. Although Vygotsky's theory, like Piaget's, is constructivist, Vygotsky's places more emphasis on the social environment as a facilitator of development and learning (Tudge & Scrimsher, 2003). The background of the theory is discussed, along with its key assumptions and principles.

Background

Lev Semenovich Vygotsky was born in Russia in 1896 and studied various subjects in school including psychology, philosophy, and literature. He received a law degree from Moscow Imperial University in 1917. Following graduation, he returned to his hometown of Gomel, which was beset with problems stemming from German occupation, famine, and civil war. Two of his brothers died, and he contracted tuberculosis—the disease that eventually killed him. He taught courses in psychology and literature, wrote literary criticism, and edited a journal. He also worked at a teacher training institution, where he founded a psychology laboratory and wrote an educational psychology book (Tudge & Scrimsher, 2003).

A critical event occurred in 1924 at the Second All-Russian Congress of Psychoneurology in Leningrad. Prevailing psychological theory at that time neglected subjective experiences in favor of Pavlov's conditioned reflexes and behaviorism's emphasis on environmental influences. Vygotsky presented a paper in which he criticized the dominant views and spoke on the relation of conditioned reflexes to human consciousness and behavior. Pavlov's experiments with dogs (Chapter 3) and Köhler's studies with apes (Chapter 7) erased many distinctions between animals and humans.

Vygotsky contended that unlike animals, which react only to the environment, humans have the adaptive capacity to alter the environment for their own purposes. His speech made such an impression on one listener—Alexander Luria (discussed later in this chapter)—that Vygotsky was invited to join the prestigious Institute of Experimental Psychology in Moscow. He helped to establish the Institute of Defektology, whose purpose was to determine ways to assist individuals with handicaps. Until his death in 1934, he wrote extensively on the social mediation of learning and the role of consciousness, often in collaboration with colleagues Luria and Leontiev (Rohrkemper, 1989).

Understanding Vygotsky's position requires keeping in mind that he was a Marxist and that his views represented an attempt to apply Marxist ideas of social change to language and development (Rohrkemper, 1989). After the 1917 Russian Revolution, an urgency among the new leaders produced rapid change in the populace. Vygotsky's strong sociocultural theoretical orientation fit well with the revolution's goals of changing the culture to a socialist system.

Vygotsky had some access to Western society such as Piaget's writings (Bredo, 1997; Tudge & Winterhoff, 1993), but little of what he wrote was published during his lifetime or for some years following his death (Gredler, 2009). A negative political climate prevailed in the former Soviet Union; among other things, the Communist Party curtailed psychological testing and publications. Vygotsky espoused revisionist thinking (Bruner, 1984). He moved from a Pavlovian view of psychology focusing on reflexes to a cultural–historical perspective that stressed language and social interaction (Tudge & Scrimsher, 2003). Some of his writings were at odds with Stalin's views and therefore were not published. References to his works were banned in the Soviet Union until the 1980s (Tudge & Scrimsher, 2003). In recent years, Vygotsky's writings have been increasingly translated and circulated, which has expanded their impact on such disciplines as education, psychology, and linguistics.

Basic Principles

One of Vygotsky's central contributions to psychological thought was his emphasis on socially meaningful activity as an important influence on human consciousness (Bredo, 1997; Gredler, 2012; Kozulin, 1986; Tudge & Winterhoff, 1993). Vygotsky attempted to explain human thought in new ways. He rejected introspection (Chapter 1) and raised many of the same objections as the behaviorists. He wanted to abandon explaining states of consciousness by referring to the concept of consciousness; similarly, he rejected behavioral explanations of action in terms of prior actions. Rather than discarding consciousness (which the behaviorists did) or the role of the environment (which the introspectionists did), he sought a middle ground of taking environmental influence into account through its effect on consciousness.

Vygotsky's theory stresses the interaction of interpersonal (social), cultural–historical, and individual factors as the key to human development (Tudge & Scrimsher, 2003). Interactions with persons in the environment (e.g., apprenticeships, collaborations) stimulate developmental processes and foster cognitive growth. But interactions are not useful in a traditional sense of providing learners with information. Rather, students transform their experiences based on their knowledge and characteristics and reorganize their mental structures.

The cultural–historical aspects of Vygotsky's theory illuminate the point that learning and development cannot be dissociated from their context. The way that learners interact with their worlds—with the persons, objects, and institutions in it—transforms their thinking. The meanings of concepts change as they are linked with the world (Gredler, 2009). Thus, "school" is not simply a word or a physical structure but also an institution that seeks to promote learning and citizenship.

There also are individual, or inherited, factors that affect development. Vygotsky was interested in children with mental and physical disabilities. He believed that their inherited characteristics produced learning trajectories different from those of children without such challenges.

Of these three influences (interpersonal, cultural–historical, individual), the one that has received the most attention—at least among Western researchers and practitioners—is the interpersonal. Vygotsky considered the social environment critical for learning and thought that social interactions transformed learning experiences. Social activity is a phenomenon that helps explain changes in consciousness and establishes a psychological theory that unifies behavior and mind (Kozulin, 1986; Wertsch, 1985).

The social environment influences cognition through its "tools"—that is, its cultural objects (e.g., cars, machines) and its language and social institutions (e.g., schools, religious institutions). Social interactions help to coordinate the three influences on development.

Cognitive change results from using cultural tools in social interactions and from internalizing and mentally transforming these interactions (Bruning et al., 2011). Vygotsky's position is a form of dialectical social constructivism because it emphasizes the interaction between persons and their environments. *Mediation* is the key mechanism in development and learning:

> All human psychological processes (higher mental processes) are mediated by such psychological tools as language, signs, and symbols. Adults teach these tools to children in the course of their joint (collaborative) activity. After children internalize these tools they function as mediators of the children's more advanced psychological processes. (Karpov & Haywood, 1998, p. 27)

Vygotsky (1962) postulated that all higher mental functions originate in the social environment. This is a powerful claim, but it has a good degree of truth to it. The most influential process involved is language. Vygotsky thought that a critical component of psychological development was mastering the external process of transmitting cultural development and thinking through symbols such as language, counting, and writing. Once this process was mastered, the next step involved using these symbols to influence and self-regulate thoughts and actions. Self-regulation uses the important function of private speech (discussed later in this chapter).

Research evidence suggests that Vygotsky's claim is too strong. Young children mentally construct some knowledge about the way the world operates before they have an opportunity to learn from the culture in which they live (Bereiter, 1994). Children also seem biologically predisposed to acquire certain concepts (e.g., understanding that adding increases quantity), which does not depend on the environment (Geary, 1995). Nonetheless, social learning affects knowledge construction and learners' cultures are critical and need to be considered in explaining learning and development. A summary of major points in Vygotsky's (1978) theory appears in Table 8.5 (Meece, 2002).

Zone of Proximal Development

A key concept in Vygotsky's theory is the *zone of proximal development (ZPD)*, defined as "the distance between the actual developmental level as determined by independent

Table 8.5
Key points in Vygotsky's theory.

■ Social interactions are critical; knowledge is co-constructed between two or more people.

■ Self-regulation is developed through internalization (developing an internal representation) of actions and mental operations that occur in social interactions.

■ Human development occurs through the cultural transmission of tools (language, symbols).

■ Language is the most critical tool. Language develops from social speech, to private speech, to covert (inner) speech.

■ The zone of proximal development (ZPD) is the difference between what children can do on their own and what they can do with assistance from others. Interactions with adults and peers in the ZPD promote cognitive development.

---

problem solving and the level of potential development as determined through problem solving under adult guidance or in collaboration with more capable peers" (Vygotsky, 1978, p. 86). The ZPD represents the amount of learning possible by a student given the proper instructional conditions (Puntambekar & Hübscher, 2005). The ZPD shows how learning and development are related (Bredo, 1997; Campione, Brown, Ferrara, & Bryant, 1984), and can be viewed as an alternative to the concept of intelligence (Belmont, 1989). In the ZPD, a teacher and learner (adult/child, tutor/tutee, model/observer, master/apprentice, expert/novice) work together on a task that the learner could not perform independently because of the difficulty level (Gredler, 2012). The ZPD reflects the Marxist idea of collective activity, in which those who know more or are more skilled share that knowledge and skill to accomplish a task with those who know less or are less skilled (Bruner, 1984).

Cognitive change occurs in the ZPD as teacher and learner share cultural tools, and this culturally mediated interaction produces cognitive change when internalized by the learner (Cobb, 1994). Working in the ZPD requires a good deal of guided participation (Rogoff, 1986); however, children do not acquire cultural knowledge passively from these interactions, nor is what they learn necessarily an automatic or accurate reflection of events. Rather, learners bring their own understandings to social interactions and construct meanings by integrating those understandings with their experiences in the context. The learning often is sudden, in the Gestalt sense of insight (Chapter 7), rather than reflecting a gradual accretion of knowledge (Wertsch, 1984).

For example, assume that a teacher (Trudy) and a child (Laura) will work on a task (making a picture of mom, dad, and Laura doing something together at home). Laura brings to the task her understandings of what the people and the home look like and the types of things they might work on, combined with knowledge of how to draw and make pictures. Trudy brings the same understandings plus knowledge of conditions necessary to work on various tasks. Suppose they decide to make a picture of the three working in the yard. Laura might draw a picture of dad cutting grass, mom trimming shrubs, and Laura raking the lawn. If Laura were to draw herself in front of dad, Trudy would explain that Laura must be behind dad to rake up the grass left behind by dad's cutting. During the interaction, Laura modifies her beliefs about working in the yard based on her current understanding and on the new knowledge she constructs.

Despite the importance of the ZPD, the overarching emphasis it has received in Western cultures has served to distort its meaning and downplay the complexity of Vygotsky's theory (Gredler, 2012).

> Moreover, the concept itself has too often been viewed in a rather limited way that emphasized the interpersonal at the expense of the individual and cultural-historical levels and treats the concept in a unidirectional fashion. As if the concept were synonymous with "scaffolding," too many authors have focused on the role of the more competent other, particularly the teacher, whose role is to provide assistance just in advance of the child's current thinking. . . . The concept thus has become equated with what sensitive teachers might do with their children and has lost much of the complexity with which it was imbued by Vygotsky, missing both what the child brings to the interaction and the broader setting (cultural and historical) in which the interaction takes place. (Tudge & Scrimsher, 2003, p. 211)

The influence of the cultural–historical setting is seen clearly in Vygotsky's belief that schooling was important not because it was where children were scaffolded but, rather, because it allowed them to develop greater awareness of themselves, their language, and their role in the world order. Participating in the cultural world transforms mental functioning rather than simply accelerating processes that would have developed anyway. Broadly speaking, the ZPD refers to new forms of awareness that occur as people interact with their societies' social institutions. The culture affects the course of one's mental development. It is unfortunate that in most discussions of the ZPD, it is conceived so narrowly (Gredler, 2012)—namely, as an expert teacher providing learning opportunities for a student (although that is part of it).

Applications

Vygotsky's ideas lend themselves to many educational applications that stress sociocultural influences (Karpov & Haywood, 1998; Moll, 2001). The field of self-regulated learning (Chapter 10) has been strongly influenced by the theory. Self-regulated learning requires metacognitive processes such as planning, checking, and evaluating. The importance of social factors is well accepted by educators and is emphasized by major organizations such as the National Association for the Education of Young Children, which stresses developmentally appropriate practices and teachers' actions and interactions with children as strong influences on their learning and development. This section and Application 8.4 discuss some examples.

APPLICATION 8.4
Applying Vygotsky's Theory

Vygotsky postulated that one's interactions with the environment assist learning. The experiences one brings to a learning situation can greatly influence the outcome.

Ice skating coaches may work with advanced students who have learned a great deal about ice skating and how they perform on the ice. Students bring with them their concepts of balance, speed, movement, and body control based on their experiences skating. Coaches take the strengths and weaknesses of these students and help them learn to alter various movements to improve their performances. For example, a skater who has trouble completing a triple axel toe loop has the height and speed needed to complete the jump, but the coach notices that

she turns her toe at an angle during the spin that alters the smooth completion of the loop. After the coach points this out to the skater and helps her learn to alter that movement, she is able to successfully complete the jump.

Veterinary students who have grown up on farms and have experienced births, illnesses, and care of various types of animals bring valuable knowledge to their training. Veterinary instructors can use these prior experiences to enhance students' learning. In teaching students how to treat an injured hoof of a cow or horse, the instructor might call on some of these students to discuss what they have observed and then build on that knowledge by explaining the latest and most effective methods of treatment.

Helping students acquire cognitive mediators (e.g., signs, symbols) through the social environment can be accomplished in many ways. A common application involves the concept of *instructional scaffolding*, which refers to the process of controlling task elements that are beyond the learners' capabilities so that they can focus on and master those features of the task that they can grasp quickly (Puntambekar & Hübscher, 2005). In construction projects, scaffolds are temporary structures erected to aid in the construction or modification of other structures. In the field of learning, scaffolding is used as a metaphor (van de Pol, Volman, & Beishuizen, 2010). Instructional scaffolding has five major functions: provide temporary support, function as a tool, extend the range of the learner, permit the attainment of tasks not otherwise possible, and use selectively only as needed.

In a learning situation, a teacher initially might take the lead, after which the teacher and the learners share responsibility. As learners become more competent, the teacher gradually withdraws the scaffolding—it is, after all, intended to be temporary—so that learners can perform independently (Campione et al., 1984). The key is to ensure that the scaffolding keeps learners in the ZPD, which is raised as they develop capabilities. Students are challenged to learn within the bounds of the ZPD. We see in the opening lesson how Anna was able to learn given the proper instructional support.

Interestingly, scaffolding is not a formal part of Vygotsky's theory (Puntambekar & Hübscher, 2005). The term was coined by Wood, Bruner, and Ross (1976). It fits nicely, however, with the ZPD. Scaffolding is part of Bandura's (1986) participant modeling technique (Chapter 4), in which a teacher initially models a skill, provides support, and gradually reduces aid as learners develop the skill. The notion also bears some relation to shaping (Chapter 3), as instructional supports are used to guide learners through various stages of skill acquisition.

Scaffolding is appropriate when a teacher wants to provide students with some information or complete parts of tasks so that learners can concentrate on the part of the task they are attempting to master. A teacher assisting children with organizing sentences in a paragraph to express ideas in a logical order initially might give them the sentences with word meanings and spellings so that these needs would not interfere with their primary task. As learners became more competent in sequencing ideas, the teacher might have students compose their own paragraphs while still assisting with word meanings and spellings. Eventually students will assume responsibility for these functions. Thus, the teacher creates a ZPD and provides the scaffolding for students to be successful (Moll, 2001; van de Pol et al., 2010).

Another application that reflects Vygotsky's ideas is *reciprocal teaching* (Chapter 7). Reciprocal teaching involves an interactive dialogue between a teacher and small group of students. Initially the teacher models the activities, after which the teacher and students take turns being the teacher. If students are learning to ask questions during reading comprehension, the instructional sequence might include the teacher modeling a question-asking strategy for determining level of understanding. From a Vygotskian perspective, reciprocal teaching comprises social interaction and scaffolding as students gradually develop skills.

An important application area is *peer collaboration*, which reflects the notion of collective activity (Bruner, 1984; Ratner, Foley, & Gimpert, 2002; see section on peer-assisted learning later in this chapter). When peers work on tasks cooperatively, the shared social interactions can serve an instructional function. Research shows that cooperative groups are most effective when each student has defined responsibilities and all learners must attain competence before any are allowed to progress (Slavin, 1995). Peer groups are commonly used during learning in fields such as mathematics, science, and language arts (Cobb, 1994; Cohen, 1994; DiPardo & Freedman, 1988; Geary, 1995; O'Donnell, 2006), which attests to the impact of the social environment during learning.

An application relevant to Vygotsky's theory and to situated cognition is social guidance through *apprenticeships* (Radziszewska & Rogoff, 1991; Rogoff, 1990). In apprenticeships, novices work closely with experts in joint work-related activities. Apprenticeships fit well with the ZPD because they occur in cultural institutions (e.g., schools, agencies) and thus help to transform learners' cognitive development. On the job, apprentices operate within a ZPD because they often work on tasks beyond their capabilities. By working with experts, novices develop a shared understanding of important processes and integrate this with their current understandings. Apprenticeships offer good examples of social constructivism in action.

Apprenticeships are used in many areas of education (Bailey, 1993). Student teachers work with cooperating teachers in schools and, once on the job, often are paired with experienced teachers for mentoring. Students conduct research with and are mentored by professors (Mullen, 2005). Counselor trainees serve internships under the direct guidance of a supervisor. On-the-job training programs use the apprentice model as students acquire skills while in the actual work setting and interacting with others. *Cognitive apprenticeships* are those aimed at teaching cognitive and metacognitive processes in academic content areas (Austin, 2009; Hunter, Laursen, & Seymour, 2006).

Some theorists contend that constructivism—and Vygotsky's theory in particular—represents a viable model for explaining how mathematics is learned (Ball et al., 2001; Cobb, 1994; Lampert, 1990). Mathematical knowledge is not passively absorbed from the environment but, rather, is constructed by individuals as a consequence of their interactions. This construction process also includes children's inventing of procedures that incorporate implicit rules.

The following unusual example illustrates rule-based procedural construction. Some time ago, I was working with a teacher to identify children in her class who might benefit from additional instruction in long division. She named several students and said that Tim also might qualify, but she was not sure. Some days he worked his problems correctly, whereas other days his work was incorrect and made no sense. I gave him problems to solve and asked him to verbalize while working because I was interested in what children thought about while they solved problems. This is what Tim said: "The problem is 17 divided into 436. I start on the side of the problem closest to the door . . . " I then knew why on some days his work was accurate and on other days it was not. It depended on which side of his body was closest to the door!

The process of constructing knowledge begins in the preschool years (Resnick, 1989). Geary (1995) distinguished *biologically primary* (biologically based) from *biologically secondary* (culturally taught) *abilities*. Biologically primary abilities are grounded in neurobiological systems that have evolved in particular ecological and social niches and that serve functions related to survival or reproduction. They should be seen cross-culturally, whereas biologically secondary abilities should show greater cultural specificity (e.g., as a function of contextual variables such as schools and other institutions). Furthermore, many of the former should be seen in very young children. Indeed, counting is a natural activity that preschoolers do without direct teaching (Resnick, 1985). Even infants may be sensitive to different properties of numbers (Geary, 1995).

Mathematical competence also depends on sociocultural influence (Cobb, 1994). Vygotsky (1978) stressed the role of competent other persons in the ZPD. The sociocultural influence is incorporated through such activities as peer teaching, instructional scaffolding, and apprenticeships.

Research supports the idea that social interactions are beneficial. Rittle-Johnson and Star (2007) found that seventh graders' mathematical proficiency was enhanced when they were allowed to compare solution methods with partners. Results of a literature review by Springer, Stanne, and Donovan (1999) showed that small-group learning significantly raised college students' achievement in mathematics and science. Kramarski and Mevarech (2003) found that combining cooperative learning with metacognitive instruction (e.g., reflecting on relevant concepts, deciding on appropriate strategies to use) raised eighth graders' mathematical reasoning more than either procedure alone. In addition to these benefits of cooperative learning (Stein & Carmine, 1999), the literature on peer and cross-age tutoring in mathematics reveals that it is effective in raising children's achievement (Robinson, Schofield, & Steers-Wentzell, 2005).

Despite its popularity and potential for application, some researchers believe it is difficult to evaluate the contributions of Vygotsky's (1978, 1987) theory to human development and learning (Tudge & Scrimsher, 2003). Educators have tended to focus on the ZPD without placing it in a larger theoretical context that is centered around cultural influence. Applications of Vygotsky's theory often are not part of the theory but rather seem to fit with it. When Wood et al. (1976) introduced the term *scaffolding*, for example, they presented it as a way for teachers to structure learning environments. As such, it has little relation to the dynamic ZPD that Vygotsky wrote about. Although reciprocal teaching also is not a Vygotskian concept, the concept (or process) captures much better this sense of dynamic, multidirectional interaction.

Debate over the theory often has focused on "Piaget versus Vygotsky," contrasting their presumably discrepant positions on the course of human development. Interestingly, however, they do not differ on many points (Duncan, 1995). While such debates may illuminate differences and provide testable research hypotheses, they are not helpful to educational practitioners seeking ways to help students learn.

Possibly the most significant implication of Vygotsky's theory for education is that the cultural–historical context is relevant to all forms of learning because learning does not occur in isolation. Student–teacher interactions are part of that context. Research has identified, for example, different interaction styles between Hawaiian, Anglo, and Navajo children (Tharp, 1989; Tharp & Gallimore, 1988). Whereas the Hawaiian culture encourages collaborative activity and more than one student talking at once, Navajo children are less acculturated to working in groups and more likely to wait to talk until the speaker is finished. Thus, the same instructional style would not be equally beneficial for all cultures. This point is especially noteworthy given the large influx of English language learners in U.S. schools. Being able to differentiate instruction to fit children's learning preferences is a key teaching skill.

PRIVATE SPEECH AND SOCIALLY MEDIATED LEARNING

A central premise of constructivism is that learning involves transforming and internalizing the social environment. This section discusses the pivotal roles of private speech and socially mediated learning.

Private Speech

Private speech is inner speech and refers to the set of speech phenomena that has a self-regulatory function but is not socially communicative (Alderson-Day & Fernyhough, 2015; Fuson, 1979). Various theories—including constructivism, cognitive–developmental, and social cognitive—establish a strong link between private speech and the development of self-regulation (Berk, 1986; Frauenglass & Diaz, 1985).

The historical impetus derives in part from work by Pavlov (1927). Recall from Chapter 3 that Pavlov distinguished the first (perceptual) from the second (linguistic) signal systems. Pavlov realized that principles of animal conditioning do not completely generalize to humans; human conditioning often occurs quickly with one or a few pairings of conditioned stimulus and unconditioned stimulus, in contrast to the multiple pairings required with animals. Pavlov believed that conditioning differences between humans and animals are largely due to the human capacity for language and thought. Stimuli may not produce conditioning automatically; people interpret stimuli in light of their prior experiences. Although Pavlov did not conduct research on the second signal system, subsequent investigations have validated his beliefs that human conditioning is complex and language plays a mediating role.

The Soviet psychologist Luria (1961) focused on the child's transition from the first to the second signal system. Luria postulated three stages in the development of verbal control of motor behavior. Initially, the speech of others is primarily responsible for directing the child's behavior (ages 1.5 to 2.5). During the second stage (ages 3 to 4), the child's overt verbalizations (i.e., self-talk) initiate motor behaviors but do not necessarily inhibit them. In the third stage, the child's private speech becomes capable of initiating, directing, and inhibiting motor behaviors (ages 4.5 to 5.5). Luria believed this private, self-regulatory speech directs behavior through neurophysiological mechanisms.

The mediating and self-directing role of the second signal system is embodied in Vygotsky's theory. Vygotsky (1962) believed private speech helps develop thought by organizing behavior. Children employ private speech to understand situations and surmount difficulties. Private speech occurs in conjunction with children's interactions in the social environment. As children's language facility develops, words spoken by others acquire meaning independent of their phonological and syntactical qualities. Children internalize meanings and use them to self-regulate their behaviors (Alderson-Day & Fernyhough, 2015; see Chapter 10).

Vygotsky hypothesized that private speech follows a curvilinear developmental pattern: Overt verbalization (self-talk or thinking aloud) increases until ages 6 to 7, after which it declines and becomes primarily covert (internal) by ages 8 to 10. However, overt verbalization can occur at any age when people encounter problems or difficulties. Research shows that although the amount of private speech decreases from approximately ages 4 or 5 to

8, the proportion of private speech that is self-regulating and goal directed increases with age (Winsler, Carlton, & Barry, 2000). In many research investigations, the actual amount of private speech is small, and many children do not verbalize at all. Thus, the developmental pattern of private speech seems more complex than originally hypothesized.

Verbalization and Achievement

Verbalization of rules, procedures, and strategies can improve student learning. Although Meichenbaum's (1977, 1986) *self-instructional training* procedure (Chapter 4) is not rooted in constructivism, it re-creates the overt-to-covert developmental progression of private speech. Types of statements modeled are *problem definition* ("What is it I have to do?"), *focusing of attention* ("I need to pay attention to what I'm doing"), *planning and response guidance* ("I need to work carefully"), *self-reinforcement* ("I'm doing fine"), *self-evaluation* ("Am I doing things in the right order?"), and *coping* ("I need to try again when I don't get it right"). Teachers can use self-instructional training to teach learners cognitive and motor skills, and it can create a positive task outlook and foster perseverance in the face of difficulties (Meichenbaum & Asarnow, 1979). The procedure need not be scripted; learners can construct their own verbalizations. Self-talk is positively associated with self-regulation (Kross et al., 2014).

Thinking aloud has been employed in many research studies (Ericsson & Fox, 2011). Verbalization seems beneficial for students who often experience learning and performance difficulties. Positive results have been obtained with children who do not spontaneously rehearse material to be learned, impulsive learners, students with learning disabilities and mental retardation, and learners who require remedial experiences (Schunk, 1986). Verbalization helps students with learning problems work at tasks systematically (Hallahan et al., 1983). It forces students to attend to tasks and rehearse content to be learned. Verbalization does not seem to facilitate learning when students can handle task demands adequately without verbalizing. Because verbalization constitutes an additional task, it might interfere with learning by distracting children from the task at hand.

Berk (1986) studied first and third graders' spontaneous private speech. Task-relevant overt speech was negatively related and faded verbalization (whispers, lip movements, muttering) was positively related to mathematical performance. These results were obtained for first graders of high intelligence and third graders of average intelligence; among third graders of high intelligence, overt and faded speech showed no relationship to achievement. For the latter students, internalized self-guiding speech apparently is the most effective. Daugherty and White (2008) found that private speech related positively to indexes of creativity among Head Start and low socioeconomic status preschoolers.

Schunk (1982b) instructed students who lacked division skills. Some students verbalized explicit statements (e.g., "check," "multiply," "copy"), others constructed their own verbalizations, a third group verbalized the statements and their own verbalizations, and students in a fourth condition did not verbalize. Self-constructed verbalizations—alone or combined with the statements—led to the highest division skill.

In summary, verbalization is more likely to promote student achievement if it is relevant to the task and does not interfere with performance. Higher proportions of task-relevant statements produce better learning (Schunk & Gunn, 1986). Private speech follows an overt-to-covert developmental cycle, and speech becomes internalized earlier in students with higher intelligence (Berk, 1986; Frauenglass & Diaz, 1985). Private speech relates positively to creativity. Allowing students to construct their verbalizations—possibly in conjunction with verbalizing steps in a strategy—is more beneficial than limiting verbalizing to specific statements. To facilitate transfer and maintenance, overt verbalization should eventually be faded to whispering or lip movements and then to a covert (silent) level. Internalization is a key feature of self-regulated learning (Schunk, 1999; Chapter 10).

These benefits of verbalization do not mean that all students ought to verbalize while learning. That practice would result in a loud classroom and would distract many students! Rather, verbalization could be incorporated into instruction for students having difficulties learning. A teacher or classroom aide could work with such students individually or in groups to avoid disrupting the work of other class members. Application 8.5 discusses ways to integrate verbalization into learning.

APPLICATION 8.5
Self-Verbalization

A teacher might use self-verbalization (self-talk) in a special education resource room or in a regular or inclusive classroom to assist students having difficulty attending to material and mastering skills. When introducing long division, a teacher might use verbalization to help children who cannot remember the steps to complete the procedure. Children can verbalize and apply the following steps:

- Will (number) go into (number)?
- Divide.
- Multiply:
  (number) × (number) = (number).
- Write down the answer.
- Subtract:
  (number) − (number) = (number).
- Bring down the next number.
- Repeat steps.

Use of self-talk helps students stay on task and builds their self-efficacy to work systematically. Once they begin to grasp the content, it is to their advantage to fade verbalizations to a covert (silent) level so they can work more rapidly.

Self-verbalization also can help students who are learning sport skills and strategies. They might verbalize what is happening and what moves they should make. A tennis coach, for example, might encourage students to use self-talk during practice matches: "high ball—overhand return," "low ball—underhand return," "cross ball—backhand return."

Aerobic and dance instructors could use self-talk during practice. A ballet teacher might have young students repeat "paint a rainbow" for a flowing arm movement, and "walk on eggs" to get them to move lightly on their toes. Participants in aerobic exercise classes also might verbalize movements (e.g., "bend and stretch," "slide right and around") as they perform them.

Socially Mediated Learning

Many forms of constructivism, and Vygotsky's theory in particular, stress the idea that learning is a socially mediated process. This focus is not unique to constructivism; many other learning theories emphasize social processes as having a significant impact on learning. Bandura's (1986, 1997) social cognitive theory (Chapter 4), for example, highlights the reciprocal relations among learners and social environmental influences, and researchers have shown that social modeling is a powerful influence on learning (Schunk, 1987). In Vygotsky's theory, however, social mediation of learning is a central construct (Karpov & Haywood, 1998; Moll, 2001; Tudge & Scrimsher, 2003). All learning is mediated by tools such as language, symbols, and signs. Children acquire these tools during their social interactions with others. They internalize these tools and then use them as mediators of more advanced learning (i.e., higher cognitive processes such as concept learning and problem solving).

As an example, let us examine how social mediation influences concept acquisition. Young children acquire concepts spontaneously by observing their worlds and formulating hypotheses. For example, they hear the noise that cars make and the noise that trucks make, and they may believe that bigger objects make more noise. They have difficulty accommodating discrepant observations (e.g., a motorcycle is smaller than a car or truck but may make more noise than either).

Through social interactions, children are taught concepts by others (e.g., teachers, parents, older siblings). This often occurs directly, as when teachers instruct students on the differences between squares, rectangles, triangles, and circles. Children use the tools of language and symbols to internalize these concepts.

It is, of course, possible to learn on one's own without social interactions. For example, Wirkala and Kuhn (2011) investigated problem-based learning among middle school students. Some learners worked individually, whereas others participated in small groups. The results showed that problem-based learning led to higher achievement compared with a lecture–discussion condition, but the problem-based learning individual and group conditions did not differ. Thus, the opportunity for socially mediated learning did not lead to greater benefits.

But even such independent learning is, in a constructivist sense, socially mediated, because it involves the tools (i.e., language, signs, symbols) that have been acquired through previous social interactions. Further, a certain amount of labeling is needed. Children may learn a concept but not have a name for it ("What do you call a thing that looks like ———?"). The label involves language and often is supplied by another person.

A central premise of contemporary learning theories that reflects constructivism is that people construct *implicit theories* about their environments and revise those theories as they encounter new evidence. Beginning at an early age, children construct theories of their minds and those of others, along with their understanding of the physical and biological worlds (Gopnik & Wellman, 2012). Children's learning and thinking occur in the context of these implicit theories.

Social interactions are critical for cognitive development. Learners may not simply build memory networks based on experience. Their understandings are situated in their theories of the world and include epistemic beliefs about the usefulness and importance of knowledge, how it relates to what else they know, and in what situations it may be appropriate. Cultural tools are essential for promoting the development of learners' implicit theories and understandings.

Tools are useful not only for learning but also for teaching. Students teach one another things they have learned. Vygotsky (1962, 1978) believed that by being used for social purposes, tools exert powerful influences on others.

These points suggest that preparation is needed for learners to effectively construct knowledge. The teaching of the basic tools to learn can be direct. There is no need for students to construct the obvious or what they can be easily taught. Constructed discoveries are the result of basic learning, not their cause (Karpov & Haywood, 1998). Teachers should prepare students to learn by teaching them the tools and then providing opportunities for learning. Applications of socially mediated learning are discussed in Application 8.6.

APPLICATION 8.6
Socially Mediated Learning

Socially mediated learning is appropriate for students of all ages. Teacher education faculty members know that success in teaching depends in part on understanding the cultures of the communities served by schools. Dr. Mayer obtains consent from the schools where her students are placed and from the parents, and she assigns each student to be a "buddy" of a schoolchild. As part of their placements, her students spend extra time with their buddies—for example, working one-to-one, eating lunch with them, riding home on the school bus with them, and visiting them in their homes. She pairs her students, and the members of each dyad meet regularly to discuss the culture of their assigned buddies, such as what their buddies like about school, what their parents or guardians do, and characteristics of the neighborhoods where their buddies live. She meets regularly with each dyad to discuss the implications of the cultural variables for school learning. Through social interactions with buddies, Dr. Mayer, and other class members, the students develop a better understanding of the role of culture in schooling.

Historical events typically are open to multiple interpretations. As part of a unit on post–World War II changes in American life, Ms. Schmitz organizes students into five teams. Each team is assigned a topic: medicine, transportation, education, technology, and housing. Teams prepare a presentation on why their topic represents a significant advance in American life. Students on each team work together to prepare the presentation, and each member presents part of it. After the presentations are finished, Ms. Schmitz leads a discussion with the class. She tries to get them to see how advances are interrelated: for example, technology influences medicine, transportation, and education; more automobiles and roads lead to growth in housing; and better education results in preventative medicine. Social mediation through discussions and presentations helps students gain a deeper understanding of changes in American life.

Peer-Assisted Learning

Peer-assisted learning methods fit well with constructivism. *Peer-assisted learning* refers to instructional approaches in which peers serve as active agents in the learning process (Rohrbeck et al., 2003). Methods emphasizing peer-assisted learning include peer tutoring (covered in Chapter 4 and this section), reciprocal teaching (Chapter 7), and cooperative learning (this section; Palincsar & Brown, 1984; Slavin, 1995; Strain et al., 1981).

Peer-assisted learning has been shown to promote achievement. In their review of the literature, Rohrbeck et al. (2003) found that peer-assisted learning was most effective with younger (first through third graders), urban, low-income, and minority children. These are promising results, given the risk to academic achievement associated with urban, low-income, and minority students. Rohrbeck et al. did not find significant differences due to content area (e.g., reading, mathematics). In addition to the learning benefits, peer-assisted learning also can foster academic and social motivation for learning (Ginsburg-Block, Rohrbeck, & Fantuzzo, 2006; Rohrbeck et al., 2003). Peers who stress academic learning convey its importance, which then can motivate others in the social environment.

As with other instructional models, teachers need to consider the desired learning outcomes in determining whether peer-assisted learning should be used. Some types of lessons (e.g., those emphasizing inquiry skills) would seem to be ideally suited for this approach, and especially if the development of social outcomes also is an objective.

Peer Tutoring. *Peer tutoring* captures many of the principles of constructivist teaching. Students are active in the learning process; tutor and tutee freely participate. The one-to-one context may encourage tutees to ask questions that they might be reluctant to ask in a large class. There is research evidence that peer tutoring can lead to greater achievement gains than traditional instruction (Fuchs, Fuchs, Mathes, & Simmons, 1997).

Peer tutoring also encourages cooperation among students and helps to diversify the class structure. A teacher might split the class into small tutoring groups while continuing to work with a different group. The content of the tutoring is tailored to the specific needs of the tutee.

Teachers likely will need to instruct peer tutors to ensure that they possess the requisite academic and tutoring skills. It also should be clear what the tutoring session is expected to accomplish. A specific goal is preferable to a general one—thus, "Work with Mike to help him understand how to regroup from the 10s column," rather than "Work with Mike to help him get better in subtraction."

Cooperative Learning. *Cooperative learning* is a form of socially mediated learning that is frequently used in classrooms (Slavin, 1994, 1995), but when it is not properly structured, it can lead to poorer learning compared with whole-class instruction. In cooperative learning, the objective is to develop in students the ability to work collaboratively with others. The task should be one that is too extensive for a single student to complete in a timely fashion. The task also should lend itself well to a group, such as by having components that can be completed by individual students who then merge their individual work into a final product.

There are certain principles that help cooperative groups be successful. One is to form groups with students who are likely to work together well and who can develop and practice cooperative skills. This does not necessarily mean allowing students to choose groups, since they may select their friends and some students may be left without a group. It also does not necessarily mean heterogeneous groupings, where different ability levels are represented. Although that strategy often is recommended, research shows that high-achieving peers do not always benefit from being grouped with lower achievers (Hogan & Tudge, 1999), and the self-efficacy of lower achievers will not necessarily improve by watching higher achievers succeed (Schunk & DiBenedetto, 2016). Whatever the means of grouping, teachers should ensure that each group can succeed with reasonable effort.

Groups also need guidance on what they are to accomplish—what is the expected product—as well as the expected mode of behavior. The task should be one that requires interdependence; no group member should be able to accomplish most of the entire task single-handedly. Ideally, the task also will allow for different approaches. For example, to address the topic of "Pirates in America," a group of middle school students might give a presentation, use posters, conduct a skit, and involve class members in a treasure hunt.

Finally, it is important to ensure that each group member is accountable. If grades are given, it is necessary for group members to document what their overall contributions were to the group. A group in which only two of six members do most of the work but everyone receives an "A" is likely to breed resentment.

Two variations of cooperative learning are the jigsaw method and STAD (student-teams-achievement divisions). In the *jigsaw method*, teams work on material that is subdivided into parts. After each team studies the material, each team member takes responsibility for one part. The team members from each group meet together to discuss their part, after which they return to their teams to help other team members learn more about their part (Slavin, 1994). This jigsaw method combines many desirable features of cooperative learning, including group work, individual responsibility, and clear goals.

STAD groups study material after it has been presented by the teacher (Slavin, 1994). Group members practice and study together but are tested individually. Each member's score contributes to the overall group score; but, because scores are based on improvement, each group member is motivated to improve—that is, individual improvements raise the overall group score. Although STAD is a form of cooperative learning, it seems best suited for material with well-defined objectives or problems with clear answers—for example, mathematical computations and social studies facts. Given its emphasis on improvement, STAD will not work as well where conceptual understanding is involved because student gains may not occur quickly.

CONSTRUCTIVIST LEARNING ENVIRONMENTS

Learning environments created to reflect constructivist principles look quite different from traditional classrooms (Brooks & Brooks, 1999). Learning in a constructivist setting is not allowing students to do whatever they want; rather, constructivist environments should create rich experiences that encourage learning. This section describes key features of constructivist learning environments to include reflective teaching.

Key Features

Constructivist classrooms have several distinctive features that differ from those of traditional classrooms (Brooks & Brooks, 1999). In traditional classes, basic skills are emphasized. The curriculum is presented in small parts (e.g., units, lessons). Teachers disseminate information to students didactically and seek answers to questions. Assessment of student learning is distinct from teaching and usually done through testing. Students often work alone.

In constructivist classrooms, the curriculum focuses on big concepts. Activities typically involve primary data sources and manipulative materials. Teachers interact with students by seeking their questions and points of view. Assessment is authentic; it is interwoven with teaching and includes teacher observations and student portfolios. Students often work in groups. The idea is to structure the learning environment such that students can effectively construct new knowledge and skills (Schuh, 2003).

Some guiding principles of constructivist learning environments are shown in Table 8.6 (Brooks & Brooks, 1999). One principle is that teachers should *pose problems of emerging relevance* to students, where relevance is pre-existing or emerges through teacher mediation. Thus, a teacher might structure a lesson around questions that challenge students' preconceptions. This takes time, which means that other critical content may not be covered. Relevance is not established by threatening to test students, but rather by stimulating their interest and helping them discover how the problem affects their lives.

A second principle is that *learning should be structured around primary concepts*. This means that teachers design activities around conceptual clusters of questions and problems so that ideas are presented holistically rather than in isolation (Brooks & Brooks, 1999). Being able to see the whole helps to understand the parts.

Holistic teaching does not require sacrificing content, but it does involve structuring content differently. A piecemeal approach to teaching history is to present information chronologically as a series of events. In contrast, a holistic method involves presenting themes that recur in history (e.g., economic hardships, disputes over territory) and structuring content so that students can discover these themes in different eras. Students then can see that although environmental features change over time (e.g., armies → air forces; farming → manufacturing), the themes remain the same.

Holistic teaching also can be done across subjects. In the middle school curriculum, for example, the theme of "courage" can be explored in social studies (e.g., courage of people to stand up and act based on their beliefs when these conflict with governments), language arts (e.g., characters in literature who display courage), and science (e.g., courage of scientists who dispute prevailing theories). An integrated curriculum in which teachers plan units together reflects this holism.

Table 8.6
Guiding principles of constructivist learning environments.

- Pose problems of emerging relevance to students.
- Structure learning around primary concepts.
- Seek and value students' points of view.
- Adapt curriculum to address students' suppositions.
- Assess student learning in the context of teaching.

Third, it is important to *seek and value students' points of view*. Understanding students' perspectives is essential for planning activities that are challenging and interesting. This requires that teachers ask questions, stimulate discussions, and listen to what students say. Teachers who make little effort to understand what students think fail to capitalize on the role of their experiences in learning. This is not to suggest that teachers should analyze every student utterance; that is not necessary, nor is there time to do it. Rather, teachers should try to learn students' conceptions of a topic.

With the current emphasis on achievement test scores, it is easy to focus only on students' correct answers. Constructivist education, however, requires that—where feasible—we go beyond the answer and learn how the students arrived at that answer. Teachers do this by asking students to elaborate on their answers; for example, "How did you arrive at that answer?" or "Why do you think that?" It is possible for a student to arrive at a correct answer through faulty reasoning and, conversely, to answer incorrectly but engage in sound thinking. Students' perspectives on a situation or theories about a phenomenon help teachers in curriculum planning.

Fourth, we should *adapt curriculum to address students' suppositions*. This means that curricular demands on students should align with the beliefs they bring to the classroom. When there is a gross mismatch, lessons will lack meaning for students. But alignment need not be perfect. Demands that are slightly above students' present capabilities (i.e., within the zone of proximal development) produce challenge and learning.

When students' suppositions are incorrect, the typical response is to inform them of such. Instead, constructivist teaching challenges students to discover the information. Recall the opening vignette describing the mystery substance experiment. Students were baffled by the substance, which seemed at the same time both a liquid and solid. The teacher did not give them answers but rather challenged them to think about the substance and construct their understanding of it. By the end of the vignette, students still are not clear what the substance is, which suggests that more experimentation and discussion will follow.

Finally, constructivist education requires that we *assess student learning in the context of teaching*. This point runs counter to the typical classroom situation where most learning assessments are disconnected from teaching—for example, end-of-grade tests, end-of-unit exams, pop quizzes. Although the content of these assessments may align well with learning objectives addressed during instruction, the assessment occasions are separate from teaching.

In a constructivist environment, assessment occurs continuously during teaching and is an assessment of both students and teacher. In the opening vignette, the teacher assesses students' thinking throughout the experiment, as well as her own success in designing an activity and guiding the students to construct their understandings.

Of course, assessment methods must reflect the type of learning (Chapter 1). Constructivist environments are best designed for meaningful, deep-structure learning, not for superficial understanding. True–false and multiple-choice tests may be inappropriate to assess learning outcomes. Authentic forms of assessment may require students to write reflective pieces, discussing what they learned and why this knowledge is useful in the world, or to demonstrate and apply skills.

Constructivist assessment is less concerned about right and wrong answers than about next steps after students answer. This type of authentic assessment guides instructional decisions, but it is difficult because it forces teachers to design activities that elicit student feedback and then alter instruction as needed. It is much easier to design and score a multiple-choice test, but encouraging teachers to teach constructively and then assess separately in a traditional manner sends a mixed message. Given the present emphasis on accountability, we may never completely move to authentic assessment, but encouraging it facilitates curricular planning and provides for more-interesting lessons than drilling students to pass tests.

APA Learner-Centered Principles

The American Psychological Association formulated a set of learner-centered psychological principles (American Psychological Association Work Group of the Board of Educational Affairs, 1997; Table 8.7) that reflect a constructivist learning approach. They were developed as guidelines for school design and reform.

The principles are grouped into four major categories: cognitive and metacognitive factors, motivational and affective factors, developmental and social factors, and individual differences. Cognitive and metacognitive factors involve the nature of the learning process, learning goals, construction of knowledge, strategic thinking, thinking about thinking, and the content of learning. Motivational and affective factors reflect motivational and emotional influences on learning, the intrinsic motivation to learn, and the effects of motivation on effort. Developmental and social factors include physical, cognitive, emotional, and social developmental differences, as well as social interactions and communications. Individual differences comprise individual difference variables, learning and diversity, and standards and assessment. These principles are reflected in current work on standards reform to address 21st century skills (White & DiBenedetto, 2015).

Application 8.7 illustrates ways to apply these principles in learning environments. In considering their application, educators should keep in mind the purpose of the instruction and the uses to which it will be put. Teacher-centered instruction often is the appropriate means of instruction and the most efficient. But when deeper student understanding is desired—along with greater student activity—the principles offer sound guidelines.

Reflective Teaching

Reflective teaching is based on thoughtful decision making that takes into account knowledge about students, contexts, psychological processes, learning and motivation, and oneself. Although reflective teaching is not part of a constructivist perspective on learning, its premises are based on the assumptions of constructivism (Armstrong & Savage, 2002).

Components. Reflective teaching stands in stark contrast to traditional teaching in which a teacher prepares a lesson, presents it to a class, gives students assignments and feedback, and evaluates their learning. Reflective teaching assumes that teaching cannot be reduced to one method to use with all students. Each teacher brings a unique set of experiences to teaching. How teachers interpret situations will differ depending on their experiences and perceptions. Professional development requires that teachers reflect on their beliefs and theories about students, content, context, and learning and check the validity of these beliefs and theories against reality.

Table 8.7
APA learner-centered principles.

1. *Nature of the learning process.* The learning of complex subject matter is most effective when it is an intentional process of constructing meaning from information and experience.

2. *Goals of the learning process.* The successful learner, over time and with support and instructional guidance, can create meaningful, coherent representations of knowledge.

3. *Construction of knowledge.* The successful learner can link new information with existing knowledge in meaningful ways.

4. *Strategic thinking.* The successful learner can create and use a repertoire of thinking and reasoning strategies to achieve complex learning goals.

5. *Thinking about thinking.* Higher-order strategies for selecting and monitoring mental operations facilitate creative and critical thinking.

6. *Context of learning.* Learning is influenced by environmental factors, including culture, technology, and instructional practices.

Motivational and Affective Factors

7. *Motivational and emotional influences on learning.* What and how much is learned is influenced by the learner's motivation. Motivation to learn, in turn, is influenced by the individual's emotional states, beliefs, interests and goals, and habits of thinking.

8. *Intrinsic motivation to learn.* The learner's creativity, higher-order thinking, and natural curiosity all contribute to motivation to learn. Intrinsic motivation is stimulated by tasks of optimal novelty and difficulty, tasks that are relevant to personal interests, and tasks that provide for personal choice and control.

9. *Effects of motivation on effort.* Acquisition of complex knowledge and skills requires extended learner effort and guided practice. Without learners' motivation to learn, the willingness to exert this effort is unlikely without coercion.

Development and Social Factors

10. *Developmental influences on learning.* As individuals develop, there are different opportunities and constraints for learning. Learning is most effective when differential development within and across physical, intellectual, emotional, and social domains is taken into account.

11. *Social influences on learning.* Learning is influenced by social interactions, interpersonal relations, and communication with others.

Individual Differences Factors

12. *Individual differences in learning.* Learners have different strategies, approaches, and capabilities for learning that are a function of prior experience and heredity.

13. *Learning and diversity.* Learning is most effective when differences in learners' linguistic, cultural, and social backgrounds are taken into account.

14. *Standards and assessment.* Setting appropriately high and challenging standards and assessing the learner as well as learning progress—including diagnostic, process, and outcome assessment—are integral parts of the learning process.

Source: Based on "Learner-Centered Psychological Principles: A Framework for School Reform and Redesign." Copyright ©1997 by the American Psychological Association.

APPLICATION 8.7
Learner-Centered Principles

Mr. Donavan applies the APA learner-centered principles in his economics classes. He knows that many students are not intrinsically motivated to learn economics, so he builds into the curriculum strategies to enhance interest. He makes use of videos, field trips, and role-playing to link economics better with real-world experiences. Mr. Donavan also does not want students to simply memorize content but rather learn to think critically. He teaches them a strategy to analyze events that includes key questions such as: What preceded the event? How might it have turned out differently? And how did this event influence future developments? Because he likes to focus on themes (e.g., economic development and policy), he has students apply these themes throughout the school year to different events.

Dr. Raimond is familiar with the APA principles and incorporates them into his teaching of educational psychology. He knows that students must have a good understanding of developmental, social, and individual difference variables if they are to be successful teachers. For their field placements, he ensures that students work in diverse settings. Students are assigned at different times to classes with younger and older students. He also ensures that students have the opportunity to work in classes where there is diversity in ethnic and socioeconomic backgrounds of students and with teachers whose methods use social interactions (e.g., cooperative learning, tutoring). Dr. Raimond understands the importance of students' reflections on their experiences. They write journals on the field placement experiences and share these in class. He helps students understand how to link these experiences to topics they study in the course (e.g., development, motivation, learning).

Henderson (1996) listed four components of reflective teaching that involve decision making (Table 8.8). Teaching decisions must be sensitive to the context, which includes the school, content, students' backgrounds, time of the year, educational expectations, and the like. Fluid planning means that instructional plans must be flexible and change as conditions warrant. When students do not understand a lesson, it makes little sense to reteach it in the same way. Rather, the plan must be modified to aid student understanding.

Henderson's model puts emphasis on teachers' personal knowledge. They should be aware of why they do what they do and be keen observers of situations. They must reflect on and process a wide variety of information about situations. Their decisions are strengthened by professional development. Teachers must have a strong knowledge base from which to draw in order to engage in flexible planning and tailor lessons to student and contextual differences.

Reflective teachers actively seek solutions to problems rather than wait for others to tell them what to do. They persist until they find the best solution rather than settle for one that is less than satisfactory. They are ethical and ask what is best for learners rather than what is best for themselves. Reflective teachers also thoughtfully consider evidence by

Table 8.8 Components of reflective teaching.	■ Sensitive to the context
	■ Guided by fluid planning
	■ Informed by professional and personal knowledge that is critically examined
	■ Enhanced by formal and informal professional growth opportunities

mentally reviewing classroom events and revising their practices to better serve students' needs. In summary, reflective teachers (Armstrong & Savage, 2002):

- Use context considerations
- Use personal knowledge
- Use professional knowledge
- Make fluid plans
- Commit to formal and informal professional growth opportunities

We can see assumptions of constructivism that underlie these points. Constructivism places heavy emphasis on the context of learning because learning is situated. People construct knowledge about themselves (e.g., their capabilities, interests, attitudes) and about their profession from their experiences. Teaching is not a lockstep function that proceeds immutably once a lesson is designed. And finally, there is no "graduation" from teaching. Conditions always are changing, and teachers must stay at the forefront in terms of content, psychological knowledge of learning and motivation, and student individual differences.

Becoming a Reflective Teacher. Being a reflective teacher is a skill, and, like other skills, it requires instruction and practice. The following suggestions are useful in developing this skill.

Being a reflective teacher requires good *personal knowledge*. Teachers have beliefs about their teaching competencies to include subject knowledge, pedagogical knowledge, and student capabilities. To develop personal knowledge, teachers reflect on and assess these beliefs. Self-questioning is helpful. For example, teachers might ask themselves: "What do I know about the subjects I teach?" "How confident am I that I can teach these subjects so that students can acquire skills?" "How confident am I that I can establish an effective classroom climate that facilitates learning?" "What do I believe about how students can learn?" "Do I hold biases (e.g., that students from some ethnic or socioeconomic backgrounds cannot learn as well as other students)?"

Personal knowledge is important because it forms the basis from which to seek improvement. For example, teachers who feel they are not well skilled in using technology to teach social studies can seek out professional development to aid them. If they find that they have biases, they can employ strategies so that their beliefs do not cause negative effects. Thus, if they believe that some students cannot learn as well as others, they can seek ways to help the former students learn better.

Being a reflective teacher also requires *professional knowledge*. Effective teachers are well skilled in their disciplines, understand classroom management techniques, and have knowledge about human development. Teachers who reflect on their professional knowledge and recognize deficiencies can correct them, such as by taking university courses or participating in staff development sessions.

Like other professionals, teachers must keep abreast of current developments in their fields. They can do this by belonging to professional organizations, attending conferences, subscribing to journals and periodicals, and discussing issues with colleagues.

Third, reflective teaching means *planning and assessing*. When reflective teachers plan, they do so with the goal of reaching all students. Many good ideas for lesson plans can be garnered from colleagues and practitioner journals. When students have difficulty grasping content presented in a certain way, reflective teachers consider other methods for attaining the same objective.

Assessment works together with planning. Reflective teachers ask how they will assess students' learning outcomes. To gain knowledge of assessment methods, teachers may need to take courses or participate in professional development. The authentic methods that are in vogue now offer many possibilities for assessing outcomes, but teachers may need to consult with assessment experts and receive training on their use.

INSTRUCTIONAL APPLICATIONS

The educational literature is replete with examples of instructional applications that reflect constructivist principles. Some are summarized in this section.

The task facing teachers who attempt to implement constructivist principles can be challenging. Many are unprepared to teach in a constructivist fashion (Elkind, 2004), especially if their preparation programs have not stressed it. There also are factors associated with schools and school systems that work against constructivism (Windschitl, 2002). For example, school administrators and teachers are held accountable for students' scores on standardized tests. These tests typically emphasize basic skills and downgrade the importance of deeper conceptual understanding. School cultures also may work against constructivism, especially if teachers have been teaching in the same fashion for many years and have standard curricula and lessons. Parents, too, may not be fully supportive of teachers using less direction in the classroom in favor of time for students to construct their understandings. And some constructivist instructional applications may work best with students who are successfully engaged in learning. Learners who experience difficulties may benefit more from direct instruction.

Despite these issues, there are many ways that teachers can incorporate constructivist teaching and learning into their instruction and especially for topics that lend themselves well (e.g., discussion issues where there is no clearly correct answer). Three applications discussed here are discovery learning, inquiry teaching, and discussions and debates.

Discovery Learning

The Process of Discovery. *Discovery learning* refers to obtaining knowledge for oneself (Bruner, 1961). Discovery involves constructing and testing hypotheses rather than simply reading or listening to teacher presentations. Discovery is a type of *inductive reasoning*, because students move from studying specific examples to formulating general rules, concepts, and principles. Discovery learning also is referred to as problem-based, inquiry, experiential, and constructivist learning (Kirschner, Sweller, & Clark, 2006).

Discovery is a form of problem solving (Klahr & Simon, 1999; Chapter 7); it is not simply letting students do what they want. Although discovery is a minimally guided instructional approach, it involves direction; teachers arrange activities in which students search, manipulate, explore, and investigate. The opening scenario represents a discovery situation. Students learn new knowledge relevant to the domain and such general problem-solving skills as formulating rules, testing hypotheses, and gathering information (Bruner, 1961).

Although some discoveries may be accidents that happen to lucky people, in fact most are planned and predictable. Consider how Pasteur developed the cholera vaccine (Root-Bernstein, 1988). Pasteur went on vacation during the summer of 1879. He had been conducting research on chicken cholera and left out germ cultures when he departed for 2 months.

> Upon his return, he found that the cultures, though still active, had become avirulent; they no longer could sicken a chicken. So he developed a new set of cultures from a natural outbreak of the disease and resumed his work. Yet he found . . . that the hens he had exposed to the weakened germ culture still failed to develop cholera. Only then did it dawn on Pasteur that he had inadvertently immunized them. (p. 26)

This exemplifies most discoveries, which are not flukes but rather a natural (albeit possibly unforeseen) consequence of systematic inquiry by the discoverer. Discoverers cultivate their discoveries by expecting the unexpected. Pasteur did not leave the germ cultures unattended but rather in the care of his collaborator, Roux. When Pasteur returned from vacation, he inoculated chickens with the germs, and they did not become sick.

> But when the same chickens were later injected with a more virulent strain, they died. No discovery here . . . Pasteur did not even initiate his first successful enfeeblement experiment until a few months later. . . . He and Roux had tried to enfeeble the germs by passing them from one animal to another, by growing them in different media . . . and only after many such attempts did one of the experiments succeed. . . . For some time, the strains that failed to kill chickens were also too weak to immunize them. But by March of 1880, Pasteur had developed two cultures with the properties of vaccines. The trick . . . was to use a mildly acidic medium, not a strong one, and to leave the germ culture sitting in it for a long time. Thus, he produced an attenuated organism capable of inducing an immune response in chickens. The discovery . . . was not an accident at all; Pasteur had posed a question—Is it possible to immunize an animal with a weakened infectious agent?—and then systematically searched for the answer. (Root-Bernstein, 1988, p. 29)

To discover knowledge, students require background knowledge (Chapter 5). Once students possess prerequisite knowledge, careful structuring of content allows them to discover important principles.

Teaching for Discovery. Teaching for discovery requires presenting questions, problems, or puzzling situations to resolve and encouraging learners to make intuitive guesses when they are uncertain. In leading a class discussion, teachers could ask questions that have no readily available answers and tell students that their answers will not be graded, which forces students to construct their understandings. Discoveries are not limited to activities within school. During a unit on ecology, students could discover why animals of a given species live in certain areas and not in others. Students might seek answers in classroom workstations, in the school media center, and on or off the school grounds. Teachers provide structure by posing questions and giving suggestions on how to search for answers. Greater teacher structure is beneficial when students are not familiar with the discovery procedure or require extensive background knowledge. Other examples are given in Application 8.8.

Discovery is not appropriate for all types of learning. Discovery can impede learning when students have no prior experience with the material or background information (Tuovinen & Sweller, 1999). Teaching for discovery learning may not be appropriate with well-structured content that is easily presented. Students could discover which historical events occurred in which years, but this is trivial learning. If they arrived at the wrong answers, time would be wasted in reteaching the content. Discovery seems more appropriate when the learning process is important, such as with problem-solving activities that motivate students to learn and acquire the requisite skills. However, establishing discovery situations (e.g., growing plants) often takes time, and experiments might not work.

As a type of minimally guided instruction, discovery learning can enhance students' problem solving and self-regulated learning (Hmelo-Silver, 2004), but it has drawn criticism.

APPLICATION 8.8
Discovery Learning

Learning becomes more meaningful when students explore their learning environments rather than listen passively to teachers. An elementary teacher used guided discovery to help her children learn animal groups (e.g., mammals, birds, reptiles). Rather than providing students with the basic animal groups and examples for each, she asked students to provide the names of types of animals. Then she helped students classify the animals by examining their similarities and differences. Category labels were assigned once classifications are made. This approach is guided to ensure that classifications are proper, but students are active contributors as they discover the similarities and differences among animals.

A high school chemistry teacher might use "mystery" liquids and have students discover the elements in each. The students could proceed through a series of tests designed to determine if certain substances are present in a sample. By using the experimental process, students learn about the reactions of substances to certain chemicals and also how to determine the contents of their substances.

A university professor uses problem-based learning activities in his class. He creates different classroom scenarios that describe situations involving student learning and behaviors, as well as teacher actions. He divides his students into small groups and asks them to work through each scenario and discover which learning principles best describe the situations presented.

Mayer (2004) reviewed research from the 1950s to the 1980s that compared pure discovery learning (i.e., unguided, problem-based learning) with guided instruction. The research showed that guided instruction produced superior learning. In a subsequent review, Alfieri, Brooks, Aldrich, and Tenenbaum (2011) found that explicit instruction promoted learning outcomes better than unassisted discovery.

Notice that these criticisms pertain to minimally guided instruction. Alfieri et al. (2011) also found in their review that assisted (guided) discovery was generally more effective than other forms of instruction. In guided discovery, teachers arrange the situation such that learners are not left to their own devices but rather receive support. Guided discovery also makes good use of the social environment—a key feature of constructivism. Supports (scaffolding) for learning can be minimized when learners have developed some skills and therefore can guide themselves. In deciding whether to use discovery, teachers should take into account the learning objectives (e.g., acquire knowledge or learn problem-solving skills), time available, and cognitive capacities of the students.

Inquiry Teaching

Inquiry teaching is a form of discovery learning, although it can be structured to have greater teacher direction. In an inquiry model based on the Socratic teaching method (Collins, 1977; Collins & Stevens, 1983), the goals are to have students reason, derive general principles, and apply them to new situations. Appropriate learning outcomes include formulating and testing hypotheses, differentiating necessary from sufficient conditions, making predictions, and determining when making predictions requires more information.

In implementing the model, the teacher repeatedly questions the student. Questions are guided by rules such as "Ask about a known case," "Pick a counterexample for an insufficient factor," "Pose a misleading question," and "Question a prediction made without enough information" (Collins, 1977). Rule-generated questions help students formulate general principles and apply them to specific problems.

The following is a sample dialogue between teacher (T) and student (S) on the topic of population density (Collins, 1977):

T: In Northern Africa, is there a large population density?

S: In Northern Africa? I think there is.

T: Well, there is in the Nile valley, but elsewhere there is not. Do you have any idea why not?

S: Because it's not good for cultivating purposes?

T: It's not good for agriculture?

S: Yeah.

T: And do you know why?

S: Why?

T: Why is the farming at a disadvantage?

S: Because it's dry.

T: Right. (p. 353)

Although this instructional approach was designed for one-to-one tutoring, with some modifications it seems appropriate with small groups of students. One issue is that persons who serve as tutors require extensive training to pose appropriate questions in response to a student's level of thinking. Also, good content-area knowledge is a prerequisite for problem-solving skills. Students who lack a decent understanding of basic knowledge are not likely to function well under an inquiry system designed to teach reasoning and application of principles. Other student characteristics (e.g., age, abilities) also may predict success under this model. As with other constructivist methods, teachers must consider the student outcomes and the likelihood that students can successfully engage in the inquiry process.

Discussions and Debates

Class discussions are useful when the objective is to acquire greater conceptual understanding or multiple sides of a topic. The topic being discussed is one for which there is no clear right answer but rather involves a complex or controversial issue. Students enter the discussion with some knowledge of the topic and are expected to gain understanding as a result of the discussion.

Discussions lend themselves well to various disciplines, such as history, literature, science, and economics. Regardless of the topic, it is critical that a class atmosphere be created that is conducive to free discussion. Students likely will have to be given rules for the discussion (e.g., do not interrupt someone who is speaking, keep arguments to the topic being discussed, do not personally attack other students). If the teacher is the facilitator of the discussion, then he or she must support multiple viewpoints, encourage students to share, and remind students of the rules when they are violated. Teachers also can ask students to elaborate on their opinions (e.g., "Tell us why you think that.").

When class size is large, small-group discussions may be preferable to whole-class ones. Students reluctant to speak in a large group may feel less inhibited in a smaller one. Teachers can train students to be facilitators of small-group discussions.

A variation of the discussion is the debate, in which students selectively argue sides of an issue. This requires preparation by the groups and, likely, some practice if they will be giving short presentations on their sides. Teachers enforce rules of the debate and ensure that all team members participate. A larger discussion with the class can follow, which allows for points to be reinforced or new points brought up.

SUMMARY AND CRITIQUE

Chapter Summary

Constructivism is an epistemology, or philosophical description of the nature of learning. Constructivist theorists reject the idea that scientific truths exist and await discovery and verification. Knowledge is not imposed from outside people but rather formed inside them. Constructivist theories vary from those that postulate complete self-construction, through those that hypothesize socially mediated constructions, to those that argue that constructions match reality. Constructivism requires that we structure teaching and learning experiences to challenge students' thinking so that they will be able to construct new knowledge. A core premise is that cognitive processes are situated (located) within physical and social contexts. The concept of situated cognition highlights these relations between persons and situations.

Piaget's theory is cognitive constructivist and postulates that children pass through a series of qualitatively different stages: sensorimotor, preoperational, concrete operational, and formal operational. The chief developmental mechanism is equilibration, which helps to resolve cognitive conflicts by changing the nature of reality to fit existing structures (assimilation) or changing structures to incorporate reality (accommodation). Neo-Piagetian theorists retain many ideas from Piaget's theories but place greater emphasis on cognitive information processing principles.

Bruner's theory of cognitive growth discusses the ways that learners represent knowledge: enactively, iconically, and symbolically. He advocated the spiral curriculum, in which subject matter is periodically revisited with increasing cognitive development and student understanding.

Vygotsky's sociocultural theory emphasizes the social environment as a facilitator of development and learning. The social environment influences cognition through its tools—cultural objects, language, symbols, and social institutions. Cognitive change results from using these tools in social interactions and from internalizing and transforming these interactions. A key concept is the zone of proximal development, which represents the amount of learning possible by a student given proper instructional conditions. Applications to learning that reflect Vygotsky's ideas are instructional scaffolding, reciprocal teaching, peer collaboration, and apprenticeships.

Private speech has a self-regulatory function, but is not socially communicative. Vygotsky believed that private speech develops thought by organizing behavior. Children employ private speech to understand situations and surmount difficulties. Private speech becomes covert with development, although overt verbalization can occur at any age. Verbalization can promote student achievement if it is relevant to the task and does not interfere with performance.

Vygotsky's theory contends that learning is a socially mediated process. Children learn many concepts during social interactions with others. Structuring learning environments to promote these interactions facilitates learning. Peer-assisted learning, which is a type of socially mediated learning, refers to instructional approaches in which peers serve as active agents in the learning.

The goal of constructivist learning environments is to provide rich experiences that encourage students to learn. Constructivist classrooms teach big concepts using much student activity, social interaction, and authentic assessments. Students' ideas are avidly sought, and, compared with traditional classes, there is less emphasis on superficial learning and more emphasis on deeper understanding. The APA learner-centered principles, which address various factors (cognitive, metacognitive, motivational, affective, developmental, social, and individual differences), reflect a constructivist learning approach. Reflective teaching is thoughtful decision making that considers such factors as students, contexts, psychological processes, learning, motivation, and self-knowledge. Becoming a reflective teacher requires developing personal and professional knowledge, planning strategies, and assessment skills.

Some instructional methods that fit well with constructivism are discovery learning, inquiry teaching, and discussions and debates. Discovery learning allows students to obtain knowledge for themselves through problem solving. Discovery requires that teachers arrange activities such that students can form and test hypotheses. It is not simply letting students do what they want. Inquiry teaching is a form of discovery learning that may follow Socratic principles with much teacher questioning of students. Discussions and debates are useful when the objective is to acquire greater conceptual understanding or multiple viewpoints of a topic. A summary of learning issues relevant to constructivism appears in Table 8.9.

Table 8.9
Summary of learning issues.

How Does Learning Occur?

Constructivism contends that learners form or construct their own understandings of knowledge and skills. Perspectives on constructivism differ as to how much influence environmental and social factors have on learners' constructions. Piaget's cognitive theory stresses equilibration, or the process of making internal cognitive structures and external reality consistent. Neo-Piagetian theories utilize many Piagetian ideas but also acknowledge the role of development of information processing capabilities. Vygotsky's sociocultural theory places a heavy emphasis on the role of social factors in learning.

How Does Memory Function?

Constructivism has not dealt explicitly with memory. Its basic principles suggest that learners are more apt to remember information if their constructions are personally meaningful to them.

What Is the Role of Motivation?

The focus of constructivism has been on learning and knowing rather than motivation, although some educators have written about motivation. Constructivists hold that learners construct motivational beliefs in the same fashion as they construct beliefs about learning. Learners also construct beliefs about their learning capabilities and other factors that affect learning.

How Does Transfer Occur?

As with memory, transfer has not been a central issue in constructivist research. The same idea applies, however: To the extent that learners' constructions are personally meaningful to them and linked with other ideas, transfer should be facilitated.

How Does Self-Regulated Learning Operate?

Self-regulated learning involves the coordination of mental functions—memory, planning, synthesis, evaluation, and so forth. Learners use the tools of their culture (e.g., language, symbols) to construct meanings. The key is for self-regulatory processes to be internalized. Learners' initial self-regulatory activities may be patterned after those of others, but as learners construct their own they become idiosyncratic.

What Are the Implications for Instruction?

The teacher's central task is to structure the learning environment so that learners can construct understandings. To this end, teachers need to provide the instructional support (scaffolding) that will assist learners to maximize their learning in their zone of proximal development. The teacher's role is to provide a supportive environment and facilitate learning.

Chapter Critique

It is difficult to determine the contributions of constructivism to the field of learning because constructivism is not a theory of learning but rather a philosophical position on knowing. Further, constructivism is not a unified perspective that offers specific hypotheses to be tested. The idea that learners construct their own knowledge is accepted by all cognitive learning theories. Cognitive theories view the mind as a repository of beliefs, values, expectations, schemata, and so forth, so any feasible explanation of how those thoughts and feelings come to reside in the mind must assume that they are formed there. In short, constructivism cannot be judged on whether its tenets are true or false. Rather, it seems imperative to determine the process whereby students construct knowledge and how social, developmental, and instructional factors may influence that process.

Another issue is how much latitude learners have in construction. People have a genetic heritage, and some competencies (e.g., mathematical) may not be constructed but rather genetically driven, which suggests that some forms of knowledge may be universally endogenous. Acquisition of other competencies (e.g., multiplying, word processing) requires environmental input. A strong cognitive perspective such as Piaget's theory downplays the importance of teaching. What we know from information processing research is that instructional methods that map better onto cognitive structures produce better learning. There is a continuing need for researchers to determine the scope of constructivist processes in the sequence of competency acquisition and how these processes change as a function of development.

Importantly, constructivism has several implications for instruction and curriculum design. The most straightforward recommendations are to involve students actively in their learning and to provide experiences that challenge their thinking and force them to re-examine their beliefs. Constructivism also underlies the current emphasis on reflective teaching. Social constructivist views (e.g., Vygotsky's) stress that social group learning and peer collaboration are useful. As students collaborate with one another, they not only teach one another skills but also improve each other's motivation for learning. The value of these benefits cannot be overestimated.

REFLECTION QUESTIONS

- The concept of situated cognition seems to run counter to the idea that we do not need a separate theory for each type of learning because there are general skills that cut across learning domains. How can this contradiction be resolved? Which aspects of learning seem situated in contexts and which aspects are likely applicable to multiple contexts?

- Allowing students to construct their understandings takes time. Given that instructional time is at a premium, it does not seem feasible to continually plan instruction to allow time for students' constructions. How can teachers make these decisions? How might teachers decide which content is most amenable to constructivist learning and which could be taught directly (and thereby conserve time)?

■ To study how learners' constructions occur and evolve over time requires a research methodology that can capture these constructions. What type of research methodologies might be well suited for constructivist research? How might researchers explore learners' constructions as they occur (i.e., in real time)?

FURTHER READING

Brainerd, C. J. (2003). Jean Piaget, learning research, and American education. In B. J. Zimmerman & D. H. Schunk (Eds.), *Educational psychology: A century of contributions* (pp. 251–287). Mahwah, NJ: Erlbaum.

Brooks, J. G., & Brooks, M. G. (1999). *In search of understanding: The case for constructivist classrooms*. Alexandria, VA: Association for Supervision and Curriculum Development.

Gredler, M. E. (2012). Understanding Vygotsky for the classroom: Is it too late? *Educational Psychology Review, 24,* 113–131.

Lutkehaus, N. C., & Greenfield, P. (2003). From *The process of education* to *The culture of education:* An intellectual biography of Jerome Bruner's contributions to education. In B. J. Zimmerman & D. H. Schunk (Eds.), *Educational psychology: A century of contributions* (pp. 409–429). Mahwah, NJ: Erlbaum.

Tudge, J. R. H., & Scrimsher, S. (2003). Lev S. Vygotsky on education: A cultural-historical, interpersonal, and individual approach to development. In B. J. Zimmerman & D. H. Schunk (Eds.), *Educational psychology: A century of contributions* (pp. 207–228). Mahwah, NJ: Erlbaum.

van de Pol, J., Volman, M., & Beishuizen, J. (2010). Scaffolding in teacher-student interaction: A decade of research. *Educational Psychology Review, 22,* 271–296.

Vygotsky, L. (1978). *Mind in society: The development of higher psychological processes.* Cambridge, MA: Harvard University Press.

9 Motivation

Kerri Townsend, an elementary teacher, has been working with her students on subtraction with regrouping. In teaching the concept, she used everyday examples, cutouts, and manipulatives, to help spark students' interest. Now as the students solve problems, Kerri walks around the room, talking with students individually and checking their work.

The first student she checks on is Margaret, who feels she is not very good in math. Kerri says to Margaret, "Margaret, you got them all correct. You're really getting good at this. That should make you feel good. I know that you'll keep doing well in math this year."

Next is Derrick, who's having a hard time concentrating and hasn't done much work. Kerri says to him, "Derrick, I know you can do much better. See how well Jason is working. (Jason and Derrick are friends.) I know that you can work just as well and do great on these problems. Let's try."

Jared likes to do better than others. As Kerri approaches, Jared says to her, "Ms. Townsend, see how good I'm doing, better than most others." Kerri says, "Yes, you are doing very well. But instead of thinking about how others are doing, think about how you're doing. See, you can do these problems now, and just a few weeks ago, you couldn't. So you really have learned a lot."

As Kerri approaches Amy, she sees that Amy is wasting time. "Amy, why aren't you working better?" Amy replies, "I don't like these problems. I'd rather be working on the computer." Kerri replies, "You'll get your chance for that. I know that you can work better on these, so let's try to finish them before the end of the period. I think you'll like subtraction more when you see how well you can solve the problems."

Matt enjoys learning and is a very hard worker. As Kerri comes up to his desk, Matt is working hard on the problems. Unfortunately, he's also making some mistakes. Kerri gives him feedback, showing him what he's doing correctly and what he needs to correct. Then she says, "Matt, you're a hard worker. I know that if you keep working on these, you will learn how to do them. I'm sure that soon you'll find that you can do them more easily."

Kerri has been working with Rosetta on setting goals for completing her work accurately. Rosetta's goal is to complete her work with at least 80% accuracy. Earlier in the year, Rosetta averaged only about 30% accuracy. Kerri checks her work and says, "Rosetta, I'm so proud of you. You did 10 problems and got 8 of them completely correct, so you made your goal. See how much better you're doing now than before? You're getting much better in math!"

We have seen that much human learning—regardless of content—has common features. Learning begins with the knowledge and skills that learners bring to the situation, which they expand and refine as a function of learning. Learning involves the use of cognitive constructivist strategies and processes such as attention, perception, rehearsal, organization, elaboration, storage, and retrieval.

This chapter discusses motivation—a topic intimately linked with learning. *Motivation* is the process of instigating and sustaining goal-directed behavior (Schunk, Meece, & Pintrich, 2014). This is a cognitive definition because it postulates that learners set goals and employ cognitive processes (e.g., planning, monitoring) and behaviors (e.g., persistence, effort) to attain their goals. Although behavioral views of motivation are reviewed, the bulk of this chapter is devoted to cognitive perspectives.

As with learning, motivation is not observed directly but, rather, inferred from behavioral indexes such as task choices, effort, persistence, and goal-directed activities. Motivation is an explanatory concept that helps us understand why people behave as they do (Graham & Weiner, 2012). In addition to an extensive learning literature showing the importance of motivation, neuroscience (Chapter 2) is increasingly supporting the link between cognition and motivation (Botvinick & Braver, 2015).

Although some simple types of learning can occur with little or no motivation, most learning is motivated. Students motivated to learn attend to instruction and engage in such activities as rehearsing information, relating it to previously acquired knowledge, and asking questions (Schunk & Zimmerman, 2008). Rather than quit when they encounter difficult material, motivated students expend greater effort. They choose to work on tasks when they are not required to do so; in their spare time, they read about topics of interest, solve problems and puzzles, and work on projects with technology. In short, motivation engages students in activities that facilitate learning. Teachers understand the importance of motivation for learning, and—as the opening vignette shows—do many things to help raise student motivation.

Cultural variables also can affect motivation. Most of the perspectives discussed in this chapter were developed against the backdrop of Western cultures that stress individual performances. In the study of cultures, a distinction is made between those that are more individualistic, stressing individual accomplishments, and those that are more collectivist, stressing group accomplishments (Klassen, 2004). The same processes may apply; for example, self-efficacy is important for individuals and groups. But how motivational processes operate and their importance in different contexts may be subject to cultural influence (e.g., individual versus collective self-efficacy).

This chapter begins by discussing some historical views of motivation; the remainder of the chapter covers cognitive perspectives. Key motivational processes are explained and linked to learning. Topics covered are achievement motivation theory, attribution theory, social cognitive theory, goal theory, perceptions of control, self-concept, and intrinsic motivation. The chapter concludes with some educational applications.

When you finish studying this chapter, you should be able to do the following:

■ Discuss the major principles of historical theories of motivation: drive, conditioning, cognitive consistency, humanistic.

■ Draw the model of motivated learning and describe its major components.

■ Explain the major features in a current model of achievement motivation.

■ Discuss the causal dimensions in Weiner's attribution theory and the effects they have in achievement situations.

- Explain how goals, expectations, social comparison, and self-concept can affect motivation.

- Distinguish between different goal orientations and describe how they can promote or undermine motivation and learning.

- Define intrinsic motivation, explain the variables that can affect it and how it can influence learning, and discuss the conditions under which rewards may increase or decrease intrinsic motivation.

- Distinguish between personal and situational interest and explain how they relate to motivation and learning.

- Describe the major findings on the role of emotions in motivation and learning.

- Discuss educational applications involving achievement motivation, attributions, and goal orientations.

BACKGROUND AND ASSUMPTIONS

Historical Perspectives

Although some variables included in historical theories are not relevant to current theories, historical views helped set the stage for current cognitive theories. Further, several historical ideas have contemporary relevance.

Some early views reflected the idea that motivation results primarily from *instincts*. Ethologists, for example, based their ideas on Darwin's theory, which postulates that instincts have survival value for organisms. Energy builds within organisms and releases itself in behaviors designed to help species survive. Other theories emphasized the individual's need for *homeostasis*, or optimal levels of physiological states. Another perspective involves *hedonism*, or the idea that humans seek to have pleasure and avoid pain. Although each of these views may explain some instances of human motivation, they are inadequate to account for a wide range of motivated activities, especially those that occur during learning (Schunk et al., 2014; Weiner, 1992). Three historical perspectives on motivation with relevance to learning are drive theory, conditioning theory, and cognitive consistency theory.

Drive Theory. *Drive theory* originated as a physiological theory; eventually, it was broadened to include psychological needs. Woodworth (1918) defined *drives* as internal forces that sought to maintain homeostatic body balance. When a person or animal is deprived of an essential element (e.g., food, air, water), this activates a drive that causes the person or animal to respond. The drive subsides when the element is obtained.

Much of the research that tested predictions of drive theory was conducted with laboratory animals (Richter, 1927; Woodworth & Schlosberg, 1954). In these experiments, animals often were deprived of food or water for some time, and their behaviors to get food or water were assessed. For example, rats might be deprived of food for varying amounts of time and placed in a maze. The time that it took them to run to the end to receive food was measured. Not surprisingly, response strength (running speed) normally varied directly with the number of prior reinforcements and with longer deprivation up to 2 to 3 days, after which it dropped off because the animals became progressively weaker.

Hull (1943) broadened the drive concept by postulating that physiological deficits were primary needs that instigated drives to reduce the needs. *Drive (D)* was the motivational force that energized and prompted people and animals into action. Behavior that obtained reinforcement to satisfy a need resulted in *drive reduction*. This process is as follows:

$$\text{Need} \rightarrow \text{Drive} \rightarrow \text{Behavior}$$

Motivation was the "initiation of learned, or habitual, patterns of movement or behavior" (Hull, 1943, p. 226). Hull believed that innate behaviors usually satisfied primary needs and that learning occurred only when innate behaviors proved ineffective. *Learning* represented one's adaptation to the environment to ensure survival.

Hull also postulated the existence of *secondary reinforcers* because much behavior was not oriented toward satisfying primary needs. Stimulus situations (e.g., work to earn money) acquired secondary reinforcing power by being paired with primary reinforcement (e.g., money buys food).

Drive theory generated much research as a consequence of Hull's writings (Weiner, 1992). As an explanation for motivated behavior, drive theory seems best applied to immediate physiological needs; for example, one lost in a desert is primarily concerned with finding food, water, and shelter. Drive theory is not an ideal explanation for much of human motivation. Needs do not always trigger drives oriented toward need reduction. Students hastily finishing an overdue paper may experience strong symptoms of hunger, yet they may not stop to eat because the desire to complete an important task outweighs a physiological need. Conversely, drives can exist in the absence of biological needs. A sex drive can lead to promiscuous behavior even though sex is not immediately needed for survival.

Drive theory may explain some behaviors directed toward immediate goals, but many human behaviors reflect long-term goals, such as finding a job, obtaining a college degree, and sailing around the world. People are not in a continuously high drive state while pursuing these goals. They typically experience periods of high, average, and low motivation. High drive is not conducive to performance over lengthy periods and especially on complex tasks (Broadhurst, 1957; Yerkes & Dodson, 1908). In short, drive theory does not offer an adequate explanation for academic motivation.

Conditioning Theory. *Conditioning theory* (Chapter 3) explains motivation in terms of responses elicited by stimuli (classical conditioning) or emitted in the presence of stimuli (operant conditioning). In the *classical conditioning* model, the motivational properties of an unconditioned stimulus (UCS) are transmitted to the conditioned stimulus (CS) through repeated pairings. Conditioning occurs when the CS elicits a conditioned response (CR) in the absence of the UCS. This is a passive view of motivation because it postulates that once conditioning occurs, the CR is elicited when the CS is presented. As discussed in Chapter 3, conditioning is not an automatic process but, rather, depends on information conveyed to the individual about the likelihood of the UCS occurring when the CS is presented.

In *operant conditioning*, motivated behavior is an increased rate of responding or a greater likelihood that a response will occur in the presence of a stimulus. Skinner (1953) contended that internal processes accompanying responding are not necessary to explain behavior. Individuals' immediate environment and their history must be examined for the causes of behavior. Labeling a student "motivated" does not explain why the student works productively. The student is motivated because of prior reinforcement for productive work and because the current environment offers effective reinforcers.

Ample evidence shows that reinforcers can influence what people do; however, what affects behavior is not reinforcement but rather beliefs about reinforcement. People engage in activities because they believe they will be reinforced and value that reinforcement (Bandura, 1986). When reinforcement history conflicts with current beliefs, people act based on their beliefs (Brewer, 1974). By omitting cognitive elements, conditioning theories offer an incomplete account of human motivation.

Cognitive Consistency Theory. *Cognitive consistency* theory assumes that motivation results from interactions of cognitions and behaviors. This theory is *homeostatic* because it predicts that when tension occurs among elements, the problem needs to be resolved by making cognitions and behaviors consistent with one another. Two prominent perspectives are balance theory and dissonance theory.

Heider's (1946) *balance theory* postulated that individuals have a tendency to cognitively balance relations among persons, situations, and events. The basic situation involves three elements, and relations can be positive or negative.

For example, assume the three elements are Janice (teacher), Ashley (student), and chemistry (subject). Balance exists when relations among all elements are positive; Ashley likes Janice, Ashley likes chemistry, Ashley believes Janice likes chemistry. Balance also exists with one positive and two negative relations: Ashley does not like Janice, Ashley does not like chemistry, Ashley believes Janice likes chemistry (Figure 9.1).

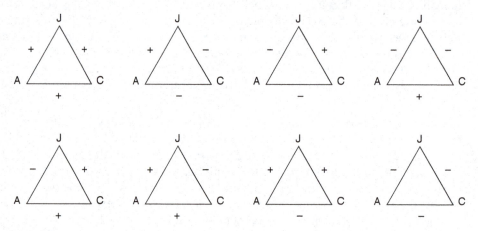

Figure 9.1
Predictions of balance theory.
Note: J = Janice (chemistry teacher); A = Ashley (student); C = chemistry. The symbols + and - stand for "likes" and "does not like," respectively, so that the top left balance can be read as follows: Ashley likes Janice, Ashley likes chemistry, Ashley believes Janice likes chemistry.

Cognitive imbalance exists with one negative and two positive relations (Ashley likes Janice, Ashley does not like chemistry, Ashley believes Janice likes chemistry) and with three negative relations. Balance theory predicts no tendency to change when the triad is balanced, but people will try cognitively and behaviorally to resolve conflicts when imbalance exists. For example, Ashley might decide that because she likes Janice and Janice likes chemistry, maybe chemistry is not so bad after all (i.e., Ashley changes her attitude about chemistry).

That people seek to restore cognitive imbalance is intuitively plausible, but balance theory contains problems. It predicts when people will attempt to restore balance but not how they will do it. Ashley might change her attitude toward chemistry, but she also could establish balance by disliking chemistry and Janice. The theory also does not adequately take into account the importance of imbalanced relationships. People care very much when imbalance exists among people and situations they value, but they may make no effort to restore balance when they care little about the elements.

Festinger (1957) formulated a theory of *cognitive dissonance*, which postulates that individuals attempt to maintain consistent relations among their beliefs, attitudes, opinions, and behaviors. Relations can be consonant, irrelevant, or dissonant. Two cognitions are *consonant* if one follows from or fits with the other; for example, "I have to give a speech in Los Angeles tomorrow morning at 9" and "I'm flying there today". Many beliefs are *irrelevant* to one another; for example, "I like chocolate" and "There is a hickory tree in my yard". *Dissonant* cognitions exist when one follows from the opposite of the other; for example, "I don't like Deborah" and "I bought Deborah a gift." Dissonance is tension with drivelike properties leading to reduction. Dissonance should increase as the discrepancy between cognitions increases. Assuming I bought Deborah a gift, the cognition "I don't like Deborah" ought to produce more dissonance than "Deborah and I are acquaintances."

Cognitive dissonance theory also takes the importance of the cognitions into account. Large discrepancies between trivial cognitions do not cause much dissonance. "Yellow is not my favorite color" and "I drive a yellow car" will not produce much dissonance if car color is not important to me.

Dissonance can be reduced in various ways:

- Change a discrepant cognition ("Maybe I actually like Deborah").
- Qualify cognitions ("The reason I do not like Deborah is because 10 years ago she borrowed $100 and never repaid it. But she's changed a lot since then and probably would never do that again").
- Downgrade the importance of the cognitions ("It's no big deal that I gave Deborah a gift; I give gifts to lots of people for different reasons").
- Alter behavior ("I'm never giving Deborah another gift").

Dissonance theory calls attention to how cognitive conflicts can be resolved. The idea that dissonance propels us into action is appealing. By dealing with discrepant cognitions, the theory is not confined to three relations as is balance theory. But dissonance and balance theories share many of the same problems. The dissonance notion is vague and difficult to verify experimentally. To predict whether cognitions will conflict in a given situation is problematic because they must be clear and important. The theory does not predict how dissonance will be reduced—by changing behavior or by altering thoughts. These problems suggest that additional processes are needed to explain human motivation. Interested readers should consult Shultz and Lepper (1996), who present a model that reconciles discrepant findings from dissonance research and integrates dissonance with other motivational variables.

Humanistic Theories

Humanistic theories as applied to learning are constructivist (Chapter 8) and emphasize cognitive and affective processes. These theories address people's capabilities and potentialities as they make choices and seek control over their lives.

Humanistic theorists make certain assumptions. One is that the study of persons is *holistic*: To understand people, we must study their behaviors, thoughts, and feelings (Weiner, 1992). Humanists disagree with behaviorists who study individual responses to discrete stimuli. Humanists emphasize individuals' self-awareness.

A second assumption is that human choices, creativity, and self-actualization are important areas to study (Weiner, 1992). To understand people, researchers should not study animals but rather people who are psychologically functioning and attempting to be creative and to maximize their capabilities and potential. Motivation is important for attaining basic needs but even more so when striving to maximize one's potential. Well-known humanistic theories are those of Maslow and Rogers.

Hierarchy of Needs. Abraham Maslow (1968, 1970) believed that human actions are unified by being directed toward goal attainment. Behaviors can serve several functions simultaneously; for example, attending a party could satisfy needs for self-esteem and social interaction. Maslow felt that conditioning theories did not capture the complexity of human behavior. To say that one socializes at a party because one previously has been reinforced for doing so fails to take into account one's current needs.

Most human actions represent strivings to satisfy needs. Needs are *hierarchical* (Figure 9.2). Lower-order needs have to be satisfied adequately before higher-order needs can influence behavior. *Physiological needs*, the lowest on the hierarchy, are needs for necessities such as food, air, and water. These needs are satisfied for most people most of the time, but they become potent when they are not satisfied. Next are *safety needs*, which involve environmental security. These needs dominate during emergencies: People fleeing from rising waters will abandon valuable property to save their lives. Safety needs are also manifested in activities such as saving money, securing a job, and taking out an insurance policy.

Once physiological and safety needs are adequately met, *belongingness (love) needs* become important. These needs involve having intimate relationships with others, belonging to groups, and having close friends and acquaintances. A sense of belonging can be attained through marriage, interpersonal commitments, volunteer groups, clubs, churches, and the like. At the fourth level are *esteem needs* that comprise self-esteem and esteem from others. These needs manifest themselves in high achievement, independence, competent work, and recognition from others.

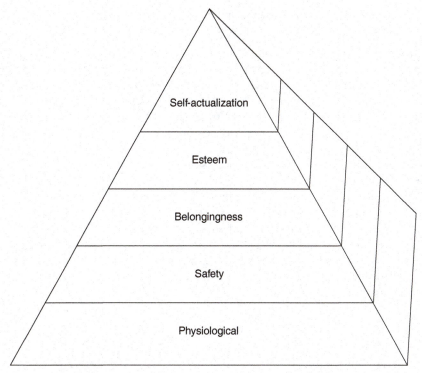

Figure 9.2
Maslow's Hierarchy of Needs.
Source: Based on *Motivation and Personality* by A. Maslow, © 1970. Pearson Education, Inc., Upper Saddle River, NJ.

The first four needs are *deprivation needs*: Their lack of satisfaction produces deficiencies that motivate people to satisfy them. At the highest level is the *need for self-actualization*, or the desire for self-fulfillment. Self-actualization manifests itself in the need to become everything that one is capable of becoming. Behavior is not motivated by a deficiency but rather by a desire for personal growth.

> Healthy people have sufficiently gratified their basic needs for safety, belongingness, love, respect, and self-esteem so that they are motivated primarily by trends to self-actualization [defined as ongoing actualization of potentials, capacities and talents, as fulfillment of mission (or call, fate, destiny, or vocation), as a fuller knowledge of, and acceptance of, the person's own intrinsic nature, as an unceasing trend toward unity, integration or synergy within the person]. (Maslow, 1968, p. 25)

Although most people go beyond the deficiency needs and strive toward self-actualization, few people ever fully reach this level—perhaps 1% of the population (Goble, 1970). Self-actualization can be manifested in various ways.

> The specific form that these needs will take will of course vary greatly from person to person. In one individual it may take the form of the desire to be an ideal mother, in another it may be

expressed athletically, and in still another it may be expressed in painting pictures or in inventions. At this level, individual differences are greatest. (Maslow, 1970, p. 46)

A strong motive to achieve is another manifestation of self-actualization (Application 9.1).

Maslow informally studied personal acquaintances and historical figures. Characteristics of self-actualized individuals included an increased perception of reality, acceptance (of self, others, nature), spontaneity, problem centering, detachment and desire for privacy, autonomy and resistance to enculturation, freshness of appreciation and richness of emotional reaction, frequency of peak experiences (loss of self-awareness), and identification with the human species (Maslow, 1968).

When self-actualized persons attempt to solve important problems, they look outside of themselves for a cause and dedicate their efforts to solving it. They also display great interest in the means for attaining their goals. The outcome (righting a wrong or solving a problem) is as important as the means to the end (the actual work involved).

Maslow's hierarchy is a useful general guide for understanding behavior. It underscores how unrealistic it is to expect students to learn in school if they have physiological or safety deficiencies. The hierarchy provides educators with clues concerning why students act as they do. Educators stress intellectual achievement, but many adolescents are preoccupied with belongingness and esteem.

APPLICATION 9.1
Maslow's Hierarchy of Needs

Maslow's hierarchy can help teachers understand students and create an environment to enhance learning. It is unrealistic to expect students to show interest in classroom activities if they have physiological or safety deficiencies. Children who come to school without having had breakfast or who have no lunch money cannot focus properly on classroom tasks. Teachers can work with counselors, principals, and social workers to assist children's families or to have children approved for free or reduced-cost meal programs.

Some students have difficulty working on tasks with nearby distractions (e.g., movement, noise). Teachers can meet with parents to assess whether home conditions are disruptive. Disruption at home can result in an unfilled safety need—a desire to feel more secure about learning. Parents can be urged to provide a favorable home

environment for studying. Teachers can teach students skills for coping with distractions (e.g., ways to concentrate and pay close attention to academic activities).

There are high schools with problems with violence (e.g., fighting) and gang behaviors. If students are afraid that they may be physically harmed or often must deal with pressures to join a gang, concentrating on academic tasks may be impossible. Teachers and administrators might consider working with students, parents, community agencies, and law enforcement officials to develop effective strategies for eliminating safety concerns. These issues must be addressed in order to create an atmosphere conducive for learning. Once the appropriate atmosphere is created, teachers should provide activities that students can complete successfully.

One problem with the theory is conceptual vagueness; what constitutes a deficiency is not clear. What one person considers a deficiency, someone else may not. Another problem is that lower-order needs are not always stronger than higher-order ones. Many people risk their safety to rescue others from danger. Third, research on the qualities of self-actualized individuals has yielded mixed results (Petri, 1986). Self-actualization can take many forms and be manifested at work, school, home, and so forth. How it may appear and how it can be influenced are unclear. Despite these problems, the idea that people strive to feel competent and lead self-fulfilling lives is a central notion in many theories of motivation.

Actualizing Tendency. Carl Rogers was a renowned psychotherapist whose approach to counseling is known as *client-centered therapy*. According to Rogers (1963), life represents an ongoing process of personal growth or achieving wholeness. This process, or *actualizing tendency*, is motivational and presumably innate (Rogers, 1963). Rogers considered this motive the only fundamental one from which all others (e.g., hunger, thirst) derive. The actualizing tendency is oriented toward personal growth, autonomy, and freedom from control by external forces.

> We are, in short, dealing with an organism which is always motivated, is always "up to something," always seeking. So I would reaffirm . . . my belief that there is one central source of energy in the human organism; that it is a function of the whole organism rather than some portion of it; and that it is perhaps best conceptualized as a tendency toward fulfillment, toward actualization, toward the maintenance and enhancement of the organism. (Rogers, 1963, p. 6)

The environment can affect the actualizing tendency. With development, individuals become more aware of their own being and functioning (*self-experience*). This awareness becomes elaborated into a self-concept through interactions with the environment and significant others (Rogers, 1959). The development of self-awareness produces a need for *positive regard*, or feelings such as respect, liking, warmth, sympathy, and acceptance. We perceive ourselves as receiving positive regard when we believe that others feel that way about us. This relation is reciprocal: When people perceive themselves as satisfying another's need for positive regard, they experience satisfaction of their need for positive regard.

People also have a need for *positive self-regard*, or positive regard that derives from self-experiences (Rogers, 1959). Positive self-regard develops when people experience positive regard from others, which creates a positive attitude toward oneself. A critical element is receiving *unconditional positive regard*, or attitudes of worthiness and acceptance with no strings attached. Unconditional positive regard is what most parents feel for their children. Parents value or accept ("prize") their children all the time, even though they do not value or accept all of their children's behaviors. People who experience unconditional positive regard believe they are valued, even when their actions disappoint others. The actualizing tendency grows because people accept their own experiences, and their perceptions of themselves are consistent with the feedback they receive.

Problems occur when people experience *conditional regard*, or regard contingent on certain actions. People act in accordance with these conditions of worth when they seek or avoid experiences that they believe are more or less worthy of regard. Conditional regard creates tension because people feel accepted and valued only when they behave appropriately.

Rogers and Education. Rogers (1969; Rogers & Frieberg, 1994) discussed education in his book *Freedom to Learn*. Meaningful, experiential learning has relevance to the whole person, has personal involvement (involves learners' cognitions and feelings), is self-initiated (impetus for learning comes from within), is pervasive (affects learners' behavior, attitudes, and personality), and is evaluated by the learner (according to whether it is meeting needs or leading to goals). Meaningful learning contrasts with meaningless learning, which does not lead to learners being invested in their learning, is initiated by others, does not affect diverse aspects of learners, and is not evaluated by learners according to whether it is satisfying their needs.

Students believe that meaningful learning will improve them personally. Learning requires active participation combined with self-criticism and self-evaluation by learners and the belief that learning is important. Rogers felt that learning that can be taught to others was of little value. Rather than imparting learning, the primary job of teachers is to act as *facilitators* who establish a classroom climate oriented toward significant learning and help students clarify their goals. Facilitators arrange resources so that learning can occur and, because they are resources, share their feelings and thoughts with students.

Instead of spending a lot of time writing lesson plans, facilitators should provide resources for students to use to meet their needs. Individual contracts are preferable to lockstep sequences in which all students work on the same material at the same time. Contracts allow students considerable freedom (i.e., self-regulation) in deciding on goals and timelines. Freedom itself should not be imposed; students who want more teacher direction should receive it. Rogers advocated greater use of inquiry, simulations, and self-evaluation as ways to provide freedom. Application 9.2 offers suggestions for applying humanistic principles.

APPLICATION 9.2
Humanistic Teaching

Humanistic principles are highly relevant to classrooms. Some important principles that can be built into instructional goals and practices are:

- Show positive regard for students.
- Separate students from their actions.
- Encourage personal growth by providing students with choices and opportunities.
- Facilitate learning by providing resources and encouragement.

Mr. Aberdon employed all four of these principles with Tony, a student in his American history class who is known to be a neighborhood troublemaker. Other teachers in the building told Mr. Aberdon negative things about Tony. He noticed, however, that Tony seemed to have an outstanding knowledge of American history. Undaunted by Tony's reputation among others, Mr. Aberdon often called on him to share in the classroom, provided him with a variety of project opportunities and resources, and praised him to further develop his interest in history. At the end of the semester, he worked with Tony to prepare a project for the state history fair, which he submitted and won second place.

Rogers's theory has seen wide psychotherapeutic application. The focus on helping people strive for challenges and maximize their potential is important for motivation and learning. The theory is developed only in general terms and the meanings of several constructs are unclear. Additionally, how one might assist students to develop self-regard is not clear. Still, the theory offers teachers principles to use to enhance learner motivation. Many of the ideas that Rogers discussed are found in other theories.

Model of Motivated Learning

Motivation is intimately linked with learning, and they affect one another. Students' motivation can influence what and how they learn. In turn, as students learn and perceive that they are becoming more skillful, they are motivated to continue to learn.

This close connection of motivation and learning is portrayed in Table 9.1 (Schunk, 1995; Schunk et al., 2014). The model is generic and is not intended to reflect any one theoretical perspective. It is a cognitive constructivist model because it views motivation arising largely from thoughts and beliefs. The model portrays three phases of pretask, during task, and posttask, which is a useful way to think about the changing role of motivation during learning. The variables included are addressed in other chapters in this text.

Pretask. Several variables influence students' initial motivation for learning. Students enter learning contexts with various goals, such as to learn the material, perform well, finish first,

Table 9.1
Model of motivated learning.

Pretask	During Task	Posttask
Goals	Instructional variables	Attributions
Expectations	Teacher feedback	Goals
Self-efficacy	Materials	Expectations
Outcome	Equipment	Values
Values	Contextual variables	Affects
Affects	Peers	Needs
Needs	Environment	Social support
Social support	Personal variables	
	Knowledge construction	
	Skill acquisition	
	Self-regulation	
	Choice of activities	
	Effort	
	Persistence	

and so on. Not all goals are academic. As Wentzel (1996, 2016) has shown, students have social goals that can integrate with their academic ones. During a group activity, Matt may want to learn the material but also become friends with Amy.

Students enter with various *expectations*. As discussed in Chapter 4, expectations may involve beliefs about capabilities for learning (self-efficacy) and consequences of learning (outcome expectations). Students differ in their *values* for learning; for example, how important it is to them. There are different types of values, as explained later.

Students differ in their *affects* associated with learning. They may be excited, anxious, or feel no particular emotions. These affects may relate closely to students' *needs*, which some theories postulate to be important.

Finally, we expect that the social support in students' lives will vary. *Social support* includes the types of assistance available at school from teachers and peers, as well as help and encouragement from parents and significant others in students' lives. Learning often requires that others provide time, money, effort, transportation, and so forth.

During Task. Instructional, contextual (social/environmental), and personal variables come into play during learning. *Instructional variables* include teachers, forms of feedback, materials, and equipment (e.g., technology). Although these variables typically are viewed as influencing learning, they also affect motivation. For instance, teacher feedback can encourage or discourage; instruction can clarify or confuse; materials and equipment can provide for many or few successes.

Contextual variables include social and environmental resources. Factors such as location, time of day, distractions, temperature, ongoing events, and the like can enhance or retard motivation for learning. Investigators have written about how highly competitive conditions can affect motivation (Ames, 1992a; Meece, 1991, 2002). Students' social comparisons of ability with peers directly link to motivation.

Personal variables include those associated with learning, such as knowledge construction and skill acquisition, self-regulation variables (Chapter 10), and motivational indexes (e.g., choices, effort, persistence). Students' perceptions of how well they are learning and of the effects of instructional, contextual, and personal variables influence motivation for continued learning.

Posttask. Posttask denotes the time when the task is completed, as well as periods of self-reflection when students pause during the task and think about their work. The same variables that are important prior to task engagement are critical during self-reflection with the addition of *attributions*, or perceived causes of outcomes. All variables, in cyclical fashion, affect future motivation and learning. Students who believe that they are progressing toward their learning goals and who make positive attributions for success are apt to sustain their self-efficacy for learning, outcome expectations, values, and positive affects. Factors associated with instruction, such as teacher feedback, provide information about goal progress and outcome expectations. Thus, students who expect to do well and receive positive outcomes from learning are apt to be motivated to continue to learn, assuming they believe they are making progress and can continue to do so by using effective learning strategies.

ACHIEVEMENT MOTIVATION

The study of achievement motivation is central to education and learning. *Achievement motivation* refers to striving to be competent in effortful activities (Elliot & Church, 1997). The next section discusses the historical foundations of achievement motivation theory, followed by contemporary perspectives.

Expectancy-Value Theory

John Atkinson (1957; Atkinson & Birch, 1978; Atkinson & Feather, 1966; Atkinson & Raynor, 1974, 1978) developed an *expectancy-value theory* of achievement motivation. The basic idea of this and other expectancy-value theories is that behavior depends on one's *expectancy* of attaining a particular outcome (e.g., goal, reinforcer) as a result of performing given behaviors and on how much one values that outcome. People judge the likelihood of attaining various outcomes. They are not motivated to attempt the impossible, so they do not pursue outcomes perceived as unattainable. Even a positive outcome expectation does not produce action if the outcome is not valued. An attractive outcome, coupled with the belief that it is attainable, motivates people to act.

Atkinson postulated that achievement behaviors represent a conflict between approach (*hope for success*) and avoidance (*fear of failure*) tendencies. Achievement actions carry with them the possibilities of success and failure. Key concepts of this mathematical model are as follows: the *tendency to approach an achievement-related goal* (T_s), the *tendency to avoid failure* (T_{af}), and the *resultant achievement motivation* (T_a). T_s is a function of the *motive to succeed* (M_s), the *subjective probability of success* (P_s), and the *incentive value of success* (I_s):

$$T_s = M_s \times P_s \times I_s$$

Atkinson believed that M_s (*achievement motivation*) is a stable disposition (characteristic trait) of the individual to strive for success. P_s (the individual's estimate of how likely goal attainment is) is inversely related to I_s: Individuals have a greater incentive to work hard at difficult tasks than at easy tasks. Greater pride is experienced in accomplishing difficult tasks.

In similar fashion, the *tendency to avoid failure* (T_{af}) is a multiplicative function of the *motive to avoid failure* (M_{af}), the *probability of failure* (P_f), and the *inverse of the incentive value of failure* ($-I_f$):

$$T_{af} = M_{af} \times P_f \times (-I_f)$$

The *resultant achievement motivation* (T_a) is represented as follows:

$$T_a = T_s - T_{af}$$

Notice that simply having a high hope for success does not guarantee achievement behavior because the strength of the motive to avoid failure must be considered. The best way to promote achievement behavior is to combine a strong hope for success with a low fear of failure (Application 9.3).

APPLICATION 9.3
Achievement Motivation

Achievement motivation theory predicts that if an academic task is perceived as too hard, students may not attempt it or may quit readily because of high fear of failure and low hope for success. Lowering fear of failure and raising hope for success enhance motivation, which can be done by conveying positive expectations for learning to students and by structuring tasks so students can successfully complete them with reasonable effort. Viewing a task as too easy is not beneficial because students may become bored. Notice in the opening vignette that Amy seems to be bored with the assignment. If lessons are not planned to meet the varying needs of students, the desired achievement behaviors will not be displayed.

Elementary teachers find that many students have difficulty with multiplication. They may need to spend the majority of their time learning facts and using manipulatives to reinforce learning of new concepts (e.g., division). Success on these activities in a nonthreatening classroom environment builds hope for success and lowers fear of failure. Students who are proficient in multiplication, have mastered the steps for

solving division problems, and understand the relationship between multiplication and division do not need to spend lots of class time on review. Instead, they can be given a brief review and then guided into more difficult skills, which maintains challenge and produces optimal achievement motivation.

College professors benefit by becoming familiar with the research knowledge and writing skills of their students prior to assigning a lengthy paper or research project. Student background factors (e.g., type of high school attended, expectations and guidance of former teachers) can influence student confidence for completing such challenging tasks. Professors also can model research and writing projects in the classroom. Initially students might complete short writing tasks and critique various research projects. Then professors can provide students with detailed feedback regarding the effectiveness of their writing. As the semester progresses, assignments can become more challenging. This approach helps to build hope for success and diminish fear of failure, which collectively raise achievement motivation and lead students to set more difficult goals.

This model predicts that students high in resultant achievement motivation will choose tasks of intermediate difficulty; that is, those they believe are attainable and will produce a sense of accomplishment. These students should avoid difficult tasks for which successful accomplishment is unlikely, as well as easy tasks for which success, although guaranteed, produces little satisfaction. Students low in resultant achievement motivation are more apt to select either easy or difficult tasks. To accomplish the former, students have to expend little effort to succeed. Although accomplishing the latter seems unlikely, students have an excuse for failure—the task is so difficult that no one can succeed at it. This excuse gives these students a reason for not expending effort, because even great effort is unlikely to produce success.

Research on task difficulty preference as a function of level of achievement motivation has yielded conflicting results (Cooper, 1983; Ray, 1982). In studies of task difficulty by Kuhl and Blankenship (1979a, 1979b), individuals repeatedly chose tasks. These researchers assumed that fear of failure would be reduced following task success, so they predicted the tendency to choose easy tasks would diminish over time. They expected this change to be most apparent among students for whom $M_{af} > M_s$. Kuhl and Blankenship found a shift toward more difficult tasks for participants in whom $M_{af} > M_s$, as well as for those in whom $M_s > M_{af}$. Researchers found no support for the notion that this tendency would be greater in the former participants.

These findings make sense when interpreted differently. Repeated success builds perceptions of competence (self-efficacy). People then are more likely to choose difficult tasks because they feel capable of accomplishing them. In short, people choose to work on easy or difficult tasks for many reasons, and Atkinson's theory may have overestimated the strength of the achievement motive.

Classical achievement motivation theory has generated much research (Trautwein et al., 2012). One problem with a global achievement motive is that it rarely manifests itself uniformly across different achievement domains. Students typically show greater motivation to perform well in some content areas than in others. Because the achievement motive varies with the domain, how well such a global trait predicts achievement behavior in specific situations is questionable. Some theorists (Elliot & Church, 1997; Elliot & Harackiewicz, 1996) have proposed an integration of classical theory with goal theory; the latter is discussed later in this chapter.

Contemporary Model of Achievement Motivation

The classical view of achievement motivation contrasts sharply with theories that stress needs, drives, and reinforcers. Atkinson and others moved the field of motivation away from a simple stimulus–response ($S \rightarrow R$) perspective to a more complex cognitive model. By stressing the person's perceptions and beliefs as influences on behavior, these researchers also shifted the focus of motivation from inner needs and environmental factors to the subjective world of the individual.

An important contribution was emphasizing both expectancies for success and perceived value of engaging in the task as factors affecting achievement. Contemporary models of achievement motivation reflect this subjective emphasis and, in addition, have incorporated other cognitive variables such as goals and perceptions of capabilities. Current models also place greater emphasis on contextual influences on achievement motivation, realizing that people alter their motivation depending on perceptions of their current situations.

This section considers a contemporary theoretical perspective on achievement motivation. Later another current view of achievement motivation—self-worth theory—is presented. These two approaches refine achievement motivation theory to incorporate additional elements.

Figure 9.3 shows the contemporary model (Eccles, 2005; Wigfield, Byrnes, & Eccles, 2006; Wigfield & Cambria, 2010; Wigfield & Eccles, 2002; Wigfield, Tonks, & Eccles, 2004; Wigfield et al., 2016). This model is complex. Only its features most germane to the present

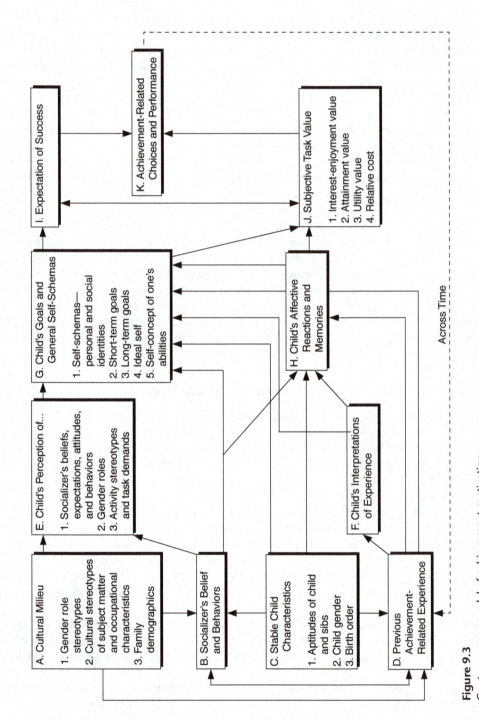

Figure 9.3

Contemporary model of achievement motivation.

Source: "Subjective task value and the Eccles et al. model of achievement-related choices," by J. S. Eccles, 2005, p. 106. In A. J. Elliott & C. S. Dweck (Eds.), *Handbook of competence and motivation* (pp. 105–121). New York: Guilford Press. Used with permission.

discussion will be described. Interested readers are referred to Eccles (2005) and the other references listed here for in-depth coverage of the model.

As the figure shows, achievement behavior is predicted by expectancy and value components. *Value* refers to the perceived importance of the task, or the belief about why one should engage in the task. Value answers the question, "Why should I do this task?" (Eccles, 2005). Answers might include interest and positive affect (e.g., "I like this and want to work on it"), perceived importance (e.g., "Doing this will help me in the future"), and perceived costs (e.g., "Doing this will take time away from playing the guitar"). In the opening vignette, Amy expresses negative affect and low value for the task.

The overall value of any task depends on four components. *Attainment value* is the importance of doing well on the task, for example, because the task conveys important information about the self, provides a challenge, or offers the opportunity to fulfill achievement or social needs. *Intrinsic* or *interest value* refers to the inherent, immediate enjoyment one derives from the task. This construct is roughly synonymous with *intrinsic motivation,* discussed later in this chapter. *Utility value* relates to task importance relative to a future goal (e.g., taking a course because it is necessary to attain a career goal). Finally, there is a *cost belief* component, defined as the perceived negative aspects of engaging in the task (Wigfield et al., 2016). When people work on one task, then they cannot work on others, and there may be associated costs (e.g., academic, social). Learners who make more connections between content to be learned and their lives tend to perform better (Hulleman, Kosovich, Barron, & Daniel, 2017).

The *expectancy* variable refers to individuals' perceptions concerning the likelihood of success on tasks—that is, their perceptions about how well they will do. The expectancy component answers the question, "Am I able to do this task?" (Eccles, 2005). In the opening vignette, Margaret feels she is not good in math and has a low expectancy of success for performing well. In contrast, Jared seems to have high expectancies for success, although he is overly concerned with doing better than others.

Expectancy is not synonymous with perceived competence; rather, it bears some resemblance to Bandura's (1986) outcome expectation in the sense that it is forward looking and reflects the person's perception of doing well. It also contrasts with task-specific self-concept, which involves current beliefs about perceived ability. Research shows that higher expectancies for success are positively related to achievement behaviors, including choice of tasks, effort, persistence, and actual achievement (Bandura, 1986, 1997; Eccles, 2005; Eccles & Wigfield, 1985; Trautwein et al., 2012; Wigfield & Eccles, 2000, 2002; Wigfield et al., 2016). Collectively, expectancies for success and task values are predicted to affect achievement-related outcomes.

The next motivational components shown in Figure 9.3 are students' goals and self-schemas and their affective reactions and memories. Affective reactions and memories refer to learners' affective experiences with this or similar tasks. Presumably these reactions can be activated by anticipation of engaging in the task when learners recall their prior experiences. Negative experiences can lead to students' avoiding tasks and low perceived value.

Goals and self-schemas include students' short- and long-term goals, as well as their self-schemas that reflect their beliefs and self-concepts. Students hold beliefs about what kind of person they are and what kind of person they want to become (possible or ideal selves). The latter include beliefs about personality and identity, as well as self-concepts about their physical attractiveness, athletic ability, academic ability, and social competence (Eccles, 2005).

Goals are cognitive representations of what students are trying to attain. They can range from short term (e.g., "Get an A on this test") to much longer term (e.g., "Become a university professor"). Goals can be shaped by self-concepts and self-schemas. For example, students whose self-schemas include the idea of being of service and helping others might set a long-term goal of becoming a teacher, doctor, or social worker.

Goals and self-schemas are influenced by students' perceptions of task demands, or their judgments of the difficulty of the task and other features of the task such as how interesting it appears. Task difficulty perceptions are relatively task specific such as school subject areas (e.g., English, biology).

Another component includes how students perceive their social and cultural environments. This includes their perceptions of socializers' beliefs (e.g., parents, teachers, peers) and how they perceive and interpret social roles such as gender roles and stereotypes about activities. Parents' or teachers' beliefs and behaviors can influence students, but these aspects of the social environment are mediated by the students' perceptions of the environment. For example, a student member of a minority group may not perceive a bias against him in a classroom. Even if there is a bias it cannot influence his motivational beliefs because he does not perceive it.

Other influential variables are learners' characteristics and experiences, as well as their cultural and social environments including the general cultural and societal milieu, gender and cultural stereotypes, and family demographics. These external factors set the context for learners as they engage in different activities and influence their motivation. These contexts also provide opportunities for and constraints on learners' beliefs and behaviors. Thus, although the model emphasizes how students construct their motivational beliefs through social cognitive processing, it is assumed that their beliefs are grounded in the larger social and cultural contexts that constitute the learners' worlds.

Research by Eccles, Wigfield, and others (e.g., Wigfield et al., 2016) demonstrates support for many of the relations depicted in the model. Studies have used both cross-sectional and longitudinal designs that assess the beliefs and achievement of upper elementary and junior high students over time. A general finding across several studies is that expectancies and task-specific self-concepts are mediators between environmental contexts and achievement, as proposed by the model. Another finding is that expectancies are closely linked to cognitive engagement and achievement and that values are strong predictors of students' choices (Schunk et al., 2014). These findings have good generalizability because the studies use students in actual classrooms and follow them over lengthy periods (Eccles, 2005; Wigfield et al., 2006). A challenge for the future is to explore in greater depth the links between variables and determine how these vary depending on the classroom context and variables associated with students (e.g., developmental status, ability level, gender).

Family Influences

Achievement motivation can be affected by home factors. An early investigation studied parents' interactions with their sons (Rosen & D'Andrade, 1959). Children were given tasks, and parents could interact in any fashion. Parents of boys with high achievement motivation interacted more, gave more rewards and punishments, and held higher expectations for their children than parents of boys with low achievement motivation. The authors concluded that parental pressure to perform well is a more important influence on achievement motivation than parental desire for child independence.

Other research, however, shows that family influences are not automatic. For example, Stipek and Ryan (1997) found that whereas economically disadvantaged preschoolers scored lower than advantaged children on cognitive measures, researchers found virtually no differences between these groups on motivation measures. Children's achievement motivation suffers when parents show little involvement in children's academics (Ratelle, Guay, Larose, & Senécal, 2004). Children who form insecure attachments with their parents are at greater risk for developing perfectionism (Neumeister & Finch, 2006).

Although families can influence children's motivation, attempts to identify parental behaviors that encourage achievement strivings are complicated because parents display many behaviors with their children. Determining which behaviors are most influential is difficult. Thus, parents may encourage their children to perform well, convey high expectations, give rewards and punishments, respond with positive affect (warmth, permissiveness), and encourage independence. These behaviors also are displayed by teachers and other significant persons in a child's life, which complicates determining the precise nature of familial influence. Another point is that although parents influence children, children also influence parents (Meece, 2002). Parents help children develop achievement behaviors when they encourage pre-existing tendencies in their children; for example, children develop independence through interactions with peers and then are praised by parents.

Self-Worth Theory

Atkinson's theory predicts that achievement behavior results from an emotional conflict between hope for success and fear of failure. This notion is intuitively appealing. Thinking about beginning a new job or taking a difficult course produces anticipated satisfaction from being successful as well as anxiety over the possibility of failing.

Self-worth theory refines this idea by combining the emotions with cognitions (Covington, 1992, 1998; 2004, 2009; Covington & Dray, 2002; De Castella, Byrne, & Covington, 2013). This theory assumes that success is valued and that failure, or the belief that one has failed, should be avoided because it implies low ability. People want to be viewed as able, but failure creates feelings of unworthiness. To preserve a sense of self-worth, individuals must feel able and demonstrate that ability to others.

One means of avoiding failure is to pursue easy goals that guarantee success. Another means is to cheat, although cheating is problematic. Shannon might copy answers from Yvonne, but if Yvonne does poorly, then Shannon will too. Shannon also might get caught copying answers by her teacher. Another way to avoid failure is to escape from a negative situation. Students who believe they will fail a course may drop it; those who are failing several courses may quit school.

Strangely, students can avoid the perception of low ability through deliberate failure. One can pursue a difficult goal, which increases the likelihood of failure. Setting high aspirations is valued, and failing to attain them does not automatically imply low ability. A related tactic is to blame failure on low effort: One could have succeeded if circumstances had allowed one to work harder. Kay cannot be faulted for failing an exam for which she did not properly study, especially if she works at a job and had inadequate study time.

Expending effort carries risk. High effort that produces success maintains the perception of ability, but high effort that results in failure implies that one has low ability. Low effort also carries risk because teachers routinely stress effort and criticize students for not expending effort (Weiner & Kukla, 1970). Effort is a "double-edged sword" (Covington & Omelich, 1979). Excuses can help students maintain the perception of ability; for example, "I would have done better had I been able to study more," "I didn't work hard enough" [when in fact the student worked very hard], or "I was unlucky—I studied the wrong material."

Self-worth theory stresses perceptions of ability as the primary influences on motivation. Research shows that perceived ability bears a strong positive relationship to students' expectations for success, motivation, and achievement (Wigfield et al., 2016). That effect, however, seems most pronounced in Western societies. Cross-cultural research shows that effort is more highly valued as a contributor to success among students from China and Japan than it is among students from the United States (Schunk et al., 2014).

Another issue is that perceived ability is only one of many influences on motivation. Self-worth predictions depend on students' developmental levels. Older students perceive ability to be a more important influence on achievement than younger students (Harari & Covington, 1981; Schunk et al., 2014). Young children do not clearly differentiate between effort and ability (Nicholls, 1978, 1979). At approximately age 8, they begin to distinguish the concepts and realize that their performances do not necessarily reflect their abilities. With development, students increasingly value ability while devaluing effort (Harari & Covington, 1981). In the opening vignette, Matt is a hard worker, and effort does not yet imply lower ability to him. Teachers and adolescents will work at cross-purposes if teachers stress working harder while adolescents (believing that hard work implies low ability) shun expending effort. A mature conception eventually emerges in which successes are attributed to a combination of ability, effort, and other factors (e.g., good strategy). Despite these limitations, self-worth theory captures the all-too-common preoccupation with ability and its negative consequences.

Task and Ego Involvement

Achievement motivation theories have shifted their focus away from general achievement motives to task-specific beliefs. Later in this chapter, goal theory is discussed, which stresses the roles of goals, conceptions of ability, and motivational patterns in achievement contexts. This section covers task and ego involvement, which are types of motivational patterns that derive largely from work in achievement motivation (Schunk et al., 2014).

Task involvement stresses learning as a goal. Task-involved students focus on task demands such as solving a problem, balancing an equation, and writing a book report. Learning is valued as a goal. In contrast, *ego involvement* is a type of self-preoccupation. Ego-involved students want to avoid looking incompetent. Learning is valued not as a goal but rather as a means to avoid appearing incapable (Nicholls, 1984).

Task and ego involvement reflect different beliefs about ability and effort (Jagacinski & Nicholls, 1984, 1987). Ego-involved students perceive ability as synonymous with *capacity*.

Ability is a relatively fixed quantity assessed by comparisons with others (norms). The role of effort is limited; effort can improve performance only to the limit set by ability. Success achieved with great effort implies high ability only if others require more effort to attain the same performance or if others perform less well with the same effort. Task-involved students perceive ability as close in meaning to *learning*, such that more effort can raise ability. Students feel more competent if they expend greater effort to succeed, because learning is their goal and implies greater ability. Feelings of competence arise when students' current performance is seen as an improvement over prior performance.

Ego and task involvement are not fixed characteristics and can be affected by contextual features (Nicholls, 1979, 1983). Ego involvement is promoted by competition, which fosters self-evaluation of abilities relative to those of others. Students typically compete for teacher attention, privileges, and grades. Elementary and middle-grades students often are grouped for reading and mathematics instruction based on ability differences; secondary students are tracked. Teacher feedback may unwittingly foster ego involvement (e.g., "Marcus, finish your work; everyone else is done"), as can teacher introductions to a lesson (e.g., "This is hard material; some of you may have trouble learning it").

Task involvement can be raised by individual learning conditions. Students evaluate their own progress relative to how they, rather than others, performed previously. Task involvement also is enhanced by cooperative learning (Chapter 8). For example, Ames (1984) found that students placed greater emphasis on ability as a determinant of outcomes in competitive contexts but stressed effort in noncompetitive (i.e., cooperative or individual) situations.

ATTRIBUTIONS

Attributions, or perceived causes of outcomes, are important motivation variables. *Attribution theory* explains how people view the causes of their behaviors and those of others (Weiner, 1985, 1992, 2000, 2004). Attribution theory has been widely applied to the study of motivation (Graham & Taylor, 2016; Graham & Weiner, 2012). The theory assumes that people seek information to form attributions. The process of assigning causes presumably is governed by rules, and much attributional research has addressed how rules are used. Attributions can influence motivational beliefs, emotions, behaviors, and, ultimately, learning.

Before discussing attributions in achievement settings, some relevant background material is described. Rotter's *locus of control* and Heider's *naïve analysis of action* incorporate attributional concepts.

Locus of Control

A central tenet of most cognitive motivation theories is that people seek to control important aspects of their lives (Schunk & Zimmerman, 2006). This tenet reflects the idea of *locus of control,* or a generalized expectancy concerning whether responses influence the attainment of outcomes (Rotter, 1966). People may believe that outcomes occur independently of how they behave (*external locus of control*) or that outcomes are contingent on their behavior (*internal locus of control*).

Other investigators have contended that locus of control can vary depending on the situation (Phares, 1976). It is not unusual to find students who generally believe they have little control over academic successes and failures but also believe they can exert much control in a particular class because the teacher and peers are helpful and because they like the content.

Locus of control is important in achievement contexts because expectancy beliefs are hypothesized to affect behavior. Students who believe they have control over their successes and failures should be more inclined to engage in academic tasks, expend effort, and persist than students who believe their behaviors have little impact on outcomes. In turn, effort and persistence promote learning and achievement (Lefcourt, 1976; Phares, 1976).

Regardless of whether locus of control is a general disposition or is situationally specific, it reflects *outcome expectations* (beliefs about the anticipated outcomes of one's actions; Chapter 4). Outcome expectations can affect achievement behaviors. Students may not work on tasks because they do not expect competent performances to produce favorable results (negative outcome expectation), as might happen if they believe the teacher dislikes them and will not reward them no matter how well they do. But positive outcome expectations do not guarantee high motivation (Bandura, 1982b, 1997). Students may believe that hard work will produce a high grade, but they will not work hard if they doubt their capability to put forth the effort (low self-efficacy).

These points notwithstanding, self-efficacy and outcome expectations usually are related (Bandura, 1986, 1997). Students who believe they are capable of performing well (high self-efficacy) expect positive reactions from their teachers following successful performances (positive outcome expectation). Outcomes, in turn, validate self-efficacy because they convey that one is capable of succeeding (Schunk & Pajares, 2005).

Naïve Analysis of Action

The origin of attribution theory generally is ascribed to Heider (1958), who referred to his theory as a *naïve analysis of action*. *Naïve* means that the average individual is unaware of the objective determinants of behavior. Heider's theory examines what ordinary people believe are the causes of important events in their lives.

Heider postulated that people attribute causes to internal or external factors. He referred to these factors, respectively, as the *effective personal force* and the *effective environmental force*, as follows:

$$Outcome = personal\ force + environmental\ force$$

Internal causes are within the individual: needs, wishes, emotions, abilities, intentions, and effort. The *personal force* is allocated to two factors: *power* and *motivation*. Power refers to abilities and motivation (trying) to intention and exertion:

$$Outcome = trying + power + environment$$

Collectively, power and environment constitute the *can factor*, which, combined with the *try factor*, is used to explain outcomes. One's power (or ability) reflects the environment. Whether Beth can swim across a lake depends on Beth's swimming ability relative to the forces of the lake (current, width, and temperature). Similarly, Jason's success or failure on a test depends on his ability relative to the difficulty of the test, along with his intentions and efforts in studying. Assuming that ability is sufficient to conquer environmental forces, then trying (effort) affects outcomes.

Although Heider sketched a framework for how people view significant events in their lives, this framework provided researchers with few empirically testable hypotheses. Investigators subsequently clarified his ideas and conducted attributional research testing refined hypotheses.

Attribution Theory of Achievement

The search for achievement causes elicits such questions as, "Why did I do well (poorly) on my social studies test?" and "Why did I get an A (D) in biology?" Studies by Weiner and his colleagues provided the empirical base for developing an attribution theory of achievement (Graham & Weiner, 2012; Weiner, 1985, 2000, 2004, 2005, 2010; Weiner et al., 1971; Weiner & Kukla, 1970). This section discusses those aspects of Weiner's theory relevant to motivated learning.

Causal Factors. Guided by Heider's work, Weiner et al. (1971) postulated that students attribute their academic successes and failures largely to ability, effort, task difficulty, and luck. These authors assumed that these factors were given general weights, and that for any given outcome, one or two factors would be judged as primarily responsible. For example, if Kara received an A on a mathematics exam, she might attribute it mostly to ability ("I'm good in math") and effort ("I studied hard for the test"), somewhat to task difficulty ("The test wasn't too hard"), and very little to luck ("I guessed right on a couple of questions"; Table 9.2).

Table 9.2
Sample attributions for grade on mathematics exam.

Grade	Attribution	Example
High	Ability	I'm good in math.
	Effort	I studied hard for the exam.
	Ability + Effort	I'm good in math, and I studied hard for the exam.
	Task ease	It was an easy test.
	Luck	I was lucky; I studied the right material for the exam.
Low	Ability	I'm no good in math.
	Effort	I didn't study hard enough.
	Ability + Effort	I'm no good in math, and I didn't study hard enough.
	Task difficulty	The test was impossible; nobody could have done well.
	Luck	I was unlucky; I studied the wrong material for the exam.

Weiner et al. (1971) did not imply that ability, effort, task difficulty, and luck are the only attributions students use to explain their successes and failures, but rather that they are commonly given by students as causes of achievement outcomes. Researchers have identified other attributions, such as people (e.g., teachers, students), mood, fatigue, illness, personality, and physical appearance (Frieze, 1980; Frieze, Francis, & Hanusa, 1983). Of the four attributions identified by Weiner et al. (1971), luck gets relatively less emphasis, although it is important in some situations (e.g., games of chance). Frieze et al. (1983) showed that task conditions are associated with particular attributional patterns. Exams tend to generate effort attributions, whereas art projects are ascribed to ability and effort. In the opening vignette, we might speculate that Margaret attributes her difficulties to low ability and Matt attributes his successes to high effort.

Causal Dimensions. Drawing on the work of Heider (1958) and Rotter (1966), Weiner et al. (1971) originally represented causes along two dimensions: (a) internal or external to the individual, and (b) relatively stable or unstable over time (Table 9.3). Ability is internal and relatively stable. Effort is internal but unstable; one can alternatively work diligently and lackadaisically. Task difficulty is external and relatively stable because task conditions do not vary much from moment to moment; luck is external and unstable—one can be lucky one moment and unlucky the next.

Weiner (1985) added a third causal dimension: controllable or uncontrollable by the individual (Table 9.3). Although effort is generally viewed as internal and unstable (immediate effort), a general effort factor (typical effort) also seems to exist: People may be typically lazy or hardworking. Effort is considered to be controllable; mood factors (to include fatigue and illness) are not. The classification in Table 9.3 has some problems (e.g., the usefulness of including both immediate and typical effort; the issue of whether an external factor can be controllable), but it has served as a framework to guide research and attributional intervention programs.

In forming attributions, people use situational cues, the meanings of which they have learned via prior experiences (Weiner et al., 1971). Salient cues for ability attributions are success attained easily or early in the course of learning, as well as many successes. With motor skills, an important effort cue is physical exertion. On cognitive tasks, effort attributions are credible when we expend mental effort or persist for a long time to succeed. Task difficulty cues include task features; for example, reading passages with fewer or easier words indicate easier tasks than those with more words or more difficult words. Task difficulty also is judged from social norms. If everyone in class fails a test, failure is

Table 9.3
Weiner's model of causal attribution.

| | Internal | | External | |
	Stable	**Unstable**	**Stable**	**Unstable**
Controllable	Typical effort	Immediate effort	Teacher bias	Help from others
Uncontrollable	Ability	Mood	Task difficulty	Luck

more likely to be attributed to high task difficulty; if everyone makes an A, then success may be attributed to task ease. A prominent cue for luck is random outcomes; how good students are (ability) or how hard they work (effort) has no obvious connection to how well they do.

Attributional Consequences. Attributions affect expectations for subsequent successes, achievement behaviors, and emotional reactions (Graham & Taylor, 2016; Graham & Weiner, 2012; Weiner, 1985, 1992, 2000). The *stability* dimension is thought to influence *expectancy of success*. Assuming that task conditions remain much the same, attributions of success to stable causes (high ability, low task difficulty) should result in higher expectations of future success than attributions to unstable causes (immediate effort, luck). Students may be uncertain whether they can sustain the effort needed to succeed or whether they will be lucky in the future. Failure ascribed to low ability or high task difficulty is apt to result in lower expectations for future success than failure attributed to insufficient effort or bad luck. Students may believe that increased effort will produce more favorable outcomes or that their luck may change in the future.

The *locus* dimension is hypothesized to influence *affective reactions*. One experiences greater pride (shame) after succeeding (failing) when outcomes are attributed to internal causes rather than to external ones. Students experience greater pride in their accomplishments when they believe they succeeded on their own (ability, effort) than when they believe external factors were responsible (teacher assistance, easy task).

The *controllability* dimension has diverse effects. Feelings of control seem to promote choosing to engage in academic tasks, effort and persistence at difficult tasks, and achievement (Schunk & Zimmerman, 2006). Students who believe they have little control over academic outcomes hold low expectations for success and display low motivation to succeed (Licht & Kistner, 1986). Researchers have shown that students who attribute failures to low ability—which is not controllable—demonstrate lower classroom engagement up to a year later (Glasgow, Dornbusch, Troyer, Steinberg, & Ritter, 1997).

Individual Differences. Some research studies indicate that attributions may vary as a function of gender and ethnic background (Graham & Taylor, 2016). With respect to gender, a common finding (although there are exceptions) is that in subjects such as mathematics and science, girls tend to hold lower expectancies for success than do boys (Bong & Clark, 1999; Meece, 2002; Meece & Courtney, 1992). Margaret exemplifies this in the opening classroom scenario. What is not clear is whether this difference is affected by different attributions, as might be predicted by attributional theories. Some researchers have found that women are more likely to attribute success to external causes (e.g., good luck, low task difficulty) or unstable causes (effort) and attribute failure to internal causes (low ability; Wolleat, Pedro, Becker, & Fennema, 1980); however, other research studies have not yielded differences (Diener & Dweck, 1978; Dweck & Repucci, 1973). It is difficult to reconcile this research because of differences in participants, instruments, and methodologies.

With respect to ethnic differences, some early research suggested that African American students use information about effort less often and less systematically than do Anglo American students and are more likely to use external attributions and hold an external locus of control (Friend & Neale, 1972; Weiner & Peter, 1973). Graham (1991, 1994) re-examined these and other findings and concluded that although many studies show greater externality among African American students, because researchers often did not control for social class, African American students were overrepresented in lower socio-economic backgrounds. When the effect of social class is controlled, researchers find few, if any, ethnic differences (Graham, 1994; Graham & Taylor, 2016; Pajares & Schunk, 2001), and some researchers have found that African American students place greater emphasis on low effort as a cause of failure—an adaptive attributional pattern (Graham & Long, 1986; Hall, Howe, Merkel, & Lederman, 1986).

Van Laar (2000) found a tendency toward external attributions in African American college students; however, these students also held high expectancies for success and felt that their efforts might not be properly rewarded (i.e., negative outcome expectations). This seeming paradox of high success expectancies amidst lower achievement outcomes has been reported by others (Graham & Hudley, 2005). In summary, research investigating ethnic differences in achievement beliefs has not yielded reliable differences (Graham & Taylor, 2002; 2016), and these inconsistent results warrant further research before conclusions are drawn.

Attribution theory has had a major impact on motivation theory, research, and practice. To ensure an optimal level of motivation for learning, students need to make facilitative attributions concerning the outcomes of achievement behaviors. Dysfunctional judgments about abilities, the importance of effort and strategies, and the role of significant others can lead to low levels of motivation and learning.

Social cognitive theory provides another important cognitive perspective on motivation, and much of Chapter 4 is relevant to motivation as well as to learning. The next section discusses influential social cognitive processes.

SOCIAL COGNITIVE PROCESSES

Although different perspectives on motivation are relevant to learning, social cognitive theorists have directed considerable attention to the relation between motivation and learning (Bandura, 1986, 1997; Pajares, 1996; Pajares & Schunk, 2001, 2002; Pintrich, 2003; Schunk, 2012; Schunk & Pajares, 2005; Schunk & Zimmerman, 2006). Important social cognitive motivational processes involved in learning are goals and expectations, social comparison, and self-concept (see Chapter 4).

Goals and Expectations

Goals and self-evaluations of goal progress are strong motivators of learning (Bandura, 1977b, 1986, 1991; Schunk & DiBenedetto, 2016; Schunk & Ertmer, 2000; Zimmerman, 2000; Chapter 4). The perceived negative discrepancy between a goal and performance creates an inducement for change. As people work toward goals, they note their progress and sustain their motivation. In the opening classroom vignette, Rosetta's goal progress should build her self-efficacy and sustain her motivation.

Goal setting works in conjunction with outcome expectations and self-efficacy. People act in ways they believe will help attain their goals. A sense of self-efficacy for performing actions to accomplish goals is necessary for goals to affect behavior (Chapter 4). One of Kerri's goals is to help build Margaret's self-efficacy. Margaret may want teacher praise (goal) and believe she will earn it if she volunteers correct answers (positive outcome expectation). But she may not volunteer answers if she doubts her capabilities to give correct ones (low self-efficacy).

Unlike conditioning theorists who believe that reinforcement is a response strengthener (Chapter 3), Bandura (1986) contended that reinforcement informs people about the likely outcomes of behaviors and motivates them to behave in ways they believe will result in positive consequences. People form expectations based on their experiences, but another important source of motivation is social comparison.

Social Comparison

Social comparison is the process of comparing ourselves with others (Wheeler & Suls, 2005). Social comparison takes some attention away from how one is performing on a task because it focuses on how well one is doing relative to how others are performing (Régner, Escribe, & Dupeyrat, 2007). Festinger (1954) hypothesized that when objective standards of behavior are unclear or unavailable, people evaluate their abilities and opinions through comparisons with others. He also noted that the most accurate self-evaluations derive from comparisons with those similar in the ability or characteristic being evaluated. The more alike observers are to models, the greater the probability that similar actions by observers are socially appropriate and will produce comparable results (Schunk, 1987). In the opening classroom scene, Jared uses social comparison as he compares his progress with that of his classmates.

Model–observer similarity in competence can improve learning (Braaksma, Rijlaarsdam, & van den Bergh, 2002). This effect on learning may result largely from the motivational effects of vicarious consequences, which depend on self-efficacy. Observing similar others succeed raises observers' self-efficacy and motivates them to try the task because they are apt to believe that if others can succeed, they will too. By comparing Derrick to Jason, Kerri hopes that Derrick's behavior will improve. Observing similar others fail can lead people to believe they also lack the competencies to succeed, which dissuades them from attempting the behavior. Similarity may be especially influential in situations in which individuals have experienced difficulties and possess self-doubts about performing well (Application 9.4).

Developmental status is important in social comparison. The ability to use comparative information depends on higher levels of cognitive development and on experience in making comparative evaluations. Festinger's hypothesis may not apply to children younger than 5 or 6, because they tend not to relate two or more elements in thought and are egocentric in that the "self" dominates their cognitive focus (Higgins, 1981; Chapter 8). This does not mean that young children cannot evaluate themselves relative to others, only that they may not automatically do so. Children show increasing interest in comparative information in elementary school, and by fourth grade, they regularly use this information to form self-evaluations of competence (Ruble, Boggiano, Feldman, & Loebl, 1980; Ruble, Feldman, & Boggiano, 1976).

APPLICATION 9.4
Social Comparison

Teachers can use social comparison to improve behavior and effort in completing assigned tasks. As a second-grade teacher works with a small reading group, she compliments students for appropriate behaviors, which emphasizes expected behaviors and instills self-efficacy in students for performing accordingly. She might say:

- "I really like the way Adrian is sitting quietly and waiting for all of us to finish reading."
- "I like the way Carrie read that sentence clearly so we could hear her."

Observing student successes leads other students to believe they are capable of succeeding. A teacher might ask a student to go to the board and write contractions for listed words. The students in the group have similar skills, so the successes of the student at the board should raise self-efficacy in the others.

A swimming coach might group swimmers with similar talents and skills when planning practices and simulated competitions. With students of like skills in the same group, a coach can use social comparison while working on improving movements and speed. The coach might say:

- "Dan is really working to keep his legs together with little bending and splashing as he moves through the water. Look at the extra momentum he is gaining from this movement. Good job, Dan!"
- "Joel is doing an excellent job of cupping his hands in a way that acts like a paddle and that pulls him more readily through the water. Good work!"

Teachers and coaches should be judicious in their use of social comparison. Students who serve as models must succeed and be perceived by others as similar in important attributes. If models are perceived as dissimilar (especially in underlying abilities) or if they fail, social comparisons will not positively motivate observers.

The meaning and function of comparative information change with development, especially after children enter school. Preschoolers actively compare at an overt level (e.g., amount of reward). Other social comparisons involve how one is similar to and different from others and competition based on a desire to be better than others (e.g., Jared) without involving self-evaluation (e.g., "I'm the general; that's higher than the captain"; Mosatche & Bragioner, 1981). As children become older, social comparisons shift to a concern for how to perform a task (Ruble, 1983). First graders engage in peer comparisons—often to obtain correct answers from peers. Providing comparative information to young children increases motivation for practical reasons. Direct adult evaluation of children's capabilities (e.g., "You can do better") influences children's self-evaluations more than comparative information.

Comparing one's current and prior performances (temporal comparison) and noting progress enhances self-efficacy and motivation. Although this capability is present in young children, they may not employ it. R. Butler (1998) found among children ages 4 to 8 that temporal comparisons increased with age, but that children most often attended only to their last outcome. In contrast, children frequently employed social comparisons and evaluated their performances higher if they exceeded those of peers. Butler's results suggest that teachers need to assist children in making temporal comparisons, such as by showing children their prior work and pointing out areas of improvement. Kerri does this with Jared, Matt, and Rosetta.

Self-Concept

Dimensions and Development. *Self-concept* refers to one's collective self-perceptions (a) formed through experiences with, and interpretations of, the environment and (b) heavily influenced by reinforcements and evaluations by significant other persons (Shavelson & Bolus, 1982). Self-concept is multidimensional and comprises elements such as self-esteem, self-confidence, self-concept stability, and self-crystallization (Pajares & Schunk, 2001, 2002). *Self-esteem* is one's perceived sense of self-worth, or whether one accepts and respects oneself. Self-esteem is the evaluative component of self-concept. *Self-confidence* denotes the extent to which one believes one can produce results, accomplish goals, or perform tasks competently (analogous to self-efficacy). Self-esteem and self-confidence are related. The belief that one is capable of performing a task can raise self-esteem. High self-esteem might lead one to attempt difficult tasks, and subsequent success enhances self-confidence.

Self-concept stability refers to the ease or difficulty of changing the self-concept. Stability depends in part on how crystallized or structured beliefs are. Beliefs become crystallized with development and repeated similar experiences. By adolescence, individuals have relatively well-structured perceptions of themselves in areas such as intelligence, sociability, and sports. Brief experiences that provide evidence conflicting with personal beliefs may not have much effect. Conversely, self-concept is modified more easily when people have poorly formed ideas about themselves, usually because they have little or no experience.

The development of self-concept proceeds from a concrete view of oneself to a more abstract one. Young children perceive themselves concretely; they define themselves in terms of their appearance, actions, name, possessions, and so forth. Children do not distinguish among behaviors and underlying abilities or personal characteristics. They also do not have a sense of enduring personality because their self-concepts are diffuse and loosely organized. They acquire a more abstract view with development and as a function of schooling. As they develop separate conceptions of underlying traits and abilities, their self-concepts become better organized and more complex.

Development also produces a differentiated self-concept. Although most investigators postulate the existence of a general self-concept, evidence indicates that it is hierarchically organized (Marsh & Shavelson, 1985; Pajares & Schunk, 2001, 2002; Schunk & Pajares, 2005; Shavelson & Bolus, 1982). A general self-concept tops the hierarchy, and specific subarea self-concepts fall below. Self-perceptions of specific behaviors influence subarea self-concepts (e.g., mathematics, social studies), which in turn combine to form the academic self-concept. For example, Chapman and Tunmer (1995) found that children's reading self-concept comprised perceived competence in reading, perceived difficulty with reading, and attitudes toward reading. General self-concept comprises self-perceptions in the academic, social, emotional, and physical domains. Vispoel (1995) examined artistic domains and found evidence for the multifaceted nature of self-concept but less support for the hierarchical framework.

Experiences that help form the self-concept emanate from personal actions and vicarious (modeled) experiences (Schunk & DiBenedetto, 2016). The role of social comparison is important, especially in school (see discussion earlier in this chapter). This idea is reflected in the *big-fish-little-pond effect* (Marsh & Hau, 2003): Students in selective schools (who have intelligent peers) may have lower self-concepts than those in less-selective schools. Marsh and Hau found evidence for this effect among students in 26 countries. Research also shows that being placed in a high-achieving group is associated with lower self-concept (Trautwein, Lüdtke, Marsh, & Nagy, 2009).

Evidence indicates that self-concept is not passively formed but rather is a dynamic structure that mediates significant intrapersonal and interpersonal processes (Cantor & Kihlstrom, 1987). Markus and colleagues (Markus & Nurius, 1986; Markus & Wurf, 1987) hypothesized that the self-concept is made up of self-schemas or generalizations formed through experiences. These schemas process personal and social information much as academic schemas process cognitive information. The multidimensional nature of self-concept is captured by the notion of *working self-concept*, or self-schemas that are mentally active at any time (presently accessible self-knowledge). Thus, a stable core (general) self-concept exists, surrounded by domain-specific self-concepts capable of being altered.

Self-Concept and Learning. The idea that self-concept is positively related to school learning is intuitively plausible. Students who are confident of their learning abilities and feel self-worthy should display greater interest and motivation in school, which enhances achievement. Higher achievement, in turn, validates self-confidence for learning and maintains high self-esteem.

Unfortunately, these ideas have not been consistently supported by research. Wylie (1979) reviewed many research studies. The general correlation between academic achievement measures (grade point averages) and measures of self-concept was $r = +.30$, which is a moderate and positive relation suggesting a direct correspondence between the two. Correlation does not imply causality, so it cannot be determined whether self-concept influences achievement, achievement influences self-concept, each influences the other, or each is influenced by other variables (e.g., factors in the home). Wylie found somewhat higher correlations when standardized measures of self-concept were employed and lower correlations with researcher-developed measures. That higher correlations were obtained between achievement and academic self-concept than between achievement and overall self-concept supports the hierarchical organization notion. The highest correlations with achievement have been found with domain-specific self-concepts (e.g., in areas such as English or mathematics; Schunk & DiBenedetto, 2016).

It is reasonable to assume that self-concept and learning affect one another. Given the general nature of self-concept, brief interventions designed to alter it may not have much effect. Rather, interventions tailored to specific domains may alter domain-specific self-concepts, which may extend up the hierarchy and influence higher-level self-concepts.

The research literature supports this proposition. The moderate relation between self-concept and achievement found in research studies may result because general self-concept measures were used. Conversely, when domain-specific self-concept measures are compared with achievement in that domain, the relation is strong and positive (Pajares & Schunk, 2001, 2002; Schunk & Pajares, 2005). As self-concept is defined more specifically, it increasingly resembles self-efficacy, and there is much evidence showing that self-efficacy predicts achievement (Bandura, 1997; Pajares, 1996; Schunk & DiBenedetto, 2016; Chapter 4).

Many of the suggestions made in this chapter have relevance for influencing self-concept. In their review of research on self-concept interventions, O'Mara, Marsh, Craven, and Debus (2006) found that domain-specific interventions had stronger effects on self-concept than did interventions designed to raise global self-concept. Teachers who show students they are capable of learning and have made academic progress in specific content areas, provide positive feedback, use models effectively, and minimize negative social comparisons can help develop students' self-concepts (see Chapter 4 for ways to enhance self-efficacy).

In summary, with its emphasis on goals, expectations, social comparisons, and self-concept, social cognitive theory offers a useful perspective on motivation. Application 9.5 gives some classroom applications of social cognitive processes. We now discuss goal orientations, which are relevant to social cognitive processes.

APPLICATION 9.5
Social Cognitive Processes

Students enter learning situations with a sense of self-efficacy for learning based on prior experiences, personal qualities, and social support mechanisms. Teachers who know their students well and incorporate various educational practices can positively affect motivation and learning.

Instruction presented such that students can comprehend it fosters self-efficacy for learning. Some students learn well in large group instruction, whereas others benefit from small group work. If a university English professor is introducing a unit on the major works of William Shakespeare, the instructor initially might provide background on Shakespeare's life and literary reputation. Then the professor could divide the students into small groups to review and discuss what had been introduced. This process would help build the self-efficacy of both

students who learn well in large groups and those who do better in small groups.

As the professor moves through the unit and introduces the major periods of Shakespeare's career, the student activities, exercises, and assignments should provide students with performance feedback. Progress made toward the acquisition of basic facts about Shakespeare and his works can be assessed through quizzes or self-checked assignments. Individual student growth as it relates to understanding specific Shakespearean works can be conveyed through written comments on essays and papers and through verbal comments during class discussions.

Students should be encouraged to share their insights and frustrations in working with interpretations of Shakespearean plays. Guiding students to serve as models during

(Continued)

APPLICATION 9.5 *(continued)*

the analysis and discussion of the plays will promote their self-efficacy better than will having a professor who has built his or her career studying Shakespeare provide the interpretation.

In working with students to develop goals toward learning and understanding Shakespeare and his works, the professor could help each student focus on short-term and specific goals. For example, the professor might have students read a portion of one major work and write a

critique, after which they could discuss their analyses with one another. Breaking the content into short segments helps to instill self-efficacy for eventually mastering it. Commenting on the quality of the critiques by students is more beneficial than rewarding them for reading a certain number of plays. Being able to interpret Shakespeare's work is more difficult than reading, and rewarding students for progress on difficult assignments strengthens self-efficacy.

GOAL ORIENTATIONS

Goal orientations are learners' reasons for engaging in academic tasks (Anderman, Austin, & Johnson, 2002). Goal orientations are central motivational variables in *goal theory*, which incorporates many variables hypothesized to be important by other theories (Schunk et al., 2014). This theory postulates that important relations exist among goals and goal orientations, expectations, attributions, conceptions of ability, social and self-comparisons, and achievement behaviors (Anderman & Wolters, 2006; Elliot, 2005; Maehr & Zusho, 2009; Meece, Anderman & Anderman, 2006; Senko, 2016).

Although goal theory bears some similarity to goal-setting theory (Bandura, 1988; Locke & Latham, 1990, 2002; Chapter 4), important differences exist. Educational and developmental psychologists developed goal theory to explain and predict students' achievement behaviors. Goal-setting theory, in contrast, has drawn from various disciplines, including social psychology, management, and clinical and health psychology. Goal-setting theory is more concerned with how goals are established and altered and with the role of their properties (e.g., specificity, difficulty, and proximity) in instigating and directing behavior. Goal theory also considers a wide array of variables in explaining goal-directed behavior, some of which may not directly involve goals (e.g., comparisons with others). Goal-setting theory typically considers a more restricted set of influences on behavior.

Types of Goal Orientations

Goal theory emphasizes that different types of goals can influence behavior in achievement situations (Anderman & Wolters, 2006; Elliot, 2005; Maehr & Zusho, 2009; Murayama, Elliot, & Friedman, 2012; Senko, 2016). Researchers have identified different orientations (Elliot & McGregor, 2001; Elliot & Thrash, 2001).

One distinction is between learning and performance goal orientations (Dweck, 1991, 1999, 2002; Dweck & Leggett, 1988; Elliott & Dweck, 1988; Schunk, 1996; Schunk & Swartz, 1993a, 1993b; Figure 9.4). A *learning goal* refers to what knowledge, behavior, skill, or strategy students are to acquire; a *performance goal* denotes what task students are to complete. Other types of goals mentioned in the literature that are conceptually similar to learning goals include *mastery, task-involved,* and *task-focused goals* (Ames & Archer, 1988; Butler, 1992; Meece, 1991; Nicholls, 1984); synonyms for performance goals include *ego-involved* and *ability-focused goals.* In the opening scenario, Matt seems to hold a learning goal orientation, whereas Jared is more performance-goal oriented.

Although these goal orientations at times may be related (e.g., learning produces faster performance), the importance of these goals for achievement behavior and learning stems from the effects they can have on learners' beliefs and cognitive processes (Pintrich, 2000a). A learning goal orientation focuses students' attention on processes and strategies that help them acquire capabilities and improve their skills (Ames, 1992a). The task focus motivates behavior and directs and sustains attention on task aspects critical for learning. Students who pursue a learning goal are apt to feel efficacious for attaining it and be motivated to engage in task-appropriate activities (e.g., expend effort, persist, and use effective strategies; Bandura, 1986; Schunk & DiBenedetto, 2016). Self-efficacy is substantiated as they work on the task and assess their progress (Wentzel, 1992). Perceived progress in skill acquisition and self-efficacy for continued learning sustain motivation and enhance skillful performance (Schunk, 1996; Figure 9.4a). Learning goals positively predict intrinsic motivation (Spinath & Steinmayr, 2012). From a related perspective, students who pursue learning goals are apt to hold a *growth mindset,* which reflects the belief that one's qualities and abilities can be developed through effort (Dweck, 2006).

In contrast, a performance goal orientation focuses attention on completing tasks (Linnenbrink-Garcia et al., 2012; Figure 9.4b). Such goals may not highlight the importance of the processes and strategies underlying task completion or raise self-efficacy for acquiring skills (Schunk & Swartz, 1993a, 1993b). As students work on tasks, they may not compare their present and past performances to determine progress. Performance goals can lead to social comparisons of one's work with that of others to determine progress. Social comparisons can result in low perceptions of ability among students who experience difficulties, which adversely affect task motivation (Schunk, 1996). Not surprisingly, competition can promote adoption of performance goals (Murayama & Elliot, 2012). Students who pursue performance goals may hold a *fixed mindset,* reflecting the idea that one's qualities and abilities are limited and cannot change very much (Dweck, 2006).

Research results support these ideas (Rolland, 2012). During science lessons, Meece, Blumenfeld, and Hoyle (1988) found that students who emphasized task-mastery goals reported more active cognitive engagement characterized by self-regulatory activities

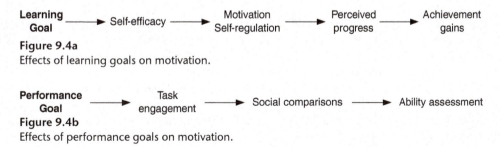

Figure 9.4a
Effects of learning goals on motivation.

Figure 9.4b
Effects of performance goals on motivation.

(e.g., reviewing material not understood). Intrinsic motivation (discussed later in this chapter) related positively to goals stressing learning and understanding.

Elliott and Dweck (1988) gave children feedback indicating they had high or low ability, along with instructions highlighting a learning goal of developing competence or a performance goal of appearing competent. Learning-goal children sought to increase competence by choosing challenging tasks and using problem-solving strategies. Performance-goal children who received high-ability feedback persisted at the task but also avoided challenging tasks that might have entailed public errors. Performance-goal children given low-ability feedback selected easier tasks, did not persist to overcome mistakes, and displayed negative affect.

During comprehension instruction with children low in reading skills, Schunk and Rice (1989) found that a process goal (e.g., learning to use a comprehension strategy) and a product (e.g., performance) goal (e.g., answering questions) led to higher self-efficacy than did a general goal of working productively; however, the process and product conditions did not differ. Schunk and Rice (1991) found that combining a process goal with feedback on progress toward the goal of learning to use a strategy promoted self-efficacy and skill better than process and product goal conditions. These two studies suggest that without progress feedback, learning goals may not be more effective than performance goals among students with reading problems.

Schunk and Swartz (1993a, 1993b) provided children in regular and gifted classes with a process goal of learning to use a paragraph-writing strategy or a product (performance) goal of writing paragraphs. Half of the process-goal students periodically received feedback on their progress in learning the strategy. Schunk and Swartz found that the process goal with feedback was the most effective and that the process goal with or without feedback led to higher achievement outcomes than did the product goal.

Schunk (1996) provided fourth graders with instruction and practice on fractions, along with either a learning goal (e.g., learning how to solve problems) or a performance goal (e.g., solving problems). In the first study, half of the students in each goal condition evaluated their problem-solving capabilities. The learning goal with or without self-evaluation and the performance goal with self-evaluation led to higher self-efficacy, skill, motivation, and task orientation than did the performance goal without self-evaluation. In the second study, all students in each goal condition evaluated their progress in skill acquisition. The learning goal led to higher motivation and achievement outcomes than did the performance goal. These findings were replicated with college students by Schunk and Ertmer (1999), who found that self-efficacy for applying computer skills was enhanced when students received a process (learning) goal and an opportunity to evaluate their learning progress.

Investigators have examined additional distinctions in the mastery–performance goal orientation dichotomy (Elliot, 2005; Elliot & McGregor, 2001; Elliot & Thrash, 2001; Maehr & Zusho, 2009; Senko, 2016). Linnenbrink and Pintrich (2002) proposed classifying mastery and performance goals according to whether they involve approach or avoidance and hypothesized that goals have different emotional consequences. Approach mastery goals are predicted to lead to positive affect, whereas both types of avoidance goals are expected to result in negative affect. The role of affect in goal choice and outcomes often is not addressed, yet the emotional consequences of motivation for schooling are important (Meyer & Turner, 2002). Murayama and Elliot (2012) found that competition promoted both performance-approach and performance-avoidance goals, which had conflicting effects on achievement: The former raised it whereas the latter undermined it. Other evidence, however, indicates that performance-approach and performance-avoidance goals are highly related (Linnenbrink-Garcia et al., 2012).

Goal orientations play a key role in self-regulated learning (Chapter 10), because they provide a framework within which learners interpret and react to events (Dweck & Leggett, 1988; Meece, 1994). Students who develop and maintain high self-efficacy for learning have higher expectancies for success, greater perceived control over learning, and more intrinsic interest in learning (Schunk & DiBenedetto, 2016). Harackiewicz, Barron, Tauer, Carter, and Elliot (2000) found that mastery goals predicted immediate and long-term interest in the discipline among college students, whereas performance goals predicted grades better. Students are more likely to adopt a task/learning-goal orientation when they believe they can improve their ability through expending effort (Dweck & Leggett, 1988; Meece, 1994; Nicholls & Miller, 1984). Purdie, Hattie, and Douglas (1996) found among Australian and Japanese students that a conception of learning as understanding was related to greater use of learning strategies. In contrast to this incremental conception of ability, students with a fixed conception believe that effort will improve ability only to a set limit. Effort becomes less important when ability is fixed.

Achievement goal patterns also can motivate self-regulated learning (Zimmerman & Cleary, 2009). Providing students with feedback stressing a learning-goal orientation can enhance self-efficacy, motivation, self-regulatory activities, and achievement more than providing feedback emphasizing performance goals (Schunk & Swartz, 1993a, 1993b). Achievement goals affect students' task persistence and effort expenditure (Elliott & Dweck, 1988). Under performance-oriented conditions, children with low perceived ability experience performance deterioration when they begin to fail (Meece, 1994); however, this pattern is not found among learning-oriented children regardless of perceived ability and among performance-oriented students with high perceived ability. Ames and Archer (1988) found that classroom mastery (learning) goal orientation related positively to students' reported use of effective learning strategies and effort attributions.

Research shows that achievement goals can affect how students study and what they learn (Dweck & Master, 2008). Learning-oriented students tend to use deep processing strategies that enhance conceptual understandings and that require cognitive effort (e.g., integrating information, monitoring comprehension; Graham & Golan, 1991; Nolen, 1996; Pintrich & Garcia, 1991). In contrast, ego-oriented goal patterns are associated with such short-term and surface-level processing strategies as rehearsal and memorization (Graham & Golan, 1991; Meece, 1994).

Factors in the home and school can affect the role of learning-goal orientation in self-regulation. Learning situations that emphasize self-improvement, discovery of new information, and usefulness of learning material can promote a learning-goal orientation (Ames & Archer, 1988; Graham & Golan, 1991; Jagacinski & Nicholls, 1984). In contrast, interpersonal competition, tests of intellectual skills, and normative evaluations can enhance performance goals. Murdock and Anderman (2006) found that performance goals related to cheating, whereas students who pursued mastery goals were less likely to cheat.

In sum, evidence demonstrates that a learning-goal orientation facilitates achievement motivation, beliefs, and skill acquisition better than a performance-goal orientation, although performance goals bear a relation to grades. The next section addresses a mechanism that may explain these effects.

Conceptions of Ability

Dweck and her colleagues hypothesized that goal orientation is intimately related to one's theory about the nature of intelligence or ability (Dweck, 1991, 1999, 2006; Dweck & Leggett, 1988; Dweck & Master, 2008; Dweck & Molden, 2005). Dweck (1991, 2006) proposed two theories of intelligence or ability: entity and incremental. People who hold an *entity theory* (or *fixed mindset*) believe that intelligence or ability is relatively fixed, stable, and unchanging over time and task conditions. Effort helps to reach one's limit, not for progressing much beyond it. Difficulties are viewed as obstacles and can lower self-efficacy and lead students to display ineffective strategies and give up or work halfheartedly.

In contrast, people who hold an *incremental theory* (or *growth mindset*) roughly equate intelligence or ability with learning. Students believe that intelligence can change and increase with experience, effort, and learning. An upper limit of intelligence—if it exists—is sufficiently high and does not preclude one from working harder to improve. Difficulties are viewed as challenges and can raise self-efficacy if students mobilize effort, persist at the task, and use effective strategies.

With some exceptions, students who hold a growth (incremental) mindset are likely to believe that learning will raise their overall ability and thus should be more apt to adopt learning goals. Conversely, students holding a fixed (entity) mindset may not adopt learning goals because they believe that learning will not raise their overall level of ability. These predictions have received research support (Dweck, 1991, 1999, 2006; Dweck & Molden, 2005; Krakovsky, 2016).

Research also shows important relations among conceptions of ability, motivation, and achievement outcomes. Wood and Bandura (1989) had adults engage in a managerial decision-making task and told them that decision-making ability was fixed (reflecting their basic cognitive capabilities) or incremental (developed through practice). Incremental decision makers maintained high self-efficacy, set challenging goals, applied rules efficiently, and performed better; entity participants showed a decline in self-efficacy. Jourden, Bandura, and Banfield (1991) obtained similar results among college students on a motor task. Participants who were led to believe that performance was an acquirable skill showed increased self-efficacy, positive self-reactions to their performance, and greater skill acquisition and task interest; those led to believe that performance reflected inherent aptitude showed no gain in self-efficacy, little increase in skill and interest, and negative self-reactions.

Implicit Theories

Constructivist theories (Chapter 8) call attention to many facets of motivation, including the cognitive and the affective. A central premise of many contemporary theories of learning and motivation, and one that fits nicely with constructivist assumptions, is that people hold *implicit theories* about issues, such as how they learn, what contributes to school achievement, and how motivation affects performance. Learning and thinking occur in the context of learners' beliefs about cognition, which differ as a function of personal, social, and cultural factors (Moll, 2001).

Research shows that implicit theories about such processes as learning, thinking, and ability can influence how students engage in learning, their achievement, and their views about what leads to success in and outside of the classroom (Dweck, 1999, 2006; Dweck & Leggett, 1988; Dweck & Molden, 2005; Yeager & Dweck, 2012). The preceding section discussed how fixed and growth mindsets can affect students' motivation differently. Evidence also shows that implicit theories and mindsets can affect the way that learners process information (Graham & Golan, 1991). Students who believe that learning outcomes are under their control (growth mindset) may expend greater mental effort, rehearse more, use organizational strategies, and employ other tactics to improve learning. In contrast, students who hold a fixed view may not expend the same type of effort.

Students differ in how they view kinds of classroom learning. Nicholls and Thorkild-sen (1989) found that elementary school students perceived learning substantive matters (e.g., mathematical logic, facts about nature) as more important than learning intellectual conventions (e.g., spelling, methods of representing addition). Students also saw didactic teaching as more appropriate for teaching of conventions than for matters of logic and fact. Nicholls, Patashnick, and Nolen (1985) found that high school students held definite beliefs about what types of activities should lead to success. A focus during learning on mastery of the task was positively associated with student perceptions that success depends on being interested in learning, working hard, trying to understand (as opposed to memorizing), and working collaboratively.

Implicit theories likely are formed as children encounter socialization influences. Dweck (1999) found evidence for implicit theories in children as young as 3.5 years. Early on, children are socialized by significant others about right and wrong, good and bad. Through what they are told and what they observe, they form implicit theories about rightness, badness, and the like. At achievement tasks, praise and criticism from others influence what they believe produce good and poor outcomes (e.g., "You worked hard and got it right," "You don't have what it takes to do this right"). As with other beliefs, these may be situated within contexts, and teachers and parents may stress different causes of achievement (effort and ability). By the time children enter school, they hold a wide range of implicit theories that they have constructed and that cover most situations. Stressing to learners that effort, good strategy use, and help from others contribute to success can help develop growth mindsets (Yeager & Dweck, 2012).

Research on implicit theories suggests that learning requires more than developing memory networks with academic content. Also important are how children refine, modify, combine, and elaborate their conceptual understandings as a function of experience. Those understandings are situated in a personal belief system and include beliefs about the usefulness and importance of knowledge, how it relates to what else one knows, and in what situations it may be appropriate.

INTRINSIC MOTIVATION

Intrinsic motivation refers to a desire to engage in an activity for no obvious reward except task engagement itself (Lepper, Corpus, & Iyengar, 2005). Intrinsic motivation contrasts with *extrinsic motivation*, or the desire to engage in an activity as a means to an end. Intrinsic and extrinsic motivation are not two ends of a continuum; there is no automatic relation between them such that the higher one is the lower the other is (Lepper et al., 2005). For any given activity, an individual may be high on both, low on both, average on one and low on the other, and so forth.

The importance of intrinsic motivation for learning is underscored by research showing that interest in learning relates positively to cognitive processing and achievement (Alexander & Murphy, 1998; Schiefele, 1996, 2009). This section examines intrinsic motivation, especially as it relates to learning.

Early Views

Early views on intrinsic motivation conceived of it as reflecting effectance motivation, mastery motivation, and incongruity and arousal.

Effectance Motivation. In a seminal paper, White (1959) defined *effectance motivation* as:

> Fitness or ability, and the suggested synonyms capability, capacity, efficiency, proficiency, and skill. It is therefore a suitable word to describe such things as grasping and exploring, crawling and walking, attention and perception, language and thinking, manipulating and changing the surroundings, all of which promote an effective—a competent—interaction with the environment. The behavior . . . is directed, selective, and persistent, and it is continued not because it serves primary drives, which indeed it cannot serve until it is almost perfected, but because it satisfies an intrinsic need to deal with the environment. (pp. 317–318)

Effectance motivation is seen in young children when they interact with environmental features that catch their attention. A youngster may reach out and grab an object, turn it over, and push it away in an effort to control it. Effectance motivation is undifferentiated in young children; it is directed toward all aspects of the environment. With development, motivation becomes increasingly specialized. Once children enter school, they show effectance motivation in achievement behaviors in various school subjects.

Effectance motivation arises when biological motives are satisfied; it also facilitates future need satisfaction. Taking the top off of a jar initially satisfies the effectance motive, but in so doing the child learns that cookies are in the jar. This knowledge may be used in the future to satisfy hunger.

Mastery Motivation. The notion of effectance motivation is intuitively appealing, but its generality limits the search for its causes and its effectiveness as an explanation for actions. How to influence such a global construct, and thereby improve academic motivation, is unclear.

Harter (1978, 1981) attempted to specify the antecedents and consequences of effectance motivation in a developmental model of *mastery motivation*. Whereas White focused on success, Harter took success and failure into account. Harter also stressed the roles of socializing agents and rewards, the process whereby children internalize mastery goals and develop a self-reward system, and the important correlates of effectance motivation (e.g., perceived competence and control).

The part of the model dealing with success is similar to White's formulation. Effectance motivation can trigger mastery attempts. White considered the motive generic, but Harter differentiated it according to domain (school, peers, athletics). Most behaviors involve optimally challenging tasks. Successes produce intrinsic pleasure and perceptions of competence and control, which in turn strengthen effectance motivation.

Also important are socializing agents. Some positive reinforcement for mastery attempts is necessary to develop and maintain motivation. Much of this reinforcement comes from primary caregivers, and eventually a self-reward system is internalized, which allows children to reinforce themselves for mastery attempts. Children acquire mastery goals by observing others, and internalization becomes more complete with development. In support of these points, researchers have shown that children from homes in which learning opportunities and activities are emphasized display higher intrinsic motivation for learning (Gottfried, Fleming, & Gottfried, 1998).

Positive outcomes result when social environments satisfy children's natural desires. Unsuccessful mastery attempts, coupled with a nonresponsive environment, can lead to low perceptions of competence, an external locus of control, and anxiety. Effectance motivation ebbs if children increasingly depend on others to set goals and reward actions.

Research supports many of the propositions of the model. For example, intrinsic motivation relates positively to perceived competence and internal control (Harter, 1981; Harter & Connell, 1984). Social models are important sources of mastery behavior and learning (Bandura, 1986, 1997; Schunk, 1987). Perceived competence relates positively to intrinsic motivation (Gottfried, 1985, 1990). Although socializing agents are important, researchers have identified other ways to foster mastery behavior, including setting learning goals, providing attributional feedback, and teaching self-regulatory strategies (Ames, 1992a; Zimmerman, 2000; Zimmerman & Cleary, 2009). Relatively little attention has been paid to educational implications of the model; for example, how an intrinsic orientation toward school can be developed.

Incongruity and Arousal. Some investigators have postulated that intrinsic motivation reflects an inherent need for a moderate amount of environmental stimulation. Hunt (1963) argued that exploratory behaviors and curiosity are intrinsically motivated and result from incongruity between prior experiences and new information. People extract information from the environment and compare it to internal representations. When incongruity exists between the input and internal knowledge or expectation, people become intrinsically motivated to reduce the incongruity. Hunt postulated that people require an optimal level of incongruity. When deprived of that level, they seek situations that provide it. Too much incongruity proves frustrating and triggers a drive to reduce frustration.

Berlyne (1963) similarly hypothesized that an optimal level of physiological incongruity (stimulation to the nervous system) is necessary and adaptive. If it becomes too low, people are intrinsically motivated to increase it; conversely, they are motivated to reduce it if it becomes too great. Berlyne's "arousal potential" may be interpreted as being approximately equivalent on a physiological level to Hunt's psychological incongruity. Properties of stimuli involving their novelty, ambiguity, incongruity, and surprise affect arousal and motivate people to explore the objects.

Although the notions of arousal and incongruity seem intuitively sensible, the idea of an optimal level of arousal or incongruity is vague, and it is unclear how much is needed to stimulate motivation. Practically speaking, we know novelty and surprise raise student interest, but how much of either is optimal? Too much may lead to frustration, attempts to escape from the situation, and lower interest in learning.

Perceived Control

Cognitive conceptions of intrinsic motivation uniformly predict that *perceived control* over task engagement and outcomes is a critical influence (Schunk & Zimmerman, 2006). Perceived control also forms the core of the belief system of learned helplessness, which is a psychological perspective on behavior relevant to motivation.

Control Beliefs. People might believe that they have greater or lesser amounts of control over many types of situations and circumstances. Recall that Bandura (1986; Chapter 4) distinguished self-efficacy from outcome expectations; the former refers to perceived capabilities to learn or perform behaviors and the latter to beliefs about the consequences of actions. Perceived control (or *agency*) is central to both of these expectations. People who believe they can control what they learn and perform, as well as the consequences of their actions, have a sense of agency. They are more apt to initiate and sustain behaviors directed toward those ends than are individuals who hold a low sense of control over their capabilities and outcomes of their actions.

Skinner, Wellborn, and Connell (1990) distinguished three types of beliefs that contribute to perceived control. *Strategy beliefs* are expectations about factors that influence success (e.g., ability, effort, other persons, luck, unknown factors). *Capacity beliefs* refer to personal capabilities with respect to ability, effort, others, and luck. For example, a strategy belief might be, "The best way for me to get good grades is to work hard"; a capacity belief could be, "I cannot seem to work very hard in school." *Control beliefs* are expectations about one's chances of doing well in school without reference to specific means (e.g., "I can do well in school if I want to"). Research by Skinner et al. (1990) showed that these three beliefs influence academic performance by promoting or decreasing active engagement in learning and that teachers contributed to students' perceptions of control by providing *contingency* (clear and consistent guidelines and feedback) and *involvement* (interest in and dedication of resources to students).

Learned Helplessness. *Learned helplessness* refers to a psychological state involving a disturbance in motivation, cognitive processes, and emotions due to previously experienced uncontrollability (Maier & Seligman, 1976; Peterson, 2000; Seligman, 1975, 1991). Learned helplessness is a psychological phenomenon that highlights perceptions of control and has implications for intrinsic motivation (Maier & Seligman, 2016). Learned helplessness can result from a perceived independence between responses and outcomes.

Helplessness was identified in laboratory studies in which dogs given inescapable shocks were moved to another location, where they could avoid shocks by jumping a hurdle. The prior inescapable shocks conditioned the dogs; they made little attempt to escape in the new setting but, rather, passively endured the shock. Dogs not previously exposed to inescapable shock easily learned to escape.

One outcome of helplessness is passivity. People may do nothing when they believe they have no control over a situation. Helplessness also retards learning. People and animals exposed to uncontrollable situations may never learn adaptive responses or may learn them more slowly than those not exposed to uncontrollability. Helplessness has emotional manifestations. Prior uncontrollable situations may initially make one respond more aggressively, but eventually behavior becomes less assertive. A sense of helplessness undermines intrinsic motivation, which is heavily dependent on perceptions of control.

Seligman's original model of learned helplessness was reformulated to incorporate attributions (Abramson, Seligman, & Teasdale, 1978). The reformulated model postulates that explanations (attributions) for outcomes influence future expectancies of outcomes and reactions to them. Explanations vary along three dimensions: *stable–unstable*, *global–specific*, and *internal–external*. One who attributes negative outcomes to stable causes (e.g., "I always arrive late for everything") is more likely to expect bad events in the future and may acquire helplessness than is one who makes attributions to unstable causes (e.g., "I arrived late when the weather was bad"). Causes can affect many areas of one's life (global) or only one area (specific). Students may believe they lack ability in all school subjects or only in one subject. Global attributions are more likely to produce helplessness. Causes for negative events may be internal to the person (low ability) or external (the teacher gives unfair tests). Internal attributions are apt to result in helplessness. Collectively, people most prone to helplessness are those who typically explain negative events with internal, global, and stable attributions (e.g., "I do poorly in school because I'm not very smart").

Learned helplessness and low intrinsic motivation characterize many students with learning problems who enter a vicious cycle in which negative beliefs reciprocally interact with academic failures (Licht & Kistner, 1986). For various reasons, students fail, begin to doubt their learning capabilities, and view academic successes as uncontrollable. These beliefs produce frustration and giving up readily on tasks. Lack of effort and persistence contribute to further failures, which reinforce negative beliefs. Eventually, students interpret their successes as externally caused; for example, the task was easy, they were lucky, or the teacher helped them. They attribute failures to low ability, which is internal, global, and stable, and which negatively affects self-efficacy, motivation, and achievement (Nolen-Hoeksema, Girgus, & Seligman, 1986). In the opening scene, Margaret may be a candidate for learned helplessness.

Compared with normal learners, students with learning problems hold lower expectations for success, judge themselves lower in ability, and emphasize lack of ability as a cause of failure (Chapman, 1988; Harris, Graham, & Mason, 2006). Such students often do not attribute failure to low effort. They give up readily when they encounter difficulties, cite uncontrollable causes for successes and failures, and hold low perceptions of control over outcomes (Licht & Kistner, 1986).

Dweck integrated learned helplessness into a model of achievement motivation (Dweck, 1986, 1999; Dweck & Leggett, 1988). Ego involvement characterizes helpless students. Their school goals are to complete tasks and avoid negative judgments of their competence. They may hold a fixed mindset and believe that intelligence is a stable quantity (Dweck, 2006). They avoid challenges, display low persistence in the face of difficulty, hold low perceptions of their capabilities, and may experience anxiety while engaged in tasks (Diener & Dweck, 1978). Variables associated with the instructional environment can prevent students with learning problems from entering this cycle and can help them overcome it (Friedman & Medway, 1987). Attributional feedback can alter students' maladaptive achievement beliefs and behaviors. Teachers also need to give students tasks they can accomplish and feedback highlighting progress toward learning goals (Schunk & DiBenedetto, 2016; Stipek, 2002). Stipek and Kowalski (1989) found that teaching task strategies to children who de-emphasized the role of effort raised their academic performance.

In contrast, mastery-oriented students are more likely to hold a growth mindset and display a task-involved achievement pattern. They believe intelligence can improve, and their goals are to learn and become more competent. They hold high perceptions of their learning capabilities, are intrinsically motivated to learn, seek challenges, and persist at difficult tasks.

These ideas fit well with the construct of *learned optimism* (Boman & Mergler, 2014; Seligman, 1991), or an explanatory style that views negative events as only temporary, not one's fault, and specific to the event (i.e., not all-encompassing). For positive events, learned optimists are apt to believe that the good outcomes are enduring and under their control. This style is learned from significant others in individuals' environments (e.g., parents), which means they can be influenced by teaching students to make more facilitative attributions for outcomes.

Self-Determination

Deci and colleagues (Deci, 1980; Deci & Moller, 2005; Grolnick, Gurland, Jacob, & Decourcey, 2002; Reeve, Deci, & Ryan, 2004; Ryan & Deci, 2000, 2009, 2016) postulated that intrinsic motivation is an innate human need and originates in infants as an undifferentiated need for competence and *self-determination*, or "the process of using one's will" (Deci, 1980, p. 26). As children develop, intrinsic motivation differentiates into specific areas (e.g., athletics, academics), and environmental interactions influence the direction of differentiation.

Self-determination theory postulates that intrinsic motivation is influenced by three basic innate psychological needs: competence, autonomy, and relatedness (Ryan & Deci, 2016). The need for competence is similar to White's (1959) need for mastery of the environment (effectance motivation). People have a need to feel competent and interact successfully with others, with tasks and activities, and within larger social contexts. The need for autonomy refers to a sense of control or agency in interactions in the environment (Ryan & Deci, 2000), which is akin to an internal locus of control. Relatedness refers to the need to belong to a group; it also is referred to as a need for belongingness. Instructional practices and environments that support these needs should lead to enhanced feelings of self-determination and higher motivation (Benita, Roth, & Deci, 2014; Jang, Kim, & Reeve, 2012).

Intrinsic motivation is "the human need to be competent and self-determining in relation to the environment" (Deci, 1980, p. 27). The need for intrinsic motivation energizes people's wills, and the will uses the energy of intrinsic motivation to satisfy needs, resolve conflicts with competing needs, and hold needs in check. Intrinsic motivation is satisfied when individuals act willfully. It is the process of self-determination that is intrinsically motivating rather than the underlying need of the demonstrated behavior. A person may have an inherent need to learn and may manifest it by reading books or exploring websites. Intrinsic motivation is satisfied when that person decides which books or web pages to read and when to read them, although the actual reading may provide further satisfaction.

This self-determination view emphasizes the internalization of social values and mores. Society contains many extrinsic rewards and controls that may not fit with children's quest for self-determination but may produce good behavior and social functioning. With development, these external motivators can become an internalized part of the self-regulatory system (Chapter 10).

Behaviors need not be completely intrinsically or extrinsically motivated; an action may reflect both forms of motivation. People may love the work they do in their jobs but also the benefits they receive (e.g., pay, health insurance). Further, the type of motivation may change. A behavior that originally was extrinsically motivated can become internalized and more self-determined. Students may want to avoid some academic activities but they work on them to obtain rewards and avoid teacher punishment. As skills develop and students believe they are becoming more competent, they perceive a sense of control and self-determination over learning.

Self-determination theory is thought provoking and has generated much research. It also has implications for educational practice because it stresses the roles of competence, autonomy, and relatedness needs in learning. Some points in the model are not clearly specified, but researchers continue to test its ideas.

Rewards and Intrinsic Motivation

Another conceptualization of intrinsic motivation was proposed by Lepper and Hodell (1989), who hypothesized four *sources of intrinsic motivation*: challenge, curiosity, control, and fantasy. The perspectives discussed earlier in this chapter support the importance of the first three sources. Fantasy contexts (e.g., involving role-playing, simulations) also seem well designed to heighten intrinsic motivation.

We typically think of intrinsic motivation increasing, but it also can diminish. A large amount of research shows that engaging in an intrinsically interesting activity to obtain an extrinsic reward can undermine intrinsic motivation (Deci, Koestner, & Ryan, 1999, 2001; Lepper et al., 2005; Lepper, Henderlong, & Gingras, 1999). This finding has important educational implications given the prevalence of rewards.

When people are *intrinsically motivated*, they engage in an activity for reasons intrinsic to the activity. The reward comes from working on the task; the task is both the means and the end. The rewards for intrinsic motivation may be feelings of competence and control, self-satisfaction, task success, or pride in one's work.

Csikszentmihalyi (1975) studied persons who engaged in intrinsically motivating activities and found that their experiences reflected total involvement or flow with the activities. *Flow* is a personal process and reflects *emergent motivation* stemming from the discovery of new goals and rewards as a consequence of interacting with the environment (Csikszentmihalyi & Rathunde, 1993; Meyer & Turner, 2002).

In contrast, *extrinsic motivation* involves engaging in an activity for reasons external to the task. This activity is a means to some end: an object, a grade, feedback or praise, or being able to work on another activity. Students are extrinsically motivated if they try to perform well in school primarily to please their parents, earn high grades, or receive teacher approval.

We engage in many activities for both intrinsic and extrinsic reasons. Many students like to feel competent in school and experience pride for a job done well, but they also may desire teacher approval and good grades. Rewards are not inherently extrinsically motivating. Deci (1980) contended that rewards have an *informational* and a *controlling* aspect. Reward systems may be primarily structured to convey information about one's capabilities or to control one's behavior, and the relative salience of each (information or control) influences subsequent behavior. A salient informational aspect indicating successful performance should promote feelings of competence, whereas a salient controlling aspect can lead to perceptions of the reward as the cause of the behavior.

For example, suppose that in a classroom reward system, the more work students accomplish, the more points they earn. Although students will want to work to earn points (because the points can be exchanged for privileges), the points convey information about their capabilities: The more points students earn, the more capable they are. In contrast, if points are given simply for time spent on a task regardless of learning or output, the task may be viewed primarily as a means to an end. The points convey nothing about capabilities; students are more likely to view the rewards as controlling their task engagement. Expected, tangible rewards offered to students for simply doing a task diminish intrinsic motivation (Cameron & Pierce, 1994, 2002).

Lepper (1983; Lepper et al., 1999) postulated that the perception of reward influences students' intrinsic motivation; that is, motivation is largely a function of one's perceptions for engaging in the task. When external conditions are salient, unambiguous, and sufficient to explain the behavior, individuals attribute their behaviors to those conditions. If external conditions are viewed as weak, unclear, or psychologically insufficient to account for their behavior, people are more likely to attribute their actions to their desires or personal dispositions.

In a classic experiment (Lepper, Greene, & Nisbett, 1973), preschoolers were observed during free play. Those who spent a lot of time drawing were selected for the study and assigned to one of three conditions. In the expected-award group, children were offered a good player certificate if they drew a picture. Unexpected-award children were not offered the certificate, but unexpectedly received it after they drew a picture. No-award children were not offered the award and did not receive it. Two weeks later children were again observed during free play.

The expected-award children engaged in drawing for a significantly shorter time following the experiment than they had prior to the study, whereas the other two conditions showed no significant change. Expected-award children spent less time drawing following the study compared with the other conditions. It was not the reward itself that was important but rather the contingency.

Lepper et al. (1973) postulated the *overjustification hypothesis*: Engaging in an intrinsically interesting activity under conditions that make it salient as a means to an end (reward) decreases subsequent interest in that activity. The overjustification hypothesis has been supported in experimental investigations with different tasks and participants of all ages (Lepper et al., 1999; Lepper & Hodell, 1989).

Rewards need not have detrimental effects on performance. Rewards can help develop skills, self-efficacy, and interest when they are linked to one's actual performance and convey that one is making progress in learning. Offering children rewards based on the amount of work they accomplish during learning activities increases self-efficacy, motivation, and skill acquisition compared with offering rewards merely for task participation or not offering rewards (Schunk, 1983e). During a subtraction instruction program, Bandura and Schunk (1981) found that higher self-efficacy related positively to the amount of intrinsic interest children subsequently showed in solving arithmetic problems. There also is evidence that rewards given for creative performances can increase subsequent creative thinking (Byron & Khazanchi, 2012).

Thus, when rewards convey that one has learned, they can increase self-efficacy and intrinsic motivation. As a form of reward, grades can function in the same way. A grade that improves shows that one is performing better in the subject, which promotes self-efficacy and motivation for further learning. Unfortunately, research shows that children's intrinsic motivation in learning declines with development (Lepper, Sethi, Dialdin, & Drake, 1997), although other research shows that interest and self-efficacy are related positively in elementary and middle-grades students (Tracey, 2002). Intrinsic motivation bears a positive relation to performance even in the absence of incentives (Cerasoli, Nicklin, & Ford, 2014). Application 9.6 demonstrates ways to enhance and sustain intrinsic motivation for learning.

APPLICATION 9.6
Intrinsic Motivation

Intrinsic motivation involves perceptions of control and competence. If elementary teachers are helping slower learners complete assigned tasks in an allotted time, they may begin by offering a reward (extrinsic motivator) and work toward building student pride in their accomplishments (intrinsic motivator). Initially teachers might reward students for increased output with time on the computer, verbal praise, or special notes home to parents. Gradually teachers could reward intermittently and then decrease it to allow students to focus more on their accomplishments. The ability to complete tasks in the appropriate time span provides students with information about their capabilities and their ability to control situations. When pride from successfully completing tasks becomes a reward, students are intrinsically motivated to continue to display the new behavior.

High school and college students often are motivated to achieve in school primarily to earn good grades (extrinsic motivators). Teachers and professors might attempt to show the connection between what is being taught in each course and the outside world and to link each student's accomplishments

(Continued)

APPLICATION 9.6 (*continued*)

with his or her ability to be successful in that world. Instructors can help move students toward wanting to learn for the sake of learning and to be able to better address future challenges (intrinsic motivator). Thus, subjects such as chemistry, physics, and biology are not stale subjects studied in artificial laboratories but have direct relevance to what we eat, wear, and do, and how we conduct our daily lives. Field experiences (internships) allow students to observe applications of motivation and learning principles during actual teaching. Enhanced perceived value of learning is apt to strengthen students' intrinsic motivation to learn.

INTEREST AND AFFECT

Interest refers to the liking of and willful engagement in an activity (Schraw & Lehman, 2001). *Affect* is a general term that includes both general moods and specific emotions (Forgas, 2000). Students' interests and affects are linked with motivation and learning in various ways.

Personal and Situational Interest

Researchers distinguish personal from situational interest. *Personal interest* is a relatively stable disposition or characteristic of the individual, whereas *situational interest* is a temporary psychological state of interest in a task or activity (Krapp, Hidi, & Renninger, 1992; Linnenbrink-Garcia, Patall, & Messersmith, 2013; Schiefele, 2009). Although both types of interest are directed toward tasks or activities, personal interest is more diffuse and enduring than situational interest. Thus, one student may have a personal interest in dance, whereas another student might have a situational interest in a particular dance lesson or activity.

Interest is intimately linked with motivation. Students who are interested in activities are more motivated to engage in them and sustain their engagement over time (Schunk et al., 2014). College students' initial interest in course content positively predicts their adoption of mastery goals and continued interest several semesters later (Harackiewicz, Durik, Barron, Linnenbrink-Garcia, & Tauer, 2008).

Interest also contributes to learning. Researchers have shown that both personal and situational interest relate positively to measures of learning such as attention, memory, comprehension, deeper cognitive processing, and achievement (Hidi, 2000; Hidi & Harackiewicz, 2000; Jones, Wilkins, Long, & Wang, 2012; Trautwein, Lüdtke, Marsh, Köller, & Baumert, 2006). This is true even among preschoolers, whose interest in different activities predicts their attention, recognition, and recall memory for these activities later on (Renninger & Wozniak, 1985).

Although young children have personal interests, these can be developed from initial situational interest. Hidi and Renninger (2006) proposed a four-stage model of the development of interest: triggered situational interest, maintained situational interest, emerging personal interest, and well-developed personal interest. This model implies that teachers should try to create situational interest in content or topics and that, over time, this situational interest may develop into personal interest. Teachers often try to do this by using fun activities, linking content to real-life applications, and using various forms of technology. Creating situational interest is much easier than attempting to determine the personal interests of all students and then trying to structure the unit to fit all the different personal interests (Hidi & Harackiewicz, 2000). The development of interest also may be enhanced by students' sense of belonging (Master, Cheryan, & Meltzoft, 2016), which suggests that a welcoming environment may help create and sustain interest in learning.

There is a difference between creating situational interest and sustaining it. Mitchell (1993) found that in high school mathematics classes group work, puzzles, and computer technologies helped to activate interest but did not necessarily sustain it. Rather, situational interest was maintained by the use of meaningful activities and the active involvement of students in learning tasks. The sustaining of interest is imperative for situational interest to develop into personal interest.

Emotions

Affect comprises moods and emotions. *Moods* are low-intensity, diffuse, and enduring affective states that have no clear causes and little cognitive content. *Emotions* are more short-lived, intense phenomena that usually have salient causes (Forgas, 2000). Thus, we might say that Jake was in a good or bad mood, or that he became emotionally upset when he received a D on his physics test.

Pekrun (1992, 2016) proposed a classification of achievement-related emotions that has relevance to motivation. Emotions can be either positive (e.g., pride) or negative (e.g., disappointment). Within each of these two categories, emotions can occur while engaged in the task (process-related; e.g., enjoyment or boredom), be prospective (forward-looking; e.g., hope or anxiety) or be retrospective (backward-looking; e.g., relief or sadness).

Pekrun (1992) also proposed that emotions can affect intrinsic motivation. Positive emotions such as enjoyment while engaged in a task or the anticipation of enjoyment may raise students' intrinsic motivation, whereas negative emotions (e.g., boredom) can lower intrinsic motivation. There is some research to support these predictions (Schunk et al., 2014). The implication for learning is that by creating and sustaining a positive emotional climate, teachers may help to raise not only students' intrinsic motivation but also their task engagement and learning (Rolland, 2012). Research shows that fifth- and sixth-grade students' achievement is predicted by classroom emotional climate and that this relation is mediated by students' engagement in learning (Reyes, Brackett, Rivers, White, & Salovey, 2012). Positive emotions also are associated with better group interactions (Linnenbrink-Garcia, Rogat, & Koskey, 2011).

A topic of much educational interest is test anxiety. Test anxiety is a normal reaction by individuals to evaluative situations. Test anxiety becomes a problem when it is overwhelming and interferes with students' thinking and performance (Zeidner, 1998).

A large body of research shows that test anxiety has negative effects on learning and achievement (Zeidner, 1998). This is not surprising. Anxiety can interfere with attention because negative thoughts and worries can distract students' attention from the learning. It also is possible that highly test-anxious students are that way in part because they use deficient learning and test-taking strategies. They do not study well or know how to take a test. Thus, their anxiety compounds the problem by contributing to low test performance. Such students enter a vicious cycle in which poor strategy use produces low performance, which leads to more anxiety and continued poor strategy use and performance.

Reducing the importance that teachers place on tests can help alleviate some anxiety. Students also can be taught effective learning and test-taking strategies, which are commonly incorporated into learning skills courses at the middle school, high school, and college levels. Teaching students relaxation techniques to use when they become anxious while studying for or taking tests (e.g., breathing exercises) also has been shown to be beneficial (Zeidner, 1998).

INSTRUCTIONAL APPLICATIONS

The material in this chapter suggests many educational applications. Three applications that are linked closely with learning involve achievement motivation training, attribution change programs, and goal orientations.

Achievement Motivation Training

The goal of achievement motivation training is for students to develop thoughts and behaviors typical of learners high in achievement motivation (de Charms, 1968, 1984). De Charms (1976) initially prepared teachers, who then worked with students to help them acquire personal responsibility for their learning outcomes.

The teacher preparation included self-study of academic motivation, realistic goal setting, development of concrete plans to accomplish goals, and evaluation of goal progress. Student motivation was integrated with academic content. Classroom activities included self-study of academic motives, achievement motivation thinking, development of self-concept, realistic goal setting, and promotion of personal responsibility. During a spelling activity designed to teach goal setting, students could choose to learn easy, moderate, or difficult words. To teach personal responsibility, teachers had students write stories about achievement, which were then used in a classroom essay contest. The results showed that the program raised teachers' and students' motivation, halted the trend among low achievers to fall increasingly behind their peers in achievement, and reduced student absenteeism and tardiness.

Integrating instruction on achievement motivation with academic content, rather than including it as an add-on activity with special content, seems imperative. The danger of the latter approach is that students may not understand how to apply achievement motivation principles to other content.

Alderman (1985, 1999) recommended several useful components of achievement motivation instruction. One is having teachers assist students to set realistic goals and provide feedback concerning their goal progress. Another aspect is self-study to examine one's motives for learning and to develop personal responsibility. The distinction between task and ego involvement seems useful. A series of questions helps students examine how they feel about tasks and what they see as their goals (e.g., learning versus pleasing others).

Attributional training (discussed next) also is relevant. One means of teaching personal responsibility is to help students place greater emphasis on effort as a cause of outcomes rather than blaming others when they fail or believing they were lucky when they succeed. As students experience successes, they should develop increased self-efficacy for continued learning and assume greater control of their learning.

Alderman (1985) applied these ideas to a senior high girls' physical education class. On the first day of class, students completed a self-evaluation of their health, physical fitness status, and competence and interest in various activities, and they set fitness goals. They took weekly self-tests in different activities (e.g., aerobics, flexibility, strength, and posture). At the end of the first grading period, students set goals for the final exam. They had various ways to accomplish the aerobic goal (running, walking, and jumping rope). The teacher met with individual students to assess goals and made suggestions if these did not seem realistic. Students established practice schedules of at least three times a week for 9 weeks and kept a record of practices. Following the final exam, students completed a self-evaluation of what they had learned. Alderman noted: "To the instructor, the most striking comment made by students on the final self-evaluation was, 'I learned to set a goal and accomplish it'" (p. 51).

Attribution Change Programs

Attribution change programs attempt to enhance motivation by altering students' attributions for successes and failures. Students commonly have some difficulties when learning new material. Some learners attribute these problems to low ability (e.g., Margaret in the opening scenario). Students who believe they lack the requisite ability to perform well may work at tasks in a lackadaisical fashion, which retards skill development. Researchers have identified students who fit this attributional pattern and have trained them to attribute failure to controllable factors (e.g., low effort, improper strategy use) rather than to low ability. Effort has received special attention; students who believe that they fail largely because of low ability may not expend much effort to succeed. Because effort is under one's control, teaching students to believe that prior difficulties resulted from low effort may lead them to work harder with the expectation that it will produce better outcomes (Application 9.7).

In an early study, Dweck (1975) identified children who had low expectations for success and whose achievement behaviors deteriorated after they experienced failure (e.g., low effort, lack of persistence). Dweck presented the children with arithmetic problems (some of which were insolvable) to assess the extent of performance decline following failure. Children largely attributed their failures to low ability. During training, children solved problems with a criterion number set for each trial. For some (*success-only*) children, the criterion was set at or below their capabilities as determined by the pretest. A similar criterion applied on most trials for *attribution retraining* children, but on some trials the criterion was set beyond their capabilities. When these children failed, they were told they did not try hard enough. On the posttest, success-only children continued to show deterioration in performance following failure, whereas attribution-retraining children showed less impairment. Success-only children continued to stress low ability; attribution-retraining students emphasized low effort.

APPLICATION 9.7
Attributional Feedback

Providing effort attributional feedback to students for their successes promotes achievement expectancies and behaviors, but the feedback must be perceived as credible. When a student is having trouble mastering difficult multiplication problems, the teacher can use past student successes and attributional feedback to build confidence in learning. If the student has mastered addition and multiplication concepts and facts, the teacher might say, "I know these new problems look hard, but you can learn how to work them because you know all the things you need to know. You just need to work hard and you'll do fine."

As the student works, the teacher can interject comments similar to the following:

- "You're doing well; you completed the first step. I was sure you knew your multiplication facts. Keep working hard."
- "Wow! Look at that! You did those so quickly. I knew you could do that because you're working hard."

- "You did it! You got it right because you worked hard."

In a nursing program, an instructor should give the future nurses positive and accurate feedback regarding their administration of various clinical procedures and their effectiveness in interacting with patients. For example, after a trainee has completed the drawing of blood for testing purposes, the instructor might say:

- "I'm glad to see you used all the correct safety procedures in handling the blood. You know what to do."
- "You did a great job of explaining the procedure to the patient before starting the process. You are really good at giving explanations!"
- "You completed the procedure very calmly and with a smile. You have real talent at this."

These types of remarks reflect positive attributional feedback concerning students' competencies, which can raise their self-efficacy and motivation for further learning.

Dweck did not assess self-efficacy or expectancies for success, so the effect of attributions on expectancies could not be determined. Other investigations have shown that teaching students to attribute failures to low effort enhances effort attributions, expectancies, and achievement behaviors (Horner & Gaither, 2004; Robertson, 2000; Schunk, 2008).

Providing effort-attributional feedback to students for their successes also promotes achievement expectancies and behaviors (Schunk, 1982a; Schunk & Cox, 1986; Schunk & Rice, 1986). In the context of subtraction instruction, Schunk (1982a) found that linking children's prior achievements with effort (e.g., "You've been working hard") enhanced task motivation, perceived competence, and skill acquisition better than linking their future achievement with effort (e.g., "You need to work hard") or not providing effort feedback. For effort feedback to be effective, students must believe that it is credible. Feedback is credible when students realistically have to work hard to succeed, as in the early stages of learning. Notice in the opening vignette how Kerri provides effort feedback to Derrick, Amy, and Matt.

Effort feedback may be especially useful for students with learning problems. Schunk and Cox (1986) provided subtraction instruction and practice opportunities to middle school students with learning disabilities. Some students received effort feedback ("You've been working hard") during the first half of a multisession instructional program, others received it during the second half, and learners in a third condition did not receive effort feedback. Each type of feedback promoted self-efficacy, motivation, and skill acquisition better than no feedback. Feedback during the first half of the program enhanced students' effort attributions for successes. Given students' learning disabilities, effort feedback for early or later successes may have seemed credible.

Attribution preferences change with development (Muenks & Miele, 2017; Sigelman, 2012). Young children attribute successes to effort, but by age 8 they begin to form a distinct conception of ability and continue to differentiate the concepts up to about age 12 (Nicholls, 1978, 1979; Nicholls & Miller, 1984). Ability attributions become increasingly important, whereas the influence of effort as a causal factor declines (Harari & Covington, 1981). During arithmetic instruction and practice, Schunk (1983a) found that providing children with ability feedback for prior successes (e.g., "You're good at this") enhanced perceived competence and skill better than providing effort feedback or ability-plus-effort (combined) feedback. Children in the latter condition judged effort expenditure greater than ability-only children and apparently discounted some of the ability information in favor of effort. In a follow-up study using a similar methodology (Schunk, 1984b), ability feedback given when children succeeded early in the course of learning raised achievement outcomes better than early effort feedback regardless of whether the ability feedback was continued or discontinued during the later stages of learning.

The *structure* of classroom activities conveys attributional information (Ames, 1992a, 1992b; see Chapter 11). Students who compete for grades and other rewards are more likely to compare their ability among one another. Students who succeed under *competitive* conditions are more likely to emphasize their abilities as contributing to their successes; those who fail believe they lack the requisite ability to succeed. These conditions create an ego-involved motivational state. Students begin to ask themselves, "Am I smart?" (Ames, 1985).

Cooperative, or *individualistic*, reward structures, on the other hand, minimize ability differences. Cooperative structures stress student effort when each student is responsible for completing some aspect of the task and for instructing other group members on that aspect, and when the group is rewarded for its collective performance. In individualistic structures, students compare their current work with their prior performances. Students in individualistic structures focus on their efforts ("Am I trying hard enough?") and on learning strategies for enhancing their achievement ("How can I do this?").

Goal Orientations

Goal theory and research suggest several ways that teachers can foster a productive learning goal orientation. Teachers might help students alter their beliefs about limits to their abilities and the usefulness of effort as a means to improve their motivation. Giving students progress feedback showing how their skills have improved (i.e., how much they have learned), along with information showing that effort has helped to produce learning, can create a growth mindset, raise self-efficacy, and motivate students to improve skills further.

Another suggestion is to use more collaborative student activities. Duda and Nicholls (1992) found for both sports and schoolwork that task orientation (growth mindset) related to high school students' beliefs that success depends on effort and collaboration with peers, whereas ego orientation (fixed mindset) was associated with beliefs that success is due to high ability and attempting to perform better than others. Goal orientations and beliefs about success were not strongly related to perceived ability. Perceived ability related better to satisfaction in sports than in school; the opposite pattern was obtained for task orientation.

A learning-goal orientation can be developed by helping students adopt learning goals. Teachers can stress acquiring skills, learning new strategies, developing problem-solving methods, and so forth. They also can de-emphasize goals such as completing work, finishing earlier than other students, and rechecking work. Assignments should involve learning; when students practice skills, teachers can stress the reasons for the practice (e.g., to retard forgetting) and inform students that skillful practice shows skills have been retained (i.e., recast practice in terms of skill acquisition). Application 9.8 gives some other suggestions for instilling a task orientation, incremental ability conception, and focus on learning goals in students.

APPLICATION 9.8
Goal Orientations

Promoting learning goal orientations in the classroom can foster self-efficacy and enhance learning. In working with elementary students on multiplication, Ms. Cataino might introduce the unit by saying, "Boys and girls, today we are going to learn some things about putting numbers together that will make you much better math students." Then she could emphasize acquisition of skills ("As we work today, you are going to learn how to multiply numbers together"), learning of new strategies ("We are going to use these manipulatives to help us figure out different ways to group numbers together and multiply"), and development of problem-solving methods ("I want all of you to put on your thinking caps as we work to figure out different numbers you can multiply together to make 20"). It

is important to stress these goals and de-emphasize goals such as completing work and finishing before other students.

Working in a large group, in small groups, or in pairs to solve problems collaboratively helps diminish competition and allows students to focus more on learning than on completing tasks. With law students, an instructor could pair them to help one another locate prior cases on child abuse and encourage them with statements such as, "I want you to put your efforts toward learning how to research a case," and "I want you to work to prepare precise short and direct opening statements." These types of statements focus students on goals for the task at hand; students can then assess learning progress against these statements.

SUMMARY AND CRITIQUE

Chapter Summary

Motivation is the process of instigating and sustaining goal-directed behavior. Some early views on motivation were drive theory, conditioning theory, cognitive consistency theory, and humanistic theory. Each of these contributed to the understanding of motivation, but none was adequate to explain human motivated behavior. Current theories view motivation as reflecting cognitive constructivist processes, although these theories differ in the importance ascribed to various processes. Models of motivated learning assume that motivation operates before, during, and after learning.

Achievement motivation theory postulates that need for achievement is a general motive leading individuals to perform their best in achievement contexts. Achievement behavior represents an emotional conflict between hope for success and fear of failure. Contemporary achievement motivation theory stresses learners' expectancies of success and the value or importance they place on learning. Self-worth theory hypothesizes that achievement behavior is a function of students' efforts to preserve the perception of high ability among themselves and others. Other researchers have focused on motivational states such as task and ego involvement.

Attribution theory incorporates Rotter's locus of control and many elements of Heider's naïve analysis of action. Weiner's attribution theory, which is relevant to achievement settings, categorizes attributions along three dimensions: internal–external, stable–unstable, and controllable–uncontrollable. Attributions are important because they affect achievement beliefs, emotions, and behaviors.

Key social cognitive processes are goals and expectations, social comparison, and self-concept. People set goals and act in ways they believe will help them attain their goals. By comparing present performance to the goal and noting progress, people experience a sense of self-efficacy for improvement. Motivation depends on believing that one will achieve desired outcomes from given behaviors (positive outcome expectations) and that one is capable of learning or performing those behaviors (high self-efficacy). Social comparison with others is an important sources of information to form outcome and efficacy expectations. Research suggests that self-concept is hierarchically organized and multifaceted. It develops from a concrete to a more abstract self-view. Self-concept and learning appear to influence one another in reciprocal fashion.

Goal orientations are the reasons that students engage in tasks. Learners may possess learning (mastery) or performance (ability-focused) goal orientations. Learning goals focus attention better on skills and competencies needed for learning and that as students perceive progress, their self-efficacy and motivation are enhanced. In contrast, performance goals may not lead to the same focus on progress but rather result in social comparison, which may not raise motivation. Goal orientations are linked with conceptions of ability that reflect an entity (fixed mindset) or incremental (growth mindset) perspective.

Intrinsically motivated activities are ends in themselves, in contrast to extrinsically motivated actions that are means to ends. Investigators have hypothesized that young children have intrinsic motivation to understand and control their environments, which becomes more specialized with development and progression in school. Harter's theory highlights the role of socializing agents and perceived competence. Other theorists hypothesize that intrinsic motivation depends on the needs for optimal levels of psychological or physiological incongruity. Many theories stress people's desire to exert control over important aspects of their lives. When people perceive independence between responses and outcomes, learned helplessness manifests itself in motivational, learning, and emotional deficits. Self-determination theory postulates that intrinsic motivation is influenced by three basic innate psychological needs: competence, autonomy, and relatedness.

Much research has addressed the effect of rewards on intrinsic motivation. Offering rewards for task engagement decreases intrinsic motivation when rewards are seen as controlling behavior. Rewards given contingent on one's level of performance are informative of capabilities and foster students' self-efficacy, interest, and skill acquisition.

Interest, or the liking and willful engagement in an activity, can affect motivation and learning. Personal interest is a stable personality variable directed toward specific activities or topics, whereas situational interest is temporary interest generated by specific features of the environment. A model of interest development postulates that personal interest can develop from initial situational interest. Affect comprises moods and emotions. Moods are low-intensity and diffuse affective states that may not have specific causes or much cognitive content. Emotions are more intense and short-lived. They can be traced to specific causes, be positive or negative, and occur before, during, or after task engagement. One emotion—test anxiety—can have negative effects on motivation and learning when it becomes excessive.

Achievement motivation, attributions, and goal orientations have important educational applications. Achievement motivation programs are designed to foster students' desire to learn and perform well at achievement tasks. Attributional change programs attempt to alter students' dysfunctional attributions for failure, such as from low ability to insufficient effort. Attributional feedback for prior successes can improve learners' motivation and learning. Teachers can foster productive goal orientations in students by teaching them to set learning goals and providing feedback on their goal progress.

Chapter Critique

In the past several years, the fields of motivation and learning have drawn closer together. Historically motivation was viewed as a process that could affect performance of previously learned actions but not necessarily learning itself. Thanks to the research of cognitive and constructivist researchers, we know today that motivation is intimately linked with learning in reciprocal fashion. Motivation can influence learning, and, in turn, the belief that one is learning can affect future motivation for learning.

Yet despite this closer theoretical and empirical integration, the role of motivation in learning needs continued research investigation. The field of motivation is fragmented with several theories (many of which are discussed in this chapter), Although these theories may appear to be distinct, they share many commonalities. Thus, most theories stress the role of expectancies/beliefs about one's competence and control. Researchers often test predictions from one theoretical perspective, and there may be little effort at relating findings to other perspectives. For the field of motivation, a better approach may be to focus on motivational processes such as expectancies, values, and attributions and to explore their operation during learning.

Motivation researchers also have tended to use motivation variables as outcomes; for example, by investigating which motivation variables affect interest—also a motivation variable. Such research is informative, but to advance the field of learning, more research needs to include learning as an outcome.

A positive change that has come from motivation research is that learning theories today incorporate motivation variables. There is widespread acceptance of the idea that learning cannot be explained wholly by referring only to cognitive variables such as attention and memory. The field of learning will continue to advance with further integration of motivation processes with learning models.

REFLECTION QUESTIONS

■ Many motivation theories stress the importance of perceived control. Yet practices of schooling often allow learners little control over environments, curricula, time, and the like. The problem may be exacerbated among students who experience learning difficulties if they believe that their academic successes are uncontrollable. What are some ways that instructional, contextual, and social conditions present in school might be adapted to provide learners with a greater sense of control over their learning and thereby promote their motivation to learn?

■ Social motivation can exert effects on learning. A common source is social comparison. Can you think of some examples of how social comparison could exert positive effects on students' motivation? Some examples of how it might exert negative effects? What are some ways that teachers can minimize negative social comparisons and use social comparisons to foster learning?

■ The interest development model discussed in this chapter offers a means for fostering students' interest in learning. Under what circumstances might this model be most effective? Can you think of some ways to integrate this model into a curriculum so that it helps to build learners' interest and motivation while they are engaged in learning?

FURTHER READING

Dweck, C. S. (2006). *Mindset: The new psychology of success.* New York: Random House.

Elliot, A. J. (2005). A conceptual history of the achievement goal construct. In A. J. Elliot & C. S. Dweck (Eds.), *Handbook of competence and motivation* (pp. 52–72). New York: Guilford Press.

Hidi, S., & Renninger, K. A. (2006). The four-phase model of interest development. *Educational Psychologist, 41*, 111–127.

Ryan, R. M., & Deci, E. L. (2016). Facilitating and hindering motivation, learning, and well-being in schools: Research and observations from self-determination theory. In K. R. Wentzel & D. B. Miele (Eds.), *Handbook of motivation at school* (2nd ed., pp. 96–119). New York: Routledge.

Weiner, B. (2005). Motivation from an attributional perspective and the social psychology of perceived competence. In A. J. Elliot & C. S. Dweck (Eds.), *Handbook of competence and motivation* (pp. 73–84). New York: Guilford Press.

Wigfield, A., Tonks, S. M., & Klauda, S. L. (2016). Expectancy-value theory. In K. R. Wentzel & D. B. Miele (Eds.), *Handbook of motivation at school* (2nd ed., pp. 55–74). New York: Routledge.

10 Self-Regulated Learning

Kim Danola, a high school sophomore, is meeting with her counselor Connie Smith. Kim is struggling in school, making C's and D's in her courses. Connie knows that Kim can do better in school. Kim's home is full of distractions and she has a hard time studying there. The two are meeting to discuss a plan to help Kim academically.

Kim: I don't know; my classes are all so different. Algebra, chemistry, history: they don't have anything in common.

Connie: Well, I agree they are different subjects. But let's think about it. Do you have a textbook in each class?

Kim: Sure.

Connie: So then, in all of them you have to do what?

Kim: Read?

Connie: Sure, read. They all involve reading right?

Kim: Yeah, but the readings are so different. It's like you have to read and study one way in math, a different way in chemistry, and another different way in history.

Connie: Yes, I understand. Kim, there are lots of students in our school who have trouble in these classes. We have student tutors at the school. I'm going to set you up with a tutor for each subject. That student will teach you learning strategies for each subject. But let's go back to what they all have in common. I'm taking a class at the university, and I've learned some general study strategies that you can use in all subjects. So I'm going to help you with those.

Kim: Such as?

Connie: Such as checking yourself when you read something to make sure you understood what you read. Then there are some other strategies, such as setting goals, taking notes, and summarizing information. These are general skills. You learn them and how to adapt them to the subject you're studying. I'll help you with those.

Kim: Do you think there's hope for me? My parents are really mad about my grades.

Connie: If I didn't think there was hope, I wouldn't be talking with you. Now let's get started!

The preceding chapters discuss learning processes that are applicable to diverse content in varied settings. For example, processes such as modeling, encoding, and metacognition apply to many types of learning; they are not unique to certain learners or a few content areas. This is what Connie says in the scenario just given.

These and other learning processes are integral components of *self-regulation*, or individuals' self-generated cognitions, affects, and behaviors that are systematically oriented toward attainment of their goals (Schunk & Greene, 2018; Sitzmann & Ely, 2011). Self-regulation includes such processes as setting goals, applying and adjusting strategies to attain them, monitoring performance and progress, maintaining motivation and positive affects and beliefs about learning, and utilizing social and environmental resources to attain goals (Lord, Diefendorff, Schmidt, & Hall, 2010; B. Zimmerman, 2000). The focus of this chapter is *self-regulated learning*, or self-regulation processes applied during a learning experience, where the goal is a desired level of achievement (Sitzmann & Ely, 2011).

Research on self-regulation during learning began as an outgrowth of psychological investigations into the development of self-control by adults and children (Zimmerman, 2001). Much early research was conducted in clinical contexts, where researchers taught participants to alter such dysfunctional behaviors as aggression, addictions, sexual disorders, interpersonal conflicts, and behavioral problems at home and in school (Mace & West, 1986). Theory and research o self-regulation has expanded to address academic learning and achievement (Schunk & Greene, 2018).

Self-regulated learning is a dynamic process that is ever changing as students are engaged in learning (Sitzmann & Ely, 2011). This chapter makes it clear that self-regulated learning can take many forms. Most notably, it involves behaviors, as individuals regulate these to stay focused on goal attainment. But self-regulated learning also involves cognitive, motivational, and affective variables. Thus, it is helpful for learners to maintain a sense of self-efficacy for learning, value the learning, believe that positive outcomes will result, and maintain a positive emotional climate (e.g., enjoy what they are doing).

The self-regulatory processes and strategies that learners apply vary in whether they are general (apply to many types of learning) or specific (apply only to a particular type of learning). This distinction is highlighted in the opening scenario. Some self-regulatory processes, such as setting goals and evaluating goal progress, can be employed generally, whereas others pertain only to specific tasks (e.g., applying the quadratic formula to solve quadratic equations).

Self-regulated learning has been addressed by theories covered in earlier chapters, and different perspectives on self-regulated learning are explained in this chapter. Lately researchers increasingly have been concerned with the self-regulation of motivation, and that topic also is addressed, as well as with self-regulated learning in various domains such as reading, writing, mathematics, science, physical education, and music (Bembenutty, Cleary, & Kitsantas, 2013; Schunk & Greene, 2018).

When you finish studying this chapter, you should be able to do the following:

- Discuss the assumptions common to theories of self-regulated learning.

- Define and exemplify the key behavioral processes of self-monitoring, self-instruction, and self-reinforcement.

- Discuss the various processes that operate during the social cognitive phases of self-regulation: forethought, performance, and self-reflection.

- Explain self-regulated learning from an information processing perspective and give examples of self-regulatory strategies used by proficient learners.

- Discuss self-regulated learning from a constructivist perspective to include the role of students' implicit theories.

- Discuss the link between motivation and self-regulated learning and explain how different motivational variables (e.g., self-efficacy, goals, values) relate to self-regulation.

- Devise a plan that students might use to improve their academic studying.

- Explain how self-regulated learning relates to writing and how technology may affect self-regulated learning.

ASSUMPTIONS

Theory and research on self-regulated learning in academic settings have been influenced by various disciplines including management, education, and psychology (e.g., organizational, clinical, cognitive). Theories of self-regulated learning differ in many ways but share common assumptions (Schunk & Greene, 2018). One is that self-regulated learning involves being behaviorally, cognitively, metacognitively, and motivationally active in one's learning and performance (Zimmerman, 2001). A second assumption is that self-regulated learning is a dynamic and cyclical process comprising feedback loops (Lord et al., 2010). Self-regulated learners set goals and metacognitively monitor their progress toward them. They respond to their monitoring, as well as to external feedback, in different ways to attain their goals, such as by working harder or changing their strategy. Attained accomplishments lead them to set new goals.

Third, goal setting triggers self-regulated learning by guiding individuals' focus on goal-directed activities and use of task-relevant strategies (Sitzmann & Ely, 2011). Goals that include learning skills and improving competencies result in better self-regulated learning than those oriented toward performing tasks. Last is an emphasis on motivation, or why persons choose to self-regulate and sustain their efforts. Motivational variables are critical for learning (Schunk & Zimmerman, 2008).

Based on theories and research, Sitzmann and Ely (2011) formulated a framework of constructs that constitute self-regulated learning, identifying three major types. Regulatory agents initiate self-regulated learning toward its objective, regulatory mechanisms help promote goal progress in an effective manner, and regulatory appraisals provide evaluative information on progress and influence continued goal striving. Sitzmann and

Ely's framework identified one regulatory agent (goal level), six regulatory mechanisms (attention, metacognitive strategies, time management, environmental structuring, motivation, and effort), and two regulatory appraisals (attributions and self-efficacy). These and other self-regulatory processes discussed in this chapter should be viewed as representative of a broader domain of potentially relevant processes.

Investigators also have addressed the development of self-regulation in groups (Hadwin, Järvelä, & Miller, 2018; Järvelä & Hadwin, 2013). *Co-regulation* refers to the coordination of self-regulation competencies among people in social contexts (Hadwin et al., 2018; Volet, Vauras, & Salonen, 2009). Learners jointly use their skills and strategies to develop new or expanded self-regulatory capabilities considered useful in group or individual contexts. Participants influence one another's self-regulated learning. Although the context and learning dynamics are social, the outcome is individual learning.

Socially shared regulation refers to interdependent regulatory processes aimed at attaining a mutual outcome (Hadwin et al., 2018). In collaborative settings, learners contribute their skills toward the goal of developing a self-regulated learning group. Although this chapter focuses on individual self-regulated learning, many of the principles discussed seem appropriate for co-regulated and socially shared regulated learning, both of which occur in educational learning environments.

BEHAVIORAL SELF-REGULATION

A behavior theory perspective on self-regulated learning derives largely from the work of Skinner (Mace, Belfiore, & Hutchinson, 2001; Chapter 3). Researchers working within the framework of operant conditioning theory apply operant principles in diverse settings (e.g., clinical, academic) with adults and children. The aim of these studies is to reduce dysfunctional behaviors and replace them with more-adaptive behaviors (Zimmerman, 2001).

Behavioral research is characterized by certain design features. Studies typically use few participants and sometimes only one. Participants are followed over time to determine behavioral changes resulting from interventions. The outcome measures are frequency and duration of the dysfunctional behaviors and the behaviors to be conditioned.

Behavior theory postulates that self-regulation involves choosing among different behaviors and deferring immediate reinforcement in favor of delayed (and usually greater) reinforcement. People self-regulate their behaviors by initially deciding which behaviors to regulate. They then establish discriminative stimuli for their occurrence, provide self-instruction as needed, and monitor their performances to determine whether the desired behavior occurs. This phase often involves self-recording the frequency or duration of behavior. When desirable behavior occurs, people administer self-reinforcement. These three key processes of self-monitoring, self-instruction, and self-reinforcement are discussed next.

Self-Monitoring

Self-monitoring refers to deliberate attention to some aspect of one's behavior and often is accompanied by recording its frequency or intensity (Mace et al., 2001; Mace & Kratochwill, 1988). People can regulate their actions only if they are aware of what they do. Behaviors can be assessed on such dimensions as quality, rate, quantity, and originality. While writing a term paper, students may periodically assess their work to determine whether it states important ideas, whether they will finish it by the due date, whether it will be too long or too short, and whether it integrates their ideas. One can engage in self-monitoring in such diverse areas as motor skills (e.g., how fast one runs the 100-meter dash), art (e.g., how original one's pen-and-ink drawings are), and social behavior (e.g., how much one interacts at social functions).

Often students must be taught self-monitoring methods (Belfiore & Hornyak, 1998; Lan, 1998; Application 10.1). Methods include narrations, frequency counts, duration

---

APPLICATION 10.1
Self-Monitoring

Self-monitoring helps students become aware of their behaviors and assists them in evaluating and improving those behaviors. In a self-contained or resource class, self-monitoring could help students improve on-task behavior, particularly if it is coupled with goal setting. The teacher might create individual charts divided into small blocks representing a short time period (e.g., 10 minutes). Once students are working independently at their seats or in centers, a signal could be given every 10 minutes. When the signal occurs, students could record on their charts what they are doing—writing, reading, daydreaming, talking with others, and so forth. The teacher could help each student set individual goals related to the number of on-task behaviors expected in a day, which should increase as the student's behavior improves.

It is important that teachers be careful about how they indicate time periods to self-monitoring students. Using a bell might disrupt other students and draw embarrassing attention to the students having difficulty. Teachers might seat their self-monitoring students close to them so that they can gently tap the students' desks at the end of each time period or otherwise quietly indicate its end.

High school teachers typically have a few students who have difficulty completing assignments and reading required material. Teachers may need to meet with these students individually to help them establish realistic goals for developing productive study habits and evaluate goal progress. Students can be taught to record how much reading (by pages), note studying, writing, and so forth, they accomplish in a set time period. Using the goals and a timer, students can monitor their progress toward achieving the goals.

Some college students in Dr. Traut's class had difficulty completing their first paper. Although he provided considerable guidance, it was clear that these students were not working in sequential steps to complete the paper by the deadline. For the next paper, he initially met individually with each of these students and created a checklist of items and timetable necessary for completing the paper. He then met with them weekly, at which time they shared their progress on the checklist and completion of the assignment. This helped the students develop a tool that they could use to self-monitor progress toward completing assignments in this and other courses.

measures, time-sampling measures, behavior ratings, and behavioral traces and archival records (Mace, Belfiore, & Shea, 1989). *Narrations* are written accounts of behavior and the context in which it occurs. Narrations can range from detailed to open-ended. *Frequency counts* are used to self-record instances of specific behaviors during a given period (e.g., number of times a student gets out of his or her seat during a 30-minute seat work exercise). *Duration measures* record the amount of time a behavior occurs during a given period (e.g., number of minutes a student studies during 30 minutes). *Time-sampling measures* divide a period into shorter intervals and record how often a behavior occurs during each interval. A 30-minute study period might be divided into six 5-minute periods; for each 5-minute period, students record whether they studied the entire time. *Behavior ratings* require estimates of how often a behavior occurs during a given time (e.g., always, sometimes, never). *Behavioral traces* and *archival records* are permanent records that exist independently of other assessments (e.g., number of Internet pages accessed, number of problems solved correctly).

In the absence of self-recording, selective memory of successes and failures can occur. Our beliefs about outcomes often do not faithfully reflect our actual outcomes (e.g., we may think we performed better than we actually did). Self-recording can yield surprising results. Students having difficulties studying who keep a written record of their activities may learn they are wasting more than half of their study time on nonacademic tasks.

There are two important criteria for self-monitoring: regularity and proximity (Bandura, 1986). *Regularity* means monitoring behavior on a continual basis instead of intermittently; for example, keeping a daily record rather than recording behavior one day per week. Nonregular observation often yields misleading results. *Proximity* means that behavior is monitored close in time to its occurrence rather than long afterward. It is better to write down what we do at the time it occurs rather than to wait until the end of the day to reconstruct events.

Self-monitoring methods place responsibility for behavioral assessment on the student (Belfiore & Hornyak, 1998). These methods often lead to significant behavioral improvements, known as reactive effects. Self-monitored responses are consequences of behaviors, and like other consequences, they affect future responding. Self-recordings are immediate responses that serve to mediate the relationship between preceding behavior and longer-term consequences (Mace & West, 1986). Students who monitor their completion of problems during seat work provide themselves with immediate reinforcers that mediate the link between seat work and such distant consequences as teacher praise and good grades.

Research supports the benefits of self-monitoring on achievement outcomes. Sagotsky, Patterson, and Lepper (1978) had children periodically monitor their performances during mathematics sessions and record whether they were working on the appropriate instructional material. Other students set daily performance goals, and students in a third condition received self-monitoring and goal setting. Self-monitoring increased time on task and mathematical achievement; goal setting had minimal effects. For goal setting to affect performance, students initially may need to learn how to set challenging but attainable goals.

Schunk (1983d) provided subtraction instruction and practice to children who failed to master subtraction operations in their classrooms. One group (self-monitoring) reviewed their work at the end of each instructional session and recorded the number of workbook pages they completed. A second group (external monitoring) had their work reviewed at the end of each session by an adult who recorded the number of pages completed. No-monitoring children received the instructional program but were not monitored or told to monitor their work.

Self- and external-monitoring conditions led to higher self-efficacy, skill, and persistence, compared with no monitoring. The effects of the two monitoring conditions were comparable. The benefits of monitoring did not depend on children's performances during the instructional sessions, because the three treatments did not produce different amounts of work completed. Monitoring progress, rather than who monitored it, enhanced children's perceptions of their learning progress and self-efficacy.

Reid, Trout, and Schartz (2005) reviewed the literature on self-regulation interventions to promote on-task behavior and academic performance and reduce disruptive behaviors among children with attention deficits and hyperactivity. Self-monitoring, alone and in combination with self-reinforcement, often was a component in effective interventions.

Self-Instruction

Self-instruction refers to establishing discriminative stimuli that set the occasion for self-regulatory responses leading to reinforcement (Mace et al., 1989). As used here, self-instruction is not the same as self-instructional training (Meichenbaum, 1977; Chapter 4). One type of self-instruction involves arranging the environment to produce discriminative stimuli. Students who realize they need to review class notes the next day might write themselves a reminder before going to bed. The written reminder serves as a cue to review, which makes reinforcement (i.e., a good grade on a quiz) more likely. Another type of self-instruction takes the form of statements (rules) that serve as discriminative stimuli to guide behavior. This type of self-instruction is included in the self-instructional training procedure.

Strategy instruction is an effective means of enhancing comprehension and self-efficacy among poor readers. Schunk and Rice (1986, 1987) taught remedial readers to use the following self-instruction strategy while reading comprehension passages:

> What do I have to do? (1) Read the questions. (2) Read the passage to find out what it is mostly about. (3) Think about what the details have in common. (4) Think about what would make a good title. (5) Reread the story if I don't know the answer to a question. (Schunk & Rice, 1987, pp. 290–291)

Children verbalized the individual steps prior to applying them to passages.

Self-instructional statements have been used to teach a variety of academic, social, and motor skills. These statements are especially helpful for students with learning disabilities or attention deficits. Verbalizing statements keeps learners focused on a task. A self-instruction procedure used to improve the handwriting of a student with learning disabilities is as follows (Kosiewicz, Hallahan, Lloyd, & Graves, 1982):

> (1) Say aloud the word to be written. (2) Say the first syllable. (3) Name each of the letters in that syllable three times. (4) Repeat each letter as it is written down. (5) Repeat steps 2 through 4 for each succeeding syllable.

This sequence appeared on a card on the student's desk. During training, the student was praised for completing the steps. Once the student learned the procedure, praise was discontinued and the sequence was maintained by the consequence of better handwriting.

Self-Reinforcement

Self-reinforcement refers to the process whereby individuals reinforce themselves contingent on their performing a desired response, which increases the likelihood of future responding (Mace et al., 1989). As discussed in Chapter 3, a reinforcer is defined on the basis of its effects. To illustrate, assume that Mitch is on a point system: He awards himself one point for each page he reads in his geography book. He keeps a record each week, and if his week's points exceed his previous week's points by 5%, he earns 30 minutes of free time on Friday. Whether this arrangement functions as self-reinforcement cannot be determined until it is known whether he regularly earns the free time. If he does (i.e., his average performance increases as the semester proceeds), then the reinforcement contingency is regulating his academic behaviors.

Much research shows that reinforcement contingencies improve academic performance (Bandura, 1986), but it is unclear whether self-reinforcement is more effective than externally administered reinforcement (such as given by the teacher). Studies investigating self-reinforcement often contain problems (Brigham, 1982). In academic settings, the reinforcement contingency typically occurs in a context that includes instruction and rules. Students usually do not work on materials when they choose but rather when told to do so by the teacher. Students may stay on task primarily because of the teacher's classroom control and fear of punishment rather than because of reinforcement.

Self-reinforcement is hypothesized to be an effective component of self-regulated behavior, but the reinforcement may be more important than the agent of reinforcement (self or others). Although self-reinforcement may enhance maintenance of behavior over time, explicitly providing reinforcement may be more important while self-regulatory skills are being learned.

Behavior theory has been widely applied to teach self-regulated behaviors. Self-monitoring, self-instruction, and self-reinforcement are self-regulatory processes that can be taught to students. At the same time, the behavioral position does not take cognitive and affective factors into consideration. This limits its applicability to self-regulated learning, because learning requires self-regulating more than just behaviors; for example, students must set goals and maintain a sense of self-efficacy for learning. These variables are considered critical in a social cognitive theoretical perspective on self-regulation, as discussed next.

SOCIAL COGNITIVE INFLUENCES

Conceptual Framework

Social cognitive theory has been applied extensively to self-regulated learning (Bandura, 1997, 2001; Pintrich, 2004; Pintrich & Zusho, 2002; Usher & Schunk, 2018; B. Zimmerman, 2000). A critical ingredient is learner choice (Zimmerman, 1994, 1998, 2000; Table 10.1). The potential for self-regulation varies depending on choices available to learners.

Table 10.1
Learner choices and self-regulatory processes.

Choice	Self-Regulatory Processes
Choose to participate	Goals, self-efficacy, values
Choose method	Strategy use, relaxation
Choose outcomes	Self-monitoring, self-judgment
Choose social and physical setting	Environmental structuring, help seeking

Table 10.1 shows choices potentially available to learners and some corresponding self-regulatory processes. One choice is whether to participate. This depends on such processes as learners' goals, values, and self-efficacy. Learners also may choose the methods they use while learning; for example, which strategies they employ and which relaxation techniques they use if they become anxious. A third type of choice involves outcomes: Which outcomes do learners desire? As they work on the task, they monitor their performances and judge whether their performances are moving them toward outcome attainment. Finally, learners may be able to choose the social and physical settings they use to work on the task. This may require that they structure their environments to make them conducive to learning and seek help when they need it.

In some classrooms, little self-regulation is possible. Suppose that a teacher tells students to write a 10-page typewritten, double-spaced paper on an assigned topic, containing at least 10 references, completed in 3 weeks, and written individually in the media center and at home. Assuming the teacher further specifies the paper format, the teacher is directing most of this assignment.

In contrast, assume Jim wants to learn to play the guitar. He chooses to engage in this task. The method he chooses is to take lessons from a teacher. He takes one 45-minute lesson per week and practices 1 hour per day. His goal is to be proficient enough to play in public. He practices the guitar at home at night. Besides his teacher, he enlists the aid of a friend who plays the guitar and asks him technical questions about finger positions and tuning. Jim has almost complete control over the situation, so it allows for maximum self-regulation.

Many situations lie somewhere between these extremes. Teachers may give a term paper assignment but allow students to choose from several topics. Students also may be able to decide on the resources they use, where they write, and how long the paper will be. High school senior graduation projects may specify some elements (e.g., research paper, oral presentation) but give students choices with other elements (e.g., topic, props). It thus makes more sense to ask to what degree one engages in self-regulation rather than whether one is self-regulated.

Interventions designed to enhance self-regulation in students often focus on one or more self-regulatory processes and provide students with instruction and practice on those processes. A wealth of evidence shows that self-regulatory competencies can be enhanced through educational interventions (Schunk & Ertmer, 2000; Schunk & Zimmerman, 2008; Usher & Schunk, 2018).

Self-Regulatory Processes

Early applications of social cognitive theoretical principles of self-regulation involved investigating the operation of three processes: self-observation (or self-monitoring), self-judgment, and self-reaction (Bandura, 1986; Table 10.2). Notice the similarity of these to the three processes espoused by behavior theory: self-monitoring, self-instruction, and self-reinforcement.

Students enter learning activities with such goals as acquiring knowledge and problem-solving strategies, finishing assignments, and performing experiments. With these goals in mind, students observe, judge, and react to their perceived progress.

Self-Observation. *Self-observation* involves judging observed aspects of one's behavior against standards and reacting positively or negatively. People's evaluations and reactions set the stage for additional observations of the same behavioral aspects or others. These processes also do not operate independently of the environment (Zimmerman, 1989, 1990, 2000). Students who judge their learning progress as inadequate may react by asking for teacher assistance, which alters their environment. In turn, teachers may instruct learners in a more efficient strategy, which students then use to promote their learning. That environmental influences (e.g., teachers) can assist the development of self-regulation is important, because educators advocate that students be taught self-regulatory skills (Usher & Schunk, 2018).

Self-observation is conceptually similar to self-monitoring and is commonly taught as part of self-regulatory instruction (Lan, 1998; Zimmerman, Bonner, & Kovach, 1996); however, by itself, self-observation usually is insufficient to self-regulate behavior over time. Standards of goal attainment and criteria in assessing goal progress are necessary.

Self-Judgment. *Self-judgment* refers to comparing present performance level with one's goal. Self-judgments depend on the type of self-evaluative standards employed, properties of the goal, importance of goal attainment, and attributions.

Self-evaluative standards may be absolute or normative. Absolute standards are fixed; normative standards are based on performances of others. Students whose goal is to read six pages in 30 minutes gauge their progress against this absolute standard. Grading systems often reflect absolute standards (e.g., A = 90 − 100, B = 80 − 89).

Normative standards frequently are acquired by observing models (Bandura, 1986). Socially comparing one's performances with those of others is an important way to determine the appropriateness of behaviors and self-evaluate performances. Social comparison becomes more probable when absolute standards are nonexistent or ambiguous (Festinger, 1954). Students have numerous opportunities to compare their work with that of their peers. Absolute

Table 10.2
Processes of self-regulation.

Self-Observation	Self-Judgment	Self-Reaction
Regularity	Types of standards	Evaluative motivators
Proximity	Goal properties	Tangible motivators
Self-recording	Goal importance	
	Attributions	

and normative standards often are employed in concert, as when students have 30 minutes to read six pages and compare their progress with peers to gauge who will be the first to finish.

Standards inform and motivate. Comparing performance with standards indicates goal progress. Students who read three pages in 10 minutes realize they have finished half of the reading in less than half of the time. The belief that they are making progress enhances their self-efficacy, which sustains their motivation to complete the task. Similar others, rather than those much higher or lower in ability, offer the best basis for comparison (Schunk, 1987).

Schunk (1983b) compared the effects of social comparative information with those of goal setting during a division training program. Half of the children were given performance goals during each instructional session; the other half were advised to work productively. Within each goal condition, half of the students were told the number of problems other similar children had completed (which matched the session goal) to convey that goals were attainable; the other half were not given comparative information. Goals enhanced self-efficacy; comparative information promoted motivation. Children who received both goals and comparative information demonstrated the highest skill acquisition.

Observation of models affects self-efficacy and achievement behaviors (Chapter 4). Zimmerman and Ringle (1981) exposed children to an adult model who unsuccessfully attempted to solve a wire puzzle for a long or short period and who verbalized statements of confidence or pessimism. Children who observed a pessimistic model persist for a long time lowered their efficacy judgments. Perceived similarity to models is especially influential when observers experience difficulties and possess self-doubts about performing well (Schunk & Hanson, 1985; Schunk et al., 1987).

Goal properties—specificity, proximity, difficulty—are especially influential with long-term tasks (Chapter 4). Teachers can assist students who have doubts about writing a good term paper by breaking the task into short-term goals (e.g., selecting a topic, conducting background research, writing an outline). Learners are apt to believe they can accomplish the subtasks, and completing each subtask develops their self-efficacy for producing a good term paper. Examples are given in Application 10.2.

APPLICATION 10.2
Goal Setting and Self-Regulation

Goal setting is a useful strategy for completing long-term tasks. Many students have doubts about finishing a project that includes a display and a research paper. Teachers can assist their students by breaking the assignment into short-term goals. If students have a 6-week period to complete the project, their first task (1 week) might be to choose a topic after researching various topics. The second week can be spent on more research and to develop a paper outline. After the outlines are submitted and feedback received, students have 2 weeks to work on the initial drafts of their papers and to draw a sketch of the items to be included in their displays. Teachers can review their progress and provide feedback. Students then revise papers and develop displays during the final 2 weeks.

Law students can become overwhelmed when trying to learn and analyze numerous landmark cases in preparing for moot court. Law professors can help throughout

APPLICATION 10.2 (*continued*)

the semester by having students set realistic goals and by helping students organize their studying. Students might begin by establishing goals to learn the cases for major categories (e.g., family, business, private, and international law) in a set time period. Within each major goal category, subgoals can be created; for example, for the major goal category of private law, subgoals can be established for ownership and use of property, contracts between individuals, and redress by way of compensation for harm inflicted on one person by another.

Allowing students to set learning goals enhances goal commitment (Locke & Latham, 1990, 2002) and promotes self-efficacy (Schunk, 1990). Schunk (1985) found support for this in a study with children with learning disabilities. Some children set mathematical subtraction problem-solving goals for themselves each session, others were assigned comparable goals by a teacher, and others received instruction but no goals. Self-set goals led to higher expectancies of goal attainment compared with goals set by others. Relative to the other two conditions, self-set goals produced the highest self-efficacy and greatest skill acquisition.

Self-judgments reflect in part the importance of goal attainment. When individuals care little about how they perform, they may not assess their performance or expend effort to improve it (Bandura, 1986). People judge their progress in learning for goals they value. Sometimes goals that originally hold little value become more important when people receive feedback indicating they are becoming skillful. Novice piano players initially may hold ill-defined goals for themselves (e.g., play better). As their skills develop, they begin to set specific goals (e.g., learn to play a particular piece) and judge progress relative to these goals.

Attributions (perceived causes of outcomes; Chapter 9), along with goal progress judgments, can affect self-efficacy, motivation, achievement, and affective reactions (Schunk, 2001, 2008). Students who believe they are not making good progress toward their goals may attribute their performances to low ability, which negatively impacts expectancies and behaviors. Students who attribute poor progress to lackadaisical effort or an inadequate learning strategy may believe they will perform better if they work harder or switch to a different strategy (Schunk, 2008). Learners take greater pride in their accomplishments when they attribute them to ability and effort than to external causes (Weiner, 1985). They are more self-critical when they believe that they failed due to personal reasons rather than to circumstances beyond their control.

Attributional feedback can enhance self-regulated learning (Schunk, 2008). Being told that one can achieve better results through harder work can motivate one to do so, because the feedback conveys that one is capable (Schunk, 2008). Providing effort feedback for prior successes supports students' perceptions of their progress, sustains their motivation, and increases their efficacy for further learning.

The timing of attributional feedback is important. Early successes constitute a prominent cue for forming ability attributions. Feedback linking early successes with ability (e.g., "That's correct; you're good at this") should enhance learning efficacy. Many times, however, effort feedback for early successes is more credible, because when students lack skills, they have to expend effort to succeed. As students develop skills, ability feedback better enhances self-efficacy (Schunk, 1983a).

Self-Reaction. *Self-reactions* to goal progress motivate behavior (Bandura, 1986; Zimmerman & Schunk, 2004). The belief that one is making acceptable progress, along with the anticipated satisfaction of accomplishing the goal, enhances self-efficacy and sustains motivation. Negative evaluations do not decrease motivation if individuals believe they are capable of improving (Schunk, 1995). If students believe they have been lackadaisical but can progress with enhanced effort, they are apt to feel efficacious and redouble their efforts. Motivation does not improve if students believe they lack the ability and will not succeed no matter how hard they try (Schunk, 2008).

Instructions to people to respond evaluatively to their performances promote motivation; people who think they can perform better persist longer and expend greater effort (Kanfer & Gaelick, 1986). Perceived progress is relative to one's goals; the same level of performance can be evaluated differently. Some students are content with a B in a course, whereas others will be dissatisfied with a B because they want an A. Assuming that people feel capable of improving, higher goals lead to greater effort and persistence than lower goals (Bandura & Cervone, 1983).

People routinely reward themselves tangibly with work breaks, new clothes, and evenings out with friends, contingent on their making progress toward goal attainment. The anticipated consequences of behavior, rather than the actual consequences, enhance motivation (Bandura, 1986). Grades are given at the end of courses, yet students typically set subgoals for accomplishing their work and reward and punish themselves accordingly.

Tangible consequences also affect self-efficacy. External rewards that are given based on actual accomplishments enhance efficacy. Telling students that they will earn rewards based on what they accomplish can instill a sense of self-efficacy for learning (Schunk, 1995). Self-efficacy is validated as students work on a task and note their progress. Receipt of the reward further validates efficacy, because it symbolizes progress. Rewards not tied to performances (e.g., given for spending time on the task regardless of what one accomplishes) may convey negative self-efficacy information; students might infer they are not expected to learn much because they are not capable (Schunk, 1983e).

Cyclical Nature of Self-Regulated Learning

Social cognitive theorists emphasize the dynamic interaction of personal, behavioral, and environmental factors (Bandura, 1986, 1997; Usher & Schunk, 2018; B. Zimmerman, 2000; Chapter 4). Self-regulated learning is a cyclical process because these factors typically change during learning and must be monitored. Such monitoring leads to changes in an individual's strategies, cognitions, affects, and behaviors.

This cyclical nature is captured in Zimmerman's (1998, 2000) three-phase model of self-regulated learning (Figure 10.1). This model also expands the classical view, which covers task engagement, because it includes self-regulatory processes performed before and after engagement. The forethought phase precedes actual performance and refers

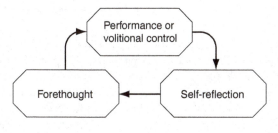

Figure 10.1
Model of self-regulated learning.
Source: Butler, D. L. (1998b). "A Strategic Content Learning Approach to Promoting Self-Regulated Learning by Students with Learning Disabilities." In D. H. Schunk and B. J. Zimmerman (Eds.)., *Self-Regulating Learning: From Teaching to Self Reflective Practice* (pp. 160) New York: Guilford Press.

to processes that set the stage for action. The performance (volitional) control phase involves processes that occur during learning and affect attention and action. During the self-reflection phase, which occurs after performance, people respond to their efforts (Zimmerman & Schunk, 2004).

Various self-regulatory processes come into play during the different phases. In the forethought phase, learners set goals, engage in strategic planning, and hold a sense of self-efficacy for attaining their goals. Performance control involves implementing learning strategies that affect motivation and learning, as well as observing and recording one's performances. During periods of self-reflection, learners engage in self-evaluation (addressed next) and make attributions for their performances, after which they return to either the forethought or performance control phase. Teaching students to engage in self-regulation in all three phases has desirable effects on strategic thinking and attributions (Cleary, Zimmerman, & Keating, 2006; DiBenedetto & Zimmerman, 2010).

Pintrich's (2000b) social cognitive model comprises four phases: forethought, planning, and activation; monitoring; control; and reaction and reflection. Within each phase, possible areas for self-regulation are cognition, motivation and affect, behavior, and context. During the forethought phase, learners set goals and activate content and metacognitive knowledge. Motivational variables during this phase are goal orientations, self-efficacy, and perceptions of task difficulty, task value, and interest. The monitoring and control phases during task engagement involve metacognitive awareness and monitoring of cognition, motivation, affect, behavior (e.g., effort, time management), and context (e.g., changes in conditions), along with strategies for learning, managing motivation, exerting behavioral self-control, and changing the task or context. Following task engagement, learners make cognitive judgments and attributions of their performance and evaluate the task and context, after which they may return to the forethought phase.

Self-Evaluation. Effective self-regulation requires goals and motivation (Bandura, 1986; B. Zimmerman, 2000). Students must regulate their actions and underlying achievement cognitions, beliefs, intentions, and affects. Research substantiates the prediction that self-monitoring of achievement beliefs sustains learning and promotes achievement (Schunk & Zimmerman, 1994, 2008; B. Zimmerman, 2000; Zimmerman et al., 1996).

Effective self-regulators develop self-efficacy for self-regulating their learning and performance (Caprara et al., 2008; Pajares, 2008; Usher & Schunk, 2018). Research shows that self-efficacy for self-regulated learning bears a significant and positive relation to students' academic achievement and grades (Caprara et al., 2008).

Of critical importance is self-evaluation of capabilities and progress in skill acquisition. *Self-evaluation* comprises self-judgments of present performance by comparing one's goal and self-reactions to those judgments by deeming performance noteworthy, unacceptable, and so forth. Positive self-evaluations lead students to feel efficacious about learning and motivated to continue to work diligently because they believe they are capable of making further progress (Usher & Schunk, 2018). Low self-judgments of progress and negative self-reactions will not necessarily diminish self-efficacy and motivation if students believe they are capable of succeeding but that their present approach is ineffective (Bandura, 1986). Such students may alter their self-regulatory processes by working harder, persisting longer, adopting what they believe is a better strategy, or seeking help from teachers and peers (Schunk, 2001; Zimmerman & Martinez-Pons, 1992).

Research substantiates the hypothesis that self-evaluations of capabilities and progress in skill acquisition affect achievement outcomes (Schunk & Ertmer, 2000). Investigations with children during learning of mathematical skills (Schunk & Hanson, 1985; Schunk et al., 1987) and writing skills (Schunk & Swartz, 1993a, 1993b) show that self-efficacy for learning or improving skills assessed prior to instruction predict motivation and skill acquisition.

Bandura and Cervone (1983) obtained benefits of goals and self-evaluative feedback among college students on motor-skill performance. A similar study showed that the greater the students' dissatisfaction with their performances and the higher their self-efficacy for performing well, the stronger was their subsequent effort expenditure (Bandura & Cervone, 1986). Cervone, Jiwani, and Wood (1991) found that providing individuals with a specific goal enhanced the effects of self-efficacy and self-evaluation on performance.

Students may not spontaneously self-evaluate their capabilities. One means of highlighting progress is to have them periodically assess their progress. Explicit capability self-evaluations constitute a type of self-monitoring because students must attend to their present performance and compare it with their prior performance to note progress. By making performance improvements salient, such self-monitoring is apt to raise self-efficacy, sustain self-regulatory activities, and promote skills. White, Kjelgaard, and Harkins (1995) noted that self-evaluation enhances the effects of goals on performance.

Schunk (1996) conducted two studies investigating how goals and self-evaluation affect achievement outcomes. Fourth graders received instruction and practice on fractions over several sessions. Students worked under conditions involving either a goal of learning how to solve problems (process goal) or a goal of merely solving them (product goal). In Study 1, half of the students in each goal condition evaluated their problem-solving capabilities. The process goal (with or without self-evaluation) and the product goal with self-evaluation led to higher self-efficacy, skill, self-directed performance, and task orientation than did the product goal without self-evaluation. In Study 2, all students in each goal condition evaluated their progress in skill acquisition. The process goal led to higher motivation and achievement outcomes than did the product goal.

Schunk and Ertmer (1999) examined how goals and self-evaluation affected self-efficacy, achievement, and self-reported competence and use of self-regulatory strategies. College undergraduates worked on computer projects over three sessions. Students received a process goal of learning computer applications or a product goal of performing them.

In the first study, half of the students in each goal condition evaluated their progress in learning after the second session. The process goal led to higher self-efficacy, self-judged learning progress, and self-regulatory competence and strategy use; the opportunity for self-evaluation promoted self-efficacy. In the second study, self-evaluation students assessed their progress after each session. Frequent self-evaluation produced comparable results when coupled with a process or product goal. Collectively, these results suggest that infrequent self-evaluation complements learning process goals, but multiple self-evaluations outweigh the benefits of process goals and raise achievement outcomes for all students.

Having students self-monitor their performance and evaluate their capabilities or progress in learning makes it clear that they have become more competent, and this perception strengthens self-efficacy and enhances self-regulated learning efforts. Given that students are not normally in the habit of evaluating their skills or learning progress, they may require instruction in self-evaluation and frequent opportunities to practice it. Suggestions for incorporating self-evaluation in learning settings are given in Application 10.3.

Learning Strategies. The opening scenario underscores the importance of learning strategies. Self-regulated learners believe acquisition of proficiency is a strategically controllable process and accept responsibility for their achievement outcomes (B. Zimmerman, 2000). According to social cognitive theory, self-regulated strategy use is influenced by students' self-belief systems. Self-regulated learners are metacognitively aware of strategic relations between self-regulatory processes and learning outcomes, feel self-efficacious about using strategies, have academic goals of learning, have control over debilitating thoughts and anxiety, and believe that strategy use will help them attain goals at higher levels (Zimmerman, 1989, 1990, 2000, 2001, 2008; Zimmerman & Cleary, 2009). Students who feel efficacious about learning select what they believe are useful learning strategies, monitor their performances, and alter their task approach when their present methods do not appear to function properly.

APPLICATION 10.3
Incorporating Self-Evaluation into Learning

Teaching students to evaluate their progress and learning can begin as early as preschool and kindergarten. Teachers initially might use simple self-checking. Children might be asked to assemble various shaped blocks to form a larger shape (rectangle, square, triangle, hexagon). Samples of various ways to combine the smaller blocks to make the shape can be drawn on cards and placed in an envelope at an activity center. Older elementary students might be given an activity sheet that accompanies a hands-on task with the answers for the sheet listed on the back so they can check their work.

For older students, self-checking can be integrated into daily activities. They also can also be taught to evaluate their learning by utilizing pretests and practice tests; for example, with the learning of spelling words and mathematical facts. More complicated and thorough practice tests can be used with middle school and high school students, allowing them to determine how much studying to do and what activities they need to complete to master the unit goals.

Table 10.3
Influence of social and self variables on self-regulated learning.

Level of Development	Social Influences	Self Influences
Observation	Modeling, verbal description	
Emulation	Social guidance and feedback	
Self-control		Internal standards, self-reinforcement
Self-regulation		Self-regulatory processes, self-efficacy beliefs

Research shows that self-efficacy relates positively to productive use of self-regulatory strategies (Pajares, 2008; Pintrich & Zusho, 2002; Zimmerman & Cleary, 2009). Results from a series of studies support the notion that altering goals and strategies is adaptive during learning (Kitsantas & Zimmerman, 1998; Zimmerman & Kitsantas, 1996, 1997). In particular, self-regulated learning is enhanced by shifting from process (strategies) to product (outcomes) goals as learning improves. Learning strategies are discussed in greater depth in the next section.

Social-Self Interaction

The dynamic nature of self-regulated learning is further highlighted in the interaction of social and self variables (Schunk, 1999; Schunk & Zimmerman, 1997; Table 10.3). Initial learning often proceeds best when learners observe social models. They then become able to perform skills in rudimentary fashion with appropriate guidance and feedback. As learners develop competence, they enter a self-control phase where they can match their actions with internal representations of the skill. At the final level, learners develop self-regulatory processes that they employ to further refine skills and select new goals.

The interaction of social and self variables helps promote internalization of self-regulatory processes. *Internalization* means that learners have these processes as part of their self-regulatory systems. They use them when they deem them necessary and can adapt them to changing task and environmental demands. Although it is possible that learners could skip early phases if they enter with some skills, this sequence is a useful instructional strategy to help learners develop skills and self-regulatory competence (Zimmerman & Kitsantas, 2005).

INFORMATION PROCESSING

Self-regulated learning has been addressed by information processing theories, which have evolved from their original formulations to incorporate cognitive and motivational self-regulatory processes. This section presents an information processing model of self-regulated learning and discusses research on and applications of learning strategies—a key feature of self-regulation from an information processing perspective.

Model of Self-Regulated Learning

Information processing theories view learning as the encoding of information in long-term memory (LTM; Chapters 5 and 6). Learners activate relevant portions of LTM and relate new knowledge to existing information in working memory (WM). Organized and meaningful information is easier to integrate with existing knowledge and more likely to be remembered.

Self-regulated learning is roughly equivalent to *metacognitive awareness* or *metacognition* (Gitomer & Glaser, 1987), where individuals monitor, direct, and regulate actions toward goals (Paris & Paris, 2001). This awareness includes knowledge of the task (e.g., what is to be learned, when and how it is to be learned), as well as self-knowledge of personal capabilities, interests, and attitudes. Self-regulated learning requires learners to have a sound knowledge base comprising task demands, personal qualities, and strategies for completing the task.

Metacognitive awareness also includes procedural knowledge that regulates learning by monitoring one's level of learning, deciding when to take a different task approach, and assessing readiness for a test. Self-regulatory (metacognitive) activities are under the learner's direction. They facilitate the construction and processing of knowledge.

One perspective is that the basic (superordinate) unit of self-regulation is a *problem-solving production system*, in which the problem is to reach the goal and the monitoring serves to ascertain whether the learner is making progress. This system compares the present situation against a standard and attempts to reduce discrepancies.

An early formulation of this system was Miller, Galanter, and Pribham's (1960) *Test-Operate-Test-Exit* (*TOTE*) model. The initial test phase compares the present situation against a standard. If they are the same, no further action is required. If they do not match, control is switched to the operate function to change behavior to resolve the discrepancy. One perceives a new state of affairs that is compared to the standard during the second test phase. Assuming that these match, one exits the model. If they do not match, further behavioral changes and comparisons are necessary.

This process can be illustrated with Lisa, who is reading her economics text and stops periodically to summarize what she has read. She recalls information from LTM pertaining to what she has read and compares the information to her internal standard of an adequate summary. This standard may be characterized by rules (e.g., be precise, include information on all topics covered, be accurate) developed through experiences in summarizing. Assuming that her summary matches her standard, she continues reading. If they do not match, Lisa evaluates where the problem lies (e.g., in her understanding of the second paragraph) and executes a correction strategy (rereads the second paragraph).

Winne and Hadwin (1998, 2008; Winne, 2001, 2011, 2018) developed an information processing model of self-regulated learning that is highly relevant to education (Greene & Azevedo, 2007). This model comprises three necessary phases (definition of task, goals and plans, studying tactics) and one optional phase (adaptations).

In the first phase, learners process information about the conditions that characterize the task to clearly define it (Winne, 2001). There are two main sources of information. Task conditions include information about the task that learners interpret based on the external environment (e.g., teacher's directions for an assignment). Cognitive conditions are those that learners retrieve from long-term memory. These include information about how they did on prior work, as well as motivational variables (e.g., perceived competence, attributions). In the second phase, learners decide on a goal and a plan for attaining it. The plan will include relevant learning strategies. As learners begin to apply these strategies, they move into the third phase (studying tactics). In the fourth phase, they make adaptations to their plans based on their evaluations of how successful they are. This phase is optional; if the original plan is successful there is no need to adapt it.

Within each phase, information processing occurs and constructs information products (new information). Information processes work on existing information and are characterized by the acronym SMART: searching, monitoring, assembling, rehearsing, translating. Working on a task requires using a schema, or script, and each script has five possible slots to fill characterized by the acronym COPES: conditions, operations, products, evaluations, standards. Figuratively speaking, these are the elements a student "copes with" to learn (Winne, 2001). Information processing outcomes are judged against standards, and these evaluations (e.g., on target, too high) serve as the basis for bringing new conditions to bear on the student's learning activities.

The importance of this model for education derives heavily from its development and use with learning content and on its inclusion of motivational variables. These motivational variables are combined with cognitive variables to determine the usefulness of a particular self-regulatory schema, or script. This model represents an advance over traditional and contemporary information processing models that emphasize cognitive components (Chapters 5 and 6). Much research supports the idea that motivational variables are important during self-regulated learning (Zimmerman & Schunk, 2001).

Information processing models emphasize the development of information processes that allow learners to engage in greater self-regulation. Two processes that are most important are working memory and inhibitory control. As children's working memories develop, they are able to process more information without being cognitively overloaded and to make better connections between information in WM and LTM. Inhibitory control refers to the ability to inhibit responding to a more immediate stimulus (e.g., a distraction) and focus on actions related to self-regulated learning. Developmental changes in both of these capabilities allow learners to stay on task better and learn more effectively.

There are other information processing models of self-regulation (e.g., Carver & Scheier, 1998), but they are in agreement in their emphasis on learning strategies. These are discussed next.

Learning Strategies

Learning strategies are cognitive plans oriented toward successful task performance (Pressley et al., 1990; Weinstein & Mayer, 1986). Strategies include methods such as selecting and organizing information, rehearsing material to be learned, relating new material to information in memory, and enhancing meaningfulness of material. Strategies also include techniques that create and maintain a positive learning climate—for example, ways to overcome test anxiety, enhance self-efficacy, appreciate the value of learning, and develop positive outcome expectations and attitudes (Weinstein & Mayer, 1986). Use of strategies is an integral part of self-regulated learning because strategies give learners better control over information processing (Winne, 2001). In the opening vignette, Connie stresses the importance of Kim using learning strategies in her courses.

Learning strategies assist encoding in each of its phases. Learners initially attend to relevant task information and transfer it from the sensory register to WM. Learners also activate related knowledge in LTM. In WM, learners build connections (links) between new information and prior knowledge and integrate these links into LTM networks.

In formulating a learning strategy, learners initially might analyze an activity or situation in terms of the goal, aspects of the situation relevant to that goal, personal characteristics that seem to be important, and potentially useful self-regulated learning methods. Learners then might develop a strategy, implement the methods, monitor their goal progress, and modify the strategy when the methods are not producing goal progress. Guiding the implementation of these methods is metacognitive knowledge, which involves knowing that one must carry out the methods, why they are important, and when and how to perform them.

Self-regulated learning methods are specific procedures or techniques included in strategies to attain goals. These methods are discussed next and are shown in Table 10.4. Learning methods are interdependent (Weinstein & Mayer, 1986). For example, procedures that elaborate information also often rehearse and organize it. Methods that organize information may relieve one's stress about learning and help one cope with anxiety. Methods are not equally appropriate with all types of tasks. Rehearsal may be the method of choice when one must memorize simple facts, but organization is more appropriate for comprehension (see Application 10.4).

APPLICATION 10.4
Learning Methods

Learning methods are useful at all educational levels. Elementary teachers might use rhyming schemes or catchy songs to teach the alphabet (e.g., the "ABC Song"). They might employ familiar words to assist children in learning the directions north, south, east, and west (e.g., learn to draw a line connecting north-east-west-south, this spells "news"). Teachers of older students can show them ways to organize material to be studied—texts, class notes, and Internet readings—as well as how to create new notes that integrate material from various sources.

In medical school, acronyms and pictures can help students memorize the terminology for parts of the body. When students learn the appropriate drugs to prescribe for various conditions, having them place the names of drugs, their uses, and their side effects into categories may assist with the learning.

Track coaches may help their broad jump and pole vault team members by asking them to close their eyes and slowly visualize every movement their bodies must make to accomplish the jumps. By visualizing their movements, team members can focus on specific positions they need to work on. Executing the actual jump happens so quickly that focusing on what one is doing is difficult, whereas the use of imagery helps to slow the action down.

College instructors could use a memory technique with students to group psychologists who have similar views by developing a catchy phrase or acronym. For example, the major behavioral theorists can be remembered with: "The (Thorndike) Sisters (Skinner) Won't (Watson) Play (Pavlov) Together (Tolman)." Students first recall the sentence, then add the names.

Rehearsal. Repeating information verbatim, underlining, and summarizing are forms of *rehearsal*. Repeating information to oneself—aloud, subvocally (whispering), or covertly—is an effective method for tasks requiring rote memorization. For example, to learn the names of the 50 state capitals, Janna might say the name of each state followed by the name of its capital. Rehearsal also can help learners memorize lines to a song or poem and learn English translations of foreign-language words.

Rehearsal that rotely repeats information does not link information with what one already knows. Nor does rehearsal organize information in hierarchical or other fashion. As a consequence, LTM does not store rehearsed information in any meaningful sense, and retrieval after some time is often difficult.

Rehearsal can be useful for complex learning, but it must involve more than merely repeating information. One useful rehearsal procedure is *underlining* (*highlighting*). This method, which is popular among students, improves learning if employed judiciously (Dembo & Seli, 2016). When too much material is underlined, underlining loses its effectiveness because less important material is underlined along with more important ideas. Underlined material should represent points most relevant to learning goals.

In *summarizing*—another popular rehearsal procedure—students put into their own words (orally or in writing) the main ideas expressed in the text. As with underlining, summarizing loses its effectiveness if it includes too much information (Snowman, 1986). Limiting the length of students' summaries forces them to identify main ideas.

The *reciprocal teaching* method of Palincsar and Brown (1984) includes summarization as a means for promoting reading comprehension (Chapter 7). Reciprocal teaching is based on Vygotsky's (1978) *zone of proximal development (ZPD)*, or the amount a student can learn given the proper instructional conditions (Chapter 8). Instruction begins with the teacher performing the activity, after which students and teacher perform together. Students gradually assume more responsibility and teach one another.

Palincsar and Brown taught children to summarize, question, clarify, and predict. Children periodically summarized what they read in the passage, asked teacher-type questions about main ideas, clarified unclear portions of text, and predicted what would happen next. Readers should note that these procedures are not unique to reading comprehension instruction; they are good problem-solving methods that can be used with effective results across domains (e.g., science, mathematics, social studies).

Elaboration. *Elaboration* procedures such as imagery, mnemonics, questioning, and note taking, expand information by adding something to make learning more meaningful. Imagery (Chapters 5 and 6) adds a mental picture. Consider the definition of a turnip: A biennial plant of the mustard family with edible hairy leaves and a roundish, light-colored fleshy root used as a vegetable. One could memorize this definition through rote rehearsal or elaborate it by looking at a picture of a turnip and forming a mental image to link with the definition.

Mnemonics are popular elaboration methods. A mnemonic makes information meaningful by relating it to what one knows. Mnemonics take various forms (Table 10.4). *Acronyms* combine the first letters of the material to be remembered into a meaningful word. "HOMES" is an acronym for the five Great Lakes (Huron, Ontario, Michigan, Erie,

Table 10.4
Learning methods.

Method	Examples
Rehearsal	Repeating information verbatim
	Underlining
	Summarizing
Elaboration	Using imagery
	Using mnemonics: acronym, sentence, narrative story, pegword, method of loci, keyword
	Questioning
	Note taking
Organization	Using mnemonics
	Grouping
	Outlining
	Mapping
Monitoring	Self-questioning
	Rereading
	Checking consistencies
	Paraphrasing
Affective	Coping with anxiety
	Holding positive beliefs: self-efficacy, outcome expectations, attitudes
	Creating a positive environment
	Managing time

Superior); "ROY G. BIV" for the colors of the spectrum (Red, Orange, Yellow, Green, Blue, Indigo, Violet). *Sentence mnemonics* use the first letters of the material to be learned as the first letters of words in a sentence. For example, "Every Good Boy Does Fine" is a sentence mnemonic for the notes on the treble clef staff (E, G, B, D, F), and "My Very Educated Mother Just Served Us Nectarines" for the order of the planets from the sun (Mercury, Venus, Earth, Mars, Jupiter, Saturn, Uranus, Neptune).

Also possible is combining material to be remembered into a *paragraph* or *narrative story*. This type of mnemonic might be useful when long lists have to be remembered (e.g., 50 state capitals). Student-generated acronyms, sentences, and stories are as effective as those supplied by others (Snowman, 1986).

The *pegword method* requires that learners first memorize a set of objects rhyming with integer names; for example, one-bun, two-shoe, three-tree, four-door, five-hive, six-sticks, seven-heaven, eight-gate, nine-wine, ten-hen. Then the learner generates an image of each item to be learned and links it with the corresponding object image. Thus, if Joan needs to buy butter, milk, and apples at the grocery store, she might imagine a buttered bun, milk in a shoe, and apples growing on a tree. To recall the shopping list, she recalls the rhyming scheme and its paired associates. Successful use of this technique requires that learners first learn the rhyming scheme.

To use the *method of loci*, learners imagine a familiar scene, such as a room in their home, after which they take a mental walk around the room and stop at each prominent object. Each new item to be learned is paired mentally with one object in the room. Assuming that the room contains (in order) a table, a lamp, and a television, and using the previous grocery list example, Joan might first imagine butter on the table, a milky-colored lamp, and apples on top of the television. To recall the grocery list, she mentally retraces the path around the room and recalls the appropriate object at each stop.

Atkinson (1975; Atkinson & Raugh, 1975) developed the *keyword method* for learning foreign language vocabulary words. For example, *pato* (pronounced "pot-o") is a Spanish word meaning "duck." Learners initially think of an English word (*pot*) that sounds like the foreign word (*pato*). Then they link an image of a pot with the English translation of the foreign word ("duck"); for example, a duck with a pot on its head. When the learners encounter *pato*, they recall the image of a duck with a pot on its head. Although the keyword method has been shown to improve self-regulated learning among children and adolescents (de Bruin, Thiede, Camp, & Redford, 2011), its success with young children often requires supplying them with the keyword and the picture incorporating the keyword and its response.

Mnemonic techniques incorporate several valid learning principles including rehearsal and relating new information to prior knowledge. Informal evidence indicates that most students have favorite memorization techniques, many of which employ mnemonics. Experiments that compare recall of students instructed in a mnemonic with recall of students not given a memory technique generally indicate that learning benefits from mnemonics instruction (Weinstein & Mayer, 1986). Students must understand how to use the technique, which often entails instruction.

Elaboration methods also are useful with complex learning tasks. For example, *questioning* requires that learners stop periodically as they read text and ask themselves questions. To address higher-order learning outcomes, learners might ask, "How does this information relate to what the author discussed in the preceding section?" (synthesis) or "How can this idea be applied in a school setting?" (application).

We might assume that questioning should improve comprehension, but research has not consistently yielded support for this relation. To be effective, questions must reflect the types of desired learning outcomes (Dembo & Seli, 2016). Questioning will not aid comprehension if questions address low-level, factual knowledge. Unfortunately, most research studies have used relatively brief passages of fewer than 1,500 words. With older students, questioning is most useful with longer passages. Among elementary children, rereading or reviewing (rehearsing) material is equally effective. This may be due to children's limited knowledge of how to construct good questions.

Note taking, another elaboration technique, requires learners to construct meaningful paraphrases of the most important ideas expressed in text. Note taking is similar to summarizing except that the former is not limited to immediately available information. While taking notes, students might integrate new textual material with other information in meaningful ways. To be effective, notes must not reflect verbatim textual information. Rote copying of material is a form of rehearsal and may improve recall, but it is not elaboration. The intent of note taking is to elaborate (integrate and apply) information. Students generally need instruction in how to take good notes for this method to be effective. Note taking works best when the notes include content relevant to the learning goals.

Organization. Organization techniques include mnemonics, grouping, outlining, and mapping. Mnemonics elaborate information and organize it in meaningful fashion. Acronyms, for example, organize information into a meaningful word. Information can be organized by grouping it before using rehearsal or mnemonics. If students are learning mammal names, they might first group the names into common families, such as apes and cats, and then rehearse or use a mnemonic. Organization imposed by learners is an effective aid to recall; learners first recall the organizational scheme and then the individual components (Weinstein & Mayer, 1986).

Organization techniques are useful with complex material. A popular one is *outlining*, which requires that learners establish headings. Outlining improves comprehension, but as with other learning methods, students usually require instruction in how to construct a good outline. One way to teach outlining is to use a text with headings that are set off from the text or that appear in the margins, along with embedded (**boldface** or *italic*) headings interspersed throughout the text. Another way is to have students identify topic sentences and points that relate to each sentence. Simply telling students to outline a passage does not facilitate learning if students do not understand the procedure.

Mapping is an organizational technique that improves learners' awareness of text structure. Mapping involves identifying important ideas and specifying their interrelationship. Concepts or ideas are identified, categorized, and related to one another. The exact nature of the map varies depending on the content and types of relationships to be specified. The following steps are useful in teaching mapping (McNeil, 1987):

- Discuss how different sentences in a paragraph relate to one another by giving the categories into which sentences will fit: main idea, example, comparison/contrast, temporal relationship, and inference.
- Model the application of this categorization with sample paragraphs.
- Give students guided practice on categorizing sentences and on explaining the reasons for their choices.
- Have students practice independently on paragraphs. Once students acquire these basic skills, more complex textual material can be used (multiple paragraphs, short sections of stories or chapters) with new categories introduced as needed (e.g., transition).

A *map* is similar to a memory network because mapping involves creating a hierarchy, with main ideas or superordinate concepts listed at the top, followed by supporting points, examples, and subordinate concepts. Branching off from the main hierarchy are lines to related points, such as might be used if a concept is being contrasted with related concepts. Figure 10.2 shows a sample cognitive concept map.

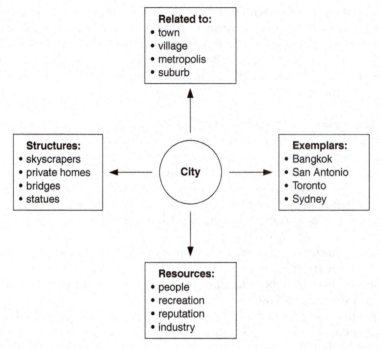

Figure 10.2
Cognitive map for "city."

Research indicates differential effectiveness for mapping as a means of improving comprehension (Snowman, 1986). The skill to discern some relationships is learned easily (main idea–example), but the skill to discern others is more difficult to acquire (cause–effect). Students often have difficulty linking ideas between sections or paragraphs. In teaching students to construct maps, having them first map each section or paragraph separately and then link the maps is helpful. Mapping is especially effective with students who experience difficulty integrating ideas (Holley, Dansereau, McDonald, Garland, & Collins, 1979).

Monitoring. *Monitoring* helps learners determine whether they are properly applying declarative and procedural knowledge to material to be learned, evaluate whether they understand the material, decide whether their strategy is effective or whether a better strategy is needed, and know why strategy use will improve learning. Teaching students comprehension monitoring is a central component of strategy-instruction programs (Dembo & Seli, 2016). *Self-questioning, rereading, checking consistencies,* and *paraphrasing* are monitoring processes. Using a hypermedia learning environment with middle- and high-school students, Greene and Azevedo (2009) found that monitoring activities (e.g., self-questioning) significantly enhanced students' understanding of complex science topics.

Some textual material periodically provides students with questions about content. Students who answer these questions as they read the material are engaging in self-questioning. When questions are not provided, students need to generate their own.

As a means of training students to ask questions, teachers can instruct students to stop periodically while reading and ask themselves a series of questions (i.e., who, what, when, where, why, how).

Rereading is often accomplished in conjunction with self-questioning; when students cannot answer questions about the text or otherwise doubt their understanding, these cues prompt them to reread. Checking for consistencies involves determining whether the text is internally consistent, that is, whether parts of the text contradict others and whether conclusions that are drawn follow from what has been discussed. A belief that textual material is inconsistent serves as a cue for rereading to determine whether the author is inconsistent or whether the reader has failed to comprehend the content. Students who periodically stop and paraphrase material are checking their level of understanding. Being able to paraphrase is a cue that rereading is unnecessary (Paris & Oka, 1986).

A useful method to teach monitoring is Meichenbaum's (1986) *self-instructional training* (Chapter 4). Cognitive modeling portrays a systematic approach to comprehension along with statements to self-check understanding and take corrective action as necessary. While presenting instruction to remedial readers, a teacher might verbalize the following (Meichenbaum & Asarnow, 1979):

> Well, I've learned three big things to keep in mind before I read a story and while I read it. One is to ask myself what the main idea of the story is. What is the story about? A second is to learn important details of the story as I go along. The order of the main events or their sequence is an especially important detail. A third is to know how the characters feel and why. So, get the main idea. Watch sequences. And learn how the characters feel and why. (p. 17)

Students learn to verbalize such statements and internalize them by gradually fading them to a covert level. To remind learners what to think about, teachers might display key ideas on a poster board (e.g., get the main idea, watch sequences, learn how the characters feel and why). Winsler and Naglieri (2003) found that between the ages of 5 and 17, children's verbal problem-solving strategies moved from overt (aloud) to partially covert (whispers) to fully covert (silent), which supports the progression in self-instructional training.

Affective Methods. *Affective methods* create a favorable psychological climate for learning (Weinstein & Mayer, 1986). These methods help one cope with anxiety, develop positive beliefs (e.g., self-efficacy, outcome expectations, attitudes), set goals, establish a regular time and place for studying, and minimize distractions (e.g., setting such rules as no talking on the phone and no watching television).

Affective techniques help learners focus and maintain attention on important task aspects, manage time effectively, and minimize anxiety. *Self-verbalization* helps keep students' attention on the academic task. At the outset of an academic activity, students might think to themselves, "This might be tough. I need to pay close attention to the teacher." If they notice their attention is waning, they might think, "Stop thinking about _____. I need to concentrate on what the teacher is saying."

Goal setting is an effective time-management strategy (Chapter 4). Learners who set overall learning goals, subdivide them into short-term goals, and periodically evaluate their goal progress are self-regulating their academic performances. The belief that they are making progress strengthens students' self-efficacy for continued learning (Schunk, 1995).

Anxiety about tests, grades, and failure interferes with learning (Dembo & Seli, 2016). Students who ruminate about potential failure waste time and strengthen doubts about their capabilities. Anxiety-reduction programs employ systematic desensitization, modeling, and guided self-talk. Models verbalize positive achievement beliefs (e.g., "I know that if I work hard, I can do well on the test") rather than dysfunctional beliefs (e.g., "I can't pass the test"). Coping models, who initially are anxious but use effective self-regulated learning methods and persist until they perform better, are important therapeutic agents of change (Schunk, 1987).

For students who have difficulties taking tests, a specific program to teach test-taking skills may prove beneficial (Kirkland & Hollandsworth, 1980). These programs typically teach students to subdivide the test, establish time limits for each part, and not spend too long on any one question. To conquer negative thoughts while taking a test, students are taught relaxation techniques and ways to refocus attention on test items. Test performance and beliefs exert reciprocal effects. Experiencing some test success creates a sense of self-efficacy for performing well, which leads to more productive studying and better performance.

Effectiveness of Strategy Instruction. There is an extensive research literature on strategy instruction (Dembo & Seli, 2016). Hattie, Biggs, and Purdie (1996) conducted an extensive review of interventions aimed at improving student learning. They concluded that most interventions were effective, and they obtained evidence for near transfer. When transfer is a goal, it is imperative that students understand the conditions under which the strategy is effective. The best strategy instruction programs are those that are integrated with academic content and implemented in classrooms that support students' self-regulated learning (Butler, 1998a, (1998b; Perry, 1998; Winne & Hadwin, 2008).

As with other aspects of learning, strategy instruction is most effective when the methods are meaningful to students and they perceive them as valuable to use. The research literature contains many examples of strategy-instruction programs with immediate effects that did not endure over time or transfer beyond the learning context (Borkowski & Cavanaugh, 1979; Borkowski, Johnston, & Reid, 1987). Strategy instruction programs with children often have participants who demonstrate production deficiencies (i.e., they fail to use a strategy that is available to them) and utilization deficiencies (i.e., they use the strategy but it does not enhance their performances; Schwenck, Bjorklund, & Schneider, 2007).

Pressley and his colleagues (Harris & Pressley, 1991; Pressley, Harris, & Marks, 1992; Pressley et al., 1990) contended that several factors should be taken into account when designing and implementing strategy-instruction programs. Strategies should not be foisted on students; teaching strategies in the hope that students will realize their benefits and use them is preferable (Pressley & McCormick, 1995).

Strategy instruction is likely to be most effective when the constructivist nature of the acquisition and use of strategies is stressed (Goldin-Meadow et al., 1993; Paris & Paris, 2001; Chapter 8). A key point is that students are motivated to construct understanding from inputs they receive. Good teaching complements this process because it provides rich inputs and the context for constructions to take place. In the opening vignette, Connie hopes that eventually Kim will adapt strategies to be most effective for her.

Pressley et al. (1992) recommended several steps to follow in strategy instruction (Table 10.5). *Introducing a few strategies at a time* does not overload students, and the strategies can be coalesced into a large package to show how they interrelate. The advantage of *providing distributed practice on diverse tasks* is to facilitate transfer and maintenance. The importance of *teachers as models* cannot be underestimated, and we must remember that the modeling is rule governed; students learn strategies and how to modify them rather than rotely copying the model's actions (Bandura, 1986). *Stressing the value of strategies* to students is necessary to encourage greater strategy use. Teachers can enhance perceived value with feedback showing how strategy use improves performance.

The importance of *feedback and personal teaching* is highlighted; teachers tailor feedback to individual student needs and developmental differences and teachers and students collaborate to work out understandings of strategies. For example, Cantrell, Almasi, Carter, Rintamaa, and Madden (2010) found that a reading strategy instruction program raised achievement for sixth graders but not for ninth graders, perhaps because the program focused on strategies to address deficiencies of immature readers. Azevedo, Greene, and Moos (2007) obtained benefits on college students' self-regulated learning by having a human tutor facilitate their use of strategies (i.e., prompt students to activate prior knowledge, plan time, monitor goal progress, summarize, use mnemonics). Teachers and students also must *determine opportunities for transfer* through discussions, prompts to students, and opportunities to practice adapting strategies to new tasks. *Sustaining student motivation*, especially by highlighting empowerment that accompanies strategy learning, is necessary. Finally, teachers encourage *habitual reflection and planning*. They model reflection, provide opportunities for students to think through problems, and create an environment that values reflection more than simply completing assignments or arriving at correct answers.

It is important that learners develop their own strategies or use strategies that are effective for them. Not all strategies work well with all learners. Learners can construct their own strategies or use or adapt ones that are available. And there are many methods that learners have found effective. For example, an effective method for studying is the SQ4R method (Survey-Question-Read-Recite-Record-Review). Before studying, you review

Table 10.5
Steps to follow in strategy instruction.

Introduce a few strategies at a time
Provide distributed practice on diverse tasks
Have teachers serve as models
Stress to students the value of strategy use
Personalize feedback and teaching
Determine opportunities for transfer
Sustain student motivation
Encourage habitual reflection and planning

the material to be studied and ask yourself one or more questions you want to be able to answer when you are finished. Then you read the material and recite material that is relevant to your questions. You record information as you study, and when finished, you review everything again. It is evident that there is a lot of rehearsal going on, as well as organization and elaboration. This and other strategies can help students become better self-regulated learners (Dembo & Seli, 2016).

CONSTRUCTIVISM

It seems natural that constructivist researchers would address self-regulated learning because a central constructivist assumption is that learners construct knowledge and ways for acquiring and applying it. There are various constructivist accounts of self-regulation, including cognitive-developmental theories (Chapter 8), precursors of contemporary cognitive theories (e.g., Gestalt psychology, memory; Chapter 5), and Vygotsky's theory (Chapter 8). Regardless of the source, constructivist views of self-regulation rest on certain assumptions, as shown in Table 10.6 (Paris & Byrnes, 1989).

Two key points underlying these assumptions are that sociocultural influences are critical and that people form implicit theories about themselves, others, and how to best manage demands. These are discussed in turn.

Sociocultural Influences

Vygotsky's (1978) sociocultural theory of human development lends itself well to self-regulation (Chapter 8). Vygotsky believed that people and their cultural environments constituted an interacting social system. Through their communications and actions, people in children's environments taught children the tools (e.g., language, symbols, signs) needed to acquire competence. Using these tools within the system, learners develop higher-level cognitive functions, such as concept acquisition and problem solving. As Vygotsky used the term *higher mental function*, he meant a consciously directed thought process. Self-regulated learning is a type of higher mental function (Henderson & Cunningham, 1994).

Self-regulated learning includes the coordination of such mental processes as memory, planning, synthesis, and evaluation (Henderson & Cunningham, 1994). These coordinated

Table 10.6
Constructivist assumptions of self-regulated learning.

- There is an intrinsic motivation to seek information.
- Understanding goes beyond the information given.
- Mental representations change with development.
- There are progressive refinements in levels of understanding.
- There are developmental constraints on learning.
- Reflection and reconstruction stimulate learning.

processes do not operate independently of the context in which they are formed. The self-regulatory processes of an individual reflect those that are valued and taught within the person's culture.

Vygotsky believed that people came to control their deliberate actions (i.e., learned to self-regulate). The primary mechanisms affecting self-regulation are language and the zone of proximal development (ZPD; see Chapter 8).

Kopp (1982) provided a useful framework for understanding the development of the self-regulatory function of speech. Self-regulation involves a transition from responding to the commands of others to the use of speech and other cognitive tools to plan, monitor, and direct one's activities.

Self-regulation also depends on learners being aware of socially approved behaviors (Henderson & Cunningham, 1994). The meaning of actions depends on both the context and the tools (language, signs, and symbols) used to describe the actions. Through inter-actions with adults in the ZPD, children make the transition from behaviors regulated by others to behaviors regulated by themselves (self-regulation).

Wertsch (1979) described four stages of intersubjectivity that correspond to the degrees of responsibility by parties in a social context. Initially the child does not understand the adult's words or gestures, so there is no intersubjectivity. With maturation of the child and greater sensitivity of the adult to the child's situation, a shared understanding of the situation develops, although responsibility for regulating behavior still lies with the adult. In the third phase, the child learns the relation between speech and activity and takes responsibility for the task. During the third phase, private speech is commonly used to self-regulate behavior. As this speech is internalized to self-directed thought, intersubjectivity becomes complete, and self-regulation occurs independently. Internalization becomes the key to use of self-regulatory processes (Schunk, 1999). Some examples of internalization are given in Application 10.5.

APPLICATION 10.5
Promoting Internalization

Many influences on students' self-regulated learning originate in their social environ-ments, such as when teachers explain and demonstrate specific strategies for students to use on academic content. But as the theo-ries covered in this chapter make clear, these external inputs are not passively received by students but rather transformed by them into personal self-regulatory influences. As learn-ers develop skills, the unidimensional social-to-self process becomes a bidirectional interactive process: Learners modify their

environments and enhance their learning. A key process is internalization of information. Internalized self-regulatory processes are under the learner's control, whereas nonin-ternalized processes are under the control of others. Internalized processes are repre-sented mentally as thoughts, beliefs, proce-dures, strategies, and so forth. Although it is possible to learn without internalization (e.g., when teachers direct students' actions), internalization is needed for skill improve-ment over time and beyond the present

(Continued)

learning setting. The net result of internalization is a set of self-regulatory influences that learners employ to promote their motivation and learning.

Mr. Cauthen works with his students to help them internalize spelling rules. For example, he teaches them the rhyme, "I before E except after C or when sounded like A as in Neighbor or Weigh." When he gives spelling words with ie or ei in them, he asks them to verbalize aloud the rhyme. Once they regularly do this, he advises them to whisper the rhyme, and eventually to say it quietly to themselves (subvocally). He uses this same procedure with other spelling rules, teaching students to internalize rules so that they can generate them in response to various spelling words.

Ms. Deutrony does not want her students to think of history as simply memorizing facts; she wants them to develop historical analysis skills. She teaches them questions to ask to analyze historical events, such as: What happened? Who were the influential people? What events led up to this event? How might this event have turned out differently if the events leading up to it had changed? Early in the course,

she has students write out the answers to these questions as they analyze events. As students develop skills of historical analysis, she asks them to formulate their own strategy that will capture the same type of information. They internalize this strategy as their own as they apply it to historical events, as well as to current events involving elections, the economy, and wars.

As part of her undergraduate educational psychology course, Dr. Mornoveny teaches her students self-regulated learning strategies to use when studying the course content. For example, she teaches them how to effectively underline and highlight information in text, how to summarize chapter content, how to budget their study time, and how to create an effective study environment. Each student formulates a study plan to use for the chapters. She provides feedback on these and asks the students to revise their plans as the semester progresses based on their evaluations of the plan's effectiveness. By the end of the semester, the goal is for students to be using their study plans routinely and adapting them as needed based on study requirements (e.g., need to consult Internet sources).

It is noteworthy that even after an adult or teacher is no longer present, the child's self-regulatory activity still may reflect that person's influence. Although the action is self-directed, it is the internalized regulation of the other's influence. Often the child may repeat the same words used by the adult. In time, the child will construct his or her self-regulatory activity.

Implicit Theories

Implicit theories (Chapters 8 and 9) are inherent features of constructivist accounts of learning, cognition, and motivation. Students also construct theories about self-regulated learning. These theories exist along with theories about others and their worlds, so self-regulated learning theories are highly contextualized (Paris, Byrnes, & Paris, 2001).

A major type of implicit theory involves children's beliefs about their academic abilities (Dweck, 2002, 2006; Chapter 9). Children who experience learning problems and who believe that these problems reflect poor ability are apt to demonstrate low motivation to succeed. The beliefs that effort leads to success and that learning produces higher ability are positively related to effective self-regulated learning. An incremental (growth) mindset (belief that abilities can be improved) predicts such self-regulatory processes as goal setting (learning goals), mastery-oriented strategies, and positive expectations (Burnette, O'Boyle, VanEpps, Pollack, & Finkel, 2013).

Children also develop theories about their competence relative to their peers. Through social comparisons with similar others, they formulate perceptions of ability and of their relative standing within their class. They also begin to differentiate their perceptions by subject area and to ascertain how smart they are in subjects such as reading and mathematics.

In line with these beliefs, children formulate theories about what contributes to success in different domains. Self-regulatory strategies may be general in nature, such as taking notes and rehearsing information to be learned, or they may be idiosyncratic to a particular area. Whether these strategies truly are useful is not the point. Because they are constructed, they may be misleading.

Learners also develop theories about agency and control that they have in academic situations. This power to act to obtain desired outcomes is central to social cognitive theory (Bandura, 1997) and to constructivist theories (Martin, 2004). Bandura contended that self-efficacy is a key influence on agency, whereas constructivist theories place greater emphasis on learners' activities in their physical and sociocultural environments (Martin, 2004). With respect to learners' theories, they may feel self-efficacious (Chapter 4) and believe that they are capable of learning what is being taught in school. Conversely, they may entertain doubts about their learning capabilities, although these beliefs may not accurately capture reality. Research has shown, for example, that children often feel highly self-efficacious about successfully solving mathematical problems even after being given feedback showing that they had failed most or all of the problems they attempted to solve (Bandura & Schunk, 1981). The correspondence between self-efficacy judgments and actual performance can be affected by many factors (Bandura, 1997; Schunk & DiBenedetto, 2016).

Another class of theories involves schooling and academic tasks (Paris et al., 2001). These theories contain information about the content and skills taught in school and what is required to learn the content and skills. The goals that students formulate for schooling may not be consistent with those of teachers and parents. For example, teachers and parents may want students to perform well, but students' goals might be to make friends and stay out of trouble. For a subject area (e.g., reading), students may have a goal of understanding the text or simply verbalizing the words on a page. A goal of writing may be to fill empty space on a page or create a short story.

Self-regulated learning, therefore, involves individuals constructing theories about themselves (e.g., abilities, capabilities, typical effort), others, and their environments. These theories are constructed partly through direct instruction from others (e.g., teachers, peers, and parents), but also largely through their personal reflections on their performances, environmental effects, and responses from others. Theories are constructed using the tools (language, signs, and symbols) and in social contexts, often through instruction in the ZPD.

The goal is for students to construct a self-identity as students. Their beliefs are influenced by parents, teachers, and peers and may include stereotypes associated with gender, culture, and ethnic background. Paris et al. (2001) contended that the separation of identity development and self-regulated learning is impossible because achievement behaviors are indicators of who students believe they are or who they want to become. Strategies cannot be taught independently of goals, roles, and identities of students. In other words, self-regulated learning is intimately linked with personal development.

Children are intrinsically motivated to construct explanatory frameworks and understand their educational experiences (Paris et al., 2001). When they are successful, they construct theories of competence, tasks, and themselves, which aid learning and use of adaptive learning strategies. But when they are not successful, they may construct inappropriate goals and strategies. In short, self-regulated learning is heavily dependent on how children perceive themselves and achievement tasks (Dweck & Master, 2008). Those who view themselves as capable and able to meet challenges are likely to develop adaptive strategies to cope with difficulties and be successful.

MOTIVATION AND SELF-REGULATED LEARNING

Motivation is intimately linked with self-regulated learning (Efklides, Schwartz, & Brown, 2018; Pintrich, 2003; Wolters, 2003). People motivated to attain a goal engage in self-regulatory activities they believe will help them (e.g., organize and rehearse material, monitor learning progress and adjust strategies). In turn, students self-regulate their motivation to learn, and the perception that one is learning sustains motivation and self-regulation to attain new goals (Schunk & Ertmer, 2000). Thus, motivation and self-regulated learning influence one another.

The link between motivation and self-regulation is seen clearly in theoretical models (Pintrich, 2000b; Vollmeyer & Rheinberg, 2006; B. Zimmerman, 2000). Pintrich's model is heavily motivation dependent, since motivation underlies learners' setting and pursuit of goals and also is a focus of self-regulation as they engage in tasks. In Zimmerman's model, motivation enters at all phases: forethought (e.g., self-efficacy, outcome expectations, interest, value, goal orientations), performance (e.g., attention focusing, self-monitoring), and self-reflection (e.g., self-evaluation of goal progress, causal attributions).

Additional evidence of this link is seen in research by Wolters (1998, 1999; Wolters, Yu, & Pintrich, 1996). In these studies, the researchers determined how various strategies designed to maintain optimal task motivation (e.g., expend effort, persist, make the task interesting, self-reward) related to self-regulatory strategy use during learning (e.g., rehearsal, elaboration, planning, monitoring, organization). The results showed that the motivation regulation activities that learners used predicted their self-regulation. Adopting a learning-goal orientation was associated with higher self-efficacy, task value, and achievement.

An aspect of self-regulated learning that has drawn increased research attention is *volition*, which is discussed next. Some researchers define volition as part of a larger self-regulatory system that includes motivation and other cognitive processes (Corno,

1993, 2001, 2008). Many other motivational components are receiving research attention for their role in self-regulated learning—for example, goal properties, goal orientations, self-efficacy, interest, attributions, values, self-schemas, and help seeking (Schunk & Zimmerman, 2008). We have examined the roles of goal properties (Zimmerman, 2008), goal orientations (Fryer & Elliot, 2008), self-efficacy (Schunk & DiBenedetto, 2016), interest (Hidi & Ainley, 2008), and attributions (Schunk, 2008) in Chapter 9. This section discusses volition, values, self-schemas, and help seeking.

Volition

Volition has been of interest for a long time. Early psychologists drew on the writings of Plato and Aristotle (Chapter 1) and conceived of the mind as comprising knowing (cognition), feeling (emotion), and willing (motivation). The will reflected one's desire, want, or purpose; volition was the act of using the will (Schunk et al., 2014).

Philosophers and psychologists have debated whether volition was an independent process or a by-product of other mental processes (e.g., perceptions). Wundt (Chapter 1) thought volition was a central, independent factor in human behavior and that it accompanied such processes as attention and perception and helped translate thoughts and emotions into actions. James (1890, 1892) also believed that volition was the process of translating intentions into actions and had its greatest effect when different intentions competed for action. Volition worked to execute intended actions by activating mental representations of them, which served as guides for behavior.

Ach (1910) pioneered the experimental study of volition. Ach considered volition the process of dealing with implementing actions designed to attain goals. This is a narrow view of motivation because it does not address the process whereby people formulate goals and commit themselves to attaining them (Heckhausen, 1991; Schunk et al., 2014). Processes that allow goals to be translated into action are *determining tendencies*; they compete with previously learned association tendencies to produce action even when the action conflicts with prior associations.

The conceptual basis for contemporary work derives from *action control theory* by Heckhausen (1991) and Kuhl (1984). These theorists proposed differentiating *predecisional processing* (cognitive activities involved in making decisions and setting goals) from *postdecisional processing* (activities engaged in subsequent to goal setting). Predecisional analyses involve decision making and are motivational; postdecisional analyses deal with goal implementation and are volitional. Volition mediates the relation between goals and actions to accomplish them. Once students move from planning and goal setting to implementation of plans, they cross a metaphorical Rubicon that protects goals by self-regulatory activities rather than reconsidering or changing them (Corno, 1993, 2001, 2008).

Debate continues over whether motivation and volition are separate constructs or whether the latter is part of the former. Nonetheless, separating pre- from postdecisional processes seems worthwhile. Some motivational outcomes used in studies of performance are not useful in learning. Choice of activities is a common outcome, yet, in school, students often do not choose to engage in tasks. There may be little predecisional activity by students. In contrast, postdecisional activity offers more latitude, especially if multiple ways are available to accomplish tasks or deal with distractions. Choice is an integral component of self-regulated learning (Zimmerman, 1994, 1998, 2000), but students still can have many choices available even when they do not choose whether to work on a task. Volitional activities presumably direct and control information processing, affects, and behaviors directed toward accomplishing goals (Corno, 1993).

Corno and her colleagues (1993, 2001, 2008; Corno & Kanfer, 1993; Corno & Mandinach, 2004) have written extensively about the role of volition in self-regulation:

> Volition can be characterized as a dynamic system of psychological control processes that protect concentration and directed effort in the face of personal and/or environmental distractions, and so aid learning and performance. (Corno, 1993, p. 16)

It is useful to distinguish two aspects of volition with respect to self-regulated learning: action control and volitional style. The *action-control* function refers to potentially modifiable regulatory skills or strategies. This function would include the focus of many interventions aimed at enhancing self-regulation, such as metacognitive monitoring (self-observation), self-arranged contingencies, redesign of tasks, strategies of emotion control, and management of environmental resources. Kuhl (1985) proposed a taxonomy of volitional strategies; Corno (1993) discussed strategies for motivation control and for emotion control. Many examples are available of successful training efforts for action-control strategies (Corno, 1994).

A second function, *volitional style*, refers to stable, individual differences in volition, as opposed to the specific skills and strategies involved in action control. Volitional style includes personality variables that should be less amenable to change through instruction—for example, impulsiveness, conscientiousness, and dependability. Corno (1994) cited research showing that these dispositions predict various student academic outcomes.

The case for treating volition as a separate construct has some merit. One problem with separating goal setting from implementation is highlighted by research studies showing that learners adjust or set new goals during task performance (Locke & Latham, 2002; Zimmerman, 2008). Another concern is how such motivationally germane processes as attributions and self-efficacy relate to volition. Researchers continue to address these issues.

Values

A central component of motivation that relates to self-regulated learning is the *value* students ascribe to learning (Wigfield, Hoa, & Klauda, 2008; Chapter 9). Students who do not value what they are learning are not motivated to improve or exercise self-regulation over their learning activities (Wigfield et al., 2004).

Wigfield et al. (2008) discussed the process whereby valuing a task can lead to better self-regulated learning. Values have a direct link to such achievement behaviors as persistence, choice, and performance. Values may relate positively to many self-regulating processes such as self-observation, self-evaluation, and goal setting. For instance, students who value history are apt to study for history tests diligently, set goals for their learning, monitor their learning progress, not be overcome by obstacles, and adjust their strategies as needed. In contrast, students who do not value history should be less likely to engage in these activities.

Research studies support the idea that valuing achievement tasks relates to the productive use of cognitive learning strategies, perceived self-regulated learning, and academic performance (Pintrich & De Groot, 1990; Wigfield et al., 2004, 2008). Pokay and Blumenfeld (1990), for example, found that students' valuing of mathematics led to their using different cognitive strategies, and in turn, strategy use influenced mathematics performance. Task values may relate positively to volitional action control strategies (Kuhl, 1985).

Unfortunately, researchers have shown that children often value academic tasks less as they get older (Eccles & Midgley, 1989). Many ways to enhance student motivation relate directly to perceptions of task value, including showing students how tasks are important in their lives and how learning these tasks helps them attain their goals (Chapter 9). In the opening scenario, Kim may not value her courses, but Connie tries to encourage her by stressing that using strategies can help her perform better, which may increase how much she values her studies. Linking learning to real-world phenomena improves perceptions of value. Teachers should incorporate methods for enhancing perceived value into their planning to ensure benefits for self-regulated learning.

Self-Schemas

Self-schemas are "cognitive manifestations of enduring goals, aspirations, motives, fears, and threats" (Markus & Nurius, 1986, p. 954). They include cognitive and affective evaluations of ability, volition, and personal agency. They essentially are conceptions of ourselves in different situations or what we might be. The theoretical importance of self-schemas is that they presumably mediate the link between situations and behavior. Individuals act in part based on their perceptions of themselves. Self-concept includes many self-schemas, only some of which are active at a given time. Those active at any time are *working self-concepts*. Self-schemas have an affective dimension (self-conceptions are positive and negatively valued), a temporal dimension (experiences result in concepts of past, present, and future possible selves), a self-efficacy dimension (beliefs about what we can do to attain our selves), and a value dimension (importance or centrality of the self to the individual).

As organized knowledge structures, possible (future) selves are ways to connect multiple motivational beliefs at a higher level (Garcia & Pintrich, 1994). Thus, goals are important motivational processes, and self-schemas are organized knowledge structures that link multiple goals. Self-schemas may provide a link between motivation and strategy use. If persons have ideas about what they can be and do, then possible selves can guide actions.

Possible selves can play an important role in self-regulated learning because the notion of what one might become underlies use of self-regulatory processes (Garcia & Pintrich, 1994). Individuals regulate their learning and performances to become their positive possible selves and to avoid becoming negative possible selves. Students self-regulate their motivation to attain selves and protect their sense of self-worth.

Help Seeking

Help seeking is a way to self-regulate the social environment to promote learning (Karabenick & Gonida, 2018). Self-regulated learners are likely to ask for assistance when they confront difficult tasks and perceive the need for help (Newman, 2000, 2002,

2008). In particular, high achievers often seek help from teachers and peers (Zimmerman & Martinez-Pons, 1990).

Newman (1994) proposed a model in which adaptive help seeking:

- Occurs following a student's lack of understanding.
- Includes the student considering the need for help, the content of the request, and the request target.
- Involves expressing the need for help in the most suitable fashion given the circumstances.
- Requires that the help seeker receive and process help in a way that will optimize the probability of success in later help-seeking attempts.

Help seeking is a relatively complex activity that includes more than the verbal request for assistance. Motivational factors come into play. Many motivational processes have been investigated for their relation to help seeking, especially the roles of self-efficacy and goal setting. Students with higher self-efficacy for learning are more apt to seek help than are those with lower efficacy (Ryan, Gheen, & Midgley, 1998). Students with a task goal orientation are more likely to seek assistance to determine the correctness of their work, whereas ego-involved students may seek help to determine how their work compares with that of others (Ryan et al., 1998).

This research suggests that different motivational patterns can prompt various forms of help seeking. With respect to self-regulated learning, the most adaptive type of help seeking is that which provides feedback on learning and progress. Teachers can encourage students to seek assistance when it is likely to help them develop academic skills.

INSTRUCTIONAL APPLICATIONS

Self-regulatory skills, like other skills, can be learned (B. Zimmerman, 2000). Effective methods for teaching these skills often include exposing students to social models, teaching them to use learning strategies, giving them practice and corrective feedback, and assisting them to evaluate their learning goal progress (Schunk & Ertmer, 2000). It is essential that students internalize the various social influences in their environments so that they become part of their self-regulatory processes (Schunk, 1999).

The principles of self-regulated learning discussed in this chapter lend themselves well to instructional applications. The most effective applications are those in which self-regulatory processes are incorporated into academic learning instruction. Three areas that are especially germane are academic studying, writing, and mathematics.

Academic Studying

Many students have problems studying. Researchers have examined students' self-regulated learning during academic studying. There are published resources that help students develop better study habits (Cleary, 2018; Dembo & Seli, 2016), as well as effective studying courses that are integrated with academic course content (Hofer, Yu, & Pintrich, 1998;

Lan, 1998). Academic studying can be improved with instruction on strategies and time management.

Strategy Instruction. Researchers have investigated how strategy instruction affects academic studying. Dansereau (1978; Dansereau et al., 1979) developed a strategy instruction program for college students. These researchers distinguished *primary strategies*, or those applied directly to the content, from *support strategies* that learners use to create and maintain a favorable psychological climate for learning. The latter strategies include affective techniques and those used to monitor and correct ongoing primary strategies.

Effective studying requires that students comprehend, retain, retrieve, and use information. In Dansereau's learning strategies program, students comprehend material by highlighting important ideas, recalling material without referring to text, digesting and expanding the information, and reviewing it. Expanding information means relating it to other information in LTM by creating links between memory networks. Students learn to ask themselves questions similar to the following: "Imagine you could talk to the author. What questions would you ask? What criticisms would you raise?" "How can the material be applied?" and "How could you make the material more understandable and interesting to other students?"

This program includes support strategies such as goal setting, concentration management, and monitoring and diagnosing. Students learn to set daily, weekly, and longer-term goals by establishing schedules. Learners monitor progress and adjust their work or goals as necessary if their performance does not match expectations. Concentration management is developed by helping students deal with frustration, anxiety, and anger. Use of self-talk is encouraged, and students can be desensitized by imagining anxiety-provoking situations when relaxing (Chapter 3). Monitoring and diagnosing require that students determine in advance where they will stop in the text to assess their level of comprehension. As they reach each stop point, they assess understanding and take corrective action (e.g., rereading) as needed. Evaluations of the strategy-instructional program have shown that it improves academic behaviors and attitudes (Dansereau et al., 1979).

Dansereau (1988) modified this program for use in cooperative learning dyads. Each member of the pair took turns reading approximately 500 words of a 2,500-word passage. One member then served as recaller and orally summarized what was read; the other listened, corrected errors in recall, and elaborated knowledge by adding imagery and links to prior knowledge. This cooperative arrangement facilitated learning and transfer better than individual studying.

Time Management. Investigators from different theoretical traditions increasingly have focused on the cognitive and behavioral processes that students use to plan and manage academic studying time (Winne, 2001; Zimmerman, Greenberg, & Weinstein, 1994). Effective time management contributes to learning and achievement (Dembo & Seli, 2016). Britton and Tesser (1991) found that the time management components of short-range planning and time attitudes were significant predictors of grade point averages among college students. Effective use of time appears partly to be a function of students' use of goal setting and planning (Weinstein & Mayer, 1986). These procedures, in turn, prompt students to engage in other self-regulatory activities such as self-monitoring of progress. Time is an important dimension of self-regulation and can be a performance outcome (e.g., how much time to devote to a task).

Poor time management may reflect problems in several areas (Zimmerman et al., 1994). It can result when students do not properly self-observe, self-evaluate, and self-react to their performance outcomes. It also may occur when students do not adequately use planning aids such as calendars and alarms. Unrealistic goals, low self-efficacy, attributions of learning difficulties to low ability, and perceptions that strategies are not all that important also affect time management (Zimmerman, 1998; Zimmerman et al., 1994).

Students can learn to manage time more effectively. Weinstein, Palmer, & Schulte, (1987) included time management as one of the areas of the *Learning and Study Strategies Inventory* (*LASSI*), a diagnostic and prescriptive self-report measure of strategic, goal-directed learning for students that focuses on thoughts, attitudes, beliefs, and behaviors that are related to academic success and can be altered. Completion of the LASSI or a similar instrument usually is necessary to ascertain the extent of a student's study problems.

Programs to facilitate better use of time typically include instruction and practice on topics such as becoming a strategic learner; the roles of goal setting and self-management; time-management planning; various study strategies including note taking, listening, underlining, summarizing, and coping with stress; test-taking strategies; and organizing a setting for learning.

An important study time issue is that students often do not realize how they really spend their time. A good assignment is to have students keep a time log for a week to show how much time they devoted to each task. Often they are surprised at how much time they wasted. Instruction must address ways to eliminate or reduce such waste.

Another common problem is failing to understand how long tasks take to complete. A student once informed me that she thought she would need about two hours to read eight chapters in her educational psychology textbook. At 15 minutes per chapter with no break, that is speed reading! A useful exercise is to have students estimate the amount of time various tasks will take, and then keep a log of the actual times and record these with the estimates to determine the correspondence between estimated and actual times.

Students often need a change in work environment. They may try to study in places with potential distractions such as friends, phones, radios, televisions, refrigerators, and so forth. Some students may benefit from light music or noise in the background, but almost everyone has difficulty concentrating when a powerful distraction or many potential distractions are present. It helps for students to complete an inventory of study preferences and present study conditions, after which they can determine whether environmental changes are necessary.

Writing

Like other forms of learning, the development of writing proficiency is affected by motivation and self-regulation (Cutler & Graham, 2008; Graham, 2006; Graham, Harris, MacArthur, & Santangelo, 2018). Bruning and Horn (2000) characterized this development as "a highly fluid process of problem solving requiring constant monitoring of progress toward task goals" (p. 25). Cognitive models of writing incorporate motivation and self-regulatory processes (Hayes, 2000; Magnifico, 2010). Students are active information processors who employ cognitive and metacognitive strategies during writing.

Goal setting, use of strategies, and self-monitoring or self-assessment of goal progress are key self-regulatory processes (Schunk, 1995). Results of a meta-analysis of studies on writing interventions with elementary students showed that strategy instruction, goal setting, and self-assessment produced significant effects (Graham, McKeown, Kiuhara, & Hanks, 2012). A meta-analysis with adolescents also showed the effectiveness of strategy instruction and goal setting on writing performance (Graham & Perin, 2007). Zimmerman and Kitsantas (1999) found that high school students who shifted their goals from process (following steps in a strategy) to outcomes (number of words in sentences) showed higher writing revision skill, self-efficacy, and interest than did students who pursued only process or only outcome goals. These results suggest that as skills develop, students can shift their focus from following a strategy to the outcomes that strategy use produces (e.g., making fewer errors). Although more research is needed on the effects of instructional procedures on motivation to write, writing motivation can be enhanced by using authentic writing tasks and by creating a supportive context for writing (e.g., the task appears doable with requisite effort).

Klassen (2002) reviewed the literature on self-efficacy for writing. Most studies found that self-efficacy was a significant predictor of writing achievement. Some studies yielded gender differences in self-efficacy with boys' judgments higher than those of girls, although there were no performance differences. Establishing a classroom environment that builds self-efficacy is conducive to improving writing. Brunstein and Glaser (2011) found that self-regulated learning improved writing self-efficacy in fourth graders.

Writing is demanding and requires attention control, self-monitoring, and volitional control. Graham and Harris (2000) noted that self-regulation affects writing in two ways. For one, self-regulatory processes (e.g., planning, monitoring, and evaluating) provide building blocks that are assembled to complete a writing task. For another, these processes can lead to strategic adjustments in writing and longer-term effects. Thus, successful planning will increase its likelihood of future use and build self-efficacy for writing, which in turn positively impacts motivation and future writing. Teaching students self-regulatory skills in the context of writing assignments can result in higher achievement and motivation (Graham & Harris, 2000; Schunk & Swartz, 1993a, 1993b). The quality and quantity of students' learning strategies (especially organization and elaboration), as determined by their writing in learning journals, positively predicts their mathematical performances (Glogger, Schwonke, Holzäpfel, Nückles, & Renkl, 2012).

The Self-Regulated Strategy Development model has been widely applied to writing (Baker, Chard, Ketterlin-Geller, Apichatabutra, & Doabler, 2009; Glaser & Brunstein, 2007; Graham et al., 2018; Graham, Harris, MacArthur, & Schwartz, 1998; Zito, Adkins, Gavins, Harris, & Graham, 2007). This model utilizes teacher modeling of writing strategies, collaborative peer group practice, and independent practice, where assistance (scaffolds) is generally faded out. The model has been used successfully with students with writing problems, learning disabilities, and attention deficit/hyperactivity disorders (Harris et al., 2006, 2013; Reid & Lienemann, 2006). The model includes general and genre-specific strategies (as emphasized in the introductory scenario), as well as motivational components (e.g., self-reinforcement). De La Paz (2005) found that applying the model with culturally diverse students helped them improve their argumentative essay writing skills.

Given that writing involves language and reflects one's thoughts and cognitive processes, writing has been viewed as a way to improve learning capabilities and academic achievement. This "writing to learn" idea stresses having students write in various disciplines. Bangert-Drowns, Hurley, and Wilkinson (2004) reviewed the research literature on writing-to-learn interventions and found a small positive effect on overall academic achievement. These researchers also found that prompting students during writing to reflect on their knowledge and learning processes was effective in raising achievement. These findings suggest that writing-to-learn has promise as a useful way to augment self-regulated learning in content areas. Some applications of self-regulated learning to writing are given in Application 10.6.

APPLICATION 10.6
Writing

Teachers can incorporate self-regulatory processes into writing lessons and activities. Ms. Nikkona wanted her third-grade students to write a paragraph describing their summer vacations; she might have students share what they did during the summer. Following this large-group activity, she and the children might jointly plan, write, and edit a paragraph about the teacher's summer vacation. This exercise would emphasize the important elements of a good paragraph and self-regulatory components of the writing process.

Students then could be paired and share orally with each other some things done during the summer. Sharing helps students generate ideas to use in writing. Following this activity, children can write their summer activities. Students will use their lists to formulate sentences of a paragraph and share their written products with their partners. Partners will provide feedback about clarity and grammar, after which students revise their paragraphs.

The faculty sponsor of the high school yearbook can incorporate self-regulatory components into producing the yearbook. When the sponsor meets with the students, the sponsor and the students plan sections and topics to be covered (e.g., school news highlights, sports, clubs), as well as who will be responsible for each section. Then the students set goals with time limits, after which they work in teams to write and revise their articles with input from the sponsor.

Dr. Smithson works with members of her class as they write their first research paper. She has each student select a topic, develop a basic outline, and compile a list of possible sources, after which she meets with students individually to plan writing strategies. Then she has students begin the first draft of the paper, giving more attention to the introduction and conclusion. She meets again with students individually to discuss their first drafts and progress and guides them toward what should be done to complete the finished product.

Technology

The impact of technology on learning is discussed in Chapter 7. Technology also can affect self-regulated learning (Moos, 2018). The use of technology in learning environments potentially involves multiple self-regulatory processes such as planning, knowledge activation, and metacognitive monitoring (Azevedo, Moos, Johnson, & Chauncey, 2010). Instructors who use technology wisely in online and blended courses can help develop their students' self-regulatory skills.

There are multiple technological tools available to instructors of online and blended courses. These include learning management systems (e.g., Blackboard) with all of their features, discussion boards, chat rooms, blogs, web conferencing, wikis, social networking platforms, cloud computing technologies, virtual worlds, and mobile technologies (Kitsantas, Dabbagh, Huie, & Dass, 2013).

A self-regulatory process that lends itself well to many tools is goal setting. Posting assignments and helping students use discussion boards can facilitate goal setting, as can the collaboration and communication tools in learning management systems (Kitsantas et al., 2013). Good time management, which is necessary for students to accomplish goals, can be fostered with calendar features such as automatic reminders about forthcoming due dates and periodic advice about how much of an assignment students should have completed by that date.

Teaching students how to effectively use online resources and giving them practice doing so can raise their self-efficacy for online learning, which contributes to their overall success using technology in online and blended courses (Kitsantas et al., 2013). Maintaining a sense of self-efficacy for learning during courses increases motivation and achievement (Schunk & DiBenedetto, 2016).

Technology tools also can help students learn and use more-effective strategies during learning. These are both general strategies, such as environmental structuring and task focusing, as well as strategies specific to the nature of the material to be learned. When well designed, online learning environments can prompt students to use effective strategies, such as by cuing students to stop periodically and summarize what they have learned.

This chapter has discussed the key role of self-monitoring in self-regulated learning. Online learning environments can assist with this, such as by prompting students to track their learning progress by using the online gradebook. Geddes (2009) found that students who more often used the online gradebook feature attained higher course grades and reported higher learning goal orientations compared with students who used this feature less often.

In similar fashion, students can monitor their progress and periodically evaluate it; that is, whether it meets or falls short of their goals. Such self-evaluation also can be cued in learning management systems, with periodic reminders to students to self-evaluate their progress. Using an online journal has been shown to be effective in helping students reflect on their learning goals and make adjustments as needed (Campbell, 2009).

Learning management systems allow instructors to personalize their courses. They can build into them materials for students to use to organize their work, check off completed assignments, ask questions, and receive feedback. This type of instructional scaffolding helps students become better self-regulators (Kitsantas et al., 2013).

Further, the adaptations described here often require little extra work by instructors. Learning management systems, for example, allow instructors to send e-mail notifications to students reminding them about forthcoming due date and expectations for assignments. Students who fail to turn work in on time can receive a notification to that effect with a reminder to turn it in as soon as possible. With lengthy assignments (e.g., research paper), instructors can e-mail reminders at various times stating how much of the project students should have completed by that date. Instructors also can suggest effective self-regulatory strategies for students to use on various parts of the assignments. These suggestions are simple and take little time, yet they can have great benefits on students' development of better self-regulated learning skills.

SUMMARY AND CRITIQUE

Chapter Summary

Self-regulated learning refers to cognitive, metacognitive, motivational, and affective processes that learners use to systematically focus their thoughts, feelings, and actions on the attainment of their learning goals. Self-regulated learning includes self-regulatory processes applied before, during, and after a learning experience, where the goal is a desired level of achievement.

The application of self-regulation to learning began as an outgrowth of psychological research on the development of self-control by adults and children. Much early self-regulation research was conducted in clinical settings, where researchers taught participants to alter dysfunctional behaviors such as aggression, addictions, sexual disorders, interpersonal conflicts, and behavioral problems at home and in school. Subsequently, researchers expanded their focus to address academic learning and achievement, as well as self-regulated learning in groups. Co-regulation refers to the coordination of self-regulation competencies among people in social contexts; socially shared regulation includes interdependent regulatory processes aimed at attaining a mutual outcome in collaborative settings.

Theories of self-regulated learning share common assumptions. One is that self-regulated learning involves being behaviorally, cognitively, metacognitively, and motivationally active in one's learning and performance. A second assumption is that self-regulated learning is a dynamic and cyclical process comprising feedback loops. Self-regulated learners set goals and metacognitively monitor their progress toward them. They respond to their monitoring, as well as to external feedback, in different ways to attain their goals, such as by working harder or changing their strategy. Accomplishments lead them to set new goals. Third, goal setting triggers self-regulated learning by guiding individuals' focus on goal-directed activities and use of task-relevant strategies. Finally, there is an emphasis on motivation, or why persons choose to self-regulate and sustain it.

Self-regulated learning involves learners' choices, such as whether to participate, which method they use, what outcomes they will pursue, and which social and physical setting they will work in. Self-regulated learning involves behaviors, as individuals regulate their actions to keep them focused on goal attainment. Individuals also regulate their cognitions and affects. While they are engaged in learning, they self-regulate cognitions, motivation, and affects by maintaining their self-efficacy for learning, valuing the learning, holding expectations for positive outcomes as a result of the learning, evaluating their goal progress, determining how effective their strategies are and altering them as necessary, and maintaining a positive emotional climate.

There are various theoretical perspectives on self-regulated learning. Behavior theories stress the setting of stimuli and conditions to which learners respond, after which they are reinforced for their efforts. Key behavioral processes are self-monitoring, self-instruction, and self-reinforcement. Learners decide which behaviors to regulate, set discriminative stimuli for their occurrence, participate in instruction as needed, monitor performance, and administer reinforcement when it matches the standard. Behavioral principles are useful for self-regulation, but by neglecting cognitive and affective processes, they offer an incomplete account of the range of self-regulation possible.

The classical social cognitive theoretical account of self-regulated learning viewed it as comprising three processes: self-observation, self-judgment, and self-reaction. Students enter learning activities with various goals such as acquiring knowledge and skills and completing assignments. With these goals in mind, they observe, judge, and react to their perceived goal progress. This classical view was broadened to emphasize the cyclical nature of self-regulation and to include activities before and after task engagement. This cyclical process reflects the social cognitive emphasis on reciprocal interactions between personal, behavioral, and social/environmental factors. The forethought phase precedes actual performance and refers to processes that set the stage for action, such as setting goals, deciding on a strategy, and assessing self-efficacy for learning. The performance control phase involves processes that occur during learning and affect attention and action, such as applying strategies and monitoring progress. During the self-reflection phase that occurs during breaks and after task completion, learners respond to their efforts by setting new goals, adjusting their strategies, and making attributions for outcomes.

Information processing theories emphasize that self-regulated learning reflects metacognitive awareness. Self-regulation requires that learners understand task demands, personal qualities, and strategies for completing the task. Metacognitive awareness also includes procedural knowledge. The basic unit of self-regulation may be a problem-solving system in which the problem is to reach the goal and through monitoring learners check progress to determine whether the learning is occurring. Information processing research historically focused on cognitive variables, but current perspectives include motivational variables.

Constructivism stresses that self-regulated learning involves the coordination of mental functions, such as memory, planning, evaluation, and synthesis. Learners use the tools of their cultures, such as language and symbols, to construct meanings of content and situations. A key feature is the internalization of self-regulatory processes. Although learners may acquire self-regulatory strategies from their environments, they alter and adapt them for use in their personal self-regulatory systems.

Self-regulated learning and motivation are related. Such processes as goal setting, self-efficacy, and outcome expectations are important motivational variables that affect self-regulated learning. In turn, engaging in successful self-regulated learning can motivate learners to set new goals and continue learning. Students also can self-regulate their motivation for learning. Researchers have examined the role of volition in achievement settings. Other motivational variables involved in self-regulated learning include values, goal orientations, self-schemas, and help seeking.

Like other skills, learners can be taught self-regulatory skills and can become better self-regulated learners. An effective teaching model begins with social (environmental) influences, such as teacher models explaining and demonstrating self-regulatory strategies. As students practice and become more skillful, they transform these social influences in idiosyncratic ways and internalize them into their personal self-regulatory systems. Self-regulation instruction is most effective when it is linked to academic content. Principles of self-regulated learning have been applied to such areas as academic studying and writing. Learning environments rich with technology can help students develop self-regulatory skills.

Chapter Critique

Since its beginnings in clinical settings as a means of helping individuals develop more-adaptive behaviors, self-regulated learning has expanded tremendously into areas involving academic, social, and motor skills. Researchers today explore self-regulated learning in such areas as mathematics, reading, physical education, and music, as well as in settings out-of-school.

The various theoretical perspectives on self-regulated learning share certain common assumptions, and there is consensus that learners can improve their self-regulatory capabilities. The field of self-regulated learning might benefit from a closer integration of theoretical perspectives. For example, greater attention might be paid by information processing and social cognitive researchers on how learners construct and adapt their self-regulatory actions, as well as how developmental factors (e.g., development of working memory) affect self-regulated learning.

Another positive direction for the field is greater exploration in relatively under-researched areas (e.g., art, music) and in out-of-school settings. It seems that there are multiple opportunities for self-regulated learning out of school, such as in internships and volunteer activities. Much learning occurs in these contexts, yet we know little about how it develops or operates.

The topics of co-regulation and socially shared regulation seem highly relevant to schooling among students and teachers, given the educational emphasis on cooperative learning, group projects, and peer-assisted learning. But to date there is little research exploring their operation. We should expect that the same self-regulatory processes important for individual learning—such as goal setting, monitoring, and self-efficacy—also pertain to group contexts, but greater research emphasis on these contexts would benefit theory, research, and practice.

REFLECTION QUESTIONS

■ Are you a self-regulated learner? How do you know if you are practicing self-regulation? What do you do when you realize you are not?

■ Self-regulated learning occurs before, during, and after task engagement. How might teachers work with students to improve their self-regulated learning at these different times? Which self-regulation skills might be easier for teachers to help students develop? Which might be more difficult?

■ Motivation is a critical aspect of self-regulated learning. Motivation can affect self-regulated learning, and in turn, the results of one's self-regulated learning efforts can influence motivation. Further, one can regulate one's motivation for self-regulated learning. What are some ways to help improve learners' motivation for self-regulated learning?

FURTHER READING

Azevedo, R., Moos, D. C., Johnson, A. M., & Chauncey, A. D. (2010). Measuring cognitive and meta-cognitive regulatory processes during hypermedia learning: Issues and challenges. *Educational Psychologist, 45,* 210–223.

Henderson, R. W., & Cunningham, L. (1994). Creating interactive sociocultural environments for self-regulated learning. In D. H. Schunk & B. J. Zimmerman (Eds.), *Self-regulation of learning and performance: Issues and educational applications* (pp. 255–281). Hillsdale, NJ: Erlbaum.

Mace, F. C., Belfiore, P. J., & Hutchinson, M. M. (2001). Operant theory and research on self-regulation. In B. J. Zimmerman & D. H. Schunk (Eds.), *Self-regulated learning and academic achievement: Theoretical perspectives* (2nd ed., pp. 39–65). Mahwah, NJ: Erlbaum.

Schunk, D. H., & Greene, J. A. (Eds.) (2018). *Handbook of self-regulation of learning and performance* (2nd ed.). New York: Routledge.

Sitzmann, T., & Ely, K. (2011). A meta-analysis of self-regulated learning in work-related training and educational attainment: What we know and where we need to go. *Psychological Bulletin, 137,* 421–442.

Winne, P. H., & Hadwin, A. F. (2008). The weave of motivation and self-regulated learning. In D. H. Schunk & B. J. Zimmerman (Eds.), *Motivation and self-regulated learning: Theory, research, and applications* (pp. 297–314). New York: Taylor & Francis.

Zimmerman, B. J. (2000). Attaining self-regulation: A social cognitive perspective. In M. Boekaerts, P. R. Pintrich, & M. Zeidner (Eds.), *Handbook of self-regulation* (pp. 13–39). San Diego: Academic Press.

11 Contextual Influences

In an undergraduate teacher education course, Dr. Richards is having a discussion with her students on student boredom. Her students are serving internships in middle and high schools. Dr. Richards asks her students why they think so many middle and high school students seem bored in school.

Tanya: I think they've just got their minds on other things. They interested in hanging out with friends, guys, and girls. They're not thinking about the learning.

Rick: The classes are boring. So many teachers just stand up in front and lecture. Students hardly ever get to talk or move around. I don't like classes like that.

Jenna: Maybe some of the problems are from home. A lot of parents don't stress education enough. How their kids do in school just isn't very important to them.

Alec: It also could be because of the friends they hang out with. If you hang out with a good crowd, you'll do better in school. But if no one in your crowd values school, then you won't either. Isn't that modeling?

Stefano: And it's not just the peers. It's in the communities where the kids live. The school where I'm doing my internship is in a bad neighborhood. Most of the people there aren't educated. So the kids don't have good role models.

Renee: And kids have different backgrounds. I heard a story on TV recently explaining cultural differences in attitudes toward schooling. What can teachers do about those?

Dr. Richards: You've made good points. All of these are possible influences on students feeling bored in school. And it's true that some influences are easier to change than others. As teachers, you can make your classrooms interesting or boring. But you also can exert some effects on parents, peers, communities, and cultural beliefs. We're going to be discussing these. Then you can look for examples at your internship sites.

Many learning principles are covered in this text. It is easy to think that these principles operate uniformly in different contexts and are relatively unaffected by contextual variables. But this is not the case. Principles of learning are not context independent. Rather, they operate in specific situations and are subject to contextual influences.

Although contextual factors are addressed by all learning theories, some theories (e.g., constructivism; Chapter 8) place great emphasis on the role of context. Contextual perspectives on learning are informed by cross-cultural comparisons showing variability in the effects of variables on learning and development. But even within societies, there is considerable variation in development and learning patterns (Meece, 2002). Clearly societal practices can affect learning.

Context has been defined in various ways. With reference to human development, Bronfenbrenner (1979) formulated a contextual model comprising a set of concentric circles with the individual at the common point of three intersecting circles: school, peers, and family (see Figure 11.1). Outside of these is a larger circle containing neighborhood, extended family, community, church, workplace, and mass media. The outermost circle contains such influences as laws, cultural values, political and economic systems, and social customs. Changes in one level can affect others. For example, physical changes in children can alter their social groups, which in turn are affected by cultural values. This model highlights the complexity of human development and, by implication, of the learning that takes place in students of different ages.

In this text, *context* is defined as the community or learning environment within which the individual is located (Cole, 2010). The community includes the people who spend time together in some institutionalized setting, such as schools, classrooms, and work settings. Researchers investigate various types of communities such as those of learners and of practice (Brown & Campione, 1996; Lave & Wenger, 1991). These researchers believe that learning cannot be studied in controlled situations because learning includes not only skill acquisition but also developing an identity as a member of a community (Lave, 1993). One's identity can motivate and give meaning to the learning that occurs.

In a wider sense, technology has led to global communities where students can interact with others who are not physically present. Such technology-assisted learning broadens the possibilities compared with what is possible in traditional communities.

This chapter addresses types of contextual influences on students' learning. Many influences come from teachers, classrooms, and schools. But other contextual influences are located outside of school structures. In the last several years, researchers increasingly have shown that parents, peers, communities, and cultures affect students' learning, motivation, and self-regulation. Educators should understand as much as possible about these contextual influences so they can use them productively to create effective learning environments for students within and outside of schools.

This chapter begins by discussing important contextual influences on student learning found within schools: teachers, classrooms, and schools. Within-school variables include classroom organization and structure, teacher–student interactions, teacher expectations, teacher support, developmentally appropriate instruction, school transitions, and school climate. Next, the key roles in learning that peers, families, communities, and cultures play are addressed. A good understanding of the topics covered in previous chapters will help readers integrate learning principles with these various influences to determine applications that promote student learning.

When you finish studying this chapter, you should be able to do the following:

■ Discuss how organization, management, and the TARGET dimensions can influence the effectiveness of learning environments for teaching and learning.

- Explain how aspects of teacher–student interactions, including teacher feedback, support, and expectations, may affect students' academic motivation and learning.

- Explain what is meant by developmentally appropriate instruction and why transitions in schooling can affect teaching and learning.

- Describe how peer modeling and peer networks may influence students' academic learning.

- Discuss the relation of socioeconomic status, home environment, parental involvement, and media influence to development and learning.

- Explain how community location and involvement may relate to students' learning and achievement beliefs.

- Describe how differences among students between and within cultures may affect their beliefs, behaviors, and learning.

- Explain some instructional implications of the literature on teacher–student interactions, learning styles, and parental and familial involvement in schooling.

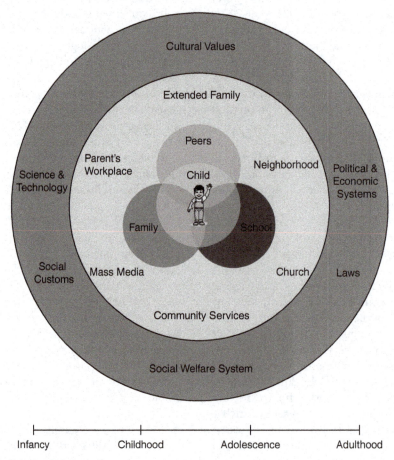

Figure 11.1
Bronfenbrenner's contextual model of human development.

TEACHERS, CLASSROOMS, AND SCHOOLS

A discussion of contextual influences on student learning should rightly begin with teachers, classrooms, and schools because those are key factors in students' lives. Several aspects of teacher, classroom, and school influences on learning are discussed in this section: effective learning environments, teacher–student interactions, developmentally appropriate instruction, transitions in schooling, and classroom and school climate.

Effective Learning Environments

Students' learning benefits from effective learning environments, or those in which teaching and learning can proceed well, and creating these is a primary responsibility of teachers. Effective learning environments reflect good organization and management, as well as the TARGET dimensions of task, authority, recognition, grouping, evaluation, and time (Levin & Nolan, 2000; Meece et al., 2006). These topics are addressed in this section.

Organization. *Organization* refers to how activities are established, students are grouped, performances are evaluated, authority is established and maintained, and time is scheduled (Stipek, 1996). Good organization of the classroom learning environment facilitates learning. Many researchers and practitioners believe that environments are complex and that to understand learning, we must take into account many factors (Marshall & Weinstein, 1984; Roeser, Urdan, & Stephens, 2009).

An important aspect of organization is *dimensionality* (Rosenholtz & Simpson, 1984). *Unidimensional classrooms* include a few activities that address a limited range of student abilities. *Multidimensional classrooms* have more activities and allow for diversity in student abilities and performances. Multidimensional classes are compatible with constructivist tenets about learning (Chapter 8).

Classroom characteristics that indicate dimensionality include differentiation of task structure, student autonomy, grouping patterns, and salience of formal performance evaluations (Table 11.1). Unidimensional classrooms have *undifferentiated task structures*. All students work on the same or similar tasks, and instruction employs a small number of

Table 11.1
Characteristics of dimensionality.

Characteristic	Unidimensional	Multidimensional
Differentiation of task structure	Undifferentiated; students work on same tasks	Differentiated; students work on different tasks
Student autonomy	Low; students have few choices	High; students have choices
Grouping patterns	Whole class; students are grouped by ability	Individual work; students are not grouped by ability
Performance evaluations	Students are graded on same assignments; grades are public; much social comparison	Students are graded on different assignments; less public grading and social comparison

materials and methods (Rosenholtz & Simpson, 1984). The less differentiated the structure, the more likely the daily activities will produce consistent performances from each student and the greater the probability that students will socially compare their work with that of others to determine relative standing. Structures become *differentiated* (and classrooms become multidimensional) when students work on different tasks at the same time.

Student autonomy refers to the extent to which students have choices about what to do and when and how to do it. Classrooms are unidimensional when autonomy is low, which can hinder self-regulation and stifle motivation. Multidimensional classrooms offer students more choices, which can enhance intrinsic motivation.

With respect to grouping patterns, social comparisons become more prominent when students work on whole-class activities or are grouped by ability. Comparisons are not as prevalent when students work individually or in mixed-ability groups. Grouping affects motivation and learning and has added influence over the long term if groups remain intact and students understand they are bound to the groups regardless of how well they perform.

Salience of formal performance evaluations refers to the public nature of grading. In unidimensional classrooms, students are graded on the same assignments and grades are public, so everyone knows the grade distribution. Those receiving low grades may not be motivated to improve. As grading becomes less public or as grades are assigned for different projects (as in multidimensional classes), grading can motivate a higher proportion of students, especially those who believe they are progressing and capable of further learning (Schunk et al., 2014).

Unidimensional classrooms have high visibility of performance (Rosenholtz & Rosenholtz, 1981), which can motivate high achievers to learn but often has a negative effect on everyone else. Multidimensional classrooms are more likely to motivate more students because they feature greater differentiation and autonomy, less ability grouping, and more flexibility in grading with less public evaluation.

Management. Good organization helps create an effective environment, but good management also is needed for learning. *Management* refers to the ways that teachers create conditions such that students behave acceptably and learning can occur. Effective classroom managers ensure that rules and procedures are established, and they organize activities to keep students productively engaged. These activities help prevent discipline problems. When problems occur, good managers deal with them quickly and fairly so they are stopped and do not interfere with other students. Collectively these activities promote learning (Levin & Nolan, 2000).

A distinction can be drawn between proactive and reactive activities. Proactive activities are those teacher actions designed to prevent discipline problems from occurring; reactive activities are teacher actions designed to deal with problems when they occur, quickly return misbehaving students to academic activities, and minimize disruptions to others. Both proactive and reactive features of management are necessary.

Seminal research by Kounin (1977) found that what distinguished classrooms with few problems and where students were involved in academic work from classrooms with more problems and less work involvement were the proactive techniques that teachers used to prevent problems. Proactive activities include the teacher being aware of everything that is occurring in the classroom at any time, being able to attend to more than one issue at a time, keeping the pace of activities moving along well, keeping students task focused, minimizing boredom, and giving students few opportunities to misbehave. To this list we might add fostering students' motivation for learning by enhancing their self-efficacy for learning (Chapter 4), positive outcome expectations (Chapter 4), perceived value of learning (Chapter 9), interest in learning (Chapter 9), and a positive classroom climate (discussed later). Kounin found that when effective teachers used reactive techniques, they did so clearly (i.e., named the misbehaving student, stated the unacceptable behavior) and firmly (i.e., an "I-mean-it" attitude with follow through until misbehavior stopped).

Good classroom management also requires that teachers establish rules and procedures and convey their expectations to students. The beginning of the school year is a desirable time to establish rules and procedures so students know them early on. A procedure for establishing rules and procedures is as follows: describe and demonstrate desired behaviors to students, have students practice behaviors repeatedly, and provide students with feedback on whether they performed behaviors correctly and suggest improvements where needed (Emmer, Evertson, & Worsham, 2000; Evertson, Emmer, & Worsham, 2000).

Research studies support the importance of teachers establishing high expectations for classroom behavior and conveying those expectations to students (Emmer et al., 2000; Evertson et al., 2000; Levin & Nolan, 2000). Effective classroom managers expect students to obey rules, and they do not tolerate excuses for disobeying them. Teachers' proactive efforts to create a productive classroom are critical for good management. Rules, procedures, and expectations are proactive techniques designed to prevent problems and promote student learning.

TARGET.   In addition to good organization and management, effective learning environments incorporate other variables that can affect learning and motivation. These variables can be summarized by the acronym *TARGET: task* design, distribution of *authority*, *recognition* of students, *grouping* arrangements, *evaluation* practices, and *time* allocation (Epstein, 1989; Table 11.2).

Table 11.2
TARGET variables affecting learning and motivation.

Factor	Characteristics
Task	Design of learning activities and assignments
Authority	Extent that students can assume leadership and develop independence and control over learning activities
Recognition	Formal and informal use of rewards, incentives, praise
Grouping	Individual, small group, large group
Evaluation	Methods for monitoring and assessing learning
Time	Appropriateness of workload, pace of instruction, time allotted for completing work

Source: Based on Epstein, J. L. (1989), "Family Structures and Student Motivation: A Development Perspective." In C. Ames & R. Ames (Eds.), *Research on Motivation in Education* (vol. 3, pp. 259–295). San Diego: Academic Press.

The task dimension involves the design of learning activities and assignments. Chapter 9 discusses ways to structure tasks to promote a mastery (learning) goal orientation in students—for example, by making learning interesting, using variety and challenge, assisting students to set realistic goals, and helping students develop organizational, management, and other strategic skills (Ames, 1992a, 1992b). Task structure is a distinguishing feature of dimensionality. In unidimensional classes, students have the same materials and assignments, so variations in ability can translate into differences in learning and motivation. In multidimensional classes, not all students work on the same task simultaneously, and thus they have fewer opportunities for social comparisons.

Authority refers to whether students can assume leadership and develop independence and control over learning activities. Teachers foster authority by allowing students to participate in decisions, giving them choices and leadership roles, and teaching them skills that allow them to take responsibility for learning. Self-efficacy tends to be higher in classes that allow students some measure of authority (Ames, 1992a, 1992b).

Recognition, which involves the formal and informal use of rewards, incentives, and praise, has important consequences for motivated learning (Schunk, 1995). Ames (1992a, 1992b) recommended that teachers help students develop mastery (learning) goal orientations by recognizing progress, accomplishments, effort, and self-regulation; providing opportunities for all learners to earn rewards; and using private forms of recognition that avoid comparing students or emphasizing the difficulties of others.

The grouping dimension focuses on students' ability to work with others. Teachers who use heterogeneous cooperative groups and peer interaction where possible help ensure that differences in ability do not translate into differences in learning and motivation. Low achievers especially benefit from small-group work because contributing to the group's success promotes self-efficacy. Group work also allows more students to share in the responsibility for learning so that a few students do not do all the work. At the same time, individual work is important because it provides clear indicators of learning progress.

Evaluation involves methods for monitoring and assessing student learning, for example, evaluating students for individual progress and mastery, giving students opportunities to improve their work (e.g., revise a paper for a better grade), using different forms of evaluation, and conducting evaluations privately. Although normative grading systems are common in schools (i.e., students compared to one another), such normative comparisons can lower self-efficacy among students who do not perform as well as their peers.

Time involves the appropriateness of workload, pace of instruction, and time allotted for completing work (Epstein, 1989). Effective strategies for enhancing learning and motivation are to adjust time or task requirements for those having difficulty and allowing students to plan their schedules and timelines for making progress. Giving students control over their time management helps allay anxiety about completing work and can promote self-efficacy for learning and the use of self-regulatory processes (Schunk & DiBenedetto, 2016; Chapter 10). Application 11.1 lists classroom applications of TARGET.

APPLICATION 11.1
TARGET in the Classroom

Incorporating TARGET components into an instructional unit can positively affect learning and motivation. As Ms. Underhill develops a unit on deserts for her elementary students, she plans part of the unit but also involves her students in planning activities. She sets up learning centers, plans reading and research assignments, organizes large- and small-group discussions, and designs unit pre- and posttests, as well as tasks for checking mastery throughout the unit. The class helps her plan a field trip to a museum with an area devoted to life in the desert, develop small-group project topics, and decide how to create a desert in the classroom. Ms. Underhill and the students then develop a calendar and timeline for working on and completing the unit. These examples incorporate the six TARGET variables of task, authority, recognition, grouping, evaluation, and time.

Teacher–Student Interactions

In typical classrooms, teachers and students continually interact. Teachers give directions, ask questions, provide feedback, respond to students' questions, correct misbehavior, and offer assistance as needed. How teachers interact with students is affected by teachers' beliefs about their teaching capabilities and students' learning capabilities (Davis, 2003; Fives & Buehl, 2016). Teachers' interactions with students can have important effects on students' learning and motivation (Martin & Dowson, 2009; Wentzel, 2010, 2016). Based on a review of the research literature, Quin (2017) found positive associations between better-quality teacher–student relationships and several indicators of greater student engagement (e.g., higher grades and attendance, fewer disruptive behaviors, lower dropout rates). This section addresses three aspects influencing interactions: teacher feedback, support, and expectations.

Teacher Feedback. Teachers provide different types of feedback to students. One type is performance feedback on the accuracy of their work (e.g., "That's correct.") and may include corrective information (e.g., "Try applying this formula."). Performance feedback is informative because from it students learn about their progress in learning. Feedback indicating accuracy and use of good strategies (e.g., "That's correct. You're using the procedure well.") helps to build students' self-efficacy and motivation, which can lead to further learning.

When students make errors, reteaching and guiding students to correct answers are effective ways to promote learning (Rosenshine & Stevens, 1986). Such corrective feedback also can raise self-efficacy and motivation because it conveys that students are capable of performing better by using a better strategy (Schunk & DiBenedetto, 2016).

Teachers often give motivational feedback. One type is attributional, where teachers link students' performances to one or more attributions (e.g., "That's correct. You're really working hard."). In Chapter 9 we saw that attributional feedback that students perceive as credible is an effective motivator. Another type of motivational feedback is using social comparison by providing vicarious information (e.g., "See how well Tanya is doing? You can do that well too."). Pointing out the performances of similar others can raise self-efficacy and motivation in observers (Schunk & DiBenedetto, 2016).

A third type is persuasory feedback, such as, "I know you can learn this." Such vicarious self-efficacy information can raise self-efficacy in students, but it is important that students subsequently experience success. Finally, teachers might provide feedback on the effectiveness of students' strategies (e.g., "See how much better you're doing now that you're using the method we discussed?"). Effective strategies promote learning because they reflect sound learning principles designed to keep students task focused. Feedback indicating that students can perform better by using a different strategy can motivate them to do so.

Teacher Support.   Teacher support refers to the social, psychological, and emotional dimensions of teacher–student relationships. Teacher support affects the classroom climate; for example, teachers who are warm, learner centered, and democratic create a positive atmosphere for learning.

Teacher support is complex. Cornelius-White (2007) conducted a meta-analysis of research studies examining the relation of teacher interaction variables (e.g., empathy, warmth, genuineness, encouraging learning, adapting to student differences) to student cognitive and affective outcomes. The affective set included student motivation, self-efficacy, satisfaction, participation, and social connection. The overall correlation was +.35, which is a moderate and positive relation and suggests that teachers who provide a more supportive environment have students who are motivated and engaged, which can lead to better learning.

Another critical dimension may be the extent that the teacher directs the group's activities. Effective teaching requires that teachers steer a middle ground between student autonomy and classroom structure (Davis, 2003). Teachers who provide strong affective and instructional support promote teacher–student relationships, student engagement in learning, and student achievement, including for students at risk for school failure (Hamre & Pianta, 2005; Sakiz, 2011). Students in learner-centered classrooms tend to display greater interest in learning and better learning compared with students in non-learner-centered classrooms (Daniels, Kalkman, & McCombs, 2001). In summary, although sound instructional content and good pedagogy are necessary for learning, the relationships that teachers form and develop with their students add a key dimension.

Teacher Expectations.   Another aspect of teacher–student interactions that is relevant to student learning involves teacher expectations, which have been the subject of research for several years. Theory and research suggest that teachers' expectations for students relate to teacher actions and student motivation and learning (Cooper & Good, 1983; Cooper & Tom, 1984; Dusek, 1985; Jussim, Robustelli, & Cain, 2009; Rosenthal, 2002).

The impetus for exploring expectations came from a study by Rosenthal and Jacobson (1968), who gave elementary school students a test of nonverbal intelligence at the start of the academic year. Teachers were told that this test predicted which students would bloom intellectually during the year. In fact, the researchers randomly identified 20% of the school population as bloomers and gave these names to the teachers. Teachers were not aware of the deception: The test did not predict intellectual blooming, and names bore no relation to test scores. Teachers taught in their usual fashion and students were retested one semester, 1 year, and 2 years later. For the first two tests, students were in the classes of teachers given bloomers' names; for the last test, students were in new classes with teachers who did not have these names.

After the first year, significant differences in intelligence were seen between bloomers and control students (those not identified as bloomers); differences were greater among children in the first and second grades. During the subsequent year, these younger children lost their advantage, but bloomers in upper grades showed an increasing advantage over control students. Differences were greater among average achievers than among high or low achievers. Similar findings were obtained for grades in reading. Overall, the differences between bloomers and control students were small, both in reading and on the intelligence test.

Rosenthal and Jacobson (1968) concluded that teacher expectations can act as *self-fulfilling prophecies* because student achievement comes to reflect the expectations. They suggested that results are stronger with young children because they have closer contact with teachers. Older students may function better after they move to a new teacher.

This study is controversial. It has been criticized on conceptual and methodological grounds, and many attempts at replication have not been successful (Cooper & Good, 1983; Jussim et al., 2009). Nonetheless, teacher expectations exist and have been found to relate to various student outcomes. A model to explain self-fulfilling prophecies is as follows:

- First, teachers develop erroneous expectations.
- Then these expectations lead teachers to treat high-expectancy students differently than they treat low-expectancy students.
- Eventually students may react to this differential treatment in such a manner as to confirm the originally erroneous expectation. (Jussim et al., 2009)

Early in the school year, teachers form expectations based on initial interactions with students and on recorded and anecdotal information. Teachers then may begin to treat students differently, consistent with these expectations. Teacher behaviors are reciprocated; for example, teachers who treat students warmly are apt to receive warmth in return. Student behaviors begin to complement and reinforce teacher behaviors and expectations. Effects will be most pronounced for rigid and inappropriate expectations. When they are appropriate or inappropriate but flexible, student behavior may substantiate or redefine expectations. When expectations are inappropriate or not easily changed, student performance might decline and become consistent with expectations.

Once teachers form expectations, they can convey them to students through climate, verbal input, verbal output, and feedback (Rosenthal, 1974). The climate includes smiles, head nods, eye contact, and supportive and friendly actions. Teachers may create a warmer climate for students for whom they hold high expectations than for those for whom expectations are lower (Cooper & Tom, 1984). Verbal input, opportunities to learn new material, and difficulty of material, varies when high-expectation students have more opportunities to interact with and learn new material and be exposed to more difficult material. Verbal output refers to number and length of academic interactions. Teachers engage in more academic interchanges with high- than with low-expectation students. They also are more persistent with highs and get them to give answers by prompting or rephrasing questions.

Feedback refers to use of praise and criticism. Teachers praise high-expectation students and criticize low-expectation students more (Cooper & Tom, 1984).

Although these factors are genuine, wide differences exist between teachers (Schunk et al., 2014). Most teachers try to encourage lower achievers and treat them much like the patterns previously described for high achievers (e.g., give more praise, get them to answer more questions). Appropriate teacher expectations for students can improve learning. Tailoring difficulty of material and level of questioning to students based on their prior performances is instructionally sound. Expecting all students to learn with requisite effort also is reasonable. Greatly distorted expectations are not credible and typically have little effect on learning. Most elementary teachers (when expectation effects may be strongest) hold positive expectations for students, provide for a lot of successes, and use praise often.

It seems likely that students construct implicit theories about what their teachers think and expect of them. How these theories might influence their achievement actions is less predictable. Our beliefs about what others expect of us may motivate ("She thinks I can do it, so I'll try"), demotivate ("She thinks I can't do it, so I won't try"), or lead us to act contrary to our theories ("She thinks I can't do it, so I'll show her I can"). The best advice is to expect that all students can learn and to support them, which should help them construct appropriate expectations for themselves. Application 11.2 gives suggestions for conveying positive expectations to students.

APPLICATION 11.2
Teacher Expectations

Expectations that teachers hold for students can positively and negatively affect their interactions with students. The following practices may help promote positive effects:

- Enforce rules fairly and consistently.
- Assume that all students can learn, and convey that expectation to them.
- Do not form differential student expectations based on qualities unrelated to performance (e.g., gender, ethnicity, socioeconomic status).
- Do not accept excuses for poor performance.
- Realize that upper limits of student ability are unknown and not relevant to school learning.

A college English professor told her class of first-year students that they would be doing a lot of writing. Some of the students looked apprehensive, and the professor assured them that it was a task they could do. "We can all work together to improve our writing. I know some of you have had different experiences in high school with writing, but I will work with each of you, and I know by the end of the semester you will be writing well."

One student waited after class and told the professor that he had been in a special education class in high school and said, "I can hardly write a good sentence; I don't think you can make a writer out of me." To which the professor replied, "Well, sentences are a good place to begin. I'll see you Wednesday morning in class."

Developmentally Appropriate Instruction

A critical contextual influence on student learning is *developmentally appropriate instruction*, or instruction that is matched (compatible) with learners' developmental levels (Eccles & Midgley, 1989). That idea sounds basic, but unfortunately instructional activities and developmental levels often are mismatched. Teaching may involve nothing more than lecturing and presenting information to students (as noted in the opening vignette). The content might be presented in such a way that students have difficulty processing it, and they also might process it in ways that produce learning different from what the teacher desires.

For example, many high school students take precalculus. Much of the content of precalculus is abstract (e.g., conic sections, trigonometric relations, limits of functions). Although high school students increasingly are able to function at a Piagetian formal operational level and cognitively handle abstract content, many students are primarily concrete operational thinkers. Teachers who make little effort to provide concrete referents for precalculus topics create a mismatch between the content and students' thinking. It is little wonder that so many students have difficulty with precalculus, which in turn can adversely affect their mathematics self-efficacy and motivation for further study of mathematics.

Developmentally appropriate instruction relies upon several assumptions. For one, students construct knowledge based on their prior experiences and present schemas. Knowledge never is transmitted automatically; the construction of knowledge and integration with current mental structures are the means whereby learning proceeds. This requires that instruction be designed to foster such knowledge construction. Piaget (Chapter 8) recommended active exploration, a notion that is compatible with instructional methods such as discovery learning and small-group projects (which Rick in the opening vignette would like to see).

For another, the social environment is important. This notion is seen clearly in Vygotsky's theory (Chapter 8). When interacting with others, children receive ideas and opinions that conflict with their own; this sets the Piagetian equilibration process into motion (Meece, 2002). The cognitive conflict that ensues is considered the impetus behind learning in many developmental theories.

Third, conflict is created when the material to be learned is just beyond students' present understandings. This creates the zone of proximal development (Chapter 8), within which learning can occur through cognitive conflict, reflection, and conceptual reorganization (Meece, 2002). Little conflict exists when material is too far advanced beyond current understandings; conflict similarly is minimized when learning is at learners' current levels.

Finally, developmentally appropriate instruction incorporates active exploration and hands-on activities. Bruner's theory (Chapter 8) recommends that enactive learning occurs first, followed by iconic and symbolic. Although children's learning is based largely on what they do, hands-on learning is beneficial at all developmental levels. Students who are learning science skills benefit from observing teachers demonstrate them (iconic) and explain them (symbolic), as well as by performing the skills themselves (enactive).

What would a developmentally appropriate classroom look like? Meece (2002) suggested several appropriate practices that are summarized in Table 11.3. Some classroom applications of developmentally appropriate instruction are provided in Application 11.3.

Table 11.3
Developmentally appropriate instructional practices.

- Teachers structure the learning environment to include adults, other children, materials, and opportunities for children to engage in active exploration and interaction.

- Children select many of their own activities from a variety.

- Children stay active as they engage in much self-regulated learning.

- Children work most of the time in small groups or individually.

- Children work with concrete, hands-on activities.

- Teachers actively monitor children's progress to ensure continued involvement.

- Teachers focus on the process children use and not insist always on one right answer.

APPLICATION 11.3
Developmentally Appropriate Instruction

Students learn best in a classroom where instruction is developmentally appropriate. Beginning in preschool and kindergarten, teachers should ensure that students have the opportunity to learn in different ways to address the learning mode that is most appropriate for each child's developmental level.

Ms. Thompson is a kindergarten teacher. For a unit on magnets, she designed a learning station where students individually use magnets of different sizes and shapes. She divided the students into small groups and had them work cooperatively to discover the differences between items that can and cannot be picked up by magnets. She worked with each small group to complete a chart looking at the differences between items attracted by magnets. For story time that day, she read a book about the uses of magnets; while she read, each student had a magnet and items to test. For homework, she asked students to bring two small items to class the next day, one of which can be picked up by a magnet and one that cannot. The next day, in groups, students tested their items and then discussed why some items were and others were not attracted; she moved around the room and interacted with each group.

Transitions in Schooling

Transitions in schooling constitute an important contextual variable and can have a major impact on student learning. In the U.S. educational system, natural transitions occur when children change schools or experience major shifts in curricula and activities; for example, preschool to elementary, elementary to middle/junior high, middle/junior high to senior high, and senior high to college.

Transitions are important because they can produce disruptions in routines and ways of thinking and because of students' developmental levels at the times they occur (Eccles & Midgley, 1989). For example, the transition from elementary school to middle school/junior high would be disruptive for anyone, but it becomes especially so for students at that age given the bodily changes they are undergoing and their typical insecurities about their sense of self and appearance. Transitional variables and development most likely interact in reciprocal fashion. Developmental variables can make a transition smooth or rough, but, in turn, factors associated with the transition might affect students' personal, social, and cognitive development (Wigfield & Wagner, 2005).

The transition to middle school/junior high school is especially problematic (Eccles & Midgley, 1989; Wigfield et al., 2006). This transition occurs at a significant period of physical change in young adolescents with its attendant personal and social changes. Furthermore, numerous changes occur in school and class structures and subject areas. In elementary school, children typically are with the same teacher and peers for most of the school day. The teacher often has a warm and nurturing relationship with the children. Instruction frequently is individualized, and teachers track and report individual progress in content areas. Ability-level differences within a class may be wide, with students ranging from those with learning disabilities to gifted.

In contrast, in middle and junior high schools students typically change classes for each subject, which results in different teachers and peers. Teachers develop close relationships with few, if any, students. Instruction is provided to the entire class and rarely individualized. Grades—whether based on absolute or normative standards—do not reflect individual progress, nor is that generally reported. Ability-level within-class differences may be minimal if students are tracked. In general, middle school and junior high classes are more formal, impersonal, evaluative, and competitive (Meece, 2002). Eccles and her colleagues (Eccles & Midgley, 1989; Wigfield et al., 2006) contended that these structural and curricular changes produce variations in students' achievement-related beliefs and motivation, often in a negative direction. The opening classroom vignette highlights the problem of student boredom, which negatively affects motivation and learning.

School transitions can be improved. The middle school configuration is designed to help ease the transition. Although some middle schools resemble junior high schools except for a different grade organization (typically grades 6 to 8 in middle schools and grades 7 to 9 in junior high schools), many middle schools attempt to ease the transition by keeping students together for much of the day and using interdisciplinary teams of teachers (e.g., four teachers, one each for language arts, social studies, mathematics, and science). Although the teachers change, most of the peers do not. These teachers work to ensure an integrated curriculum. Greater efforts also may be made to report individual progress. Less emphasis on evaluative comparisons among peers helps to lighten young adolescents' self-concerns typical at this time. Application 11.4 gives additional suggestions for ways to ease transitions in schooling.

APPLICATION 11.4
Transitions in Schooling

Making the transition from one school level to another is difficult for many students. Ability and socioemotional levels vary widely, and students differ in their ability to cope with the numerous organizational changes that occur. The transition from elementary to middle school/junior high level can be especially troublesome.

Ms. Appleton is a sixth-grade social studies teacher at a middle school. She understands that students become accustomed to having one teacher for most content areas. She works with fifth-grade teachers to suggest activities that they might incorporate (e.g., using planners) that will help students when they are faced with changing classes and being responsible for remembering and completing assignments

for each class. She also spends time at the start of the school year helping her students set up their assignment books and organize their materials. She makes herself available during lunch and after school to give students assistance they might need about transition issues.

Ms. Vanaman, a high school science teacher, asks eighth-grade science teachers about their policies for assigning classwork and homework, giving tests, grading projects, receiving late work, allowing students to make up missed work, and so forth. She tries to incorporate some of the same approaches in her ninth-grade science classes so that these class procedures will be familiar and will reduce student concerns that could impede learning.

Classroom and School Climate

The climate that exists in classrooms and schools can have a major impact on students' learning and achievement (Bryk, Sebring, Allensworth, Luppescu, & Easton, 2010; Lee & Shute, 2010). *Climate* refers to the atmosphere, tone, or culture associated with the classroom or school environment (Wolters & Gonzalez, 2008). Climate arises from the shared understandings and interactions, common practice, and accepted routines within the classroom and school. Climate is a function of the teachers, students, curricula, and other important elements in the environment. Most of the six TARGET dimensions (covered earlier in this chapter) would be included in climate. Discussed in this section are three affective aspects of climate that are relevant to learning: sense of community, warmth and civility, and safety and security.

Sense of Community. A sense of community includes individuals' feelings that they belong to a group or organization, that they are committed to the organization's goals and values, and that there is reciprocity in the relation such that people in the organization care about and are concerned about individual group members. Lee, Bryk, and Smith (1993) stressed the importance of a community perspective on school organization that focuses on the quality of the social relations among the individuals in the organization. They noted that schools where the administrators, faculty, and students demonstrate mutual respect and concern for each other are linked to positive outcomes for teachers and students.

Noddings (1992) proposed that caring for others is an important component that should be present in all relations in a school and taught in the curriculum. The student dropout and at-risk literatures also suggest that the absence of teacher concern and care is a major factor mentioned by students who leave school (Lee & Smith, 1999; National Research Council, 2004; Natriello, 1986; Rumberger & Lim, 2008).

Self-determination theory (Ryan & Deci, 2016) stresses the idea that individuals have a basic need for belongingness or relatedness and that organizational structures that support or satisfy this need will result in more intrinsic motivation and engagement (see Chapter 9). Research studies document the contributions of students' sense of belonging and connection to learning, motivation, engagement, and academic performance (Juvonen, 2006; Master et al., 2016; Osterman, 2000; Voelkl, 1997). A sense of belonging may be particularly important for students entering new school environments or attending schools with diverse student populations (Eccles & Roeser, 2011; Garcia-Reid, Reid, & Peterson, 2005).

Warmth and Civility.   Warmth and civility are aspects of the relations among individuals in the classroom and school. Researchers have shown that civil and collegial relations between teachers and administrators are associated with positive organizational effectiveness outcomes (Lee et al., 1993). Bryk et al. (2010) refer to this school dimension as *relational trust,* and they view it as critical for experimenting with instructional practices to improve student engagement and achievement. In addition, friendly and collegial relations among teachers help ease the isolation of teaching and are associated with greater teacher satisfaction (Lee et al., 1993).

As discussed earlier, feelings of concern, care, support, and respect between teachers and students are associated with better learning, motivation, and achievement (Wentzel, 2016; Wentzel, Battle, Russel, & Looney, 2010). Lee et al. (1993) suggested that a concern for the welfare of others or the creation of a caring community can have positive effects on all students including those at risk for school failure. The literature on middle schools shows that they are more bureaucratic, less personal, and engender fewer positive teacher–student interactions than elementary schools. These differences have been linked to declines in student motivation as the students make the transition to middle schools (Eccles, Midgley, Wigfield, Reuman, Mac Iver, & Feldlaufer, 1993).

In their review of research on teaching, Brophy and Good (1986) noted that the emotional climate of the classroom (as defined by teacher criticism and teacher and student negative affect) often is associated with student achievement. Although a negative emotional climate can decrease achievement, a warm emotional climate is not necessarily associated with better achievement. Neutral climates may be just as supportive of achievement as warm climates. Overall, however, the research suggests that positive teacher–student interactions can create a desirable climate for all members of the school community.

Safety and Security.   Feelings of safety and security can refer to individuals' feelings about taking risks and feeling secure in expressing different ideas and opinions. Given the tragic school violence in recent years, this aspect of climate also refers to feelings of physical safety and being free from the fear and anxiety of physical harm.

Despite efforts to increase school safety over the last decades, a significant number of U.S. youth (20%–30%) enrolled in public schools report involvement in physical fights or bullying incident at least once during the school year (Simone, Zhang, & Truman, 2010). Concerns about physical or psychological safety at school has important consequences for students' perceptions of the school climate, as well as for school engagement, learning, and academic achievement (Crosnoe, Johnson, & Elder, 2004; Eccles & Roeser, 2011; Wentzel et al., 2010). Accordingly, it is necessary that schools offer a safe and secure environment for staff and students and have a plan for dealing with incidents involving violence.

PEERS

There is considerable research investigating the influence of peers on learning, motivation, and other achievement-related outcomes (Juvonen & Knifsend, 2016; Ladd, Herald-Brown, & Kochel, 2009; Wentzel, 2005). This section reviews theory and research on peers and student learning, the role of peer networks, and how peers may affect school adjustment and dropout.

Peers and Learning

Peer influence operates largely through *modeling*, or behavioral, cognitive, and affective changes that result from observing one or more models (Schunk, 2012; Chapter 4). Three important functions of modeling are inhibition/disinhibition, response facilitation, and observational learning.

Observers' inhibitions about engaging in certain acts can be strengthened and weakened by observing models. When models are punished for their actions, observers' inhibitions may be strengthened, and they are unlikely to perform the same actions because they believe they will be punished if they do. When models go unpunished or are rewarded, observers' inhibitions may be weakened, and they may perform the same actions. In these cases, models convey information about consequences and the modeled effects are motivational.

Response facilitation occurs when modeled actions serve as social prompts for observers to behave accordingly. As with inhibition and disinhibition, response facilitation actions have been learned; models convey information, and their effects on observers are motivational. Response facilitation can be seen in forms of dress. Students who aspire to be valued by a certain peer group may wear the same type of clothes as those worn by members of that group.

Whereas response facilitation behaviors typically are neutral, inhibited/disinhibited actions are rule governed or have moral or legal overtones. A student walking down a hall who sees a group of students looking into a classroom might stop and also look into the classroom. This is a response facilitation effect; the behavior is neutral. Conversely, inhibition occurs when a teacher disciplines one misbehaving student and misbehavior among others stops. Misbehavior is not neutral; it is prohibited. Another difference is that inhibition and disinhibition are more likely to involve emotions (e.g., anxiety, exhilaration), whereas response facilitation rarely does.

Observational learning through modeling occurs when observers display new behaviors that, prior to modeling, had no likelihood of occurring, even with motivational inducements in effect (Schunk, 2012). Observational learning expands the range and rate of learning over what could occur if each response had to be performed and reinforced.

Observational learning comprises attention, retention, production, and motivation. Observers who are motivated to learn modeled actions are likely to attend to models, attempt to retain the modeled actions, perform them when necessary, and be motivated to do so.

These three forms of modeling are easily discerned among students and highlight peer effects on students' learning and achievement. Altermatt and Pomerantz (2003) found high consistency among best friends' report card grades. When a child's friends value school and engage in scholastic activities, these models can have a positive effect on academic learning and motivation. The opposite may occur when peers express negative attitudes and withdraw from school (Ladd et al., 2009).

Model similarity affects observers' self-efficacy. Observing similar others (e.g., peers) succeed can raise observers' self-efficacy and motivate them to perform the task; they believe that if others can succeed, they can as well. Observing others fail can lead students to believe that they lack the competence to succeed and dissuade them from attempting the task. Similarity is most influential when students are uncertain about their performance capabilities, when they lack task familiarity, have little information to use in judging self-efficacy, or when they previously experienced difficulties and hold self-doubts (Schunk, 2012).

Students who have positive peer relations perform better in school, and these associations are found across the school years (Juvonen, Espinoza, & Knifsend, 2012; Wentzel, 2005). Jones, Audley-Piotrowski, and Kiefer (2012) found that tenth-grade students' mathematics self-concepts aligned well with their perceptions of their friends' academic behaviors. Mathematics self-concepts, in turn, related positively to mathematics performance. Teachers also attribute positive academic characteristics (e.g., high achievement, confidence) to children who are popular with peers (Wentzel, 2005). By contrast, less popular or socially rejected children are at risk for lower academic achievement.

To explain the potential influence of peer relations on learning, Wentzel (2005) postulated that social competence involves displaying such behaviors as helping, sharing, cooperating, and avoiding problem behaviors. These behaviors involve self-regulatory processes (e.g., goal setting, self-monitoring; see Chapter 10) that contribute to learners' academic and intellectual development.

Research studies indicate that school engagement increases when students feel a sense of belonging (Juvonen, 2006; Osterman, 2000), which also acts as a protective factor against nonacademic risk behaviors such as depression and pregnancy (Anderman, 2002). Given this research evidence, measures of classroom social climate often include items to assess feelings of support, care, and encouragement from peers. Students' perceptions of peer emotional and academic support are positively related to several achievement-related behaviors, including mastery goals, selection of self-regulation strategies, and classroom engagement and learning (Patrick, Ryan, and Kaplan, 2007). Supportive peer relations may provide a secure base for learners to engage in academic learning and take risks without fear of ridicule.

Peer Networks

Researchers have examined the role of *peer networks*, or large groups of peers with whom students associate. Students in peer networks tend to be similar to one another in many ways (Cairns, Cairns, & Neckerman, 1989), which enhances the likelihood of influence by modeling. Networks help define students' opportunities for social interactions and access to activities (Ryan, 2000). Over time, network members become more similar to one another.

Kindermann (1993; Kindermann, McCollam, and Gibson, 1996; Sage & Kindermann, 1999) examined motivation in peer selection and socialization among children (grades 4–5) and adolescents (grades 9–12). Adolescent peer networks were more complex than children's. Among children, most peer networks were dyads; average network size was 2.2 students. Large networks were uncommon. Among adolescents, there were many dyads and triads, as well as larger networks (average size was 3.2 students). Among both children and adolescents, some students were not connected with a network.

Kindermann's research also identified gender differences. Among children, groups were composed exclusively of members of the same sex. Among adolescents, there were some groups that included boys and girls. A significant decline in motivation was reported by students, although teachers reported comparable levels of student motivation across grades. Older students expressed lower motivation than did younger ones.

Comparisons of individual academic motivation scores with peer group motivation scores showed that among ninth graders, students who were more academically motivated had larger peer networks. Adolescents who were less motivated had fewer classmates in their peer networks. Across the school year and grade levels, students' motivation scores remained consistent.

There was evidence of motivational selection and socialization through peer groups. Changes in children's motivational engagement across the school year were predicted by their peer group membership at the start of the year. There also were effects due to peer networks containing students from different grades. Students in highly motivated peer groups that contained members from across grades tended to increase in motivation across the school year. Students in low-motivation peer networks that had little grade diversity tended to decrease in motivation across time.

Sage and Kindermann (1999) found that peer groups approved or disapproved of peers' behaviors depending on whether the behaviors were consistent with group norms. Students with higher academic motivation were likely to be members of groups more motivated for academics, and they received group approval for positive academic behaviors. Students with lower motivation tended to be members of less motivated groups; their approval for positive behaviors mostly came from teachers. Children affiliated with highly motivated groups changed positively across the school year; children in less motivated groups changed negatively. Among adolescents, the evidence for change was strongest in peer groups that included peers from different grades.

Kindermann (2007) found that sixth-graders' peer networks were homogeneous in their academic (behavioral and emotional) engagement and that such homogeneity persisted during the school year even where there was member turnover. Students who initially shared networks with engaged peers maintained or increased their engagement; those in less engaged networks showed less engagement.

Other studies have obtained similar findings (Ryan, 2000). Ryan (2001) found that students typically end up in peer networks with similar motivational beliefs to theirs at the beginning of a school year. During the year, the peer group influenced the members of the group so that group members became more homogeneous. The peer group socialization influence depended on the nature of the outcome. Students' intrinsic interest in school and their academic performances (grades) were influenced by the peer group. The utility value that students had for school (how useful they thought school work was) was not related to peer influence but rather was more a function of selection into certain peer groups from the beginning of the year.

These findings are supported by longitudinal research by Steinberg, Brown, and Dornbusch (1996), who followed students over 3 years from when they entered high school until their senior year. Steinberg et al. determined whether students who began high school equivalent academically (grades) but who became affiliated with different crowds (i.e., like-minded students who have some common attributes but are not friends with everyone else) remained stable academically. Crowds influenced academic performance and delinquency. Students in higher academically oriented crowds achieved better grades during high school compared with those in lower academically oriented crowds. Students in crowds in which delinquency occurred more often became increasingly delinquent (i.e., experienced more conduct problems and drug and alcohol use). Students in less delinquent crowds did not develop the same problems.

Steinberg et al. also found developmental patterns in the influence of peer pressure on many activities, including academic motivation and performance. Peer pressure rose during childhood and peaked around the eighth or ninth grade but then declined through high school. A key time of influence was roughly from ages 12 through 16. Interestingly, it is around this time that parental involvement in children's activities declines. As parents' role declines and peers' role ascends among adolescents in grades 6 through 10, they become especially vulnerable to peer pressure.

Steinberg et al. noted that parents typically set their children onto trajectories by establishing goals for them and involving them in groups and activities. Thus, parents who want their child to be academically oriented are likely to involve their child in activities that stress academics. If the peer crowd in those settings also is academically focused, the peer influence complements that of the parents. But if there are other types of crowds in those settings, the child may come under the influence of a less academically oriented crowd, with negative consequences for academic learning.

Peers and School Adjustment

School adjustment often is defined in terms of students' academic progress or achievement (Birch & Ladd, 1996). On a broader level, adjustment can be viewed as comprising not only students' progress and achievement but also their attitudes toward and identification with school, anxieties, loneliness, social support, and academic motivation (e.g., engagement, avoidance, absences; Birch & Ladd, 1996; Roeser, Eccles, & Strobel, 1998; Voelkl, 2012).

Involvement refers to the quality of a student's relationships with peers and teachers. Ryan and Powelson (1991) contended that school learning can be promoted by learning environments that enhance student involvement with others. Research shows that children's loneliness and social dissatisfaction relate negatively to school achievement (Galanski & Kalantzi-Azizi, 1999).

Berndt and Keefe (1992) found that peer pressure can affect adjustment and that peer pressure operated more often in a positive rather than a negative manner. Friends often discourage negative behavior, drug and alcohol use, and poor academic performance, and encourage prosocial behavior, good studying behaviors, and academic motivation (Berndt & Keefe, 1996; Juvonen et al., 2012). Friendships can affect students' success in the transition from elementary to junior high school. Berndt, Hawkins, and Jiao (1999) found that students with high-quality friendships across the transition demonstrated increased leadership and sociability. But students' behavior problems increased across the transition if they had stable friendships with peers high in behavior problems.

Researchers have shown that children and adolescents whose friendships have a positive quality display greater prosocial behavior, are more popular, hold higher self-esteem, have fewer emotional problems, have better attitudes toward school, and achieve at a higher level in school, compared with other students (Berndt & Keefe, 1996). Wentzel, Barry, and Caldwell (2004) found that friends' prosocial behaviors predicted changes in peers' prosocial behaviors as a function of changes in goals to behave prosocially. Friendships with negative qualities lead to less student classroom involvement and more disruptive behavior. Interestingly, number of friends is weakly correlated with school adjustment, which implies that relationship quality is more influential than quantity.

Poor school adjustment also can lead to dropout, which is a major problem confronting schools and society (Rumberger, 2010). Many researchers have investigated the influence of such variables as early academic achievement, socioeconomic status, and family influences, but peers also play a role. Feelings of relatedness contribute to motivation and learning, and students' relations with peers are part of this influence (Juvonen et al., 2012).

Hymel, Comfort, Schonert-Reichl, and McDougall (1996) suggested that students' involvement and participation in school depend partly on how much the school environment contributes to their perceptions of autonomy and relatedness (Chapter 9), which in turn influence perceptions of competence (self-efficacy; Chapter 4) and academic achievement. Hymel et al. (1996) identified four critical aspects of peer influence. One is prior social acceptance within a peer group. Students rejected by peers are at a greater risk for adjustment problems than those who are socially accepted. Research studies also show that students who are not socially accepted by peers are more likely to drop out of school than those with greater social acceptance (Hymel et al., 1996; Jimerson, Egeland, Sroufe, & Carlson, 2000).

A second factor is social isolation. Not all socially rejected youth drop out of school. What seems more important is students' perception of rejection or isolation within the peer group. Students who are socially rejected but do not perceive themselves that way are at lower risk for dropping out.

A third factor is the negative influence of peers. The peer crowd can affect students' motivation and learning (Juvonen et al., 2012; Newman, 2000). Students who quit school are more likely than others to be part of a crowd that is at risk for dropping out (Cairns et al., 1989). The crowd may collectively disengage from school. Even when students are not socially isolated, they are affected by negative peer influence.

Finally, aggression and antisocial behavior contribute to dropping out. Compared with students who graduate, those who drop out are rated by teachers and peers as displaying more aggressive behaviors (Farmer et al., 2003; Hymel et al., 1996). Strong associations between poor peer relations and later high school dropout are found as early as elementary school (Jimerson et al., 2000). Research that explores the link between adjustment and learning will contribute to our understanding of this relation and potentially offer guidelines for educators to improve students' adjustment and diminished chances for dropping out.

FAMILIES

Of the many contextual factors that can influence learning, several are found in the family environment (Raftery, Grolnick, & Flamm, 2012). Although we should expect that families have profound influences on children's development and learning, some contend that the family's role has been overstated (Harris, 1998). Researchers are increasingly showing, however, that families make a difference and often a great one (Collins, Maccoby, Steinberg, Hetherington, & Bornstein, 2000; Masten & Coatsworth, 1998; Raftery et al., 2012). Some of the key family influences on learning are socioeconomic status, home environment, parental involvement, and electronic media.

Socioeconomic Status

Definition. *Socioeconomic status (SES)* has been defined in various ways, with definitions typically comprising social status (position, rank) and economic indicators (wealth, education). Many researchers consider three prime indicators in determining SES: parental income, education, and occupation (Sirin, 2005). Increasingly, investigators are stressing the idea of *capital* (resources, assets; Bradley & Corwyn, 2002). Capital includes such indices as financial or material resources (e.g., income and assets), human or nonmaterial resources (e.g., education), and social resources (e.g., those obtained through social networks and connections; Putnam, 2000). Each of these would seem to potentially affect children's learning.

However SES is defined, it is important to remember that it is a descriptive variable, not an explanatory one (Schunk et al., 2014). To say that students have learning difficulties because they are from needy families does not explain why they have learning difficulties. Rather, the conditions that often are found in needy families may be responsible for the learning difficulties. Conversely, not all children from needy families have learning difficulties. There are countless stories of successful adults who were raised in impoverished conditions. It is more meaningful to speak of a relation between SES and learning and then look for the responsible conditions.

SES and Learning.   Much correlational research evidence shows that poverty and low parental education relate to poorer development and learning (Bradley & Corwyn, 2002). What is less clear is which aspects of SES are responsible for this relation.

Family resources seem critical. Families with less education, money, and social connections cannot provide many resources that can promote students' cognitive development and learning. For example, students from wealthier families have greater access to computers, books, games, travel, and cultural experiences, compared with students from needy families. These and other resources can stimulate cognitive development and learning.

Another important factor is socialization. Schools and classrooms typically have a middle-class orientation with accepted rules and procedures that children must follow to succeed (e.g., pay attention, do your work, study, work cooperatively with others). Socialization influences in lower-SES homes may not prepare students adequately for these conditions (Schunk et al., 2014). As a consequence, lower-SES children may have more discipline and behavior problems in school and not learn as well.

SES also relates to school attendance and years of schooling (Bradley & Corwyn, 2002). SES is related positively to school achievement (Sirin, 2005) and is, unfortunately, one of the best predictors of school dropout. Lower SES children may not understand the benefits of schooling (Meece, 2002); they may not realize that more education leads to better jobs, more income, and a better lifestyle than they have experienced. They may be drawn by immediate short-term benefits of leaving school (e.g., money from working full-time) and not be swayed by potential long-term assets. In their home environments, they may not have positive role models displaying the benefits of schooling or parental encouragement to stay in school.

The relation of SES to cognitive development seems complex, with some factors contributing directly and others serving a moderating influence (Bradley & Corwyn, 2002). Its predictive value also may vary by group. For example, SES is a stronger predictor of academic achievement for White students than for minority students (Sirin, 2005). SES has been implicated as a factor contributing to the achievement gap between White and minority children. Gaps exist when children enter kindergarten. The White–Hispanic American gap narrows in kindergarten and first grade (perhaps because of Hispanic American children's increasing English language proficiency) and then stays steady through fifth grade; however, the White–African American gap continues to widen through fifth grade (Reardon & Galindo, 2009).

While the effects of material, human, and social capital seem clear, the influence of other factors may be indirect. For example, large families are not inherently beneficial or harmful to cognitive development and learning. But in deprived conditions, they may be harmful as already scarce resources are spread among more children.

The literature suggests that early educational interventions for children from low-SES families are critical to ensuring their preparation for schooling. A review of the literature revealed that effective educational interventions for low-SES students were tutoring, feedback and learning progress monitoring, and cooperative learning (Dietrichson, Bøg, Filges, & Jørgensen, 2017).

One of the best-known early intervention efforts is Project Head Start, a federally funded program for preschool children (3- to 5-year-olds) from low income families across the United States. Head Start programs provide preschool children with intensive educational experiences, as well as social, medical, and nutritional services. Most programs also include a parent education and involvement component (Washington & Bailey, 1995).

Early evaluations of Head Start indicated that programs were able to produce short-term gains in intelligence test scores. Compared to comparable groups of children who had not attended Head Start, they also performed better on cognitive measures in kindergarten and first grade (Lazar, Darlington, Murray, Royce, & Snipper, 1982). Although Head Start children lost this advantage by ages 10 and 17, other measures of program effectiveness indicated that participants were less likely to be retained, to receive special education, and to drop out of high school than nonparticipants (Lazar et al., 1982).

Other research shows that gains in children's motivation and attentional persistence can endure after the transition from Head Start to kindergarten (McDermott, Rikoon, & Fantuzzo, 2014) and that Head Start children can benefit from exposure to advanced content prior to kindergarten entry (Claessens, Engel, & Curran, 2014). Providing Head Start teachers with training and professional development on practices to enhance children's literacy and socioemotional skills can lead to gains in children's social problem-solving skills (Bierman et al., 2008).

Home and family factors can affect outcomes for Head Start participants. Robinson, Lanzi, Weinberg, Ramey, and Ramey (2002) identified at the end of third grade the top-achieving 3% of 5,400 children in the National Head Start/Public School Early Childhood Transition Demonstration Project. Compared with the remaining children, these children came from families that had more resources (capital). These families also endorsed more positive parenting attitudes, more strongly supported and encouraged their children's academic progress, and volunteered more often in their children's schools. Teachers reported these children as more motivated to succeed academically. Although there were not strong differences in children's ratings of motivational variables, fewer children in the top 3% group rated school negatively compared with the remaining children. Thus, among low income groups as well as the general population, greater parental support and better home resources are associated with achievement and motivational benefits for children.

Encouraged by the success of Head Start, states operate prekindergarten programs for 3- and 4-year-olds under the auspices of public schools to reduce the number of children failing in the early grades (Clifford, Early, & Hill, 1999). Most programs are half day and vary with regard to teacher–student ratios, socioeconomic and ethnic diversity, quality, and curricula. Early evaluations of these programs are promising. Children enrolled in prekindergarten programs tend to improve on standardized measures of language and mathematics skills (FPG Child Development Institute, 2005). The long-term benefits of these programs are not yet known.

One highly effective preschool program for low income children was the High/Scope Perry Preschool Project. Initiated in 1962, this program predated Head Start. In this two-year program, 3- and 4-year-old children received a half-day cognitively oriented program based on Piaget's principles (Oden, Schweinhart, & Weikart, 2000; Chapter 8). Teachers also made weekly 90-minute home visits to each mother and child to review classroom activities and to discuss similar activities in the home. Longitudinal data collected over 25 years revealed that the High/Scope program improved children's school achievement, reduced their years in special education, reduced the likelihood of grade retention, and increased the years of school completed (Oden et al., 2000; Schweinhart & Weikart, 1997).

Unfortunately, the effects of such early interventions do not always persist over time as children progress in school, but there are promising results. Campbell, Pungello, Miller-Johnson, Burchinal, and Ramey (2001) evaluated the Abecedarian Project, a full-time educational child care project for children from low income families. These researchers found that the benefits of the intervention persisted through the last evaluation when many of the children had attained age 21. Given the longitudinal nature of this project (it began when the participants were infants), it is difficult to determine when and how it prepared them to be successful in educational environments. SES is an active area of research, and we are sure to learn more about the roles of SES variables in learning.

Home Environment

There is much variability in the richness of home environments, and usually (but not always) this richness matches SES. Some homes provide experiences replete with economic capital (computers, games, and books), human capital (parents help children with homework, projects, and studying), and social capital (through social contacts, parents get children involved in activities and teams). Other homes lack in one or more of these respects.

The effects of the home environment on cognitive development seem most pronounced in infancy and early childhood (Meece, 2002). Children's social networks expand as they grow older, especially as a consequence of schooling and participation in activities. Peer influence becomes increasingly important with development.

The quality of children's early home learning relates positively to the development of intelligence (Schunk et al., 2014). Important home factors include mother's responsiveness, discipline style, and child involvement; organization present in the home; availability of stimulating materials; and opportunities for interaction. Parents who provide a warm and responsive home environment tend to encourage children's explorations and stimulate their curiosity and play, which accelerate intellectual development (Meece, 2002).

As discussed earlier, the increasing role of peer influence was found in longitudinal research by Steinberg et al. (1996). Over a 10-year period, these researchers surveyed more than 20,000 adolescents from high schools in different states and interviewed many teachers and parents. Although parents do not have full control over the crowds with which their children associate, they can exert indirect influence by steering children in appropriate directions. Parents who urge their children to participate in activities in which the children of other like-minded parents participate steer them toward appropriate peer influence regardless of whom they select as friends. Parents who offer their home as a place where friends are welcome further guide their children in positive directions.

Parental Involvement

Harris (1998) downplayed the influence of parents on children past infancy and concluded that peers exert a much greater effect; however, there is substantial evidence that parental influence continues to be strong well past infancy (Rowe, Ramani, & Pomerantz, 2016; Vandell, 2000). This section considers the role of parental involvement in children's cognitive development and learning.

Parental involvement occurs in and away from the home, such as in school and activities. Research studies show that parental involvement in schools has a positive impact on children, teachers, and the school itself (Englund, Luckner, Whaley, & Egeland, 2004; Gonzalez-DeHass, Willems, & Doan Holbein, 2005; Hill & Craft, 2003; Sénéchal & LeFevre, 2002). These effects may vary by group; parent involvement effects seem stronger among White students than among minority students (Lee & Bowen, 2006).

One effect of parent involvement, as noted previously, is that parents can be influential in launching their children onto particular trajectories by involving them in groups and activities (Steinberg et al., 1996). For example, parents who want their children to be academically focused are likely to involve them in activities that stress academics.

Fan and Chen (2001) conducted a meta-analysis of research on the relation of parental involvement to children's academic attainments. The results showed that parents' expectations for their children's academic successes bore a positive relation to their actual cognitive achievements. The relation was strongest when academic attainment was assessed globally (e.g., grade point average) than by subject-specific indicators (e.g., grade in a particular class). There also is evidence that parental involvement effects on children's achievement are greatest when there is a high level of parental involvement in the neighborhood (Collins et al., 2000).

Parental involvement is a critical factor influencing children's self-regulation, which is central to the development of cognitive functioning. Research by Stright, Neitzel, Sears, and Hoke-Sinex (2001) found that the type of instruction parents provide and how they provide it relate to children's self-regulated learning in school. Children of parents who provided understandable metacognitive information displayed greater classroom monitoring, participation, and metacognitive talk. Children's seeking and attending to classroom instruction also were related to whether parents' instruction was given in an understandable manner. These authors suggested that parental instruction helps to create the proper conditions for their children to develop self-regulatory competence. Some suggestions for parents working with their children are given in Application 11.5.

APPLICATION 11.5
Parental Involvement

McGowan Elementary School holds an open house for parents early in the school year. When meeting with parents, McGowan teachers explain the many ways that parents can become involved. Teachers ask for volunteers for three groups: school learning, out-of-school learning, and planning. School-learning parents volunteer a half-day per week to work in class, assisting with small-group and individual work.

Out-of-school-learning parents accompany the class on field trips and organize and work with children on community projects (e.g., a walk through the neighborhood to identify types of trees). Planning-group parents periodically meet as a group with teachers who explain upcoming units and ask parents to help design activities. McGowan's goal is 100% involvement of at least one parent or guardian per child.

(Continued)

APPLICATION 11.5 (*continued*)

Parents can be a valuable resource in history classes because they have lived through some of the events students study. Mr. Sakizch contacts parents at the start of the year and provides them with a list of events in the past several years that students will study in class (e.g., Vietnam War, fall of the Berlin Wall, World Trade Center terrorist attack). He seeks the assistance of every family on at least one event, such as by the parent coming to class to discuss it (i.e., what they remember about it, why it was important, how it affected their lives). When several parents volunteer for the same event, he forms them into a panel to discuss the event. If there are living grandparents in the area, Mr. Sakizch asks them to share their experiences about such events as World War II and the Eisenhower presidency. His students set up a website containing information about key events and excerpts from parents and grandparents about these events.

Positive effects of parental involvement have been obtained in research with ethnic minority children and those from impoverished environments (Hill & Craft, 2003; Masten & Coatsworth, 1998; Masten et al., 1999). Some forms of parents' involvement that make a difference are contacting the school about their children, attending school functions, communicating strong educational values to their children, conveying the value of effort, expecting children to perform well in school, and monitoring or helping children with homework and projects. Researchers have shown that the more children perceive their parents as involved in schooling, the stronger they believe that their parents value education (Cheung & Pomerantz, 2015). The latter student perceptions, in turn, predict students' subsequent value of achievement. Miliotis, Sesma, and Masten (1999) found that after families left homeless shelters, high parent involvement in children's education was one of the best predictors of children's school success.

Researchers have investigated the role of parenting styles on children's development. Baumrind (1989) distinguished three styles: authoritative, authoritarian, permissive. Authoritative parents provide children with warmth and support. They have high demands (e.g., expectations for achievement) but support these through good communication, explanations, and encouragement of independence. Authoritarian parents are strict and assert power. They are neither warm nor responsive. Permissive parents are moderately responsive but are lax in demands (e.g., expectations) and tolerant of misbehavior. Not surprisingly, many research studies have found a positive relation between authoritative parenting and student achievement (Spera, 2005).

One of the strongest advocates of community and parental involvement in education has been James Comer. Comer and his colleagues began the *School Development Program* in two schools, and it has spread to more than 500. The SDP (or Comer Program) is based on the principles shown in Table 11.4 (Comer, 2001; Comer & Haynes, 1999; Emmons, Comer, & Haynes, 1996). Students need positive interactions with adults because these help to form their behaviors. Planning for student development should be a collaborative effort between professionals and community members.

Table 11.4
Principles of the School Development Program.

- Students' behaviors are determined by their interactions with the physical, social, and psychological environments.

- Students need positive interactions with adults to develop adequately.

- Student-centered planning and collaboration among adults facilitate positive interactions.

- Planning for student development should be done collaboratively by professional and community members.

Three guiding principles of SDP are consensus, collaboration, and no-fault. Decisions are arrived at by consensus to discourage taking sides for critical votes. Collaboration means working as part of a team. No-fault implies that everyone is responsible for change.

School staff and community members are grouped into teams. The School Planning and Management Team includes the building principal, teachers, parents, and support staff. This team plans and coordinates activities. The Parent Team involves parents in all school activities. The Student and Staff Support Team is responsible for schoolwide prevention issues and individual student cases.

At the core of the SDP is a comprehensive school plan with such components as curriculum, instruction, assessment, social and academic climate, and information sharing. This plan provides structured activities addressing academics, social climate, staff development, and public relations. The School Planning and Management Team establishes priorities and coordinates school improvement.

Comer and his colleagues report impressive effects on student achievement due to implementation of the SDP (Haynes, Emmons, Gebreyesus, & Ben-Avie, 1996). Comer schools typically show gains in student achievement and often outperform school district averages in reading, mathematical, and language skills. Cook, Murphy, and Hunt (2000) evaluated the Comer SDP in 10 inner-city Chicago schools over four years. Using students in grades 5 through 8, these authors found that by the last years, Comer program students showed greater gains in reading and mathematics compared with control students. Cook et al. (1999) found that Comer schools do not always implement all of the program's elements, which can limit gains. Regardless of whether schools adopt the Comer program, it contains many points that should facilitate students' cognitive development and learning.

Electronic Media

The advent of electronic media began in the middle of the twentieth century when televisions became common household items. In recent years, the potential influence of electronic media has expanded with increased television programming, audio and video players, radios, video game players, computers (e.g., applications, Internet), and handheld devices (e.g., phones, iPods). It is not unusual for children to spend 25% or more of their daily time engaged with some form of electronic media. Often they multitask and use more than one media source at once (Roberts & Foehr, 2008).

Researchers have investigated the potential ways that exposure to electronic media relates to children's cognitive development, learning, and achievement. Most research has investigated the link between children's television viewing and measures of cognitive development and achievement and found no relationship or a negative relationship between the time children spend watching television and their school achievement (Schmidt & Vandewater, 2008). When negative associations are found, they typically are weak. But these results are misleading because the relation may not be linear. Compared with no television viewing, moderate viewing (1–10 hours) per week is positively associated with achievement, whereas heavier viewing is negatively associated.

The relation between television viewing and achievement also is difficult to interpret because the data are correlational and therefore causality cannot be determined. Several causal explanations are possible. It is possible that heavy television viewing lowers achievement because it takes children away from studying and completing assignments. It also is possible that children with academic problems are less motivated to learn academic content and thus are drawn more strongly to television. The link between television viewing and achievement may be mediated by a third variable, such as SES. In support of this possibility, children from lower-class homes tend to watch more television and demonstrate lower achievement (Kirkorian, Wartella, & Anderson, 2008).

Young children's learning from television also may depend on the extent that they interact with the televised characters and believe that these characters exist outside of television. The latter belief is associated with children believing the characters are socially relevant and thus are reliable sources of information (Richert, Robb, & Smith, 2011).

Examining the relation between time spent watching television and academic achievement does not consider the content of what children watch. Television programming varies; some programs are educational, whereas others are entertaining or violent. A general finding from research is that watching educational programming is positively related to achievement, whereas watching entertainment is negatively linked (Kirkorian et al., 2008). This varies as a function of amount of television watched, because moderate viewers are more apt to watch educational programming whereas heavier viewers watch extensive entertainment. Correlational research has demonstrated a positive relation between exposure to *Sesame Street* and school readiness (Kirkorian et al., 2008). Ennemoser and Schneider (2007) found a negative association between the amount of entertainment television watched by children at age 6 and reading achievement at age 9, after controlling for intelligence, SES, and prior reading ability. Watching educational television was positively associated with reading achievement. Other research has shown that educational television can help prepare at-risk children in low-SES families to read (Linebarger & Piotrowski, 2010), especially when the televised content is integrated with learning strategies that help children process the content (e.g., showing a word that breaks into individual sounds then reassembles into the word).

The findings on the link between interactive media (e.g., digital games, Internet) and school achievement are mixed. Some research has obtained a positive relation between computer use and achievement and a negative association between game use and achievement (Kirkorian et al., 2008). Nietfeld (2018) reviewed the literature and found that current research shows a positive association between digital game use and student achievement, motivation, and self-regulated learning. In this analysis, self-regulated learning is both an influence on game use and a positive outcome of it. It is possible that the same result obtained with television also may hold for other media; that is, education-related content may link positively with achievement and entertaining content negatively.

With respect to measures of cognitive development, research has identified a *video deficit* among infants and toddlers such that they learn better from real-life experiences than from video. This deficit disappears by around age 3, after which children can learn just as well from video experiences (Kirkorian et al., 2008). It may be that young children are less attentive to dialogue and do not fully integrate content portrayed across different scenes, which may change rapidly. This does not imply that viewing is negatively associated with the development of attention. Again, the critical variable may be the content of the programming. Educational programs have been shown to actually help children develop attention skills, in contrast to entertaining programs (Kirkorian et al., 2008).

Some research has investigated links between electronic media and the development of spatial skills. Most of this research has involved games. There is some evidence that games can have short-term benefits on spatial reasoning and problem-solving skills (Schmidt & Vandewater, 2008). However, long-term benefits depend on whether students generalize those skills to learning contexts outside of game play. To date, evidence is mixed whether such transfer occurs (Nietfeld, 2018; Schmidt & Vandewater, 2008). Hofferth (2010) reported that game use was associated with increased aggression among boys.

Parents and other adults can have important influences on children's learning and cognitive development from electronic media. Adults can control what media children interact with and how much time they do so. This control can help ensure that children do not spend an excessive amount of time engaged with media but rather only a moderate amount (1–10 hours per week; Schmidt & Vandewater, 2008). Further, parent coviewing seems to be a critical variable. Adults who interact with media while their children are engaged (e.g., watch television programs together) can enhance benefits from electronic media by pointing out important aspects of the program and linking those with what children previously have learned. Some research studies have found benefits from coviewing on children's learning and development of attention (Kirkorian et al., 2008).

In summary, it is clear that use of electronic media is associated with children's learning, achievement, and cognitive development. Determining causal links is difficult because data are correlational and there are potential mediating variables. Content is of utmost importance. Moderate exposure to televised educational content is associated with benefits for children, entertaining content is not, and the same results may hold for other forms of media (Kirkorian et al., 2008). Coviewing adults can further enhance the educational links. While games may have some benefits for spatial and problem-solving skills, evidence does not show transfer to academic learning settings. Although electronic media can be a valuable means of learning, they will be effective to the extent that they are designed with sound instructional principles in mind, just like any other teaching method. Some applications of instructional uses of electronic media are given in Application 11.6.

APPLICATION 11.6
Electronic Media

At the parent meeting at the start of the school year, fourth-grade teacher Mr. Simonian discusses how parents can help their children. He explains research findings showing that children who watch television for a moderate amount of time per week (up to 10 hours) and whose television viewing is primarily educational content actually can benefit from it. Engaging with other educational media (e.g., computers) is similarly beneficial. He advises parents to monitor children's use of electronic media. He also demonstrates how parents might interact with children while they view television programs together. Mr. Simonian presents film clips from children's shows and then demonstrates to parents the types of questions to ask children. At individual parent meetings later in the school year, he asks parents how they are engaging with their children with media.

Middle school science teacher Ms. Wolusky gives students assignments to watch science programs on television (e.g., PBS). For each program, students are to write a short essay that answers questions that she gives them in advance. By giving these assignments, she feels that she can help to focus their attention on those aspects of the programs that are most germane to the content of his course and thereby promote students' learning.

COMMUNITIES

Contextual influences on students' learning also arise from communities. Although the influence of communities is typically acknowledged, there is not a lot of systematic research examining its effects. Fortunately, this topic is drawing increased research attention. This section discusses contextual influences from school location and involvement.

Location

Students' experiences with schools are influenced by the schools' physical (geographic) locations. Most students in the United States attend urban or suburban schools (Provasnik et al., 2007). When these two types of school communities are compared, urban students generally trail their suburban peers in standardized achievement, school attendance, high school completion, and college attendance.

Urban schools present many challenges for learning (Bryk et al., 2010). They tend to be large and often serve a high percentage of ethnic minority, non-native-English language speaking, and low income students. Urban students also may face challenges regarding school safety, access to highly qualified teachers, and teacher absenteeism and turnover (National Research Council, 2004). These and other factors can make students at risk for poor school performance, school disengagement, and educational attainment. For these reasons, educational reform efforts have focused largely on urban schools (Balfanz, Herzog, & Mac Iver, 2007; Bryk et al., 2010; Letgers, Balfanz, Jordon, & McPartland, 2002; National Research Council, 2004).

But rural communities also face challenges in meeting the academic learning needs of their students, although rural schools have received less attention in the national conversation on school reform. One third of public schools in the U.S. are located in rural areas (Provasnik et al., 2007). Poverty rates actually are higher for students in rural than in non-rural areas, and poverty tends to be intergenerational, long-term, and concentrated in ethnic minority populations in remote geographical areas. Like their urban peers, rural students encounter economic hardship, but they also experience difficulties related to geographical location, limited community resources, low parental education, and teacher recruitment and retention. Rural students in impoverished communities have high dropout rates (Provasnik et al., 2007).

Researchers investigating the role of school location on student learning are facilitating the discussion on how community resources, values, and norms may affect students' schooling experiences related to important learning and motivation variables such as engagement, belonging, self-efficacy, and school valuing. The availability of large national data sets should stimulate further research and understanding of ways to offset potential negative effects of school location on students' educational outcomes.

Community Involvement

Community involvement in education is not new. Schools attempt to involve their communities in many ways. The social institutions within a community (e.g., families, schools, churches, workplaces) are considered forms of *community social capital* (Israel & Beaulieu, 2004), which may help alleviate family and school resource constraints. For example, research indicates that participation in school-based extracurricular activities positively influences students' educational aspirations, especially for those who struggle to maintain a connection to their school (Finn, 1989).

There are various forms of community involvement. The most common form is parent volunteers who work in schools, are active in parent organizations, assist with after-school activities, and help organize events. Community members may be invited to talk with children and visit classrooms.

Research suggests that to improve student motivation, learning, and achievement, community involvement must go beyond assisting schools with tutoring and field trips. It is important for community members to serve on school boards, share in school governance, and support school improvement initiatives. Community involvement in school governance is a critical component of the School Development Program (Comer, 2001). Shared community–school governance contributed to important achievement gains in efforts to improve Chicago's elementary schools (Bryk et al., 2010).

Another form of involvement is taking students into the community, such as when students go on field trips. Field trips are most beneficial for learning when there are clear learning goals and when teachers help prepare students in advance of the trips (e.g., by providing information and engaging students in hands-on activities), which reduces novelty on the trips and helps students focus on the learning objectives (Pugh & Bergin, 2005). Apprentice programs with community businesses often are established, where students spend part of the day receiving training in business procedures. Various community agencies provide programs for children and youth when they are not in school; for example, Boy or Girl Scouts of America, YMCA/YWCA, and 4-H clubs. Over the last several years, community-sponsored organizations have expanded to include little league teams, soccer teams, church youth groups, and so on. Youth programs can be found in libraries, museums, and community centers.

Many schools provide before- and after-school programs with an explicit academic focus. With federal funding for 21st Century Community Learning Centers, these initiatives help create partnerships between schools and nonprofit community agencies to provide safe, drug-free, supervised environments for students during nonschool hours. Many of these programs include tutoring and educational enhancements, as well as opportunities for enrichment and recreation (Mahoney, Parente, & Zigler, 2010).

Whether students benefit from these out-of-school activities depends on the quality of program and its content (National Research Council and Institute of Medicine, 2002). Community-based programs are linked to positive student development outcomes, academic learning and achievement, attitudes toward schools, and classroom behaviors, when the following features are present: safety, structure, skill-building opportunities, supportive relations, positive social norms, opportunities to belong, and integration of family, school, and community initiatives (National Research Council and Institute of Medicine, 2002). Out-of-school activities should be most beneficial when they are linked with academic material and promote students' identification with the school (Valentine, Cooper, Bettencourt, & DuBois, 2002). Such activities are apt to improve students' motivational beliefs (e.g., self-efficacy), which can raise learning (Schunk & DiBenedetto, 2016). The benefits of participating in high-quality community- or school-based programs are particularly strong for low income children (Mahoney et al., 2005).

CULTURES

As societies become increasingly diverse, schools become less homogeneous. Contextual influences stemming from students' cultural backgrounds can affect learning and other educational outcomes.

Culture refers to the shared norms, traditions, behaviors, languages, and perceptions of a group (King, 2002). Cultural differences are found not only between communities but also within them. Cultural differences can arise from many factors discussed in this text including ethnicity, SES, home environments, and group identities and experiences. Students also can be affected by different cultures when they identify with overlapping groups.

Researchers often have investigated differences in students' learning, motivation, and other outcomes, as a function of cultural background (McInerney & King, 2018), but many studies have found little if any evidence of them. A lack of obtained cultural differences can be found when cultural variables are treated as control variables; that is, their effects are controlled statistically so that the effects of other variables on educational outcomes can be studied. Cultural identities and differences are often merged, and researchers provide general interpretations of data (Portes, 1996).

It is important to examine potential cultural differences in motivation and learning. Such research contributes to our understanding and provides a basis for offering suggestions for teaching diverse learners. Although researchers have shown that many of the findings discussed in this text are robust across cultures, this is not always the case. Thus, we should not assume that findings obtained with students in Western cultures apply to those from other cultural backgrounds (McInerney & King, 2018).

With respect to goal orientations (Chapter 9), for example, we might ask whether students from other cultures are as concerned with appearing competent to others, performing better than peers, and pursuing academic and social goals. McInerney, Hinkley, Dowson, and Van Etten (1998) assessed mastery, performance, and social goals among three groups of Australian high school students: Anglo Australian, Aboriginal Australian, and immigrant-background Australian. The results showed that the three groups were similar in their goal beliefs. Groups placed greatest emphasis on satisfying mastery needs, whereas satisfying social and performance-goal needs were judged as less important. But the effects were greatest for the Anglo and immigrant-background Australian students; Aboriginal Australian students were less likely to believe that their success depended on satisfying mastery and performance-goal needs. The Aboriginal Australian group was more socially oriented and less individually oriented than the other groups.

These findings can be interpreted in light of cultural knowledge. Many Australian Aboriginal students come from families that emphasize traditional values (e.g., affiliation, social concern). Thus, it is not surprising that these students might place greater importance on that goal. The implications for education are that for these students (and for others who might respond similarly) more activities should be incorporated into instruction that include social links (e.g., cooperative learning). This does not mean that the emphasis on mastery should be abandoned; McInerney et al. (1998) found that all groups espoused a mastery goal orientation. Rather, the two goal orientations can be linked in creative ways.

Another study on cross-cultural differences was conducted by Kinlaw, Kurtz-Costes, and Goldman-Fraser (2001), who compared the attribution (Chapter 9) beliefs of European American and Chinese American mothers of preschool children. These researchers found that Chinese American mothers placed greater emphasis on effort-related beliefs. On a test of school readiness, Chinese American children scored higher on readiness and autonomy. Although these data are correlational and thus do not imply causality, the results show that cultural differences in mothers' attribution beliefs are present before children enter school and suggest that when children get to school, their attribution beliefs may relate to their motivation and learning.

A cultural dimension that has been explored in research is individualism and collectivism. Individualistic cultures tend to stress independence and individual initiative, whereas collectivist cultures emphasize group identify and "we" consciousness (Klassen, 2004).

The United States and Western European countries are high in individualism; Asian cultures tend to be more collectivist. Researchers comparing these cultures often find that individuals from collectivist cultures judge self-efficacy (Chapter 4) lower than do those from more individualistic cultures including when performances are equivalent or higher. Further, lower self-efficacy beliefs typically are better aligned with actual performances (Klassen, 2004). These results suggest that collectivist cultures may promote modesty in self-efficacy judgments, and they raise the issue of whether collective self-efficacy (Chapter 4) may be a better predictor of performance among students from these cultures than individual self-efficacy (Klassen, 2004). They also suggest that persons in individualistic cultures may be more self-efficacious when they feel they have more control over personal actions.

In contrast, persons from collectivist societies may feel more self-efficacious when they believe they can work with others for the betterment of the group. Group activities (e.g., peer teaching, cooperative learning) may be more favorably received by students from collectivist cultures than by those from more individualistic cultures. Clearly, more research is needed on this issue as theory and research suggest that group activities may be differentially effective for teaching and learning depending on students' cultural backgrounds.

Future research on cultures will contribute greatly to the learning literature. It is imperative that principles of learning be tested for cross-cultural consistency to promote a better understanding of learning in all contexts and cultures (McInerney, 2008).

We must remember that there is much variability within any culture (Zusho & Clayton, 2011). Further, it is well known that cultures change—often in the course of one's lifetime—as a result of societal elements becoming incorporated into cultural norms (Gauvain & Munroe, 2012). Thus, it may be misleading to compare learners from different cultures and discuss between-culture differences. Unfortunately this often is done, as there is much research comparing Eastern and Western cultures. Even if between-group differences are obtained, it is difficult to determine the causes of the differences. To better understand learning differences among learners in different cultures and within the same culture, researchers may need to focus more on contextual variations including those found in the experiences, settings, and ecological conditions of individuals (Zusho & Clayton, 2011).

INSTRUCTIONAL APPLICATIONS

Learning theories and principles suggest many ways to take contextual variables into account in instruction. Instructional applications derive from theory and research on teacher–student interactions, learning styles, and parental and familial involvement.

Teacher–Student Interactions

Teacher–student interactions are critically important for effective teaching and learning. Interactions will vary with students' developmental levels. Young children's attention can be captured by novel, interesting displays while minimizing unnecessary distractions.

It helps to provide opportunities for physical movement and to keep activities short to maintain children's concentration. Young students also benefit from physical objects and visual displays (e.g., manipulatives, pictures). Teachers may need to point out how what students are learning relates to what they already know. Children should be encouraged to use outlines and pictures to help them organize information. The opening vignette suggests that making learning meaningful, such as by relating it to real-life experiences, helps to build children's memory networks. Other important aspects of interactions involve feedback and classroom climate.

Feedback. Rosenshine and Stevens (1986) recommended that teachers provide performance feedback (e.g., "Correct," "Good") and maintain lesson momentum when students make mistakes by giving corrective feedback but not completely re-explaining the process. Reteaching is called for when many students do not understand the material. When leading lessons, teachers should keep interactions with younger students brief (30 or fewer seconds) when such interactions are geared to leading them toward the correct answer with hints or simple questions. Longer contacts lose other students' attention.

Reteaching and leading students to correct answers are effective ways to promote learning (Rosenshine & Stevens, 1986). Asking simpler questions and giving hints are useful when contacts can be kept short. Reteaching is helpful when many students make errors during a lesson. Feedback informing students that answers are correct motivates because it indicates the students are becoming more competent and are capable of further learning (Schunk, 1995). Feedback indicating an error also can build self-efficacy if followed by corrective information on how to perform better. Younger students benefit from frequent feedback.

Similarly, other interactions involving rewards, goals, contracts, and so forth must be linked with student progress. For example, rewards linked to learning progress build self-efficacy (Schunk, 1983e). With children, progress is best indicated with short-term tasks. Rewards given merely for participation regardless of level of performance actually may convey negative efficacy information. Students may wonder whether they are capable of performing better.

Classroom Climate. As discussed earlier, teachers help to establish a climate that affects interactions. Emotional aspects of teacher–student interactions are important. A positive classroom climate that reflects teacher warmth and sensitivity is associated with higher achievement and better self-regulation among elementary students (Pianta, Belsky, Vandergrift, Houts, & Morrison, 2008).

A classic study by Lewin, Lippitt, and White (1939) showed that a *democratic (collaborative) leadership style* is effective. The teacher works cooperatively with students, motivating them to work on tasks, posing questions, and having them share their ideas. Although an *authoritarian style* (strict with rigid rules and procedures) can raise achievement, high anxiety levels characterize such classrooms, and productivity drops off when the teacher is absent. A *laissez-faire style* with the teacher providing little classroom direction results in wasted time and aimless activities. Democratic leadership encourages independence and initiative in students, who continue to work productively in the teacher's absence.

Teacher–student interactions often include praise and criticism. *Praise* goes beyond simple feedback on accuracy of work or appropriateness of behavior because it conveys positive teacher affect and provides information about the worth of students' behaviors. Thus, a teacher who says, "Correct, your work is so good," is providing both performance feedback ("Correct") and praise ("Your work is so good").

Brophy (1981) reviewed research on teacher praise and found that it does not always reinforce desirable behavior (Chapter 3) because teachers often do not give it based on student responses. Rather, it may be infrequent, noncontingent, general, and highly dependent on teachers' perceptions of students' need for praise. Many studies also show that praise is not strongly related to student achievement. The effects of praise may depend on SES and ability level. In the early elementary grades, praise correlates weakly but positively with achievement among low SES and low-ability students but weakly and negatively or not at all with achievement among high SES and high-ability students (Brophy & Good, 1986).

After the first few grades in school, praise is a weak reinforcer. Up to approximately age 8, children want to please adults, which makes praise effects powerful; but this desire to please weakens with development. Praise also can have unintended effects. Because it conveys information about teachers' beliefs, teachers who praise students for success may convey that they do not expect students to learn much. Students might believe that the teacher thinks they have low ability, and this negatively affects motivation and learning.

When linked to progress in learning, praise substantiates students' beliefs that they are becoming more competent and raises self-efficacy and motivation for learning. Praise used indiscriminately carries no information about capabilities and has little effect on behavior (Schunk & DiBenedetto, 2016).

Criticism provides information about undesirability of student behaviors. Criticism ("I'm disappointed in you") is distinguished from performance feedback ("That's wrong"). Criticism is not necessarily bad. We might expect that criticism's effect on achievement will depend on the extent to which it conveys that students are competent and can perform better with more effort or better use of strategies. Thus, a statement such as, "I'm disappointed in you. I know you can do better if you work harder," might motivate students to learn because it contains positive self-efficacy information. As with praise, other variables temper the effects of criticism. Some research shows that criticism is given more often to boys, African American students, students for whom teachers hold low expectations, and students of lower SES status (Brophy & Good, 1986).

As a motivational technique to aid learning, criticism probably is not a good choice because it can have variable effects. Younger children may misinterpret academic criticism to mean that the teacher does not like them or is mean. Some students respond well to criticism. In general, however, teachers are better advised to provide positive feedback about ways to improve performance than to criticize present performance. Application 11.7 offers ways to use praise and criticism in learning settings.

APPLICATION 11.7
Using Praise and Criticism

The praise and criticism teachers use as they interact with their students can affect student performance. Teachers must be careful to use both appropriately and remember that criticism generally is not a good choice because it can have variable effects.

Praise is most effective when it is simple, direct, and linked with accomplishment of specific actions. For example, a teacher who is complimenting a student for sitting quietly, concentrating, and completing his or her work accurately that day should not say, "You really have been good today" (too general). Instead, the teacher might say something such as, "I really like the way you worked hard at your seat and finished all of your math work today. It paid off because you got all of the division problems correct. Great job!"

When a student answers a question in a class during a discussion about a chapter, it is desirable that the teacher let him or her know why the answer was a good one. Instead of simply replying, "Good answer," the teacher might add, "You outlined very well the main points in that chapter."

If criticism is used, it should convey that students are competent and can perform better, which may motivate performance. For example, assume that a capable undergraduate student submitted a poor project that did not fulfill the assignment. The professor might say to the student, "John, I am disappointed in your project. You are one of the best students in our class. You always share a great deal in class and perform well on the tests. I know you are capable of completing an outstanding project. I want you to work some more on this and try harder as you redo this project."

Learning Styles

Taking learning style differences into account helps make instruction more developmentally appropriate. *Learning styles* (or *preferences*) are stable individual variations in perceiving, organizing, processing, and remembering information (Shipman & Shipman, 1985). Styles are people's preferred ways to process information and handle tasks (Sternberg & Grigorenko, 1997; Zhang & Sternberg, 2005). Although some have questioned whether learning styles really exist (Riener & Willingham, 2010), it is important to note that styles are not synonymous with abilities. Abilities refer to capacities to learn and execute skills; styles are habitual (preferred) ways of processing and using information.

Styles are inferred from one's preferred ways of organizing and processing information on different tasks (Dunn & Honigsfeld, 2013). To the extent that preferences affect cognition, affects, and behavior, they help link cognitive, affective, and social functioning (Messick, 1994). In turn, stylistic differences are associated with differences in learning and receptivity to various forms of instruction (Messick, 1984).

This section discusses three styles (field dependence–independence, categorization, cognitive tempo) that have substantial research bases and educational implications. There are many other styles including *leveling* or *sharpening* (blurring or accentuating differences among stimuli), *risk taking* or *cautiousness* (high or low willingness to take chances to achieve goals), and *sensory modality preference* (enactive or kinesthetic, iconic or visual, symbolic or auditory; Sternberg & Grigorenko, 1997). A popular style inventory is the *Myers-Briggs Type Indicator* (Myers & McCaulley, 1988), which purports to identify individuals' preferred ways of seeking out learning environments and attending to elements in them. Its four dimensions are: extroversion–introversion, sensing–intuitive, thinking–feeling, and judging–perceiving. Readers are referred to Zhang and Sternberg (2005) for in-depth descriptions of other styles.

Styles provide information about cognitive development. One also can relate styles to larger behavioral patterns to study personality development (e.g., Myers-Briggs). Educators investigate styles to determine ways to provide developmentally appropriate instruction and to teach students more adaptive styles to enhance learning and motivation. Styles also seem relevant to brain development and functions (Chapter 2).

Field Dependence–Independence.   *Field dependence–independence* (also called psychological differentiation, *global* and *analytical functioning*) refers to the extent that one depends on or is distracted by the context or perceptual field in which a stimulus or event occurs (Sternberg & Grigorenko, 1997). The construct was identified and researched by Witkin (1969; Witkin, Moore, Goodenough, & Cox, 1977; Application 11.8)

APPLICATION 11.8
Learning Styles

To ensure that instruction is developmentally appropriate, elementary teachers should address the cognitive differences of their children in designing classroom activities, particularly because young children are more field dependent (global) than field independent (analytical). For early elementary children, emphasis should be placed on designing activities that address global understanding, while at the same time taking analytical thinking into account.

For example, when Ms. Banner implements a unit on the neighborhood, she and her third graders might initially talk about the entire neighborhood and all the people and places in it (global thinking).

The children might build replicas of their homes, the school, churches, stores, and so forth—which could tap analytical thinking—and place these on a large floor map to get an overall picture of the neighborhood (global). Children could think about people in the neighborhood and their major features (analytical thinking) and then put on a puppet show portraying them interacting with one another without being too precise about exact behaviors (global). Ms. Banner could show a real city map to provide a broad overview (global) and then focus on that section of the map detailing their neighborhood (analytical).

APPLICATION 11.8 (*continued*)

Secondary teachers also can take preferences into account in instructional planning. In teaching about World War II, Mr. Teague should emphasize both global and analytical thinking by discussing overall themes and underlying causes of the war and by creating lists of important events and characters. Student activities can include discussions of important issues underlying the war (global) and making time lines showing dates of important battles and other activities (analytical). If Mr. Teague were to stress only one type, students who process and construct knowledge differently may doubt their ability to understand material, which will have a negative impact on self-efficacy and motivation for learning.

Young children primarily are field dependent, but an increase in field independence begins during preschool and extends into adolescence. Children's individual preferences remain reasonably consistent over time. The data are less clear on gender differences. Although some data suggest that older male students are more field independent than older female students, research on children shows that girls are more field independent than boys. Whether these differences reflect cognitive preference or some other variable that contributes to test performance (e.g., activity–passivity) is not clear.

Because field-dependent persons may be more sensitive to and attend carefully to aspects of the social environment, they are better at learning material with social content; however, field-independent learners can easily learn such content when it is brought to their attention. Field-dependent learners seem sensitive to teacher praise and criticism. Field-independent persons are more likely to impose structure when material lacks organization; field-dependent learners consider material as it is. With poorly structured material, field-dependent learners may be at a disadvantage. They use salient features of situations in learning, whereas field-independent learners also consider less salient cues. The latter students may be at an advantage with concept learning when relevant and irrelevant attributes are contrasted.

These differences suggest ways for teachers to alter instruction to make it developmentally appropriate. If field-dependent learners miss cues, teachers should highlight them to help students distinguish relevant features of concepts. This may be especially important with children who are beginning readers as they focus on letter features. Field-dependent learners may have more trouble during early stages of reading.

Categorization Style. *Categorization style* refers to criteria used to perceive objects as similar to one another (Sigel & Brodzinsky, 1977). Style is assessed with a grouping task in which one must group objects on the basis of perceived similarity. This is not a cut-and-dried task because objects can be categorized in many ways. From a collection of animal pictures, one might select a cat, dog, and rabbit and give as the reason for the grouping that they are mammals, have fur, run, and so forth. Categorization style reveals information about how the individual prefers to organize information.

Three types of categorization styles are relational, descriptive, and categorical (Kagan, Moss, & Sigel, 1960). A *relational (contextual) style* links items on a theme or function (e.g., spatial, temporal); a *descriptive (analytic) style* involves grouping by similarity according to some detail or physical attribute; a *categorical (inferential) style* classifies objects as instances of a superordinate concept. In the preceding example, "mammals," "fur," and "run," reflect categorical, descriptive, and relational styles, respectively.

Preschoolers' categorizations tend to be descriptive; however, relational responses of the thematic type also are prevalent (Sigel & Brodzinsky, 1977). Researchers note a developmental trend toward greater use of descriptive and categorical classifications along with a decrease in relational responses.

Learning preference and academic achievement are related, but the causal direction is unclear (Shipman & Shipman, 1985). Reading, for example, requires perception of analytic relations (e.g., fine discriminations); however, the types of discriminations made are as important as the ability to make such discriminations. Students are taught the former. Style and achievement may influence each other. Certain styles may lead to higher achievement, and the resulting rewards, perceptions of progress, and self-efficacy may reinforce one's continued use of the style.

Cognitive Tempo.   *Cognitive (conceptual, response) tempo* was extensively investigated by Kagan (1966). Kagan was investigating categorization when he observed that some children responded rapidly whereas others were more reflective and took their time. Cognitive tempo refers to the willingness "to pause and reflect upon the accuracy of hypotheses and solutions in a situation of response uncertainty" (Shipman & Shipman, 1985, p. 251).

Children become more reflective with development, particularly in the early school years (Sigel & Brodzinsky, 1977). Evidence suggests different rates of development for boys and girls, with girls showing greater reflectivity at an earlier age. A moderate positive correlation between scores over a 2-year period indicates reasonable stability (Brodzinsky, 1982).

Differences in tempo are unrelated to intelligence scores but correlate with school achievement. Messer (1970) found that children not promoted to the next grade were more impulsive than peers who were promoted. Reflective children tend to perform better on moderately difficult perceptual and conceptual problem-solving tasks and make mature judgments on concept attainment and analogical reasoning tasks (Shipman & Shipman, 1985). Reflectivity bears a positive relationship to prose reading, serial recall, and spatial perspective-taking (Sigel & Brodzinsky, 1977). Impulsive children often are less attentive and more disruptive than reflective children, oriented toward quick success, and demonstrate low performance standards and mastery motivation (Sternberg & Grigorenko, 1997).

Given the educational relevance of cognitive tempo, many have suggested training children to be less impulsive. Meichenbaum and Goodman (1971; Chapter 4) found that self-instructional training decreased errors among impulsive children. Modeled demonstrations of reflective cognitive style, combined with student practice and feedback, seem important as a means of change.

Preferences seem important for teaching and learning, and a fair amount of developmental research exists that may help guide attempts by practitioners to apply findings to make instruction more developmentally appropriate. For example, learners with a visual-spatial preference are better able to process and learn from graphical displays (Vekiri, 2002). At the same time, drawing instructional conclusions from the literature can be difficult. The distinction between cognitive styles and abilities is tenuous and controversial (Tiedemann, 1989); field independence may be synonymous with aspects of intelligence (Sternberg & Grigorenko, 1997). Researchers have investigated the organization of styles within information processing frameworks and within the structure of human personality (Messick, 1994; Sternberg & Grigorenko, 1997; Zhang & Sternberg, 2005).

Ideally the conditions of instruction will match learners' preferences; however, this match often does not occur. And the research evidence does not uniformly show that matching instructional modes to learners' preferences improves their learning. For example, Rogowsky, Calhoun, and Tallal (2015) found no significant relations between instructional methods (audiobook, e-text) and learning style preferences (auditory, visual word) among adult learners. Learners may need to adapt their preferred modes of learning to instructional conditions involving content and teaching methods. Self-regulation methods (Chapter 10) help learners adapt to changing instructional conditions.

Instructional conditions can be tailored to individual differences to provide equal learning opportunities for all students despite differences in aptitudes, styles, and so forth. Teachers control many aspects of the instructional environment, which they can tailor to student differences. These aspects include organizational structure (whole-class, small-group, individual), regular and supplementary materials, use of technology, type of feedback, and type of material presented (tactile, auditory, visual). Teachers also make adaptations when they provide remedial instruction to students who have difficulty grasping new material.

Parental and Familial Involvement

As we have seen in this chapter, parents and other family members can affect their children's learning directly through such activities as helping them with homework and studying and offering advice. But they also can affect children's learning indirectly; for example, by steering them to desirable activities and people. Some instructional applications are given in this section.

One application is for parents and others to encourage children to take part in activities in which most participants will display positive achievement beliefs (e.g., self-efficacy) and behaviors (e.g., studying), such as school clubs, athletic teams, and musical groups. For students to remain involved in activities, they must maintain good grades, which can help students develop time management and study skills. Parents and other family members cannot control who will be their children's friends, but they can help steer children into groups where the participants value learning and achieving.

Parents can assist children with course planning. Especially with high school students, parents can discuss courses and electives and encourage children to talk with school counselors. Learning is aided because such course counseling helps ensure that children end up in courses that are neither too easy nor too difficult. Learners with self-efficacy for learning will be motivated to learn in these courses.

Children's learning benefits when parents and family members help them determine their work requirements and schedule the appropriate amount of time to complete them.

Goal-setting research underscores the importance of setting realistic goals (Locke & Latham, 2002). Parents can establish a routine; for example, before dinner, children write down what they need to accomplish that evening and then set a rough schedule for completing the work. Children may be unrealistic about how much time is required; parents can help them set realistic time limits. Children can check off tasks as they complete them. The perception of progress helps build their self-efficacy for learning.

Parental participation in school activities is important because this conveys that school is important and that they are willing to spend some of their time engaged in these activities. The belief that activities are valued is a key motivation variable and higher motivation leads to better learning (Schunk & DiBenedetto, 2016). As children get older, they may not want parents too overtly involved in the school, but there are many forms of involvement that do not draw attention to parents' presence (e.g., attend PTA meetings, school performances, athletic events).

Media's effects on learning are beneficial when activities are limited and of the educational variety. It also helps for parents to coview televised programs. Through coviewing, parents can discuss the program with children and ask them questions to help stimulate their learning (e.g., "Why do you think she did that?"). Coviewing also conveys the attitude that programs are beneficial and that parents think learning is important because they are spending time doing it. By checking channel listings, parents might identify some programs that sound educationally important and plan time to watch the programs with their children.

Parental and familial involvement is important during periods when children are not in school, such as summer vacations. Children can lose learning gains and motivation for learning during these times, especially when there are many activities competing for their time. It is desirable for parents to talk with children about ways they might keep up some academic learning. Setting a few goals (e.g., number of books to read) can help sustain children's academic focus and motivation for learning.

SUMMARY AND CRITIQUE

Chapter Summary

The context of learning, or the community or learning environment within which the student is located, can have important effects on student learning. Context comprises many aspects such as teachers, classrooms, schools, peers, families, communities, and cultures.

Teachers are responsible for creating effective learning environments where teaching and learning can proceed well. Good classroom organization and management practices enhance the effectiveness of learning environments. Also important are the implementation of the six TARGET variables: task, authority, recognition, grouping, evaluation, and time.

Another critical aspect of classrooms is how teachers and students interact. To facilitate positive interactions and student motivation and learning, teachers should provide feedback indicating student progress and ways to improve, support students' learning, and hold reasonable expectations based on the idea that all students are capable of learning.

Peers can have important effects on students' achievement beliefs, motivation, and learning. Peers exert their influence through modeling with its functions of inhibition/

disinhibition, response facilitation, and observational learning. Similarity to models enhances their influence. Peers' similarity in background and experiences can affect observers' motivation and learning.

Peer networks, or large groups of peers with whom students associate, are composed of students similar to one another in many ways. Networks help define opportunities for social interactions, allow students to observe others' interactions, and provide access to activities. Members of networks tend to become more similar over time. Parents may try to direct their children into activities where the members hold similar beliefs about the importance of learning.

Family influences on learning include socioeconomic status (SES), home environment, parental involvement, and electronic media. SES relates to school socialization, attendance, and years of schooling. Higher SES families have greater capital and provide more and richer opportunities for children. Early interventions for low-SES families help prepare children for school. Home environment effects are most pronounced in infancy and early childhood. As children become older, their social networks expand and peers become more important. Parents can launch children onto trajectories by involving them in groups and activities. Parents' expectations for children relate positively to their achievement. Comer's School Development Program involves parents and community members in school planning. Children learn from electronic media, and moderate exposure to educational media is associated with better cognitive development and achievement. Parents and caregivers who view media with children can help to promote children's learning.

Families are critical for children's motivation and learning. Children benefit from authoritative parenting practices that provide guidance and limits while assisting children to regulate and assume responsibility for their behaviors. Family involvement in children's education is important. Homes that that are rich in resources and in which parents assist children with educational activities bear a positive relation to student learning and achievement.

Community influences include location and involvement. Learning benefits when students' communities have access to resources and stimulating educational experiences. Community members often are involved in education by participating in school events and field trips in the community. It is important that schools partner with community agencies to enhance involvement.

Cultural differences often are found in learning and achievement. The attitudes, beliefs, and practices of cultures must be examined to determine causes of differences. There often are wide differences within cultures, so generalizations about cross-cultural differences may be misleading. When reliable cultural differences are found, students may benefit from programs aimed at enhancing their learning potential.

Some important instructional applications pertain to the areas of teacher–student interactions, learning styles or preferences, and parental and familial involvement. Teachers who structure feedback and provide a positive classroom climate—which includes effectively using praise and criticism—help motivate students and improve their learning. Students differ in their preferred learning styles. Teachers can take stylistic differences into account by ensuring that information is conveyed in multiple ways and that student activities are varied. Parents can be involved in children's schooling in and out of school, by participating in school activities, ensuring that children complete work, assisting with planning, and monitoring media usage to help ensure that it may facilitate academic learning.

Chapter Critique

The topic of contextual influences on learning seems somewhat antithetical to a central message of this text that learning principles are general and intended to apply to diverse contexts. For example, the central processes of information processing—attention, perception, working and long-term memories—are postulated to apply to learning in different contexts, and research supports their operation across contexts.

Although learning processes are general in the sense of applying to multiple contexts, how they apply is subject to adaptation depending on variables associated with the context. Continuing with this example, how learners apply information processing principles will vary depending on the conditions under which they apply them.

The research evidence on contextual influences is somewhat uneven. A great deal of research exists on the topics of teachers, classrooms, schools, peers, and families, whereas much less research has been conducted on the roles of communities and cultures. We should expect that investigations on these under-researched areas will increase in the future.

Contextual influences should not be viewed simply as variables that can affect learning but rather as opportunities for educators to use these variables to improve learning. Peer influence on learning, for example, may be positive, neutral, or negative. The key is to use peers in educationally desirable ways to foster learning among all students.

This chapter also calls attention to some variables that often are overlooked in discussions of teaching and learning, such as school climate and students' feelings of belongingness. These and other variables should be attended to because the same lesson delivered in different classrooms may have different effects on student learning. Discussions of context bring together environmental/social, behavioral, cognitive, and affective variables, which is desirable because learning is not a simple process, and researchers have demonstrated its influence by multiple variables.

REFLECTION QUESTIONS

- Many students experience difficulties with school transitions. These difficulties often manifest themselves in emotional issues, but they also can negatively affect students' motivation and learning. An underlying cause of transition problems may be poor person–environment fit. Many of the instructional, social, and environmental aspects of schooling are not well matched to students' changing needs and goals. What are some ways of altering instructional, social, and environmental aspects of schooling so that they are better matched to students' needs and therefore help students during transitions? Can you think of examples of how to assist students in the transition from elementary to middle school, from middle to high school, and from high school to college?

- As children develop, parents find that they have less control over their children's activities. On the one hand, this lessened control is adaptive as it can help children develop a sense of self and agency for being able to control many outcomes in their lives. But children's greater independence also can lead to problems. Two problematic areas that have been identified are peer influence and media/social networking. Social groups with whom students associate can influence their motivation and learning, and students' excessive interactions with media and social networking bear a negative relationship to motivation and learning. How might teachers productively use peer influence and media/social networking to help motivate students for learning? And how might teachers work with parents so that parents also can use these influences productively?

■ Cultural differences can affect learning. This is a key point to keep in mind given the rapid influx of non-native-English-speaking students into educational systems. Educators strive to accommodate students' cultural differences but may not fully understand how to do so. What advice would you give to educators for ways to learn about cultural differences and take these into account in planning for teaching and learning?

FURTHER READING

Bradley, R. H., & Corwyn, R. F. (2002). Socioeconomic status and child development. *Annual Review of Psychology, 53*, 371–399.

Cole, M. (2010). Education as an intergenerational process of human learning, teaching, and development. *American Psychologist, 65*, 796–807.

Cornelius-White, J. (2007). Learner-centered teacher-student relations are effective: A meta-analysis. *Review of Educational Research, 77*, 113–143.

Kirkorian, H. L., Wartella, E. A., & Anderson, D. R. (2008). Media and young children's learning. *The Future of Children, 18*(1), 39–61.

McInerney, D. M., & King, R. B. (2018). Culture and self-regulation in educational contexts. In D. H. Schunk & J. A. Greene (Eds.), *Handbook of self-regulation of learning and performance* (2nd ed., pp. 485–502). New York: Routledge.

Rumberger, R. (2010). *Why students drop out of school and what can be done about it.* Cambridge, MA: Harvard University Press.

Wentzel, K. R. (2016). Teacher-student relationships. In K. R. Wentzel & D. B. Miele (Eds.), *Handbook of motivation at school* (2nd ed., pp. 211–230). New York: Routledge.

12 Next Steps

The setting is the same as the opening vignette in Chapter 1—Russ Nyland's graduate course on learning and cognition. In that scenario, three students—Jeri Kendall, Matt Bowers, and Trisha Pascella— talked with Russ after class because they were confused about whether they should accept one theory or draw from different theories. Russ advised them not to worry about what type of theorist they were but rather to determine what they believe about learning and what types of learning they are interested in. Now, after the last class of the semester, the same three students talk with him again.

Russ: Well, tell me, what did you think about the class?

Jeri: Dr. Nyland, we want to say we think you're an awesome teacher! You have opened our minds to so much and given us lots to think about. This is a great course for anyone in education.

Russ: Thank you for the kind words! College instructors don't have many students give them feedback like that. Let me ask you, what did you decide about what you believe about learning for the type of learning you're interested in?

Matt: I teach high school math. For me, constructivism makes a lot of sense, especially the idea that students construct memory networks. I see how important these are for problem-solving.

Trisha: I work with a lot of children with learning and behavior problems. Social cognitive theory speaks to this with its emphasis on modeling and self-efficacy. These kids are so influenced by peers, and many have such a low sense of efficacy for being able to learn.

Jeri: For me, the role of motivation in learning is critical. Concepts like interest, values, goals, and others are perfect for my teaching. I'm going to pay more attention to how what I do affects motivation as well as learning.

Russ: I'm pleased to hear what you've said. You've begun with your interests and then found relevant ideas in theories. And you can keep revising your ideas as you learn more and reflect on your teaching. Good luck to you!

You are about to finish your study of learning theories in educational contexts. As Russ Nyland advised and his students did, it is time for you to examine your beliefs and assumptions about learning. Once it is clear in your mind where you stand on learning in general, then the theoretical perspective or perspectives that are most relevant will emerge. Examining your beliefs and assumptions about learning and seeing how these align with theoretical perspectives are your next steps.

LEARNING QUESTIONS

A good place to begin is by addressing the six questions about learning raised in Chapter 1, along with what you believe about some other issues. For starters, you might focus on the setting where you work. You may be teaching children, adolescents, or adults. You may be in a school or a different setting. Your students may or may not have normal learning capabilities. You may be working on different types of content. Thinking about your present setting, you might try to address the issues summarized in the next section, and in doing so formulate your philosophy of learning.

How Does Learning Occur?

This is the central question in understanding learning. How does a learner move from an unknowing to a knowing state? Learning processes can be internal to the learner (e.g., beliefs, cognitions) and external (e.g., instructional and environmental factors). Which of these are important in your situation? Think of your learners, content, and setting. What do your learners bring with them? Is your content factual, or does it require reasoning? How is your content best learned? What instructional variables are important? For example, do students learn better from teacher or peer models? Do they learn better individually or in groups? What other environmental factors facilitate learning (e.g., graphics, technology, discussions)? Write down your assumptions about learning and what learning processes you believe are important in your situation.

How Does Memory Function?

Some questions to ask are the following: How much do students have to remember? How demanding is the content (i.e., the cognitive load) on their working and long-term memories? Are there ways you can organize the material to facilitate memory? What other ways might students build good memory networks? Instructional content differs in the amount and type of demands it makes on memory. Write down what you assume about the role of memory in your learning setting.

What Is the Role of Motivation?

People can learn without being motivated to do so, but motivation improves learning. In your setting, how important is it that students be motivated to learn? If motivation is important, what are some ways that you can build students' motivation? Will you use rewards or goals? How can you increase their self-efficacy for learning? How can you ensure that students make desirable attributions for their successes and difficulties? How can you increase their perceptions of value of the learning? If social comparisons will occur in your learning setting how might they affect motivation? Write down what you believe about motivation in your learning setting.

How Does Transfer Occur?

Transfer is critical, because without it all learning becomes subject and location specific. We want students to transfer what they have learned to other content and settings. In your setting, how can you enhance students' transfer of skills, strategies, and beliefs? Are they apt to see other uses for the learning on their own, or will they need assistance? If the latter, what will you do? Will you tell them about other uses, plan activities where they can apply knowledge in new ways, work with other teachers, or what? Write down what you believe facilitates transfer in your learning setting.

How Does Self-Regulated Learning Operate?

Self-regulated learning is a key educational goal, yet often it is overlooked and students are allowed few choices in learning. Do you want your learners to develop self-regulatory skills? If self-regulated learning is important in your setting, what do you feel are its important components, and how can you incorporate those into your teaching? Are there impediments to developing self-regulated learning in your environment? If so, how might you minimize those? Write down what you believe about self-regulated learning in your setting.

What Are the Implications for Instruction?

After summarizing what you believe about the preceding five questions, your beliefs about the sixth question should fall into line. Your assumptions about learning processes, memory, motivation, transfer, and self-regulated learning will suggest some instructional strategies to use with your learners. These implications will address various instructional facets, such as the organization of content, how it is presented, the use of technology, student grouping for learning, student activities, forms of feedback and evaluation, and so forth. Write down what you believe are effective instructional approaches in your learning setting.

LEARNING THEORIES

Once you have completed the previous section, you are ready to see where your philosophy fits with the various theories discussed in this text. Although many theories of learning have been discussed, they can be conveniently grouped into four major categories (keeping in mind that there is some overlap): conditioning, social cognitive, cognitive information processing, and constructivist.

Conditioning

Conditioning (behavior) theories focus on environmental variables. Behavior is a function of its consequences. Learning is a change in behavior brought about through conditioning. To facilitate learning, you structure the environment so that students can respond correctly and reinforce those responses. Organization of material is critical, because the learning must proceed in small steps for students to respond correctly. Although students' thoughts and beliefs exist, they are not necessary to explain learning.

Social Cognitive

Social cognitive theories assume that learning can occur by doing or by observing others. Models who explain and demonstrate skills and strategies can greatly facilitate the learning process. Learning can occur without reinforcement. Reinforcement is a type of feedback that informs students about the accuracy of their work and motivates them to continue to improve. Motivation leads to better learning. Critical personal variables that facilitate learning include self-efficacy, outcome expectations, goals, values, and self-regulatory processes.

Information Processing

Information processing theories contend that learning involves the forming of networks in memory. Information is attended to, perceived, transferred to working memory, and related to information in long-term memory. Processes such as organization, elaboration, and rehearsal help to form memory networks. These theories are highly compatible with findings from brain research. The focus is on the acquisition, storage, and retrieval of information. Relatively less attention is given to motivational processes.

Constructivist

Constructivist theories, like social cognitive and information processing theories, are cognitive in nature. Constructivism places greater emphasis on learners' construction of knowledge and beliefs. Learning is the process whereby learners take in information from the environment and combine it with their present knowledge. Learners' constructions are aided by instructional conditions that stress social interactions.

FUTURE DEVELOPMENTS

Learning is a dynamic field. It is ever changing to address the many complexities and to better understand the operation of learning. Like learning research, your philosophy is evolving and likely to change over time.

Based on recent history of learning research, seven trends and directions for future research are briefly summarized. Some of these contemporary trends may affect your philosophy.

■ *Neuroscience.* Neuroscience research increasingly is exploring the operation of neural processes in contexts involving learning. Advances in technology make possible more-naturalistic experimentation. A goal is to determine whether neuroscience and learning research findings are compatible and support one another. We should expect a closer integration of neuroscientific explanations for learning with those from learning theories (e.g., information processing).

■ *Context.* The role of contextual variables in learning cannot be overstated. While we know quite a bit about some contextual influences, others have been under-researched—for example, the roles of communities, cultures, and learning in out-of-school contexts (e.g., homes, volunteer activities, internships). An important trend is greater research in these types of authentic settings.

■ *Operation.* Expect to see more research on the operation of learning as it occurs. Prior research often has used assessments before and after learning, which does not capture the dynamic way it changes. Researchers increasingly are using real-time measures to study learning, such as think-alouds, observations, and assessments at different points during learning.

■ *Motivation.* Researchers should continue to investigate the role of motivation before, during, and after learning. It is now accepted that motivation and learning bear a reciprocal influence on one another. How this dynamic plays out will be the subject of continuing research. The findings have implications for practice and should suggest ways to maintain learners' motivation.

■ *Self-regulated learning.* Research on self-regulated learning is increasing. Researchers will continue to examine influences on it and how variables associated with instruction and the learning context may help develop self-regulated learning among students. More research is expected on the role of self-regulation among groups and in out-of-school contexts.

■ *Methodology.* In addition to more real-time assessment as noted previously, learning research is likely to address methodological points that have not received much attention. For example, we need to know more about learning in various student populations, such as students with disabilities, homeless students, and students whose native language is not English.

■ *Technology.* To say that technology has had a major impact on learning is an understatement. Research will continue to address how technology can affect learning processes and especially in areas that have not seen extensive research activity such as social media and gaming. The prevalence of online learning creates many venues in which to conduct research.

CONCLUSION

In addition to the factors discussed in this chapter and possible future developments, there undoubtedly are other factors you want to consider in developing your theoretical philosophy of learning. These other factors will differ according to the context. For example, we know that developmental factors place constraints on what students are capable of learning.

The type of learning possible with adults differs from what we can expect from children. If your learning environment is technologically rich, you also will want to consider how students learn best from the available technologies. If your students have cognitive limitations, then you will need to determine how instruction can be differentiated to take those into account.

As you construct your personal theory of learning, keep in mind that this is not a one-time activity. Theories of learning are not formulated and then left unchanged. As explained in Chapter 1, by conducting research, we test theoretical predictions. Those predictions that are not supported by research require re-examination and possibly modification of the theory. The same is true for you. You may hold a set of beliefs but then find that some of your beliefs do not produce desired learning. That is a call for you to re-examine your beliefs. Future research and theory development will bring about yet-to-be-determined changes.

Best of luck on your next steps. When you complete this task, you will have a clearer idea about how to improve teaching and student learning in your setting. This knowledge is sure to influence your life and the lives of your students!

Glossary

Accommodation The process of changing internal structures to provide consistency with external reality.

Accretion Encoding new information in terms of existing schemata.

Achievement Motivation The striving to be competent in effortful activities.

Act A class of movements that produces an outcome.

Action Control Potentially modifiable self-regulatory volitional skills and strategies.

Action Control Theory Theory stressing the role of volitional processes in behavior.

Activation Level Extent that information in memory is being processed or is capable of being processed quickly; information in an active state is quickly accessible.

Actualizing Tendency Innate motive that is a precursor to other motives and is oriented toward personal growth, autonomy, and freedom from external control.

Adaptation See *Equilibration*.

Adapting Instruction Tailoring instructional conditions at the system, course, or individual class level to match important individual differences to ensure equal learning opportunities for all students.

Advance Organizer Device that helps connect new material with prior learning, usually with a broad statement presented at the outset of a lesson.

Affect General term that includes both diffuse moods and specific emotions.

Affective Learning Technique Specific procedure included in a learning strategy to create a favorable psychological climate for learning by helping the learner cope with anxiety, develop positive beliefs, set work goals, establish a place and time for working, or minimize distractions.

Agency The belief that one can exert a large degree of control over the important events in one's life.

All-or-None Learning View that a response is learned by proceeding from zero or low strength to full strength rapidly (e.g., during one trial).

Amygdala Part of the brain involved in regulating emotion and aggression.

Analogical Reasoning Problem-solving strategy in which one draws an analogy between the problem situation and a situation with which one is familiar, works through the problem in the familiar domain, and relates the solution to the problem situation.

Apprenticeship Situation in which novice works with expert in joint work-related activities.

Artificial Intelligence Programming computers to engage in human activities such as thinking, using language, and solving problems.

Assessment The process of determining students' status with respect to educational variables.

Assimilation The process of fitting external reality to existing cognitive structures.

Associative Shifting Process of changing behavior whereby responses made to a particular stimulus eventually are made to a different stimulus as a consequence of altering the stimulus slightly on repeated trials.

Associative Strength Strength of association between a stimulus and a response.

Asynchronous Learning Nonreal-time interactions.

Attention The process of selecting some environmental inputs for further information processing.

Attribution Perceived cause of an outcome.

Attribution Retraining Intervention strategy aimed at altering students' attributional beliefs, usually from dysfunctional attributions (e.g., failure attributed to low ability) to those conducive to motivation and learning (failure attributed to low effort).

Automaticity Cognitive processing with little or no conscious awareness.

Autonomic Nervous System (ANS) The part of the nervous system that regulates involuntary behaviors involving the heart, lungs, glands, and muscles.

Axon Long thread of brain tissue in a neuron that sends messages.

Backup Reinforcer A reinforcer that one receives in exchange for a generalized reinforcer.

Backward-Reaching Transfer Abstracting transfer context features to integrate with previously learned ideas.

Balance Theory Theory postulating the tendency for people to balance relations between persons, situations, and events.

Behavior Modification (Therapy) Systematic application of behavioral learning principles to facilitate adaptive behaviors.

Behavior Rating An estimate of how often a behavior occurs in a given time.

Behavioral Objective Statement describing the behaviors a student will perform as a result of instruction, the conditions under which behaviors will be performed, and the criteria for assessing behaviors to determine whether the objective has been accomplished.

Behavior Theory Theory that views learning as a change in the form or frequency of behavior as a consequence of environmental events.

Big-Fish-Little-Pond Effect Students in selective schools having lower self-concepts than students in less-selective schools.

Blended Model Instruction that combines face-to-face instruction with e-learning.

Bottom-Up Processing Pattern recognition of visual stimuli that proceeds from analysis of features to building a meaningful representation.

Brain The primary organ in the nervous system that regulates cognition, motivation, and emotions.

Brain Stem That part of the central nervous system that links the lower brain with the middle brain and hemispheres.

Brainstorming Problem-solving strategy that comprises defining the problem, generating possible solutions, deciding on criteria to use in judging solutions, and applying criteria to select the best solution.

Branching Program Type of programmed instruction in which students complete different sequences depending on how well they perform.

Broca's Area Brain part in the left frontal lobe that controls speech production.

Buggy Algorithm An incorrect rule for solving a mathematical problem.

Capital Socioeconomic indicator that includes one's financial, material, human, and social resources.

CAT Scan Computerized axial tomography; technology that provides three-dimensional images used to detect body abnormalities.

Categorical Clustering Recalling items in groups based on similar meaning or membership in the same category.

Categorization Style Cognitive style referring to the criteria used to perceive objects as similar to one another.

Cell Assembly In Hebb's theory, a structure that includes cells in the cortex and subcortical centers.

Central Executive Information processing component that directs processing of information in working memory and movement of knowledge in and out of working memory.

Central Nervous System (CNS) The part of the nervous system that includes the spinal cord and the brain.

Cerebellum Part of the brain that regulates body balance, muscular control, movement, and body posture.

Cerebral Cortex The thin, outer covering of the cerebrum.

Cerebrum The largest part of the brain that includes left and right hemispheres; involved in cognition and learning.

Chaining The linking of three-term contingencies so that each response alters the environment and the altered condition serves as a stimulus for the next response.

Chameleon Effect Nonconscious mimicking of behaviors and mannerisms of persons in one's social environment.

Chunking Combining information in a meaningful fashion.

Classical Conditioning Descriptive term for Pavlov's theory in which a neutral stimulus becomes conditioned to elicit a response through repeated pairing with an unconditioned stimulus.

Climate The atmosphere, tone, or culture associated with the classroom or school environment.

Closed-Loop Theory Theory of motor skill learning postulating that people develop perceptual traces of motor movements through practice and feedback.

Cognitive Apprenticeship Apprenticeship aimed at teaching cognitive and metacognitive processes in academic content areas.

Cognitive Behavior Modification Behavior modification techniques that incorporate learners' thoughts (overt and covert) as discriminative and reinforcing stimuli.

Cognitive Consistency Idea that people have a need to make behaviors and cognitions consistent.

Cognitive Constructivism Constructivist perspective that focuses heavily on cognitive processes.

Cognitive Dissonance Mental tension that is produced by conflicting cognitions and has drivelike properties leading to reduction.

Cognitive Load The demands placed on the information processing system, especially on working memory (WM).

Cognitive Map Internal plan comprising expectancies of which actions are required to attain one's goal.

Cognitive Modeling Modeled explanation and demonstration incorporating verbalizations of the model's thoughts and reasons for performing given actions.

Cognitive Style See *Learning Style*.

Cognitive (Conceptual, Response) Tempo Cognitive style referring to the willingness to pause and reflect on the accuracy of information in a situation of response uncertainty.

Cognitive Theory Theory that views learning as the acquisition of knowledge and cognitive structures due to information processing.

Collective Self-Efficacy Perceived capabilities of group members to produce outcomes.

Collective Teacher Efficacy Perceptions of teachers in a school that their efforts as a whole will positively affect students.

Comer Program See *School Development Program*.

Comparative Organizer Type of advance organizer that introduces new material by drawing an analogy with familiar material.

Comprehension Attaching meaning to verbal (printed or spoken) information and using it for a particular purpose.

Comprehension Monitoring Cognitive activity directed toward determining whether one is properly applying knowledge to material to be learned, evaluating whether one understands the material, deciding that the strategy is effective or that a better strategy is needed, and knowing why strategy use improves learning. Monitoring procedures include self-questioning, rereading, paraphrasing, and checking consistencies.

Computer-Adaptive System Computer system that delivers instruction or assessment items based on how students respond.

Computer-Based (-Assisted) Instruction Interactive instruction in which a computer system provides information and feedback to students and receives student input.

Computer-Based Learning Environment Setting that includes computer technology used for learning in various ways, including with simulations, computer-based instruction, and hypermedia/multimedia.

Computer Learning Learning that occurs with the aid of a computer.

Computer-Mediated Communication (CMC) Technological applications that allow users to communicate with one another (e.g., distance education, computer conferencing).

Concept Labeled set of objects, symbols, or events sharing common characteristics (critical attributes).

Concept Learning Identifying attributes, generalizing them to new examples, and discriminating examples from nonexamples.

Conception of Ability One's belief/theory about the nature of intelligence (ability) and how it changes over time.

Concrete Operational Stage Third of Piaget's stages of cognitive development, encompassing roughly ages 7 to 11.

Conditional Knowledge Knowledge of when to employ forms of declarative and procedural knowledge and why doing so is important.

Conditional Regard Regard that is contingent on certain actions.

Conditioned Response (CR) The response elicited by a conditioned stimulus.

Conditioned Stimulus (CS) A stimulus that, when repeatedly paired with an unconditioned stimulus, elicits a conditioned response similar to the unconditioned response.

Conditioning Theory See *Behavior Theory*.

Conditions of Learning Circumstances that prevail when learning occurs and that include internal conditions (prerequisite skills and cognitive processing requirements of the learner) and external conditions (environmental stimuli that support the learner's cognitive processes).

Connectionism Descriptive term for Thorndike's theory postulating learning as the forming of connections between sensory experiences (perceptions of stimuli or events) and neural impulses that manifest themselves behaviorally.

Connectionist Model Computer simulation of learning processes in which learning is linked with neural system processing, where impulses fire across synapses to form connections.

Consolidation The process of stabilizing and strengthening neural (synaptic) connections.

Constructivism Doctrine stating that learning takes place in contexts and that learners form or construct much of what they learn and understand as a function of their experiences in situations.

Constructivist Theory See *Constructivism*.

Context The community or learning environment within which the individual is located.

Contiguity (Contiguous Conditioning) The basic principle of Guthrie's theory, which refers to learning that results from a pairing close in time to a response with a stimulus or situation.

Contingency Contract Written or oral agreement between teacher and student specifying what work the student must accomplish to earn a particular reinforcer.

Continuous Reinforcement Reinforcement for every response.

Control (Executive) Processes Cognitive activities that regulate the flow of information through the processing system.

Cooperative Learning Situation in which a group of students work on a task that is too great for any one student to complete and in which an objective is to develop in students the ability to work collaboratively.

Coping Model Model that initially demonstrates the typical fears and deficiencies of observers but gradually demonstrates improved performance and self-confidence in his or her capabilities.

Co-Regulation Coordination of self-regulatory competencies among people in social contexts.

Corpus Callosum Band of fibers in the brain that connects the right and left hemispheres.

Correlational Research A study in which an investigator explores naturally existing relations among variables.

Cortex See *Cerebral Cortex*.

Cortisol Bodily hormone that can retard brain development in babies when elevated.

Creativity Development of a novel idea, problem solution, or product that is of value and appropriate for the individual and larger social group.

Critical Thinking Reflective cognitive activity focused on deciding what to do or what to believe.

Cue-Dependent Forgetting Forgetting due to an absence of cues associated with the original learning.

Culture The shared norms, traditions, behaviors, languages, and perceptions of a group.

Declarative Knowledge Knowledge that something is the case; knowledge of facts, beliefs, organized passages, and events of a story.

Decoding Deciphering printed symbols or making letter–sound correspondences.

Deductive Reasoning Process of deriving specific points from general principles.

Deep Structure The meaning of the speech and syntax of a language.

Dendrite Elongated brain tissue surrounding a neuron that receives messages.

Development Changes in people over time that follow an orderly pattern and enhance survival.

Developmental Status What an individual is capable of doing given his or her present level of development.

Developmentally Appropriate Instruction Instruction matched to students' developmental levels.

Dialectical Constructivism Constructivist perspective stating that knowledge derives from interactions between persons and their environments.

Dialogue   Conversation between two or more persons while engaged in a learning task.

Dichotic Listening   Hearing two verbal inputs simultaneously.

Differentiated Instruction   Instructional activities tailored to individual student needs.

Differentiated Task Structure   Class situation in which all students work on different tasks and materials or methods are tailored to students' needs.

Direct Observations   Instances of behavior that are observed.

Discovery Learning   A type of inductive reasoning in which one obtains knowledge by formulating and testing hypotheses through hands-on experiences.

Discrimination   Responding differently, depending on the stimulus.

Discriminative Stimulus   The stimulus to which one responds in the operant model of conditioning.

Disinhibition   See *Inhibition/Disinhibition*.

Distance Learning (Education)   Instruction that originates at one site and is transmitted to students at one or more remote sites; it may include two-way interactive capabilities.

Distributed Practice   Study trials apart in time.

Domain Specificity   Discrete declarative and procedural knowledge structures.

Dopamine   A chemical neurotransmitter that can lead to the brain being more sensitive to the pleasurable effects of drugs and alcohol.

Drive   Internal force that energizes and propels one into action.

Dual-Code Theory   The view that long-term memory represents knowledge with a verbal system that includes knowledge expressed in language and an imaginal system that stores visual and spatial information.

Dual-Memory Model of Information Processing   See *Two-Store (Dual) Memory Model of Information Processing*.

Duration Measure   Amount of time a behavior occurs during a given period.

Dynamic Visualization   A visualization that portrays change such as a video or animation.

Echo   Sensory memory for auditory sounds.

Educational Data Mining   The tools and techniques used to find meanings in large data repositories generated during learners' activities.

EEG   Electroencephalograph; measures electrical patterns caused by movement of neurons and used to investigate brain disorders.

Effectance Motivation (Mastery Motivation)   Motivation to interact effectively with one's environment and control critical aspects.

Efficacy Expectations   See *Self-Efficacy*.

Effortful Control   Voluntary control of behavior and emotions.

Ego Involvement   Motivational state characterized by self-preoccupation, a desire to avoid looking incompetent, and viewing learning as a means to the end of avoiding the appearance that one lacks ability.

Egocentrism   Cognitive inability to take the perspective of another person.

Elaboration   The process of expanding upon new information by adding to it or linking it to what one already knows.

Elaboration Theory of Instruction   Means of presenting instruction in which one begins with a general view of the content, moves to specific details, and returns later to the general view with review and practice.

E-Learning   Learning through electronic means.

Electronic Bulletin Board (Conference)   Electronic means for posting messages and participating in a discussion (chat group).

Electronic Media   Media that operate through electronic means including televisions, cell phones, video games, Web social networks, and e-mail.

Emotion   A feeling that often is short-lived, intense, and specific.

Empiricism   The doctrine that experience is the only source of knowledge.

Enactive Learning   Learning through actual performance.

Enactive Representation   Representing knowledge through motor responses.

Encoding   The process of putting new, incoming information into the information processing system and preparing it for storage in long-term memory.

Encoding–Retrieval Similarity   See *Encoding Specificity Hypothesis*.

Encoding Specificity Hypothesis   The idea that retrieval of information from long-term memory is maximized when retrieval cues match those present during encoding.

Endogenous Constructivism   Constructivist perspective stating that people construct mental structures out of pre-existing structures and not directly from environmental information.

Entity Theory   The belief that abilities represent fixed traits over which one has little control.

Episodic Buffer   Information processing component where information from multiple modalities is integrated.

Epistemic Thinking   Cognitive and metacognitive processes involving learners' beliefs about how they learn.

Epistemology   Study of the origin, nature, limits, and methods of knowledge.

Equilibration   A biological drive to produce an optimal state of equilibrium; it includes the complementary processes of assimilation and accommodation.

Event-Related Potentials   Changes in brain waves measured while individuals are engaged in various tasks.

Evoked Potentials   See *Event-Related Potentials*.

Executive Attention Network   Neural network that allows one to control and shift attention relevant to goals and control distractions.

Executive Control   The capability to maintain attentional control.

Executive Function   The brain's goal-directed activities involved in planning, attention, self-control, monitoring, mental flexibility, and management of working memory.

Executive Processes   See *Control (Executive) Processes*.

Exogenous Constructivism   Constructivist perspective stating that the acquisition of knowledge represents a reconstruction of structures that exist in the external world.

Expectancy-Value Theory   Psychological theory postulating that behavior is a function of how much one values a particular outcome and one's expectation of obtaining that outcome as a result of performing that behavior.

Experimental Research   A study in which an investigator systematically varies conditions (independent variables) and observes changes in outcomes (dependent variables).

Expert   A person who has attained a high level of competence in a domain.

Expert System   Computer system that is programmed with a large knowledge base and that behaves intelligently by solving problems and providing instruction.

Explicit Instruction   Instructional approach where students are informed of the purpose and importance of learning, given explanations and demonstrations of skills, and engage in guided and independent practice.

Expository Organizer   Type of advance organizer that introduces new material with concept definitions and generalizations.

Extinction   Decrease in intensity and disappearance of a conditioned response due to repeated presentations of the conditioned stimulus without the unconditioned stimulus.

Extrinsic (Extraneous) Cognitive Load   The demands placed on the information processing system (especially on working memory) by unnecessary content, distractions, or difficulties with the instructional presentation.

Extrinsic Motivation   Engaging in a task as a means to the end of attaining an outcome (reward).

Facilitator   One who arranges resources and shares feelings and thoughts with students in order to promote learning.

False Memory   Memory of something that did not happen.

Far Transfer   Transfer to a different context unlike that involved in original learning.

Fatigue Method of Behavioral Change   Altering behavior by transforming the cue for engaging in the behavior into a cue for avoiding it through repeated presentation.

Fear of Failure   The tendency to avoid an achievement goal that derives from one's belief concerning the anticipated negative consequences of failing.

Feature Analysis   Theory of perception postulating that people learn the critical features of stimuli, which are stored in long-term memory as images or verbal codes and compared with environmental inputs.

Field Dependence and Independence   Cognitive style referring to the extent that one is dependent on or distracted by the context in which a stimulus or event occurs. Also called global and analytical functioning.

Field Expectancy   Perceived relation between two stimuli or among a stimulus, response, and stimulus.

Field Research   Study conducted where participants live, work, or go to school.

Figural Transfer   Transfer using metaphors, analogies, or comparable situations.

Figure–Ground Relation   See *Gestalt Principles*.

Filter (Bottleneck) Theory   Theory of attention contending that information not perceived is not processed beyond the sensory register.

Fixed Mindset   Belief that one's qualities and abilities are limited and cannot change much.

Flipped Classroom   Learning environment where content is studied at home with multimedia and the next class focuses on discussion and other activities based on homework and explores concepts at a deeper level.

Flow   Total involvement in an activity.

fMRI   See *Functional Magnetic Resonance Imaging*.

Forgetting   Loss of information from memory or inability to recall information due to interference or improper retrieval cues.

Formal Operational Stage   Fourth of Piaget's stages of cognitive development, encompassing roughly ages 11 to adult.

Forward-Reaching Transfer   Abstracting knowledge from learning situations to potential transfer situations.

Free Recall   Recalling stimuli in any order.

Frequency Count   Frequency of a behavior in a given time period.

Frontal Lobe   Brain lobe responsible for processing information relating to memory, planning, decision making, goal setting, and creativity; also contains the primary motor cortex regulating muscular movements.

Functional Analysis of Behavior   Process of determining the external variables of which behavior is a function.

Functional Fixedness   Failure to perceive different uses for objects or new configurations of elements in a situation.

Functional Magnetic Resonance Imaging (fMRI)   Technology measuring magnetic flow in the brain caused by performance of mental tasks that fires neurons and causes blood flow; image compared to that of the brain at rest to show responsible regions.

Functionalism   Doctrine postulating that mental processes and behaviors of living organisms help them adapt to their environments.

Game   Activity that creates an enjoyable learning context by linking material to sport, adventure, or fantasy.

General Skill   Skill applying to many domains (e.g., goal setting).

Generalization   Occurrence of a response to a new stimulus or in a situation other than that present during original learning. See also *Transfer*.

Generalized Reinforcer A secondary reinforcer that becomes paired with more than one primary or secondary reinforcer.

Generate-and-Test Strategy Problem-solving strategy in which one generates (thinks of) a possible problem solution and tests its effectiveness.

Germane Cognitive Load Intrinsic cognitive load plus necessary extrinsic cognitive load due to situational factors.

Gestalt Principles *Figure–ground relationship*: A perceptual field is composed of a figure against a background. *Proximity*: Elements in a perceptual field are viewed as belonging together according to their closeness in space or time. *Similarity*: Perceptual field elements similar in such respects as size or color are viewed as belonging together. *Common direction*: Elements of a perceptual field appearing to constitute a pattern or flow in the same direction are perceived as a figure. *Simplicity*: People organize perceptual fields in simple, regular features. *Closure*: People fill in incomplete patterns or experiences.

Gestalt Psychology Psychological theory of perception and learning stressing the organization of sensory experiences.

Glial Cell Brain cell that serves to nourish and cleanse neurons.

Global and Analytical Functioning See *Field Dependence and Independence.*

Goal The behavior (outcome) that one is consciously trying to perform (attain).

Goal Orientations Reasons for engaging in academic tasks.

Goal Progress Feedback Feedback providing information about progress toward a goal.

Goal Setting Process of establishing a standard or objective to serve as the aim of one's actions.

Grammar The underlying abstract set of rules governing a language.

Grouping Structure Instructional method for linking attainment of students' goals. *Cooperative*—positive link; *competitive*—negative link; *individualistic*—no link.

Growth Mindset Belief that one's qualities and abilities can be developed.

Habit Behavior established to many cues.

Hedonism Philosophical position that humans seek pleasure and avoid pain.

Heuristic A method for solving problems in which one employs principles (rules of thumb) that usually lead to a solution.

High-Road Transfer Transfer that is mindful and abstract.

Higher-Order Conditioning Use of a conditioned stimulus to condition a new, neutral stimulus by pairing the two stimuli.

Hill Climbing See *Working Forward.*

Hippocampus Brain structure responsible for memory of the immediate past; it helps to establish information in long-term memory.

Holistic Idea that we must study people's behaviors, thoughts, and feelings together and not in isolation.

Homeostasis Optimal levels of physiological states.

Hope for Success The tendency to approach an achievement goal that derives from one's subjective estimate of the likelihood of succeeding.

Humanistic Theory Theory emphasizing people's capabilities to make choices and seek control over their lives.

Hypermedia See *Multimedia.*

Hypothalamus Part of the autonomic nervous system that controls body functions needed to maintain homeostasis and also is involved in emotional reactions.

Hypothesis Assumption that can be empirically tested.

Icon Sensory memory for visual inputs.

Iconic Representation Representing knowledge with mental images.

Identical Elements View of transfer postulating that application of a response in a situation other than the one in which it was learned depends on the number of features (stimuli) common to the two situations.

Imitation Copying the observed behaviors and verbalizations of others.

Implicit Theories Students' beliefs about themselves, others, and their environments.

Inclusion Process of integrating students with disabilities into regular classroom instruction.

Incompatible Response Method of Behavioral Change Altering behavior by pairing the cue for the undesired behavior with a response incompatible with (i.e., that cannot be performed at the same time as) the undesired response.

Incremental Learning View that learning becomes established gradually through repeated performances (exemplified by Thorndike's theory).

Incremental Theory The belief that abilities are skills that can improve through learning.

Inductive Reasoning Process of formulating general principles based on specific examples.

Information Processing Sequence and execution of cognitive events.

Inhibition In Pavlov's theory, a type of neural excitation that works antagonistically to an excitation producing conditioning and that diminishes the conditioned response in intensity or extinguishes it.

Inhibition/Disinhibition Strengthening/weakening of inhibitions over behaviors previously learned, which results from observing consequences of the behaviors performed by models.

Inquiry Teaching Socratic teaching method in which learners formulate and test hypotheses, differentiate necessary from sufficient conditions, make predictions, and decide when more information is needed.

Insight A sudden perception, awareness of a solution, or transformation from an unlearned to a learned state.

Instinct A natural behavior or capacity.

Instructional Quality The degree to which instruction is effective, efficient, appealing, and economical in promoting student performance and attitude toward learning.

Instructional Scaffolding See *Scaffolding*.

Instructional Self-Efficacy Personal beliefs about one's capabilities to help students learn.

Interest Liking of and willful engagement in an activity.

Interference Blockage of the spread of activation across memory networks.

Interleaved Practice Intermixing different examples with practice.

Intermittent Reinforcement Reinforcement for some but not all responses.

Internalization Transforming information acquired from the social environment into mechanisms of self-regulating control.

Internet International collection of computer networks.

Interval Schedule Reinforcement is contingent on the first response being made after a specific time period.

Interview Situation in which interviewer presents questions or points to discuss and respondent answers orally.

Intrinsic Cognitive Load The demands placed on the information processing system (especially on working memory) by the unalterable properties of the knowledge to be acquired.

Intrinsic Motivation Engaging in a task for no obvious reward except for the activity itself (the activity is the means and the end).

Introspection Type of self-analysis in which individuals verbally report their immediate perceptions following exposure to objects or events.

Irreversibility The cognitive belief that once something is done it cannot be changed.

Keyword Method Mnemonic technique in which one generates an image of a word sounding like the item to be learned and links that image with the meaning of the item to be learned.

Laboratory Research Study conducted in a controlled setting.

Lateralization See *Localization*.

Law of Disuse That part of the Law of Exercise postulating that the strength of a connection between a situation and response is decreased when the connection is not made over a period of time.

Law of Effect The strength of a connection is influenced by the consequences of performing the response in the situation: Satisfying consequences strengthen a connection; annoying consequences weaken a connection. Eventually modified by Thorndike to state that annoying consequences do not weaken connections.

Law of Exercise Learning (unlearning) occurs through repetition (nonrepetition) of a response. Eventually discarded by Thorndike.

Law of Readiness When an organism is prepared to act, to do so is satisfying and not to do so is annoying. When an organism is not prepared to act, forcing it to act is annoying.

Law of Use That part of the Law of Exercise postulating that the strength of a connection between a situation

and response is increased when the connection is made.

Learned Helplessness Psychological state involving a disturbance in motivation, cognition, and emotions due to previously experienced uncontrollability (lack of contingency between action and outcome).

Learned Optimism Explanatory style that views negative events as temporary, not one's fault, and specific to the event.

Learning An enduring change in behavior or in the capacity to behave in a given fashion resulting from practice or other forms of experience.

Learning Analytics Process of using learner-generated data and analysis models to discover how students learn and connect with one another for the purpose of predicting future learning.

Learning Goal A goal of acquiring knowledge, behaviors, skills, or strategies.

Learning Hierarchy Organized set of intellectual skills.

Learning Method Specific procedure or technique included in a learning strategy and used to attain a learning goal.

Learning Strategy Systematic plan oriented toward regulating academic work and producing successful task performance.

Learning Style Stable individual variations in perceiving, organizing, processing, and remembering information.

Levels (Depth) of Processing Conceptualization of memory according to the type of processing that information receives rather than the processing's location.

Linear Program Programmed instructional materials that all students complete in the same sequence.

Literal Transfer Transfer of intact skills to new contexts.

Localization Control of specific functions by different sides of the brain or in different areas of the brain.

Locus of Control Motivational concept referring to generalized control over outcomes; individuals may believe that outcomes occur independently of how they act (external control) or are highly contingent on their actions (internal control).

Long-Term Memory (LTM) Stage of information processing corresponding to the permanent repository of knowledge.

Low-Road Transfer Transfer of well-established skills spontaneously.

Magnetic Resonance Imaging (MRI) Magnetic resonance imaging; technology in which radio waves cause the brain to produce signals that are mapped, which can detect tumors, lesions, and other abnormalities.

Mapping Learning technique in which one identifies important ideas and specifies how they are related.

Massed Practice Study trials close together in time.

Mastery Learning A systematic instructional plan that has as its objective students demonstrating high achievement and that includes the components of defining mastery, planning for mastery, teaching for mastery, and grading for mastery.

Mastery Model   Model who demonstrates faultless performance and high self-confidence throughout the modeled sequence.

Mastery Motivation   See *Effectance Motivation*.

Matched-Dependent Behavior   Behavior matched to (the same as) that of the model and dependent on (elicited by) the model's action.

Meaningful Reception Learning   Learning of ideas, concepts, and principles when material is presented in final form and related to students' prior knowledge.

Means–Ends Analysis   Problem-solving strategy in which one compares the current situation with the goal to identify the differences between them, sets a subgoal to reduce one of the differences, performs operations to reach the subgoal, and repeats the process until the goal is attained.

Mediation   Mechanism that bridges the link between external reality and mental processes and affects the development of the latter.

Mental Discipline   The doctrine that learning certain subjects in school enhances mental functioning better than does studying other subjects.

Mental Imagery   See *Visual Memory*.

Mentoring   Situation involving the teaching of skills and strategies to students or other professionals within advising and training contexts.

Metacognition   Deliberate conscious control of one's cognitive activities.

Method of Loci   Mnemonic technique in which information to be remembered is paired with locations in a familiar setting.

Mimesis   See *Imitation*.

Min Model   Counting method in which one begins with the larger addend and counts in the smaller one.

Mindset   Set of beliefs about the individual's capability to change intelligence and abilities.

Mnemonic   A type of learning method that makes to-be-learned material meaningful by relating it to information that one already knows.

Modeling   Behavioral, cognitive, and affective changes deriving from observing one or more models.

Molar Behavior   A large sequence of behavior that is goal-directed.

Mood   A diffuse general feeling that often has no specific antecedent.

Motivated Learning   Motivation to acquire new knowledge, skills, and strategies, rather than merely to complete activities.

Motivation   The process of instigating and sustaining goal-directed activities.

Motivational State   A complex neural connection that includes emotions, cognitions, and behaviors.

Movement   Discrete behavior that results from muscle contractions.

Multidimensional Classroom   Classroom having many activities and allowing for diversity in student abilities.

Multimedia   Technology that combines the capabilities of computers with other media such as film, video, sound, music, and text.

Multitasking   Process of aligning attention with various sources of sensory input.

Myelin Sheath   Brain tissue surrounding an axon and facilitating travel of signals.

Naïve Analysis of Action   The way that common people interpret events.

Narration   Written account of behavior and the context in which it occurs.

Near-Infrared Optical Topography   Noninvasive technique for investigating higher-order brain functions in which near-infrared light is radiated on and penetrates the scalp, then is reflected by the cortex and passes back through the scalp.

Near Transfer   Transfer between overlapping situations.

Negative Reinforcer   A stimulus that, when removed by a response, increases the future likelihood of the response occurring in that situation.

Negative Transfer   Prior learning that makes subsequent learning more difficult.

Network   A set of interrelated propositions in long-term memory.

Networking   Computers in various locations connected to one another and to central peripheral devices.

Neural Assemblies   Collections of neurons synoptically connected with one another.

Neuron   Brain cell that sends and receives information across muscles and organs.

Neuroplasticity   See *Plasticity*.

Neuroscience   Science of the relation of the nervous system to learning and behavior.

Neuroscience of Learning   See *Neuroscience*.

Neurotransmitter   Chemical secretions that travel along a brain axon to dendrites of the next cell.

NIR-OT   See *Near-Infrared Optical Topography*.

Nonsense Syllable   Three-letter (consonant-vowel-consonant) combination that makes a nonword.

Novice   A person who has some familiarity with a domain but performs poorly.

Novice-to-Expert Methodology   Means of analyzing learning by comparing behaviors and reported thoughts of skilled individuals (experts) with those of less-skilled persons (novices) and deciding on an efficient means of moving novices to the expert level.

Observational Learning   Display of a new pattern of behavior by one who observes a model; prior to the modeling, the behavior has a zero probability of occurrence by the observer even with motivational inducements in effect.

Occipital Lobe   Brain lobe primarily concerned with processing visual information.

Online Social Media   Internet tools used to collaborate, communicate, and distribute information.

Operant Behavior   Behavior that produces an effect on the environment.

Operant Conditioning   Presenting reinforcement contingent on a response emitted in the presence of a stimulus to increase the rate or likelihood of occurrence of the response.

Operational Definition Definition of a phenomenon in terms of the operations or procedures used to measure it.

Oral Responses Verbalized questions or answers to questions.

Outcome Expectation Belief concerning the anticipated outcome of actions.

Overjustification Decrease in intrinsic interest (motivation) in an activity subsequent to engaging in it under conditions that make task engagement salient as a means to some end (e.g., reward).

Paired-Associate Recall Recalling the response of a stimulus–response item when presented with the stimulus.

Paradigm Model for research.

Parietal Lobe Brain lobe responsible for the sense of touch; helps determine body position and integrates visual information.

Parsing Mentally dividing perceived sound patterns into units of meaning.

Participant Modeling Therapeutic treatment (used by Bandura) comprising modeled demonstrations, joint performance between client and therapist, gradual withdrawal of performance aids, and individual mastery performance by the client.

Pattern Recognition See *Perception*.

Peer Collaboration Learning that occurs when students work together and their social interactions serve an instructional function.

Peer Network Large group of peers with whom students associate.

Peer Tutoring Situation in which a student who has learned a skill teaches it to one who has not.

Pegword Method Mnemonic technique in which the learner memorizes a set of objects rhyming with integer names (e.g., one is a bun, two is a shoe, etc.), generates an image of each item to be learned, and links it with the corresponding object image. During recall, the learner recalls the rhyming scheme with its associated links.

Perceived Control Belief that one can influence task engagement and outcomes.

Perceived Self-Efficacy See *Self-Efficacy*.

Perception Process of recognizing and assigning meaning to a sensory input.

Performance Goal A goal of completing a task.

PET Scan Positive emission tomography scan; assesses gamma rays produced by mental activity and provides overall picture of brain activity.

Phase Sequence In Hebb's theory, a series of cell assemblies.

Phi Phenomenon Perceptual phenomenon of apparent motion caused by lights flashing on and off at short intervals.

Phonemes The smallest unit of a speech sound.

Plasticity Capability of the brain to change its structure and function as a result of experience.

Positive Behavior Supports Components of a system designed to identify and remediate problem behaviors.

Positive Regard Feelings such as respect, liking, warmth, sympathy, and acceptance.

Positive Reinforcer A stimulus that, when presented following a response, increases the future likelihood of the response occurring in that situation.

Positive Self-Regard Positive regard that derives from self-experiences.

Positive Transfer Prior learning that facilitates subsequent learning.

Postdecisional Processes Cognitive activities engaged in subsequent to goal setting.

Predecisional Processes Cognitive activities involved in making decisions and setting goals.

Prefrontal Cortex Front part of the frontal lobe of the brain.

Premack Principle A principle stating that the opportunity to engage in a more-valued activity reinforces engaging in a less-valued activity.

Preoperational Stage Second of Piaget's stages of cognitive development, encompassing roughly ages 2 to 7.

Primacy Effect Tendency to recall the initial items in a list.

Primary Motor Cortex Area of the brain that controls bodily movements.

Primary Reinforcement Behavioral consequence that satisfies a biological need.

Primary Signals Environmental events that can become conditioned stimuli and produce conditioned responses.

Private Events Thoughts or feelings accessible only to the individual.

Private Speech The set of speech phenomena that has a self-regulatory function but is not socially communicative.

Proactive Interference Old learning makes new learning more difficult.

Problem A situation in which one is trying to reach a goal and must find a means of attaining it.

Problem Solving One's efforts to achieve a goal for which one does not have an automatic solution.

Problem Space The problem-solving context that comprises a beginning state, a goal state, and possible solution paths leading through subgoals and requiring application of operations.

Procedural Knowledge Knowledge of how to do something: employ algorithms and rules, identify concepts, solve problems.

Process–Product Research Study that relates changes in teaching processes to student products or outcomes.

Production Translating visual and symbolic conceptions of events into behaviors.

Production Deficiency The failure to generate task-relevant verbalizations when they could improve performance.

Production System (Production) Memory network of condition–action sequences (rules), where the condition is the set of circumstances that activates the system and the action is the set of activities that occurs.

Productive Thinking   See *Problem Solving.*

Programmed Instruction (PI)   Instructional materials developed in accordance with behavioral learning principles.

Proposition   The smallest unit of information that can be judged true or false.

Propositional Network   Interconnected associative structure in long-term memory comprising nodes or bits of information.

Prototype   Abstract form stored in memory that contains the basic ingredients of a stimulus and is compared with an environmental input during perception.

Punishment   Withdrawal of a positive reinforcer, or presentation of a negative reinforcer contingent on a response, which decreases the future likelihood of the response being made in the presence of the stimulus.

Purposive Behaviorism   Descriptive term for Tolman's theory emphasizing the study of large sequences of (molar) goal-directed behaviors.

Qualitative Research   Study characterized by depth and quality of analysis and interpretation of data through the use of methods such as classroom observations, use of existing records, interviews, and think-aloud protocols.

Questionnaire   Situation in which respondents are presented with items or questions asking about their thoughts and actions.

Ratings by Others   Evaluations of students on quality or quantity of performance.

Ratio Schedule   A schedule where reinforcement is contingent on the number of responses.

Rationalism   The doctrine that knowledge derives from reason without the aid of the senses.

Readiness   What children are capable of doing or learning at various points in development.

Reasoning   Mental processes involved in generating and evaluating logical arguments.

Recency Effect   Tendency to recall the last items in a list.

Reciprocal Teaching   Interactive dialogue between teacher and students in which teacher initially models activities, after which teacher and students take turns being the teacher.

Reflective Teaching   Thoughtful teacher decision making that takes into account knowledge about students, the context, psychological processes, learning and motivation, and self-knowledge.

Rehearsal   Repeating information to oneself aloud or subvocally.

Reinforcement   Any stimulus or event that leads to response strengthening.

Reinforcement History   Extent that an individual has been reinforced previously for performing the same or similar behavior.

Reinforcement Theory   See *Behavior Theory.*

Reinforcing Stimulus   The stimulus in the operant model of conditioning that is presented contingent on a response and increases the probability of the response being emitted in the future in the presence of the discriminative stimulus.

Relearning   Learning material for the second or subsequent time after it previously had been learned.

Research   Systematic investigation designed to develop or contribute to generalizable knowledge.

Respondent Behavior   Response made to an eliciting stimulus.

Response Facilitation   Previously learned behaviors of observers are prompted by the actions of models.

Response Tempo   See *Cognitive (Response) Tempo.*

Restructuring   Process of forming new schemata.

Retention   Storage of information in memory.

Reticular Formation   Part of the brain that handles autonomic nervous systems functions, controls sensory inputs, and is involved in awareness.

Retrieval-Induced Forgetting   Forgetting of some knowledge due to retrieval of other knowledge.

Retroactive Interference   New learning makes recall of old knowledge and skills more difficult.

Reversibility   Cognitive ability to sequence operations in opposite order.

Satiation   Fulfillment of reinforcement that results in decreased responding.

Savings Score   Time or trials necessary for relearning as a percentage of time or trials required for original learning.

Scaffolding   Process of controlling task elements that are beyond the learner's capabilities so that the learner can focus on and master those task features that he or she can grasp quickly.

Schedule of Reinforcement   When reinforcement is applied.

Schema   A cognitive structure that organizes large amounts of information into a meaningful system.

School Development Program   System of community and parental involvement in schools; stresses consensus, collaboration, and no-fault.

Script   A mental representation of an often-repeated event.

Second Signal System   Words and other features of language that are used by humans to communicate and that can become conditioned stimuli.

Secondary Reinforcement   Process whereby a behavioral consequence (e.g., money) becomes reinforcing by being paired with a primary reinforcer (e.g., food).

Self-Actualization   The desire for self-fulfillment or for becoming everything one is capable of becoming; the highest level in Maslow's hierarchy of needs.

Self-Concept   One's collective self-perceptions that are formed through experiences with, and interpretations of, the environment and that are heavily influenced by reinforcements and evaluations by significant other persons.

Self-Confidence   The extent that one believes one can produce results, accomplish goals, or perform tasks competently (analogous to *Self-Efficacy*).

Self-Determination   Motive aimed at developing competence, which begins as undifferentiated but eventually differentiates into specific areas.

Self-Efficacy (Efficacy Expectations)   Personal beliefs concerning one's capabilities to organize and implement actions necessary to learn or perform behaviors at designated levels.

Self-Esteem One's perceived sense of self-worth; whether one accepts and respects oneself.

Self-Evaluation Process involving self-judgments of current performance by comparing it to one's goal and self-reactions to these judgments by deeming performance noteworthy, unacceptable, and so forth.

Self-Evaluative Standards Standards people use to evaluate their performances.

Self-Instruction In a learning setting, discriminative stimuli that are produced by the individual and that set the occasion for responses leading to reinforcement.

Self-Instructional Training Instructional procedure that comprises cognitive modeling, overt guidance, overt self-guidance, faded overt self-guidance, and covert self-instruction.

Self-Judgment Comparing one's current performance level with one's goal.

Self-Modeling Changes in behaviors, thoughts, and affects that derive from observing one's own performances.

Self-Monitoring(-Observation,-Recording) Deliberate attention to some aspect of one's behavior, often accompanied by recording its frequency or intensity.

Self-Reaction Changes in one's beliefs and behaviors after judging performance against a goal.

Self-Regulation (Self-Regulated Learning) The process whereby students personally activate and sustain behaviors, cognitions, and affects that are systematically oriented toward the attainment of learning goals.

Self-Reinforcement The process whereby individuals, after performing a response, arrange to receive reinforcement that increases the likelihood of future responding.

Self-Reports People's judgments and statements about themselves.

Self-Schema Manifestation of enduring goals, aspirations, motives, and fears, which includes cognitive and affective evaluations of ability, volition, and personal agency.

Self-Worth Perceptions of one's value, grounded largely in beliefs about ability.

Semantic Memory Memory of general information and concepts available in the environment and not tied to a particular individual or context.

Sense Making Determining whether task goals have been accomplished based on coordination of prior knowledge with information about the environment and task.

Sensitive Period Time period when a type of development proceeds well.

Sensorimotor Stage First of Piaget's stages of cognitive development, encompassing birth to roughly age 2.

Sensory Register State of information processing concerned with receiving inputs, holding them briefly in sensory form, and transferring them to working memory.

Serial Recall Recalling stimuli in the order in which they are presented.

Shaping Differential reinforcement of successive approximations to the desired rate or form of behavior.

Short-Term Memory (STM) See *Working Memory*.

Simulation Real or imaginary situation that cannot be brought into a learning setting.

Situated Cognition (Learning) Idea that thinking is situated (located) in physical and social contexts.

Social Cognitive Theory Cognitive theory that emphasizes the role of the social environment in learning.

Social Comparison Process of comparing one's beliefs and behaviors with those of others.

Social Constructivism Constructivist perspective emphasizing the importance of social interactions and sociocultural factors.

Socially Mediated Learning Learning influenced by aspects of the sociocultural environment.

Socioeconomic Status (SES) Descriptive term denoting one's capital (resources, assets).

Specific Skill Skill applying only to certain domains (e.g., regrouping in subtraction).

Speech Act Speaker's purpose in uttering a communication.

Spinal Cord That part of the central nervous system that connects the brain to the rest of the body.

Spiral Curriculum Building on prior knowledge by presenting the same topics at increasing levels of complexity as students move through schooling.

Spontaneous Recovery Sudden recurrence of the conditioned response following presentation of the conditioned stimulus after a time lapse in which the conditioned stimulus is not presented.

Spreading Activation Activation in long-term memory of propositions that are associatively linked with material currently in one's working memory.

SQ4R Method Reading comprehension method emphasizing the following steps: survey, question, read, recite, relate, review.

Steroid A type of hormone that can affect various functions including sexual development and stress reactions.

Stimulated Recall Research procedure in which people work on a task and afterward recall their thoughts at various points; the procedure may include videotaping.

Stimulus–Response (S–R) Theory Learning theory emphasizing associations between stimuli and responses.

Strategy Value Information Information linking strategy use with improved performance.

Structuralism Doctrine postulating that the mind is composed of associations of ideas and that studying the complexities of the mind requires breaking associations into single ideas.

Successive Approximations See *Shaping*.

Sum Model Counting method in which one counts in the first addend and then the second one.

Suppression Process of decreasing a response but not eliminating it.

Surface Structure The speech and syntax of a language.

Syllogism Deductive reasoning problem that includes premises and a conclusion containing *all, no,* or *some.*

Symbolic Representation Representing knowledge with symbol systems (e.g., language, mathematical notation).

Synapse Point where axons and dendrites meet in the brain.

Synaptic Gap Space between axons and dendrites into which neurotransmitters are released.

Synchronous Learning Real-time interactions.

Systematic Desensitization Therapeutic procedure used to extinguish fears by pairing threatening stimuli with cues for relaxation.

Tabula Rasa Native state of a learner (blank tablet).

TARGET Acronym representing classroom motivation variables: task, authority, recognition, grouping, evaluation, time.

Task Involvement Motivational state characterized by viewing learning as a goal and focusing on task demands rather than on oneself.

Technology The designs and environments that engage learners.

Template Matching Theory of perception postulating that people store templates (miniature copies of stimuli) in memory and compare these templates with environmental stimuli during perception.

Temporal Lobe Brain lobe responsible for processing auditory information.

Teratogen A foreign substance that can cause abnormalities in a developing embryo or fetus.

Testing Effect Positive effect on learning and retention that occurs from previously taking tests or quizzes.

Thalamus Part of the brain that sends sensory inputs (except for smell) to the cortex.

Theory Scientifically acceptable set of principles offered to explain a phenomenon.

Think-Aloud Research procedure in which participants verbalize aloud their thoughts, actions, and feelings while performing a task.

Three-Term Contingency The basic operant model of conditioning: A discriminative stimulus sets the occasion for a response to be emitted, which is followed by a reinforcing stimulus.

Threshold Method of Behavioral Change Altering behavior by introducing the cue for the undesired response at a low level and gradually increasing its magnitude until it is presented at full strength.

Time Needed for Learning Amount of academically engaged time required by a student to learn a task.

Time Out (From Reinforcement) Removal of an individual from a situation where reinforcement can be obtained.

Time-Sampling Measure Measure of how often a behavior occurs during an interval of a longer period.

Time Spent in Learning Amount of academically engaged time expended to learn.

Tools The objects, language, and social institutions of a culture.

Top-Down Processing Pattern recognition of stimuli that occurs by forming a meaningful representation of the context, developing expectations of what will occur, and comparing features of stimuli to expectations to confirm or disconfirm one's expectations.

Trace Decay Loss of a stimulus from the sensory register over time.

Transfer (Generalization) Application of skills or knowledge in new ways or situations.

Translation Aspect of writing involving putting one's ideas into print.

Triadic Reciprocality Reciprocal interactions (causal relations) among behaviors, environmental variables, and cognitions and other personal factors.

Trial and Error Learning by performing a response and experiencing the consequences.

Tuning Modification and refinement of schemata as they are used in various contexts.

Tutoring A situation in which one or more persons serve as the instructional agents for another, usually in a specific subject or for a particular purpose.

Two-Store (Dual) Memory Model of Information Processing Conceptualization of memory as involving stages of processing and having two primary areas for storing information (short- and long-term memory).

Type R Behavior See *Operant Behavior.*

Type S Behavior See *Respondent Behavior.*

Unconditional Positive Regard Attitudes of worthiness and acceptance with no conditions attached.

Unconditioned Response (UCR) The response elicited by an unconditioned stimulus.

Unconditioned Stimulus (UCS) A stimulus that when presented elicits a natural response from the organism.

Undifferentiated Task Structure Class situation in which all students work on the same or similar tasks and instruction uses a small number of materials or methods.

Unidimensional Classroom Classroom having few activities that address a limited range of student abilities.

Unitary Theory Theory postulating that all information is represented in long-term memory in verbal codes.

Unlearning See *Forgetting.*

Utilization The use made of parsed sound patterns (e.g., store in memory, respond if a question, or seek additional information).

Utilization Deficiency Failure to use a strategy of which one is cognitively aware.

Value The perceived importance or usefulness of learning.

Value-Added Assessment Model An assessment model that attempts to determine the causes of students' learning progress.

Verbal Behavior Vocal responses shaped and maintained by the actions of other persons.

Vicarious Learning Learning that occurs without overt performance, such as by observing live or symbolic models.

Video Deficit Poorer learning by young children from video compared with real-life experiences.

Virtual Reality Computer-based technology that incorporates input and output devices and that allows students to experience and interact with an artificial environment as if it were the real world.

Visual Cortex   Occipital lobe of the brain.

Visual Imagery   See *Visual Memory*.

Visual Memory   Mental representation of visual/spatial knowledge.

Visualization   A nonverbal symbolic or pictorial illustration such as a graph, realistic diagram, or picture.

Volition   The act of using the will; the process of dealing with the implementation of actions to attain goals.

Volitional Style   Stable individual differences in volition.

Wernicke's Area   Brain part in the left hemisphere that is involved in speech comprehension and use of proper syntax when speaking.

Will   That part of the mind that reflects one's desire, want, or purpose.

Worked Example   Step-by-step problem solution that may include diagrams.

Worked-Example Effect   The advantage on learning and transfer from studying worked examples before solving problems compared with problem solving alone.

Working Backward   Problem-solving strategy in which one starts with the goal and asks which subgoals are necessary to accomplish it, what is necessary to accomplish these subgoals, and so forth, until the beginning state is reached.

Working Forward   Problem-solving strategy in which one starts with the beginning problem state and decides how to alter it to progress toward the goal.

Working Memory (WM)   Information processing stage corresponding to awareness, or what one is conscious of at a given moment.

Working Self-Concept   Those self-schemas that are mentally active at any time; currently accessible self-knowledge.

Written Responses   Performances on tests, quizzes, homework, term papers, reports, and computer documents.

X-Ray   High frequency electromagnetic waves used to determine abnormalities in solid body structures.

Zero Transfer   One type of learning has no obvious effect on subsequent learning.

Zone of Proximal Development (ZPD)   The amount of learning possible by a student given the proper instructional conditions.

References

Abrami, P. C., Bernard, R. M., Borokhovski, E., Waddington, D. I., Wade, C. A., & Persson, T. (2015). Strategies for teaching students to think critically: A meta-analysis. *Review of Educational Research, 85,* 275–314.

Abramson, L. Y., Seligman, M. E. P., & Teasdale, J. D. (1978). Learned helplessness in humans: Critique and reformulation. *Journal of Abnormal Psychology, 87,* 49–74.

Ach, N. (1910). *Uber den Willensakt und das Temperament* [On the will and the temperament.] Leipzig, Germany: Quelle & Meyer.

Adesope, O. O., & Nesbit, J. C. (2012). Verbal redundancy in multimedia learning environments: A meta-analysis. *Journal of Educational Psychology, 104,* 250–263.

Alderman, M. K. (1985). Achievement motivation and the preservice teacher. In M. K. Alderman & M. W. Cohen (Eds.), *Motivation theory and practice for preservice teachers* (pp. 37–51). Washington, DC: ERIC Clearinghouse on Teacher Education.

Alderman, M. K. (1999). *Motivation for achievement: Possibilities for teaching and learning.* Mahwah, NJ: Erlbaum.

Alderson-Day, B., & Fernyhough, C. (2015). Inner speech: Development, cognitive functions, phenomenology, and neurobiology. *Psychological Bulletin, 141,* 931–965.

Alexander, J. E., Carr, M., & Schwanenflugel, P. J. (1995). Development of metacognition in gifted children: Directions for future research. *Developmental Review, 15,* 1–37.

Alexander, P. A., & Murphy, P. K. (1998). Profiling the differences in students' knowledge, interest, and strategic planning. *Journal of Educational Psychology, 90,* 435–447.

Alexander, P. A., Schallert, D. L., & Reynolds, R. E. (2009). What is learning anyway? A topographical perspective considered. *Educational Psychologist, 44,* 176–192.

Alfieri, L., Brooks, P. J., Aldrich, N. J., & Tenenbaum, H. R. (2011). Does discovery-based instruction enhance learning? *Journal of Educational Psychology, 103, 1–18.*

Altermatt, E. R., & Pomerantz, E. M. (2003). The development of competence-related and motivational beliefs: An investigation of similarity and influence among friends. *Journal of Educational Psychology, 95,* 1–13.

American Educational Research Association (2007). Time to learn. *Research Points: Essential Information for Education Policy, 5(2),* 1–4.

American Educational Research Association (2015). AERA statement on use of value-added models (VAM) for the evaluation of educators and educator preparation programs. *Educational Researcher, 44,* 448–452.

American Psychological Association (1992). Special issue: Reflections on B. F. Skinner and psychology. *American Psychologist, 47,* 1269–1533.

American Psychological Association Work Group of the Board of Educational Affairs (1997). *Learner-centered psychological principles.* Washington, DC: Author.

Ames, C. (1984). Competitive, cooperative, and individualistic goal structures: A cognitive-motivational analysis. In R. Ames & C. Ames (Eds.), *Research on motivation in education* (Vol. 1, pp. 177–208). New York: Academic Press.

Ames, C. (1985). Attributions and cognitions in motivation theory. In M. K. Alderman & M. W. Cohen (Eds.), *Motivation theory and practice for preservice teachers* (pp. 16–21). Washington, DC: ERIC Clearinghouse on Teacher Education.

Ames, C. (1992a). Achievement goals and the classroom motivational climate. In D. H. Schunk & J. L. Meece (Eds.), *Student perceptions in the classroom* (pp. 327–348). Hillsdale, NJ: Erlbaum.

Ames, C. (1992b). Classrooms: Goals, structures, and student motivation. *Journal of Educational Psychology, 84,* 261–271.

Ames, C., & Archer, J. (1988). Achievement goals in the classroom: Student learning strategies and motivation processes. *Journal of Educational Psychology, 80,* 260–267.

Anand, P. G., & Ross, S. M. (1987). Using computer-assisted instruction to personalize arithmetic materials for elementary school children. *Journal of Educational Psychology, 79,* 72–78.

Anderman, E. M. (2002). School effects on psychological outcomes during adolescence. *Journal of Educational Psychology, 94,* 795–809.

Anderman, E. M., Anderman, L. H., Yough, M. S., & Gimbert, B. G. (2010). Value-added models of assessment: Implications for motivation and accountability. *Educational Psychologist, 45,* 123–137.

Anderman, E. M., Austin, C. C., & Johnson, D. M. (2002). The development of goal orientation. In A. Wigfield & J. S. Eccles (Eds.), *Development of achievement motivation* (pp. 197–220). San Diego: Academic Press.

Anderman, E. M., & Wolters, C. A. (2006). Goals, values, and affects: Influences on student motivation. In P. A. Alexander & P. H. Winne (Eds.), *Handbook of educational psychology* (2nd ed., pp. 369–389). Mahwah, NJ: Erlbaum.

Anderson, J. R. (1982). Acquisition of cognitive skill. *Psychological Review, 89,* 369–406.

Anderson, J. R. (1983). A spreading activation theory of memory. *Journal of Verbal Learning and Verbal Behavior, 22,* 261–295.

Anderson, J. R. (1984). Spreading activation. In J. R. Anderson & S. M. Kosslyn (Eds.), *Tutorials in learning and memory: Essays in honor of Gordon Bower* (pp. 61–90). San Francisco: Freeman.

Anderson, J. R. (1990). *Cognitive psychology and its implications* (3rd ed.). New York: Freeman.

Anderson, J. R. (1993). Problem solving and learning. *American Psychologist, 48,* 35–44.

Anderson, J. R. (1996). ACT: A simple theory of complex cognition. *American Psychologist, 51,* 355–365.

Anderson, J. R. (2000). *Learning and memory: An integrated approach* (2nd ed.). New York: Wiley.Ander

Anderson, J. R., Bothell, D., Byrne, M. D., Douglass, S., Lebiere, C., & Qin, Y. (2004). An integrated theory of the mind. *Psychological Review, 111,* 1036–1060.

Anderson, J. R., & Fincham, J. M. (2014). Extending problem-solving procedures through reflection. *Cognitive Psychology, 74,* 1–34.

Anderson, J. R., Fincham, J. M., & Douglass, S. (1997). The role of examples and rules in the acquisition of a cognitive skill. *Journal of Experimental Psychology: Learning, Memory, and Cognition, 23,* 932–945.

Anderson, J. R., Reder, L. M., & Lebiere, C. (1996). Working memory: Activation limitations on retrieval. *Cognitive Psychology*, 30, 221–256.

Anderson, J. R., Reder, L. M., & Simon, H. A. (1996). Situated learning and education. *Educational Researcher*, 25(4), 5–11.

Anderson, J. R., Zhang, Q., Borst, J. P., & Walsh, M. M. (2016). The discovery of processing stages: Extension of Sternberg's method. *Psychological Review*, 123, 481–509.

Anderson, L. W. (1976). An empirical investigation of individual differences in time to learn. *Journal of Educational Psychology*, 68, 226–233.

Anderson, L. W. (2003). Benjamin S. Bloom: His life, his works, and his legacy. In B. J. Zimmerman & D. H. Schunk (Eds.), *Educational psychology: A century of contributions* (pp. 367–389). Mahwah, NJ: Erlbaum.

Anderson, R. C. (1982). Allocation of attention during reading. In A. Flammer & W. Kintsch (Eds.), *Discourse processing* (pp. 292–305). Amsterdam: North Holland Publishing Company.

Anderson, R. C., & Pichert, J. W. (1978). Recall of previously unrecallable information following a shift in perspective. *Journal of Verbal Learning and Verbal Behavior*, 17, 1–12.

Anderson, R. C., Reynolds, R. E., Schallert, D. L., & Goetz, T. E. (1977). Frameworks for comprehending discourse. *American Educational Research Journal*, 14, 367–381.

Andersson, U., & Lyxell, B. (2007). Working memory deficit in children with mathematical difficulties: A general or specific deficit? *Journal of Experimental Child Psychology*, 96, 197–228.

Andre, T. (1986). Problem solving and education. In G. D. Phye & T. Andre (Eds.), *Cognitive classroom learning: Understanding, thinking, and problem solving* (pp. 169–204). Orlando: Academic Press.

Antonenko, P., Paas, F., Grabner, R., & van Gog, T. (2010). Using electroencephalography to measure cognitive load. *Educational Psychology Review*, 22, 425–438.

Archer, A. L., & Hughes, C. A. (2011). *Explicit instruction: Effective and efficient teaching*. New York: Guilford Press.

Armstrong, D. G., & Savage, T. V. (2002). *Teaching in the secondary school: An introduction* (5th ed.). Upper Saddle River, NJ: Merrill/Prentice Hall.

Asher, J. W. (2003). The rise to prominence: Educational psychology 1920–1960. In B. J. Zimmerman & D. H. Schunk (Eds.), *Educational psychology: A century of contributions* (pp. 189–205). Mahwah, NJ: Erlbaum.

Ashton, P. T., & Webb, R. B. (1986). *Making a difference: Teachers' sense of efficacy and student achievement*. New York: Longman.

Assor, A., & Connell, J. P. (1992). The validity of students' self-reports as measures of performance affecting self-appraisals. In D. H. Schunk & J. L. Meece (Eds.), *Student perceptions in the classroom* (pp. 25–47). Hillsdale, NJ: Erlbaum.

Atkinson, J. W. (1957). Motivational determinants of risk-taking behavior. *Psychological Review*, 64, 359–372.

Atkinson, J. W., & Birch, D. (1978). *Introduction to motivation* (2nd ed.). New York: D. Van Nostrand.

Atkinson, J. W., & Feather, N. T. (1966). *A theory of achievement motivation*. New York: Wiley.

Atkinson, J. W., & Raynor, J. O. (1974). *Motivation and achievement*. Washington, DC: Hemisphere.

Atkinson, J. W., & Raynor, J. O. (1978). *Personality, motivation, and achievement*. Washington, DC: Hemisphere.

Atkinson, R. C. (1975). Mnemotechnics in second-language learning. *American Psychologist*, 30, 828–921.

Atkinson, R. C., & Raugh, M. R. (1975). An application of the mnemonic keyword method to the acquisition of a Russian vocabulary. *Journal of Experimental Psychology: Human Learning and Memory*, 104, 126–133.

Atkinson, R. C., & Shiffrin, R. M. (1968). Human memory: A proposed system and its control processes. In K. W. Spence & J. T. Spence (Eds.), *The psychology of learning and motivation: Advances in research and theory* (Vol. 2, pp. 89–195). New York: Academic Press.

Atkinson, R. C., & Shiffrin, R. M. (1971). The control of short-term memory. *Scientific American*, 225, 82–90.

Atkinson, R. K., Derry, S. J., Renkl, A., & Wortham, D. (2000). Learning from examples: Instructional principles from the worked examples research. *Review of Educational Research*, 70, 181–214.

Atkinson, R. K., & Renkl, A. (2007). Interactive example-based learning environments: Using interactive elements to encourage effective processing of worked examples. *Educational Psychology Review*, 19, 375–386.

Atkinson, R. K., Renkl, A., & Merrill, M. M. (2003). Transitioning from studying examples to solving problems: Effects of self-explanation prompts and fading worked-out steps. *Journal of Educational Psychology*, 95, 774–783.

Austin, A. E. (2009). Cognitive apprenticeship theory and its implications for doctoral education: A case example from a doctoral program in higher and adult education. *International Journal for Academic Development*, 14, 173–183.

Austin, J. L. (1962). *How to do things with words*. Oxford, England: Oxford University Press.

Ausubel, D. P. (1963). *The psychology of meaningful verbal learning: An introduction to school learning*. New York: Grune & Stratton.

Ausubel, D. P. (1968). *Educational psychology: A cognitive view*. New York: Holt, Rinehart & Winston.

Ausubel, D. P. (1977). The facilitation of meaningful verbal learning in the classroom. *Educational Psychologist*, 12, 162–178.

Ausubel, D. P. (1978). In defense of advance organizers: A reply to the critics. *Review of Educational Research*, 48, 251–257.

Ausubel, D. P., & Robinson, F. G. (1969). *School learning: An introduction to educational psychology*. New York: Holt, Rinehart & Winston.

Azevedo, R. (2005a). Computer environments as metacognitive tools for enhancing learning. *Educational Psychologist*, 40, 193–197.

Azevedo, R. (2005b). Using hypermedia as a metacognitive tool for enhancing student learning? The role of self-regulated learning. *Educational Psychologist*, 40, 199–209.

Azevedo, R. (2009). Theoretical, conceptual, methodological, and instructional issues in research on metacognition and self-regulated learning: A discussion. *Metacognition & Learning*, 4, 87–95.

Azevedo, R., & Cromley, J. G. (2004). Does training on self-regulated learning facilitate students' learning with hypermedia? *Journal of Educational Psychology*, 96, 523–535.

Azevedo, R., Greene, J. A., & Moos, D. C. (2007). The effect of a human agent's external regulation upon college students' hypermedia learning. *Metacognition & Learning*, 2, 67–87.

Azevedo, R., Guthrie, J. T., & Seibert, D. (2004). The role of self-regulated learning in fostering students' conceptual understanding of complex systems with hypermedia. *Journal of Educational Computing Research*, 30, 85–109.

Azevedo, R., Moos, D. C., Johnson, A. M., & Chauncey, A. D. (2010). Measuring cognitive and metacognitive regulatory processes during hypermedia learning: Issues and challenges. *Educational Psychologist*, 45, 210–223.

Azevedo, R., Taub, M., & Mudrick, N. (2018). Understanding and reasoning about real-time cognitive, affective, and meta-cognitive processes to foster self-regulation with advanced learning technologies. In D. H. Schunk & J. A. Greene (Eds.), *Handbook of self-regulation of learning and performance* (2nd ed., pp. 254–270). New York: Routledge.

Baddeley, A. D. (1978). The trouble with levels: A reexamination of Craik and Lockhart's framework for memory research. *Psychological Review*, 85, 139–152.

Baddeley, A. D. (1992). Working memory. *Science*, 255, 556–559.

Baddeley, A. D. (1998). *Human memory: Theory and practice* (Rev. ed.). Boston: Allyn and Bacon.

Baddeley, A. D. (2001). Is working memory still working? *American Psychologist*, 56, 851–864.

BaBBaddeley, A. D. (2007). *Working memory: Thought and action*. Oxford, England: Oxford University Press.

Baddeley, A. D. (2012). Working memory: Theories, models, and controversies. *Annual Review of Psychology*, 63, 1–29.

Bailey, T. (1993). Can youth apprenticeship thrive in the United States? *Educational Researcher*, 22(3), 4–10.

Baker, L. (1989). Metacognition, comprehension monitoring, and the adult reader. *Educational Psychology Review*, 1, 3–38.

Baker, L., & Brown, A. L. (1984). Metacognitive skills and reading. In P. D. Pearson (Ed.), *Handbook of reading research* (pp. 353–394). New York: Longman.

Baker, S. K., Chard, D. J., Ketterlin-Geller, L. R., Apichatabutra, C., & Doabler, C. (2009). Teaching writing to at-risk students: The quality of evidence for self-regulated strategy development. *Exceptional Children*, 75, 303–318.

Balcetis, E., & Dunning, D. (2006). See what you want to see: Motivational influences on visual perception. *Journal of Personality and Social Psychology*, 91, 612–625.

Balfanz, R., Herzog, L., & Mac Iver, D. (2007). Preventing student disengagement and keeping students on the graduation path in urban middle-grades schools: Early identification and effective interventions. *Educational Psychologist*, 42, 223–235.

Ball, D. L., Lubienski, S. T., & Mewborn, D. S. (2001). Mathematics. In V. Richardson (Ed.), *Handbook of research on teaching* (4th ed., pp. 433–456). Washington, DC: American Educational Research Association.

Bandura, A. (1969). *Principles of behavior modification*. New York: Holt, Rinehart & Winston.

Bandura, A. (1973). *Aggression: A social learning analysis*. Englewood Cliffs, NJ: Prentice Hall.

Bandura, A. (1977a). Self-efficacy: Toward a unifying theory of behavioral change. *Psychological Review*, 84, 191–215.

Bandura, A. (1977b). *Social learning theory*. Englewood Cliffs, NJ: Prentice Hall.

Bandura, A. (1981). Self-referent thought: A developmental analysis of self-efficacy. In J. H. Flavell & L. Ross (Eds.), *Social cognitive development: Frontiers and possible futures* (pp. 200–239). Cambridge, England: Cambridge University Press.

Bandura, A. (1982a). The self and mechanisms of agency. In J. Suls (Ed.), *Psychological perspectives on the self* (Vol. 1, pp. 3–39). Hillsdale, NJ: Erlbaum.

Bandura, A. (1982b). Self-efficacy mechanism in human agency. *American Psychologist*, 37, 122–147.

Bandura, A. (1986). *Social foundations of thought and action: A social cognitive theory*. Englewood Cliffs, NJ: Prentice Hall.

Bandura, A. (1988). Self-regulation of motivation and action through goal systems. In V. Hamilton, G. H. Bower, & N. H. Frijda (Eds.), *Cognitive perspectives on emotion and motivation* (pp. 37–61). Dordrecht, The Netherlands: Kluwer Academic Publishers.

Bandura, A. (1991). Self-regulation of motivation through anticipatory and self-reactive mechanisms. In R. A. Dienstbier (Ed.), *Nebraska Symposium on Motivation*, 1990 (Vol. 38, 69–164). Lincoln, NE: University of Nebraska Press.

Bandura, A. (1993). Perceived self-efficacy in cognitive development and functioning. *Educational Psychologist*, 28, 117–148.

Bandura, A. (1994). Social cognitive theory and the exercise of control over HIV infection. In R. DiClemente & J. Peterson (Eds.), *Preventing AIDS: Theories and methods of behavioral interventions* (pp. 25–59). New York: Plenum.

Bandura, A. (1997). *Self-efficacy: The exercise of control*. New York: Freeman.

Bandura, A. (2001). Social cognitive theory: An agentic perspective. *Annual Review of Psychology*, 52, 1–26.

Bandura, A. (2005). The primacy of self-regulation in health promotion. *Applied Psychology: An International Review*, 54, 245–254.

Bandura, A. (2006). Toward a psychology of human agency. *Perspectives on Psychological Science*, 1, 164–180.

Bandura, A. (2016). *Moral disengagement: How people do harm and live with themselves*. New York: Worth Publishers.

Bandura, A., & Adams, N. E. (1977). Analysis of self-efficacy theory of behavioral change. *Cognitive Therapy and Research*, 1, 287–308.

Bandura, A., Adams, N. E., & Beyer, J. (1977). Cognitive processes mediating behavioral change. *Journal of Personality and Social Psychology*, 35, 125–139.

Bandura, A., Barbaranelli, C., Caprara, G. V., & Pastorelli, C. (1996). Multifaceted impact of self-efficacy beliefs on academic functioning. *Child Development*, 67, 1206–1222.

Bandura, A., Barbaranelli, C., Caprara, G. V., & Pastorelli, C. (2001). Self-efficacy beliefs as shapers of children's aspirations and career trajectories. *Child Development*, 72, 187–206.

Bandura, A., & Bussey, K. (2004). On broadening the cognitive, motivational, and sociostructural scope of theorizing about gender development and functioning: Comment on Martin, Ruble, and Szkrybalo (2002). *Psychological Bulletin*, 130, 691–701.

Bandura, A., & Cervone, D. (1983). Self-evaluative and self-efficacy mechanisms governing the motivational effects of goal systems. *Journal of Personality and Social Psychology*, 45, 1017–1028.

Bandura, A., & Cervone, D. (1986). Differential engagement of self-reactive influences in cognitive motivation. *Organizational Behavior and Human Decision Processes*, 38, 92–113.

Bandura, A., & Jeffery, R. W. (1973). Role of symbolic coding and rehearsal processes in observational learning. *Journal of Personality and Social Psychology*, 26, 122–130.

Bandura, A., Ross, D., & Ross, S. A. (1963). Imitation of film-mediated aggressive models. *Journal of Abnormal and Social Psychology*, 66, 3–11.

Bandura, A., & Schunk, D. H. (1981). Cultivating competence, self-efficacy, and intrinsic interest through proximal self-motivation. *Journal of Personality and Social Psychology*, 41, 586–598.

Bandura, A., & Walters, R. H. (1963). *Social learning and personality development*. New York: Holt, Rinehart & Winston.

Bangert, R. L., Kulik, J. A., & Kulik, C. C. (1983). Individualized systems of instruction in secondary schools. *Review of Educational Research*, 53, 143–158.

Bangert-Drowns, R. L., Hurley, M. M., & Wilkinson, B. (2004). The effects of school-based writing-to-learn interventions on academic achievement: A meta-analysis. *Review of Educational Research*, 74, 29–58.

Bargh, J. A., & Ferguson, M. J. (2000). Beyond behaviorism: On the automaticity of higher mental processes. *Psychological Bulletin*, 126, 925–945.

Barnett, S. M., & Ceci, S. J. (2002). When and where do we apply what we learn? A taxonomy for far transfer. *Psychological Bulletin*, 128, 612–637.

Barrouillet, P., Portrat, S., & Camos, V. (2011). On the law relating processing to storage in working memory. *Psychological Review*, 118, 175–192.

Bartlett, F. C. (1932). *Remembering: A study in experimental and social psychology*. Cambridge, England: Cambridge University Press.

Bartlett, T. (2012, February 10). The sad saga of "little Albert" gets far worse for a researcher's reputation. *The Chronicle of Higher Education*, 58(23), A26.

Barzilai, S., & Zohar, A. (2016). Epistemic (meta)cognition: Ways of thinking about knowledge and knowing. In J. A. Greene, W. A. Sandoval, & I. Bråten (Eds.), *Handbook of epistemic cognition* (pp. 409–424). New York: Routledge.

Basden, B. H., Basden, D. R., Devecchio, E., & Anders, J. A. (1991). A developmental comparison of the effectiveness of encoding tasks. *Genetic, Social, and General Psychology Monographs*, 117, 419–436.

Baumrind, D. (1989). Rearing competent children. In W. Damon (Ed.), *Child development today and tomorrow* (pp. 349–378). San Francisco: Jossey-Bass.

Beal, C. R., & Belgrad, S. L. (1990). The development of message evaluation skills in young children. *Child Development*, 61, 705–712.

Bear, G. G., & Manning, M. A. (2014). Positive psychology and school discipline. In M. J. Furlong, R. Gilman, & E. S. Huebner, (Eds.), *Handbook of positive psychology in schools* (2nd ed., pp. 347–364). New York: Routledge.Bear

Beaudoin, M., & Desrichard, O. (2011). Are memory self-efficacy and memory performance related? A meta-analysis. *Psychological Bulletin*, 137, 211–241.

Beaudoin, M., & Desrichard, O. (2011)Beck, H. P., Levinson, S., & Irons, G. (2009). Finding little Albert: A journey to John B. Watson's infant laboratory. *American Psychologist*, 64, 605–614.

Becker, W. C. (1971). *Parents are teachers: A child management program*. Champaign, IL: Research Press.

Belfiore, P. J., & Hornyak, R. S. (1998). Operant theory and application to self-monitoring in adolescents. In D. H. Schunk & B. J. Zimmerman (Eds.), *Self-regulated learning: From teaching to self-reflective practice* (pp. 184–202). New York: Guilford Press.

Bellini, S., & Akullian, J. (2007). A meta-analysis of video modeling and video self-modeling interventions for children and adolescents with autism spectrum disorders. *Exceptional Children*, 73, 264–287.

Belmont, J. M. (1989). Cognitive strategies and strategic learning: The socio-instructional approach. *American Psychologist*, 44, 142–148.

Bembenutty, H., Cleary, T. J., & Kitsantas, A. (Eds.) (2013). *Applications of self-regulated learning across diverse disciplines: A tribute to Barry J. Zimmerman*. Charlotte, NC: Information Age Publishing.

Benenson, J. F., Quinn, A., & Stella, S. (2012). Boys affiliate more than girls with a familiar same-sex peer. *Journal of Experimental Child Psychology*, 113, 587–593.

Benight, C. C., & Bandura, A. (2004). Social cognitive theory of posttraumatic recovery: The role of perceived self-efficacy. *Behaviour Research and Therapy*, 42, 1129–1148.

Benita, M., Roth, G., & Deci, E. L. (2014). When are mastery goals more adaptive? It depends on experiences of autonomy support and autonomy. *Journal of Educational Psychology*, 106, 258–267.Ben

Benjamin, L. T., Jr. (1988). A history of teaching machines. *American Psychologist*, 43, 703–712.

Benjamin, L. T., Jr. (2000). The psychological laboratory at the turn of the 20th century. *American Psychologist*, 55, 318–321.

Benjamin, L. T., Jr., Durkin, M., Link, M., Vestal, M., & Acord, J. (1992). Wundt's American doctoral students. *American Psychologist*, 47, 123–131.

Bereiter, C. (1994). Constructivism, socioculturalism, and Popper's World 3. *Educational Researcher*, 23(7), 21–23.

Berk, L. E. (1986). Relationship of elementary school children's private speech to behavioral accompaniment to task, attention, and task performance. *Developmental Psychology*, 22, 671–680.

Berlyne, D. E. (1963). Motivational problems raised by exploratory and epistemic behavior. In S. Koch (Ed.), *Psychology: A study of a science* (Vol. 5, pp. 284–364). New York: McGraw-Hill.

Bernard, R. M., Abrami, P. C., Borokhovski, E., Wade, C. A., Tamim, R. M., Surkes, M. A., & Bethel, E. C. (2009). A meta-analysis of three types of interaction treatments in distance education. *Review of Educational Research*, 79, 1243–1289.

Bernard, R. M., Abrami, P. C., Lou, Y., Borokhovski, E., Wade, A., Wozney, L., Wallet, P. A., Fiset, M., & Huang, B. (2004). How does distance education compare with classroom instruction? A meta-analysis of the empirical literature. *Review of Educational Research*, 74, 379–439.

Berndt, T. J., Hawkins, J. A., & Jiao, Z. (1999). Influences of friends on adjustment to junior high school. *Merrill-Palmer Quarterly*, 45, 13–41.

Berndt, T. J., & Keefe, K. (1992). Friends' influence on adolescents' perceptions of themselves at school. In D. H. Schunk & J. L. Meece (Eds.), *Student perceptions in the classroom* (pp. 51–73). Hillsdale, NJ: Erlbaum.

Berndt, T. J., & Keefe, K. (1996). Friends' influence on school adjustment: A motivational analysis. In J. Juvonen & K. R. Wentzel (Eds.), *Social motivation: Understanding children's school adjustment* (pp. 248–278). Cambridge, UK: Cambridge University Press.

Bernier, M., & Avard, J. (1986). Self-efficacy, outcome, and attrition in a weight-reduction program. *Cognitive Therapy and Research*, 10, 319–338.

Betz, N. E., & Hackett, G. (1981). The relationship of career-related self-efficacy expectations to perceived career options in college women and men. *Journal of Counseling Psychology*, 28, 399–410.

Betz, N. E., & Hackett, G. (1983). The relationship of mathematics self-efficacy expectations to the selection of science-based college majors. *Journal of Vocational Behavior*, 23, 329–345.

Bierman, K L., Domitrovich, C. E., Nix, R. L., Gest, S. D., Welsh, J. A., Greenberg, M. T., Blair, C., Nelson, K. E., & Gill, S. (2008). Promoting academic and social-emotional school readiness: The Head Start REDI Program. *Child Development*, 79, 1802–1817.

Binney, R., & Janson, M. (Eds.) (1990). *Atlas of the mind and body*. London: Mitchell Beazley Publishers.

Birch, S. H., & Ladd, G. W. (1996). Interpersonal relationships in the school environment and children's early school adjustment: The role of teachers and peers. In J. Juvonen & K. R. Wentzel (Eds.), *Social motivation: Understanding children's school adjustment* (pp. 199–225). Cambridge, UK: Cambridge University Press.

Biswas, G., Baker, R. S., & Paquette, L. (2018). Data mining methods for assessing self-regulated learning. In D. H. Schunk & J. A. Greene (Eds.), *Handbook of self-regulation of learning and performance* (2nd ed., pp. 388–403). New York: Routledge.

Black, J. B. (1984). Understanding and remembering stories. In J. R. Anderson & S. M. Kosslyn (Eds.), *Tutorials in learning and memory: Essays in honor of Gordon Bower* (pp. 235–255). San Francisco: Freeman.

Block, J. H., & Burns, R. B. (1977). Mastery learning. In L. S. Shulman (Ed.), *Review of research in education* (Vol. 4, pp. 3–49). Itasca, IL: Peacock.

Blok, H., Oostdam, R., Otter, M. E., & Overmaat, M. (2002). Computer-assisted instruction in support of beginning reading instruction: A review. *Review of Educational Research*, 72, 101–130.

Bloom, B. S. (1976). *Human characteristics and school learning*. New York: McGraw-Hill.

Bloom, B. S., Hastings, J. T., & Madaus, G. F. (1971). *Handbook on formative and summative evaluation of student learning*. New York: McGraw-Hill.

Blunt, J. R., & Karpicke, J. D. (2014). Learning with retrieval-based concept mapping. *Journal of Educational Psychology*, 106, 849–858.Bl

Bokosmaty, S., Sweller, J., & Kalyuga, S. (2015). Learning geometry problem solving by studying worked examples: Effects of learner guidance and expertise. *American Educational Research Journal*, 52, 307–333.

Boman, P., & Mergler, A. (2014). Optimism: What it is and its relevance in the school context. In M. J. Furlong, R. Gilman, & E. S. Huebner (Eds.), *Handbook of positive psychology in schools* (2nd ed., pp. 31–66). New York: Routledge.

Bong, M., & Clark, R. (1999). Comparisons between self-concept and self-efficacy in academic motivation research. *Educational Psychologist*, 34, 139–154.

Borkowski, J. G., & Cavanaugh, J. C. (1979). Maintenance and generalization of skills and strategies by the retarded. In N. R. Ellis (Ed.), *Handbook of mental deficiency, psychological theory and research* (2nd ed., pp. 569–617). Hillsdale, NJ: Erlbaum.

Borkowski, J. G., Johnston, M. B., & Reid, M. K. (1987). Metacognition, motivation, and controlled performance. In S. J. Ceci (Ed.), *Handbook of cognitive, social, and neuropsychological aspects of learning disabilities* (Vol. 2, pp. 147–173). Hillsdale, NJ: Erlbaum.

Borowsky, R., & Besner, D. (2006). Parallel distributed processing and lexical-semantic effects in visual word recognition: Are a few stages necessary? *Psychological Review*, 113, 181–195.

Botvinick, M., & Braver, T. (2015). Motivation and cognitive control: From behavior to neural mechanism. *Annual Review of Psychology*, 66, 83–113.

Bourne, L. E., Jr. (1992). Cognitive psychology: A brief overview. *Psychological Science Agenda*, 5(5), 5, 20.

Bouton, M. E., Nelson, J. B., & Rosas, J. M. (1999). Stimulus generalization, context change, and forgetting. *Psychological Bulletin*, 125, 171–186.

Bower, G. H., & Hilgard, E. R. (1981). *Theories of learning* (5th ed.). Englewood Cliffs, NJ: Prentice Hall.

Bower, G. H., & Morrow, D. G. (1990). Mental models in narrative comprehension. *Science*, 247, 44–48.

Bowers, J. S. (2009). On the biological plausibility of grandmother cells: Implications for neural network theories in psychology and neuroscience. *Psychological Review*, 116, 220–251.

Bowers, J. S. (2016). The practical and principled problems with educational neuroscience. *Psychological Review*, 123, 600–612.

Braaksma, M. A. H., Rijlaarsdam, G., & van den Bergh, H. (2002). Observational learning and the effects of model-observer similarity. *Journal of Educational Psychology*, 94, 405–415.

Bradley, R. H., & Corwyn, R. F. (2002). Socioeconomic status and child development. *Annual Review of Psychology*, 53, 371–399.

Brainerd, C. J. (2003). Jean Piaget, learning research, and American education. In B. J. Zimmerman & D. H. Schunk (Eds.), *Educational psychology: A century of contributions* (pp. 251–287). Mahwah, NJ: Erlbaum.

Bransford, J. D., & Johnson, M. K. (1972). Contextual prerequisites for understanding: Some investigations of comprehension and recall. *Journal of Verbal Learning and Verbal Behavior*, 11, 717–726.

Bransford, J. D., & Stein, B. S. (1984). *The IDEAL problem solver: A guide for improving thinking, learning, and creativity*. New York: Freeman.

Bredo, E. (1997). The social construction of learning. In G. Phye (Ed.), *Handbook of academic learning: The construction of knowledge* (pp. 3–45). New York: Academic Press.

Bredo, E. (2003). The development of Dewey's psychology. In B. J. Zimmerman & D. H. Schunk (Eds.), *Educational psychology: A century of contributions* (pp. 81–111). Mahwah, NJ: Erlbaum.

Bredo, E. (2006). Conceptual confusion and educational psychology. In P. A. Alexander & P. H. Winne (Eds.), *Handbook of educational psychology* (2nd ed., pp. 43–57). Mahwah, NJ: Erlbaum.

Bredo, E. (2016). Philosophical perspectives on mind, nature, and educational psychology. In L. Corno & E. M. Anderman (Eds.), *Handbook of educational psychology* (3rd ed., pp. 3–15). New York: Routledge.

Brewer, W. F. (1974). There is no convincing evidence for operant or classical conditioning in adult humans. In W. B. Weimer & D. S. Palermo (Eds.), *Cognition and the symbolic processes* (pp. 1–42). Hillsdale, NJ: Erlbaum.

Brewer, W. F., & Treyens, J. C. (1981). Role of schemata in memory for places. *Cognitive Psychology*, 13, 207–230.

Brigham, T. A. (1982). Self-management: A radical behavioral perspective. In P. Karoly & F. H. Kanfer (Eds.), *Self-management and behavior change: From theory to practice* (pp. 32–59). New York: Pergamon.

Britton, B. K., & Tesser, A. (1991). Effects of time-management practices on college grades. *Journal of Educational Psychology*, 83, 405–410.

Broadbent, D. E. (1958). *Perception and communication*. London: Pergamon.

Broadhurst, P. L. (1957). Emotionality and the Yerkes-Dodson Law. *Journal of Experimental Psychology*, 54, 345–352.

Brody, G. H., & Stoneman, Z. (1985). Peer imitation: An examination of status and competence hypotheses. *Journal of Genetic Psychology*, 146, 161–170.

Brodzinsky, D. M. (1982). Relationship between cognitive style and cognitive development: A 2-year longitudinal study. *Developmental Psychology*, 18, 617–626.

Bronfenbrenner, U. (1979). *The ecology of human development: Experiments by nature and design*. Cambridge, MA: Harvard University Press.

Brooks, J. G., & Brooks, M. G. (1999). *In search of understanding: The case for constructivist classrooms*. Alexandria, VA: Association for Supervision and Curriculum Development.

Brophy, J. E. (1981). Teacher praise: A functional analysis. *Review of Educational Research*, 51, 5–32.

Brophy, J. E., & Good, T. L. (1986). Teacher behavior and student achievement. In M. L. Wittrock (Ed.), *Handbook of research on teaching* (3rd ed., pp. 328–375). New York: Macmillan.

Brown, A. L. (1980). Metacognitive development and reading. In R. J. Spiro, B. C. Bruce, & W. F. Brewer (Eds.), *Theoretical issues in reading comprehension* (pp. 453–481). Hillsdale, NJ: Erlbaum.

Brown, A. L., & Campione, J. C. (1996). Psychological theory and the design of innovative learning environments: On procedures, principles, and systems. In L. Schauble & R. Glaser (Eds.), *Innovations in learning: New environments for education* (pp. 289–325). Hillsdale, NJ: Erlbaum.

Brown, A. L., Palincsar, A. S., & Armbruster, B. B. (1984). Instructing comprehension-fostering activities in interactive learning situations. In H. Mandl, N. L. Stein, & T. Trabasso (Eds.), *Learning and comprehension of text* (pp. 255–286). Hillsdale, NJ: Erlbaum.

Brown, G. D. A., Neath, I., & Chater, N. (2007). A temporal ratio model of memory. *Psychological Review*, 114, 539–576.

Brown, I., Jr., & Inouye, D. K. (1978). Learned helplessness through modeling: The role of perceived similarity in competence. *Journal of Personality and Social Psychology*, 36, 900–908.

Brown, J. (1968). Reciprocal facilitation and impairment of free recall. *Psychonomic Science*, 10, 41–42.

Brown, J. S. (2006, September/October). New learning environments for the 21st century: Exploring the edge. *Change*, 38, 18–24.

Brown, J. S., & Burton, R. R. (1978). Diagnostic models for procedural bugs in basic mathematical skills. *Cognitive Science*, 2, 155–192.

Brown, S. C., & Craik, F. I. M. (2000). Encoding and retrieval of information. In E. Tulving & F. I. M. Craik (Eds.), *The Oxford handbook of memory* (pp. 93–108). New York: Oxford University Press.

Bruner, J. S. (1960). *The process of education*. New York: Vintage.

Bruner, J. S. (1961). The act of discovery. *Harvard Educational Review*, 31, 21–32.

Bruner, J. S. (1964). The course of cognitive growth. *American Psychologist*, 19, 1–15.

Bruner, J. S. (1966). *Toward a theory of instruction*. New York: Norton.

Bruner, J. S. (1984). Vygotsky's zone of proximal development: The hidden agenda. In B. Rogoff & J. V. Wertsch (Eds.), *Children's learning in the "zone of proximal development"* (pp. 93–97). San Francisco: Jossey-Bass.

Bruner, J. S. (1985). Models of the learner. *Educational Researcher*, 14(6), 5–8.

Bruner, J. S., Goodnow, J., & Austin, G. A. (1956). *A study of thinking*. New York: Wiley.

Bruner, J. S., Olver, R. R., & Greenfield, P. M. (1966). *Studies in cognitive growth*. New York: Wiley.

Bruning, R. H., Dempsey, M., Kauffman, D. F., McKim, C., & Zumbrunn, S. (2013). Examining dimensions of self-efficacy for writing. *Journal of Educational Psychology*, 105, 25–38.

Bruning, R. H., & Horn, C. (2000). Developing motivation to write. *Educational Psychologist*, 35, 25–37.

Bruning, R. H., Schraw, G. J., & Norby, M. M. (2011). *Cognitive psychology and instruction* (5th ed.). Boston: Pearson Education.

Brunstein, J. C., & Glaser, C. (2011). Testing a path-analytic mediation model of how self-regulated writing strategies improve fourth graders' composition skills: A randomized controlled trial. *Journal of Educational Psychology*, 103, 922–938.

Brunton, M. (2007, January 29). What do babies know? *Time*, 169, 94–95.

Bryan, J. H., & Bryan, T. H. (1983). The social life of the learning disabled youngster. In J. D. McKinney & L. Feagans (Eds.), *Current topics in learning disabilities* (Vol. 1, pp. 57–85). Norwood, NJ: Ablex.

Bryce, D., & Whitebread, D. (2012). The development of metacognitive skills: Evidence from observational analysis of young children's behavior during problem-solving. *Metacognition and Learning*, 7, 197–217.Bryce

Bryk, A. S., Sebring, P. B., Allensworth, E., Luppescu, S., & Easton, J. Q. (2010). *Organizing schools for improvement: Lessons from Chicago*. Chicago: University of Chicago Press.

Burnette, J. L., O'Boyle, E. H., VanEpps, E. M., Pollack, J. M., & Finkel, E. J. (2013). Mind-sets matter: A meta-analytic review of implicit theories and self-regulation. *Psychological Bulletin*, 139, 655–701.

Butler, A. C., Godbole, N., & Marsh, E. J. (2013). Explanation feedback is better than correct answer feedback for promoting transfer of learning. *Journal of Educational Psychology*, 105, 290–298.

Butler, D. L. (1998a). The strategic content learning approach to promoting self-regulated learning: A report of three studies. *Journal of Educational Psychology*, 90, 682–697.

Butler, D. L. (1998b). A strategic content learning approach to promoting self-regulated learning by students with learning disabilities. In D. H. Schunk & B. J. Zimmerman (Eds.), *Self-regulated learning: From teaching to self-reflective practice* (pp. 160–183). New York: Guilford Press.

Butler, R. (1992). What young people want to know when: Effects of mastery and ability goals on interest in different kinds of social comparisons. *Journal of Personality and Social Psychology*, 62, 934–943.

Butler, R. (1998). Age trends in the use of social and temporal comparison for self-evaluation: Examination of a novel developmental hypothesis. *Child Development*, 69, 1054–1073.

Byrnes, J. P. (2001). *Minds, brains, and learning: Understanding the psychological and educational relevance of neuroscientific research*. New York: Guilford Press.

Byrnes, J. P. (2012). How neuroscience contributes to our understanding of learning and development in typically developing and special-needs students. In K. R. Harris, S. Graham & T. Urdan (Eds.), *APA educational psychology handbook. Vol. 1: Theories, constructs, and critical issues* (pp. 561–595). Washington, DC: American Psychological Association.

Byrnes, J. P., & Dunbar, K. N. (2014). The nature and development of critical-analytic thinking. *Educational Psychology Review, 26,* 477–493,

Byrnes, J. P., & Fox, N. A. (1998). The educational relevance of research in cognitive neuroscience. *Educational Psychology Review, 10,* 297–342.

Byron, K., & Khazanchi, S. (2012). Rewards and creative performance: A meta-analytic test of theoretically derived hypotheses. *Psychological Bulletin, 138,* 809–830.

Cairns, R. B., Cairns, B. D., & Neckerman, J. J. (1989). Early school dropout: Configurations and determinants. *Child Development, 60,* 1437–1452.

Calfee, R., & Drum, P. (1986). Research on teaching reading. In M. C. Wittrock (Ed.), *Handbook of research on teaching* (3rd ed., pp. 804–849). New York: Macmillan.

Cameron, J., & Pierce, W. D. (1994). Reinforcement, reward, and intrinsic motivation: A meta-analysis. *Review of Educational Research, 64,* 363–423.

Cameron, J., & Pierce, W. D. (2002). *Rewards and intrinsic motivation: Resolving the controversy.* Westport, CT: Bergin & Garvey.

Campbell, C. (2009). Middle years students' use of self-regulating strategies in an online journaling environment. *Educational Technology & Society, 12*(3), 98–106.

Campbell, F. A., Pungello, E. P., Miller-Johnson, S., Burchinal, M., & Ramey, C. T. (2001). The development of cognitive and academic abilities: Growth curves from an early childhood educational experiment. *Developmental Psychology, 37,* 231–242.

Campbell, G. (2006, September/October). Education, information technologies, and the augmentation of human intellect. *Change, 38,* 26–31.

Campione, J. C., Brown, A. L., Ferrara, R. A., & Bryant, N. R. (1984). The zone of proximal development: Implications for individual differences and learning. In B. Rogoff & J. V. Wertsch (Eds.), *Children's learning in the "zone of proximal development"* (pp. 77–91). San Francisco: Jossey-Bass.

Cantor, N., & Kihlstrom, J. F. (1987). *Personality and social intelligence.* Englewood Cliffs, NJ: Prentice Hall.

Cantrell, S. C., Almasi, J. F., Carter, J. C., Rintamaa, M., & Madden, A. (2010). The impact of a strategy-based intervention on the comprehension and strategy use of struggling adolescent readers. *Journal of Educational Psychology, 102,* 257–280.

Caprara, G. V., Barbaranelli, C., Borgogni, L., & Steca, P. (2003). Efficacy beliefs as determinants of teachers' job satisfaction. *Journal of Educational Psychology, 95,* 821–832.

Caprara, G. V., Fida, R., Vecchione, M., Del Bove, G., Vecchio, G. M., Barbaranelli, C., & Bandura, A. (2008). Longitudinal analysis of the role of perceived self-efficacy for self-regulated learning in academic continuance and achievement. *Journal of Educational Psychology, 100,* 515–534.

Carlson, R., Chandler, P., & Sweller, J. (2003). Learning and understanding science instructional material. *Journal of Educational Psychology, 95,* 629–640.

Carney, R. N., & Levin, J. R. (2002). Pictorial illustrations *still* improve students' learning from text. *Educational Psychology Review, 14,* 5–26.

Carpenter, P. A., Miyake, A., & Just, M. A. (1995). Language comprehension: Sentence and discourse processing. *Annual Review of Psychology, 46,* 91–120.

Carr, M. (2012). Critical transitions: Arithmetic to algebra. In K. R. Harris, S. Graham, & T. Urdan (Eds.), *APA educational psychology handbook. Vol. 3: Application to learning and teaching* (pp. 229–255). Washington, DC: American Psychological Association.

Carr, N. (2011). *The shallows: What the internet is doing to our brains.* New York: Norton.

Carrington, V. (2009). From Wikipedia to the humble classroom Wiki: Why we should pay attention to Wikis. In V. Carrington & M. Robinson (Eds.), *Digital literacies: Social learning and classroom practices* (pp. 65–80). Los Angeles: SAGE.

Carrington, V., & Robinson, M. (2009). *Digital literacies: Social learning and classroom practices.* Los Angeles: SAGE.

Carroll, J. B. (1963). A model of school learning. *Teachers College Record, 64,* 723–733.

Carroll, J. B. (1965). School learning over the long haul. In J. D. Krumboltz (Ed.), *Learning and the educational process* (pp. 249–269). Chicago: Rand McNally.

Carroll, J. B. (1989). The Carroll model: A 25-year retrospective and prospective view. *Educational Researcher, 18*(1), 26–31.

Carroll, W. R., & Bandura, A. (1982). The role of visual monitoring in observational learning of action patterns: Making the unobservable observable. *Journal of Motor Behavior, 14,* 153–167.

Carver, C. S., & Scheier, M. F. (1998). *On the self-regulation of behavior.* New York: Cambridge University Press.

Case, R. (1978a). A developmentally based theory and technology of instruction. *Review of Educational Research, 48,* 439–463.

Case, R. (1978b). Piaget and beyond: Toward a developmentally based theory and technology of instruction. In R. Glaser (Ed.), *Advances in instructional psychology* (Vol. 1, pp. 167–228). Hillsdale, NJ: Erlbaum.

Case, R. (1981). Intellectual development: A systematic reinterpretation. In F. H. Farley & N. J. Gordon (Eds.), *Psychology and education: The state of the union* (pp. 142–177). Berkeley, CA: McCutchan.

Case, R. (1993). Theories of learning and theories of development. *Educational Psychologist, 28,* 219–233.

Case, R., & Mueller, M. P. (2001). Differentiation, integration, and covariance mapping as fundamental processes in cognitive and neurological growth. In J. L. McClelland & R. S. Siegler (Eds.), *Mechanisms of cognitive development: Behavioral and neural perspectives* (pp. 185–219). Mahwah, NJ: Erlbaum.

Ceci, S. J. (1989). On domain specificity . . . More or less general and specific constraints on cognitive development. *Merrill-Palmer Quarterly, 35,* 131–142.

Ceci. S. J., Fitneva, S. A., & Williams, W. M. (2010). Representational constraints on the development of memory and metamemory: A developmental-representational theory. *Psychological Review, 117,* 464–495,C

Centre for Educational Research and Innovation (2007). *Understanding the brain: The birth of a learning science.* Paris: Organisation for Economic Co-operation and Development.

Cerasoli, C. P., Nicklin, J. M., & Ford, M. T. (2014). Intrinsic motivation and extrinsic incentives jointly predict performance: A 40-year meta-analysis. *Psychological Bulletin, 140,* 980–1008.

Cervone, D., Jiwani, N., & Wood, R. (1991). Goal setting and the differential influence of self-regulatory processes on complex decision-making performance. *Journal of Personality and Social Psychology, 61,* 257–266.

Chan, W., Lau, S., Nie, Y., Lim, S., & Hogan, D. (2008). Organizational and personal predictors of teacher commitment: The mediating role of teacher efficacy and identification with school. *American Educational Research Journal*, 45, 597–630.

Chapman, J. W. (1988). Learning disabled children's self-concepts. *Review of Educational Research*, 58, 347–371.

Chapman, J. W., & Tunmer, W. E. (1995). Development of young children's reading self-concepts: An examination of emerging subcomponents and their relationship with reading achievement. *Journal of Educational Psychology*, 87, 154–167.

Chartrand, T. L., & Bargh, J. A. (1999). The Chameleon Effect: The perception-behavior link and social interaction. *Journal of Personality and Social Psychology*, 76, 893–910.

Chen, O., Kalyuga, S., & Sweller, J. (2015). The worked example effect, the generation effect, and element interactivity. *Journal of Educational Psychology*, 107, 689–704.

Chen, Z. (1999). Schema induction in children's analogical problem solving. *Journal of Educational Psychology*, 91, 703–715.

Cherry, E. C. (1953). Some experiments on the recognition of speech with one and two ears. *Journal of the Acoustical Society of America*, 25, 975–979.

Cheung, C. S-S., & Pomerantz, E. M. (2015). Value development underlies the benefits of parents' involvement in children's learning: A longitudinal investigation in the United States and China. *Journal of Educational Psychology*, 107, 309–320.

Chi, M. T. H., Bassok, M., Lewis, M. W., Reimann, P., & Glaser, R. (1989). Self-explanations: How students study and use examples in learning to solve problems. *Cognitive Science*, 13, 145–182.

Chi, M. T. H., Feltovich, P. J., & Glaser, R. (1981). Categorization and representation of physics problems by experts and novices. *Cognitive Science*, 5, 121–152.

Chi, M. T. H., & Glaser, R. (1985). Problem-solving ability. In R. J. Sternberg (Ed.), *Human abilities: An information-processing approach* (pp. 227–250). New York: Freeman.

Chi, M. T. H., Glaser, R., & Farr, M. J. (Eds.). (1988). *The nature of expertise*. Hillsdale, NJ: Erlbaum.

Chi, M. T. H., Glaser, R., & Rees, E. (1982). Expertise in problem solving. In R. J. Sternberg (Ed.), *Advances in the psychology of human intelligence* (Vol. 1, pp. 7–75). Hillsdale, NJ: Erlbaum.

Chi, M. T. H., & VanLehn, K. A. (2012). Seeing deep structure from the interactions of surface features. *Educational Psychologist*, 47, 177–188/

Chinn, C. A., & Samarapungavan, A. (2009). Conceptual change—multiple routes, multiple mechanisms: A commentary on Ohlsson (2009). *Educational Psychologist*, 44, 48–57.

Chomsky, N. (1957). *Syntactic structures*. The Hague: Mouton.

Claessens, A., Engel, M., & Curran, F. C. (2014). Academic content, student learning, and the persistence of preschool effects. *American Educational Research Journal*, 51, 403–434.C

Clark, D. B., Tanner-Smith, E. E., & Killingsworth, S. S. (2016). Digital games, design, and learning: A systematic review and meta-analysis. *Review of Educational Research*, 86, 79–122.

Clark, H. H., & Clark, E. V. (1977). *Psychology and language: An introduction to psycholinguistics*. New York: Harcourt Brace Jovanovich.

Clark, H. H., & Haviland, S. E. (1977). Psychological processes as linguistic explanation. In R. O. Freedle (Ed.), *Discourse production and comprehension* (pp. 1–40). Norwood, NJ: Ablex.

Clark, J. M., & Paivio, A. (1991). Dual coding theory and education. *Educational Psychology Review*, 3, 149–210.

Clark, K. (2008, January 21). New answers for e-learning. *U. S. News & World Report*, 144, 46, 48–50.

Cleary, T. J. (2018). *The self-regulated learning guide: Teaching students to think in the language of strategies*. New York: Routledge.

Cleary, T. J., Zimmerman, B. J., & Keating, T. (2006). Training physical education students to self-regulate during basketball free throw practice. *Research Quarterly for Exercise and sport*, 77, 251–262.

Clerc, J., Miller, P. H., & Cosnefroy, L. (2014), Young children's transfer of strategies: Utilization deficiencies, executive function, and metacognition. *Developmental Review*, 34, 378–393.

Clifford, R. M., Early, D. M., & Hill, T. (1999). About a million children in school before kindergarten. *Young Children*, 54, 48–51.

Cobb, P. (1994). Where is the mind? Constructivist and sociocultural perspectives on mathematical development. *Educational Researcher*, 23(7), 13–20.

Cobb, P., & Bowers, J. (1999). Cognitive and situated learning perspectives in theory and practice. *Educational Researcher*, 28(2), 4–15,

Cohen, E. G. (1994). Restructuring the classroom: Conditions for productive small groups. *Review of Educational Research*, 64, 1–35.

Cole, M. (2010). Education as an intergenerational process of human learning, teaching, and development. *American Psychologist*, 65, 796–807.

Collie, R. J., Shapka, J. D., & Perry, N. E. (2012). School climate and social-emotional learning: Predicting teacher stress, job satisfaction, and teaching efficacy. *Journal of Educational Psychology*, 104, 1189–1204.

Collins, A. (1977). Processes in acquiring knowledge. In R. C. Anderson, R. J. Spiro, & W. E. Montague (Eds.), *Schooling and the acquisition of knowledge* (pp. 339–363). Hillsdale, NJ: Erlbaum.

Collins, A., & Loftus, E. F. (1975). A spreading-activation theory of semantic processing. *Psychological Review*, 82, 407–428.

Collins, A., & Quillian, M. R. (1969). Retrieval time from semantic memory. *Journal of Verbal Learning and Verbal Behavior*, 8, 240–247.

Collins, A., & Stevens, A. L. (1983). A cognitive theory of inquiry teaching. In C. M. Reigeluth (Ed.), *Instructional-design theories and models: An overview of their current status* (pp. 247–278). Hillsdale, NJ: Erlbaum.

Collins, J. L. (1982, March). *Self-efficacy and ability in achievement behavior*. Paper presented at the annual meeting of the American Educational Research Association, New York.

Collins, W. A., Maccoby, E. E., Steinberg, L., Hetherington, E. M., & Bornstein, M. H. (2000). Contemporary research on parenting: The case for nature and nurture. *American Psychologist*, 55, 218–232.

Comer, J. P. (2001, April 23). Schools that develop children. *The American Prospect*, 30–35.

Comer, J. P., & Haynes, N. M. (1999). The dynamics of school change: Response to the article, "Comer's School Development Program in Prince George's County, Maryland: A theory-based evaluation," by Thomas D. Cook et al. *American Educational Research Journal*, 36, 599–607.

Cook, T. D., Habib, F., Phillips, M., Settersten, R. A., Shagle, S. C., & Degirmencioglu, S. M. (1999). Comer's School Development Program in Prince George's County, Maryland: A theory-based evaluation. *American Educational Research Journal*, 36, 543–597.

Cook, T. D., Murphy, R. F., & Hunt, H. D. (2000). Comer's School Development Program in Chicago: A theory-based evaluation. *American Educational Research Journal*, 37, 535–597.

Cooper, H. M., & Good, T. L. (1983). *Pygmalion grows up: Studies in the expectation communication process.* New York: Longman.

Cooper, H. M., Robinson, J. C., & Patall, E. A. (2006). Does homework improve academic achievement? A synthesis of research, 1987–2003. *Review of Educational Research*, 76, 1–62.

Cooper, H. M., & Tom, D. Y. H. (1984). Teacher expectation research: A review with implications for classroom instruction. *Elementary School Journal*, 85, 77–89.

Cooper, L. A., & Shepard, R. N. (1973). Chronometric studies of the rotation of mental images. In W. G. Chase (Ed.), *Visual information processing* (pp. 95–176). New York: Academic Press.

Cooper, R. P., & Shallice, T. (2006). Hierarchical schemas and goals in the control of sequential behavior. *Psychological Review*, 113, 887–916.

Cooper, W. H. (1983). An achievement motivation nomological network. *Journal of Personality and Social Psychology*, 44, 841–861.

Corballis, M. C. (2006). Language. In K. Pawlik & G. d'Ydewalle (Eds.), *Psychological concepts: An international historical perspective* (pp. 197–221). New York: Psychology Press.

Cordova, J. R., Sinatra, G. M., Jones, S. H., Taasoobshirazi, G., & Lombardi, D. (2014). Confidence in prior knowledge, self-efficacy, interest and prior knowledge: Influences on conceptual change. *Contemporary Educational Psychology*, 39, 164–174.

Cornelius-White, J. (2007). Learner-centered teacher-student relationships are effective: A meta-analysis. *Review of Educational Research*, 77, 113–143.

Corno, L. (1993). The best-laid plans: Modern conceptions of volition and educational research. *Educational Researcher*, 22(2), 14–22.

Corno, L. (1994). Student volition and education: Outcomes, influences, and practices. In D. H. Schunk & B. J. Zimmerman (Eds.), *Self-regulation of learning and performance: Issues and educational applications* (pp. 229–251). Hillsdale, NJ: Erlbaum.

Corno, L. (2001). Volitional aspects of self-regulated learning. In B. J. Zimmerman & D. H. Schunk (Eds.), *Self-regulated learning and academic achievement: Theoretical perspectives* (2nd ed., pp. 191–225). Mahwah, NJ: Erlbaum.

Corno, L. (2008). Work habits and self-regulated learning: Helping students to find a "will" from a "way." In D. H. Schunk & B. J. Zimmerman (Eds.), *Motivation and self-regulated learning: Theory, research, and applications* (pp. 197–222). New York: Taylor & Francis.

Corno, L., & Kanfer, R. (1993). The role of volition in learning and performance. In L. Darling-Hammond (Ed.), *Review of research in education* (Vol. 19, pp. 301–341). Washington, DC: American Educational Research Association.

Corno, L., & Mandinach, E. B. (2004). What we have learned about student engagement in the past twenty years. In D. M. McInerney & S. Van Etten (Eds.), *Big theories revisited* (pp. 299–328). Greenwich, CT: Information Age Publishing.

Courage, M. L., & Setliff, A. E. (2009). Debating the impact of television and video material on very young children: Attention, learning, and the developing brain. *Child Development Perspectives*, 3, 72–78.

Covey, S. R. (1989). *The seven habits of highly effective people: Restoring the character ethic.* New York: Simon and Schuster.

Covington, M. V. (1992). *Making the grade: A self-worth perspective on motivation and school reform.* Cambridge, England: Cambridge University Press.

Covington, M. V. (1998). *The will to learn: A guide for motivating young people.* New York: Cambridge University Press.

Covington, M. V. (2004). Self-worth theory goes to college: Or do our motivation theories motivate? In D. M. McInerney & S. Van Etten (Eds.), *Big theories revisited* (pp. 91–114). Greenwich, CT: Information Age Publishing.

Covington, M. V. (2009). Self-worth theory: Retrospection and prospects. In K. R. Wentzel & A. Wigfield (Eds.), *Handbook of motivation at school* (pp. 141–169). New York: Routledge.

Covington, M. V., & Dray, E. (2002). The developmental course of achievement motivation: A need-based approach. In A. Wigfield & J. S. Eccles (Eds.), *Development of achievement motivation* (pp. 33–56). San Diego: Academic Press.

Covington, M. V., & Omelich, C. L. (1979). Effort: The double-edged sword in school achievement. *Journal of Educational Psychology*, 71, 688–700.

Cowan, N. (1999). An embedded-processes model of working memory. In A. Miyake & P. Shah (Eds.), *Models of working memory: Mechanisms of active maintenance and executive control.* Cambridge, England: Cambridge University Press.Cow

Cowan, N. (2014). Working memory underpins cognitive development, learning, and education. *Educational Psychology Review*, 26, 197–223.Cowan

Cowan, N., Hismjatullina, A., AuBuchon, A. M., Saults, J. S., Horton, N., Leadbitter, K., & Towse, J. (2010). With development, list recall includes more chunks, not just larger ones. *Developmental Psychology*, 46, 1119–1131.

Cowan, N., Rouder, J. N., Blume, C. L., & Saults, J. S. (2012). Models of verbal working memory capacity: What does it take to make them work? *Psychological Review*, 119, 480–499.

Cowey, A. (1998). Localization of brain function and cortical maps. In R. L. Gregory (Ed.), *The Oxford companion to the mind* (pp. 436–438). Oxford, England: Oxford University Press.

Cox, B. D. (1997). The rediscovery of the active learner in adaptive contexts: A developmental-historical analysis of transfer of training. *Educational Psychologist*, 32, 41–55.

Craig, S. D., Chi, M. T. H., & VanLehn, K. (2009). Improving classroom learning by collaboratively observing human tutoring videos while problem solving. *Journal of Educational Psychology*, 101, 779–789.

Craik, F. I. M. (1979). Human memory. *Annual Review of Psychology*, 30, 63–102.

Craik, F. I. M., & Lockhart, R. S. (1972). Levels of processing: A framework for memory research. *Journal of Verbal Learning and Verbal Behavior*, 11, 671–684.

Craik, F. I. M., & Tulving, E. (1975). Depth of processing and the retention of words in episodic memory. *Journal of Experimental Psychology: General*, 104, 268–294.

Creswell, J. W., & Plano-Clark, V. L. (2007). *Designing and conducting mixed methods research.* Thousand Oaks, CA: SAGE Publications.

Crisafi, M. A., & Brown, A. L. (1986). Analogical transfer in very young children: Combining two separately learned solutions to reach a goal. *Child Development*, 57, 953–968.

Crosnoe, R., Johnson, M. K., & Elder, G. H. (2004). School size and the interpersonal side of education. *Social Science Quarterly*, 85, 1259–1274.

Crowley, K., & Siegler, R. S. (1999). Explanation and generalization in young children's strategy learning. *Child Development*, 70, 304–316.

Csikszentmihalyi, M. (1975). *Beyond boredom and anxiety*. San Francisco: Jossey-Bass.

Csikszentmihalyi, M., & Rathunde, K. (1993). The measurement of flow in everyday life: Toward a theory of emergent motivation. In J. E. Jacobs (Ed.), *Nebraska symposium on motivation 1992* (Vol. 40, pp. 57–97). Lincoln, NE: University of Nebraska Press.

Cummins, D. D., Kintsch, W., Reusser, K., & Weimer, R. (1988). The role of understanding in solving word problems. *Cognitive Psychology*, 20, 405–438.

Cutler, L., & Graham, S. (2008). Primary grade writing instruction: A national survey. *Journal of Educational Psychology*, 100, 907–919.

Daniels, D. H., Kalkman, D. L., & McCombs, B. L. (2001). Young children's perspectives on learning and teacher practices in different classroom contexts: Implications for motivation. *Early Education and Development*, 12, 253–273.

Dansereau, D. F. (1978). The development of a learning strategies curriculum. In H. F. O'Neil, Jr. (Ed.), *Learning strategies* (pp. 1–29). New York: Academic Press.

Dansereau, D. F. (1988). Cooperative learning strategies. In C. E. Weinstein, E. T. Goetz, & P. A. Alexander (Eds.), *Learning and study strategies: Issues in assessment, instruction, and evaluation* (pp. 103–120). San Diego: Academic Press.

Dansereau, D. F., McDonald, B. A., Collins, K. W., Garland, J., Holley, C. D., Diekhoff, G. M., & Evans, S. H. (1979). Evaluation of a learning strategy system. In H. F. O'Neil, Jr., & C. D. Spielberger (Eds.), *Cognitive and affective learning strategies* (pp. 3–43). New York: Academic Press.

Darling-Hammond, L., Amrein-Beardsley. A., Haertel, E., & Rothstein, J. (2012). Evaluating teacher evaluation. *Phi Delta Kappan*, 93(6), 8–15.

Darwin, C. J., Turvey, M. T., & Crowder, R. G. (1972). An auditory analogue of the Sperling partial report procedure: Evidence for brief auditory storage. *Cognitive Psychology*, 3, 255–267.

Daugherty, M., & White, C. S. (2008). Relationships among private speech and creativity in Head Start and low-socioeconomic status preschool children. *Gifted Child Quarterly*, 52, 30–39.

Davelaar, E. J., Goshen-Gottstein, Y., Ashkenazi, A., Haarmann, H. J., & Usher, M. (2005). The demise of short-term memory revisited: Empirical and computational investigations of recency effects. *Psychological Review*, 112, 3–42.

Davis, H. A. (2003). Conceptualizing the role and influence of student-teacher relationships on children's social and cognitive development. *Educational Psychologist*, 38, 207–234.

Debowski, S., Wood, R. E., & Bandura, A. (2001). Impact of guided exploration and enactive exploration on self-regulatory mechanisms and information acquisition through electronic search. *Journal of Applied Psychology*, 86, 1129–1141.

de Bruin. A. B. H., Thiede, K. W., Camp, G., & Redford, J. (2011). Generating keywords improves metacomprehension and self-regulation in elementary and middle school children. *Journal of Experimental Child Psychology*, 109, 294–310.

De Castella, K., Byrne, D., & Covington, M. (2013). Unmotivated or motivated to fail? A cross-cultural study of achievement motivation, fear of failure, and student disengagement. *Journal of Educational Psychology*, 105, 861–880.

de Charms, R. (1968). *Personal causation: The internal affective determinants of behavior*. New York: Academic Press.

de Charms, R. (1976). *Enhancing motivation: Change in the classroom*. New York: Irvington.

de Charms, R. (1984). Motivation enhancement in educational settings. In R. Ames & C. Ames (Eds.), *Research on motivation in education* (Vol. 1, pp. 275–310). Orlando: Academic Press.

Deci, E. L. (1975). *Intrinsic motivation*. New York: Plenum.

Deci, E. L. (1980). *The psychology of self-determination*. Lexington, MA: D. C. Heath.

Deci, E. L., Koestner, R., & Ryan, R. M. (1999). A meta-analytic review of experiments examining the effects of extrinsic rewards on intrinsic motivation. *Psychological Bulletin*, 125, 627–668.

Deci, E. L., Koestner, R., & Ryan, R. M. (2001). Extrinsic rewards and intrinsic motivation in education: Reconsidered once again. *Review of Educational Research*, 71, 1–27.

Deci, E. L., & Moller, A. C. (2005). The concept of competence: A starting place for understanding intrinsic motivation and self-determined extrinsic motivation. In A. J. Elliot & C. S. Dweck (Eds.), *Handbook of competence and motivation* (pp. 579–597). New York: Guilford Press.

DeGrandpre, R. J. (2000). A science of meaning: Can behaviorism bring meaning to psychological science? *American Psychologist*, 55, 721–739.

de Jong, P. F. (1998). Working memory deficits of reading disabled children. *Journal of Experimental Child Psychology*, 70, 75–96.

de Jong, T., & van Joolingen, W. R. (1998). Scientific discovery learning with computer simulations of conceptual domains. *Review of Educational Research*, 68, 179–201.

De La Paz, S. (2005). Effects of historical reasoning instruction and writing strategy mastery in culturally and academically diverse middle school classrooms. *Journal of Educational Psychology*, 97, 139–156.

DeLeeuw, K. E., & Mayer, R. E. (2008). A comparison of three measures of cognitive load: Evidence for separable measures of intrinsic, extraneous, and germane load. *Journal of Educational Psychology*, 100, 223–234.

Dembo, M. H., & Seli, H. (2016). *Motivation and learning strategies for college success: A focus on self-regulated learning*. New York: Routledge.

Dempster, F. N., & Corkill, A. J. (1999). Interference and inhibition in cognition and behavior: Unifying themes for educational psychology. *Educational Psychology Review*, 11, 1–88.

Dermitzaki, I. (2005). Preliminary investigation of relations between young students' self-regulatory strategies and their metacognitive experiences. *Psychological Reports*, 97, 759–768.

D'Esposito, M., & Postle, B. R. (2015). The cognitive neuroscience of working memory. *Annual Review of Psychology*, 66, 115–142.

Dewey, J. (1896). The reflex arc concept in psychology. *Psychological Review*, 3, 357–370.

Dewey, J. (1900). Psychology and social practice. *Psychological Review*, 7, 105–124.

Dewsbury, D. A. (2000). Introduction: Snapshots of psychology circa 1900. *American Psychologist*, 55, 255–259.

DiBenedetto, M. K., & Zimmerman, B. J. (2010). Differences in self-regulatory processes among students studying science: A microanalytic investigation. *International Journal of Educational and Psychological Assessment*, 5(1), 2–24.

Dick, W., & Carey, L. (1985). *The systematic design of instruction* (2nd ed.). Glenview, IL: Scott, Foresman.

DiClemente, C. C. (1981). Self-efficacy and smoking cessation maintenance: A preliminary report. *Cognitive Therapy and Research*, 5, 175–187.

DiClemente, C. C., Prochaska, J. O., & Gilbertini, M. (1985). Self-efficacy and the stages of self-change in smoking. *Cognitive Therapy and Research, 9*, 181–200.

Diener, C. I., & Dweck, C. S. (1978). An analysis of learned helplessness: Continuous changes in performance, strategy, and achievement cognitions following failure. *Journal of Personality and Social Psychology, 36*, 451–462.

Dietrich, A., & Kanso, R. (2010). A review of EEG, ERP, and neuroimaging studies of creativity and insight. *Psychological Bulletin, 136*, 822–848.

Dietrichson, J., Bøg, M., Filges, T., & Jørgensen, A-M. K. (2017). Academic interventions for elementary and middle school students with low socioeconomic status: A systematic review and meta-analysis. *Review of Educational Research, 87*, 243–282.

Dijksterhuis, A., & Aarts, H. (2010). Goals, attention, and (un)consciousness. *Annual Review of Psychology, 61*, 467–490.

Dillon, A., & Gabbard, R. (1998). Hypermedia as an educational technology: A review of the quantitative research literature on learner comprehension, control, and style. *Review of Educational Research, 68*, 322–349.

Dimmitt, C., & McCormick, C. B. (2012). Metacognition in education. In K. R. Harris, S. Graham, & T. Urdan (Eds.), *APA educational psychology handbook. Vol.1: Theories, constructs, and critical issues* (pp. 157–187). Washington, DC: American Psychological Association.

Dinsmore, D. L., Alexander, P. A., & Loughlin, S. M. (2008). Focusing the conceptual lens on metacognition, self-regulation, and self-regulated learning. *Educational Psychology Review, 20*, 391–409.

DiPardo, A., & Freedman, S. W. (1988). Peer response groups in the writing classroom: Theoretical foundations and new directions. *Review of Educational Research, 58*, 119–149.

Dowrick, P. W. (1983). Self-modelling. In P. W. Dowrick & S. J. Biggs (Eds.), *Using video: Psychological and social applications* (pp. 105–124). Chichester, England: Wiley.

Dowrick, P. W. (1999). A review of self modeling and related interventions. *Applied & Preventive Psychology, 8*, 23–39.

Dragoi, V., & Staddon, J. E. R. (1999). The dynamics of operant conditioning. *Psychological Review, 106*, 20–61.

Driver, R., Asoko, H., Leach, J., Mortimer, E., & Scott, P. (1994). Constructing scientific knowledge in the classroom. *Educational Researcher, 23*(7), 5–12.

Dubinsky, J. M., Roehrig, G., & Varma, S. (2013). Infusing neuroscience into teacher professional development. *Educational Researcher, 42*, 317–329.

Duchastel, P., & Brown, B. R. (1974). Incidental and relevant learning with instructional objectives. *Journal of Educational Psychology, 66*, 481–485.

Duda, J. L., & Nicholls, J. G. (1992). Dimensions of achievement motivation in schoolwork and sport. *Journal of Educational Psychology, 84*, 290–299.

Duell, O. K. (1986). Metacognitive skills. In G. D. Phye & T. Andre (Eds.), *Cognitive classroom learning: Understanding, thinking, and problem solving* (pp. 205–242). Orlando: Academic Press.

Duncan, R. M. (1995). Piaget and Vygotsky revisited: Dialogue or assimilation? *Developmental Review, 15*, 458–472.

Duncker, K. (1945). On problem-solving (L. S. Lees, Trans.). *Psychological Monographs, 58*(5, Whole No. 270).

Dunham, P. (1977). The nature of reinforcing stimuli. In W. K. Honig & J. E. R. Staddon (Eds.), *Handbook of operant behavior* (pp. 98–124). Englewood Cliffs, NJ: Prentice Hall.

Dunn, R., & Honigsfeld, A. (2013). Learning styles: What we know and what we need. *The Educational Forum, 77*, 225–232.

Dusek, J. B. (Ed.) (1985). *Teacher expectancies*. Hillsdale, NJ: Erlbaum.

Dweck, C. S. (1975). The role of expectations and attributions in the alleviation of learned helplessness. *Journal of Personality and Social Psychology, 31*, 674–685.

Dweck, C. S. (1986). Motivational processes affecting learning. *American Psychologist, 41*, 1040–1048.

Dweck, C. S. (1991). Self-theories and goals: Their role in motivation, personality, and development. In R. A. Dienstbier (Ed.), *Nebraska Symposium on Motivation, 1990* (Vol. 38, pp. 199–235). Lincoln, NE: University of Nebraska Press.

Dweck, C. S. (1999). *Self-theories: Their role in motivation, personality, and development*. Philadelphia: Taylor & Francis.

Dweck, C. S. (2002). The development of ability conceptions. In A. Wigfield & J. S. Eccles (Eds.), *Development of achievement motivation* (pp. 57–88). San Diego: Academic Press.

Dweck, C. S. (2006). *Mindset: The new psychology of success*. New York: Random House.

Dweck, C. S., & Leggett, E. L. (1988). A social-cognitive approach to motivation and personality. *Psychological Review, 95*, 256–273.

Dweck, C. S., & Master, A. (2008). Self-theories motivate self-regulated learning. In D. H. Schunk & B. J. Zimmerman (Eds.), *Motivation and self-regulated learning: Theory, research, and applications* (pp. 31–51). New York: Taylor & Francis.

Dweck, C. S., & Molden, D. C. (2005). Self-theories: Their impact on competence motivation and acquisition. In A. J. Elliot & C. S. Dweck (Eds.), *Handbook of competence and motivation* (pp. 122–140). New York: Guilford Press.

Dweck, C. S., & Repucci, N. D. (1973). Learned helplessness and reinforcement responsibility in children. *Journal of Personality and Social Psychology, 25*, 109–116.

Eby, L. T., Rhodes, J. E., & Allen, T. D. (2007). Definition and evolution of mentoring. In T. D. Allen & L. T. Eby (Eds.), *The Blackwell handbook of mentoring: A multiple perspectives approach* (pp. 7–20). Malden, MA: Blackwell.

Eccles, J. S. (2005). Subjective task value and the Eccles et al. model of achievement-related choices. In A. J. Elliot & C. S. Dweck (Eds.), *Handbook of competence and motivation* (pp. 105–121). New York: Guilford Press.

Eccles, J. S., & Midgley, C. (1989). Stage-environment fit: Developmentally appropriate classrooms for young adolescents. In C. Ames & R. Ames (Eds.), *Research on motivation in education* (Vol. 3, pp. 139–186). San Diego: Academic Press.

Eccles, J. S., Midgley, C., Wigfield, A., Reuman, D., Mac Iver, D., & Feldlaufer, H. (1993). Negative effects of traditional middle schools on students' motivation. *Elementary School Journal, 93*, 553–574.

Eccles, J. S., & Roeser, R. W. (2011). Schools as developmental contexts during adolescence. *Journal of Research on Adolescence, 21*, 225–241.

Eccles, J. S., & Wigfield, A. (1985). Teacher expectations and student motivation. In J. B. Dusek (Ed.), *Teacher expectancies* (pp. 185–226). Hillsdale, NJ: Erlbaum.

Efklides, A. (2006). Metacognitive experiences: The missing link in the self-regulated learning process. A rejoinder to Ainley and Patrick. *Educational Psychology Review, 18*, 287–291.

Efklides, A., Schwartz, B. L., & Brown, V. (2018). Motivation and affect in self-regulated learning: Does metacognition play a role? In D. H. Schunk & J. A. Greene (Eds.), *Handbook of self-regulation of learning and performance* (2nd ed., pp. 64–82). New York: Routledge.

Elkind, D. (2004). The problem with constructivism. *The Educational Forum, 68,* 306–312.

Elliot, A. J. (2005). A conceptual history of the achievement goal construct. In A. J. Elliot & C. S. Dweck (Eds.), *Handbook of competence and motivation* (pp. 52–72). New York: Guilford Press.

Elliot, A. J., & Church, M. A. (1997). A hierarchical model of approach and avoidance achievement motivation. *Journal of Personality and Social Psychology, 72,* 218–232.

Elliot, A. J., & Harackiewicz, J. M. (1996). Approach and avoidance achievement goals and intrinsic motivation: A mediational analysis. *Journal of Personality and Social Psychology, 70,* 461–475.

Elliot, A. J., & McGregor, H. A. (2001). A 2 x 2 achievement goal framework. *Journal of Personality and Social Psychology, 80,* 501–519.

Elliot, A. J., & Thrash, T. M. (2001). Achievement goals and the hierarchical model of achievement motivation. *Educational Psychology Review, 13,* 139–156,

Elliott, E. S., & Dweck, C. S. (1988). Goals: An approach to motivation and achievement. *Journal of Personality and Social Psychology, 54,* 5–12.

Ellis, S., & Rogoff, B. (1982). The strategies and efficacy of child versus adult teachers. *Child Development, 53,* 730–735.

Elstein, A. S., Shulman, L. S., & Sprafka, S. A. (1978). *Medical problem solving.* Cambridge, MA: Harvard University Press.

Emmer, E. T., Evertson, C., & Worsham, M. E. (2000). *Classroom management for secondary teachers* (5th ed.). Boston: Allyn & Bacon.

Emmons, C. L., Comer, J. P., & Haynes, N. M. (1996). Translating theory into practice: Comer's theory of school reform. In J. P. Comer, N. M. Haynes, E. T. Joyner, & M. Ben-Avie (Eds.), *Rallying the whole village: The Comer process for reforming education* (pp. 27–41). New York: Teachers College Press.

Englund, M. M., Luckner, A. E., Whaley, G. J. L., & Egeland, B. (2004). Children's achievement in early elementary school: Longitudinal effects of parental involvement, expectations, and quality of assistance. *Journal of Educational Psychology, 96,* 723–730.

Ennemoser, M., & Schneider, W. (2007). Relations of television viewing and reading: Findings from a 4-year longitudinal study. *Journal of Educational Psychology, 99,* 349–368.

Ennis, R. H. (1987). A taxonomy of critical thinking dispositions and abilities. In J. B. Baron & R. J. Sternberg (Eds.), *Teaching thinking skills: Theory and practice* (pp. 9–26). New York: Freeman.

Epstein, J. L. (1989). Family structures and student motivation: A developmental perspective. In C. Ames & R. Ames (Eds.), *Research on motivation in education* (Vol. 3, pp. 259–295). San Diego: Academic Press.

Erdelyi, M. H. (2010). The ups and downs of memory. *American Psychologist, 65,* 623–633.

Erickson, F. (1986). Qualitative methods in research on teaching. In M. C. Wittrock (Ed.), *Handbook of research on teaching* (3rd ed., pp. 119–161). New York: Macmillan.

Ericsson, K. A., & Fox, M. C. (2011). Thinking aloud is not a form of introspection but a qualitatively different methodology: Reply to Schooler (2011). *Psychological Bulletin, 137,* 351–354.

Ericsson, K. A., Krampe, R. T., & Tesch-Römer, C. (1993). The role of deliberate practice in the acquisition of expert performance. *Psychological Review, 100,* 363–406.

Ertmer, P. A. (1999). Addressing first- and second-order barriers to change: Strategies for technology integration. *Educational Technology Research & Development, 47,* 47–61.

Ertmer, P. A., Driscoll, M. P., & Wager, W. W. (2003). The legacy of Robert Mills Gagné. In B. J. Zimmerman & D. H. Schunk (Eds.), *Educational psychology: A century of contributions* (pp. 303–330). Mahwah, NJ: Erlbaum.

Estes, W. K. (1970). *Learning theory and mental development.* New York: Academic Press.

Estes, W. K. (1997). Processes of memory loss, recovery, and distortion. *Psychological Review, 104,* 148–169.

Evans, R. B. (2000). Psychological instruments at the turn of the century. *American Psychologist, 55,* 322–325.

Evenson, D. H., Salisbury-Glennon, J. D., & Glenn, J. (2001). A qualitative study of six medical students in a problem-based curriculum: Toward a situated model of self-regulation. *Journal of Educational Psychology, 93,* 659–676.

Evertson, C., Emmer, E. T., & Worsham, M. E. (2000). *Classroom management for elementary teachers* (5th ed.). Boston: Allyn & Bacon.

Evrard, M. R., Annese, J., & Ludvik, M. J. B. (2016). Basic brain parts and their functions. In M. J. B. Ludvik (Ed.), *The neuroscience of learning and development* (pp. 27–53). Sterling, VA: Stylus Publishing.

Evrard, M. R., & Ludvik, M. J. B. (2016). Unpacking neuroplasticity and neurogenesis. In M. J. B. Ludvik (Ed.), *The neuroscience of learning and development* (pp. 54–72). Sterling, VA: Stylus Publishing.

Eysink, T. H. S., de Jong, T., Berthold, K., Kolloffel, B., Opfermann, M., & Wouters, P. (2009). Learner performance in multimedia learning arrangements: An analysis across instructional approaches. *American Educational Research Journal, 46,* 1107–1149.

Fabos, B., & Young, M. D. (1999). Telecommunication in the classroom: Rhetoric versus reality. *Review of Educational Research, 69,* 217–259.

Falmagne, R. J., & Gonsalves, J. (1995). Deductive inference. *Annual Review of Psychology, 46,* 525–559.

Fan, X., & Chen, M. (2001). Parental involvement and students' academic achievement: A meta-analysis. *Educational Psychology Review, 13,* 1–22.

Farmer, T. W., Estell, D. B., Leung, M. C., Trotte, H., Bishop, J., & Cairns, B. D. (2003). Individual characteristics, early adolescent peer affiliations, and school dropout: An examination of aggressive and popular group types. *Journal of School Psychology, 41,* 217–232.

Farnham-Diggory, S. (1992). *Cognitive processes in education* (2nd ed.). New York: HarperCollins.

Faw, H. W., & Waller, T. G. (1976). Mathemagenic behaviours and efficiency in learning from prose materials: Review, critique and recommendations. *Review of Educational Research, 46,* 691–720.

Feldon, D. F. (2007). Cognitive load and classroom teaching: The double-edged sword of automaticity. *Educational Psychologist, 42,* 123–137.

Feltz, D. L., Chase, M. A., Moritz, S. E., & Sullivan, P. J. (1999). A conceptual model of coaching efficacy: Preliminary investigation and instrument development. *Journal of Educational Psychology*, 91, 765–776.

Fenesi, B., Sana, F., Kim, J. A., & Shore, D. L. (2015). Reconceptualizing working memory in educational research. *Educational Psychology Review*, 27, 333–351.

Ferster, C. S., & Skinner, B. F. (1957). *Schedules of reinforcement*. New York: Appleton-Century-Crofts.

Festinger, L. (1954). A theory of social comparison processes. *Human Relations*, 7, 117–140.

Festinger, L. (1957). *A theory of cognitive dissonance*. Stanford, CA: Stanford University Press.

Fillmore, L. W., & Valadez, C. (1986). Teaching bilingual learners. In M. W. Wittrock (Ed.), *Handbook of research on teaching* (3rd ed., pp. 648–685). New York: Macmillan.

Finn, J. D. (1989). Withdrawing from school. *Review of Educational Research*, 59, 117–142.

Fiorella, L., & Mayer, R. E. (2012). Paper-based aids for learning with a computer-based game. *Journal of Educational Psychology*, 104, 1074–1082.

Fiorella, L., & Mayer, R. E. (2016). Effects of observing the instructor draw diagrams on learning from multimedia messages. *Journal of Educational Psychology*, 108, 528–546.

Fischer, K. W., & Bidell, T. R. (1991). Constraining nativist inferences about cognitive capacities. In S. Carey & R. Gelman (Eds.), *The epigenesis of mind: Essays on biology and cognition* (pp. 199–236). Hillsdale, NJ: Erlbaum.

Fives, H., & Buehl, M. M. (2016). Teacher motivation: Self-efficacy and goal orientation. In K. R. Wentzel & D. B. Miele (Eds.), *Handbook of motivation at school* (2nd ed., pp. 340–360). New York: Routledge.

Flavell, J. H. (1985). *Cognitive development* (2nd ed.). Englewood Cliffs, NJ: Prentice Hall.

Flavell, J. H., Friedrichs, A. G., & Hoyt, J. D. (1970). Developmental changes in memorization processes. *Cognitive Psychology*, 1, 324–340.

Flavell, J. H., Green, F. L., & Flavell, E. R. (1995). Young children's knowledge about thinking. *Monographs of the Society for Research in Child Development*, 60(1) (Serial No. 243).

Flavell, J. H., & Wellman, H. M. (1977). Metamemory. In R. B. Kail, Jr., & J. W. Hagen (Eds.), *Perspectives on the development of memory and cognition* (pp. 3–33). Hillsdale, NJ: Erlbaum.

Fletcher, S., & Mullen, C. A. (Eds.) (2012). *The SAGE handbook of mentoring and coaching in education*. Thousand Oaks, CA: SAGE.

Floden, R. E. (2001). Research on effects of teaching: A continuing model for research on teaching. In V. Richardson (Ed.), *Handbook of research on teaching* (4th ed., pp. 3–16). Washington, DC: American Educational Research Association.

Ford, D. Y. (2016). Black and Hispanic students: Cultural differences within the context of education. In L. Corno & E. M. Anderman (Eds.), *Handbook of Educational Psychology* (3rd ed., pp. 364–377). New York: Routledge.

Forgas, J. (2000). The role of affect in social cognition. In J. Forgas (Ed.), *Feeling and thinking: The role of affect in social cognition* (pp. 1–28). New York: Cambridge University Press.

FPG Child Development Institute. (2005). *Early developments. NCEDL pre-kindergarten study, 9(1)*. Chapel Hill, NC: Author. Available online at: http://www.fpg.unc.edu/~ncdel.

Franks, J. J., & Bransford, J. D. (1971). Abstraction of visual patterns. *Journal of Experimental Psychology*, 90, 65–74.

Frauenglass, M. H., & Diaz, R. M. (1985). Self-regulatory functions of children's private speech: A critical analysis of recent challenges to Vygotsky's theory. *Developmental Psychology*, 21, 357–364.

Friedman, D. E., & Medway, F. J. (1987). Effects of varying performance sets and outcome on the expectations, attributions, and persistence of boys with learning disabilities. *Journal of Learning Disabilities*, 20, 312–316.

Friend, R., & Neale, J. (1972). Children's perceptions of success and failure: An attributional analysis of the effects of race and social class. *Developmental Psychology*, 7, 124–128.

Frieze, I. H. (1980). Beliefs about success and failure in the classroom. In J. H. McMillan (Ed.), *The social psychology of school learning* (pp. 39–78). New York: Academic Press.

Frieze, I. H., Francis, W. D., & Hanusa, B. H. (1983). Defining success in classroom settings. In J. M. Levine & M. C. Wang (Eds.), *Teacher and student perceptions: Implications for learning* (pp. 3–28). Hillsdale, NJ: Erlbaum.

Fryer, J. W., & Elliot, A. J. (2008). Self-regulation of achievement goal pursuit. In D. H. Schunk & B. J. Zimmerman (Eds.), *Motivation and self-regulated learning: Theory, research, and applications* (pp. 53–75). New York: Taylor & Francis.

Fuchs, D., Fuchs, L. S., Mathes, P. G., & Simmons, D. C. (1997). Peer-assisted learning strategies: Making classrooms more responsive to diversity. *American Educational Research Journal*, 34, 174–206.

Fuchs, L. S., Fuchs, D., Finelli, R., Courey, S. J., & Hamlett, C. L. (2004). Expanding schema-based transfer instruction to help third graders solve real-life mathematical problems. *American Educational Research Journal*, 41, 419–445.

Fuchs, L. S., Fuchs, D., Prentice, K., Burch, M., Hamlett, C. L., Owen, R., Hosp, M., & Jancek, D. (2003). Explicitly teaching for transfer: Effects on third-grade students' mathematical problem solving. *Journal of Educational Psychology*, 95, 293–305.

Fukkink, R. G., Trienekens, N., & Kramer, L. J. C. (2011). Video feedback in education and training: Putting learning in the picture. *Educational Psychology Review*, 23, 45–63.

Furth, H. G. (1970). *Piaget for teachers*. Englewood Cliffs, NJ: Prentice Hall.

Fuson, K. C. (1979). The development of self-regulating aspects of speech: A review. In G. Zivin (Ed.), *The development of self-regulation through private speech* (pp. 135–217). New York: Wiley.

Fyfe, E. R., Rittle-Johnson, B., & DeCaro, M. S. (2012). The effects of feedback during exploratory mathematics problem solving: Prior knowledge matters. *Journal of Educational Psychology*, 104, 1094–1108.

Gage, N. L. (1978). *The scientific basis of the art of teaching*. New York: Teachers College Press.

Gagné, R. M. (1984). Learning outcomes and their effects: Useful categories of human performance. *American Psychologist*, 39, 377–385.

Gagné, R. M. (1985). *The conditions of learning* (4th ed.). New York: Holt, Rinehart & Winston.

Gagné, R. M., & Briggs, L. J. (1979). *Principles of instructional design* (2nd ed.). New York: Holt, Rinehart & Winston.

Gagné, R. M., & Dick, W. (1983). Instructional psychology. *Annual Review of Psychology*, 34, 261–295.

Gagné, R. M., & Glaser, R. (1987). Foundations in learning research. In R. M. Gagné (Ed.), *Instructional technology: Foundations* (pp. 49–83). Hillsdale, NJ: Erlbaum.

Gaillard, V., Barrouillet, P., Jarrold, C., & Camos, V. (2011). Developmental differences in working memory: Where do they come from? *Journal of Experimental Child Psychology*, 110, 469–479.Gai

Gais, S., & Born, J. (2004). Declarative memory consolidation: Mechanisms acting during human sleep. *Learning and Memory*, 11, 679–685.

Galanski, E., & Kalantzi-Azizi, A. (1999). Loneliness and social dissatisfaction: Its relation with children's self-efficacy for peer interaction. *Child Study Journal*, 29, 1–22.

Gallo, D. A. (2010). False memories and fantastic beliefs: 15 years of the DRM illusion. *Memory & Cognition*, 38, 833–848.

Garcia, T., & Pintrich, P. R. (1994). Regulating motivation and cognition in the classroom: The role of self-schemas and self-regulatory strategies. In D. H. Schunk & B. J. Zimmerman (Eds.), *Self-regulation of learning and performance: Issues and educational applications* (pp. 127–153). Hillsdale, NJ: Erlbaum.

Garcia-Reid, P., Reid, R. J., & Peterson, N. A. (2005). School engagement among Latino youth in an urban middle school context. *Education and Urban Society*, 37, 257–275.

Gauvain, M., & Munroe, R. L. (2012). Cultural change, human activity, and cognitive development. *Human Development*, 55, 205–228.

Gazzaniga, M., Bogen, J., & Sperry, R. (1962). Some functional effects of sectioning the cerebral commissures in man. *Proceedings of the National Academy of Science, USA*, 48, 1765–1769.

Gazzaniga, M., Ivry, R., & Mangun, R. (1998) *Cognitive neuroscience*. New York: Norton.

Geary, D. C. (1995). Reflections of evolution and culture in children's cognition: Implications for mathematical development and instruction. *American Psychologist*, 50, 24–37.

Geary, D. C. (2009). The *why* of learning. *Educational Psychologist*, 44, 198–201.Geary, D

Geary, D. C. (2011). Cognitive predictors of achievement growth in mathematics: A 5-year longitudinal study. *Developmental Psychology*, 47, 1539–1552.

Geary, D. C., Hoard, M. K., Byrd-Craven, J., Nugent, L., & Numtee, C. (2007). Cognitive mechanisms underlying achievement deficits in children with mathematical learning disability. *Child Development*, 78, 1343–1359.

Geddes, D. (2009). How am I doing? Exploring on-line guidebook monitoring as a self-regulated learning practice that impacts academic achievement. *Academy of Management Learning & Education*, 8, 494–510.

Gentner, D., Loewenstein, J., & Thompson, L. (2003). Learning and transfer: A general role for analogical encoding. *Journal of Educational Psychology*, 95, 393–408.

George, T. R., Feltz, D. L., & Chase, M. A. (1992). Effects of model similarity on self-efficacy and muscular endurance: A second look. *Journal of Sport and Exercise Psychology*, 14, 237–248.

Gersten, R., Chard, D. J., Jayanthi, M., Baker, S. K., Morphy, P., & Flojo, J. (2009). Mathematics instruction for students with learning disabilities: A meta-analysis of instructional components. *Review of Educational Research*, 79, 1202–1242.

Geschwind, N. (1998). Language areas in the brain. In R. L. Gregory (Ed.), *The Oxford companion to the mind* (pp. 425–426). Oxford, England: Oxford University Press.

Gick, M. L., & Holyoak, K. J. (1980). Analogical problem solving. *Cognitive Psychology*, 12, 306–355.

Gick, M. L., & Holyoak, K. J. (1983). Schema induction and analogical transfer. *Cognitive Psychology*, 15, 1–38.

Ginsburg, H., & Opper, S. (1988). *Piaget's theory of intellectual development* (2nd ed.). Englewood Cliffs, NJ: Prentice Hall.

Ginsburg-Block, M. D., Rohrbeck, C. A., & Fantuzzo, J. W. (2006). A meta-analytic review of social, self-concept, and behavioral outcomes of peer-assisted learning. *Journal of Educational Psychology*, 98, 732–749.

Gitomer, D. H., & Glaser, R. (1987). If you don't know it work on it: Knowledge, self-regulation and instruction. In R. E. Snow & M. J. Farr (Eds.), *Aptitude, learning, and instruction* (Vol. 3, pp. 301–325). Hillsdale, NJ: Erlbaum.

Glaser, C., & Brunstein, J. C. (2007). Improving fourth-grade students' composition skills: Effects of strategy instruction and self-regulation procedures. *Journal of Educational Psychology*, 99, 297–310.

Glaser, M., & Schwan. S. (2015). Explaining pictures: How verbal cues influence processing of pictorial learning material. *Journal of Educational Psychology*, 107, 1006–1018.

Glasgow, K. L., Dornbusch, S. M., Troyer, L., Steinberg, L., & Ritter, P. L. (1997). Parenting styles, adolescents' attributions, and educational outcomes in nine heterogeneous high schools. *Child Development*, 68, 507–529.

Glogger, I., Schwonke, R., Holzäpfel, L., Nückles, M., & Renkl, A. (2012). Learning strategies assessed by journal writing: Prediction of learning outcomes by quantity, quality, and combinations of learning strategies. *Journal of Educational Psychology*, 104, 452–468.

Glover, J. A., Plake, B. S., Roberts, B., Zimmer, J. W., & Palmere, M. (1981). Distinctiveness of encoding: The effects of paraphrasing and drawing inferences on memory from prose. *Journal of Educational Psychology*, 73, 736–744.

Goble, F. G. (1970). *The third force: The psychology of Abraham Maslow*. New York: Grossman.

Goddard, R. D., Hoy, W. K., & Woolfolk Hoy, A. (2000). Collective teacher efficacy: Its meaning, measure, and impact on student achievement. *American Educational Research Journal*, 37, 479–512.

Goddard, R. D., Hoy, W. K., & Woolfolk Hoy, A. (2004). Collective efficacy beliefs: Theoretical developments, empirical evidence, and future directions. *Educational Researcher*, 33(3), 3–13.

Godden, D. R., & Baddeley, A. D. (1975). Context-dependent memory in two natural environments: On land and underwater. *British Journal of Psychology*, 66, 325–332.

Godding, P. R., & Glasgow, R. E. (1985). Self-efficacy and outcome expectations as predictors of controlled smoking status. *Cognitive Therapy and Research*, 9, 583–590.

Goldin-Meadow, S., Alibali, M. W., & Church, R. B. (1993). Transitions in concept acquisition: Using the hand to read the mind. *Psychological Review*, 100, 279–297.

Goldin-Meadow, S., Levine, S. C., Hedges, L. V., Huttenlocher, J., Raudenbush, S. W., & Small, S. L. (2014). New evidence about language and cognitive development based on a longitudinal study. *American Psychologist*, 69, 588–599.

Gonzalez-DeHass, A. R., Willems, P. P., & Doan Holbein, M. F. (2005). Examining the relationship between parental involvement and student motivation. *Educational Psychology Review*, 17, 99–123.

Gopnik, A., & Wellman, H. M. (2012). Reconstructing constructivism: Causal models, Bayesian learning mechanisms, and the theory theory. *Psychological Bulletin*, 138, 1085–1108.

Gottfried, A. E. (1985). Academic intrinsic motivation in elementary and junior high school students. *Journal of Educational Psychology, 77,* 631–645.

Gottfried, A. E. (1990). Academic intrinsic motivation in young elementary school children. *Journal of Educational Psychology, 82,* 525–538.

Gottfried, A. E., Fleming, J. S., & Gottfried, A. W. (1998). Role of cognitively stimulating home environment in children's academic intrinsic motivation: A longitudinal study. *Child Development, 69,* 1448–1460.

Gould, D., & Weiss, M. (1981). The effects of model similarity and model talk on self-efficacy and muscular endurance. *Journal of Sport Psychology, 3,* 17–29.

Grabe, M. (1986). Attentional processes in education. In G. D. Phye & T. Andre (Eds.), *Cognitive classroom learning: Understanding, thinking, and problem solving* (pp. 49–82). Orlando: Academic Press.

Graesser, A. C., Conley, M. W., & Olney, A. (2012). Intelligent tutoring systems. In K. R. Harris, S. Graham, & T. Urdan (Eds.), *APA educational psychology handbook. Vol. 3: Application to learning and teaching* (pp. 451–473). Washington, DC: American Psychological Association.

Graham, S. (1991). A review of attribution theory in achievement contexts. *Educational Psychology Review, 3,* 5–39.

Graham, S. (1994). Motivation in African Americans. *Review of Educational Research, 64,* 55–117.

Graham, S. (2006). Writing. In P. A. Alexander & P. H. Winne (Eds.), *Handbook of educational psychology* (2nd ed., pp. 457–478). Mahwah, NJ: Erlbaum.

Graham, S., & Golan, S. (1991). Motivational influences on cognition: Task involvement, ego involvement, and depth of information processing. *Journal of Educational Psychology, 83,* 187–194.

Graham, S., & Harris, K. R. (2000). The role of self-regulation and transcription skills in writing and writing development. *Educational Psychologist, 35,* 3–12.

Graham, S., & Harris, K. R. (2003). Students with learning disabilities and the process of writing: A meta-analysis of SRSD studies. In H. L. Swanson, K. R. Harris, & S. Graham (Eds.), *Handbook of learning disabilities* (pp. 323–344). New York: Guilford Press.

Graham, S., Harris, K. R., MacArthur, C., & Santangelo, T. (2018). Self-regulation and writing. In D. H. Schunk & J. A. Greene (Eds.), *Handbook of self-regulation of learning and performance* (2nd ed., pp. 138–152). New York: Routledge.

Graham, S., Harris, K. R., MacArthur, C. A., & Schwartz, S. S. (1998). Writing instruction. In B. Y. L. Wong (Ed.), *Learning about learning disabilities* (2nd ed., pp. 391–424). New York: Academic Press.

Graham, S., & Hudley, C. (2005). Race and ethnicity in the study of motivation and competence. In A. J. Elliot & C. S. Dweck (Eds.), *Handbook of competence and motivation* (pp. 392–413). New York: Guilford Press.

Graham, S., & Long, A. (1986). Race, class, and the attributional process. *Journal of Educational Psychology, 78,* 4–13.

Graham, S., McKeown, D., Kiuhara, S., & Harris, K. R. (2012). A meta-analysis of writing instruction for students in the elementary grades. *Journal of Educational Psychology, 104,* 879–896.

Graham, S., & Perin, D. (2007). A meta-analysis of writing instruction for adolescent students. *Journal of Educational Psychology, 99,* 445–476.

Graham, S., & Taylor, A. Z. (2002). Ethnicity, gender, and the development of achievement values. In A. Wigfield & J. S. Eccles (Eds.), *Development of achievement motivation* (pp. 121–146). San Diego: Academic Press.

Graham, S., & Taylor, A. Z. (2016). Attribution theory and motivation in school. In K. R. Wentzel & D. B. Miele (Eds.), *Handbook of motivation at school* (2nd ed., pp. 11–33). New York: Routledge.

Graham, S., & Weiner, B. (2012). Motivation: Past, present, and future. In K. R. Harris, S. Graham, & T. Urdan (Eds.), *APA educational psychology handbook. Vol. 1: Theories, constructs, and critical issues* (pp. 367–397). Washington, DC: American Psychological Association.

Granic, I., Lobel, A., & Engels, R. C. M. E. (2014). The benefits of playing video games. *American Psychologist, 69,* 66–78.

Gredler, M. E. (2009). Hiding in plain sight: The stages of mastery/self-regulation in Vygotsky's cultural-historical theory. *Educational Psychologist, 44,* 1–19.

Gredler, M. E. (2012). Understanding Vygotsky for the classroom: Is it too late? *Educational Psychology Review, 24,* 113–131.

Green, C. D. (2009). Darwinian theory, functionalism, and the first American psychological revolution. *American Psychologist, 64,* 75–83.

Greene, J. A. (2016). Interacting epistemic systems within and beyond the classroom. In J. A. Greene, W. A. Sandoval, & I. Bråten (Eds.), *Handbook of epistemic cognition* (pp. 265–277). New York: Routledge.

Greene, J. A., & Azevedo, R. (2007). A theoretical review of Winne and Hadwin's model of self-regulated learning: New perspectives and directions. *Review of Educational Research, 77,* 334–372.

Greene, J. A., & Azevedo, R. (2009). A macro-level analysis of SRL processes and their relations to the acquisition of a sophisticated mental model of a complex system. *Contemporary Educational Psychology, 34,* 18–29.

Greene, J. A., Deekens, V. M., Copeland, D. Z., & Yu, S. (2018). Capturing and modeling self-regulated learning using think-aloud protocols. In D. H. Schunk & J. A. Greene (Eds.), *Handbook of self-regulation of learning and performance* (2nd ed., pp. 323–337). New York: Routledge.

Greene, J. A., Sandoval, W. A., & Bråten, I. (Eds.) (2016). *Handbook of epistemic cognition.* New York: Routledge.

Greeno, J. G. (1989). A perspective on thinking. *American Psychologist, 44,* 134–141.

Greeno, J. G., & the Middle School Mathematics Through Applications Project Group (1998). The situativity of knowing, learning, and research. *American Psychologist, 53,* 5–26.

Gregory, S. (2013, April 15). Practice, made perfect? An amateur's golf quest sheds light on how we learn. *Time, 181,* 56–57.

Griffin, M. M. (1995). You can't get there from here: Situated learning, transfer, and map skills. *Contemporary Educational Psychology, 20,* 65–87.

Grimaldi, P. J., & Karpicke, J. D. (2014). Guided retrieval practice of educational materials using automated scoring. *Journal of Educational Psychology, 106,* 58–68.

Grolnick, W. S., Gurland, S. T., Jacob, K. F., & Decourcey, W. (2002). The development of self-determination in middle childhood and adolescence. In A. Wigfield & J. S. Eccles (Eds.), *Development of achievement motivation* (pp. 147–171). San Diego: Academic Press.

Grossen, B. (1991). The fundamental skills of higher order thinking. *Journal of Learning Disabilities, 24,* 343–353.

Gunnar, M. R. (1996). *Quality of care and buffering of stress physiology: Its potential for protecting the developing human brain.* Minneapolis: University of Minnesota Institute of Child Development.

Gupta, P., & Cohen, N. J. (2002). Theoretical and computational analysis of skill learning, repetition priming, and procedural memory. *Psychological Review, 109,* 401–448.

Guskey, T. R., & Passaro, P. D. (1994). Teacher efficacy: A study of construct dimensions. *American Educational Research Journal, 31,* 627–643.

Guthrie, E. R. (1930). Conditioning as a principle of learning. *Psychological Review, 37,* 412–428.

Guthrie, E. R. (1940). Association and the law of effect. *Psychological Review, 47,* 127–148.

Guthrie, E. R. (1942). Conditioning: A theory of learning in terms of stimulus, response, and association. In N. B. Henry (Ed.), *The psychology of learning: The forty-first yearbook of the National Society for the Study of Education* (Part II, pp. 17–60). Chicago: University of Chicago Press.

Guthrie, E. R. (1952). *The psychology of learning* (Rev. ed.). New York: Harper & Brothers.

Guthrie, E. R. (1959). Association by contiguity. In S. Koch (Ed.), *Psychology: A study of a science* (Vol. 2, pp. 158–195). New York: McGraw-Hill.

Guthrie, J. T., Wigfield, A., Barbosa, P., Perencevich, K. C., Taboada, A., Davis, M. H., Scafiddi, N. T., & Tonks, S. (2004). Increasing reading comprehension and engagement through concept-oriented reading instruction. *Journal of Educational Psychology, 96,* 403–423.

Guthrie, J. T., Wigfield, A., & Perencevich, K. C. (Eds.) (2004). *Motivating reading comprehension: Concept-oriented reading instruction.* Mahwah, NJ: Erlbaum.

Guthrie, J. T., Wigfield, A., & VonSecker, C. (2000). Effects of integrated instruction on motivation and strategy use in reading. *Journal of Educational Psychology, 92,* 331–341.

Hackett, G., & Betz, N. E. (1981). A self-efficacy approach to the career development of women. *Journal of Vocational Behavior, 18,* 326–339.

Hadwin, A., Järvelä, S., & Miller, M. (2018). Self-regulation, co-regulation, and shared regulation in collaborative learning environments. In D. H. Schunk & J. A. Greene (Eds.), *Handbook of self-regulation of learning and performance* (2nd ed., pp. 83–106). New York: Routledge.

Halgren, E., & Marinkovic, K. (1995). Neurophysiological networks integrating human emotions. In M. S. Gazzaniga (Ed.), *The cognitive neurosciences* (pp. 1137–1151). Cambridge, MA: MIT Press.

Hall, V., Howe, A., Merkel, S., & Lederman, N. (1986). Behavior, motivation, and achievement in desegregated junior high school science classes. *Journal of Educational Psychology, 78,* 108–115.

Hall, V. C. (2003). Educational psychology from 1890 to 1920. In B. J. Zimmerman & D. H. Schunk (Eds.), *Educational psychology: A century of contributions* (pp. 3–39). Mahwah, NJ: Erlbaum.

Hallahan, D. P., Kneedler, R. D., & Lloyd, J. W. (1983). Cognitive behavior modification techniques for learning disabled children: Self-instruction and self-monitoring. In J. D. McKinney & L. Feagans (Eds.), *Current topics in learning disabilities* (Vol. 1, pp. 207–244). Norwood, NJ: Ablex.

Halliday, A. M. (1998). Evoked potential. In R. L. Gregory (Ed.), *The Oxford companion to the mind* (pp. 231–233). Oxford, England: Oxford University Press.

Halpern, D. F. (1998). Teaching critical thinking for transfer across domains. *American Psychologist, 53,* 449–455.

Halpern, D. F., & Hakel, M. D. (2003). Applying the science of learning to the university and beyond: Teaching for long-term retention and transfer. *Change, 35*(4), 36–41.

Halpern, D. F., Hansen, C., & Riefer, D. (1990). Analogies as an aid to understanding and memory. *Journal of Educational Psychology, 82,* 298–305.

Hamilton, R. J. (1985). A framework for the evaluation of the effectiveness of adjunct questions and objectives. *Review of Educational Research, 55,* 47–85.

Hamre, B. K., & Pianta, R. C. (2005). Can instructional and emotional support in the first-grade classroom make a difference for children at risk of school failure? *Child Development, 76,* 949–967.

Hancock, C. R. (2001). The teaching of second languages: Research trends. In V. Richardson (Ed.), *Handbook of research on teaching* (4th ed., pp. 358–369). Washington, DC: American Educational Research Association.

Hannus, M., & Hyönä, J. (1999). Utilization of illustrations during learning of science textbook passages among low- and high-ability children. *Contemporary Educational Psychology, 24,* 95–123.

Harackiewicz, J. M., Barron, K. E., Tauer, J. M., Carter, S. M., & Elliot, A. J. (2000). Short-term and long-term consequences of achievement goals: Predicting interest and performance over time. *Journal of Educational Psychology, 92,* 316–330.

Harackiewicz, J. M., Durik, A. M., Barron, K. E., Linnenbrink-Garcia, L., & Tauer, J. M. (2008). The role of achievement goals in the development of interest: Reciprocal relations between achievement goals, interest, and performance. *Journal of Educational Psychology, 100,* 105–122.

Harari, O., & Covington, M. V. (1981). Reactions to achievement behavior from a teacher and student perspective: A developmental analysis. *American Educational Research Journal, 18,* 15–28.

Hardiman, P. T., Dufresne, R., & Mestre, J. P. (1989). The relation between problem categorization and problem solving among experts and novices. *Memory & Cognition, 17,* 627–638.

Harlow, S., Cummings, R., & Aberasturi, S. M. (2006). Karl Popper and Jean Piaget: A rationale for constructivism. *The Educational Forum, 71,* 41–48.

Harris, B. (1979). Whatever happened to Little Albert? *American Psychologist, 34,* 151–160.

Harris, J. A. (2006). Elemental representations of stimuli in associative learning. *Psychological Review, 113,* 584–605.

Harris, J. R. (1998). *The nurture assumption: Why children turn out the way they do.* New York: Free Press.

Harris, K. R., Graham, S., & Mason, L. H. (2006). Improving the writing, knowledge, and motivation of struggling young writers: Effects of self-regulated strategy development with and without peer support. *American Educational Research Journal, 43,* 295–340.

Harris, K. R., Graham, S., & Santangelo, T. (2013). Self-regulated strategies development in writing: Development, implementation, and scaling up. In H. Bembenutty, T. J. Cleary, & A. Kitsantas (Eds.), *Applications of self-regulated learning across diverse disciplines: A tribute to Barry J. Zimmerman* (pp. 59–87). Charlotte, NC: Information Age Publishing.

Harris, K. R., & Pressley, M. (1991). The nature of cognitive strategy instruction: Interactive strategy construction. *Exceptional Children, 57*, 392–404.

Harter, S. (1978). Effectance motivation reconsidered: Toward a developmental model. *Human Development, 21*, 34–64.

Harter, S. (1981). A model of mastery motivation in children: Individual differences and developmental change. In W. A. Collins (Ed.), *Aspects on the development of competence: The Minnesota symposia on child psychology* (Vol. 14, pp. 215–255). Hillsdale, NJ: Erlbaum.

Harter, S., & Connell, J. P. (1984). A comparison of children's achievement and related self-perceptions of competence, control, and motivational orientation. In J. G. Nicholls (Ed.), *Advances in motivation and achievement* (Vol. 3, pp. 219–250). Greenwich, CT: JAI Press.

Hartley, E. T., Bray, M. A., & Kehle, T. J. (1998). Self-modeling as an intervention to increase student classroom participation. *Psychology in the Schools, 35*, 363–372.

Hattie, J. (2012). Know thy impact. *Educational Leadership, 70*(1), 18–23.

Hattie, J., Biggs, J., & Purdie, N. (1996). Effects of learning skills interventions on student learning: A meta-analysis. *Review of Educational Research, 66*, 99–136.

Hattie, J., & Timperley, H. (2007). The power of feedback. *Review of Educational Research, 77*, 81–112.

Haviland, S. E., & Clark, H. H. (1974). What's new? Acquiring new information as a process in comprehension. *Journal of Verbal Learning and Verbal Behavior, 13*, 512–521.

Hayes, J. R. (2000). A new framework for understanding cognition and affect in writing. In R. Indrisano & J. R. Squire (Eds.), *Perspectives on writing: Research, theory, and practice* (pp. 6–44). Newark, DE: International Reading Association.

Hayes-Roth, B., & Thorndyke, P. W. (1979). Integration of knowledge from text. *Journal of Verbal Learning and Verbal Behavior, 18*, 91–108.

Haynes, N. M., Emmons, C. L., Gebreyesus, S., & Ben-Avie, M. (1996). The School Development Program evaluation process. In J. P. Comer, N. M. Haynes, E. T. Joyner, & M. Ben-Avie (Eds.), *Rallying the whole village: The Comer process for reforming education* (pp. 123–146). New York: Teachers College Press.

Heatherton, T. F. (2011). Neuroscience of self and self-regulation. *Annual Review of Psychology, 62*, 363–390.

Hebb, D. O. (1949). *The organization of behavior: A neuropsychological theory.* New York: Wiley.

Heckhausen, H. (1991). *Motivation and action.* Berlin: Springer-Verlag.

Hegarty, M., Mayer, R. E., & Monk, C. A. (1995). Comprehension of arithmetic word problems: A comparison of successful and unsuccessful problem solvers. *Journal of Educational Psychology, 87*, 18–32.

Heidbreder, E. (1933). *Seven psychologies.* New York: Appleton-Century-Crofts.

Heider, F. (1946). Attitudes and cognitive organization. *Journal of Psychology, 21*, 107–112.

Heider, F. (1958). *The psychology of interpersonal relations.* New York: Wiley.

Hélie, S., & Sun, R. (2010). Incubation, insight, and creative problem solving: A unified theory and a connectionist model. *Psychological Review, 117*, 994–1024.

Henderson, J. G. (1996). *Reflective teaching: The study of your constructivist practices* (2nd ed.). Englewood Cliffs, NJ: Merrill/Prentice Hall.

Henderson, R. W., & Cunningham, L. (1994). Creating interactive sociocultural environments for self-regulated learning. In D. H. Schunk & B. J. Zimmerman (Eds.), *Self-regulation of learning and performance: Issues and educational applications* (pp. 255–281). Hillsdale, NJ: Erlbaum.

Hennessey, B. A., & Amabile, T. M. (2010). Creativity. *Annual Review of Psychology, 61*, 569–598.

Henson, R. K. (2002). From adolescent angst to adulthood: Substantive implications and measurement dilemmas in the development of teacher efficacy research. *Educational Psychologist, 37*, 137–150.

Heward, W. L., Alber-Morgan, S. R., & Konrad, M. (2017). *Exceptional children: An introduction to special education* (11th ed.). Boston: Pearson Education.Hew

Hickendorff, M., van Putten, C. M., Verhelst, N. D., & Heiser, W. J. (2010). Individual differences in strategy use on division problems: Mental versus written computation. *Journal of Educational Psychology, 102*, 438–452.

Hidi, S. (2000). An interest researcher's perspective: The effects of extrinsic and intrinsic factors on motivation. I C. Sansone & J. Harackiewicz (Eds.), *Intrinsic and extrinsic motivation: The search for optimal motivation and performance* (pp. 309–339). San Diego: Academic Press.

Hidi, S. E., & Ainley, M. (2008). Interest and self-regulation: Relationships between two variables that influence learning. In D. H. Schunk & B. J. Zimmerman (Eds.), *Motivation and self-regulated learning: Theory, research, and applications* (pp. 77–109). New York: Taylor & Francis.

Hidi, S., & Harackiewicz, J. (2000). Motivating the academically unmotivated: A critical issue for the 21st century. *Review of Educational Research, 70*, 151–179.

Hidi, S., & Renninger, K. A. (2006). The four-phase model of interest development. *Educational Psychologist, 41*, 111–127.

Higgins, E. T. (1981). Role taking and social judgment: Alternative developmental perspectives and processes. In J. H. Flavell & L. Ross (Eds.), *Social cognitive development: Frontiers and possible futures* (pp. 119–153). Cambridge, England: Cambridge University Press.

Highet, G. (1950). *The art of teaching.* New York: Vintage.

Hilgard, E. R. (1956). *Theories of learning* (2nd ed.). New York: Appleton-Century-Crofts.

Hilgard, E. R. (1996). Perspectives on educational psychology. *Educational Psychology Review, 8*, 419–431.

Hill, N. E., & Craft, S. A. (2003). Parent-school involvement and school performance: Mediated pathways among socioeconomically comparable African American and Euro-American families. *Journal of Educational Psychology, 95*, 74–83.

Hirsch, E. D., Jr. (1987). *Cultural literacy: What every American needs to know.* New York: Houghton Mifflin.

Hirt, E. R., Erickson, G. A., & McDonald, H. E. (1993). Role of expectancy timing and outcome consistency in expectancy-guided retrieval. *Journal of Personality and Social Psychology, 65*, 640–656.

Hitchcock, C. H., Dowrick, P. W., & Prater, M. A. (2003). Video self-modeling intervention in school-based settings, *Remedial and Special Education, 24*, 36–45, 56.

Hmelo-Silver, C. E. (2004). Problem-based learning: What and how do students learn? *Educational Psychology Review, 16*, 235–266.

Hofer, B. K., Yu, S. L., & Pintrich, P. R. (1998). Teaching college students to be self-regulated learners. In D. H. Schunk & B. J. Zimmerman (Eds.), *Self-regulated learning: From teaching to self-reflective practice* (pp. 57–85). New York: Guilford Press.

Hofferth, S. L. (2010). Home media and children's achievement and behavior. *Child Development, 81,* 1598–1619.

Höffler, T. N. (2010). Spatial ability: Its influence on learning with visualizations—a meta-analytic review. *Educational Psychology Review, 22,* 245–269.

Hogan, D. M., & Tudge, J. R. H. (1999). Implications of Vygotsky's theory for peer learning. In A. M. O'Donnell & A. King (Eds.), *Cognitive perspectives on peer learning* (pp. 39–65). Mahwah, NJ: Erlbaum.

Holland, J. G. (1992). Obituary: B. F. Skinner (1904–1990). *American Psychologist, 47,* 665–667.

Holland, J. G., & Skinner, B. F. (1961). *The analysis of behavior.* New York: McGraw-Hill.

Holley, C. D., Dansereau, D. F., McDonald, B. A., Garland, J. C., & Collins, K. W. (1979). Evaluation of a hierarchical mapping technique as an aid to prose processing. *Contemporary Educational Psychology, 4,* 227–237.

Hollis, K. L. (1997). Contemporary research on Pavlovian conditioning: A "new" functional analysis. *American Psychologist, 52,* 956–965.

Holyoak, K. J. (1984). Mental models in problem solving. In J. R. Anderson & S. M. Kosslyn (Eds.), *Tutorials in learning and memory: Essays in honor of Gordon Bower* (pp. 193–218). San Francisco: Freeman.

Holyoak, K. J., & Thagard, P. (1997). The analogical mind. *American Psychologist, 52,* 35–44.

Hom, H. L., Jr., & Murphy, M. D. (1985). Low need achievers' performance: The positive impact of a self-determined goal. *Personality and Social Psychology Bulletin, 11,* 275–285.

Homme, L., Csanyi, A. P., Gonzales, M. A., & Rechs, J. R. (1970). *How to use contingency contracting in the classroom.* Champaign, IL: Research Press.

Hopkins, S. L., & Lawson, M. J. (2002). Explaining the acquisition of a complex skill: Methodological and theoretical considerations uncovered in the study of simple addition and the moving-on process. *Educational Psychology Review, 14,* 121–154.

Horner, S. L. (2004). Observational learning during shared book reading: The effects on preschoolers' attention to print and letter knowledge. *Reading Psychology, 25,* 1–22.

Horner, S. L., & Gaither, S. M. (2004). Attribution retraining instruction with a second-grade class. *Early Childhood Education Journal, 31,* 165–170.

Horowitz, F. D. (1992). John B. Watson's legacy: Learning and environment. *Developmental Psychology, 28,* 360–367.

HuHuang, S., Zhang, Y., & Broniarczyk, S. M. (2012). So near and yet so far: The mental representation of goal progress. *Journal of Personality and Social Psychology, 103,* 225–241.

HuHübner, R., Steinhauser, M., & Lehle, C. (2010). A dual-stage two-phase model of selective attention. *Psychological Review, 117,* 759–784.

Hull, C. L. (1943). *Principles of behavior: An introduction to behavior theory.* New York: Appleton-Century-Crofts.

Hulleman, C. S., Kosovich, J. J., Barron, K. E., & Daniel, D. B. (2017). Making connections: Replicating and extending the utility value intervention in the classroom. *Journal of Educational Psychology, 109,* 387–404.

Hunt, E. (1989). Cognitive science: Definition, status, and questions. *Annual Review of Psychology, 40,* 603–629.

Hunt, J. McV. (1963). Motivation inherent in information processing and action. In O. J. Harvey (Ed.), *Motivation and social interaction* (pp. 35–94). New York: Ronald.

Hunt, M. (1993). *The story of psychology.* New York: Doubleday.

Hunter, A. B., Laursen, S. L., & Seymour, E. (2006). Becoming a scientist: The role of undergraduate research in students' cognitive, personal, and professional development. *Science Education, 91,* 36–74.

Hymel, S., Comfort, C., Schonert-Reichl, K., & McDougall, P. (1996). Academic failure and school dropout: The influence of peers. In J. Juvonen & K. R. Wentzel (Eds.), *Social motivation: Understanding children's school adjustment* (pp. 313–345). Cambridge, UK: Cambridge University Press.

Hyslop-Margison, E. J., & Strobel, J. (2008). Constructivism and education: Misunderstandings and pedagogical implications. *The Teacher Educator, 43,* 72–86.

Isaksen, S. G., & Gaulin, J. P. (2005). A reexamination of brainstorming research: Implications for research and practice. *Gifted Child Quarterly, 49,* 315–329.

Israel, G. D., & Beaulieu, L. J. (2004). Investing in communities: Social capital's role in keeping youth in school. *Journal of the Community Development Society, 34*(2), 35–57.

Jacoby, L. L., Bartz, W. H., & Evans, J. D. (1978). A functional approach to levels of processing. *Journal of Experimental Psychology: Human Learning and Memory, 4,* 331–346.

Jagacinski, C. M., & Nicholls, J. G. (1984). Conceptions of ability and related affects in task involvement and ego involvement. *Journal of Educational Psychology, 76,* 909–919.

Jagacinski, C. M., & Nicholls, J. G. (1987). Competence and affect in task involvement and ego involvement: The impact of social comparison information. *Journal of Educational Psychology, 79,* 107–114.

Jairam, D., & Kiewra, K. A. (2010). Helping students soar to success on computers: An investigation of the SOAR study method for computer-based learning. *Journal of Educational Psychology, 102,* 601–614.

James, W. (1890). *The principles of psychology* (Vols. I & II). New York: Henry Holt.

James, W. (1892). *Psychology: Briefer course.* New York: Henry Holt.

Jang, H., Kim, E. J., & Reeve, J. (2012). Longitudinal test of self-determination theory's motivation mediation model in a naturally occurring classroom context. *Journal of Educational Psychology, 104,* 1175–1188.J

Jarrold, C., & Hall, D. (2013). The development of rehearsal in verbal short-term memory. *Child Development Perspectives, 7*(3), 182–186.

Järvelä, S., & Hadwin, A. F. (2013). New frontiers: Regulating learning in CSCL. *Educational Psychologist, 48,* 25–39.

Jensen, E. (2005). *Teaching with the brain in mind* (2nd ed.). Alexandria, VA: ASCD.

Jensen, J. L., McDaniel, M. A., Woodard, S. M., & Kummer, T.A. (2014). Teaching to the test . . . or testing to teach: Exams requiring higher order thinking skills encourage greater conceptual understanding. *Educational Psychology Review, 26,* 307–329.

Jimerson, S. Egeland, B., Sroufe, A. A., & Carlson, B. (2000). A prospective longitudinal study of high school dropouts examining multiple predictors across development. *Journal of School Psychology, 38,* 525–549.

Johnson, C. I., & Mayer, R. E. (2009). A testing effect with multimedia learning. *Journal of Educational Psychology*, 101, 621–629.

Johnson, W. B. (2007). *On being a mentor: A guide for higher education faculty*. Mahwah, NJ: Erlbaum.

Johnson-Laird, P. N. (1972). The three-term series problem. *Cognition*, 1, 57–82.

Johnson-Laird, P. N. (1985). Deductive reasoning ability. In R. J. Sternberg (Ed.), *Human abilities: An information-processing approach* (pp. 173–194). New York: Freeman.

Johnson-Laird, P. N. (1999). Deductive reasoning. *Annual Review of Psychology*, 50, 109–135.

Johnson-Laird, P. N., Byrne, R. M. J., & Schaeken, W. (1992). Propositional reasoning by model. *Psychological Review*, 99, 418–439.

Johnson-Laird, P. N., Byrne, R. M. J., & Tabossi, P. (1989). Reasoning by model: The case of multiple quantification. *Psychological Review*, 96, 658–673.

Jonassen, D. H. (1996). *Computers in the classroom: Mind tools for critical thinking*. Englewood Cliffs, NJ: Merrill/Prentice Hall.

Jonassen, D. H., & Hung, W. (2006). Learning to troubleshoot: A new theory-based design architecture. *Educational Psychology Review*, 18, 77–114.

Jonassen, D. H., Peck, K. L., & Wilson, B. G. (1999). *Learning with technology: A constructivist perspective*. Upper Saddle River, NJ: Merrill/Prentice Hall.

Jones, B. D., Wilkins, J. L. M., Long, M. H., & Wang, F. (2012). Testing a motivational model of achievement: How students' mathematical beliefs and interests are related to their achievement. *European Journal of Psychology in Education*, 27, 1–20.Jo

Jones, M. H., Audley-Piotrowski, S. R., & Kiefer, S. M. (2012). Relationships among adolescents' perceptions of friends' behaviors, academic self-concept, and math performance. *Journal of Educational Psychology*, 104, 19–31.

Jonker, T. R., Seli, P., & MacLeod, C. M. (2013). Putting retrieval-induced forgetting in context: An inhibition-free, context-based account. *Psychological Review*, 120, 852–872.

Jourden, F. J., Bandura, A., & Banfield, J. T. (1991). The impact of conceptions of ability on self-regulatory factors and motor skill acquisition. *Journal of Sport and Exercise Psychology*, 8, 213–226.

Joussemet, M., & Koestner, R. (1999). Effect of expected rewards on children's creativity. *Creativity Research Journal*, 12, 231–239.

Jussim, L., Robustelli, S. L., & Cain, T. R. (2009). Teacher expectations and self-fulfilling prophecies. In K. R. Wentzel & A. Wigfield (Eds.), *Handbook of motivation at school* (pp. 349–380). New York: Routledge.

Just, M. A., & Carpenter, P. A. (1992). A capacity theory of comprehension: Individual differences in working memory. *Psychological Review*, 99, 122–149.

Justice, E. M., Baker-Ward, L., Gupta, S., & Jannings, L. R. (1997). Means to the goal of remembering: Developmental changes in awareness of strategy use-performance relations. *Journal of Experimental Child Psychology*, 65, 293–314.

Juvonen, J. (2006). Sense of belonging, social relationships, and school functioning. In P. A. Alexander & P. H. Winne (Eds.), *Handbook of educational psychology* (2nd ed., pp. 255–274). Mahwah, NJ: Erlbaum.

Juvonen, J., Espinoza, G., & Knifsend, C. (2012). He role of peer relationships in student academic and extracurricular engagement. In S. L. Christenson, A. L. Reschly, & C. Wylie (Eds.), *Handbook of research on student engagement* (pp. 387–401). New York: Springer.

Juvonen, J., & Knifsend, C. (2016). School-based peer relationships and achievement motivation. In K. R. Wentzel & D. B. Miele (Eds.), *Handbook of motivation at school* (2nd ed., pp. 231–250). New York: Routledge.

Kagan, J. (1966). Reflection-impulsivity: The generality and dynamics of conceptual tempo. *Journal of Abnormal Psychology*, 71, 17–24.

Kagan, J., Moss, H. A., & Sigel, I. E. (1960). Conceptual style and the use of affect labels. *Merrill-Palmer Quarterly*, 6, 261–278.

Kail, R. (2002). Developmental change in proactive interference. *Child Development*, 73, 1703–1714.

Kail, R. B., Jr., & Hagen, J. W. (1982). Memory in childhood. In B. B. Wolman (Ed.), *Handbook of developmental psychology* (pp. 350–366). Englewood Cliffs, NJ: Prentice Hall.

Kalyuga, S. (2007). Enhancing instructional efficiency of interactive e-learning environments: A cognitive load perspective. *Educational Psychology Review*, 19, 387–399.

Kalyuga, S., Renkl, A., & Paas, F. (2010). Facilitating flexible problem solving: A cognitive load perspective. *Educational Psychology Review*, 22, 175–186.

Kanfer, F. H., & Gaelick, L. (1986). Self-management methods. In F. H. Kanfer & A. P. Goldstein (Eds.), *Helping people change: A textbook of methods* (3rd ed., pp. 283–345). New York: Pergamon.

Kanfer, R., & Ackerman, P. L. (1989). Motivation and cognitive abilities: An integrative/aptitude-treatment interaction approach to skill acquisition. *Journal of Applied Psychology*, 74, 657–690.

Kanfer, R., & Kanfer, F. H. (1991). Goals and self-regulation: Applications of theory to work settings. In M. L. Maehr & P. R. Pintrich (Eds.), *Advances in motivation and achievement* (Vol. 7, pp. 287–326). Greenwich, CT: JAI Press.

Karabenick, S. A., & Gonida, E. N. (2018). Academic help seeking as a self-regulated learning strategy: Current issues, future directions. In D. H. Schunk & J. A. Greene (Eds.), *Handbook of self-regulation of learning and performance* (2nd ed., pp. 421–433). New York: Routledge.

Kardash, C. A. M., Royer, J. M., & Greene, B. A. (1988). Effects of schemata on both encoding and retrieval of information from prose. *Journal of Educational Psychology*, 80, 324–329.

Karpicke, J. D., & Aue, W. R. (2015). The testing effect is alive and well with complex materials. *Educational Psychology Review*, 27, 317–326.K

Karpicke, J. D., & Grimaldi, P. J. (2012). Retrieval-based learning: A perspective for enhancing meaningful learning. *Educational Psychology Review*, 24, 401–418.

Karpov, Y. V., & Haywood, H. C. (1998). Two ways to elaborate Vygotsky's concept of mediation: Implications for instruction. *American Psychologist*, 53, 27–36.

Kartal, G. (2010). Does language matter in multimedia learning: Personalization principle revisited. *Journal of Educational Psychology*, 102, 615–624.

Katona, G. (1940). *Organizing and memorizing*. New York: Columbia University Press.

Katzir, T., & Paré-Blagoev, J. (2006). Applying cognitive neuroscience research to education: The case of literacy. *Educational Psychologist*, 41, 53–74.

Kauffman, D. F. (2004). Self-regulated learning in web-based environments: Instructional tools designed to facilitate cognitive strategy use, metacognitive processing, and motivational beliefs. *Journal of Educational Computing Research*, 30, 139–161.

Kauffman, D. F., Ge, X., Xie, K., & Chen, C-H. (2008). Prompting in web-based environments: Supporting self-monitoring and problem solving skills in college students. *Journal of Educational Computing Research*, 38, 115–137.

Kauffman, D. F., & Kiewra, K. A. (2010). What makes a matrix so effective? An empirical test of the relative benefits of signaling, extraction, and localization. *Instructional Science*, 38, 679–705.

Kauffman, D. F., Zhao, R., & Yang, Y-S. (2011). Effects of online note taking formats and self-monitoring prompts on learning from online text: Using technology to enhance self-regulated learning. *Contemporary Educational Psychology*, 36, 313–322.

Keen, R. (2011). The development of problem solving in young children: A critical cognitive skill. *Annual Review of Psychology*, 62, 1–21.

Keller, F. S., & Ribes-Inesta, E. (1974). *Behavior modification: Applications to education*. New York: Academic Press.

Kempermann, G., & Gage, F. (1999, May). New nerve cells for the adult brain. *Scientific American*, 280(6), 48–53.

Kerst, S. M., & Howard, J. H., Jr. (1977). Mental comparisons for ordered information on abstract and concrete dimensions. *Memory & Cognition*, 5, 227–234.

Khemlani, S., & Johnson-Laird, P. N. (2012). Theories of the syllogism: A meta-analysis. *Psychological Bulletin*, 138, 427–457.

Kimmerle, J., Moskaliuk, J., Oeberst, A., & Cress, U. (2015). Learning and collective knowledge construction with social media: A process-oriented perspective. *Educational Psychologist*, 50, 120–137.

Kindermann, T. A. (1993). Natural peer groups as contexts for individual development: The case of children's motivation in school. *Developmental Psychology*, 29, 970–977.

Kindermann, T. A. (2007). Effects of naturally existing peer groups on changes in academic engagement in a cohort of sixth graders. *Child Development*, 78, 1186–1203.

Kindermann, T. A., McCollam, T. L., & Gibson, E., Jr. (1996). Peer networks and students' classroom engagement during childhood and adolescence. In J. Juvonen & K. R. Wentzel (Eds.), *Social motivation: Understanding children's school adjustment* (pp. 279–312). Cambridge, UK: Cambridge University Press.

King, E. W. (2002). Ethnicity. In D. L. Levinson, P. W. Cookson, Jr., & A. R. Sadovnik (Eds.), *Education and sociology: An encyclopedia* (pp. 247–253). New York: Routledge.

Kinlaw, C. R., Kurtz-Costes, B., & Goldman-Fraser, J. (2001). Mothers' achievement beliefs and behaviors and their children's school readiness: A cultural comparison. *Applied Developmental Psychology*, 22, 493–506.

Kintsch, W. (1974). *The representation of meaning in memory*. Hillsdale, NJ: Erlbaum.

Kintsch, W. (1979). On modeling comprehension. *Educational Psychologist*, 14, 3–14.

Kirkland, K., & Hollandsworth, J. G. (1980). Effective test taking: Skills-acquisition versus anxiety-reduction techniques. *Journal of Consulting and Clinical Psychology*, 48, 431–439.

Kirkorian, H. L., Wartella, E. A., & Anderson, D. R. (2008). Media and young children's learning. *The Future of Children*, 18(1), 39–61.

Kirschner, F., Paas, F., & Kirschner, P. A. (2009). A cognitive load approach to collaborative learning: United brains for complex tasks. *Educational Psychology Review*, 21, 31–42.

Kirschner, P. A., Sweller, J., & Clark, R. E. (2006). Why minimal guidance during instruction does not work: An analysis of the failure of constructivist, discovery, problem-based, experiential, and inquiry-based teaching. *Educational Psychologist*, 41, 75–86.

Kirshner, P., & Karpinski, A. (2010). Facebook and academic performance. *Computers in Human Behavior*, 26, 1237–1245.

Kitsantas, A., Dabbagh, N., Huie, F. C., & Dass, S. (2013). Learning technologies and self-regulated learning: Implications for practice. In H. Bembenutty, T. J. Cleary, & A. Kitsantas (Eds.), *Applications of self-regulated learning across diverse disciplines: A tribute to Barry J. Zimmerman* (pp. 325–354). Charlotte, NC: Information Age Publishing.

Kitsantas, A., & Zimmerman, B. J. (1998). Self-regulation of motoric learning: A strategic cycle view. *Journal of Applied Sport Psychology*, 10, 220–239.

Klahr, D., & Simon, H. A. (1999). Studies of scientific discovery: Complementary approaches and convergent findings. *Psychological Bulletin*, 125, 524–543.

Klassen, R. (2002). Writing in early adolescence: A review of the role of self-efficacy beliefs. *Educational Psychology Review*, 14, 173–203.

Klassen, R. (2004). Optimism and realism: A review of self-efficacy from a cross-cultural perspective. *International Journal of Psychology*, 39, 205–230.

Klauer, K. J., & Phye, G. D. (2008). Inductive reasoning: A training approach. *Review of Educational Research*, 78, 85–123.

Klausmeier, H. J. (1990). Conceptualizing. In B. F. Jones & L. Idol (Eds.), *Dimensions of thinking and cognitive instruction* (pp. 93–138). Hillsdale, NJ: Erlbaum.

Klausmeier, H. J. (1992). Concept learning and concept teaching. *Educational Psychologist*, 27, 267–286.

Kluger, J. (2013, July 29). The power of the bilingual brain. *Time*, 182(5), 42–47.

Kluger, J. (2013, September 23). The art of living. *Time*, 182(13), 44–46, 48, 50.

Koenig, M. A., & Sabbagh, M. A. (2013). Selective social learning: New perspectives on learning from others. *Developmental Psychology*, 49, 399–403.

Koffka, K. (1922). Perception: An introduction to the Gestalttheorie. *Psychological Bulletin*, 19, 531–585.

Koffka, K. (1924). *The growth of the mind* (R. M. Ogden, Trans.). London: Kegan Paul, Trench, Trubner.

Koffka, K. (1926). Mental development. In C. Murchison (Ed.), *Psychologies of 1925* (pp. 129–143). Worcester, MA: Clark University Press.

Köhler, W. (1925). *The mentality of apes* (E. Winter, Trans.). New York: Harcourt, Brace & World.

Köhler, W. (1926). An aspect of Gestalt psychology. In C. Murchison (Ed.), *Psychologies of 1925* (pp. 163–195). Worcester, MA: Clark University Press.

Köhler, W. (1947). *Gestalt psychology: An introduction to new concepts in modern psychology*. New York: Liveright. (Reprinted 1959, New American Library, New York)

Kolodner, J. L. (1997). Educational implications of analogy: A view from case-based reasoning. *American Psychologist*, 52, 57–66.

Kopp, C. B. (1982). Antecedents of self-regulation: A developmental perspective. *Developmental Psychology*, 18, 199–214.

Kosiewicz, M. M., Hallahan, D. P., Lloyd, J., & Graves, A. W. (1982). Effects of self-instruction and self-correction procedures on handwriting performance. *Learning Disability Quarterly, 5,* 71–78.

Kosslyn, S. M. (1980). *Image and mind.* Cambridge, MA: Harvard University Press.

Kosslyn, S. M. (1984). Mental representation. In J. R. Anderson & S. M. Kosslyn (Eds.), *Tutorials in learning and memory: Essays in honor of Gordon Bower* (pp. 91–117). San Francisco: Freeman.

Kosslyn, S. M. (1988). Aspects of a cognitive neuroscience of mental imagery. *Science, 240,* 1621–1626.

Kosslyn, S. M., & Pomerantz, J. P. (1977). Imagery, propositions, and the form of internal representations. *Cognitive Psychology, 9,* 52–76.

Kounin, J. S. (1977). *Discipline and group management in classrooms.* Huntington, NY: Krieger.

Kozulin, A. (1986). The concept of activity in Soviet psychology: Vygotsky, his disciples and critics. *American Psychologist, 41,* 264–274.

Krakovsky, M. (2016). When success sours: Public acclaim can distort research applications. *Stanford, 45*(6), 34–35.

Kramarski, B., & Mevarech, Z. R. (2003). Enhancing mathematical reasoning in the classroom: The effects of cooperative learning and metacognitive training. *American Educational Research Journal, 40,* 281–310.

Krämer, N. C., & Bente, G. (2010). Personalizing e-learning. The social effects of pedagogical agents. *Educational Psychology Review, 22,* 71–87.

Krapp, A., Hidi, S., & Renninger, K. A. (1992). Interest, learning, and development. In K. A. Renninger, S. Hidi, & A. Krapp (Eds.), *The role of interest in learning and development* (pp. 3–25). Hillsdale, NJ: Erlbaum.

Kross, E., Bruehlman-Senecal, E., Park, J., Burson, A., Dougherty, A., Shablack, H., Bremner, R., Moser, J., & Ayduk, O. (2014). Self-talk as a regulatory mechanism: How you do it matters. *Journal of Personality and Social Psychology, 106,* 304–324.

Kubovy, M., & van den Berg, M. (2008). The whole is equal to the sum of its parts: A probabilistic model of grouping by proximity and similarity in regular patterns. *Psychological Review, 115,* 131–154.

Kuhl, J. (1984). Volitional aspects of achievement motivation and learned helplessness: Toward a comprehensive theory of action control. In B. A. Maher (Ed.), *Progress in experimental personality research* (Vol. 13, pp. 99–171). New York: Academic Press.

Kuhl, J. (1985). Volitional mediators of cognition-behavior consistency: Self-regulatory processes and action versus state orientation. In J. Kuhl & J. Beckmann (Eds.), *Action control: From cognition to behavior* (pp. 101–128). New York: Springer-Verlag.

Kuhl, J., & Blankenship, V. (1979a). Behavioral change in a constant environment: Shift to more difficult tasks with constant probability of success. *Journal of Personality and Social Psychology, 37,* 549–561.

Kuhl, J., & Blankenship, V. (1979b). The dynamic theory of achievement motivation: From episodic to dynamic thinking. *Psychological Review, 86,* 141–151.

Kuhn, D. (1999). A developmental model of critical thinking. *Educational Researcher, 28*(2), 16–25, 46.

Kulik, C. C., Kulik, J. A., & Bangert-Drowns, R. L. (1990). Effectiveness of mastery learning programs: A meta-analysis. *Review of Educational Research, 60,* 265–299.

Kulik, J. A., & Fletcher, J. D. (2016). Effectiveness of intelligent tutoring systems: A meta-analytic review. *Review of Educational Research, 86,* 42–78.

Kulik, J. A., Kulik, C. C., & Cohen, P. A. (1980). Effectiveness of computer-based college teaching: A meta-analysis of findings. *Review of Educational Research, 50,* 525–544.

Ladd, G. W., Herald-Brown, S. L., & Kochel, K. P. (2009). Peers and motivation. In K. R. Wentzel & A. Wigfield (Eds.), *Handbook of motivation at school* (pp. 323–348). New York: Routledge.

Lajoie, S. P. (2003). Transitions and trajectories for studies of expertise. *Educational Researcher, 32*(8), 21–25.

Laming, D. (2010). Serial position curves in free recall. *Psychological Review, 117,* 93–133.

Lampert, M. (1990). When the problem is not the question and the solution is not the answer: Mathematical knowing and teaching. *American Educational Research Journal, 27,* 29–63.

Lan, W. Y. (1998). Teaching self-monitoring skills in statistics. In D. H. Schunk & B. J. Zimmerman (Eds.), *Self-regulated learning: From teaching to self-reflective practice* (pp. 86–105). New York: Guilford Press.

Lange, P. C. (1972). What's the score on: Programmed instruction? *Today's Education, 61,* 59.

Larkin, J. H., McDermott, J., Simon, D. P., & Simon, H. A. (1980). Models of competence in solving physics problems. *Cognitive Science, 4,* 317–345.

Larrauri, J. A., & Schmajuk, N. A. (2008). Attentional, associative, and configural mechanisms in extinction. *Psychological Review, 115,* 640–676.

Larreamendy-Joerns, J., & Leinhardt, G. (2006). Going the distance with online education. *Review of Educational Research, 76,* 567–605.

Lattal, K. A. (1992). B. F. Skinner and psychology: Introduction to the special issue. *American Psychologist, 47,* 1269–1272.

Lauer, P. A., Akiba, M., Wilkerson, S. B., Apthorp, H. S., Snow, D., & Martin-Glenn, M. L. (2006). Out-of-school-time programs: A meta-analysis of effects for at-risk students. *Review of Educational Research, 76,* 275–313.

Lave, J. (1993). Situating learning in communities of practice. In L. B. Resnick, J. M. Levine, & S. D. Teasley (Eds.), *Perspectives on socially shared cognition* (pp. 63–82). Washington, DC: American Psychological Association.

Lave, J., & Wenger, E. (1991). *Situated learning: Legitimate peripheral participation.* New York: Cambridge University Press.

Lazar, I., Darlington, R., Murray, H., Royce, J., & Snipper, A. (1982). Lasting effects of early education: A report from the Consortium for Longitudinal Studies. *Monograph of the Society for Research in Child Development* (Serial no. 195).

Ledford, J. R., & Wolery, M. (2013). Peer modeling of academic and social behaviors during small-group direct instruction. *Exceptional Children, 79,* 439–458.

Lee, F. J., & Anderson, J. R. (2001). Does learning a complex task have to be complex? A study in learning decomposition. *Cognitive Psychology, 42,* 267–316.

Lee, H., Plass, J. L., & Homer, B. D. (2006). Optimizing cognitive load for learning from computer-based science simulations. *Journal of Educational Psychology, 98,* 902–913.

Lee, J., & Bowen, N. K. (2006). Parent involvement, cultural capital, and the achievement gap among elementary school children. *American Educational Research Journal, 43,* 193–218.

Lee, J., & Shute, V. J. (2010). Personal and social-contextual factors in K-12 academic performance: An integrative perspective on student learning. *Educational Psychologist*, 45, 185–202.

Lee, V. E., Bryk, A. S., & Smith, J. B. (1993). The organization of effective secondary schools. In L. Darling-Hammond (Ed.), *Review of research in education* (Vol. 19, pp. 171–267). Washington, DC: American Educational Research Association.

Lee, V. E., & Smith, J. B. (1999). Social support and achievement for young adolescents in Chicago: The role of school academic press. *American Educational Research Journal*, 36, 907–945.

Leeper, R. (1935). A study of a neglected portion of the field of learning—The development of sensory organization. *Pedagogical Seminary and Journal of Genetic Psychology*, 46, 41–75.

Lefcourt, H. M. (1976). *Locus of control: Current trends in theory and research*. Hillsdale, NJ: Erlbaum.

Lehman, M., & Hasselhorn, M. (2010). The dynamics of free recall and their relation to rehearsal between 8 and 10 years of age. *Child Development*, 81, 1006–1020.

Lehman, M., & Malmberg, K. J. (2013). A buffer model of memory encoding and temporal correlations in retrieval. *Psychological Review*, 120, 155–189.

Lemonick, M. D. (2003, February 17). A twist of fate. *Time*, 161, 48–58.

Lemonick, M. D. (2007a, January 29). The flavor of memories. *Time*, 169, 102–104.

Lemonick, M. D. (2007b, July 16). The science of addiction. *Time*, 170, 42–48.

Lemonick, M. D., & Dorfman, A. (2006, October 9). What makes us different? *Time*, 168, 44–50, 53.

Lent, R. W., Brown, S. D., & Hackett, G. (2000). Contextual supports and barriers to career choice: A social cognitive analysis. *Journal of Counseling Psychology*, 47, 36–49.

Leopold, C., & Mayer, R. E. (2015). An imagination effect in learning from scientific text. *Journal of Educational Psychology*, 107, 47–63.

Lepper, M. R. (1983). Extrinsic reward and intrinsic motivation: Implications for the classroom. In J. M. Levine & M. C. Wang (Eds.), *Teacher and student perceptions: Implications for learning* (pp. 281–317). Hillsdale, NJ: Erlbaum.

Lepper, M. R., Corpus, J. H., & Iyengar, S. S. (2005). Intrinsic and extrinsic motivational orientations in the classroom: Age differences and academic correlates. *Journal of Educational Psychology*, 97, 184–196.

Lepper, M. R., Greene, D., & Nisbett, R. E. (1973). Undermining children's intrinsic interest with extrinsic rewards: A test of the "overjustification" hypothesis. *Journal of Personality and Social Psychology*, 28, 129–137.

Lepper, M. R., Henderlong, J., & Gingras, I. (1999). Understanding the effects of extrinsic rewards on intrinsic motivation—uses and abuses of meta-analysis: Comment on Deci, Koestner, and Ryan (1999). *Psychological Bulletin*, 125, 669–676.

Lepper, M. R., & Hodell, M. (1989). Intrinsic motivation in the classroom. In C. Ames & R. Ames (Eds.), *Research on motivation in education* (Vol. 3, pp. 73–105). San Diego: Academic Press.

Lepper, M. R., Sethi, S., Dialdin, D., & Drake, M. (1997). Intrinsic and extrinsic motivation: A developmental perspective. In S. S. Luthar, J. A. Burack, D. Cicchetti, & J. R. Weisz (Eds.), *Developmental psychopathology: Perspectives on adjustment,*

risk, and disorder (pp. 23–50). New York: Cambridge University Press.

Lesgold, A.M. (2001). The nature and methods of learning by doing. *American Psychologist*, 56, 964–973.

Letgers, N. E., Balfanz, R., Jordan, W. J., & McPartland, M. M. (2002). *Comprehensive reform for urban high schools: A talent development approach*. New York: Teachers College Press.

Leung, K. C. (2015). Preliminary empirical model of crucial determinants of best practice for peer tutoring on academic achievement. *Journal of Educational Psychology*, 107, 558–589.

Levin, J., & Nolan, J. F. (2000). *Principles of classroom management: A professional decision-making model*. Boston: Allyn & Bacon.

Lewin, K., Lippitt, R., & White, R. K. (1939). Patterns of aggressive behavior in experimentally created "social climates." *Journal of Social Psychology*, 10, 271–299.

Li, Q., & Ma, X. (2010). A meta-analysis of the effects of computer technology on school students' mathematics learning. *Educational Psychology Review*, 22, 215–243.

Licht, B. G., & Kistner, J. A. (1986). Motivational problems of learning-disabled children: Individual differences and their implications for treatment. In J. K. Torgesen & B. W. L. Wong (Eds.), *Psychological and educational perspectives on learning disabilities* (pp. 225–255). Orlando: Academic Press.

Lin, L. (2009). Breadth-based versus focused cognitive control in media multitasking. *Proceedings of the National Academy of Sciences of the United States of America*, 106, 15521–15522.

Linebarger, D. L., & Piotrowski, J. T. (2010). Structure and strategies in children's educational television: The roles of program type and learning strategies in children's learning. *Child Development*, 81, 1582–1597.

Linn, M. C., & Eylon, B. (2006). Science education: Integrating views of learning and instruction. In P. A. Alexander & P. H. Winne (Eds.), *Handbook of educational psychology* (2nd ed., pp. 511–544). Mahwah, NJ: Erlbaum.

Linnenbrink, E. A., & Pintrich, P. R. (2002). Achievement goal theory and affect: An asymmetrical bi-directional model. *Educational Psychologist*, 37, 69–78.

Linnenbrink-Garcia, L., Middleton, M. J., Ciani, K. D., Easter, M. A., O'Keefe, P. A., & Zusho, A. (2012). The strength of the relation between performance-approach and performance-avoidance goal orientations: Theoretical, methodological, and instructional implications. *Educational Psychologist*, 47, 281–301.

Linnenbrink-Garcia, L., Patall, E. A., & Messersmith, E. E. (2013). Antecedents and consequences of situational interest. *British Journal of Educational Psychology*, 83, 591–614.

Linnenbrink-Garcia, L., Rogat, T. K., & Koskey, K. L. K. (2011). Affect and engagement during small group instruction. *Contemporary Educational Psychology*, 36, 13–24.

Lipowski, S. L., Pyc, M. A., Dunlosky, J., & Rawson, K. A. (2014). Establishing and explaining the testing effect in free recall for young children. *Developmental Psychology*, 50, 994–1000.

Locke, E. A., & Latham, G. P. (1990). *A theory of goal setting and task performance*. Englewood Cliffs, NJ: Prentice Hall.

Locke, E. A., & Latham, G. P. (2002). Building a practically useful theory of goal setting and task motivation: A 35-year odyssey. *American Psychologist*, 57, 705–717.

Lockhart, R. S., Craik, F. I. M., & Jacoby, L. (1976). Depth of processing, recognition and recall. In J. Brown (Ed.), *Recall and recognition* (pp. 75–102). London: Wiley.

Loftus, E. F. (2003). Make believe memories. *American Psychologist*, 58, 867–873.

Loftus, E. F. (2004). Memories of things unseen. *Current Directions in Psychological Science*, 13, 145–147.

Logan, G. D. (2002). An instance theory of attention and memory. *Psychological Review*, 109, 376–400.

Lord, R. G., Diefendorff, J. M., Schmidt, A. M., & Hall, R. J. (2010). Self-regulation at work. *Annual Review of Psychology*, 61, 543–568.

Lovaas, O. I. (1977). *The autistic child: Language development through behavior modification*. New York: Irvington.

Love, S. Q. (1983). *Prediction of bulimic behaviors: A social learning analysis*. Unpublished doctoral dissertation, Virginia Polytechnic Institute and State University.

Luchins, A. S. (1942). Mechanization in problem solving: The effect of Einstellung. *Psychological Monographs*, 54(6, Whole No. 248).

Ludvik, M. J. B. (Ed.) (2016). *The neuroscience of learning and development*. Sterling, VA: Stylus Publishing.

Luria, A. R. (1961). *The role of speech in the regulation of normal and abnormal behavior* (J. Tizard, Trans.). New York: Liveright.

Lutkehaus, N. C., & Greenfield, P. (2003). From *The process of education* to *The culture of education*: An intellectual biography of Jerome Bruner's contributions to education. In B. J. Zimmerman & D. H. Schunk (Eds.), *Educational psychology: A century of contributions* (pp. 409–430). Mahwah, NJ: Erlbaum.

Ma, W., Adesope, O. O., Nesbit, J. C., & Liu, Q. (2014). Intelligent tutoring systems and learning outcomes: A meta-analysis. *Journal of Educational Psychology*, 106, 901–918.

Maag, J. W. (2001). Rewarded by punishment: Reflections on the disuse of positive reinforcement in schools. *Exceptional Children*, 67, 173–186.

Mabbott, D. J., & Bisanz, J. (2003). Developmental change and individual differences in children's multiplication. *Child Development*, 74, 1091–1107.

MacDonald, M. C., Just, M. A., & Carpenter, P. A. (1992). Working memory constraints on the processing of syntactic ambiguity. *Cognitive Psychology*, 24, 56–98.

Mace, F. C., Belfiore, P. J., & Hutchinson, J. M. (2001). Operant theory and research on self-regulation. In B. J. Zimmerman & D. H. Schunk (Eds.), *Self-regulated learning and academic achievement: Theoretical perspectives* (2nd ed., pp. 39–65). Mahwah, NJ: Erlbaum.

Mace, F. C., Belfiore, P. J., & Shea, M. C. (1989). Operant theory and research on self-regulation. In B. J. Zimmerman & D. H. Schunk (Eds.), *Self-regulated learning and academic achievement: Theory, research, and practice* (pp. 27–50). New York: Springer-Verlag.

Mace, F. C., & Kratochwill, T. R. (1988). Self-monitoring: Applications and issues. In J. Witt, S. Elliott, & F. Gresham (Eds.), *Handbook of behavior therapy in education* (pp. 489–502). New York: Pergamon.

Mace, F. C., & West, B. J. (1986). Unresolved theoretical issues in self-management: Implications for research and practice. *Professional School Psychology*, 1, 149–163.

Maddux, J. E. (1993). Social cognitive models of health and exercise behavior: An introduction and review of conceptual issues. *Journal of Applied Sport Psychology*, 5, 116–140.

Maddux, J. E., Brawley, L., & Boykin, A. (1995). Self-efficacy and healthy behavior: Prevention, promotion, and detection. In J. E. Maddux (Ed.), *Self-efficacy, adaptation, and adjustment: Theory, research, and application* (pp. 173–202). New York: Plenum.

Maehr, M. L., & Zusho, A. (2009). Achievement goal theory: The past, present, and future. In K. R. Wentzel & A. Wigfield (Eds.), *Handbook of motivation at school* (pp. 77–104). New York: Routledge.

Maes, S., & Gebhardt, W. (2000). Self-regulation and health behavior: The health behavior goal model. In M. Boekaerts, P. R. Pintrich, & M. Zeidner (Eds.), *Handbook of self-regulation* (pp. 343–368). San Diego: Academic Press.

Maes, S., & Karoly, P. (2005). Self-regulation assessment and intervention in physical health and illness: A review. *Applied Psychology: An International Review*, 54, 245–277.

Mager, R. (1962). *Preparing instructional objectives*. Palo Alto, CA: Fearon.

Magnifico, A. M. (2010). Writing for whom? Cognition, motivation, and a writer's audience. *Educational Psychologist*, 45, 167–184.

Mahoney, J. L., Lord, H., & Carryl, E. (2005). An ecological analysis of after-school program participation and the development of academic performance and motivational attributes for disadvantaged children. *Child Development*, 76, 811–825.

Mahoney, J. L., Parente, M. E., & Zigler, E. F. (2010). After-school program participation and children's development. In J. L. Meece & J. S. Eccles (Eds.), *Handbook of research on schools, schooling, and human development* (pp. 379–397). New York: Routledge.

Maier, S. F., & Seligman, M. E. P. (1976). Learned helplessness: Theory and evidence. *Journal of Experimental Psychology*, 105, 3–46.

Maier, S. F., & Seligman, M. E. P. (2016). Learned helplessness at fifty: Insights from neuroscience. *Psychological Review*, 123, 349–367.

Manderlink, G., & Harackiewicz, J. M. (1984). Proximal versus distal goal setting and intrinsic motivation. *Journal of Personality and Social Psychology*, 47, 918–928.

Mandler, J. M. (1978). A code in the node: The use of a story schema in retrieval. *Discourse Processes*, 1, 14–35.

Mandler, J. M., & Johnson, N. S. (1976). Some of the thousand words a picture is worth. *Journal of Experimental Psychology: Human Learning and Memory*, 2, 529–540.

Mandler, J. M., & Ritchey, G. H. (1977). Long-term memory for pictures. *Journal of Experimental Psychology: Human Learning and Memory*, 3, 386–396.

Marcovitch, S., Boseovski, J. J., Knapp, R. J., & Kane, M. J. (2010). Goal neglect and working memory capacity in 4- to 6-year-old children. *Child Development*, 81, 1687–1695.

Markman, A. B. (1999). *Knowledge representation*. Mahwah, NJ: Erlbaum.

Markus, H., & Nurius, P. (1986). Possible selves. *American Psychologist*, 41, 954–969.

Markus, H., & Wurf, E. (1987). The dynamic self-concept: A social psychological perspective. *Annual Review of Psychology*, 38, 299–337.

Marsh, H. W., & Hau, K. (2003). Big-fish-little-pond effect on academic self-concept: A cross-cultural (26-country) test of the negative effects of academically selective schools. *American Psychologist*, 58, 364–376.

Marsh, H. W., & Shavelson, R. (1985). Self-concept: Its multifaceted, hierarchical structure. *Educational Psychologist*, 20, 107–123.

Marshall, H. H., & Weinstein, R. S. (1984). Classroom factors affecting students' self-evaluations: An interactional model. *Review of Educational Research, 54*, 301–325.

Martin, A. J., & Dowson, M. (2009). Interpersonal relationships, motivation, engagement, and achievement: Yields for theory, current issues, and educational practice. *Review of Educational Research, 79*, 327–365.

Martin, J. (2004). Self-regulated learning, social cognitive theory, and agency. *Educational Psychologist, 39*, 135–145. Martin, J

Mashburn, A. J., Justice, L. M., Downer, J. T., & Pianta, R. C. (2009). Peer effects on children's language achievement during pre-kindergarten. *Child Development, 80*, 686–702.

Maslow, A. H. (1968). *Toward a psychology of being* (2nd ed.). New York: Van Nostrand Reinhold.

Maslow, A. H. (1970). *Motivation and personality* (2nd ed.). New York: Harper & Row.

Mason, L. H. (2004). Explicit self-regulated strategy development versus reciprocal questioning: Effects on expository reading comprehension among struggling readers. *Journal of Educational Psychology, 96*, 283–296.

Masten, A. S., & Coatsworth, J. D. (1998). The development of competence in favorable and unfavorable environments: Lessons from research on successful children. *American Psychologist, 53*, 205–220.

Masten, A. S., Hubbard, J. J., Gest, S. D., Tellegen, A., Garmezy, N., & Ramirez, M. (1999). Competence in the context of adversity: Pathways to resilience and maladaptation from childhood to late adolescence. *Development and Psychopathology, 11*, 143–169.

Master, A., Cheryan, S., & Meltzoff, A. N. (2016). Computing whether she belongs: Stereotypes undermine girls' interest and sense of belonging in computer science. *Journal of Educational Psychology, 108*, 424–437.

Mastropieri, M. A., & Scruggs, T. E. (2018). *The inclusive classroom: Strategies for effective differentiated instruction* (6th ed.). New York: Pearson Education.

Matlin, M. W. (2009). *Cognition* (7th ed.). Hoboken, NJ: Wiley.

Mautone, P. D., & Mayer, R. E. (2001). Signaling as a cognitive guide in multimedia learning. *Journal of Educational Psychology, 93*, 377–389.

Mautone, P. D., & Mayer, R. E. (2007). Cognitive aids for guiding graph comprehension. *Journal of Educational Psychology, 99*, 640–652.

Mayer, R. E. (1984). Aids to text comprehension. *Educational Psychologist, 19*, 30–42.

Mayer, R. E. (1985). Mathematical ability. In R. J. Sternberg (Ed.), *Human abilities: An information-processing approach* (pp. 127–150). New York: Freeman.

Mayer, R. E. (1992). *Thinking, problem solving, cognition* (2nd ed.). New York: Freeman.

Mayer, R. E. (1996). Learners as information processors: Legacies and limitations of educational psychology's second metaphor. *Educational Psychologist, 31*, 151–161.

Mayer, R. E. (1997). Multimedia learning: Are we asking the right questions? *Educational Psychologist, 32*, 1–19.

Mayer, R. E. (1999). *The promise of educational psychology: Learning in the content areas*. Upper Saddle River, NJ: Merrill/Prentice Hall.

Mayer, R. E. (2003). E. L. Thorndike's enduring contributions to educational psychology. In B. J. Zimmerman & D. H. Schunk (Eds.), *Educational psychology: A century of contributions* (pp. 113–154). Mahwah, NJ: Erlbaum.

Mayer, R. E. (2004). Should there be a three-strikes rule against pure discovery learning? The case for guided methods of instruction. *American Psychologist, 59*, 14–19.

Mayer, R. E. (2012). Information processing. In K. R. Harris, S. Graham, & T. Urdan (Eds.), *APA educational psychology handbook. Vol. 1: Theories, constructs, and critical issues* (pp. 85–99). Washington, DC: American Psychological Association.

Mayer, R. E., & Chandler, P. (2001). When learning is just a click away: Does simple user interaction foster deeper understanding of multimedia messages? *Journal of Educational Psychology, 93*, 390–397.

Mayer, R. E., Dow, G. T., & Mayer, S. (2003). Multimedia learning in an interactive self-explaining environment: What works in the design of agent-based microworlds? *Journal of Educational Psychology, 95*, 806–813.

Mayer, R. E., Fennell, S., Farmer, L., & Campbell, J. (2004). A personalization effect in multimedia learning: Students learn better when words are in conversational style rather than formal style. *Journal of Educational Psychology, 96*, 389–395.

Mayer, R. E., Heiser, J., & Lonn, S. (2001). Cognitive constraints on multimedia learning: When presenting more material results in less understanding. *Journal of Educational Psychology, 93*, 187–198.

Mayer, R. E., & Johnson, C. I. (2008). Revising the redundancy principle in multimedia learning. *Journal of Educational Psychology, 100*, 380–386.

Mayer, R. E., & Moreno, R. (2003). Nine ways to reduce cognitive load in multimedia learning. *Educational Psychologist, 38*, 43–52.

Mayer, R. E., Moreno, R., Boire, M., & Vagge, S. (1999). Maximizing constructivist learning from multimedia communications by minimizing cognitive load. *Journal of Educational Psychology, 91*, 638–643.

Mayer, R. E., Sobko, K., & Mautone, P. D. (2003). Social cues in multimedia learning: Role of speaker's voice. *Journal of Educational Psychology, 95*, 419–425.

Mayrath, M. C., Nihalani, P. K., & Robinson, D. H. (2011). Varying tutorial modality and interface restriction to maximize transfer in a complex simulation environment. *Journal of Educational Psychology, 103*, 257–268.

McCloskey, M., & Kaiser, M. (1984). The impetus impulse: A medieval theory of motion lives on in the minds of children. *The Sciences, 24*(6), 40–45.

McCullagh, P. (1993). Modeling: Learning, developmental, and social psychological considerations. In R. N. Singer, M. Murphey, & L. K. Tennant (Eds.), *Handbook of research on sport psychology* (pp. 106–126). New York: Macmillan.

McDermott, P. A., Rikoon, S. H., & Fantuzzo, J. W. (2014). Tracing children's approaches to learning through Head Start, kindergarten, and first grade: Different pathways to different outcomes. *Journal of Educational Psychology, 106*, 200–213.

McDougall, W. (1926). *An introduction to social psychology* (Rev. ed.). Boston: John W. Luce.

McInerney, D. M. (2008). The motivational role of cultural differences and cultural identity in self-regulated learning. In D. H. Schunk & B. J. Zimmerman (Eds.), *Motivation and self-regulated learning: Theory, research, and applications* (pp. 369–400). New York: Taylor & Francis.

McInerney, D. M., Hinkley, J., Dowson, M., & Van Etten, S. (1998). Aboriginal, Anglo, and immigrant Australian students' motivational beliefs about personal academic success: Are there cultural differences? *Journal of Educational Psychology*, 90, 621–629.

McInerney, D. M., & King, R. B. (2018). Culture and self-regulation in educational contexts. In D. H. Schunk & J. A. Greene (Eds.), *Handbook of self-regulation of learning and performance* (2nd ed., pp. 485–502). New York: Routledge.

McKeachie, W. J. (1990). Learning, thinking, and Thorndike. *Educational Psychologist*, 25, 127–141.

McNeil, J. D. (1987). *Reading comprehension: New directions for classroom practice* (2nd ed.). Glenview, IL: Scott, Foresman.

McVee, M. B., Dunsmore, K., & Gavelek, J. R. (2005). Schema theory revisited. *Review of Educational Research*, 75, 531–566.

Medin, D. L., Lynch, E. B., & Solomon, K. O. (2000). Are there kinds of concepts? *Annual Review of Psychology*, 51, 121–147.

Meece, J. L. (1991). The classroom context and students' motivational goals. In M. L. Maehr & P. R. Pintrich (Eds.), *Advances in motivation and achievement* (Vol. 7, pp. 261–285). Greenwich, CT: JAI Press.

Meece, J. L. (1994). The role of motivation in self-regulated learning. In D. H. Schunk & B. J. Zimmerman (Eds.), *Self-regulation of learning and performance: Issues and educational applications* (pp. 25–44). Hillsdale, NJ: Erlbaum.

Meece, J. L. (2002). *Child and adolescent development for educators* (2nd ed.). New York: McGraw-Hill.

Meece, J. L., Anderman, E. M., & Anderman, L. H. (2006). Classroom goal structure, student motivation, and academic achievement. *Annual Review of Psychology*, 57, 487–504.

Meece, J. L., Blumenfeld, P. C., & Hoyle, R. H. (1988). Students' goal orientations and cognitive engagement in classroom activities. *Journal of Educational Psychology*, 80, 514–523.

Meece, J. L., & Courtney, D. P. (1992). Gender differences in students' perceptions: Consequences for achievement-related choices. In D. H. Schunk & J. L. Meece (Eds.), *Student perceptions in the classroom* (pp. 209–228). Hillsdale, NJ: Erlbaum.

Meece, J. L., & Miller, S. D. (2001). A longitudinal analysis of elementary school students' achievement goals in literacy activities. *Contemporary Educational Psychology*, 26, 454–480.

Meichenbaum, D. (1977). *Cognitive behavior modification: An integrative approach*. New York: Plenum.

Meichenbaum, D. (1986). Cognitive behavior modification. In F. H. Kanfer & A. P. Goldstein (Eds.), *Helping people change: A textbook of methods* (3rd ed., pp. 346–380). New York: Pergamon.

Meichenbaum, D., & Asarnow, J. (1979). Cognitive-behavior modification and metacognitive development: Implications for the classroom. In P. C. Kendall & S. D. Hollon (Eds.), *Cognitive behavioral interventions: Theory, research, and procedures* (pp. 11–35). New York: Academic Press.

Meichenbaum, D., & Goodman, J. (1971). Training impulsive children to talk to themselves: A means of developing self-control. *Journal of Abnormal Psychology*, 77, 115–126.

Merrill, P. F. (1987). Job and task analysis. In R. M. Gagné (Ed.), *Instructional technology: Foundations* (pp. 141–173). Hillsdale, NJ: Erlbaum.

Messer, S. (1970). Reflection-impulsivity: Stability and school failure. *Journal of Educational Psychology*, 61, 487–490.

Messick, S. (1984). The nature of cognitive styles: Problems and promise in educational practice. *Educational Psychologist*, 19, 59–74.

Messick, S. (1994). The matter of style: Manifestations of personality in cognition, learning, and teaching. *Educational Psychologist*, 29, 121–136.

Meyer, D. E., & Schvaneveldt, R. W. (1971). Facilitation in recognizing pairs of words: Evidence of a dependence between retrieval operations. *Journal of Experimental Psychology*, 90, 227–234.

Meyer, D. K., & Turner, J. C. (2002). Discovering emotion in classroom motivation research. *Educational Psychologist*, 37, 107–114.

Mickelson, R. (1990). The attitude-achievement paradox among Black adolescents. *Sociology of Education*, 63, 44–61.

Miele, D. B., Son, L. K., & Metcalfe, J. (2013). Children's naïve theories of intelligence influence their metacognitive judgments. *Child Development*, 84, 1879–1886.

Miliotis, D., Sesma, A., Jr., & Masten, A. S. (1999). Parenting as a protective process for school success in children from homeless families. *Early Education & Development*, 10, 111–133.

Miller, G. A. (1956). The magical number seven, plus or minus two: Some limits on our capacity for processing information. *Psychological Review*, 63, 81–97.

Miller, G. A. (1988). The challenge of universal literacy. *Science*, 241, 1293–1299.

Miller, G. A., Galanter, E., & Pribham, K. H. (1960). *Plans and the structure of behavior*. New York: Holt, Rinehart & Winston.

Miller, N. E., & Dollard, J. (1941). *Social learning and imitation*. New Haven, CT: Yale University Press.

Mitchell, M. (1993). Situational interest: Its multifaceted structure in the secondary school mathematics classroom. *Journal of Educational Psychology*, 85, 424–436.

Molfese, D. L., Key, A. F., Kelly, S., Cunningham, N., Terrell, S., Ferguson, M., Molfese, V. J., & Bonebright, T. (2006). Below-average, average, and above-average readers engage different and similar brain regions while reading. *Journal of Learning Disabilities*, 39, 352–363.

Moll, L. C. (2001). Through the mediation of others: Vygotskian research on teaching. In V. Richardson (Ed.), *Handbook of research on teaching* (4th ed., pp. 111–129). Washington, DC: American Educational Research Association.

Montague, M., Krawec, J., Enders, C., & Dietz, S. (2014). The effects of cognitive strategy instruction on math problem solving of middle-school students of varying ability. *Journal of Educational Psychology*, 106, 469–481.

Moore, M. T. (1990). Problem finding and teacher experience. *Journal of Creative Behavior*, 24, 39–58.

Moors, A., & De Houwer, J. (2006). Automaticity: A theoretical and conceptual analysis. *Psychological Bulletin*, 132, 297–326.

Moos, D. C. (2018). Emerging classroom technology: Using self-regulation principles as a guide for effective implementation. In D. H. Schunk & J. A. Greene (Eds.), *Handbook of self-regulation of learning and performance* (2nd ed., pp. 243–253). New York: Routledge.

Moos, D. C., & Azevedo, R. (2009). Learning with computer-based learning environments: A literature review of computer self-efficacy. *Review of Educational Research*, 79, 576–600.

Moreno, R., & Mayer, R. E. (2000). Engaging students in active learning: The case for personalized multimedia messages. *Journal of Educational Psychology*, 92, 724–733.

Moreno, R., & Mayer, R. E. (2004). Personalized messages that promote science learning in virtual environments. *Journal of Educational Psychology*, 96, 165–173.

Moreno, R., & Mayer, R. E. (2007). Interactive multimodal learning environments. *Educational Psychology Review*, 19, 309–326.

Moreno, R., Ozogul, G., & Reisslein, M. (2011). Teaching with concrete and abstract visual representations: Effects on students' problem solving, problem representations, and learning perceptions. *Journal of Educational Psychology*, 103, 32–47.

Morgan, P. L., & Fuchs, D. (2007). Is there a bidirectional relationship between children's reading skills and reading motivation? *Exceptional Children*, 73, 165–183.

Morra, S., Gobbo, C., Marini, Z., & Sheese, R. (2008). *Cognitive development: Neo-Piagetian perspectives*. New York: Erlbaum.

Morris, C. D., Bransford, J. D., & Franks, J. J. (1977). Levels of processing versus transfer-appropriate processing. *Journal of Verbal Learning and Verbal Behavior*, 16, 519–533.

Morris, E. K. (2003). B. F. Skinner: A behavior analyst in educational psychology. In B. J. Zimmerman & D. H. Schunk (Eds.), *Educational psychology: A century of contributions* (pp. 229–250). Mahwah, NJ: Erlbaum.

Morse, W. H., & Kelleher, R. T. (1977). Determinants of reinforcement and punishment. In W. K. Honig & J. E. R. Staddon (Eds.), *Handbook of operant behavior* (pp. 174–200). Englewood Cliffs, NJ: Prentice Hall.

Mosatche, H. S., & Bragonier, P. (1981). An observational study of social comparison in preschoolers. *Child Development*, 52, 376–378.

Moscovitch, M., & Craik, F. I. M. (1976). Depth of processing, retrieval cues, and uniqueness of encoding as factors in recall. *Journal of Verbal Learning and Verbal Behavior*, 15, 447–458.

Motl, R. W., Dishman, R. K., Saunders, R. P., Dowda, M., & Pate, R. R. (2007). Perceptions of physical and social environment variables and self-efficacy as correlates of self-reported physical activity among adolescent girls. *Journal of Pediatric Psychology*, 32, 6–12.

Motl, R. W., Dishman, R. K., Ward, D. S., Saunders, R. P., Dowda, M., Felton, G., & Pate, R. R. (2005). Perceived physical environment and physical activity across one year among adolescent girls: Self-efficacy as a possible mediator? *Journal of Adolescent Health*, 37, 403–408.

Muenks, K., & Miele, D. B. (2017). Students' thinking about effort and ability: The role of developmental, contextual, and individual difference factors. *Review of Educational Research*, 87, 707–735.

Muldner, K., Lam, R., & Chi, M. T. H. (2014). Comparing learning from observing and from human tutoring. *Journal of Educational Psychology*, 106, 69–85.

Mullen, C. A. (2005). *Mentorship primer*. New York: Peter Lang.

Mullen, C. A. (2011). Facilitating self-regulated learning using mentoring approaches with doctoral students. In B. J. Zimmerman & D. H. Schunk (Eds.), *Handbook of self-regulation of learning and performance* (pp. 137–152). New York: Routledge.

Multon, K. D., Brown, S. D., & Lent, R. W. (1991). Relation of self-efficacy beliefs to academic outcomes: A meta-analytic investigation. *Journal of Counseling Psychology*, 38, 30–38.

Murayama, K., & Elliot, A. J. (2012). The competition-performance relation: A meta-analytic review and test of the opposing processes model of competition and performance. *Psychological Bulletin*, 138, 1035–1070.

Murayama, K., Elliot, A. J., & Friedman, R. (2012). Achievement goals. In R. M. Ryan (Ed.), *The Oxford handbook of human motivation* (pp. 191–207). Oxford, England: Oxford University Press.

Murayama, K., Miyatsu, T., Buchli, D., & Storm, B. C. (2014). Forgetting as a consequence of retrieval: A meta-analytic review of retrieval-induced forgetting. *Psychological Bulletin*, 140, 1383–1409.

Murayama, K., Pekrun, R., Lichtenfeld, S., & vom Hofe, R. (2013). Predicting long-term growth in students' mathematics achievement: The unique contributions of motivation and cognitive strategies. *Child Development*, 84, 1475–1490.

Murdock, T. B., & Anderman, E. M. (2006). Motivational perspectives on student cheating: Toward an integrated model of academic dishonesty. *Educational Psychologist*, 41, 129–145.

Murray, D. J., Kilgour, A. R., & Wasylkiw, L. (2000). Conflicts and missed signals in psychoanalysis, behaviorism, and Gestalt psychology. *American Psychologist*, 55, 422–426.

Muth, K. D., Glynn, S. M., Britton, B. K., & Graves, M. F. (1988). Thinking out loud while studying text: Rehearsing key ideas. *Journal of Educational Psychology*, 80, 315–318.

Myers, I. B., & McCaulley, M. H. (1988). *Manual: A Guide to the Development and Use of the Myers-Briggs Type Indicator*. Palo Alto, CA: Consulting Psychologists.

Myers, M., II, & Paris, S. G. (1978). Children's metacognitive knowledge about reading. *Journal of Educational Psychology*, 70, 680–690.

Nairne, J. S. (2002). Remembering over the short-term: The case against the standard model. *Annual Review of Psychology*, 53, 53–81.

Nandagopal, K., & Ericsson, K. A. (2012). Enhancing students' performance in traditional education: Implications from the expert performance approach and deliberate practice. In K. R. Harris, S. Graham, & T. Urdan (Eds.), *APA educational psychology handbook. Vol. 1: Theories, constructs, and critical issues* (pp. 257–293). Washington, DC: American Psychological Association.

National Governors Association Center for Best Practices and Council of Chief State School Officers (2010). *Common Core State Standards for English language arts and mathematics*. Washington, DC: Author.

National Research Council (2000). *How people learn: Brain, mind, experience, and school*. Washington, DC: National Academy Press.

National Research Council (2004). *Engaging schools: Fostering high school students' motivation to learn*. Washington, DC: National Academy Press.

National Research Council and Institute of Medicine. (2002). *Community programs to promote youth development*. Washington, DC: National Academy Press.

Natriello, G. (1986). *School dropouts: Patterns and policies*. New York: Teachers College Press.

Neisser, U. (1967). *Cognitive psychology*. Englewood Cliffs, NJ: Prentice Hall.

Nelson, T. O. (1977). Repetition and depth of processing. *Journal of Verbal Learning and Verbal Behavior*, 16, 151–171.

Nesbit, J. C., & Adesope, O. O. (2006). Learning with concept and knowledge maps: A meta-analysis. *Review of Educational Research*, 76, 413–448.

Neumeister, K. L. S., & Finch, H. (2006). Perfectionism in high-ability students: Relational precursors and influences on achievement motivation. *Gifted Child Quarterly*, 50, 238–251.

Neuringer, A., & Jensen, G. (2010). Operant variability and voluntary action. *Psychological Review*, 117, 972–993.

Newcombe, N. S., Ambady, N., Eccles, J., Gomez, L., Klahr, K., Linn, M., Miller, K., & Mix, K. (2009). Psychology's role in mathematics and science education. *American Psychologist, 64*, 538–550.

Newell, A., & Simon, H. A. (1972). *Human problem solving.* Englewood Cliffs, NJ: Prentice Hall.

Newman, R. S. (1994). Adaptive help seeking: A strategy of self-regulated learning. In D. H. Schunk & B. J. Zimmerman (Eds.), *Self-regulation of learning and performance: Issues and educational applications* (pp. 283–301). Hillsdale, NJ: Erlbaum.

Newman, R. S. (2000). Social influences on the development of children's adaptive help seeking: The role of parents, teachers, and peers. *Developmental Review, 20*, 350–404.

Newman, R. S. (2002). What do I need to do to succeed ... when I don't understand what I'm doing!?: Developmental influences on students' adaptive help seeking. In A. Wigfield & J. S. Eccles (Eds.), *Development of achievement motivation* (pp. 285–306). San Diego: Academic Press.

Newman, R. S. (2008). The motivational role of adaptive help seeking in self-regulated learning. In D. H. Schunk & B. J. Zimmerman (Eds.), *Motivation and self-regulated learning: Theory, research, and applications* (pp. 315–337). New York: Taylor & Francis.

Ng, W. (2015). *New digital technology in education: Conceptualizing professional learning for educators.* Cham, Switzerland: Springer International Publishing.

Nicholls, J. G. (1978). The development of the concepts of effort and ability, perception of academic attainment, and the understanding that difficult tasks require more ability. *Child Development, 49*, 800–814.

Nicholls, J. G. (1979). Development of perception of own attainment and causal attribution for success and failure in reading. *Journal of Educational Psychology, 71*, 94–99.

Nicholls, J. G. (1983). Conceptions of ability and achievement motivation: A theory and its implications for education. In S. G. Paris, G. M. Olson, & H. W. Stevenson (Eds.), *Learning and motivation in the classroom* (pp. 211–237). Hillsdale, NJ: Erlbaum.

Nicholls, J. G. (1984). Achievement motivation: Conceptions of ability, subjective experience, task choice, and performance. *Psychological Review, 91*, 328–346.

Nicholls, J. G., & Miller, A. T. (1984). Reasoning about the ability of self and others: A developmental study. *Child Development, 55*, 1990–1999.

Nicholls, J. G., Patashnick, M., & Nolen, S. B. (1985). Adolescents' theories of education. *Journal of Educational Psychology, 77*, 683–692.

Nicholls, J. G., & Thorkildsen, T. A. (1989). Intellectual conventions versus matters of substance: Elementary school students as curriculum theorists. *American Educational Research Journal, 26*, 533–544.

Nielsen, M. (2006). Copying actions and copying outcomes: Social learning through the second year. *Developmental Psychology, 42*, 555–565.

Nietfeld, J. L. (2018). The role of self-regulated learning n digital games. In D. H. Schunk & J. A. Greene (Eds.), *Handbook of self-regulation of learning and performance* (2nd ed., pp. 271–284). New York: Routledge.

Noddings, N. (1992). *The challenge to care in schools.* New York: Teachers College Press.

Nokes, J. D., Dole, J. A., & Hacker, D. J. (2007). Teaching high school students to use heuristics while reading historical texts. *Journal of Educational Psychology, 99*, 492–504.

Nokes-Malach, T. J., & Mestre, J. P. (2013). Toward a model of transfer as sense-making. *Educational Psychology Review, 48*, 184–207.

Nolen, S. B. (1996). Why study? How reasons for learning influence strategy selection. *Educational Psychology Review, 8*, 335–355.

Nolen-Hoeksema, S., Girgus, J. S., & Seligman, M. E. P. (1986). Learned helplessness in children: A longitudinal study of depression, achievement, and explanatory style. *Journal of Personality and Social Psychology, 51*, 435–442.

Norman, D. A. (1976). *Memory and attention: An introduction to human information processing* (2nd ed.). New York: Wiley.

Nussbaum, E. M., & Kardash, C. M. (2005). The effects of goal instructions and text on the generation of counterarguments during writing. *Journal of Educational Psychology, 97*, 157–169.

Oberauer, K., & Lewandowsky, S. (2008). Forgetting in immediate serial recall: Decay, temporal distinctiveness, or interference? *Psychological Review, 115*, 544–576.

O'Day, E. F., Kulhavy, R. W., Anderson, W., & Malczynski, R. J. (1971). *Programmed instruction: Techniques and trends.* New York: Appleton-Century-Crofts.

Oden, S., Schweinhart, L., & Weikart, D. (2000). *Into adulthood: A study of the effects of Head Start.* Ypsilanti, MI: High/Scope Educational Research Foundation.

O'Donnell, A. M. (2006). The role of peers and group learning. In P. A. Alexander & P. H. Winne (Eds.), *Handbook of educational psychology* (2nd ed., pp. 781–802). Mahwah, NJ: Erlbaum.

O'Donnell, A. M. (2012). Constructivism. In K. R. Harris, S. Graham, & T. Urdan (Eds.), *APA educational psychology handbook. Vol. 1: Theories, constructs, and critical issues* (pp. 61–84). Washington, DC: American Psychological Association.

O'Donnell, A. M., Dansereau, D. F., & Hall, R. H. (2002). Knowledge maps as scaffolds for cognitive processing. *Educational Psychology Review, 14*, 71–86.

Ohlsson, S. (1993). The interaction between knowledge and practice in the acquisition of cognitive skills. In S. Chipman & A. L. Meyrowitz (Eds.), *Foundations of knowledge acquisition: Cognitive models of complex learning* (pp. 147–208). Boston: Kluwer.

Ohlsson, S. (1996). Learning from performance errors. *Psychological Review, 103*, 241–262.

Ohlsson, S. (2009). Resubsumption: A possible mechanism for conceptual change and belief revision. *Educational Psychologist, 44*, 20–40.

O'Leary, K. D., & Drabman, R. (1971). Token reinforcement programs in the classroom: A review. *Psychological Bulletin, 75*, 379–398.

Olson, K. R., & Dweck, C. S. (2009). Social cognitive development: A new look. *Child Development Perspectives, 3*(1), 60–65.

O'Mara, A. J., Marsh, H. W., Craven, R. G., & Debus, R. L. (2006). Do self-concept interventions make a difference? A synergistic blend of construct validation and meta-analysis. *Educational Psychologist, 41*, 181–206.

Ornstein, R. (1997). *The right mind.* Orlando: Harcourt Brace.

Osborn, A. F. (1963). *Applied imagination.* New York: Scribner's.

Osterman, K. (2000). Students' need for belonging in the school community. *Review of Educational Research, 70*, 323–367.

Overskeid, G. (2007). Looking for Skinner and finding Freud. *American Psychologist, 62*, 590–595.

Paas, F., & Ayres, P. (2014). Cognitive load theory: A broader view on the role of memory in learning and education. *Educational Psychology Review, 26*, 191–195.

Paas, F., & Sweller, J. (2012). An evolutionary upgrade of cognitive load theory: Using the human motor system and collaboration to support the learning of complex cognitive tasks. *Educational Psychology Review*, 24, 27–45.Paas,

Paas, F., van Gog, T., & Sweller, J. (2010). Cognitive load theory: New conceptualizations, specifications, and integrated research perspectives. *Educational Psychology Review*, 22, 115–121.

Packer, M. J., & Goicoechea, J. (2000). Sociocultural and constructivist theories of learning: Ontology, not just epistemology. *Educational Psychologist*, 35, 227–241.

Padilla, A. M. (2006). Second language learning: Issues in research and teaching. In P. A. Alexander & P. H. Winne (Eds.), *Handbook of educational psychology* (2nd ed., pp. 571–591). Mahwah, NJ: Erlbaum.

Pai, H-H., Sears, D. A., & Maeda, Y. (2015). Effects of small-group learning on transfer: A meta-analysis. *Educational Psychology Review*, 27, 79–102.

Paivio, A. (1970). On the functional significance of imagery. *Psychological Bulletin*, 73, 385–392.

Paivio, A. (1971). *Imagery and verbal processes*. New York: Holt, Rinehart & Winston.

Paivio, A. (1978). Mental comparisons involving abstract attributes. *Memory & Cognition*, 6, 199–208.

Paivio, A. (1986). *Mental representations: A dual-coding approach*. New York: Oxford University Press.

Pajares, F. (1996). Self-efficacy beliefs in achievement settings. *Review of Educational Research*, 66, 543–578.

Pajares, F. (1997). Current directions in self-efficacy research. In M. Maehr & P. R. Pintrich (Eds.), *Advances in motivation and achievement* (Vol. 10, pp. 1–49). Greenwich, CT: JAI Press.

Pajares, F. (2003). William James: Our father who begat us. In B. J. Zimmerman & D. H. Schunk (Eds.), *Educational psychology: A century of contributions* (pp. 41–64). Mahwah, NJ: Erlbaum.

Pajares, F. (2008). Motivational role of self-efficacy beliefs in self-regulated learning. In D. H. Schunk & B. J. Zimmerman (Eds.), *Motivation and self-regulated learning: Theory, research, and applications* (pp. 111–139). New York: Taylor & Francis.

Pajares, F., & Schunk, D. H. (2001). Self-beliefs and school success: Self-efficacy, self-concept, and school achievement. In R. J. Riding & S. G. Rayner (Eds.), *Self-perception* (pp. 239–265). Westport, CT: Ablex.

Pajares, F., & Schunk, D. H. (2002). Self and self-belief in psychology and education: A historical perspective. In J. Aronson (Ed.), *Improving academic achievement: Impact of psychological factors on education* (pp. 3–21). San Diego, CA: Academic Press.

Palincsar, A. S., & Brown, A. L. (1984). Reciprocal teaching of comprehension-fostering and comprehension-monitoring activities. *Cognition and Instruction*, 1, 117–175.

Pan, S. C., Gopal, A., & Rickard, T. C. (2016). Testing with feedback yields potent, but piecewise, learning of history and biology facts. *Journal of Educational Psychology*, 108, 563–575.

Papini, M. R., & Bitterman, M. E. (1990). The role of contingency in classical conditioning. *Psychological Review*, 97, 396–403.

Paris, S. G., & Byrnes, J. P. (1989). The constructivist approach to self-regulation and learning in the classroom. In B. J. Zimmerman & D. H. Schunk (Eds.), *Self-regulated learning and academic achievement: Theory, research, and practice*, (pp. 169–200). New York: Springer-Verlag.

Paris, S. G., Byrnes, J. P., & Paris, A. H. (2001). Constructing theories, identities, and actions of self-regulated learners. In B. J.

Zimmerman & D. H. Schunk (Eds.), *Self-regulated learning and academic achievement: Theoretical perspectives* (2nd ed., pp. 253–287). Mahwah, NJ: Erlbaum.

Paris, S. G., Lipson, M. Y., & Wixson, K. K. (1983). Becoming a strategic reader. *Contemporary Educational Psychology*, 8, 293–316.

Paris, S. G., & Oka, E. R. (1986). Children's reading strategies, metacognition, and motivation. *Developmental Review*, 6, 25–56.

Paris, S. G., & Paris, A. H. (2001). Classroom applications of research on self-regulated learning. *Educational Psychologist*, 36, 89–101.

Pascual-Leone, J. (1970). A mathematical model for the transition rule in Piaget's development stages. *Acta Psychologica*, 32, 301–345.

Patrick, H., Ryan, A. M., & Kaplan, A. (2007). Early adolescents' perceptions of the classroom social environment, motivational beliefs, and engagement. *Journal of Educational Psychology*, 99, 83–98.

Paul, A. M. (2010, October 4). The womb. Your mother. Yourself. *Time*, 176, 50–55.

Pavlov, I. P. (1927). *Conditioned reflexes* (G. V. Anrep, Trans.). London: Oxford University Press.

Pavlov, I. P. (1928). *Lectures on conditioned reflexes* (W. H. Gantt, Trans.). New York: International Publishers.

Pavlov, I. P. (1932a). Neuroses in man and animals. *Journal of the American Medical Association*, 99, 1012–1013.

Pavlov, I. P. (1932b). The reply of a physiologist to psychologists. *Psychological Review*, 39, 91–127.

Pavlov, I. P. (1934). An attempt at a physiological interpretation of obsessional neurosis and paranoia. *Journal of Mental Science*, 80, 187–197.

Pekrun, R. (1992). The impact of emotions on learning and achievement: Towards a theory of cognitive/motivational mediators. *Applied Psychology: An International Review*, 41, 359–376.

Pekrun, R. (2006). The control-value theory of achievement emotions: Assumptions, corollaries, and implications for educational research and practice. *Educational Psychology Review*, 18, 315–341.

Pekrun, R. (2016). Academic emotions. In K. R. Wentzel & D. B. Miele (Eds.), *Handbook of motivation at school* (2nd ed., pp. 120–144). New York: Routledge.

Péladeau, N., Forget, J., & Gagné, F. (2003). Effect of paced and unpaced practice on skill application and retention: How much is enough? *American Educational Research Journal*, 40, 769–801.

Pellegrino, J. W. (1985). Inductive reasoning ability. In R. J. Sternberg (Ed.), *Human abilities: An information-processing approach* (pp. 195–225). New York: Freeman.

Pellegrino, J. W., Baxter, G. P., & Glaser, R. (1999). Addressing the "two disciplines" problem: Linking theories of cognition and learning with assessment and instructional practice. In A. Iran-Nejad & P. D. Pearson (Eds.), *Review of Research in Education* (Vol. 24, pp. 307–353). Washington, DC: American Educational Research Association.

Peltier, C., & Vannest, K. J. (2017). A meta-analysis of schema instruction on the problem-solving performance of elementary school students. *Review of Educational Research*, 87, 899–920.

Perkins, D. N., & Salomon, G. (1989). Are cognitive skills context-bound? *Educational Researcher*, 18(1), 16–25.

Perkins, D. N., & Salomon, G. (2012). Knowledge to go: A motivational and dispositional view of transfer. *Educational Psychologist*, 47, 248–258.

Perry, D. G., & Bussey, K. (1979). The social learning theory of sex differences: Imitation is alive and well. *Journal of Personality and Social Psychology*, 37, 1699–1712.

Perry, N. E. (1998). Young children's self-regulated learning and contexts that support it. *Journal of Educational Psychology*, 90, 715–729.

Peterson, C. (2000). The future of optimism. *American Psychologist*, 55, 44–55.

Peterson, L. R., & Peterson, M. J. (1959). Short-term retention of individual verbal items. *Journal of Experimental Psychology*, 58, 193–198.

Petri, H. L. (1986). *Motivation: Theory and research* (2nd ed.). Belmont, CA: Wadsworth.

Phares, E. J. (1976). *Locus of control in personality*. Morristown, NJ: General Learning Press.

Phelps, E. A. (2006). Emotion and cognition: Insights from studies of the human amygdale. *Annual Review of Psychology*, 57, 27–53.

Phillips, D. C. (1995). The good, the bad, and the ugly: The many faces of constructivism. *Educational Researcher*, 24(7), 5–12.

Phillips, J. L., Jr. (1969). *The origins of intellect: Piaget's theory*. San Francisco: Freeman.

Phye, G. D. (1989). Schemata training and transfer of an intellectual skill. *Journal of Educational Psychology*, 81, 347–352.

Phye, G. D. (1990). Inductive problem solving: Schema inducement and memory-based transfer. *Journal of Educational Psychology*, 82, 826–831.

Phye, G. D. (1992). Strategic transfer: A tool for academic problem solving. *Educational Psychology Review*, 4, 393–421.

Phye, G. D. (1997). Inductive reasoning and problem solving: The early grades. In G. D. Phye (Ed.), *Handbook of academic learning: The construction of knowledge* (pp. 451–471). San Diego: Academic Press.

Phye, G. D. (2001). Problem-solving instruction and problem-solving transfer: The correspondence issue. *Journal of Educational Psychology*, 93, 571–578.

Phye, G. D., & Sanders, C. E. (1992). Accessing strategic knowledge: Individual differences in procedural and strategy transfer. *Contemporary Educational Psychology*, 17, 211–223.

Phye, G. D., & Sanders, C. E. (1994). Advice and feedback: Elements of practice for problem solving. *Contemporary Educational Psychology*, 19, 286–301.

Piaget, J. (1952). *The origins of intelligence in children*. New York: International Universities Press.

Piaget, J. (1962). *Play, dreams and imitation*. New York: Norton.

Piaget, J. (1970). Piaget's theory. In P. Mussen (Ed.), *Carmichael's manual of child psychology* (3rd ed., Vol. 1, pp. 703–732). New York: Wiley.

Piaget, J., & Inhelder, B. (1969). *The psychology of the child*. New York: Basic Books.

Pianta, R. C., Belsky, J., Vandergrift, N., Houts, R., & Morrison, F. J. (2008). Classroom effects on children's achievement trajectories in elementary school. *American Educational Research Journal*, 45, 365–397.

Pianta, R.C., & Hamre, B. K. (2009). Conceptualization, measurement, and improvement of classroom processes: Standardized observation can leverage capacity. *Educational Researcher*, 38, 109–119.

Pimperton, H., & Nation, K. (2014). Poor comprehenders in the classroom: Teacher ratings of behavior in children with poor reading comprehension and its relationship with individual differences in working memory. *Journal of Learning Disabilities*, 47, 199–207.P

Pine, D. S. (2006). A primer on brain imaging in developmental psychopathology: What is it good for? *Journal of Child Psychology and Psychiatry*, 47, 983–986.

Pintrich, P. R. (2000a). Multiple goals, multiple pathways: The role of goal orientation in learning and achievement. *Journal of Educational Psychology*, 92, 544–555.

Pintrich, P. R. (2000b). The role of goal orientation in self-regulated learning. In M. Boekaerts, P. R. Pintrich, & M. Zeidner (Eds.), *Handbook of self-regulation* (pp. 451–502). San Diego: Academic Press.

Pintrich, P. R. (2003). A motivational science perspective on the role of student motivation in learning and teaching contexts. *Journal of Educational Psychology*, 95, 667–686.

Pintrich, P. R. (2004). A conceptual framework for assessing motivation and self-regulated learning in college students. *Educational Psychology Review*, 16, 385–407.

Pintrich, P. R., & De Groot, E. V. (1990). Motivational and self-regulated learning components of classroom academic performance. *Journal of Educational Psychology*, 82, 33–40.

Pintrich, P. R., & Garcia, T. (1991). Student goal orientation and self-regulation in the college classroom. In M. L. Maehr & P. R. Pintrich (Eds.), *Advances in motivation and achievement* (Vol. 7, pp. 371–402). Greenwich, CT: JAI Press.

Pintrich, P. R., Marx, R. W., & Boyle, R. A. (1993). Beyond cold conceptual change: The role of motivational beliefs and classroom contextual factors in the process of conceptual change. *Review of Educational Research*, 63, 167–199.

Pintrich, P. R., & Zusho, A. (2002). The development of academic self-regulation: The role of cognitive and motivational factors. In A. Wigfield & J. S. Eccles (Eds.), *Development of achievement motivation* (pp. 249–284). San Diego: Academic Press.

Plass, J. L., Homer, B. D., & Kinzer, C. K. (2015). Foundations of game-based learning. *Educational Psychologist*, 50, 258–283.

Plato (1965). *Plato's Meno: Text and criticism* (A. Sesonske & N. Fleming, Eds.). Belmont, CA: Wadsworth.

Poag-DuCharme, K. A., & Brawley, L. R. (1993). Self-efficacy theory: Use in the prediction of exercise behavior in the community setting. *Journal of Applied Sport Psychology*, 5, 178–194.

Pokay, P., & Blumenfeld, P. C. (1990). Predicting achievement early and late in the semester: The role of motivation and use of learning strategies. *Journal of Educational Psychology*, 82, 41–50.

Polk, T. A., & Newell, A. (1995). Deduction as verbal reasoning. *Psychological Review*, 102, 533–566.

Polya, G. (1945). *How to solve it*. Princeton, NJ: Princeton University Press. (Reprinted 1957, Doubleday, Garden City, NY)

Popham, W. J. (2014). *Classroom assessment: What teachers need to know* (7th ed.). Boston: Pearson Education.

Popkewitz, T. S. (1998). Dewey, Vygotsky, and the social administration of the individual: Constructivist pedagogy as systems of ideas in historical spaces. *American Educational Research Journal*, 35, 535–570.

Portes, P. R. (1996). Ethnicity and culture in educational psychology. In D. C. Berliner & R. C. Calfee (Eds.), *Handbook of educational psychology* (pp. 331–357). New York: Macmillan.

Posner, M. I., & Keele, S. W. (1968). On the genesis of abstract ideas. *Journal of Experimental Psychology, 77,* 353–363.

Postman, L. (1961). The present status of interference theory. In C. N. Cofer (Ed.), *Verbal learning and verbal behavior* (pp. 152–179). New York: McGraw-Hill.

Postman, L., & Stark, K. (1969). Role of response availability in transfer and interference. *Journal of Experimental Psychology, 79,* 168–177.

Powell, R. A., Digdon, N., Harris, B., & Smithson, C. (2014). Correcting the record on Watson, Rayner, and Little Albert. *American Psychologist, 69,* 600–611.

Premack, D. (1962). Reversibility of the reinforcement relation. *Science, 136,* 255–257.

Premack, D. (1971). Catching up with common sense or two sides of a generalization: Reinforcement and punishment. In R. Glaser (Ed.), *The nature of reinforcement* (pp. 121–150). New York: Academic Press.

Pressley, M., & Harris, K. R. (2006). Cognitive strategy instruction: From basic research to classroom instruction. In P. A. Alexander & P. H. Winne (Eds.), *Handbook of educational psychology* (2nd ed., pp. 265–286). Mahwah, NJ: Erlbaum.

Pressley, M., Harris, K. R., & Marks, M. B. (1992). But good strategy instructors are constructivists! *Educational Psychology Review, 4,* 3–31.

Pressley, M., & McCormick, C. B. (1995). *Advanced educational psychology for educators, researchers, and policymakers.* New York: HarperCollins.

Pressley, M., Woloshyn, V., Lysynchuk, L. M., Martin, V., Wood, E., & Willoughby, T. (1990). A primer of research on cognitive strategy instruction: The important issues and how to address them. *Educational Psychology Review, 2,* 1–58.

Presti, D. E. (2016). *Foundational concepts in neuroscience: A brain-mind odyssey.* New York: Norton.

Provasnik, S., Kewal Ramani, A., Coleman, M. M., Gilbertson, L., Herring, W., & Xie, Q. (2007). *Status of education in rural America (NCES 2007-040).* Washington, DC: National Center for Education Statistics.

Pugh, K. J., & Bergin, D. A. (2005). The effect of schooling on students' out-of-school experience. *Educational Researcher, 34*(9), 15–23.

Pugh, K. J., & Bergin, D. A. (2006). Motivational influences on transfer. *Educational Psychologist, 41,* 147–160.

Puntambekar, S., & Hübscher, R. (2005). Tools for scaffolding students in a complex learning environment: What have we gained and what have we missed? *Educational Psychologist, 40,* 1–12.

Purdie, N., Hattie, J., & Douglas, G. (1996). Student conceptions of learning and their use of self-regulated learning strategies: A cross-cultural comparison. *Journal of Educational Psychology, 88,* 87–100.

Putnam, R. D. (2000). *Bowling alone: The collapse and revival of American community.* New York: Simon & Schuster.

Pylyshyn, Z. W. (1973). What the mind's eye tells the mind's brain: A critique of mental imagery. *Psychological Bulletin, 80,* 1–24.

Quellmalz, E. S. (1987). Developing reasoning skills. In J. B. Baron & R. J. Sternberg (Eds.), *Teaching thinking skills: Theory and practice* (pp. 86–105). New York: Freeman.

Quin, D. (2017). Longitudinal and contextual associations between teacher-student relationships and student engagement: A systematic review. *Review of Educational Research, 87,* 345–387.Qu

Radvansky, G. A., & Ashcraft, M. H. (2014). *Cognition* (6th ed.). Boston: Pearson Education.

Radziszewska, B., & Rogoff, B. (1991). Children's guided participation in planning imaginary errands with skilled adult or peer partners. *Developmental Psychology, 27,* 381–389.

Raftery, J. N., Grolnick, W. S., & Flamm, E. S. (2012). Families as facilitators of student engagement: Toward a home-school partnership model. In S. L. Christenson, A. L. Reschly, & C. Wylie (Eds.), *Handbook of research on student engagement* (pp. 343–364). New York: Springer.R

Ramsburg, J. T., & Ohlsson, S. (2016). Category change in the absence of cognitive conflict. *Journal of Educational Psychology, 108,* 98–113.

Ramsel, D., & Grabe, M. (1983). Attentional allocation and performance in goal-directed reading: Age differences in reading flexibility. *Journal of Reading Behavior, 15,* 55–65.

Randall, J. G., Oswald, F. L., & Beier, M. E. (2014). Mind-wandering, cognition, and performance: A theory-driven meta-analysis of attention regulation. *Psychological Bulletin, 140,* 1411–1431,

Ratelle, C. F., Guay, F., Larose, S., & Senécal, C. (2004). Family correlates of trajectories of academic motivation during a school transition: A semiparametric group-based approach. *Journal of Educational Psychology, 96,* 743–754.

Ratner, H. H., Foley, M. A., & Gimpert, N. (2002). The role of collaborative planning in children's source-monitoring errors and learning. *Journal of Experimental Child Psychology, 81,* 44–73.

Ray, J. J. (1982). Achievement motivation and preferred probability of success. *Journal of Social Psychology, 116,* 255–261.

Reardon, S. F., & Galindo, C. (2009). The Hispanic-White achievement gap in math and reading in the elementary grades. *American Educational Research Journal, 46,* 853–891.

Redish, A. D., Jensen, S., Johnson, A., & Kurth-Nelson, Z. (2007). Reconciling reinforcement learning models with behavioral extinction and renewal: Implications for addiction, relapse, and problem gambling. *Psychological Review, 114,* 784–805.

Reed, S. K. (2006). Cognitive architectures for multimedia learning. *Educational Psychologist, 41,* 87–98.

Reeve, J., Deci, E. L., & Ryan, R. M. (2004). Self-determination theory: A dialectical framework for understanding sociocultural influences on student motivation. In D. M. McInerney & S. Van Etten (Eds.), *Big theories revisited* (pp. 31–60). Greenwich, CT: Information Age Publishing.

Reeve, J., & Lee, W. (2016). Neuroscientific contributions to motivation in education. In K. R. Wentzel & D. B. Miele (Eds.), *Handbook of motivation at school* (2nd ed., pp. 424–439). New York: Routledge.

Régner, I., Escribe, C., & Dupeyrat, C. (2007). Evidence of social comparison in mastery goals in natural academic settings. *Journal of Educational Psychology, 99,* 575–583.

Reid, R., & Lienemann, T. O. (2006). Self-regulated strategy development for written expression with students with attention deficit/hyperactivity disorder. *Exceptional Children, 73,* 53–68.

Reid, R., Trout, A. L., & Schartz, M. (2005). Self-regulation interventions for children with attention deficit/hyperactivity disorder. *Exceptional Children, 71,* 361–377.

Reigeluth, C. M. (Ed.) (1999). *Instructional design theories and models.* Mahwah, NJ: Erlbaum.

Relich, J. D., Debus, R. L., & Walker, R. (1986). The mediating role of attribution and self-efficacy variables for treatment effects on achievement outcomes. *Contemporary Educational Psychology, 11,* 195–216.

Reimann, P., & Bannert, M. (2018). Self-regulation of learning and performance in computer-supported collaborative learning environments. In D. H. Schunk & J. A. Greene (Eds.), *Handbook of self-regulation of learning and performance* (2nd ed., pp. 285–303). New York: Routledge.

Renkl, A., & Atkinson, R. K. (2003). Structuring the transition from example study to problem solving in cognitive skill acquisition: A cognitive load perspective. *Educational Psychologist*, 38, 15–22.

Renkl, D., Hilbert, T., & Schworm, S. (2009). Example-based learning in heuristic domains: A cognitive load theory account. *Educational Psychology Review*, 21, 67–78.

Renninger, K. A., & Wozniak, R. H. (1985). Effect of interest on attentional shift, recognition, and recall in young children. *Developmental Psychology*, 21, 624–632.

Rescorla, R. A. (1972). Informational variables in conditioning. In G. H. Bower (Ed.), *The psychology of learning and motivation* (Vol. 6, pp. 1–46). New York: Academic Press.

Rescorla, R. A. (1976). Pavlovian excitatory and inhibitory conditioning. In W. K. Estes (Ed.), *Handbook of learning and cognitive processes* (Vol. 2, pp. 7–35). Hillsdale, NJ: Erlbaum.

Rescorla, R. A. (1987). A Pavlovian analysis of goal-directed behavior. *American Psychologist*, 42, 119–129.

Resnick, L. B. (1981). Instructional psychology. *Annual Review of Psychology*, 32, 659–704.

Resnick, L. B. (1985). Cognition and instruction: Recent theories of human competence. In B. L. Hammonds (Ed.), *Psychology and learning: The master lecture series* (Vol. 4, pp. 127–186). Washington, DC: American Psychological Association.

Resnick, L. B. (1989). Developing mathematical knowledge. *American Psychologist*, 44, 162–169.

Reyes, M. R., Brackett, M. A., Rivers, S. E., White, M., & Salovey, P. (2012). Classroom emotional climate, student engagement, and academic achievement. *Journal of Educational Psychology*, 104, 700–712.

Reynolds, R., & Anderson, R. (1982). Influence of questions on the allocation of attention during reading. *Journal of Educational Psychology*, 74, 623–632.

Rhodes, M. G., & Tauber, S. K. (2011). The influence of delaying judgments of learning on metacognitive accuracy: A meta-analytic review. *Psychological Bulletin*, 137, 131–148.

Richert, R. A., Robb, M. B., & Smith, E. J. (2011). Media as social partners: The social nature of young children's learning from screen media. *Child Development*, 82, 82–95.

Richland, L. E., Morrison, R. G., & Holyoak, K. J. (2006). Children's development of analogical reasoning: Insights from scene analogy problems. *Journal of Experimental Child Psychology*, 94, 249–273.

Richter, C. P. (1927). Animal behavior and internal drives. *Quarterly Review of Biology*, 2, 307–343.

Riener, C., & Willingham, D. (2010). The myth of learning styles. *Change*, 42, 32–35.

Rips, L. J., Shoben, E. J., & Smith, E. E. (1973). Semantic distance and the verification of semantic relations. *Journal of Verbal Learning and Verbal Behavior*, 12, 1–20.

Rissman, J., & Wagner, A. D. (2012). Distributed representations in memory: Insights from functional brain imaging. *Annual Review of Psychology*, 63, 101–128.

Rittle-Johnson, B. (2006). Promoting transfer: Effects of self-explanation and direct instruction. *Child Development*, 77, 1–15.

Rittle-Johnson, B., & Star, J. (2007). Does comparing solution methods facilitate conceptual and procedural knowledge? An experimental study on learning to solve equations. *Journal of Educational Psychology*, 99, 561–574.

Roberts, D. F., & Foehr, U. G. (2008). Trends in media use. *The Future of Children*, 18(1), 11–37.

Robertson, J. S. (2000). Is attribution training a worthwhile classroom intervention for K-12 students with learning difficulties? *Educational Psychology Review*, 12, 111–134.

Robinson, D. R., Schofield, J. W., & Steers-Wentzell, K. L. (2005). Peer and cross-age tutoring in math: Outcomes and their design implications. *Educational Psychology Review*, 17, 327–362.

Robinson, N. M., Lanzi, R. G., Weinberg, R. A., Ramey, S. L., & Ramey, C. T. (2002). Family factors associated with high academic competence in former Head Start children at third grade. *Gifted Child Quarterly*, 46, 278–290.

Robinson, T. R., Smith, S. W., Miller, M. D., & Brownell, M. T. (1999). Cognitive behavior modification of hyperactivity-impulsivity and aggression: A meta-analysis of school-based studies. *Journal of Educational Psychology*, 91, 195–203.

Roblyer, M. D. (2006). *Integrating educational technology into teaching* (4th ed.). Upper Saddle River, NJ: Merrill/Prentice Hall.

Roediger, H. L., & Karpicke, J. D. (2006). Test enhanced learning: Taking memory tests improves long-term retention. *Psychological Science*, 17, 249–255.

Roeser, R. W., Eccles, J. S., & Strobel, K. (1998). Linking the study of schooling and mental health: Selected issues and empirical illustrations at the level of the individual. *Educational Psychologist*, 33, 153–176.

Roeser, R. W., Urdan, T. C., & Stephens, J. M. (2009). School as a context of student motivation and achievement. In K. R. Wentzel & A. Wigfield (Eds.), *Handbook of motivation at school* (pp. 381–410). New York: Routledge.

Rogers, C. R. (1959). A theory of therapy, personality, and interpersonal relationships, as developed in the client-centered framework. In S. Koch (Ed.), *Psychology: A study of a science* (Vol. 3, pp. 184–256). New York: McGraw-Hill.

Rogers, C. R. (1963). The actualizing tendency in relation to "motives" and to consciousness. In M. R. Jones (Ed.), *Nebraska symposium on motivation* (Vol. 11, pp. 1–24). Lincoln, NE: University of Nebraska Press.

Rogers, C. R. (1969). *Freedom to learn*. Columbus, OH: Merrill.

Rogers, C. R., & Freiberg, H. J. (1994). *Freedom to learn* (3rd ed.). Columbus, OH: Merrill/Prentice Hall.

Rogoff, B. (1986). Adult assistance of children's learning. In T. E. Raphael (Ed.), *The contexts of school-based literacy* (pp. 27–40). New York: Random House.

Rogoff, B. (1990). *Apprenticeship in thinking: Cognitive development in the social context*. New York: Oxford University Press.

Rogowsky, B. A., Calhoun, B. M., & Tallal, P. (2015). Matching learning style to instructional method: Effects on comprehension. *Journal of Educational Psychology*, 107, 64–78.

Rohrbeck, C. A., Ginsburg-Block, M. D., Fantuzzo, J. W., & Miller, T. R. (2003). Peer-assisted learning interventions with elementary school students: A meta-analytic review. *Journal of Educational Psychology*, 95, 240–257.

Rohrer, D., Dedrick, R. F., & Stershic, S. (2015). Interleaved practice improves mathematics learning. *Journal of Educational Psychology*, 107, 900–908.

Rohrer, D., & Pashler, H. (2010). Recent research on human learning challenges conventional instructional strategies. *Educational Researcher*, 39, 406–412.

Rohrkemper, M. M. (1989). Self-regulated learning and academic achievement: A Vygotskian view. In B. J. Zimmerman & D. H. Schunk (Eds.), *Self-regulated learning and academic achievement: Theory, research, and practice* (pp. 143–167). New York: Springer-Verlag.

Rolland, R. G. (2012). Synthesizing the evidence on classroom goal structures in middle and secondary schools: A meta-analysis and narrative review. *Review of Educational Research*, 82, 396–435.

Romberg, T. A., & Carpenter, T. P. (1986). Research on teaching and learning mathematics: Two disciplines of scientific inquiry. In M. C. Wittrock (Ed.), *Handbook of research on teaching* (3rd ed., pp. 850–873). New York: Macmillan.

Root-Bernstein, R. S. (1988). Setting the stage for discovery. *The Sciences*, 28(3), 26–34. © The New York Academy of Sciences 1988. Reproduced with the permission of John Wiley & Sons, Inc.

Rosch, E. (1973). Natural categories. *Cognitive Psychology*, 4, 328–350.

Rosch, E. (1975). Cognitive representations of semantic categories. *Journal of Experimental Psychology: General*, 104, 192–233.

Rosch, E. (1978). Principles of categorization. In E. Rosch & B. Lloyd (Eds.), *Cognition and categorization* (pp. 9–31). Hillsdale, NJ: Erlbaum.

Roscoe, R. D., & Chi, M. T. H. (2007). Understanding tutor learning: Knowledge-building and knowledge-telling in peer tutors' explanations and questions. *Review of Educational Research*, 77, 534–574.

Rosen, B., & D'Andrade, R. C. (1959). The psychosocial origins of achievement motivation. *Sociometry*, 22, 185–218.

Rosenholtz, S. J., & Rosenholtz, S. H. (1981). Classroom organization and the perception of ability. *Sociology of Education*, 54, 132–140.

Rosenholtz, S. J., & Simpson, C. (1984). The formation of ability conceptions: Developmental trend or social construction? *Review of Educational Research*, 54, 31–63.

Rosenshine, B., & Stevens, R. (1986). Teaching functions. In M. C. Wittrock (Ed.), *Handbook of research on teaching* (3rd ed., pp. 376–391). New York: Macmillan.

Rosenthal, R. (1974). *On the social psychology of the self-fulfilling prophecy: Further evidence for Pygmalion effects and their mediating mechanisms.* New York: MSS Modular Publications.

Rosenthal, R. (2002). Covert communication in classrooms, clinics, courtrooms, and cubicles. *American Psychologist*, 57, 839–849.

Rosenthal, R., & Jacobson, L. (1968). *Pygmalion in the classroom.* New York: Holt, Rinehart & Winston.

Rosenthal, T. L., & Bandura, A. (1978). Psychological modeling: Theory and practice. In S. L. Garfield & A. E. Bergin (Eds.), *Handbook of psychotherapy and behavior change: An empirical analysis* (2nd ed., pp. 621–658). New York: Wiley.

Rosenthal, T. L., & Zimmerman, B. J. (1978). *Social learning and cognition.* New York: Academic Press.

Ross, S. M., McCormick, D., Krisak, N., & Anand, P. (1985). Personalizing context in teaching mathematical concepts: Teacher-managed and computer-assisted models. *Educational Communication and Technology Journal*, 33, 169–178.

Rothbart, M. K., & Posner, M. I. (2015). The developing brain in a multitasking world. *Developmental Review*, 35, 42–63.

Rotter, J. B. (1966). Generalized expectancies for internal versus external control of reinforcement. *Psychological Monographs*, 80(1, Whole No. 609).

Rowe, M. L., Ramani, G. B., & Pomerantz, E. M. (2016). Parental involvement and children's motivation and achievement: A domain-specific perspective. In K. R. Wentzel & D. B. Miele (Eds.), *Handbook of motivation at school* (2nd ed., pp. 459–476). New York: Routledge.R

Rowland, C. A. (2014). The effect of testing versus restudy on retention: A meta-analytic review of the testing effect. *Psychological Bulletin*, 140, 1432–1463.

Royer, J. M. (1986). Designing instruction to produce understanding: An approach based on cognitive theory. In G. D. Phye & T. Andre (Eds.), *Cognitive classroom learning: Understanding, thinking, and problem solving* (pp. 83–113). Orlando: Academic Press.

Royer, J. M., Tronsky, L. N., Chan, Y., Jackson, S. J., & Marchant, H., III. (1999). Math-fact retrieval as the cognitive mechanism underlying gender differences in math test performance. *Contemporary Educational Psychology*, 24, 181–266.

Ruble, D. N. (1983). The development of social-comparison processes and their role in achievement-related self-socialization. In E. T. Higgins, D. N. Ruble, & W. Hartup (Eds.), *Social cognition and social development* (pp. 134–157). New York: Cambridge University Press.

Ruble, D. N., Boggiano, A. K., Feldman, N. S., & Loebl, J. H. (1980). Developmental analysis of the role of social comparison in self-evaluation. *Developmental Psychology*, 16, 105–115.

Ruble, D. N., Feldman, N. S., & Boggiano, A. K. (1976). Social comparison between young children in achievement situations. *Developmental Psychology*, 12, 191–197.

Rumberger, R. W. (2010). *Dropping out of school.* Cambridge, MA: Harvard University Press.

Rumberger, R. W., & Lim, S. A. (2008). *Why students drop out of school.* Santa Barbara, CA: California Dropout Research Project. Retrieved January 10, 2010, from http://www.lmri.ucsb.edu/dropouts.

Rumelhart, D. E. (1975). Notes on a schema for stories. In D. G. Bobrow & A. M. Collins (Eds.), *Representation and understanding: Studies in cognitive science* (pp. 211–236). New York: Academic Press.

Rumelhart, D. E. (1977). Understanding and summarizing brief stories. In D. Laberge & S. J. Samuels (Eds.), *Basic processes in reading* (pp. 265–303). Hillsdale, NJ: Erlbaum.

Rumelhart, D. E., & McClelland, J. L. (1986). *Parallel distributed processing: Explorations in the microstructure of cognition.* Cambridge, MA: MIT Press.

Rumelhart, D. E., & Norman, D. A. (1978). Accretion, tuning, and restructuring: Three modes of learning. In J. W. Cotton & R. L. Klatzky (Eds.), *Semantic factors in cognition* (pp. 37–53). Hillsdale, NJ: Erlbaum.

Rundus, D. (1971). Analysis of rehearsal processes in free recall. *Journal of Experimental Psychology*, 89, 63–77.

Ryan, A. M. (2000). Peer groups as a context for the socialization of adolescents' motivation, engagement, and achievement in school. *Educational Psychologist*, 35, 101–111.

Ryan, A. M. (2001). The peer group as a context for the development of young adolescents' motivation and achievement. *Child Development*, 72, 1135–1150.

Ryan, A. M., Gheen, M. H., & Midgley, C. (1998). Why do some students avoid asking for help? An examination of the interplay among students' academic efficacy, teachers' social-emotional role, and the classroom goal structure. *Journal of Educational Psychology*, 90, 528–535.

Ryan, R. M., & Deci, E. L. (2000). Self-determination theory and the facilitation of intrinsic motivation, social development, and well-being. *American Psychologist*, 55, 68–78.

Ryan, R. M., & Deci, E. L. (2009). Promoting self-determined school engagement: Motivation, learning, and well-being. In K. R. Wentzel & A. Wigfield (Eds.), *Handbook of motivation at school* (pp. 171–195). New York: Routledge.

Ryan, R. M., & Deci, E. L. (2016). Facilitating and hindering motivation, learning, and well-being in schools: Research and observations from self-determination theory. In K. R Wentzel & D. B. Miele (Eds.), *Handbook of motivation at school* (2nd ed., pp. 96–119). New York: Routledge.Ryan, R. M., & Deci, E. L.(2016). Facililtating and hindering motivation, learning, and well-being in schools: Research and observations from self-determination theory. In K. R. Wentzel & D. B> Miele (Eds.), *Handbook of motivation at school* (2nd ed., pp. 96-119). New York: ROutledge.

Ryan, R. M., & Powelson, C. L. (1991). Autonomy and relatedness as fundamental to motivation and education. *Journal of Experimental Education*, 60, 49–66.

Sadoski, M., & Paivio, A. (2001). *Imagery and text: A dual coding theory of reading and writing*. Mahwah, NJ: Erlbaum.

Sage, N. A., & Kindermann, T. A. (1999). Peer networks, behavior contingencies, and children's engagement in the classroom. *Merrill-Palmer Quarterly*, 45, 143–171.

Sagotsky, G., Patterson, C. J., & Lepper, M. R. (1978). Training children's self-control: A field experiment in self-monitoring and goal-setting in the classroom. *Journal of Experimental Child Psychology*, 25, 242–253.

Sakitt, B. (1976). Iconic memory. *Psychological Review*, 83, 257–276.

Sakitt, B., & Long, G. M. (1979). Spare the rod and spoil the icon. *Journal of Experimental Psychology: Human Perception and Performance*, 5, 19–30.

Sakiz, G. (2011). Mastery and performance approach goal orientations in relation to academic self-efficacy belies and academic help seeking behaviors of college students in Turkey. *Educational Research*, 2, 771–778.

Salden, R. J. C. M., Koedinger, K. R., Renkl, A., Aleven, V., & McLaren, B. M. (2010). Accounting for beneficial effects of worked examples in tutored problem solving. *Educational Psychology Review*, 22, 379–392.

Salen, K., & Zimmerman, E. (2004). *Rules of play: Game design fundamentals*. Cambridge, MA: MIT Press.

Salomon, G. (1984). Television is "easy" and print is "tough": The differential investment of mental effort in learning as a function of perceptions and attributions. *Journal of Educational Psychology*, 76, 647–658.

Salomon, G., & Perkins, D. N. (1989). Rocky roads to transfer: Rethinking mechanisms of a neglected phenomenon. *Educational Psychologist*, 24, 113–142.

Sandoval, J. (1995). Teaching in subject matter areas: Science. *Annual Review of Psychology*, 46, 355–374.

Scalise, K., & Felde, M. (2017). *Why neuroscience matters in the classroom: Principles of brain-based instructional design for teachers*. Boston: Pearson Education.

Scheiter, K., & Gerjets, P. (2007). Learner control in hypermedia environments. *Educational Psychology Review*, 19, 285–307.

Schiefele, U. (1996). Topic interest, text representation, and quality of experience. *Contemporary Educational Psychology*, 21, 3–18.

Schiefele, U. (2009). Situational and individual interest. In K. R. Wentzel & A. Wigfield (Eds.), *Handbook of motivation at school* (pp. 197–222). New York: Routledge.

Schmidt, M. E., & Vandewater, E. A. (2008). Media and attention, cognition, and school achievement. *The Future of Children*, 18(1), 63–85.

Schnotz, W., & Kürschner, C. (2007). A reconsideration of cognitive load theory. *Educational Psychology Review*, 19, 469–508.

Schoenfeld, A. H. (2006). Mathematics teaching and learning. In P. A. Alexander & P. H. Winne (Eds.), *Handbook of educational psychology* (2nd ed., pp. 479–510). Mahwah, NJ: Erlbaum.

Schraw, G., & Lehman, S. (2001). Situational interest: A review of the literature and directions for future research. *Educational Psychology Review*, 13, 23–52.

Schraw, G., & Moshman, D. (1995). Metacognitive theories. *Educational Psychology Review*, 7, 351–371.

Schuh, K. L. (2003). Knowledge construction in the learner-centered classroom. *Journal of Educational Psychology*, 95, 426–442.

Schüler, A., Scheiter, K., & van Genuchten, E. (2011). The role of working memory in multimedia instruction: Is working memory working during learning from text and pictures? *Educational Psychology Review*, 23, 389–411.

Schultz, W. (2006). Behavioral theories and the neurophysiology of reward. *Annual Review of Psychology*, 57, 87–115.

Schulz, L. E., Hooppell, C., & Jenkins, A. C. (2008). Judicious imitation: Children differentially imitate deterministically and probabilistically effective actions. *Child Development*, 79, 395–410.

Schunk, D. H. (1981). Modeling and attributional effects on children's achievement: A self-efficacy analysis. *Journal of Educational Psychology*, 73, 93–105.

Schunk, D. H. (1982a). Effects of effort attributional feedback on children's perceived self-efficacy and achievement. *Journal of Educational Psychology*, 74, 548–556.

Schunk, D. H. (1982b). Verbal self-regulation as a facilitator of children's achievement and self-efficacy. *Human Learning*, 1, 265–277.

Schunk, D. H. (1983a). Ability versus effort attributional feedback: Differential effects on self-efficacy and achievement. *Journal of Educational Psychology*, 75, 848–856.

Schunk, D. H. (1983b). Developing children's self-efficacy and skills: The roles of social comparative information and goal setting. *Contemporary Educational Psychology*, 8, 76–86.

Schunk, D. H. (1983c). Goal difficulty and attainment information: Effects on children's achievement behaviors. *Human Learning*, 2, 107–117.

Schunk, D. H. (1983d). Progress self-monitoring: Effects on children's self-efficacy and achievement. *Journal of Experimental Education*, 51, 89–93.

Schunk, D. H. (1983e). Reward contingencies and the development of children's skills and self-efficacy. *Journal of Educational Psychology*, 75, 511–518.

Schunk, D. H. (1984a). Enhancing self-efficacy and achievement through rewards and goals: Motivational and informational effects. *Journal of Educational Research*, 78, 29–34.

Schunk, D. H. (1984b). Sequential attributional feedback and children's achievement behaviors. *Journal of Educational Psychology*, 76, 1159–1169.

Schunk, D. H. (1985). Participation in goal setting: Effects on self-efficacy and skills of learning disabled children. *Journal of Special Education*, 19, 307–317.

Schunk, D. H. (1986). Verbalization and children's self-regulated learning. *Contemporary Educational Psychology*, 11, 347–369.

Schunk, D. H. (1987). Peer models and children's behavioral change. *Review of Educational Research*, 57, 149–174.

Schunk, D. H. (1990). Goal setting and self-efficacy during self-regulated learning. *Educational Psychologist*, 25, 71–86.

Schunk, D. H. (1995). Self-efficacy and education and instruction. In J. E. Maddux (Ed.), *Self-efficacy, adaptation, and adjustment: Theory, research, and applications* (pp. 281–303). New York: Plenum.

Schunk, D. H. (1996). Goal and self-evaluative influences during children's cognitive skill learning. *American Educational Research Journal*, 33, 359–382.

Schunk, D. H. (1999). Social-self interaction and achievement behavior. *Educational Psychologist*, 34, 219–227.

Schunk, D. H. (2001). Social cognitive theory and self-regulated learning. In B. J. Zimmerman & D. H. Schunk (Eds.), *Self-regulated learning and academic achievement: Theoretical perspectives* (2nd ed., pp. 125–151). Mahwah, NJ: Erlbaum.

Schunk, D. H. (2008). Attributions as motivators of self-regulated learning. In D. H. Schunk & B. J. Zimmerman (Eds.), *Motivation and self-regulated learning: Theory, research, and applications* (pp. 245–266). New York: Taylor & Francis.

Schunk, D. H. (2012). Social cognitive theory. In K. R. Harris, S. Graham, & T. Urdan (Eds.), *APA educational psychology handbook. Vol. 1: Theories, constructs, and critical issues* (pp. 101–123). Washington, DC: American Psychological Association.

Schunk, D. H., & Cox, P. D. (1986). Strategy training and attributional feedback with learning disabled students. *Journal of Educational Psychology*, 78, 201–209.

Schunk, D. H., & DiBenedetto, M. K. (2016). Self-efficacy theory in education. In K. R. Wentzel & D. B. Miele (Eds.), *Handbook of motivation at school* (2nd ed., pp. 34–54). New York: Routledge.

Schunk, D. H., & Ertmer, P. A. (1999). Self-regulatory processes during computer skill acquisition: Goal and self-evaluative influences. *Journal of Educational Psychology*, 91, 251–260.

Schunk, D. H., & Ertmer, P. A. (2000). Self-regulation and academic learning: Self-efficacy enhancing interventions. In M. Boekaerts, P. R. Pintrich, & M. Zeidner (Eds.), *Handbook of self-regulation* (pp. 631–649). San Diego: Academic Press.

Schunk, D. H., & Greene, J. A. (Eds.) (2018). *Handbook of self-regulation of learning and performance* (2nd ed.). New York: Routledge.

Schunk, D. H., & Gunn, T. P. (1986). Self-efficacy and skill development: Influence of task strategies and attributions. *Journal of Educational Research*, 79, 238–244.

Schunk, D. H., & Hanson, A. R. (1985). Peer models: Influence on children's self-efficacy and achievement. *Journal of Educational Psychology*, 77, 313–322.

Schunk, D. H., & Hanson, A. R. (1989a). Influence of peer-model attributes on children's beliefs and learning. *Journal of Educational Psychology*, 81, 431–434.

Schunk, D. H., & Hanson, A. R. (1989b). Self-modeling and children's cognitive skill learning. *Journal of Educational Psychology*, 81, 155–163.

Schunk, D. H., Hanson, A. R., & Cox, P. D. (1987). Peer-model attributes and children's achievement behaviors. *Journal of Educational Psychology*, 79, 54–61.

Schunk, D. H., Meece, J. L., & Pintrich, P. R. (2014). *Motivation in education: Theory, research, and applications* (4th ed.). Boston: Pearson Education.

Schunk, D. H., & Mullen, C. A. (2013). Toward a conceptual model of mentoring research: Integration with self-regulated learning. *Educational Psychology Review*, 25, 361–389.

Schunk, D. H., & Pajares, F. (2002). The development of academic self-efficacy. In A. Wigfield & J. S. Eccles (Eds.), *Development of academic motivation* (pp. 15–31). San Diego: Academic Press.

Schunk, D. H., & Pajares, F. (2005). Competence perceptions and academic functioning. In A. J. Elliot & C. S. Dweck (Eds.), *Handbook of competence and motivation* (pp. 85–104). New York: Guilford Press.

Schunk, D. H., & Rice, J. M. (1986). Extended attributional feedback: Sequence effects during remedial reading instruction. *Journal of Early Adolescence*, 6, 55–66.

Schunk, D. H., & Rice, J. M. (1987). Enhancing comprehension skill and self-efficacy with strategy value information. *Journal of Reading Behavior*, 19, 285–302.

Schunk, D. H., & Rice, J. M. (1989). Learning goals and children's reading comprehension. *Journal of Reading Behavior*, 21, 279–293.

Schunk, D. H., & Rice, J. M. (1991). Learning goals and progress feedback during reading comprehension instruction. *Journal of Reading Behavior*, 23, 351–364.

Schunk, D. H., & Rice, J. M. (1993). Strategy fading and progress feedback: Effects on self-efficacy and comprehension among students receiving remedial reading services. *Journal of Special Education*, 27, 257–276.

Schunk, D. H., & Richardson, K. (2011). Motivation and self-efficacy in mathematics education. In D. J. Brahier & W. R. Speer (Eds.), *Motivation and disposition: Pathways to learning mathematics* (pp. 13–30). Reston, VA: National Council of Teachers of Mathematics.

Schunk, D. H., & Swartz, C. W. (1993a). Goals and progress feedback: Effects on self-efficacy and writing achievement. *Contemporary Educational Psychology*, 18, 337–354.

Schunk, D. H., & Swartz, C. W. (1993b). Writing strategy instruction with gifted students: Effects of goals and feedback on self-efficacy and skills. *Roeper Review*, 15, 225–230.

Schunk, D. H., & Zimmerman, B. J. (Eds.) (1994). *Self-regulation of learning and performance: Issues and educational applications*. Hillsdale, NJ: Erlbaum.

Schunk, D. H., & Zimmerman, B. J. (1997). Social origins of self-regulatory competence. *Educational Psychologist*, 32, 195–208.

Schunk, D. H., & Zimmerman, B. J. (2006). Competence and control beliefs: Distinguishing the means and ends. In P. A. Alexander & P. H. Winne (Eds.), *Handbook of educational psychology* (2nd ed., pp. 349–367). Mahwah, NJ: Erlbaum.

Schunk, D. H., & Zimmerman, B. J. (Eds.) (2008). *Motivation and self-regulated learning: Theory, research, and applications*. New York: Taylor & Francis.

Schwaighofer, M., Fischer, F., & Bühner, M. (2015). Does working memory training transfer? A meta-analysis including training conditions as moderators. *Educational Psychologist*, 50, 138–166.

Schwartz, D. L., & Goldstone, R. (2016). Learning as coordination: Cognitive psychology and education. In L. Corno & E. M. Anderman (Eds.), *Handbook of educational psychology* (3rd ed., pp. 61–75). New York: Routledge.S

Schwartz, S. J., Lilienfeld, S. O., Meca, A., & Sauvigné, K. C. (2016). The role of neuroscience within psychology: A call for inclusiveness over exclusiveness. *American Psychologist*, 71, 52–70.

Schweinhart, L. J., & Weikart, D. (1997). *Lasting differences: The High/Scope Perry Preschool curriculum comparison study through age 23.* (Monographs of the High/Scope Educational Research Foundation, 12). Ypsilanti, MI: High/Scope Press.

Schwenck, C., Bjorklund, D. F., & Schneider, W. (2007). Factors influencing the incidence of utilization deficiencies and other patterns of recall/strategy-use relations in a strategic memory task. *Child Development, 78,* 1771–1787.

Schweppe, J., & Rummer, R. (2014). Attention, working memory, and long-term memory in multimedia learning: An integrated perspective based on process models of working memory. *Educational Psychology Review, 26,* 285–306.

Searle, J. R. (1969). *Speech acts.* Cambridge, England: Cambridge University Press.

Sederberg, P. B., Howard, M. W., & Kahana, M. J. (2008). A context-based theory of recency and contiguity in free recall. *Psychological Review, 115,* 893–912.

Seidel, T., & Shavelson, R. J. (2007). Teaching effectiveness research in the past decade: The role of theory and research design in disentangling meta-analysis results. *Review of Educational Research, 77,* 454–499.

Seligman, M. E. P. (1975). *Helplessness: On depression, development, and death.* San Francisco: Freeman.

Seligman, M. E. P. (1991). *Learned optimism.* New York: Knopf.

Sénéchal, M., & LeFevre, J. (2002). Parental involvement in the development of children's reading skill: A five-year longitudinal study. *Child Development, 73,* 445–460.

Senko, C. (2016). Achievement goal theory. A story of early promises, eventual discords, and future possibilities. In K. R. Wentzel & D. B. Miele (Eds.), *Handbook of motivation at school* (2nd ed., pp. 75–95). New York: Routledge.Senko, C. (2016).

Seo, K. K-J., Pellegrino, D. A., & Engelhard, C. (2012). *Designing problem-driven instruction with online social media.* Charlotte, NC: Information Age Publishing.

Shanks, D. R. (2010). Learning: From association to cognition. *Annual Review of Psychology, 61,* 273–301.

Shaul, M. S., & Ganson, H. C. (2005). The No Child Left Behind Act of 2001: The Federal Government's role in strengthening accountability for student performance. In L. Parker (Ed.), *Review of Research in Education* (Vol. 29, pp. 151–165). Washington, DC: American Educational Research Association.

Shavelson, R. J., & Bolus, R. (1982). Self-concept: The interplay of theory and methods. *Journal of Educational Psychology, 74,* 3–17.

Shell, D. F., Murphy, C. C., & Bruning, R. H. (1989). Self-efficacy and outcome expectancy mechanisms in reading and writing achievement. *Journal of Educational Psychology, 81,* 91–100.

Shepard, R. N. (1978). The mental image. *American Psychologist, 33,* 125–137.

Shepard, R. N., & Cooper, L. A. (1983). *Mental images and their transformations.* Cambridge, MA: MIT Press.

Shipman, S., & Shipman, V. C. (1985). Cognitive styles: Some conceptual, methodological, and applied issues. In E. W. Gordon (Ed.), *Review of research in education* (Vol. 12, pp. 229–291). Washington, DC: American Educational Research Association.

Shipstead, Z., Redick, T. S., & Engle, R. W. (2012). Is working memory training effective? *Psychological Bulletin, 138,* 628–654.

Shore, N. (1997). *Rethinking the brain: New insights into early development.* New York: Families and Work Institute.

Short, E. J., Friebert, S. E., & Andrist, C. G. (1990). Individual differences in attentional processes as a function of age and skill level. *Learning and Individual Differences, 2,* 389–403.

Shuell, T. J. (1986). Cognitive conceptions of learning. *Review of Educational Research, 56,* 411–436.

Shuell, T. J. (1988). The role of the student in learning from instruction. *Contemporary Educational Psychology, 13,* 276–295.

Shultz, T. R., & Lepper, M. R. (1996). Cognitive dissonance reduction as constraint satisfaction. *Psychological Review, 103,* 219–240.

Shute, N. (2009, February). The amazing teen brain. *U. S. News & World Report, 146,* 37–39.

Siegler, R. S. (1989). Mechanisms of cognitive development. *Annual Review of Psychology, 40,* 353–379.

Siegler, R. S. (1991). *Children's thinking* (2nd ed.). Englewood Cliffs, NJ: Prentice Hall.

Siegler, R. S. (2000). The rebirth of children's learning. *Child Development, 71,* 26–35.

Siegler, R. S. (2005). Children's learning. *American Psychologist, 60,* 769–778.

Sigel, I. E., & Brodzinsky, D. M. (1977). Individual differences: A perspective for understanding intellectual development. In H. Hom & P. Robinson (Eds.), *Psychological processes in early education* (pp. 295–329). New York: Academic Press.

Sigelman, C. K. (2012). Rich man, poor man: Developmental differences in attributions and perceptions. *Journal of Experimental Child Psychology, 113,* 415–429.

Silver, E. A. (1981). Recall of mathematical problem information: Solving related problems. *Journal for Research in Mathematics Education, 12,* 54–64.

Simmering, V. R. (2012). The development of visual working memory capacity during early childhood. *Journal of Experimental Child Psychology, 111,* 695–707.

Simon, H. A. (1974). How big is a chunk? *Science, 183,* 482–488.

Simon, H. A. (1979). Information processing models of cognition. *Annual Review of Psychology, 30,* 363–396.

Simone, R., Zhang, L., & Truman, J. (2010). *Indicators of school crime and safety: 2010.* Washington, DC: U.S. Department of Education, National Center for Education Statistics (NCES 2011-002). Retrieved November 14, 2011, from http://nces.ed.gov.

Simpson, T. L. (2002). Dare I oppose constructivist theory? *The Educational Forum, 66,* 347–354.

Sirin, S. R. (2005). Socioeconomic status and academic achievement: A meta-analytic review of research. *Review of Educational Research, 75,* 417–453.

Sitzmann, T., & Ely, K. (2011). A meta-analysis of self-regulated learning in work-related training and educational attainment: What we know and where we need to go. *Psychological Bulletin, 137,* 421–442.

Sivan, E. (1986). Motivation in social constructivist theory. *Educational Psychologist, 21,* 209–233.

Skinner, B. F. (1938). *The behavior of organisms.* New York: Appleton-Century-Crofts.

Skinner, B. F. (1948). *Walden two.* New York: Macmillan.

Skinner, B. F. (1953). *Science and human behavior.* New York: Free Press.

Skinner, B. F. (1954). The science of learning and the art of teaching. *Harvard Educational Review, 24,* 86–97.

Skinner, B. F. (1958). Teaching machines. *Science, 128,* 969–977.

Skinner, B. F. (1961). Why we need teaching machines. *Harvard Educational Review, 31,* 377–398.

Skinner, B. F. (1968). *The technology of teaching*. New York: Appleton-Century-Crofts.

Skinner, B. F. (1970). B. F. Skinner An autobiography. In P. B. Dews (Ed.), *Festschrift for B. F. Skinner* (pp. 1–21). New York: Appleton-Century-Crofts.

Skinner, B. F. (1971). *Beyond freedom and dignity*. New York: Knopf.

Skinner, B. F. (1984). The shame of American education. *American Psychologist*, 39, 947–954.

Skinner, B. F. (1987). Whatever happened to psychology as the science of behavior? *American Psychologist*, 42, 780–786.

Skinner, B. F. (1990). Can psychology be a science of mind? *American Psychologist*, 45, 1206–1210.

Skinner, E. A., Wellborn, J. G., & Connell, J. P. (1990). What it takes to do well in school and whether I've got it: A process model of perceived control and children's engagement and achievement in school. *Journal of Educational Psychology*, 82, 22–32.

Slavin, R. E. (1994). *Using team learning* (4th ed.). Baltimore: Johns Hopkins University, Center for Research on Elementary Schools.

Slavin, R. E. (1995). *Cooperative learning* (2nd ed.). Boston: Allyn & Bacon.

Slavin, R. E., & Cheung, A. (2005). A synthesis of research on language of reading instruction for English language learners. *Review of Educational Research*, 75, 247–284.

Small, G. W., Moody, T. D., Siddarth, P., & Bookheimer, S. Y. (2009). Your brain on Google: Patterns of cerebral activation during Internet searching. *American Journal of Geriatric Psychiatry*, 17, 116–126.

Small, G. W., & Vorgan, G. (2008). *iBrain: Surviving the technological alteration of the modern mind*. New York: Collins.

Smith, E. E., & Medin, D. L. (1981). *Categories and concepts*. Cambridge, MA: Harvard University Press.

Smith, E. R. (1996). What do connectionism and social psychology offer each other? *Journal of Personality and Social Psychology*, 70, 893–912.

Smith, P. L., & Fouad, N. A. (1999). Subject-matter specificity of self-efficacy, outcome expectancies, interests, and goals: Implications for the social-cognitive model. *Journal of Counseling Psychology*, 46, 461–471.

Smith, R. E. (1989). Effects of coping skills training on generalized self-efficacy and locus of control. *Journal of Personality and Social Psychology*, 56, 228–233.

Snowman, J. (1986). Learning tactics and strategies. In G. D. Phye & T. Andre (Eds.), *Cognitive classroom learning: Understanding, thinking, and problem solving* (pp. 243–275). Orlando: Academic Press.

Snyder, K. E., Nietfeld, J. L., & Linnenbrink-Garcia, L. (2011). Giftedness and metacognition: A short-term longitudinal investigation of metacognitive monitoring in the classroom. *Gifted Child Quarterly*, 55, 181–193.

Spanjers, I. A. E., van Gog, T., & van Merriënboer, J. J. G. (2010). A theoretical analysis of how segmentation of dynamic visualizations optimizes students' learning. *Educational Psychology Review*, 22, 411–423.

Spence, J. T. (1984). Gender identity and its implications for the concepts of masculinity and femininity. In T. B. Sonderegger (Ed.), *Nebraska Symposium on Motivation*, 1984 (Vol. 32, pp. 59–95). Lincoln, NE: University of Nebraska Press.

Spera, C. (2005). A review of the relationship among parenting practices, parenting styles, and adolescent school achievement. *Educational Psychology Review*, 17, 125–146.

Sperling, G. (1960). The information available in brief visual presentations. *Psychological Monographs*, 74(Whole No. 498).

Spinath, B., & Steinmayr, R. (2012). The roles of competence beliefs and goal orientations for change in intrinsic motivation. *Journal of Educational Psychology*, 104, 1135–1148.

Springer, L., Stanne, M. E., & Donovan, S. S. (1999). Effects of small-group learning on undergraduates in science, mathematics, engineering, and technology: A meta-analysis. *Review of Educational Research*, 69, 21–51.

Steenbergen-Hu, S., & Cooper, H. (2014). A meta-analysis of the effectiveness of intelligent tutoring systems on college students' academic learning. *Journal of Educational Psychology*, 106, 331–347.

Stein, B. S., Littlefield, J., Bransford, J. D., & Persampieri, M. (1984). Elaboration and knowledge acquisition. *Memory & Cognition*, 12, 522–529.

Stein, M., & Carnine, D. (1999). Designing and delivering effective mathematics instruction. In R. J. Stevens (Ed.), *Teaching in American schools* (pp. 245–269). Upper Saddle River, NJ: Merrill/Prentice Hall.

Stein, N. L., & Glenn, C. G. (1979). An analysis of story comprehension in elementary school children. In R. O. Freedle (Ed.), *New directions in discourse processing* (pp. 53–120). Norwood, NJ: Ablex.

Stein, N. L., & Trabasso, T. (1982). What's in a story: An approach to comprehension and instruction. In R. Glaser (Ed.), *Advances in instructional psychology* (Vol. 2, pp. 213–267). Hillsdale, NJ: Erlbaum.

Steinberg, L., Brown, B. B., & Dornbusch, S. M. (1996). *Beyond the classroom: Why school reform has failed and what parents need to do*. New York: Simon & Schuster.

Stenhoff, D. M., & Lignugaris/Kraft, B. (2007). A review of the effects of peer tutoring on students with mild disabilities in secondary settings. *Exceptional Children*, 74, 8–30.

Sternberg, R. J. (1986). Cognition and instruction: Why the marriage sometimes ends in divorce. In R. F. Dillon & R. J. Sternberg (Eds.), *Cognition and instruction* (pp. 375–382). Orlando: Academic Press.

Sternberg, R. J. (2008). Applying psychological theories to educational practice. *American Educational Research Journal*, 45, 150–165.

Sternberg, R. J., & Grigorenko, E. L. (1997). Are cognitive styles still in style? *American Psychologist*, 52, 700–712.

Sternberg, R. J., & Horvath, J. A. (1995). A prototype view of expert teaching. *Educational Researcher*, 24(6), 9–17.

Sternberg, S. (1969). Memory-scanning: Mental processes revealed by reaction-time experiments. *American Scientist*, 57, 421–457.

Stipek, D. J. (2002). Good instruction is motivating. In A. Wigfield & J. S. Eccles (Eds.), *Development of achievement motivation* (pp. 309–332). San Diego: Academic Press.

Stipek, D. J., & Kowalski, P. S. (1989). Learned helplessness in task-orienting versus performance-orienting testing conditions. *Journal of Educational Psychology*, 81, 384–391.

Stipek, D. J., & Ryan, R. H. (1997). Economically disadvantaged preschoolers: Ready to learn but further to go. *Developmental Psychology*, 33, 711–723.

Strain, P. S., Kerr, M. M., & Ragland, E. U. (1981). The use of peer social initiations in the treatment of social withdrawal. In P. S. Strain (Ed.), *The utilization of classroom peers as behavior change agents* (pp. 101–128). New York: Plenum.

Stright, A. D., Neitzel, C., Sears, K. G., & Hoke-Sinex, L. (2001). Instruction begins in the home: Relations between parental instruction and children's self-regulation in the classroom. *Journal of Educational Psychology*, 93, 456–466.

Stull, A. T., & Mayer, R. E. (2007). Learning by doing versus learning by viewing: Three experimental comparisons of learner-generated versus author-provided graphic organizers. *Journal of Educational Psychology*, 99, 808–820.

Sugai, G., & Horner, R. H. (2002). The evolution of discipline practices: School-wide positive behavior supports. *Child and Family Behavior Therapy*, 24, 23–50.

Surprenant, A. M., & Neath, I. (2009). *Principles of memory: Essays in cognitive psychology*. New York: Taylor & Francis.

Swanson, H. L. (2008). Working memory and intelligence in children: What develops? *Journal of Educational Psychology*, 100, 581–602.

Swanson, H. L. (2011). Working memory, attention, and mathematical problem solving: A longitudinal study of elementary school children. *Journal of Educational Psychology*, 103, 821–837.

Swanson, H. L. (2016). Cognition and cognitive disabilities. In L. Corno & E. M. Anderman (Eds.), *Handbook of educational psychology* (3rd ed., pp. 135–145). New York: Routledge.

Swanson, H. L., & Fung, W. (2016). Working memory components and problem-solving accuracy: Are there multiple pathways? *Journal of Educational Psychology*, 108, 1153–1177.

Sweller, J. (2009). Cognitive bases of human creativity. *Educational Psychology Review*, 21, 11–19.

Sweller, J. (2010). Element interactivity and intrinsic, extraneous, and germane cognitive load. *Educational Psychology Review*, 22, 123–138.

Sztajn, P., Confrey, J., Wilson, P. H., & Edgington, C. (2012). Learning trajectory based instruction: Toward a theory of teaching. *Educational Researcher*, 41, 147–156.

Taatgen, N. A. (2013). The nature and transfer of cognitive skills. *Psychological Review*, 120, 439–471.

Tallent-Runnels, M. K., Thomas, J. A., Lan, W. Y., Cooper, S., Ahern, T. C., Shaw, S. M., & Liu, X. (2006). Teaching courses online: A review of the research. *Review of Educational Research*, 76, 93–135.

Tallis, R. (2014, November 15–16). Does Pavlov's name ring a bell? *The Wall Street Journal*, 264(117), C5–C6.

Tamim, R. M., Bernard, R. M., Borokhovski, E., Abrami, P. C., & Schmid, R. F. (2011). What forty years of research says about the impact of technology on learning: A second-order meta-analysis and validation study. *Review of Educational Research*, 81, 4–28.

Tarde, G. (1903). *The laws of imitation*. New York: Henry Holt.

Tennyson, R. D. (1980). Instructional control strategies and content structure as design variables in concept acquisition using computer-based instruction. *Journal of Educational Psychology*, 72, 525–532.

Tennyson, R. D. (1981). Use of adaptive information for advisement in learning concepts and rules using computer-assisted instruction. *American Educational Research Journal*, 18, 425–438.

Tennyson, R. D., & Park, O. (1980). The teaching of concepts: A review of instructional design research literature. *Review of Educational Research*, 50, 55–70.

Terry, W. S. (2009). *Learning and memory: Basic principles, processes, and procedures* (4th ed.). Boston: Allyn & Bacon.

Tharp, R. G. (1989). Psychocultural variables and constants: Effects on teaching and learning in schools. *American Psychologist*, 44, 349–359.

Tharp, R. G., & Gallimore, R. (1988). *Rousing minds to life: Teaching, learning, and schooling in social context*. New York: Cambridge University Press.

Thompson, V. A., Turner, J. A. P., & Pennycook, G. (2011). Intuition, reason, and metacognition. *Cognitive Psychology*, 63, 107–140.

Thomson, D. M., & Tulving, E. (1970). Associative encoding and retrieval: Weak and strong cues. *Journal of Experimental Psychology*, 86, 255–262.

Thorndike, E. L. (1906). *The principles of teaching: Based on psychology*. New York: A. G. Seiler.

Thorndike, E. L. (1911). *Animal intelligence: Experimental studies*. New York: Macmillan.

Thorndike, E. L. (1912). *Education: A first book*. New York: Macmillan.

Thorndike, E. L. (1913a). *Educational psychology: Vol. 1. The original nature of man*. New York: Teachers College Press.

Thorndike, E. L. (1913b). *Educational psychology: Vol. 2. The psychology of learning*. New York: Teachers College Press.

Thorndike, E. L. (1914). *Educational psychology: Vol. 3. Mental work and fatigue and individual differences and their causes*. New York: Teachers College Press.

Thorndike, E. L. (1924). Mental discipline in high school studies. *Journal of Educational Psychology*, 15, 1–22, 83–98.

Thorndike, E. L. (1932). *The fundamentals of learning*. New York: Teachers College Press.

Thorndike, E. L., & Gates, A. I. (1929). *Elementary principles of education*. New York: Macmillan.

Thorndike, E. L., & Woodworth, R. S. (1901). The influence of improvement in one mental function upon the efficiency of other functions. *Psychological Review*, 8, 247–261, 384–395, 553–564.

Thorndyke, P. W., & Hayes-Roth, B. (1979). The use of schemata in the acquisition and transfer of knowledge. *Cognitive Psychology*, 11, 82–106.

Thorne, S. L., & May, S. (Eds.) (2017). *Language, education and technology* (3rd ed.), Cham, Switzerland: Springer International Publishing.

Tiedemann, J. (1989). Measures of cognitive styles: A critical review. *Educational Psychologist*, 24, 261–275.

Titchener, E. B. (1909). *Lectures on the experimental psychology of the thought processes*. New York: Macmillan.

Tolman, E. C. (1932). *Purposive behavior in animals and men*. New York: Appleton-Century-Crofts. (Reprinted 1949, 1951, University of California Press, Berkeley, CA)

Tolman, E. C. (1949). There is more than one kind of learning. *Psychological Review*, 56, 144–155.

Tolman, E. C. (1951). *Collected papers in psychology*. Berkeley, CA: University of California Press.

Tolman, E. C. (1959). Principles of purposive behavior. In S. Koch (Ed.), *Psychology: A study of a science* (Vol. 2, pp. 92–157). New York: McGraw-Hill.

Tolman, E. C., Ritchie, B. F., & Kalish, D. (1946a). Studies in spatial learning. I. Orientation and the short-cut. *Journal of Experimental Psychology*, 36, 13–24.

Tolman, E. C., Ritchie, B. F., & Kalish, D. (1946b). Studies in spatial learning. II. Place learning versus response learning. *Journal of Experimental Psychology*, 36, 221–229.

Tolson, J. (2006, October 23). Is there room for the soul? New challenges to our most cherished beliefs about self and the human spirit. *U. S. News & World Report*, 141, 56–63.

Tracey, T. J. G. (2002). Development of interests and competency beliefs: A 1-year longitudinal study of fifth- to eighth-grade students using the ICA-R and structural equation modeling. *Journal of Counseling Psychology*, 49, 148–163.

Trautwein, U., Lüdtke, O., Marsh, H. W., Köller, O., & Baumert, J. (2006). Tracking, grading, and student motivation: Using group composition and status to predict self-concept and interest in ninth-grade mathematics. *Journal of Educational Psychology*, 98, 788–806.

Trautwein, U., Lüdtke, O., Marsh, H. W., & Nagy, G. (2009). Within-school social comparison: How students perceive the standing of their class predicts academic self-concept. *Journal of Educational Psychology*, 101, 853–866.

Trautwein, U., Marsh, H. W., Nagengast, B., Lüdtke, O., Nagy, G., & Jonkmann, K. (2012). Probing for the multiplicative term in modern expectancy-value theory: A latent interaction modeling study. *Journal of Educational Psychology*, 104, 763–777.

Trawick-Smith, J. (2003). *Early childhood development: A multi-cultural perspective* (3rd ed.). Upper Saddle River, NJ: Merrill/Prentice Hall.

Treffinger, D. J. (1985). Review of the Torrance Tests of Creative Thinking. In J. Mitchell (Ed.), *Ninth Mental Measurements Yearbook* (pp. 1633–1634). Lincoln, NE: Buros Institute of Mental Measurement.

Treffinger, D. J. (1995). Creative problem solving: Overview and educational implications. *Educational Psychology Review*, 7, 301–312.

Treffinger, D. J., & Isaksen, S. G. (2005). Creative problem solving: The history, development, and implications for gifted education and talent development. *Gifted Child Quarterly*, 49, 342–353.

Treisman, A. M. (1960). Contextual cues in selective listening. *Quarterly Journal of Experimental Psychology*, 12, 242–248.

Treisman, A. M. (1964). Verbal cues, language, and meaning in selective attention. *American Journal of Psychology*, 77, 206–219.

Treisman, A. M. (1992). Perceiving and re-perceiving objects. *American Psychologist*, 47, 862–875.

Treisman, A. M., & Gelade, G. (1980). A feature-integration theory of attention. *Cognitive Psychology*, 12, 97–136.

Tricot, A., & Sweller, J. (2014). Domain-specific knowledge and why teaching generic skills does not work. *Educational Psychology Review*, 26, 265–283.

Tucker, D. M., & Luu, P. (2007). Neurophysiology of motivated learning: Adaptive mechanisms underlying cognitive bias in depression. *Cognitive Therapy and Research*, 31, 189–209.

Tudge, J. R. H., & Scrimsher, S. (2003). Lev S. Vygotsky on education: A cultural-historical, interpersonal, and individual approach to development. In B. J. Zimmerman & D. H. Schunk (Eds.), *Educational psychology: A century of contributions* (pp. 207–228). Mahwah, NJ: Erlbaum.

Tudge, J. R. H., & Winterhoff, P. A. (1993). Vygotsky, Piaget, and Bandura: Perspectives on the relations between the social world and cognitive development. *Human Development*, 36, 61–81.

Tulving, E. (1974). Cue-dependent forgetting. *American Scientist*, 62, 74–82.

Tulving, E. (1983). *Elements of episodic memory*. Oxford, England: Clarendon Press.

Tuovinen, J. E., & Sweller, J. (1999). A comparison of cognitive load associated with discovery learning and worked examples. *Journal of Educational Psychology*, 91, 334–341.

Tweney, R. D., & Budzynski, C. A. (2000). The scientific status of American psychology in 1900. *American Psychologist*, 55, 1014–1017.

Underwood, B. J. (1961). Ten years of massed practice on distributed practice. *Psychological Review*, 68, 229–247.

Underwood, B. J. (1983). *Attributes of memory*. Glenview, IL: Scott, Foresman.

Unsworth, N., & Engle, R. W. (2007). The nature of individual differences in working memory capacity: Active maintenance in primary memory and controlled search from secondary memory. *Psychological Review*, 114, 104–132.

Usher, E. L., & Schunk, D. H. (2018). Social cognitive theoretical perspective of self-regulation. In D. H. Schunk & J. A. Greene (Eds.), *Handbook of self-regulation of learning and performance* (2nd ed., pp. 19–35). New York: Routledge.

Valentine, C. W. (1930a). The innate base of fear. *Journal of Genetic Psychology*, 37, 394–419.

Valentine, C. W. (1930b). The psychology of imitation with special reference to early childhood. *British Journal of Psychology*, 21, 105–132.

Valentine, J. C., Cooper, H., Bettencourt, B. A., & DuBois. D. L. (2002). Out-of-school activities and academic achievement: The mediating role of self-beliefs. *Educational Psychologist*, 37, 245–256.

Valentine, J. C., DuBois, D. L., & Cooper, H. (2004). The relation between self-beliefs and academic achievement: A meta-analytic review. *Educational Psychologist*, 39, 111–133.

Vandell, D. L. (2000). Parents, peer groups, and other socializing influences. *Developmental Psychology*, 36, 699–710.

van de Pol, J., Volman, M., & Beishuizen, J. (2010). Scaffolding in teacher-student interaction: A decade of research. *Educational Psychology Review*, 22, 271–296.van de Pol, J., Volman, M., & Beishuizen, J. (2010). Scaffolding in teacher-student interaction: A decade of research. *Educational Psychology Review, 22*, 271–296.

Van der Kleij, F. M., Feskens, R. C. W., & Eggen, T. J. H. M. (2015). Effects of feedback in a computer-based learning environment on students' learning outcomes: A meta-analysis. *Review of Educational Research*, 85, 475–511.

van Drie, J., & van Boxtel, C. (2008). Historical reasoning: Towards a framework for analyzing students' reasoning about the past. *Educational Psychology Review*, 20, 87–110.

van Gog, T., Paas, F., Marcus, N., Ayres, P., & Sweller, J. (2009). The mirror neuron system and observational learning: Implications for the effectiveness of dynamic visualizations. *Educational Psychology Review*, 21, 21–30.

van Gog, Tvan Gog, T., Paas, F., & Sweller, J. (2010). Cognitive load theory: Advances in research on worked examples, animations, and cognitive load measurement. *Educational Psychology Review*, 22, 375–378.

van Gog, T., & Rummel, N. (2010). Example-based learning: Integrating cognitive and social-cognitive research perspectives. *Educational Psychology Review*, 22, 155–174.

van Laar, C. (2000). The paradox of low academic achievement but high self-esteem in African American students: An attributional account. *Educational Psychology Review*, 12, 33–61.

VanLehn, K. (1996). Cognitive skill acquisition. *Annual Review of Psychology*, 47, 513–539.

VanLehn, K. (2011). The relative effectiveness of human tutoring, intelligent tutoring systems, and other tutoring systems. *Educational Psychologist*, 46, 197–221.

van Merriënboer, J. J. G., Kirschner, P. A., & Kester, L. (2003). Taking the load off a learner's mind: Instructional design for complex learning. *Educational Psychologist*, 38, 5–13.

van Merriënboer, J. J. G., & Sweller, J. (2005). Cognitive load theory and complex learning: Recent developments and future directions. *Educational Psychology Review*, 17, 147–177.

Varma, S., McCandliss, B. D., & Schwartz, D. L. (2008). Scientific and pragmatic challenges for bridging education and neuroscience. *Educational Researcher*, 37, 140–152.

Vekiri, I. (2002). What is the value of graphical displays in learning? *Educational Psychology Review*, 14, 261–312.

Vellutino, F. R., & Denckla, M. B. (1996). Cognitive and neuropsychological foundations of word identification in poor and normally developing readers. In R. Barr, M. L. Kamil, P. B. Mosenthal, & P. D. Pearson (Eds.), *Handbook of reading research* (Vol. 2, pp. 571–608). Mahwah, NJ: Erlbaum.

Verdi, M. P., & Kulhavy, R. W. (2002). Learning with maps and texts: An overview. *Educational Psychology Review*, 14, 27–46.

Vispoel, W. P. (1995). Self-concept in artistic domains: An extension of the Shavelson, Hubner, and Stanton (1976) model. *Journal of Educational Psychology*, 87, 134–153.

Voelkl, K. E. (1997). Identification with school. *American Journal of Education*, 105, 294–318.

Voelkl, K. E. (2012). School identification. In S. L. Christenson, A. L. Reschly, & C. Wylie (Eds.), *Handbook of research on student engagement* (pp. 193–218). New York: Springer.

Volet, S., Vauras, M., & Salonen, P. (2009). Self- and social regulation in learning contexts: An integrative perspective. *Educational Psychologist*, 44, 215–226.

Vollmeyer, R., & Rheinberg, F. (2006). Motivational effects on self-regulated learning with different tasks. *Educational Psychology Review*, 18, 239–253.

Voss, J. F., Wiley, J., & Carretero, M. (1995). Acquiring intellectual skills. *Annual Review of Psychology*, 46, 155–181.

Vygotsky, L. (1962). *Thought and language*. Cambridge, MA: MIT Press.

Vygotsky, L. (1978). *Mind in society: The development of higher psychological processes*. Cambridge, MA: Harvard University Press.

Vygotsky, L. (1987). *The collected works of L. S. Vygotsky: Vol. 1. Problems of general psychology* (R. W. Rieber & A. S. Carton, Vol. Eds.; N. Minick, Trans.). New York: Plenum.

Wadsworth, B. J. (1996). *Piaget's theory of cognitive and affective development* (5th ed.). White Plains, NY: Longman.

Wagemans, J., Elder, J. H., Kubovy, M., Palmer, S. E., Peterson, M. A., Singh, M., & von der Heydt, R. (2012a). A century of Gestalt psychology in visual perception: I. Perceptual grouping and figure-ground organization. *Psychological Bulletin*, 138, 1172–1217.

Wagemans, J., Feldman, J., Gepshtein, S., Kimchi, R., Pomerantz, J. R., van der Helm, P. A., & van Leeuwen, C. (2012b). A century of Gestalt psychology in visual perception: II. Conceptual and theoretical foundations. *Psychological Bulletin*, 138, 1218–1252.

Wallas, G. (1921). *The art of thought*. New York: Harcourt, Brace, & World.

Wallis, C. (2004, May 10). What makes teens tick. *Time*, 163, 56–62, 65.

Wang, S-H., & Morris, R. G. M. (2010). Hippocampal-neurocortical interactions in memory formation, consolidation, and reconsolidation. *Annual Review of Psychology*, 61, 49–79.

Washington, V., & Bailey, U. J. O. (1995). *Project Head Start: Models and strategies for the twenty-first century*. New York: Garland.

Wason, P. C. (1966). Reasoning. In B. M. Foss (Ed.), *New horizons in psychology* (pp. 135–151). Harmondsworth, England: Penguin.

Wason, P. C., & Johnson-Laird, P. N. (1972). *The psychology of deduction: Structure and content*. Cambridge, MA: Harvard University Press.

Wass, S. V., Scerif, G., & Johnson, M. H. (2012). Training attentional control and working memory – is younger better? *Developmental Review*, 32, 360–387.

Watson, J. B. (1916). The place of the conditioned-reflex in psychology. *Psychological Review*, 23, 89–116.

Watson, J. B. (1924). *Behaviorism*. New York: Norton.

Watson, J. B. (1926a). Experimental studies on the growth of the emotions. In C. Murchison (Ed.), *Psychologies of 1925* (pp. 37–57). Worcester, MA: Clark University Press.

Watson, J. B. (1926b). What the nursery has to say about instincts. In C. Murchison (Ed.), *Psychologies of 1925* (pp. 1–35). Worcester, MA: Clark University Press.

Watson, J. B., & Rayner, R. (1920). Conditioned emotional reactions. *Journal of Experimental Psychology*, 3, 1–14.

Webley, K. (2013, June 17). A is for adaptive. *Time*, 181(23), 40–45.

Weiner, B. (1985). An attributional theory of achievement motivation and emotion. *Psychological Review*, 92, 548–573.

Weiner, B. (1992). *Human motivation: Metaphors, theories, and research*. Newbury Park, CA: SAGE Publications.

Weiner, B. (2000). Intrapersonal and interpersonal theories of motivation from an attributional perspective. *Educational Psychology Review*, 12, 1–14.

Weiner, B. (2004). Attribution theory revisited: Transforming cultural plurality into theoretical unity. In D. M. McInerney & S. Van Etten (Eds.), *Big theories revisited* (pp. 13–29). Greenwich, CT: Information Age Publishing.

Weiner, B. (2005). Motivation from an attributional perspective and the social psychology of perceived competence. In A. J. Elliot & C. S. Dweck (Eds.), *Handbook of competence and motivation* (pp. 73–84). New York: Guilford Press.

Weiner, B. (2010). The development of an attribution-based theory of motivation: A history of ideas. *Educational Psychologist*, 45, 28–36.

Weiner, B., Frieze, I. H., Kukla, A., Reed, L., Rest, S., & Rosenbaum, R. M. (1971). *Perceiving the causes of success and failure*. Morristown, NJ: General Learning Press.

Weiner, B., & Kukla, A. (1970). An attributional analysis of achievement motivation. *Journal of Personality and Social Psychology*, 15, 1–20.

Weiner, B., & Peter, N. (1973). A cognitive-developmental analysis of achievement and moral judgments. *Developmental Psychology*, 9, 290–309.

Weinstein, C. E., & Mayer, R. E. (1986). The teaching of learning strategies. In M. C. Wittrock (Ed.), *Handbook of research on teaching* (3rd ed., pp. 315–327). New York: Macmillan.

Weinstein, C. E., Palmer, D. R., & Schulte, A. C. (1987). *LASSI: Learning and Study Strategies Inventory*. Clearwater, FL: H & H Publishing Company.

Weiss, M. R. (1983). Modeling and motor performance: A developmental perspective. *Research Quarterly for Exercise and Sport*, 54, 190–197.

Weiss, M. R., Ebbeck, V., & Wiese-Bjornstal, D. M. (1993). Developmental and psychological factors related to children's observational learning of physical skills. *Pediatric Exercise Science*, 5, 301–317.

Weiss, M. R., & Klint, K. A. (1987). "Show and tell" in the gymnasium: An investigation of developmental differences in modeling and verbal rehearsal of motor skills. *Research Quarterly for Exercise and Sport*, 58, 234–241.

Wellman, H. M. (1977). Tip of the tongue and feeling of knowing experiences: A developmental study of memory monitoring. *Child Development*, 48, 13–21.

Wellman, H. M. (1990). *The child's theory of mind*. Cambridge, MA: MIT Press.

Wentzel, K. R. (1992). Motivation and achievement in adolescence: A multiple goals perspective. In D. H. Schunk & J. L. Meece (Eds.), *Student perceptions in the classroom* (pp. 287–306). Hillsdale, NJ: Erlbaum.

Wentzel, K. R. (1996). Social goals and social relationships as motivators of school adjustment. In J. Juvonen & K. R. Wentzel (Eds.), *Social motivation: Understanding children's school adjustment* (pp. 226–247). Cambridge, England: Cambridge University Press.

Wentzel, K. R. (2005). Peer relationships, motivation, and academic performance at school. In A. J. Elliot & C. S. Dweck (Eds.), *Handbook of competence and motivation* (pp. 279–296). New York: Guilford Press.

Wentzel, K. R. (2010). Students' relationships with teachers. In J. L. Meece & J. S. Eccles (Eds.), *Handbook of research on schools, schooling, and human development* (pp. 75–91). New York: Routledge.

Wentzel, K. R. (2016). Teacher-student relationships. In K. R. Wentzel & D. B. Miele (Eds.), *Handbook of motivation at school* (2nd ed., pp. 211–230). New York: Routledge.

Wentzel, K. R., Barry, C. M., & Caldwell, K. A. (2004). Friendships in middle school: Influences on motivation and school adjustment. *Journal of Educational Psychology*, 96, 195–203.

Wentzel, K. R., Battle, A., Russel, S. L., & Looney, L. B. (2010). Social supports from teachers and peers as predictors of academic and social motivation. *Contemporary Educational Psychology*, 35, 193–202.

Wertheimer, M. (1945). *Productive thinking*. New York: Harper & Row.

Wertsch, J. V. (1979). From social interaction to higher psychological processes: A clarification and application of Vygotsky's theory. *Human Development*, 22, 1–22.

Wertsch, J. V. (1984). The zone of proximal development: Some conceptual issues. In B. Rogoff & J. V. Wertsch (Eds.), *Children's learning in the "zone of proximal development"* (pp. 7–18). San Francisco: Jossey-Bass.

Wertsch, J. V. (1985). *Culture, communication, and cognition: Vygotskian perspectives*. New York: Cambridge University Press.

Wheeler, L., & Suls, J. (2005). Social comparison and self-evaluations of competence. In A. J. Elliot & C. S. Dweck (Eds.), *Handbook of competence and motivation* (pp. 566–578). New York: Guilford Press.

White, M. C., & DiBenedetto, M. K. (2015). *Self-regulation and the Common Core: Application to ELA standards*. New York: Routledge.

White, P. H., Kjelgaard, M. M., & Harkins, S. G. (1995). Testing the contribution of self-evaluation to goal-setting effects. *Journal of Personality and Social Psychology*, 69, 69–79.

White, R. (2001). The revolution in research on science teaching. In V. Richardson (Ed.), *Handbook of research on teaching* (4th ed., pp. 457–471). Washington, DC: American Educational Research Association.

White, R. T., & Tisher, R. P. (1986). Research on natural sciences. In M. C. Wittrock (Ed.), *Handbook of research on teaching* (3rd ed., pp. 874–905). New York: Macmillan.

White, R. W. (1959). Motivation reconsidered: The concept of competence. *Psychological Review*, 66, 297–333.

Wickelgren, W. A. (1979). *Cognitive psychology*. Englewood Cliffs, NJ: Prentice Hall.

Wigfield, A., Byrnes, J. P., & Eccles, J. S. (2006). Development during early and middle adolescence. In P. A. Alexander & P. H. Winne (Eds.), *Handbook of educational psychology* (2nd ed., pp. 87–113). Mahwah, NJ: Erlbaum.

Wigfield, A., & Cambria, J. (2010). Students' achievement values, goal orientations, and interest: Definitions, development, and relations to achievement outcomes. *Developmental Review*, 30, 1–35.

Wigfield, A., & Eccles, J. S. (1992). The development of achievement task values: A theoretical analysis. *Developmental Review*, 12, 265–310.

Wigfield, A., & Eccles, J. S. (2000). Expectancy-value theory of motivation. *Contemporary Educational Psychology*, 25, 68–81.

Wigfield, A., & Eccles, J. S. (2002). The development of competence beliefs, expectancies for success, and achievement values from childhood through adolescence. In A. Wigfield & J. S. Eccles (Eds.), *Development of achievement motivation* (pp. 91–120). San Diego: Academic Press.

Wigfield, A., Hoa, L. W., & Klauda, S. L. (2008). The role of achievement values in the regulation of achievement behaviors. In D. H. Schunk & B. J. Zimmerman (Eds.), *Motivation and self-regulated learning: Theory, research, and applications* (pp. 169–195). New York: Taylor & Francis.

Wigfield, A., Tonks, S., & Eccles, J. S. (2004). Expectancy value theory in cross-cultural perspective. In D. M. McInerney & S. Van Etten (Eds.), *Big theories revisited* (pp. 165–198). Greenwich, CT: Information Age Publishing.

Wigfield, A., Tonks, S. M., & Klauda, S. L. (2016). Expectancy-value theory. In K. R. Wentzel & D. B. Miele (Eds.), *Handbook of motivation at school* (2nd ed., pp. 55–74). New York: Routledge.

Wigfield, A., & Wagner, A. L. (2005). Competence, motivation, and identity development during adolescence. In A. J. Elliot & C. S. Dweck (Eds.), *Handbook of competence and motivation* (pp. 222–239). New York: Guilford Press.

Williams, J. M., & Tolmie, A. (2000). Conceptual change in biology: Group interaction and the understanding of inheritance. *British Journal of Developmental Psychology*, 18, 625–649.

Windholz, G. (1997). Ivan P. Pavlov: An overview of his life and psychological work. *American Psychologist*, 52, 941–946.

Windschitl, M. (2002). Framing constructivism in practice as the negotiation of dilemmas: An analysis of the conceptual, pedagogical, cultural, and political challenges facing teachers. *Review of Educational Research*, 72, 131–175.

Windschitl, M., & Thompson, J. (2006). Transcending simple forms of school science investigation: The impact of preservice instruction on teachers' understandings of model-based inquiry. *American Educational Research Journal*, 43, 783–835.

Winett, R. A., & Winkler, R. C. (1972). Current behavior modification in the classroom: Be still, be quiet, be docile. *Journal of Applied Behavior Analysis*, 5, 499–504.

Winne, P. H. (2001). Self-regulated learning viewed from models of information processing. In B. J. Zimmerman & D. H. Schunk (Eds.), *Self-regulated learning and academic achievement: Theoretical perspectives* (2nd ed., pp. 153– 189). Mahwah, NJ: Erlbaum.

Winne, P. H. (2011). A cognitive and metacognitive analysis of self-regulated learning. In B. J. Zimmerman & D. H. Schunk (Eds.), *Handbook of self-regulation of learning and performance* (pp. 15–32). New York: Routledge.

Winne, P. H. (2018). Cognition and metacognition within self-regulated learning. In D. H. Schunk & J. A. Greene (Eds.), *Handbook of self-regulation of learning and performance* (2nd ed., pp. 36–48). New York: Routledge.

Winne, P. H., & Hadwin, A. F. (1998). Studying as self-regulated learning. In D. J. Hacker, J. Dunlosky, & A. C. Graesser (Eds.), *Metacognition in educational theory and practice* (pp. 277–304). Hillsdale, NJ: Erlbaum.

Winne, P. H., & Hadwin, A. R. (2008). The weave of motivation and self-regulated learning. In D. H. Schunk & B. J. Zimmerman (Eds.), *Motivation and self-regulated learning: Theory, research, and applications* (pp. 297–314). New York: Taylor & Francis.

Winne, P. H., & Nesbit, J. C. (2010). The psychology of academic achievement. *Annual Review of Psychology*, 61, 653–678.

Winsler, A., Carlton, M. P., & Barry, M. J. (2000). Age-related changes in preschool children's systematic use of private speech in a natural setting. *Journal of Child Language*, 27, 665–687.

Winsler, A., & Naglieri, J. (2003). Overt and covert verbal problem-solving strategies: Developmental trends in use, awareness, and relations with task performance in children aged 5 to 17. *Child Development*, 74, 659–678.

Wirkala, C., & Kuhn, D. (2011). Problem-based learning in K-12 education: Is it effective and how does it achieve its effects? *American Educational Research Journal*, 48, 1157–1186.

Witkin, H. A. (1969). Social influences in the development of cognitive style. In D. A. Goslin (Ed.), *Handbook of socialization theory and research* (pp. 687–706). Chicago: Rand McNally.

Witkin, H. A., Moore, C. A., Goodenough, D. R., & Cox, P. W. (1977). Field-dependent and field-independent cognitive styles and their educational implications. *Review of Educational Research*, 47, 1–64.

Wittwer, J., & Renkl, A. (2010). How effective are instructional explanations in example-based learning? A meta-analytic review. *Educational Psychology Review*, 22, 393–409.

Wolfe, P. (2010). *Brain matters: Translating research into classroom practice* (2nd ed.). Alexandria, VA: ASCD.

Wolleat, P. L., Pedro, J. D., Becker, A. D., & Fennema, E. (1980). Sex differences in high school students' causal attributions of performance in mathematics. *Journal for Research in Mathematics Education*, 11, 356–366.

Wolpe, J. (1958). *Psychotherapy by reciprocal inhibition*. Stanford, CA: Stanford University Press.

Wolters, C. A. (1998). Self-regulated learning and college students' regulation of motivation. *Journal of Educational Psychology*, 90, 224–235.

Wolters, C. A. (1999). The relation between high school students' motivational regulation and their use of learning strategies, effort, and classroom performance. *Learning and Individual Differences*, 11, 281–299.

Wolters, C. A. (2003). Regulation of motivation: Evaluating an underemphasized aspect of self-regulated learning. *Educational Psychologist*, 38, 189–205.

Wolters, C. A., & Daugherty, S. G. (2007). Goal structures and teachers' sense of efficacy: Their relation and association to teaching experience and academic level. *Journal of Educational Psychology*, 99, 181–193.

Wolters, C. A., & Gonzalez, A-L. (2008). Classroom climate and motivation: A step toward integration. In T. Urdan, S. Karabenick, & M. Maehr (Eds.), *Advances in motivation and achievement* (Vol. 15, pp. 493–519). Bingley, UK: Emerald Group Publishing.

Wolters, C. A., Yu, S. L., & Pintrich, P. R. (1996). The relation between goal orientation and students' motivational beliefs and self-regulated learning. *Learning and Individual Differences*, 8, 211–238.

Wood, D. A., Rosenberg, M. S., & Carran, D. T. (1993). The effects of tape-recorded self-instruction cues on the mathematics performance of students with learning disabilities. *Journal of Learning Disabilities*, 26, 250–258, 269.

Wood, D. J., Bruner, J. S., & Ross, G. (1976). The role of tutoring in problem solving. *Journal of Child Psychology and Psychiatry*, 17, 89–100.

Wood, L. A., Kendal, R. L., & Flynn, E. G. (2013). Whom do children copy? Model-based biases in social learning. *Developmental Review*, 33, 341–356.

Wood, R., & Bandura, A. (1989). Impact of conceptions of ability on self-regulatory mechanisms and complex decision-making. *Journal of Personality and Social Psychology*, 56, 407–415.

Wood, W., & Neal, D. T. (2007). A new look at habits and the habit-goal interface. *Psychological Review*, 114, 843–863.

Woodward, J., Carnine, D., & Gersten, R. (1988). Teaching problem solving through computer simulations. *American Educational Research Journal*, 25, 72–86.

Woodworth, R. S. (1918). *Dynamic psychology*. New York: Columbia University Press.

Woodworth, R. S., & Schlosberg, H. (1954). *Experimental psychology* (Rev. ed.). New York: Holt, Rinehart & Winston.

Woolfolk-Hoy, A. E., Hoy, W. K., & Davis, H. A. (2009). Teachers' self-efficacy beliefs. In K. R. Wentzel & A. Wigfield (Eds.), *Handbook of motivation at school* (pp. 627–653). New York: Routledge.

Wouters, P., Paas, F., & van Merriënboer, J. J. G. (2008). How to optimize learning from animated models: A review of guidelines based on cognitive load. *Review of Educational Research*, 78, 645–675.

Wurtele, S. K. (1986). Self-efficacy and athletic performance: A review. *Journal of Social and Clinical Psychology*, 4, 290–301.

Wüstenberg, S., Greiff, S., Vainikainen, M-P., & Murphy, K. (2016). Individual differences in students' complex problem solving skills: How they evolve and what they imply. *Journal of Educational Psychology*, 108, 1028–1044.

Wylie, R. C. (1979). *The self-concept* (Vol. 2). Lincoln, NE: University of Nebraska Press.

Yeager, D. S., & Dweck, C. S. (2012). Mindsets that promote resilience: When students believe that personal characteristics can be developed. *Educational Psychologist*, 47, 302–314.

Yerkes, R. M., & Dodson, J. D. (1908). The relation of strength of stimulus to rapidity of habit-formation. *Journal of Comparative Neurology and Psychology*, 18, 459–482.

Zeidner, M. (1998). *Test anxiety: The state of the art*. New York: Plenum.

Zepeda, C. D., Richey, J. E., Ronevich, P., & Nokes-Malach, T. J. (2015). Direct instruction of metacognition benefits adolescent science learning, transfer, and motivation: An in vivo study. *Journal of Educational Psychology*, 107, 954–970.

Zepeda, S. J., & Mayers, R. S. (2006). An analysis of research on block scheduling. *Review of Educational Research*, 76, 137–170.

Zhang, L., & Sternberg, R. J. (2005). A threefold model of intellectual styles. *Educational Psychology Review*, 17, 1–53.

Zheng, B., Warschauer, M., Lin, C-H., & Chang, C. (2016). Learning in one-to-one laptop environments: A meta-analysis and research synthesis. *Review of Educational Research*, 86, 1052–1084.

Zimmerman, B. J. (1989). Models of self-regulated learning and academic achievement. In B. J. Zimmerman & D. H. Schunk (Eds.), *Self-regulated learning and academic achievement: Theory, research, and practice* (pp. 1–25). New York: Springer-Verlag.

Zimmerman, B. J. (1990). Self-regulating academic learning and achievement: The emergence of a social cognitive perspective. *Educational Psychology Review*, 2, 173–201.

Zimmerman, B. J. (1994). Dimensions of academic self-regulation: A conceptual framework for education. In D. H. Schunk & B. J. Zimmerman (Eds.), *Self-regulation of learning and performance: Issues and educational applications* (pp. 3–21). Hillsdale, NJ: Erlbaum.

Zimmerman, B. J. (1998). Developing self-fulfilling cycles of academic regulation: An analysis of exemplary instructional models. In D. H. Schunk & B. J. Zimmerman (Eds.), *Self-regulated learning: From teaching to self-reflective practice* (pp. 1–19). New York: Guilford Press.

Zimmerman, B. J. (2000). Attaining self-regulation: A social cognitive perspective. In M. Boekaerts, P. R. Pintrich, & M. Zeidner (Eds.), *Handbook of self-regulation* (pp. 13–39). San Diego: Academic Press.

Zimmerman, B. J. (2001). Theories of self-regulated learning and academic achievement: An overview and analysis. In B. J. Zimmerman & D. H. Schunk (Eds.), *Self-regulated learning and academic achievement: Theoretical perspectives* (2nd ed., pp. 1–38). Mahwah, NJ: Erlbaum.

Zimmerman, B. J. (2008). Goal setting: A key proactive source of academic self-regulation. In D. H. Schunk & B. J. Zimmerman (Eds.), *Motivation and self-regulated learning: Theory, research, and applications* (pp. 267–295). New York: Taylor & Francis.

Zimmerman, B. J. (2013). From cognitive modeling to self-regulation: A social cognitive career path. *Educational Psychologist*, 48, 135–147.

Zimmerman, B. J., & Bandura, A. (1994). Impact of self-regulatory influences on writing course achievement. *American Educational Research Journal*, 31, 845–862.

Zimmerman, B. J., & Blom, D. E. (1983a). On resolving conflicting views of cognitive conflict. *Developmental Review*, 3, 62–72.

Zimmerman, B. J., & Blom, D. E. (1983b). Toward an empirical test of the role of cognitive conflict in learning. *Developmental Review*, 3, 18–38.

Zimmerman, B. J., Bonner, S., & Kovach, R. (1996). *Developing self-regulated learners: Beyond achievement to self-efficacy.* Washington, DC: American Psychological Association.

Zimmerman, B. J., & Cleary, T. J. (2009). Motives to self-regulate learning: A social cognitive account. In K. R. Wentzel & A. Wigfield (Eds.), *Handbook of motivation at school* (pp. 247–264). New York: Routledge.

Zimmerman, B. J., & DiBenedetto, M. K. (2008). Mastery learning and assessment: Implications for students and teachers in an era of high-stakes testing. *Psychology in the Schools*, 45, 206–216.

Zimmerman, B. J., Greenberg, D., & Weinstein, C. E. (1994). Self-regulating academic study time: A strategy approach. In D. H. Schunk & B. J. Zimmerman (Eds.), *Self-regulation of learning and performance: Issues and educational applications* (pp. 181–199). Hillsdale, NJ: Erlbaum.

Zimmerman, B. J., & Kitsantas, A. (1996). Self-regulated learning of a motoric skill: The role of goal setting and self-monitoring. *Journal of Applied Sport Psychology*, 8, 60–75.

Zimmerman, B. J., & Kitsantas, A. (1997). Developmental phases in self-regulation: Shifting from process goals to outcome goals. *Journal of Educational Psychology*, 89, 29–36.

Zimmerman, B. J., & Kitsantas, A. (1999). Acquiring writing revision skill: Shifting from process to outcome self-regulatory goals. *Journal of Educational Psychology*, 91, 241–250.

Zimmerman, B. J., & Kitsantas, A. (2005). The hidden dimension of perceived competence: Self-regulated learning and practice. In A. J. Elliot & C. S. Dweck (Eds.), *Handbook of competence and motivation* (pp. 509–526). New York: Guilford Press.

Zimmerman, B. J., & Martinez-Pons, M. (1990). Student differences in self-regulated learning: Relating grade, sex, and giftedness to self-efficacy and strategy use. *Journal of Educational Psychology*, 82, 51–59.

Zimmerman, B. J., & Martinez-Pons, M. (1992). Perceptions of efficacy and strategy use in the self-regulation of learning. In D. H. Schunk & J. L. Meece (Eds.), *Student perceptions in the classroom* (pp. 185–207). Hillsdale, NJ: Erlbaum.

Zimmerman, B. J., & Ringle, J. (1981). Effects of model persistence and statements of confidence on children's self-efficacy and problem solving. *Journal of Educational Psychology*, 73, 485–493.

Zimmerman, B. J., & Schunk, D. H. (Eds.) (2001). *Self-regulated learning and academic achievement: Theoretical perspectives* (2nd ed.). Mahwah, NJ: Erlbaum.

Zimmerman, B. J., & Schunk, D. H. (2003). Albert Bandura: The scholar and his contributions to educational psychology. In B. J. Zimmerman & D. H. Schunk (Eds.), *Educational psychology: A century of contributions* (pp. 431–457). Mahwah, NJ: Erlbaum.

Zimmerman, B. J., & Schunk, D. H. (2004). Self-regulating intellectual processes and outcomes: A social cognitive perspective. In D. Y. Dai & R. J. Sternberg (Eds.), *Motivation, emotion, and cognition: Integrative perspectives on intellectual functioning and development* (pp. 323–350). Mahwah, NJ: Erlbaum.

Zimmerman, B. J., & Schunk, D. H. (Eds.) (2011). *Handbook of self-regulation of learning and performance.* New York: Routledge.

Zimmerman, B. J., & Tsikalas, K. E. (2005). Can computer-based learning environments (CBLEs) be used as self-regulatory tools to enhance learning? *Educational Psychologist*, 40, 267–271.

Zimmerman, C. (2000). The development of scientific reasoning skills. *Developmental Review*, 20, 99–149.

Zito, J. R., Adkins, M., Gavins, M., Harris, K. R., & Graham, S. (2007). Self-regulated strategy development: Relationship to the social-cognitive perspective and the development of self-regulation. *Reading & Writing Quarterly*, 23, 77–95.

Zusho, A., & Clayton, K. (2011). Culturalizing achievement goal theory and research. *Educational Psychologist*, 46, 239–260.

Name Index

Weikart, D., 485
Weimer, R., 307
Weinberg, R. A., 485
Weiner, B., 361, 362, 363, 366, 381, 383, 384, 385, 427
Weinstein, C. E., 434, 435, 438, 439, 441, 453, 454
Weinstein, R. S., 465
Weiss, M., 156
Weiss, M. R., 137, 138
Wellborn, J. G., 400
Wellman, H. M., 261, 263, 264, 341
Welsh, J. A., 485
Wenger, E., 463
Wentzel, K. R., 372, 393, 469, 477, 478, 479, 482
Wertheimer, M., 173–174, 275, 276, 277
Wertsch, J. V., 331, 333, 445
West, B. J., 417, 421
Whaley, G. J. L., 487
Wheeler, L., 387
White, M., 407
White, M. C., 15, 347
White, P. H., 430
White, R., 257
White, R. K., 497
White, R. T., 257
White, R. W., 398, 402
Whitebread, D., 264
Wickelgren, W. A., 230
Wiese-Bjornstal, D. M., 137
Wigfield, A., 139, 149, 150, 267, 375, 377, 378, 380, 450, 451, 475, 477
Wiley, J., 254, 257
Wiliam, D., 21
Wilkerson, S. B., 112
Wilkins, J. L. M., 406
Wilkinson, B., 456
Willems, P. P., 487
Williams, J. M., 273

Williams, W. M., 229
Willingham, D., 499
Willoughby, T., 243, 255, 273, 434, 442
Wilson, B. G., 292, 293
Wilson, P. H., 21, 23
Windholz, G., 85, 86
Windschitl, M., 273, 351
Winett, R. A., 106
Winkler, R. C., 106
Winne, P. H., 210, 433, 434, 442, 453
Winsler, A., 339, 441
Winterhoff, P. A., 330, 331
Wirkala, C., 341
Witkin, H. A., 500
Wittwer, J., 302
Wixson, K. K., 197, 201, 259
Wolery, M., 140
Wolfe, P., 32, 33, 34, 37, 38, 39, 42, 43, 44, 45, 47, 49, 53, 61, 65, 73, 181, 182, 184, 186, 189, 232
Wolleat, P. L., 385
Woloshyn, V., 243, 255, 273, 434, 442
Wolpe, J., 88
Wolters, C. A., 157, 392, 448, 476
Wood, D. A., 137
Wood, D. J., 335, 337
Wood, E., 243, 255, 273, 434, 442
Wood, L. A., 140, 142, 154
Wood, R., 273, 396, 430
Wood, R. E., 298
Wood, W., 90
Woodard, S. M., 269
Woodward, J., 295
Woodworth, R. S., 82, 362
Woolfolk Hoy, A., 158
Woolfolk-Hoy, A. E., 157
Worsham, M. E., 467
Wortham, D., 161, 162, 271, 302, 303
Wouters, P., 297, 303
Wozney, L., 301
Wozniak, R. H., 406

Wundt, W., 7–9, 449
Wurf, E., 390
Wurtele, S. K., 156
Wüstenberg, S., 284
Wylie, R. C., 151, 390

Xie, K., 298
Xie, Q., 492, 493

Yang, Y-S., 298
Yeager, D. S., 397
Yerkes, R. M., 363
Yough, M. S., 21
Young, M. D., 301
Yu, S., 18
Yu, S. L., 448, 452

Zeidner, M., 407, 408
Zepeda, C. D., 263
Zepeda, S. J., 112
Zhang, L., 478, 499, 500, 503
Zhang, Q., 196
Zhang, Y., 144, 146
Zhao, R., 298
Zheng, B., 294
Zigler, E. F., 494
Zimmer, J. W., 179
Zimmerman, B. J., 26, 114, 126, 129, 130, 131, 133, 135, 136, 147, 150, 151, 154, 246, 259, 263, 273, 298, 322, 361, 381, 385, 386, 395, 399, 400, 417, 418, 419, 423, 424, 425, 426, 428, 429, 430, 431, 432, 434, 448, 449, 450, 452, 453, 454, 455
Zimmerman, C., 257
Zimmerman, E., 295
Zito, J. R., 455
Zohar, A., 263, 264, 265
Zumbrunn, S., 153
Zusho, A., 392, 393, 394, 395, 423, 432, 496

Subject Index

Page numbers followed by f and t indicate figures and tables, respectively.